HOTEL HOSPITALITY, & TOURISM LAW

FIFTH EDITION

John R. Goodwin
Professor Emeritus,
University of Nevada, Las Vegas

Jolie R. Gaston
University of Nevada, Las Vegas

Holcomb Hathaway, Publishers
Scottsdale, Arizona

To Matthew, Mark, Luke, John, and Elizabeth Ann
John R. Goodwin

To J.D.C.
Jolie R. Gaston

Publisher	Gay L. Pauley
Editor	Shari Jo Hehr
Developmental Editor	Katie E. Bradford
Production Editor	Ann Waggoner Aken
Cover Design	John Wincek/Aerocraft Charter Art Service
Typesetting	Andrea Reider

Holcomb Hathaway, Publishers
6207 N. Cattletrack Rd., Ste. 5
Scottsdale, AZ 85250

10 9 8 7 6

ISBN 0-89787-201-0

Copyright © 1997 by Holcomb Hathaway, Publishers, Inc.

All rights reserved. No part of this publication may be reproduced, stored in a retrieval system, or transmitted in any form or by any means, electronic, mechanical, photocopy, recording, or otherwise, without the prior written permission of the publisher.

Printed in the United States of America

Library of Congress Cataloging-in-Publication Data

Goodwin, John R.,
    Hotel, hospitality, and tourism law.—5th ed. / by John R. Goodwin and Jolie R. Gaston.
        p.   cm.
    Rev. ed. of: Hotel and hospitality law. 4th ed. ©1992.
    Includes bibliographical references and index.
    ISBN 0-89787-201-0 (alk. paper)
    1. Hotels—Law and legislation—United States. 2. Hospitality industry—Law and legislation—United States. 3. Tourist trade—Law and legislation—United States. I. Gaston, Jolie R. II. Goodwin, John R., Hotel and hospitality law. III. Title.
KF951.G65 1996
343.73'07891—dc20
[347.3037891]
                                                                96-34141
                                                                CIP

BRIEF CONTENTS

For the complete Contents, see p. iv.

CONTENTS

PREFACE

Hotel, Hospitality, and Tourism Law, Fifth Edition, is written to meet the needs of students in courses such as hotel law, travel law, travel agent law, tourism law, and the laws of innkeepers and hotel managers. The development of the new edition is based on two decades of legal research, writing, and appraisal; teaching; personal experiences in hotels, motels, and inns across the nation; and suggestions offered by many of you who have used the book in previous editions.

The objectives of this new edition are, first, to examine the laws that regulate the travel, lodging, and tourism industry and, second, to set forth management principles that must be developed and followed in those industries. In serving this dual purpose, the book emphasizes the relationship between the science of business management and the laws governing the industries in question. Students are provided with effective application of business law topics as they relate to the travel and lodging industry.

Litigation in the hotel, hospitality, and tourism world literally exploded in the 1990s; thus, study of the legal aspects of the industry is timely and of the utmost importance. Issues that must be considered include: computer literacy, access to technological information resources that enhance profits, travel expenditures of businesses, and payrolls of the direct and indirect travel and tourism workforce. This all points to specialized industry performance analysis and the need for higher education standards.

Taken together, the chapters in this book deal with the heavy legal burden on hotels, inns, and others in the hospitality, travel, and tourism industry to keep abreast of both current and former legal matters. To help meet that burden, the traditional, yet viable, cases of past decades have been included in abbreviated form to allow for the addition of more recent cases, where appropriate. This new edition represents a continuing effort to prepare students for the legal needs of a vast worldwide industry now poised to enter the twenty-first century. The book will serve as a firm legal base for the countless management decisions that will be made in this industry in the future.

ACKNOWLEDGMENTS

A textbook is never the sole effort of its authors, and that is certainly true of this one. Many people have contributed, not only in the form of material supplied, but also by their critical, constructive comments and reviews.

I wish to thank two reviewers whose detailed suggestions were a great help to us in revising this edition. First, thanks to Ted Carlton, MGM Grand Hotel and Casino, Las Vegas, whose valuable comments and perceptions are strongly industry-oriented. Second, Dr. Debara Cannon, Ph.D., Georgia State University, who took the time to write one of the finest reviews that the authors have seen in reference to a college textbook. This in-depth review contributed many clear, constructive ideas for further improving the text.

A special word of thanks to Professor Steven A. Hammel, Roosevelt University, Chicago, and Professor David W. Howell, Niagara University, New York, for their detailed observations and suggestions. Their individual contributions, influenced by the programs they teach, added considerable strength to the book.

Next, a debt of gratitude is due to two practicing lawyers. Thanks to Lawrence I. Drath of the New York firm of Feigen Post Holm & Drath, and James O. Eiler of the Los Angeles firm of Chase, Rotchford, Drukker & Bogust, both of whom have made major contributions to our efforts.

Many other lawyers and teachers have played an active role in the life of this book; their individual contributions, although invaluable, are too numerous to mention. My appreciation to the following: Bruce R. Maughan, Michigan State University; Valerie Larson, Endicott College; Frank Pauze, Mercyhurst College; Edward J. Martin, Georgetown Technical College; S. K. Wagner, St. Phillips College; Arthur A. Lebow, Nassau Community College; John E. Sherry, Cornell University; John I. Schensul, Grand Valley State College; and Paul D. Rompf, University of Southern Mississippi.

Sincere thanks to Thomas J. Lynch, New York University, for his sales contract chapter suggestions; and Professor Roberta Alison, Newberry College, for her thought-provoking inquiry about the differences between common-law and UCC sales contracts. Finally, my sincere thanks to my son, Matthew E. Goodwin, who did all of the typing and also offered many helpful suggestions as the new edition developed.

Note:

This publication was designed to provide accurate, authoritative information about the laws that regulate the hotel, hospitality, and tourism industry. Although the authors hold law degrees, the publisher is not engaged in the rendering of legal services in any form.

All quotes from the Uniform Commercial Code were taken from the West Virginia Code and not from the uniform draft. Legal terms and phrases are listed to assist students in their study of the cases. Many of these are defined in the cases by special notation, but some are not.

John R. Goodwin

Legal Terms and Phrases

Ab initio: From the beginning.

Addendum (plural, *addenda*): Material added to a document.

Ad hoc: "For this." A special purpose such as a committee.

Ad valoreum: Literally, "according to the value."

Annum: Year.

Appellant: The one taking an appeal in court.

Appellee: The one against whom an appeal is taken.

A priori: A conclusion based on what went before.

Arguendo: In the course of the argument.

Bifurcated: Splitting of a trial into separate issues.

Bill of lading: A transportation document that lists goods received for shipment.

Bona fide: Honestly and without fraud.

Causa mortis: In contemplation of approaching death.

Caveat: A warning to be careful.

Caveat emptor: Let the buyer beware.

Certiorari: Proceedings in which a higher court reviews what a lower court has done.

Circa: About, around, with relation to.

Common law: That body of law that has grown from the rulings of courts over the centuries.

Constructione juris: The origin of "contructive notice" or knowledge.

Cui bono?: Who benefits?

Cum testamento annexo: With the will annexed.

De bene esse: Conditionally, provisionally.

Defacto: In actual fact.

Dehors: Out of, without, beyond.

De jure: By right of lawful authority.

De novo: Anew, fresh, a second time.

Diem: Day. (*per diem:* by the day)

Ejusdem generis: Of the same kind, class, or nature.

Emptor: Buyer.

En masse: In a mass or lump.

Escritoire: A writing desk or "secretary."

Estoppel: Stopping or closing one's mouth; a technique that the courts can use to correct an inconsistent position that one may attempt to use against another.

Et al.: Abbreviation for et alia; "and others."

Et uxor: And wife.

Ex contractu: From the contract.

Facto: Fact.

Femme: Woman.

Femme sole: A single woman.

Fiat: A sanction or decree; an order "let it be done."

Fides: Faith.

Fructus: Fruits of a thing.

Habeas corpus: "You have the body."

In camera: In chambers, in private.

Infra hospitium ("hospis-e-em"): Within the inn.

In limine: In the very beginning; on or at the threshold.

Innamium: In old English, a pledge.

In personam: Against the person.

In re: In regard to or with reference to.

In rem: Against the thing (property).

Inter alia enactatum fuit: "Among other things, it was enacted." An ancient phrase found in the old pleadings (court papers) to refer to statutes.

Inter vivos: Between the living.

"Invenian viam aut facium": "I shall find a way or make one."

Ipso facto: By the fact itself.

Ipso jure: By law.

Judex: A private person appointed by the Praetor, with the consent of the parties, to try a case brought before that person in ancient Rome.

Judex ad quem: A judge to whom an appeal was taken in ancient Rome.

Jure: By right or law.

Jurisprudence: A term that describes the legal system and its supporting laws.

Jus: Right, justice, law.

"Laus deo": "Praise be to God." A phrase used as a heading on old bills of exchange.

Lex fori: Law of the place.

Lex loci: Where the contract was made.

Liability: Responsibility under law.

Liber: Book.

Lis pendens: Pending litigation.

Locus sigilli: Place of the seal, also "LS."

Mala fides: Done with bad intention.

Malfeasance: Evil doing. The commission of an act that is unlawful. Ill conduct.

Misfeasance: The improper performance of an act that a person has the legal power to do.

Mote: A meeting or assembly.

Moteer: A service or payment at the court of the lord, from which some were exempt by charter or privilege.

Nexus: Connection.

Nihil: Not at all.

Nonfeasance: Nonperformance of an act that should be performed.

Non obstante verdicto: Not withstanding the verdict. In spite of the verdict.

Pendens: Pending; "lis pendens": pending litigation.

Per annum: Per year.

Per curium: By the court.

Per se: By himself, herself, or itself.

Praetor: A municipal officer of the ancient city of Rome.

Prima facie: Such as will prevail until contradicted. On the face of it.

Pro: Acting as.

Pro facto: Held to be a fact.

Pro forma: A matter of form.

Prohibition: Inhibition, intradiction.

Pro indiviso: In common.

Pro rata: In proportion.

Pro se: For himself (or herself) in his or her own behalf.

Quasi: Almost, as in contract law.

Quasi-contract: Not a true contract, but close to it.

Quid pro quo: This for that, something for something.

"Qui facit per alium facit per se": "He who acts through another, acts himself." (The basis for the law of agency.)

Quo warranto: An ancient writ used to force one to show by what authority he or she holds a public office.

Re: In the matter of.

Remittitur: A subtraction from a jury verdict.

Res ipsa loquitur: The thing speaks for itself.

Respondent: The party who must reply or answer an appeal in court.

Scienter: Knowingly.

Sequester: To separate or isolate.

Seriatim: In succession.

Situs: Place or site.

Stare decisis: To abide by or adhere to decisions. "Let the decision stand."

Statute: An act of a legislative body.

Statutory law: Law that comes from acts of legislative bodies.

Subjudice: Under judicial consideration.

Summary judgment: Judgment given to one party where the other fails to reply to the complaint filed in court.

Supercedas: A writ commanding a stay of legal proceedings.

Suzerainty (French): A nation that exercises potential control over nations in relation to which it is sovereign.

Ultra vires: Beyond its powers.

Vadium: A pledge of property as security.

Venditor: Seller.

Veni-vidi-vici: "I came, I saw, I overcame." (Julius Caesar)

Venire facias de novo: A new trial in which some error occurred that prevents a judgment from being entered.

Via: Way.

Vis: That is to say.

1

The Laws of Hotels,
Hospitality, and Tourism

OVERVIEW

IN THIS, OUR first chapter, we want to offer a preliminary discussion of what law is and begin learning some of the legal terminology.

The hotel, hospitality, and tourism industries are maturing rapidly and are becoming more and more sophisticated as measured by the standards of American business. Our legal system has played an important role in the development of this sophistication and will continue to do so in the future.

Thus, we have to broaden the legal knowledge of all employees, agents, and managers; to create a clear-cut way in which the complaints of every employee or agent can be heard; to take a strong approach to issues that have to be communicated effectively; and to actively address the benefits of continuous legal education—all of which must be implemented against the legal environment within which each business must operate.

BOUNDARIES OR ENVIRONMENT OF LEGAL AND RELATED BEHAVIOR

positive

The phrase "boundaries of legal behavior" identifies one of the positive aspects of the American legal system. It tells us that, as long as our business practices comply with the law, the standards of industry, the nuances of custom and the usage of trade, we occupy a position that is "legal" and, thus, of economic value to us.

On the other hand, if we cross these boundaries, and if loss occurs to guests, patrons, invitees, or third parties, we could well be called upon to make good those losses out of business assets, even as individuals in some instances. "Law," then, becomes of more than casual importance no matter at what level we function in these industries.

What Is Law, and What Are Its Purposes?

The overriding purpose of law is to structure our society. Law establishes a level of social conduct that permits us to relate to each other at a satisfactory level of safety and decency. In this manner, law creates a legal environment built around

establishes a level of social conduct

1

order rather than conflict. Nothing or no one is favored in the American legal system, and the key to its success is balance, or evenness. All persons are entitled to equal treatment under the law.

Because of the complexity of the affairs in our society, law must be reasonable. The law must be definite so it has some precision when it is applied in court. The law must be practical and not philosophical, because time seldom is available to ponder the issues at any length. The law must be flexible so it can be adapted to changing conditions and times, and it must be final. The legal disputes of today must not be allowed to continue indefinitely. (This is why the law provides Statutes of Limitations: time constraints in which legal matters must be completed.)

The mission of law, among other things, is to enforce legal contracts; answer legal questions placed before it; maintain peace and order; protect property; protect each of us from each other, and facilitate commercial transactions. Gayle Binion, Chair of the Law and Society Program at the University of California at Santa Barbara, tells us what undergraduate law students must come to understand:[1]

> Students should understand that law has the most ancient of origins, that it is shaped by powerful evolutionary forces of history and social turbulence, and that it is the arena in which a society's most conflicted values get played out. Among results of such an inquiry can be the knowledge that society, in the pursuit of justice, can commit injustices; that in the resolution of conflict the law court is increasingly regarded as the forum of last resort; and that the supposed safety of law as a body of precedents and rules is illusive in the face of the unmet perplexities we will face in such domains as medicine, the environment, family relations and the scope of personal liberties.

Indeed, we must hasten to add to her statement the dominions of the hotel, hospitality, and tourism industries.

Preliminary Areas of Law

Five basic legal areas, events, or circumstances, may bring the law, lawyers, and courts into play (See Figure 1.1.).

First, a breach of a common law, or conventional contract, involves an agreement between two parties in which one or the other of the parties refuses in whole or in part, to do what the two had agreed to do. An example is a person with a confirmed room reservation who is turned away at the hotel front desk because no rooms are available because of overbooking (selling more rooms than are available).

Second, a breach of a sales contract arises when there is a dispute between merchant buyers and sellers of goods. Sales contracts are covered by Article 2, Uniform Commercial Code (UCC). An example is a hotel's purchase of a new carpet that is found to be defective. The hotel wants the carpet replaced but the merchant seller refuses to do so, claiming the defect in the carpet was due to abnormal foot traffic at the hotel.

Third are those instances in which a guest, a patron, an invitee, or a passerby is injured or killed at a hotel, motel, inn, restaurant, bar, or other industry property because of negligence. These occurrences are called *torts*. An example is an incident in which an elderly woman sustains a serious fall after dark as she attempts to reach her motel room. She claims that the cause of her fall was the

FIGURE 1.1 Areas of legal liability and the severity of them.

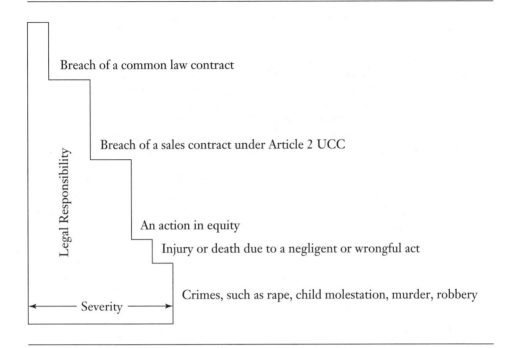

Breach of a common law contract

Breach of a sales contract under Article 2 UCC

An action in equity

Injury or death due to a negligent or wrongful act

Crimes, such as rape, child molestation, murder, robbery

Legal Responsibility

Severity

failure of the inn to replace burned-out spotlights that should have lighted her passageway. Such a claim raises the issue of negligence.

Fourth, a criminal act occurs that causes injury or loss of property. Although such an act is a tort, it is also a crime. An example is the theft of a small bag containing jewelry from a couple who had just checked out of a hotel and were preparing to enter a cab to go to the airport.

The fifth area has to do with "equity," closely related to law, yet distinguished from it. Law has to do with rules, customs, and usages. Equity has to do with what is fair, just, or right. Background information on equity is found later. An example is a travel group that has confirmed reservations but is denied admittance; these people then petition a court (judge) to order the hotel to admit them.

THE HISTORICAL PERSPECTIVE

The principles of travel and lodging law have been recognized for centuries as a unique, specialized body of jurisprudence, designed to control a specific industry. Yet the subject has only recently—as legal history goes—made its formal appearance in the colleges of hotel administration.

Increased litigation over the past decade has made it clear that those who are preparing for a career in the hotel, hospitality, and tourism industries must study law as it is applied to the segments of these industries because they have special requirements that have been forced upon them by court decisions.

The English Common Law

The imposition of strict liability [no excuses accepted] on the innkeeper found its origin in the conditions existing in England in the fourteenth and fifteenth centuries. Inadequate means of travel, the sparsely settled country, and the constant exposure to robbers left the traveler with the inn practically his only hope for protection. Innkeepers themselves, and their servants, were often as dishonest as the highwaymen roaming the countryside and were not beyond joining forces with the outlaws to relieve travelers and guests, by connivance or force, of their valuables and goods. Under such conditions, it was purely a matter of necessity and policy for the law to require the innkeeper to exert his utmost efforts to protect his guests' property and to ensure results by imposing legal liability for loss without regard to fault.[2]

With the court control of innkeepers came the realization that the travel itself was of key importance to the welfare and development of the nations of the world. Indeed, the *right* to travel came to be recognized in the courts and was given effect by those tribunals.

The right to travel is a part of the "liberty" of which the citizen cannot be deprived without due process of law under the Fifth Amendment. . . . In Anglo-Saxon law that right was emerging at least as early as the Magna Carta. . . . Freedom of movement across frontiers in either direction, and inside frontiers as well, was a part of our heritage. Travel abroad, like travel within the country, may be necessary for a livelihood. It may be as close to the heart of the individual as the choice of what he eats, or wears, or reads. Freedom of movement is basic in our scheme of values. . . . Freedom to travel is, indeed, an important aspect of the citizen's liberty. . . .[3]

Promoting Travel

Several things are needed to promote travel:

1. The courts must recognize travel as a matter of right.
2. Reliable and safe transportation must be readily available.
3. Home-away-from-home living accommodations must await the traveler.
4. Access to accommodations must be open to all travelers without restriction or discrimination.
5. Accommodation costs must be reasonable.
6. Controls and guidelines must be in place to regulate travel and lodging.
7. A means of redress for the traveler must be available for transgressions of the controls and guidelines.
8. A body of reliable law must be in place to assist the courts in providing such redress for the benefit of the traveler.

Thus, it became imperative that laws be created or be in existence, to ensure that travel could be engaged in with a minimum of loss and inconvenience to travelers. There was a corresponding need to protect those who were engaged in serving the traveling public. History shows us that development of these laws fell principally upon the shoulders of the early English courts. Thus, most of our industry laws today come from "court-made" or "common" law and not from acts of legislative bodies. The relatively late establishment of the English Parliament also can be cited as a reason for this. Figure 1.2 traces the development of travel and lodging laws.

FIGURE 1.2   Development of travel and lodging laws.

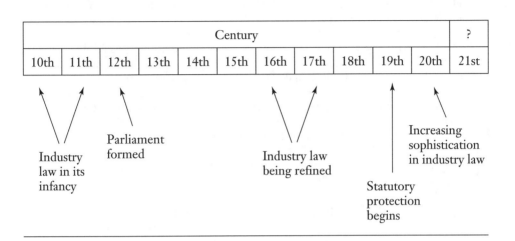

The courts began the creation of a body of unique law that still is being developed. These laws placed upon those in the "travel chain" increasing legal responsibilities for the safety of travelers, for their comfort, and for protection of their goods and valuables. In this manner the law began to forge standard travel practices.

Many of these practices have come down to us today in the form of custom. To illustrate, when a modern innkeeper greets a guest, the innkeeper is acting out an age-old policy forced upon inns by early court decisions. These decisions made the innkeeper an "insurer" of the property of the guest, and so the guests were greeted for security purposes and escorted personally to their rooms for the night.

In this legal process another feature of hospitality industry law had its birth. Because the inn and the tavern were so important to the needs of the traveling public, the courts came to treat them as public houses.

> The supply of food and shelter to a traveler was a matter of public concern, and the house which offered such food and shelter was [recognized to be] engaged in a public service. The law must make injustice to the individual traveler impossible: the caprice of the host could not be permitted to leave a subject of the king hungry and shelterless. In a matter of such importance the public had an interest, and must see that, so far as was consistent with justice to the innkeeper, his [her] inn was carried on for the benefit of the whole public, and so it became in an exact sense a public house."[4]

Shaped by the courts, nurtured by the public need, the law of innkeeping developed into a finely honed body of law that forms the basis of our study. The legal picture has now become more complicated.

INDUSTRIES RIPE FOR LITIGATION

That the study of legal requirements of the basic industries is necessary is illustrated by a full-page ad that appeared in a national law journal published for the legal profession.[5]

> FOR YEARS LAWYERS HAVE THOUGHT OF TRAVEL LITIGATION AS UNREWARDING. IT'S JUST NOT TRUE.
> [These paragraphs follow:]
> For years lawyers have operated under the illusion that they should avoid travel litigation as not worth the time and trouble. Nothing could be further from the truth! Increasingly, attorneys and the courts are discovering that spoiled travel plans involve more than superficial injuries. Awareness of consumer rights has resulted in sizeable recoveries against those responsible for destroying the travel plans of vacationers and businessmen.
> Consider: A vacation is ruined because an individual was "bumped" from his airline flight, his baggage was lost, his hotel was overbooked, and the hotel he was forced to stay in was unfinished and miles from the area he wanted to visit. Do you take the case?

The legal upshot is clear: The travel and lodging business has become a "legal-target industry." This has happened in the past in automobile-injury cases, products-liability cases against manufacturers of defective products, and malpractice cases against medical doctors. It is now the turn of the hospitality industry, and future managers in this industry have to prepare themselves to minimize or avoid this legal assault.

Two cases decided in federal courts in 1993 illustrate today's changing legal environment. The first case involves an employee fired from a restaurant. The second involves an employee at a hotel/casino who was involved with the injury of a person heading for the hotel, and the death of a third party as well.

First Case

In this case, a restaurant employee filed suit against six restaurant managers, claiming that the (male) innkeeper denied her equal pay, did not promote her because of her age and sex, and subjected her to a hostile and sexually discriminatory work environment. As we will see in Chapter 9, these allegations, if proven true, violate federal statutes. These statutes include Title VII of the Civil Rights Act of 1964 and the federal Age Discrimination in Employment Act. There is an exception, though, in that the federal laws do not apply to companies that have fewer than fifteen employees.

The legal issue raised in this case was whether Title VII and ADEA did or did not apply to the six managers as individuals (the restaurant company was exempt, since it had fewer than fifteen employees).

The federal trial court, and later the appeals court, held that no legal liability would be imposed on the managers as individuals. Liability, if any, could be only against the restaurant company, and it was exempt.[6]

In reference to this case, it should be observed that the managers could have state-statutory liability or common-law liability if their acts had been unlawful under common-law rules or state statutes. What the court held was that the *federal statutes* did not apply. The distinction between statutes, both federal and state, and the common law will be explored as we proceed.

Second Case

The Showboat Hotel and Casino in Atlantic City, New Jersey, hires limousines from independent companies to transport incoming guests to the hotel from the Philadelphia International Airport. In November 1988, the hotel hired Jiffy Executive Limousine Company to transport a wealthy gambler from the airport to the hotel. During the trip the limousine driver suffered a heart attack, causing an accident that injured the passenger and killed the driver of another vehicle.

The limousine service was found to be not insured and also was severely undercapitalized. The issue in this case was whether the Showboat Hotel and Casino was liable for hiring an "incompetent, independent contractor," rendering the hotel liable for the injuries and the death. The federal court declined to hold the hotel responsible.[7]

Even though the outcomes of these two cases were favorable to the businesses in question, they still form part of the legal mosaic that is being developed constantly in the courts. The results of these cases will play a role when similar cases come before the federal courts in the future.

Turning from the examples of emerging case law, we now must learn something about legislative enactments—acts of legislatures. Although such acts have been noticeably absent in the past, that will not be true in the future.

ABSENCE OF LEGISLATIVE CONTROLS

At the present time statutes (legislation) in our states that apply specifically to the hospitality industry are lacking. Although while some exist, notably in the area of health and safety regulation, most of the legal controls are found in the common law.

Yet the industries undoubtedly are heading toward an era of increasing legislative controls. It is a time of increasing business sophistication, and the law will have to adjust to meet the new needs. This trend can be seen in the airline industry, as well as in the travel-agent business. More and more legislation is coming into being to regulate those two areas. The same will come to pass in the hotel business, particularly in reference to "overbooking." If this practice continues, legislation can be expected to discourage it. This also will be true with practices at theme parks, restaurants, bars, and other businesses that will cause problems in the future and, thus, not meet legal muster. Many examples will be seen in the coming chapters, yet, at the present time, the lack of statutory controls continues.

INDUSTRY TERMINOLOGY

Hotel

The word is of French origin, being derived from *hostel*, and more remotely from the Latin word *hospes*, a word having a double signification, as it was used by the

Romans both to denote a stranger who lodges at the house of another and the master of the house who entertains travelers or guests.[8]

Another definition states:

A hotel is a building held out to the public as a place where all transient persons who come will be received and entertained as guests for compensation and it opens its facilities to the public as a whole rather than limited accessibility to well-defined private groups.[9]

The definition of a hotel under New Jersey law is important to those who want to enter the casino business in Atlantic City. Such persons must, as a condition precedent to the issuance of a gaming license, construct a hotel that meets the specifications of New Jersey law. A portion of the New Jersey casino-control law follows.

A hotel is:
 A single building under one ownership, located within the limits of the city of Atlantic City as said limits were defined as of November 2, 1976, and containing not fewer than 500 sleeping units, each of at least 325 square feet measured to the center of perimeter walls, including bathroom and closet space and excluding hallways, balconies and lounges; each containing private bathroom facilities; and each held available and used regularly for the lodging of tourists and convention guests and conforming in all respects to the facilities requirements contained in this act.

Under Virginia law a hotel is a public lodging house that can accommodate five or more transient guests. A "transient guest" is one who puts up for less than one week.[10]

The courts, by legal interpretation, have expanded the word *hotel* to include private schools. In *Blair Academy et al. v. Patricia Q. Sheehan*,[11] the Superior Court of New Jersey had this to say:

The hearing examiner who conducted the Department hearing on the requests for an administrative determination made findings and conclusions and recommended to the Commissioner that the three appellant schools "be ordered to permit the Department to inspect their dormitories as 'multiple dwellings,'" and that they "be ordered to register their buildings with the Department and pay the required fee." The Commissioner modified the first part of "the recommended decision and order of [the] hearing examiner," by providing that the schools "be ordered to permit the Department to inspect their dormitories as 'hotels' rather than 'multiple dwellings,'" and adopted the recommended decision and order as thus modified.

In Nevada the statutory definition enlarges the word *hotel* to include rooming-houses and lodginghouses that solicit transient trade.

Every building or structure kept as, used as, maintained as, or held out to the public to be, a place where sleeping or rooming accommodations are furnished to the transient public, whether with or without meals, shall, for the purpose of this chapter, be deemed to be a hotel; and whenever the word "hotel" shall occur in this chapter, it shall be deemed to include a lodginghouse or roominghouse where transient trade is solicited.[12]

Under the "Hotel Keeper's Contract," which is a draft by the International Institute for the Unification of Private Law, *hotel* is defined to include a business with the following attributes:

1. It acts on a regular basis to serve travelers.
2. It undertakes its activities for a reward (payment).
3. It provides temporary accommodations to travelers.
4. It provides ancillary services to travelers.
5. It is under the supervision of an innkeeper.

The student should know that the Hotel Keeper's Contract is a treaty that is being offered to the nations of the world to control the law of hotels and to make these laws uniform worldwide. About one dozen nations now follow this international hotel law, but presently the United States is not one of them.

A word closely associated with *hotel* is *motel*. Often in ordinances or zoning restrictions, the distinction between them becomes important.

Motel

The word *motel*, a product of the last fifty years, is a blend of "motorist" and "hotel." As the motel industry began to develop, notably in the 1950s, the word identified a small hotel-type structure with rooms for hire by the day, with a minimum amount of service provided by management.

Today, the word *motel* is associated with some of the most luxurious travel accommodations on the face of the earth. Some of the larger motel chains are advertising their units as "hotels." A word closely associated with hotels and motels is the old word "inn."

Inn

The forerunner of the hotel and the motel was, of course, the inn.

> An inn is a house where all who conduct themselves properly, and who are able and ready to pay for their entertainment, are received, if there is accommodation for them, and who, without any stipulated engagement as to the duration of the stay or as to the rate of compensation, are, while there, supplied at a reasonable charge for their meals, their lodging, and such services and attention as are necessarily incident to the use of the house as a temporary home.[13]

Guests at Hotels, Motels, and Inns

Another industry word that requires definition is *guest*. A person who is a *guest* at a lodging facility is given greater rights by law than one who is not a guest. To determine if one is a *guest* in the innkeeping sense, the courts will look *to the intention of the parties.* A townsperson who stops at the cigar stand in the lobby to buy a newspaper would not be a guest.

This intention of the traveler to become a guest is treated at law as being an "offer." If this offer is accepted by the innkeeper, the innkeeper-guest relationship has arisen. The offer of the traveler is most often accepted by front-desk personnel who are agents of the innkeeper.

The status of guest at an inn never can be established unilaterally by the traveler. Thus, if a traveler, intending to pay later, takes a room key from an unattended front desk and gains admittance to a room, he or she is not a guest at that inn. For the inn-guest relationship to arise, an opportunity must arise for the innkeeper to receive or reject that person. If received, the innkeeper-guest relationship comes into being. The law of innkeeping then will control the relationship.

Inn/Guest Relationship

The responsibility of an innkeeper for the safety of a traveler's property [as well as the traveler] begins at the moment when the relation of guest and host arises, and that relation begins as soon as the traveler enters the inn with the intention of using it as an inn, and is so received by the host. It does not matter that no food or lodging has been supplied or found up to the time of the loss. It is sufficient if the circumstances show an intention on the one hand to provide and on the other hand to accept such accommodation . . . .[14]

The ordinary laws of supply and demand would lead to the establishment of such houses by the roadside at places which would sufficiently serve the public convenience, but those laws could not be trusted to secure to each individual the benefit of the food and shelter therein provided . . . . The law must make injustice to the individual traveler impossible . . . .[15]

Special Relationships

At law, there exists between an innkeeper and a guest a special relationship. This relationship determines the nature of the duties involved between A and B in a given situation. If a court finds such a relationship, then, as a matter of law, the court can set the standards the jury must follow in determining "questions of fact." This happens when a case ends up in court.

Special relationships are routinely found by the courts between innkeepers and their guests, carriers and their passengers—and often between restaurant and bar operators and their patrons.[16]

Terminating Guest Status

Guest status may end in a variety of ways: A guest may check out and end it, or an innkeeper may eject a guest for immoral conduct. A problem in determining the beginning rather than the ending of the relationship arises in instances where travelers use the services of an inn for food and drink, but not for lodging. The courts may say that if such use is in furtherance of the travel and if the innkeeper knowingly serves the traveler, the inn-guest relationship *is* in being until the traveler moves on. Locals generally cannot gain guest status, as they are not "travelers." Yet, if a local is received by the innkeeper with the intention of having that person as a guest, the status has arisen.[17]

Does the inn-guest relationship apply to an *employee* who, as part of his or her employment contract, occupies a room at the inn? Or how about an employee who stays overnight at an inn because of a severe snowstorm? In both instances the courts have held that no inn-guest relationship exists. The reason is, of course, that the employee does not meet the "traveler" test.[18] A *guest* must be distinguished from a *tenant*.

Tenant

A *tenant*, under landlord and tenant law, gains a right of exclusive possession of the leased premises. This right is an enforceable property interest, and legal process is required to terminate the status. A guest at an inn, on the other hand, gains a mere license or right to *use* the inn room. This is a temporary right and ends as the guest resumes his or her travels. Of course, a guest who remains at an inn on an extended basis could become a tenant and then would have a property interest in the room. The counterpart of the tenant is the "landlord."

Landlord

Landlords, as distinguished from innkeepers, serve tenants who intend to remain in a certain locale on an extended basis. Tenants traditionally have not needed the same legal protection as travelers. For this reason, the law allows a landlord to bargain, select, and use his/her own judgment in deciding who will or will not be acceptable as a tenant.

In addition, the rates landlords charge are a matter of contract between the parties. In the absence of rent controls, no rule says the rates a landlord charges must be reasonable, whereas that is the rule in innkeeping law. Closely related to inns are taverns.

Tavern

At common law a *taverner* was a person who sold wines to the public. From that word came the word *tavern*. Though inns and taverns share common points, they are not the same legally. An inn is an establishment designed to provide rest, shelter, and entertainment for the traveler. A tavern, on the other hand, primarily serves those who live in the immediate area and thus have access to their homes at night.

Innkeeper

An *innkeeper* is one who assumes the responsibilities of operating an inn, as that word developed at common law. In practice, there have been cases in which the keeper of rooms has denied that he or she was in fact an innkeeper. This could happen when an attempt was made to escape innkeeping liability to a guest or roomer. The defense often seen in such cases is that only shelter was furnished, not food and drink; at common law, to be an innkeeper within the legal meaning of that word, both shelter and food and drink had to be furnished.[19]

In *Doe v. Bridgton*[20] the judge provided a summary of what an innkeeper is.

> He (the innkeeper) was bound by the common law to receive and lodge all comers in the absence of a reasonable ground of refusal. 21 *Halsbury's Laws of England* 445–446, 3d ed. (1957). A valid refusal had to be related to the inn's operations as an inn. *White's Case*, 2 Dyer 158, 73 Eng. Reports 343 (K.B. 1558). Full occupancy or the traveler's

condition, such as drunkenness, which might offend other guests, constituted good
cause for exclusion. On the other hand, arrival at a late hour or on a Sunday was held
to be insufficient to deny lodging. *Rex v. Ivens.* There had to be a rational relationship, a causal nexus, between the reason for the refusal and the function of the inn.

One who only occasionally receives travelers and provides food and shelter for
them is not an innkeeper. In addition, one who receives and provides for those
who are not travelers or transients is not an innkeeper and cannot be held to
innkeeper liability.

To render one responsible as an innkeeper,

> . . . a person must make [innkeeping] to some extent a regular business, a means of
> livelihood. He should hold himself out to the world as an *innkeeper*. It is not neces-
> sary that he should have a sign, or a license (although he will usually have both), pro-
> vided that he has in any other manner authorized the general understanding that his
> was a public house, where strangers had the right to require accommodation.[21]

The courts are consistent in holding that the basic duty of innkeepers to provide reasonable safe premises for guests cannot be delegated to the independent
contractors the innkeepers employ. For example, when an inn contracted with an
outside company to maintain its lawns and shrubbery, the inn was held liable to a
guest for the slip and fall that resulted from improper maintenance.[22]

An early California case had this to say about the standard of conduct that an
innkeeper should follow in that state: "the innkeeper should be held to the
responsibilities which by his [her] representations, induced . . . the guest . . . to
believe he [she] would assume."[23] The rule is as valid fifteen decades later as it was
then. It also should be pointed out that "representations" can include not only
what an innkeeper says but also what is done and what can reasonably be implied
from the surrounding facts and circumstances.

In *Lorio v. San Antonio Inn*, a guest slipped on accumulated water on unlit
stairs at the inn and was injured. The court set down a concise summary of the
basic legal duties of innkeepers:[24]

> The rule applicable to this case is that while an innkeeper does not insure his guests
> against the risk of injury, he nonetheless owes his guest a high degree of care, *Kraaz v.
> La Quinta Motor Inns, Inc.*, 410 So. 2d 1048 (Louisiana 1982). A basic element of this
> duty is to maintain the premises in a reasonably safe condition. To this end, reason-
> able inspections of the premises and mechanical equipment are required, *Brasseaux
> v. Stand-By Corp.*, 402 So. 2d 140 (La. App. 1st Cir. 1981). In addition, an innkeep-
> er is held to have constructive knowledge of a dangerous condition if that condition
> has existed for such a time as to reasonably have been discovered by the innkeeper,
> *Kauffmann v. Royal Orleans, Inc.*, 216 So. 2d 394 (La. App. 4th Cir. 1968) . . . .

The common law, speaking through a thousand years of English and
American court decisions, tells the innkeeper to receive guests, up to the capacity
of the inn; charge them a reasonable price (because to charge them an unreasonable price might force some of them back onto the highway); safeguard guests and
their property in a reasonable manner while they remain as guests; provide them
with food and drink at reasonable prices (at times that one would normally expect
to be served at the inn); give them sleeping accommodations that are fit, fair, and

suitable in relation to the price charged; make all reasonable house rules known to them by direct statement or by the placement of suitable signs; warn them of known dangers that may exist at the inn; keep a constant eye open for dangers that may be perceived later and which must then be told to the guests; treat all guests in a courteous and kind manner while they remain on the premises, and facilitate the resumption of their travels without hindrance or restraint.

Leaving these definitions, it is useful to examine briefly an area of concern to all hotel, hospitality, and tourism businesses. This has to do with injuries to employees, agents, guests, patrons, and third parties.

INJURY TO GUESTS AND OTHERS

A variety of injuries can occur in the businesses under discussion. An in-depth discussion will follow about them in Chapters 15, 16, and 17. Statistics show that the most frequent cases brought against hotels, motels, inns, and others involve injuries caused by falls on the premises of the business.

For example, a patron leaving a fast food restaurant in Michigan, stepped forward expecting her foot to fall on an even surface. Instead, at that point an inclined ramp had been installed so wheelchair-bound persons would have access to the restaurant. This resulted in a fall, causing severe injuries to the departing patron.

The Court of Appeals of Michigan decided the case in favor of the restaurant. The court was of the opinion that the patron should have observed an inclined ramp by casual inspection. The court found this reason enough to excuse the restaurant from a duty to warn of the existence of the incline.[25] It is not often as simple as that, however.

In contemplating this incline, and other possible falls, the careful manager must reflect upon some legal points:

1. If the incline lacked a handrail upon which the patron could have caught herself as she fell forward, the result could have been much different.
2. If this incident had occurred after dark, and the patron had reason to expect a flat surface to walk on, the result also would have been different.
3. If it had been daylight and the patron had been blind, it then would have become a question of fact for a jury to decide if the injured patron had used tools available to her with which to detect dangers that confronted her.[26]

In recent years a variety of injury and death cases have arisen in the hotel, hospitality, and tourism industries. Examples include guest poisoning cases in New Mexico, a hotel parking lot car highjacking case in Scottsdale, Arizona, the murder of German tourists in Florida, and the outbreak of Legionnaire's disease on a cruise ship, to mention a few. Injuries and deaths of this nature will form the basis for a myriad of new laws for the industries in the future.

SUMMARY

The modern legal nature of the hotel, hospitality, and tourism industries is such that there are "boundaries of the law" that must constantly be followed. Distinctions must be made in regard to the terms "hotel," "motel," and "inns" because while they perform similar functions as far as housing guests for the night, they may not be the same regarding tax laws, sanitation ordinances, and other laws.

At the heart of the hospitality industry is the "hotel/motel/inn-guest relationship." The courts have long labeled this to be a "special," and not an ordinary, relationship. In this manner, the laws place heavier responsibilities upon those who serve travelers. Selling a traveler a room for the night is vastly different from selling a tire to a local at a service station.

The special relationship does not always end when one checks out of a hotel and settles the account there. For example, the person who is about to resume travel is robbed while in or near the hotel. A court may well find that innkeeper obligations continued during the robbery and that the relationship had not ended even though it in fact had.

Finally, the distinctions between common law contracts and sales contracts is important to remember. When one sells a room at an inn, one has created a common law contract. When one buys food supplies for a restaurant, a sales contract has been created. The rules that govern these two classes of contracts are vastly different as we will learn in Chapters 5 and 6.

QUESTIONS

1. The travel industry has become ripe for litigation. Although not discussed specifically in this chapter, can you give a reason why this is happening?
2. A traveler in the "King's realm" was extended a preferred status by the courts. List three reasons for this.
3. Why, as a matter of law, was it important that the early courts recognize inns as public houses? What might have happened if the courts had not done so?
4. In the past, the travel industry was fragmented and, thus, invisible—at least in the contemplation of legal minds. Why?
5. The travel industry has few statutory controls upon it at the present time. Is this likely to change? Why?
6. The state of Virginia defines a "transient guest" as one who puts up at an inn for less than one week. What might a person be who stays at an inn in that state for *more* than a week?
7. Can you see the legal problem created by having no set definition of a "traveler?" Would a succinct definition be of legal use?
8. Name three reasons why the early courts of England extended protection to the traveler.
9. When does the inn-guest relationship come into being as a matter of law?
10. Why is a landlord not an innkeeper in the operation of an apartment building or condominium?

NOTES

1. Writing in *Focus on Legal Studies*, Fall 1994, Vol. X, No. 1.
2. *Minneapolis Fire & Marine Insurance Co. v. Matson Navigation Co.*, 44 Hawaii 59, 61, 352 P. 2d 335, 337 (1960).

3. *Kent v. Dulles*, 357 U.S. 116, 78 S. Ct. 1113, 2 L. Ed. 2d 1204 (1957).

4. John E. H. Sherry, *The Laws of Innkeepers, Revised Edition*, Cornell University Press, Ithica, New York, 1981, p. 9.

5. *The National Law Journal*, Monday, May 11, 1981, p. 36, advertising *Travel Law* by Thomas A. Dickerson, who cites the first edition of *Travel and Lodging Law* many times.

6. *Miller v. Maxwell's International*, 991 F. 2d 583 (9th Cir 1993).

7. *Robinson v. Jiffy Executive Limousine Co.*, 4 F. 3d 237 (3rd Circuit 1993).

8. *Cromwell v. Stephens*, 2 Daly 15 (N.Y. 1867).

9. *Ambassador Athletic Club v. Utah State Tax Commissioner*, 27 Utah 2d 377, 496 P. 2d 883.

10. 373 A. 2d 418.

11. 149 *N. J. Super.* 113 (April 7, 1977).

12. Nevada Revised Statutes, 447.010.

13. *Cromwell v. Stephens, supra*.

14. *Wright v. Anderson*, 1 King's Bench 209.

15. *State v. Stone*, 6 Vt. 295, 298 (Vermont 1834).

16. *Hopkinson v. Chicago Transit Authority*, 570 N.E. 2d 717 (Illinois 1991).

17. *Orchard v. Bush*, 2 Q.B. 284 (1898).

18. *Powers v. Raymond*, 197 Cal. 126, 239 P. 1089 (1925).

19. *Pinkerton v. Woodward*, 33 Cal. 557 (1867).

20. 71 N.J. 478, 483, 366 A. 2d 641 (1976).

21. *Lyon v. Smith*, 1 Iowa 244 (1843).

22. *Simons v. San Antonio Marriott Riverwalk Hotel*, 1993. See also *Robertson v. Travelers Inn*, 613 So. 2d 376 (Alabama 1993).

23. *Pinkerton v. Woodward*, 33 Cal. 557, 559 (California 1867).

24. 454 So. 2d 844 (Louisiana 1984).

25. *Novotney v. Burger King*, 499 N.W. 2d 379 (Michigan 1993).

26. *Cohen v. McDonald's*, 537 A. 2d 549 (Delaware 1987).

Sources and Classifications of Hotel, Hospitality, and Tourism Law

OVERVIEW

OUR PURPOSE HERE is, first, to learn something about the sources or origins of the law that plays such a large part in the American legal system. The second is to classify these laws so that we can learn to distinguish them for purposes of applying them in the industries under discussion.

For the most part, other than the common law, the hotel, hospitality, and tourism industries are unregulated by law and, indeed, sometimes unlicensed. For industry components to protect themselves from legal claims from guests, patrons, or third parties, they often turned to an old doctrine of the common law, *caveat emptor*—"let the buyer beware." This caveat often was useful in court, but sometimes it was not. On the other hand, the person claiming loss relied upon another ancient legal doctrine, *caveat venditor*—"let the seller beware."

Having to rely upon either of these old principles of the common law ran counter to what was needed. The courts recognized this and, in a lesser fashion, so did the legislatures. It is now useful to look first at the sources or origins of law to see what developed over the centuries, and, second, to examine the classifications found within these sources.

SOURCES OF LAW

We will examine five major sources of law: history, written law (constitutions and statutes), common law, rulings of administrative agencies, and public policy.

History

History, in the simplest sense, is what has been done in the past, a record of humanity and what has been done by others in prior centuries. Thus, the rulings of the Pharaohs in ancient Egypt, procedures followed in the early Greek and Babylonian courts, the practices of lawyers following the Norman Conquest and the actions of the arbitrators in Colonial times in America are all sources of law. One who studies legal history finds modern rules or principles of law constantly that have their roots in antiquity. As a striking example of this, the modern definition of a partnership is almost word for word the same as that found in the

Justinian Code. Thus, what has gone before us in the courts, in law offices and in early law-making bodies is a primary and ongoing source of law.

Written Law

Our next two sources of law often are spoken of as being "written" so as to distinguish them from court-made law. Law that is written is law that, at the time of its inception, is placed in written (today, printed) form. The two categories of written law are constitutions and their amendments, and statutes. The word *statute* refers to formal law created in a prescribed manner, by a law-making body. As we use the term here, it will be synonymous with *ordinances*, created at the municipal level, and *acts of Congress*, created at the congressional level.

Constitutions

A constitution is the supreme law of the state or nation for which it was created. It follows that amendments to constitutions supplement or alter the basic law and become part of that supreme law.

Today, in the United States, we have fifty-one constitutions: one U. S. Constitution and fifty state constitutions. The U. S. Constitution has been amended twenty-six times. The number of amendments in our state constitutions vary from state to state.

Although each constitution is supreme in its own area of jurisdiction, this is qualified in reference to our states. The U. S. Constitution provides:

> This Constitution and the laws of the United States which shall be made in pursuance thereof, and all treaties made, or which shall be made under the authority of the United States, shall be the supreme law of the land; and the judges of every state shall be bound thereby, anything in the Constitution or laws of any state to the contrary notwithstanding.[1]

Clearly, then, state laws and constitutions must be *subordinate* to the U. S. Constitution. With this exception, each state constitution is supreme within the state itself, and all other laws of the state must, in turn, conform to it. For example, a city cannot create an ordinance that would violate the state constitution. In turn, a state legislature cannot create a law that would violate the U. S. Constitution or its amendments. Perhaps it isn't precise to say that such laws "cannot be created." It is better to say that if they are created, they are "unconstitutional" and are subject to being struck down by a court.

While the U. S. Constitution is and will remain the fountainhead of law for the United States, the Amendments to that Constitution have an impact on all businesses in the United States and its territories. The first ten Amendments became effective on December 15, 1791, and are known today as the Bill of Rights. The First Amendment protects religious freedom and arises in some hotel cases.

Particularly applicable to the industries under discussion is the Fourth Amendment, which prohibits unlawful searches and seizures. The courts have held this amendment applicable to searches of hotel rooms and lockers of employees.

Following the Bill of Rights came the other Amendments. The Thirteenth Amendment abolished slavery and prohibited "involuntary servitude." This Amendment has direct application when an innkeeper tries to get a prosecuting attorney to get an indictment against a former guest for not paying a bill at a hotel. In short, the Amendment says that not paying a civil debt is not a crime.

The Fourteenth Amendment also is of particular interest to us. It requires "due process" and "equal protection," and makes clear that no state shall deny these protections to any guest, patron, invitee, or other person. This issue has come up in many cases where innkeepers have detained property of guests so as to enforce debts that are due. This is known informally as the "innkeeper's lien."

By the *absorption principle*, the courts have held that, because the Fifth and Fourteenth Amendments both include the words "due process," the Fifth Amendment is absorbed, or made a part of, the Fourteenth Amendment.

The Eighteenth Amendment prohibits the ". . . manufacture, sale, or transportation of intoxicating liquors within, the importation thereof from the United States . . . ." Authored by Senator Andrew J. Volstead, it now is known as Prohibition or the Volstead Act. It became effective January 16, 1919, and was repealed by the Twenty-First Amendment in 1933. The Twenty-First Amendment, Section 1, said in fifteen words: "The eighteenth article of amendment to the Constitution of the United States is hereby repealed."

Section 2 of the Twenty-First Amendment has direct application to the hotel and hospitality industries. It says that the laws of the *states* shall control the sale of "intoxicating liquors." Thus, today, state laws control such sales in all fifty states. These laws may permit, limit, or prohibit sales of intoxicating beverages. This topic will be discussed further in Chapter 21, under the topic of dram-shop laws.

Constitutions are supreme because they emanate from a people and create the "state" itself. Thus, the U. S. Constitution created the United States, and each state constitution created each state. In Figure 2.1 we first see "a people" who have evolved over some span of time, bringing with them their customs, usages, and history. By organizing these people, such as was done in the Continental Congress in 1787, a constitution can be drafted and ratified by representatives of the people. In this manner the state is created. The state consists of three branches of government: executive, legislative, and judicial. Now a workable political entity exists that can begin carrying out the functions of government. From the diagram we see that "administrative agencies" are created by the legislative branch. These agencies carry out the day-to-day functions of running a government for the people—and, as we shall see, these agencies also create law.

The executive branch can issue executive orders, and it operates under the "executive privilege," which in the past included the power to declare war. The legislative branch not only creates agencies but, in turn, creates new laws called statutes (discussed next). The judicial branch provides the forum where the constitutionality and legality of these statutes can be tested; it is here that controversies can be litigated. The judicial branch also can create law through the common-law process, as we have discussed it before.

Thus, by tracing a political entity backward, we come to the constitution, and beyond this document, we find the people themselves. If amending the constitution should become desirable, it cannot be done by a unilateral act of a law-making body, nor by executive order, nor by court ruling. It can be done only by the people through the constitutional-ratification process.

We must point out, however, that a court can *interpret* constitutional provisions and, by doing so, place new meanings on the words. This power of the courts was recognized by Justice John Marshall in 1819 in an opinion of the U. S.

Figure 2.1   Constitutions and the separation of powers.

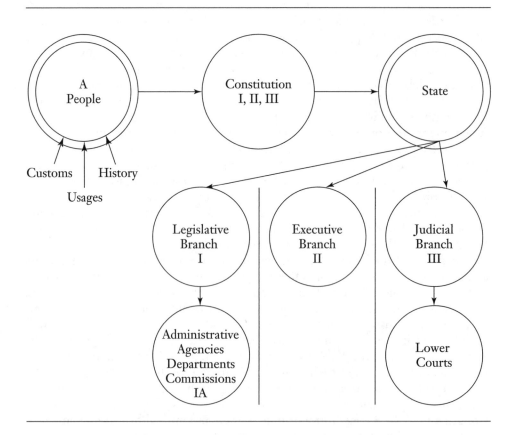

Supreme Court in which he wrote: "We must never forget that it is a constitution that we are expounding, intended to endure for ages to come, and consequently to be adapted to the various crises of human affairs."[2] Since that time, our courts have called upon this thought to place new meanings upon the old words of our national constitution, as well as those of our state constitutions.

In the trilogy of government (legislative, executive, and judicial), we see the separation-of-powers principle. No division is superior over any other. "The doctrine of the separation of powers was adopted by the Convention of 1787, not to promote efficiency but, rather, to preclude the exercise of arbitrary power. The purpose was not to avoid friction but, instead, by means of the inevitable friction incident to the distribution of the governmental powers among three departments, to save the people from autocracy."[3]

Statutes

The second type of written law are statutes, or "legislation." Written laws created by law-making bodies make up the largest body of written law. Statutes can be standard or they may be uniform.

Standard statutes. A constant need arises to place new regulations upon businesses, individuals, and others within our society. For example, the state may see a need for a new law to regulate the motel industry. The federal government may find it necessary to create a new law to regulate the airlines. As these needs arise, statutes are created to meet them. Thus, we have a constantly increasing body of statutory laws that regulates business, sets standards of personal conduct of citizens, and provides new regulatory measures in an ever-changing variety of situations. Statutes affect the travel and lodging industry. All are important and require constant awareness of the ongoing creation of the usual or standard statutory law. As noted, however, there is a noticeable lack of statutory law regarding the hospitality and tourism industries at this time.

The second kind of statutes we encounter are "uniform" in nature. Unfortunately, few uniform laws are in place with the exception of the Uniform Commercial Code.

Uniform statutes. In the past, the law-making bodies of our states acted independently of one another. No state concerned itself with what the lawmakers were doing in other states. Because of this, we wound up with fifty separate codes of laws. No particular harm resulted as long as business and industry remained on a purely local basis. When X corporation had one motel in Memphis, the manager had to be concerned with one body of state law. But with thousands of inns today, the opposite is true for that corporation. Thus, as all forms of business began to expand, the need for uniformity in laws, especially the laws of business, became apparent.

A National Conference of Commissioners on Uniform State Laws was created earlier in this century. Its job was to modernize, update, and make uniform the various bodies of business law; to draft uniform acts; and to encourage the state legislatures to adopt them after they were created. The most important accomplishment of the National Commissioners was the creation and subsequent adoption of the Uniform Commercial Code (UCC) by our states. The UCC replaced the Uniform Sales Act and the Negotiable Instruments Law, which were pioneer uniform laws.

Unfortunately, each state legislature maintains independence, even with uniform laws, and often makes changes in the uniform drafts. As a result, even with the UCC, the law varies somewhat in minor instances from state to state. In spite of this, the effort being made with uniform laws is a vast improvement over the situation that existed sixty years ago. When Congress enacts a law, it comes close to true uniformity, as it is a single law that binds fifty states as one. Uniformity could be achieved in the UCC by adopting it as a *federal* law. There is no indication, however, that this will be done in the near future.

The Common Law

The fourth source of law is the *common law*. This term has two meanings. The first is that body of law that was brought to the American Colonies from England in the 1600s. This was the English Common Law, and much of it is with us today. For example, any rule of law found in an American Colony in the 1600s that has not been altered or replaced is still the law of the state that developed from that colony.

The second meaning of the term *common law*—the one that we are concerned with here—is law created by *court decisions* as contrasted with law created by *law-making bodies*.

A general principle of the common law is to let such decisions or cases stand once they are created, that is, to follow such cases in the future and not disturb them until a good reason to do so arises. This is true only in the jurisdiction where the case was decided. Case decisions have no binding power outside of the state within which they have been decided. On the other hand, these "foreign" cases are often persuasive in other jurisdictions and for this reason are cited in court by lawyers.

Stare Decisis

"Let the decision stand" said the old-time judges. "It is not so important that a matter be decided correctly as it is that it simply be decided." The doctrine of *stare decisis* is a part of our common-law system today, and its existence tends to encourage litigants to tailor their affairs to fit within existing common-law rules, because the doctrine holds that the rule of law from a case should stand in a similar current case. (This is the rule of "precedent.")

Rejecting Stare Decisis

Even though the doctrine of *stare decisis* is firm in American law, it can be altered or rejected in two ways:

1. A legislature may enact a statute that negates or cancels how a prior court ruled.
2. A higher court may overrule the decision of a lower court.

If a common-law principle becomes "too old" or if it no longer serves a rational purpose, a court can reject it. In the area of "public law," however, the doctrine is ignored frequently. This often happens in cases involving interpretations of a constitution, as the following illustrates:

> A judge looking at a constitutional decision may have compulsions to revere past history and accept what was once written. But he remembers above all else that it is the Constitution which he swore to support and defend, not the gloss which his predecessors may have put on it. So he comes to formulate his own views, rejecting some earlier ones as false and embracing others. He cannot do otherwise unless he lets men long dead and unaware of the problems of the age in which he lives do his thinking for him.
>
> This reexamination of precedent in constitutional law is a personal matter for each judge who comes along. When only one new judge is appointed during a short period, the unsettling effect in constitutional law may not be great. But when a majority of a Court is suddenly reconstituted, there is likely to be substantial unsettlement. There will be unsettlement until the new judges have taken their positions on constitutional doctrine. During that time—which may extend a decade or more—constitutional law will be in flux. That is the necessary consequence of our system and to my mind a healthy one. The alternative is to let the Constitution freeze in the pattern which one generation gave it. But the Constitution was designed for the vicissitudes of time. It must never become a code which carries the overtones of one period that may be hostile to another.
>
> So far as constitutional law is concerned *stare decisis* must give way before the dynamic component of history. Once it does, the cycle starts again. Today's new and startling decision quickly becomes a coveted anchorage for new vested interests. The former proponents of change acquire an acute conservatism in their new *status quo*. It will then take an oncoming group from a new generation to catch the broader vision which may require an undoing of the work of our present and their past. . . .[4]

Administrative Agencies and Their "Law"

A fifth source of law is found in the rulings of administrative agencies in cases that come before them. The population of the United States 130 years ago was a fraction of what it is today. Business was agriculture-oriented and, for the most part, localized. Our nation was only partially settled, and life still had a rural, local, personal atmosphere to it. All of this changed with the coming of the first "war to end all wars."

An industrial expansion started that has not ceased in growth. Life changed to one of increasing complexities, and the courts and law were caught up in the change. Although the courts had been adequate to regulate society in that other age of 130 years ago, it became increasingly evident that they no longer could fill this role in such changing times.

When this came to pass, large gaps existed in the laws needed to make certain that an orderly process of business—life itself—would be available to our society today and tomorrow. One hundred years ago one could challenge a business practice or seek protection by bringing a lawsuit and then patiently waiting for the court-legal process to run its course. Today it would be impossible for our courts to regulate the growing airline, travel, radio, television, computer, video, and other industries that have had their inception in recent times. Something else was needed to provide such regulation.

The device selected had its beginning when legislative bodies began to enact laws designed to create *administrative agencies*. These laws would grant certain powers to a *commission*, the membership of which then would be filled by the executive officer at the state or federal level.

At the federal level we find the Federal Trade Commission (FTC), Interstate Commerce Commission (ICC), and numerous other "alphabet agencies." At the state level we find public service commissions, departments of public safety, banking commissions, alcohol control commissions, insurance commissions, and others. At the municipal level we find water and sanitation commissions, parking authorities, and city police forces.

As a practical matter, the day-to-day impact of agencies and commissions is as great as that of the courts, and they play a direct and important part in the regulation of business. Administrative agencies and their rulings have been challenged as an unconstitutional intrusion upon the three-part separation of powers, but the courts uphold them as *an extension of the legislative power* as it is there that they were created in the first instance.

Other sources of law include executive orders at the state and federal levels, and rulings of attorney generals. They will not be discussed, but we will look at a final source that involves the wishes of the people.

Public Policy

Public policy can find expression through political actions. To illustrate, the voters of a state reject a candidate for governor who campaigns on the grounds of legalization of gambling. The rejection expresses the wishes of the voters; thus, this becomes part of the public policy of that state. The courts will give effect to this policy when matters involving gambling come before them.

The doctrine of *stare decisis* is in itself a matter of public policy. Other matters of public policy involve things that are against the interests of the public. Some examples include contracts that restrain trade, agreements that affect the administration of justice, contracts never to compete in a certain business, and similar areas.

CLASSIFICATIONS OF LAW

It is an axiom of the legal profession that "law is a seamless web." The thought behind that statement has strong truth to it. Yet, for our purposes here, dividing law (and equity) into classifications will allow us to gain a better overall understanding of law and our legal system.

The balance of the chapter will discuss seven classifications of law:

1. judicial and administrative law
2. common and statutory law
3. common and civil law
4. public and private law
5. substantive and procedural law
6. contract law
7. tort and criminal law

Judicial and Administrative Law

Many things that become the subject matter of court action involve matters that are "legal" or judicial in nature. They involve law that is created in our constitutions, in the statutes, by common-law rulings, or by interpretations of judges. On the other hand, administrative law has as its source an agency that exists outside of the legal system.

The long, but not always so colorful, development of administrative agencies began in the second half of the nineteenth century. The first two agencies were the Civil Service Commission, created in 1883, and the Interstate Commerce Commission, in 1887. Then came departments: The Department of Labor in 1888, followed by The Department of Agriculture in 1889.

Giving commissions and departments rule-making power over business created the tendency for them to assume the role of judge, jury, and prosecutor over their assigned areas. To overcome this, Congress enacted the Administrative Procedure Act earlier in this century. This federal statute provides the groundwork upon which administrative procedures must be carried out at the federal level and sets forth procedures that must be followed.

The following newspaper item illustrates an administrative action at the state level:[5]

> BEER TOO STRONG—Miller Icehouse is being sent to the doghouse, and other ice-brewed beers could join it. The Alabama Alcoholic Beverage Control Board is sending letters to brewers, telling them to remove from stores any new beers that contain more than the 5 percent alcohol allowed by state law. Miller Icehouse has an alcohol level of 5.5 percent.

An example of an administrative agency at the federal level is the Occupational Safety and Health Administration (OSHA).

Common and Statutory Law

Common law is created by court rulings while statutory law is created by acts of law-making bodies.

Common Law

As was stated previously, the common law is created by actions taken and decided by the courts. The English common law was created in English courts, and the American common law in the American courts.

In a 1988 court case in Tennessee, the status of the common law of Tennessee came into question. The state of Tennessee had enacted the Tennessee Code in 1858. This Code repealed all public and general statutes in effect at that time, including "ancient English statutes" as well as statutes of North Carolina that had been in force in Tennessee. This left open the question of validity of Tennessee court decisions prior to 1858, which had been decided under English and North Carolina statutes. Were they too abolished along with the older statutes under which they had been decided? *Shepherd Fleets, Inc., v. Opryland* held that Tennessee court decisions, even though based on English and North Carolina statutes that the Code abolished, were part of the Tennessee common law and these decisions remain part of the common law of Tennessee today.[6]

Statutory Law

Statutory law must be distinguished from the common law, as the source of it is not the same. Statutory law comes from acts, bills, ordinances, or legislation of properly constituted law-making bodies. To say it another way, the common law is created by actions of the judicial branch, whereas statutes are created by the legislative branch of government. Common law, of course, can be created by court actions in which statutes are involved. This often happens when a court hears a controversy involving a statute and the result of the court action creates a new interpretation of the statute. Some examples of statutory action follow.

Incentives to install sprinklers. In 1980 the Alaska legislature enacted a law giving incentives to hospitality businesses to install sprinkler systems. The law allowed an exemption of 2 percent on property tax on the assessed value of the business property. In addition, this legislation encouraged lenders to lend money at reduced rates to encourage the installation of sprinkler systems at hotels, motels, and other hospitality and tourism operations.

Signage. One of the allures of the hospitality industry, especially to travelers who are seeking sleeping accommodations, are the welcome brilliant lights of signs that guide them to these accommodations. In designing the signs, however, legal issues must be considered.

1. Does the state have statutes that set standards for such signs? In Nevada, for example, room rates cannot be advertised on outdoor signs. In Florida, room rates can be placed on signs, but all details about double occupancy and other variations of prices must be included on the signs.

2. Are there city ordinances or county regulations that apply to proposed signs? Palm Springs, California, for example, has a longstanding ordinance that

prohibits use of the word "motel" on signs within the city limits. When Motel 6 wanted to operate a business in Palm Springs, the property name was changed to Hotel 6. The city council of Palm Springs, upon the urging of the Motel 6 organization, decided that travelers might consider that name to be a cheap imitation on Motel 6 that is recognized nationwide, and it allowed the name to be changed back to Motel 6 in spite of the city ordinance.

Moving from these examples, we encounter another classification of common law that varies from the previous classification.

Common and Civil Law

While common law exists because of court decisions, civil law exists solely because of legislative acts. Where we find a civil-law system, ancient Roman law has had an influence on that system. The law of Europe and South America alike is civil—a statutory or codified system as contrasted with one that uses precedent from case decisions to create new law. Thus a civil-law system operates primarily on statutes; a common-law system operates on case precedent.

Louisiana, Texas, California, and five other states follow a civil-law system. If a common-law state would reduce its law to a code (codification), it could become a civil-law state.

Public and Private Law

Public law affects us collectively as a people. This heading can be subdivided into constitutional law, administrative law, and criminal law. Private law, on the other hand, is law that relates directly to legal relationships between one individual and another. Examples include contract, tort, and property.

A ruling of a Public Service Commission is a public-law ruling. An interpretation of a constitutional principle—even if it concerns only one person—is also public. This is true because that interpretation will affect society *en masse* just as does the Constitution itself. If A kills B, that act is public in nature even though it is a highly personal matter to B. If C enters into a contract with D, or if E injures F in a car accident, those acts are private between C and D, and between E and F.

Substantive and Procedural Law

Substantive law is the substance of the law itself. Substantive law deals with rights, duties, and responsibilities. It may be a statutory or civil-law rule of law. It may be a common-law precedent. Statutes that set forth health regulations for lodging facilities are substantive. So are case decisions that establish liability standards for innkeepers. Likewise, rulings of an administrative agency are substantive because they are part of the matrix or substance of the law.

Procedural law, on the other hand, concerns matters *other* than substantive law. Here we encounter the methods by which lawsuits are started, the way wages are attached, and countless other matters of procedure including actions of administrative agencies as contrasted to their rulings.

One must look to substantive law to determine if a *cause of action* exists. This is the right to use a court in an attempt to obtain relief. If a cause of action does *not* exist, or if in the opinion of a lawyer it does not exist, then, in most instances, the matter ends there. If a cause of action does exist, or, if in the opinion of a lawyer there is at least a fair chance of success, one can begin to use procedural law in a court or before an administrative agency.

Procedural law includes filing suits, serving papers, calling jurors, serving subpoenas on witnesses, taking testimony in court and before agencies, enforcing judgments, and all of the other functions carried out by courts and administrative bodies. Procedural law may be thought of as the "machinery" of the legal system.

Contract Law

Contract law is the body of law that regulates the creation of private agreements between two or more parties. These agreements almost always arise from promises. These promises may be to build a theme park, to remodel a restaurant, or to serve as a manager in a travel agency. The promises may be to supply materials, to construct specially designed equipment, or to pave a parking lot.

The principal feature of a contract is that two persons, firms, or any combination of persons and firms have brought into play an obligation on the part of each that had no existence before the contract was made. Thus, a contract is a voluntary relationship.

Tort and Criminal Law

A tort is a negligent, careless, or deliberate act of one person that results in injury to another person, his or her reputation, the other person's property, or all three. The word evolved from the French word *torquere* which means "twisted" or wrong. The parties to a tort often do not intend for a tort to come into being; therefore, it is usually involuntary. An exception exists when one *intends* to harm another. In a deliberate assault by C on D, it can be assumed that C intended to injure D or the assault would not have occurred. Regardless of the intention, however, the assault or attack is a tort. Because the act was deliberate, it also would be a crime. A crime is some conduct that is recognized as being undesirable to society collectively. Therefore, criminal law involves duties owed to the state. For this reason, the state prosecutes those who commit crimes.

In the absence of intention to commit harm, torts are treated as violations of duties owed to the injured party. Thus, they are private between those parties. A owes a duty to the *state* not to rob B with a gun. C owes a duty to D not to operate his (C's) car in such a careless manner as to injure D. Thus, tort and crime can be distinguished by the duties owed.

Tort liability can arise in a variety of ways. *Negligence* is the most common basis upon which tort actions are based. Negligence, or neglect, is the failure to use due care in doing an act, such as driving a car. Or it can be the failure to do something that a reasonable person *should* have done under the same circumstances. An example is the failure to replace burned-out lights in a motel parking lot.

Many other grounds for tort actions are possible, and they will be discussed at appropriate places in later chapters.

LAW AND EQUITY

Law, as we have looked at it up to this point, is concerned with legal matters—matters of litigation in the law courts. Although equity is administered in the courts by judges, it is not "law" in the broad sense. A historical illustration will help put this into perspective.

A thousand years ago, the English courts used a writ system. This was a procedural arrangement whereby the litigants had to fashion their pending cases to match the available writs. There were writs in contract, tort, conversion, debt, covenant, and other areas that are still a part of our modern court systems. Today, they are called "common-law forms of action." In those early centuries a potential litigant often could not fit his or her case into one of the established writs. When this happened, there could be no court relief in that case. This was the old doctrine of "no writ, no remedy." In short, the law was deficient in certain areas.

At some point in history, such matters began to come to the attention of the King or Queen, who in turn would refer them to the spiritual advisor, the "chancellor." When the King or Queen began issuing orders based upon the chancellor's advice, "equity" was born. This became that side of our courts that deals in what is just or right—in short, what is equitable.

From the birth of equity, equitable actions were handled by the issuance of orders from an appropriate person. Today, the same is true, and all equitable matters are heard and decided by a judge sitting without a jury. Some examples of modern equity matters include specific performance (ordering one to do an act promised), rescission (canceling a contract), and injunctions (ordering someone to stop doing something).

If one refuses to obey an equitable order, that person can be held in "contempt of court" and may be jailed until the order is obeyed. Many courts today list their equity cases on the "chancery docket," a modern remembrance of the ancient chancellor who had a hand in the development of equity.

Today, most courts call both legal and equitable cases "civil actions," yet all modern courts handle equitable matters without a jury. Figure 2.2 presents a summary of the relationship of law and equity.

FIGURE 2.2   Law and equity.

		Purpose	**Who hears?**	**Enforcing rulings**
Civil actions	Law	To recover damages (dollars)	Jury and (or) judge	Levy of execution
	Equity	To force action or inaction	Judge (no jury)	Contempt of court

Because the historical role of equity was to cover areas of social and business conflict wherein the law was deficient or nonexistent, equity has been concerned with ethics, reason, what is fair and what is just.

When a court (judge) allows equity to come into play, equity overrides both common and statutory law. This is true because once the court decides that equity is the proper remedy for the issue at hand, law must step aside, as the court has given the nod to equity. On the other hand, the judges consistently hold that if a legal remedy is available, equity cannot intervene. The use of equity in our courts is a special remedy that will be used only when a legal remedy is not available. That squares up with the historical reason for equity coming into being centuries ago.

A situation that arose at a major hotel in Las Vegas will illustrate the difference between law and equity. On the weekend in question, an electronics show was in town and all hotel and motel rooms were sold out. A group of 100 persons with reservations arrived at the hotel and were informed that no rooms were available. Las Vegas is an isolated city; the closest rooms available would have been at Kingman, Arizona, or St. George, Utah, more than 100 miles away in each direction.

The travel agent traveling with the group contacted a Law Vegas lawyer who, by petition, brought the matter before one of the sixteen circuit judges in Las Vegas. This was done within a few hours. Upon seeing proof of the reservations, and upon posting by the travel agent of a suitable bond to protect the hotel, the court issued an order for the hotel to provide rooms for the group. This order was served on the hotel by the sheriff of the county, and guests in 100 rooms who had not had reservations, were forced out of the hotel. These guests had no alternative

FIGURE 2.3 Summary of legal classifications.

I. Contract law
  A. Conventional contracts
    1. Front-of-the-house contracts
      a. Room reservations
      b. Check-in
    2. Realty contracts
    3. Employment contracts
  B. Sales contracts, Article 2, UCC
    1. Back-of-the-house contracts
      a. Ordering supplies
      b. Buying food and drink
    2. Selling food and drink
II. Tort law
  A. Law of negligence
    1. Contributory negligence
    2. Comparative negligence
  B. Breach of common-law duty
    to receive
  C. Injury to person, property, or
    reputation

III. Law of business organizations
  A. Corporation law
  B. Partnership law
IV. Bailment law
  A. Gratuitous bailments
  B. Bailments for hire
  C. Professional and nonprofessional
    bailments
V. Treaties
  A. Warsaw Convention
  B. Travel compacts
VI. Criminal law
  A. Felonies
  B. Misdemeanors
  C. Petty offenses
    1. Assault
    2. Assault and battery
    3. Invasion of privacy
    4. False imprisonment
    5. Robbery

but to travel elsewhere. Equity was not available to them. The people with reservations thus used *equity* to gain admittance to the hotel. Those forced out then had the right to turn to *law* to recover money for their inconvenience and losses. This case was settled out of court for the purported sum of $500,000 paid to the 100 guests who were forced out. Thus, equity provides action; law provides money.

Figure 2.3 provides a synopsis of legal areas that are of concern to us now and later. Leaving our discussion of classifications of law, we will examine two cases so as to see these classifications in use.

CASE INTRODUCTION: OWEN CASE

In this case we see several of the classifications of law in use. First is the contract by which the old hotel structure was to be demolished. This was followed by the tort that damaged the restaurant. Then came the administrative action of the appraisers in setting values on the land and building. The matter went to a lower court in New Mexico and ended up in a higher court, where the error of the two lower courts was corrected. This was done by "directing a verdict" to a lower judge. This means that the lower court must do what the higher court has told it to do.

The case illustrates how something that started out as a routine business matter developed into a legal tangle. A good question to ask is, "How could the litigation have been avoided in the beginning?"

OWEN V. BURN CONST. CO.
563 P. 2d 919 (New Mexico 1977)

EASLEY, Justice.

Plaintiffs A. A. Owen and his wife, Rubye (Owen), owners of a restaurant building in Las Cruces, sued Burn Construction Company, Inc. (Burn) in damages for the negligent destruction of the building. The jury returned a verdict of $3,500 in favor of Owen. Both parties filed motions for judgment notwithstanding the verdict, and both motions were denied by the trial court. [This means that in spite of the verdict, neither party is satisfied with the verdict and wants it set aside, or adjusted to favor one or the other of the parties. In the usual case, only one party to a case makes this motion for the winning party is usually satisfied. This motion is seen in other cases under the abbreviation "N.O.V."—*non obstante verdicto.*]

Both parties appealed to the Court of Appeals and that court reversed the trial court, directing that judgment be entered in favor of defendant notwithstanding the verdict. Owen petitioned for *certiorari*. We reverse the Court of Appeals and the trial court.

Burn held a contract with Las Cruces Urban Renewal Agency (Agency) to demolish a two-story hotel building immediately adjacent to Owen's restaurant building. While the work was in progress part of the second story of the hotel toppled onto Owen's structure completely destroying its usefulness. The Agency agreed to complete the demolition of the Owen building and to remove the debris. Part of the agreement was that the action of the Agency in clearing Owen's lot would not prejudice Owen's right to seek damages against Burn for the destruction of the building.

Two months after the hotel collapsed on the Owen structure and after the debris had been removed, the Agency filed suit to condemn the vacant lot. The Agency and Owen stipulated to the entry of judgment whereby Owen would receive $59,072.00 for the vacant lot. The judgment signed by the court specifically set forth that the settlement was based on the value of the lot at the time the condemnation action was filed, i.e., without the building, and that the settlement would in no way affect any claim which Owen might have against Burn for the prior damage to the building.

Owen later filed this case against Burn to recover $26,000.00 in damages for the total destruction of the building. It was undisputed that the damage to the building was the fault of Burn. The evidence was also uncontested that the value of Owen's building at the time the damage occurred was $26,000.00.

On the theory that Owen had already been fully compensated by the Agency for both the lot and the building, Burn induced the trial court to take judicial notice of the entire file in the prior condemnation action. Over Owen's objections and in derogation of the express terms of the judgment entered pursuant to the stipulation of the parties, testimony and written opinions of the court-appointed appraisers were admitted into evidence to attempt to prove that the $59,072.00 appraised value included both the building and the land.

The jury returned a verdict for Owen in the inexplicable amount of $3,500.00. Both parties moved for judgment which motions were denied; judgment was entered; both parties appealed.

The Court of Appeals held that the trial court should have entered judgment n. o. v. in favor of Burn, and remanded with instructions to set aside the $3,500.00 judgment for Owen and to enter judgment for Burn. This court granted Owen's petition for writ of *certiorari*.

Owen makes three contentions: (1) the judgment in the condemnation matter was clear and unambiguous; therefore, it was error for the trial court to permit evidence which varied and contradicted the judgment and it was error for the court to refuse an instruction that the building had not been paid for in the condemnation case; (2) the admission of written appraisals made by persons who were not called as witnesses and were not subject to cross-examination was violative of N.M.R. Evid. 802 [§20-4-802, N.M.S.A. 1953 (Supp. 1975)]; and (3) the Court of Appeals' direction of a verdict for Burn was improper because the record shows that Owen was entitled to that relief.

Owen first contends that the two lower courts were in error in deciding that evidence of the condemnation suit and the appraisals made in conjunction therewith were admissible in this cause for the purpose of proving that Owen had already been paid for his building.

The consent judgment entered by stipulation of the Agency and Owen was in no way ambiguous. It provided:

> The compensation is based upon the value of the premises . . . on the date of the commencement of this action, and such award is not intended to affect any claim which the defendants, Owen, may have against any person, firm or corporation who may have damaged said premises prior to the commencement of this proceeding, and the stipulation on file herein and this judgment shall not constitute a settlement or release of any claim which the defendants may have by reason of damage that may have occurred to the condemned premises prior to the commencement of this action; . . .

The written stipulation that was filed was even more explicit as to the parties' intent that the $59,072.00 be considered payment for the vacant lot.

However, the trial court permitted testimony and written opinions from the appraisers that their evaluations in the condemnation suit included both the land and the building. The Court of Appeals held that the consent judgment was binding on the Agency and Owen but was not binding on Burn, that since the appraisers considered the value of the land and the building in arriving at their evaluations that Owen had already been justly compensated, that assessment of damages is the exclusive function of the jury and that "duplication of damages is not proper." We disagree that these principles of law are dispositive of the case.

It is true, as pointed out by the Court of Appeals, that a stipulated judgment is not considered to be a judicial determination; "rather it is a contract between the parties," *State v. Clark*, 79 N.M. 29, 439 P.2d 547 (1968); but this legal principle is not controlling and does not diminish the legitimacy of the claim or preclude the relief prayed for by Owen.

The rules to be followed in arriving at the meaning of judgments and decrees are not dissimilar to those relating to other written documents. Where the decree is clear and unambiguous, neither pleadings, findings nor matters *dehors* the record may be used to change or even to construe its meaning, *Chavez v. Chavez* 82 N.M. 624, 485 P.2d 735 (1971).

Considering this consent judgment as a mere contract between Owen and the Agency affords no comfort to Burn. "It is well settled in New Mexico that where the language of a contract is clear and unambiguous, the intent of the parties must be ascertained from the language and terms of the agreement," *Hondo Oil & Gas Co. v. Pan American Petroleum Corp.*, 73 N.M. 241, 245, 387 P.2d 342, 345 (1963). It is not the province of the court to amend or alter the contract by construction and the court must interpret and enforce the contract which the parties made for themselves.

[Citations omitted.]

In this case the words cannot be misconstrued; they spell out clearly that the parties intended that Owen should have the right to preserve this action against Burn for damages. There can be no legitimate claim of ambiguity; therefore, there was no need for the court to resort to evidence extrinsic to the agreement.

We are confronted with the specious reasoning of Burn, which corporation was not a party to the suit, that we should go behind the judgment and the specific stipulation signed by the parties and adopt unsworn testimony to emasculate these solemn documents. Who would know what was bought and sold and at what price better than the buyer and seller; and how much better can the bargain be sealed than by a lucid stipulation and judgment?

We hold that it was error to admit the evidence *dehors* the record to vary the terms of the judgment in condemnation; and, as a necessary corollary, we hold that it was error for the court to refuse Owen's instruction that he had not received compensation for his building in the first suit.

Owen claims that the trial court was in error in admitting into evidence written appraisals of the property in question without the appraisers being present for cross-examination. The trial court held that the evidence was admissible under N.M.R. Evid. 803(6), [§20–4–803(6), N.M.S.A. 1953 (Supp. 1975) as an exception to the hearsay rule because it was a record of a regularly conducted activity. The rule provides that a report setting forth an opinion in the course of a regularly conducted activity, "as shown by the testimony of the custodian or other qualified witness," is admissible even though the declarant is not available.

The evidence shows that the written appraisals were prepared for use in the condemnation proceedings, i.e., for purposes of litigation. The Agency did not prepare them but engaged outside parties, whom they did not supervise, to make the appraisals. The Agency would not vouch for the accuracy of the reports and did not know what factors were considered by the appraisers. The evaluation of one of the appraisers was based on the erroneous assumption that the building was forty years old rather than ten years old. There was no opportunity for Owen to cross-examine, the appraisers not being present at the trial.

Owen claims that the circumstances under which the appraisals were prepared and presented provide none of the circumstantial guarantees of trustworthiness which are normally required to justify an exception to the hearsay rule. We agree.

[Citations omitted.]

The prejudice inherent in the admission of such hearsay evidence is readily apparent. It is even questionable, although we need not decide, that the evidence qualifies as a "record of a regularly conducted activity."

Therefore, even if Burn had the legal right to challenge the efficacy of the judgment in question, the entire evidentiary basis of his challenge was inadmissible hearsay. The trial court and the Court of Appeals were in error in holding otherwise.

Owen's third issue on appeal is that the two lower courts were in error in failing to hold that Owen's motion for judgment n.o.v. should have been granted, and was in error in giving the same relief to Burn. We agree. The issues as to Burn are heretofore set forth. There is no rational basis to support the $3,500.00 verdict awarded by the jury. Furthermore, as to Burn's liability and the amount of $26,000.00 as the damages suffered by Owen there are no issues of material fact disclosed by the record.

In a case such as this where the evidence on an issue of fact is undisputed, and the inferences to be drawn therefrom are plain and not open to doubt by reasonable men, the issue is no longer one of fact to be submitted to the jury, but becomes a question of law. If reasonable minds cannot differ, then a directed verdict is not only proper but the court has a duty to direct a verdict.

We have no hesitancy in holding that reasonable minds could not differ as to the liability of Burn or as to the amount of damages, since there literally is no evidence disputing either of these factual issues. The same holding pertains to the wholly unsubstantiated award of damages in the verdict of the jury.

It necessarily follows that we dismiss the cross-appeal of Burn, reverse the Court of Appeals and the trial court on issues above indicated, affirm the Court of Appeals' decision ordering that the award to Owen of $3,500.00 be set aside, and direct that judgment be entered, notwithstanding the verdict, awarding Owen $26,000.00 in damages plus his costs.

IT IS SO ORDERED.

McMANUS, C.J., and SOSA and PAYNE, J.J., concur.

To conclude, we will examine an administrative-law case that was appealed to a state supreme court. It gives us a chance to see how administrative actions create "law" in the broad sense.

CASE INTRODUCTION: MARKANTONATOS CASE

Two brothers in Portland applied to the Oregon Liquor Control Commission for a license to sell alcoholic beverages at their restaurant. To qualify for the license, the brothers had to produce sufficient evidence to convince the commission that granting a liquor license would be "a judicious use" of the limited licenses that the commission could issue. The evidence they produced did not convince the hearings officer, however. The brothers then went before the commission, where the findings of the hearings officer were confirmed. The brothers then appealed to the courts in an attempt to overturn the ruling of the commission. They failed there, too, thus ending their restaurant venture.

As you read the case, pay close attention to the conclusions of the administrative agency, because these rulings create law. Also ask this question: What additional evidence might the brothers have brought before the commission to have increased their chances of getting the license?

MARKANTONATOS V. OREGON LIQUOR CONTROL COMMISSION
Oregon App. 562 P. 2d 570 (1977)

THORNTON, Judge.

Petitioners seek judicial review of the Oregon Liquor Control Commission's (OLCC) refusal to grant them a Dispenser Class "A" (DA) license for their restaurant, Zorba the

Greek. Petitioners assert that the OLCC's findings of fact and ultimate findings of fact are not supported by substantial evidence and that therefore the conclusions of law, on which the license refusal ultimately depends, are unsupported.

Petitioners at the hearing before the hearings officer introduced, in support of their application for a DA license, a petition signed by about 650 supporters, various documents indicating that petitioners' credit is sound, photographs of the decor of the restaurant, an Economic Analysis of the Portland Downtown Guidelines Plan conducted by a Portland consulting firm, a letter from the mayor of Portland indicating a need for more downtown liquor licenses and testimony by eight favorable witnesses. OLCC presented evidence in opposition in the form of testimony by three witnesses and the results of an informal survey.

After a hearing, the hearings officer recommended denial of a DA license. At the hearing before OLCC, the denial was affirmed based on the following ultimate findings of fact, which are generalized restatements of findings of fact, and conclusions of law:

"ULTIMATE FINDINGS OF FACT

"1. There is some opposition in the community to the issuance of the license, and there is likewise some support.

"2. The area in which applicants' outlet is located is heavily saturated with DA outlets, with seven in a radius of 1½ blocks. These outlets offer reasonably adequate service to the public. Applicants' witnesses referred in significant numbers to the shortcomings of only three of the outlets, and a generalized statement to the effect that 'all the outlets' in the area have similar problems does not adequately demonstrate that the witness was in fact aware of the existence of each of the seven outlets' names. The fact that three outlets in the area have replaced seven previously licensed is as indicative of lack of demand leading to the closure of the other outlets, as it is an opportunity for additional licenses in the area. Issuance of licenses to Rian's and L'Omelette was made on the basis of saturation at that time, together with all other factors present, and these outlets are more centrally located.

"3. A gross volume of food sales averaging approximately $60 a day is indicative of the lack of demand at the location, and the adequacy of present outlets to meet the public demand. A change of menu may possibly increase food sales, but the fact and extent of this change cannot be determined on the present record.

"4. Demand for Dispenser outlets in the downtown Portland core area in general may well continue to be present, and increase in the future, but there is no basis in the record that this demand requires an additional DA outlet at this time, or if so, such demand exists at applicants' specific location. The testimony of a small number of witnesses is not persuasive on the issue of demand by the entire public, especially when the sales of the establishment indicate that large numbers of persons choose not to patronize the outlet.

"5. The fact that the number of DA licenses in downtown Portland exceed its ratable allocation indicates that the citizens of the state would be better served by issuance of the license to establishments better able to serve a greater number of the citizens of the community and state.

"From the foregoing Findings of Fact, the following Conclusions of Law are entered:

"CONCLUSIONS OF LAW

"1. Seven premises licensed to serve liquor by the drink are available within a radius of 1½ blocks from applicants' premises, [10–715(1)].

"2. Applicants' low gross food sales indicate a lack of demand at that location, and the adequacy of the seven outlets mentioned previously to provide service to the public, [10–720(5)].

"3. The granting of a Dispenser license to applicants' outlet would not be a judicious use of the limited number of such licenses available statewide, [10–715(10)]."

***

Since the actual grounds for denial of the license in this case are the conclusions of law, findings of fact not relevant to those conclusions are superfluous and we need not consider them on appeal.

Petitioners maintain that the findings of saturation in the area and that other outlets adequately serve the public are not based on substantive evidence. The evidence is uncontroverted that there are seven DA licensed outlets within one and one-half blocks of applicants' premises. Applicants and six of their supporting witnesses testified that other establishments in the area generally provided bad service, were overcrowded and charged high prices. The OLCC found that the applicants had failed to establish that the other outlets were inadequate and gleaned the opposite conclusion from the testimony, i.e., the fact that the witnesses patronized the other establishments was evidence that the prices were not too high and the service was adequate. The applicants in this case did not introduce specific evidence tending to establish the inadequacy of other outlets in the area. The OLCC's conclusions that there is a heavy saturation in the area and that these outlets offer reasonably adequate service to the public, are rationally supported by the evidence.

Petitioners challenge the OLCC's findings on food sales but do not contend that they are not based on the evidence. They maintain that the average per-day food sales figure is misleading because petitioners are only open six days a week and not seven days a week. The commission's arithmetical method may have been questionable, but that does not affect the operative fact that the applicants' food sales are low and that fact led the OLCC to conclude that there is a lack of demand for a DA license at the subject location. The finding that applicants' food sales are low is supported by the evidence.

Petitioners also object to the commission's rejection of their argument that present food sales are not pertinent since petitioners intend to change their menu to offer specialty Greek cuisine which would, according to their testimony, increase food sales by 100 percent to 400 percent. The OLCC need not accept petitioners' speculative predictions.

Contrary to petitioners' argument, the OLCC's third conclusion of law referred to above was not a holding that the 1:2000 ratio (ORS 472.110(4)) precludes issuance of the license, but that issuance of the license to these applicants would not be judicious given low food sales and a saturation in the immediate area.

In their third assignment of error, petitioners maintain that the decision of the OLCC must be reversed because the members of the commission did not personally hear the case or consider the record, contrary to the provisions of former ORS 183.460. That portion of former ORS 183.460 on which petitioners rely was deleted from the statute by Oregon Laws 1975, ch. 759, §13, p. 2092, effective October 8, 1975. The final order in this proceeding was issued November 18, 1975. The requirement that the OLCC members personally consider the record before issuing a final order does not, therefore, apply in this case.

Affirmed.

Summary

The laws of ancient civilizations are a primary source of modern law since rules and regulations have always been necessary to regulate the affairs of human beings. In many instances, these early rules of law have not changed greatly but remain much as they were thousands of years ago. Statutory law, as created by legislative bodies over the centuries, is constantly being modified to meet the changing needs of society. Computer law, for example, was nonexistent a few decades ago, but today it is a very dynamic topic.

The two court cases contained in this chapter permit us to see the primary sources of law and their various classifications as they are used in our legal system. These cases demonstrate a vehicle by which various legal objectives can be sought. They also show that desired business goals are not always met when "law" is applied to them.

"Statutes" are the written laws that come into play at the local (courts/city), state, and federal levels. All such written laws must be in compliance with the U.S. Constitution.

The age-old doctrine of *stare decisis* is as important today as it has been over the centuries. When the judge allows a "decision to stand," precedent has been created; this in turn provides legal stability. The doctrine also allows judges to refuse to follow an undesirable precedent; thus, flexibility in the law is provided.

The role of administrative agencies, such as the Interstate Commerce Commission, is constantly expanding. These agencies can meet the expanding needs of society, such as in the computer area, and can do it a thousand times faster than the courts.

Eight states in the United States are civil law states meaning that their laws are based on statutes, ordinances, and other written law. The balance of the states are common law states and follow the precedents of case law. The common law system, by necessity, develops much slower than civil law systems.

Finally, we must distinguish between "law" and "equity." Cases brought in both law and equity are "civil actions"; this distinguishes them from "criminal actions" which have to do with punishment for the commissions of crimes.

QUESTIONS

1. What are some examples of *substantive* law and *procedural* law?
2. Why does a contract have to be voluntary? Why is a tort usually involuntary?
3. Can you give five examples of personal property and five of real property?
4. How can some modern rules of law be more than 1,000 years old and, in some instances, even much older?
5. How can a law be "unconstitutional"?
6. How can something be "unlawful" but *not* "unconstitutional"?
7. Why must a judge wait for a "justiciable controversy" (lawsuit) before a matter can be declared unconstitutional or unlawful?
8. What is an example of law-making in each of the three branches of government? (Make-up fictitious examples).

NOTES

1. U.S. Constitution, Article IV.
2. *McCullough v. Maryland*, 4 Wheat 316, 407, L. Ed. 579 (1819)
3. *Myers v. United States*, 272 U.S. 52.
4. Justice William O. Douglas, Eighth Annual Benjamin Cardozo Lectures, 1931.
5. *Las Vegas Sun*, Wednesday, March 2, 1994, p. 1B.
6. 759 S.W. 2d 914 (Tennessee App., 1988).

3

Lawyers, Judges, and Juries

OVERVIEW

OUR PURPOSE HERE is to learn enough about the legal role of lawyers, judges, and juries so as to give us a better understanding of the cases that we have seen and will be working with as we go along in our study.

The only time the typical citizen goes near a courthouse is as a party or witness to litigation or when called for jury duty. In these instances, which are infrequent, one finds himself or herself in a foreign world of armed guards, court reporters, jurors, and in an arena where the watchwords are "tort," *habeas corpus*, "depositions," "cross examination," and countless other unusual words. There is nothing comparable in our society, and thus there is no way to prepare oneself for it. It has just not been part of most people's lives, nor have we as a public been taught very much about the court system.

Cases are brought under the American *adversary process*, which means that for every lawyer who would seek money damages, another would just as forcibly deny that recovery. That brings judges, lawyers, and juries into the picture as these disputes go to court for resolution. It means that there are different points of view in the legal process. The plaintiff's (the party bringing the suit) lawyer sees things one way, the defense lawyer another. Quite frequently the judge disagrees with both, and what juries do is almost always unpredictable.

The interplay of the three—judge, jury, and lawyers—is a meshing of interests, and the results are often unsatisfactory. Such results are more often than not a detriment to the defendant (the one against whom litigation is brought). Let's learn something about lawyers.

LAWYERS

A lawyer is a person who is learned in the law: ". . . who, for fee or reward, prosecutes or defends causes in courts of records or other judicial tribunals of the United States, or of any of the states, or whose business it is to give legal advice in relation to any cause or matter whatever."[1] Thus, we see at the outset that lawyers function both in and out of court. In England and Australia, lawyers are divided into "solicitors" and "barristers." The former confine their legal activities to their offices and rarely are seen in court. The latter specialize in trial work.

Although there is no such formal distinction in the United States, as a practical matter we have "office lawyers" and "trial lawyers." Many of our 800,000-plus lawyers engage in both activities; others specialize in office consultation and some in trial work. A few have gained national reputations for criminal defense work, tort work, contract work, or other specific area of law.

About half of the American lawyers belong to the American Bar Association (ABA), and all practicing lawyers are members of their state bar associations. In addition, all states have local bar associations. Through these organizations, standards of conduct are established and rules of court procedure are developed.

Legal Profession Under Fire

In recent years, the profession has been subjected to closer scrutiny than ever before by the public, as well as by the courts. For example, the U. S. Supreme Court in *Goldfarb v. Virginia State Bar*, ruled that fee schedules of local bar associations are a form of price fixing and thus are illegal.[2] In addition, many of the practices of the profession have been challenged successfully, and this can be expected to continue in the future. Although considerable publicity has been directed toward lawyers who have plundered estates or who have been held to be incompetent in the courts, the vast majority of American lawyers are intelligent, honest, hard-working men and women, who give value for the fees they are paid.

Rules of Professional Conduct

The primary code is the Rules of Professional Conduct (RPC). Set forth in the RPC are detailed guidelines establishing standards of conduct for lawyers. Even though the RPC is a product of the ABA, which represents only about 50 percent of American lawyers, all lawyers are expected to comply with its standards. The supreme courts of most of our states have approved the RPC, in effect making it state law. Failure to comply with the rules can result in disciplinary action, such as a reprimand or, in severe cases, disbarment of the offending lawyer. Some states, such as West Virginia, have adopted a separate code to supplement the RPC.

Code of Professional Courtesy

The purpose of the Code of Professional Courtesy is to stress professionalism for all lawyers in the adopting states. The West Virginia Code has thirteen sections, and three of them follow.

1. My first obligation as a lawyer is to represent my client in a professional manner.

6. While my duty is to zealously represent my client, I will treat opposing counsel with courtesy and respect. I will refrain from unnecessary or unjustified criticism of the Court, my adversary or my adversary's client.

9. I recognize that professional courtesy requires promptness and attention to necessary detail. I will be punctual, both in Court and out. I will respond to telephone calls and correspondence in a timely fashion. I will make myself available to those whom I represent and to opposing counsel.

Services of Lawyers

Most of a practicing attorney's time is spent in the office. Consulting touches all phases of business and other activities and is perhaps the most important service the legal profession can provide. Proper legal advice, timely sought and wisely given, can avoid the necessity of going to court.

Lawyers who consult with business persons and others will admit that the necessity of using the courts often means that something went wrong along the way. Of course, if one's business is sued, it is necessary to use lawyers for defensive purposes. As part of the court function, lawyers will prepare the papers needed to start and defend lawsuits, research and prepare trial briefs, uncover evidence to be produced at trial, present and defend cases before judges and juries, and file appeals if they are warranted.

A Cause of Action

Before any lawyer will bring court proceedings in contract, tort, or property, it must be determined if a "cause of action" exists.

This is a legal phrase that lawyers use routinely, but others, unfortunately, often do not know what it means. "Causes" are reasons for which the legal system may be turned to for redress (compensation). Some examples are a breach of contract; a question involving ownership of property; a question involving injury or death of a guest, patron, or other person by negligence of the business in question; or a civil rights violation. "Action" involves legal steps available after it is determined that a "cause" exists. Some examples of "action" include:

1. Suit to recover for breach of a conventional contract.
2. Suit to recover for breach of a sales contract under Article 2 of the Uniform Commercial Code.
3. Suit to recover for a tort that results in injury to the plaintiff.
4. Suit to recover for losses related to property ownership.

Will the Lawyer Take the Case?

Once it is determined that there is a "cause of action," the question arises: Will the lawyer take the case? Lawyers do not automatically take each law or equity matter brought to them by potential clients. Many factors influence the decision of whether to take the case.

1. Was there a clear absence of care at the business where the person was injured? If proof on this point will be doubtful, the lawyer may decline to take the case.[3]
2. Was the injured party led to believe the premises were safe?
3. Is there more than an average possibility of prevailing for the plaintiff?
4. Were the actions of the injured person such that they substantially contributed to the loss?
5. Are ethical issues involved that go against the person wanting to sue?

Legal Fees

Once the decision by the lawyer is made to proceed, the question of cost arises. Before the Goldfarb case, it was a practice for local bar associations to publish and circulate "minimum bar fee schedules." The fees set forth were what would be charged for the services listed. For example, a name change might be $300, a will $200, and a deed $200. Now, because of the Goldfarb decision, lawyers charge what they think clients will bear, which is often *higher* than the minimum fees. A vestige of the minimum fees, however, remain in "flat fees."

Flat Fees

Certain legal services become so standardized that lawyers tend to charge a flat fee for them. This is true of adoption, divorce, and title-search fees. These often remain uniform in spite of the abolition of the fee schedules.

Hourly Fees

Many lawyers work on an hourly basis. At appropriate times the hours are billed at a rate that may begin at $100 per hour or may be much higher. Surprisingly enough, this is often the cheapest way that legal services can be provided. The client can obtain lawyer contact, split into a series of relatively short time periods, that may add up to only an hour or two. Administrative matters, such as OSHA or EEOC complaints, or worker's compensation matters, usually are best handled on an hourly basis.

In the much publicized 1994–95 O. J. Simpson criminal case, the defense lawyers reportedly charged Mr. Simpson $600 per hour minimum.

Retainers

Some business persons prefer to place lawyers on "retainers." A retainer is the "act of a client in employing his or her attorney or counsel, and also denotes the fee which the client pays when he [or she] retains the lawyer to work for him [or her], and thereby prevents the attorney from acting for his adversary."[4] Retainers can be general or special.

A *general retainer* gives one the right to expect legal services when requested. It binds the one retained not to take a fee from another that would be contrary to that retainer.[5]

A *special retainer* is an engagement for a designated purpose, such as to defend one on a criminal charge.[6]

Annual general retainers may run into the hundreds of thousands of dollars, or be as low as $100 in small-business situations. Their value is in gaining the assurance that the services of a particular lawyer or firm will be available if needed. If services are provided, the client will pay for services beyond the amount of the retainer.

Contingent Fees

Legal fees can be based upon the "contingency of recovery." These fees represent one of the more spectacular arrangements between lawyers and clients. These arrangements enable those who may not be able to afford an attorney to obtain legal representation.

These arrangements are encountered frequently in tort (negligence) cases but are seen in contract and property disputes. They are not permitted in criminal defense cases, however. There can be no monetary award beyond the fees agreed upon for criminal defense work. Public policy and court decisions in the past require this rule.

Contingent legal fees have led to some spectacular results. In the 1982 MGM fire case in Las Vegas, recoveries totaled $138 million, more than $41 million of which went for lawyers' fees.

Prepaid Legal Plans

One final way in which legal fees can be paid is by the use of prepaid legal service plans. These plans are a product of the 1970s. When they are in operation, covered employees contribute so much per hour, week, or month toward a prepaid legal service plan. This is matched by employer contributions. Funds are administered by a board of trustees usually made up of company employees elected for that purpose.

To implement these plans, prearrangements are made with specific lawyers in "closed plans" or the general bar in "open plans." The scope of the services available per year is spelled out, such as six hours of office consultation, one will, one contested court action. As an employee draws upon his or her plan, the fees are paid out of the fund. Some plans have deductibles. These plans have found wide acceptance and now can be bargained for collectively just as other fringe benefits.

Settling Legal Disputes

Once the attorney-client relationship is formed—which is much like the innkeeper-guest relationship in its formation, it is good legal business to make an honest attempt to settle the dispute. In attempting to settle, both before and after the litigation, papers are filed and served on the defendant. Lawyers are engaged in art involving human skills. Successful efforts in this regard can be of benefit to clients and have the practical effect of reducing the workload of the courts. Lawyers from both sides attempt to work out a mutually agreeable settlement, but if agreement cannot be reached, the court is available.

The Lawyer as a Means of Control

While the hotel, hospitality, and tourism industries have a legal obligation to regulate themselves, for protection of guests, patrons, third parties, and themselves as well, they often do not do so. Lawyers, through court actions on behalf of clients, can force compensation to be paid by the hospitality industry. Thus, the lawyer becomes an agency of control.

The lawyer who accepts cases will examine the marketing and delivery practices of the target business. In doing so, the lawyer will look for active or passive negligence, fraud, illegality, puffing, overreaching, breach of contract, and other actionable areas. If one or more of these has been involved, a cause of action exists and legal action may follow. It may come by a demand for payment, or it may come in a lawsuit that seeks compensation for loss or damage.

Through this *legal observation and action* process, the lawyer brings life to the law, as it is used to seek satisfaction for the client. Lawyers serve as watchdogs who remain passive when all goes well but who become active when things do not. Lawyer now have others to look to for legal assistance.

The Paralegal Movement

There has been a growing movement to delegate "lawyer-like" duties to non-lawyers. "Paralegals" are not secretaries but, rather, persons who have been trained to handle routine legal matters. They frequently are business-trained persons who have degrees from paralegal schools or who are provided special training by law firms. They are used to make investigations, to prepare corporate minutes and resolutions, to handle filing work in the courts, and to do legal matters that have become a drain on the lawyers' time. They do not try cases, except in limited situations. In California, for example, paralegals are permitted to make limited court appearances.

Some of the paralegal programs offered at the universities require a candidate to have completed an undergraduate degree in some other subject. Other programs do not have that requirement, and some are set up in training steps. Step one creates the "document technician," who is learning the basic requirements of the paralegal profession and performing clerical duties not required of secretaries. The second step comes when that person is accepted as an official paralegal and is given more duties to assume. The third step comes when a paralegal specializes at the law firm where he or she is employed and thus gains senior paralegal status.

JUDGES

Judges, while often lawyers, are given by law a position of power and consequent respect that rivals the governors of our states and even the president of our nation. The primary function of judges is to decide questions of law—for example, to determine what statutes apply to the case at hand.

Orders and Judgments

Although judges never can bring matters before themselves by unilateral action, once a controversy is there, they can hold hearings, issue orders, and render judgments.

When a court enters an *order* directing that something be done, that order must be obeyed. Failure to obey court orders permits judges to issue contempt citations in both legal and equitable matters. This can lead to a fine or imprisonment, or both. This power gives our courts "teeth" or power over the matters that come before them.

Other orders issued by the courts are routine, such as those that overrule motions, those that permit papers and motions to be filed, and many others. The nature of the judgment must be understood.

A *judgment* has been defined as "the official and authentic decisions of a court of justice upon the respective rights and claims of the parties to an action or suit therein litigated and submitted to its determination."[7] "The conclusion (of the judge) is a syllogism having for its major and minor premises issues raised by the pleadings and the proofs thereon."[8]

Forms of Judgments

Various forms of judgments are found in our courts, and a few follow.

1. A *confession of judgment* means that one admits the truth of the charges against her or him.

2. A *consent judgment* is one in which the parties have agreed upon the terms.

3. A *default judgment* is one entered by the court when one of the parties fails to defend the lawsuit.

4. A *final judgment* puts an end to a lawsuit.

5. An *interlocutory judgment* is of a preliminary nature, with something yet to be done in the court.

Following are some terms that relate to court judgments.

Judgment Terms

A *judgment book* is where judgments are recorded and indexed. A *judgment debtor* is one who has had judgment entered against him or her. A *judgment creditor* is the one to whom the judgment debt is owed. Judgments can be *in personam*, against the person, or *in rem*, against a particular thing or subject matter. The latter would take the form of a *judgment lien* against the property once the judgment is placed on record.

Turning from forms and terms of judgments, it is important to look at qualifications of judges as well as the legal reasoning applied by them in the courts.

Qualifications of Judges

The qualifications of judges vary from state to state, but most state constitutions establish minimum age and residency requirements. Most states require that judges be lawyers except, perhaps, at the municipal or city level. Yet here, judges frequently are found that are, in fact, lawyers. In the federal system, because judges must be nominated by the President of the United States and confirmed by the U.S. Senate, they must be lawyers or they would not be considered for appointment.

The state of Missouri has a bifurcated (split) system by which judges are first selected and later elected. This has been called the "Missouri Nonpartisan Court Plan." The governor fills all vacancies by appointments on the state supreme court, the court of appeals, and the circuit courts of Kansas City, Missouri, and the courts of St. Louis, Missouri. These judges then face the voters at designated times in a "yes" or "no" ballot as to whether or not to retain them.

Schools of Thought

Once on the bench, judges, federal and state alike, are influenced not only by their personal backgrounds by but the way in which they think as well.

Some judges give weight to the evolutionary process of ideas and prior case decisions. They tend to be influenced by history and custom and frequently do *not* exercise independent judgment.

Other judges are "natural-law" thinkers. These judges view humanity as a grouping of persons who seek ideal rights and justice and who are concerned about "good" and "evil." Law rests on reason and is something more than what humans made as law. The latter may be held by such a thinker to be unfair, unjust, or unreasonable. One who thinks this way may find ways to circumvent existing laws when rendering decisions.

An "analytical thinker" views law as something that is made up of rules and principles that the *state* thinks is mandatory for its citizens—even if those rules may seem unjust or unreasonable to the judge. One who is influenced by this type of thinking has a need for certainty, and law is considered to be a series of commands or orders from the state. Under this thinking, the less control by law, the wider latitude those in business have in which to conduct their affairs. If the state does not consider certain acts to be unjust, the judge will not interfere with those acts. These judges often say, "If that should be the law, then it is for the legislature to say so, not me."

Other judges are "sociological thinkers." To them, law is a means to an end, and it is a matter of striking a balance between conflicting interests. Law thus becomes a generalization and is based on experience.

Many judges are affected, of course, by different combinations of these schools of legal thought. This tells us that "law" often can be what a judge says it is. In practice, judges become identified with certain forms of thinking, and are sought or avoided by lawyers and litigants for that reason.

Judicial Notice

An important power the law allows judges to exercise is that of *judicial notice*. Earlier English courts recognized this principle, and it is now widespread in American law. This rule reduces the requirements of proof in court on both sides of an issue.

To illustrate, assume that a hospitality case is before a federal court in Massachusetts and that it involves an injury that occurred to a guest at an inn in Texas near the Louisiana border. The case is in the Massachusetts court on the grounds of "diversity jurisdiction": that is, the injured plaintiff is a resident of Massachusetts, while the inn in Texas is "diverse" [different] to the plaintiff. The plaintiff has chosen to bring suit in her home state, and she has the right to do this if the sum in controversy exceeds $50,000.

The issue now arises as to whether the inn is, in fact, in Texas. If it is in Louisiana, for example, the Massachusetts federal court would have to dismiss the case for lack of jurisdiction because the plaintiff has asserted in her lawsuit that the inn is in Texas. The court, which by common knowledge knows the inn is in fact located in Texas, can take judicial notice that it is there and, as a matter of law, cut off the need for formal proof of the location of the inn.

The doctrine of judicial notice came into play in a unique manner in California in 1991. A court (judge) there ruled that " . . . we take judicial notice that the immune systems of a substantial number of San Francisco residents have been compromised by alcoholism, cancer, HIV infection, and other diseases . . . ." The court then labeled those in the above categories as being a part of " . . . an at risk population. . . ."[9]

Before we leave judges, a few words are in order about the companion of both lawyers and judges in our courts: the jury.

JURIES

The word *jurata* in old English law referred to those persons chosen by their peers to hear and decide questions of fact in court. After being sworn to "truly try the facts," they would hear evidence from all parties involved and then "declare the truth" of the matter before them. The term "jury" today includes grand juries, trial or petit juries, coroner's juries, and others.

A jury is selected by the parties to the lawsuit and, at common law, was made up of twelve persons. Today the six-person jury is used in some states and in the federal courts in civil cases.

"Trial by jury" means a trial by the designated number of

> competent men and women, disinterested and impartial, not of kin, nor personal dependents of either of the parties, having their homes within the jurisdictional limits of the court, drawn and selected by officers free from all bias in favor of or against either party, duly empaneled and sworn to render a true verdict according to the law and the evidence."[10]

These are the *trial juries*, as contrasted to the grand juries, and their function is to decide "questions of fact," not law. The latter questions are reserved for the judge.

A *grand jury* is one that hears preliminary evidence in a pending criminal case and must decide if "probable cause" has been produced that shows that the person or business entity has committed a crime. If the grand jury so believes, it can return a *true bill*, known as an *indictment*. These juries do not decide questions of fact, because that is the function of the trial jury.

Once trial juries are selected, empaneled, and sworn, they will hear the evidence given to them by the testimony of witnesses. They will examine photos and other documents that the judge allows to "come into evidence" and will then decide questions of fact.

Fact Finders

The role of our trial or petit juries as "finders of fact" presents an interesting situation. If A claims that facts UV&W control the oral contract that he has entered into with B, but if B claims that facts XY&Z control, then a finding must be made of the "true facts." This is done by the presentation of evidence to the jury under the judge's guidelines.

It is often difficult to distinguish questions of fact, which must be decided by juries, from questions of law, which must be decided by judges.

Questions of Fact and Law

One of the fundamental tenets of the American legal system is that questions of fact must be decided by a trial jury—unless both parties agree to waive the jury—and questions of law must be decided by the court (judge). What is not as clear is what "questions of fact" and "questions of law" are.

In dispute resolution in courts, it becomes necessary to decide what the facts are in the case at hand. One side gives its version of what the facts are, and the other gives a different version.

Someone must determine which version to adopt, and that job historically has been given to the jury. When a jury says the facts are as the plaintiff claims, that decision controls the case. This is true even if the actual facts are as the defendant claims. This illustrates one of the hazards of litigating a matter before a jury.

Three examples of questions of fact are taken form *Whitley v. Hulon*.[11] The jury in that case had to answer these questions before the case could be concluded:

1. Should the restaurant operator have painted the edges of the stairs yellow inside the restaurant so the plaintiff, who fell, would have been more likely to have seen them?
2. Should handrails have been installed for patrons of the restaurant to use when going up and down the stairs?
3. Should warning signs have been erected at the top and bottom of the stairs?

Let's assume the jury answers "yes" to these questions. If these things had not been done at the restaurant, the jury can find that the restaurant is guilty of negligence.

Other questions of fact are: Is the plaintiff guilty of contributory negligence? Did the travel agent act in a reasonable manner with the traveler? Did the hotel fail to exercise reasonable care for the autos of guests parked at the hotel parking lot?[12] Should the business have discovered defects on the premises and warned of them? These questions must be answered by the jury.

Determination of the controlling law in each particular case is the job of the court (judge).

Legal Instructions by the Court (Judge)

Questions of law are determined in the following manner: The lawyers will submit to the judge their versions of what the controlling law should be. These versions usually are diametrically opposed to each other. It then is the job of the judge to decide which of these differing versions of the law should be read to the jury.

The instructions, called a *charge* in federal courts, then are read to the jury. Armed with the power to decide questions of fact, backed by the law as the judge has given it to them, the jury is allowed to deliberate and decide the case.

Following are examples of instructions given to a jury in two hotel cases.

1. The duty of the owner or operator of a business that is open to the public is to exercise reasonable care in keeping that part of the sidewalk in proper condition for the passage of customers rightfully using it.

2. The operator or owner of a parking ramp facility has a duty to use reasonable care to deter criminal activity on its premises. The care to be provided is that care which a prudent operator or owner would provide under like circumstances. Among the circumstances to be considered are the location and construction of the ramp, the feasibility and cost of various security measures, and the risk to customers which the owner or operator knows, or in the exercise of due care should know, presents a reasonable likelihood of happening. In this connection, the owner or operator is not an insurer of the safety of its premises and cannot be expected to prevent all criminal activity. The fact that a criminal assault occurs on the premises is not evidence that the duty to deter criminal acts has been breached.[13]

Once a jury decides a case by its "verdict," an appeal may be taken. If the upper court (appellate court) believes, from the record brought before it, that the case was presented fairly and impartially to the jury, the upper court seldom will set aside that verdict or amend it.

In that way, the higher court gives recognition to the work done by the trial jury. On the other hand, if the trial jury is misled or makes errors of its own, the upper courts have a duty to make necessary adjustments leading to justice in the matter at hand.

CASE INTRODUCTION: FREEMAN CASE

In the case that follows, a New York lawyer attempted to use an 1883 statute to force an innkeeper to forfeit treble damages. The theory was that the guest was not provided the services under the minimum-period contract between the parties. Recovery was denied, however, as explained by the judge. The case does contain a good discussion of the evolution of the laws of innkeeping and should be read carefully.

FREEMAN V. KIAMESHA CONCORD, INC.,
76 Misc. 2d 915, 351 N.Y.S. 2d 541 (1974).

SHANLEY N. EGETH, Judge

The Statutory Language

The relevant portion of General Business Law Sec. 206, reads as follows:

> . . . no charge or sum shall be collected or received by any . . . hotel keeper or inn keeper for any service not actually rendered or for a longer time than the person so charged actually remained at such hotel or inn . . . provided such guest shall have given such hotel keeper or inn keeper notice at the office of his departure. For any violation of this section the offender shall forfeit to the injured party three times the amount so charged, and shall not be entitled to receive any money for meals, services, or time charged.

The Facts

Plaintiff, a lawyer, has commenced this action against the defendant, the operator of the Concord Hotel (Concord), one of the more opulent of the resort hotels in the Catskill Mountain resort area, to recover the sum of $424.00. Plaintiff seeks the return of charges paid at the rate of $84.80 per day for two days spent at the hotel ($169.60) plus three times said daily rate ($254.40) for a day charged, and not refunded after he and his wife checked out before the commencement of the third day of a reserved three-day Memorial Day weekend. Plaintiff asserts that he is entitled to this sum pursuant to the provisions of Sec. 206, General Business Law.

The testimony adduced at trial reveals that, in early May 1973, after seeing an advertisement in the New York Times indicating that Joel Gray would perform at the (Concord) during the forthcoming Memorial Day weekend, plaintiff contacted a travel agent and solicited a reservation for his wife and himself at the hotel. In response he received an offer of a reservation for a "three-night minimum stay" which contained a request for a $20.00 deposit. He forwarded the money confirming the reservation, which was deposited by the defendant.

While driving to the hotel the plaintiff observed a billboard, located about 20 miles from his destination which indicated that Joel Gray would perform at the Concord only on the Sunday of the holiday weekend. The plaintiff was disturbed because he had understood the advertisement to mean that the entertainer would be performing on each day of the weekend. He checked into the hotel notwithstanding this disconcerting information, claiming that he did not wish to turn back and ruin a long anticipated weekend vacation. The plaintiff later discovered that two subsequent New York Times

Advertisements, not seen by him before checking in, specified that Gray would perform on the Sunday of that weekend.

After staying at the hotel for two days, the plaintiff advised the management that he wished to check out because of his dissatisfaction with the entertainment. He claims to have told them that he had made his reservation in reliance upon what he understood to be a representation in the advertisement to the effect that Joel Gray would perform throughout the holiday weekend. The management suggested that, since Gray was to perform that evening, he should remain. The plaintiff refused and again asserted his claim that the advertisement constituted a misrepresentation. The defendant insisted upon full payment for the entire three-day guaranteed weekend in accordance with the reservation. Plaintiff then told the defendant's employees that he was an attorney and that they had no right to charge him for the third day of the reserved period if he checked out. He referred them to the text of Sec. 206, General Business Law, which he had obviously read in his room where it was posted on the door, along with certain other statutory provisions and the schedule of rates and charges. The plaintiff was finally offered a one-day credit for a future stay, if he made full payment. He refused, paid the full charges under protest and advised the defendant of his intention to sue them for treble damages. This is that action.

Subsidiary Issue: The Claimed Misrepresentation

I find that the advertisement relied upon by the plaintiff did not contain a false representation. It announced that Joel Gray would perform at the hotel during the Memorial Day weekend. Gray did actually appear during that weekend. The dubious nature of the plaintiff's claim is demonstrated by the fact that when he checked in at the hotel he had been made aware of the date of Gray's performance and remained at the hotel for two days and then checked out prior to the performance that he had allegedly travelled to see.

The Claimed Violation of Sec. 206

We now reach plaintiff's primary contention. Simply put, plaintiff asserts that by requiring him to pay the daily rate for the third day of the holiday weekend (even though he had given notice of his intention to leave and did not remain for that day), the defendant violated the provisions of Sec. 206, General Business Law, and thereby became liable for the moneys recoverable thereunder. Plaintiff contends that the language of the statute is clear, and that under its terms he is entitled to the relief sought irrespective of whether he had a fixed weekend, week, or monthly reservation, or even if the hotel services were available to him.

It must be noted at the outset that the plaintiff checked into the defendant's hotel pursuant to a valid, enforceable contract for a three-day stay. The solicitation of a reservation, the making of a reservation by the transmittal of a deposit, and the acceptance of the deposit constituted a binding contract in accordance with traditional contract principles of offer and acceptance. Unquestionably the defendant would have been liable to the plaintiff had it not had an accommodation for plaintiff upon his arrival. The plaintiff is equally bound under the contract for the agreed minimum period.

The testimony reveals that the defendant was ready, willing, and able to provide all of the services contracted for, but that plaintiff refused to accept them for the third day of the three-day contract period. These services included lodging, meals, and the use of the defendant's recreational and entertainment facilities. In essence, plaintiff maintains that under the terms of the statute, his refusal, for any reason, to accept or utilize these facilities for part of the contract period precludes the defendant from charging him the contract price.

Section 206 is silent as to its applicability to circumstances which constitute a breach of contract or a conscious refusal to accept offered services. This is one of those instances in which, upon analysis, a statute which appears to be clear and unambiguous is sought to be applied to a situation not envisioned by its framers. Nothing contained in the statute provides assistance in answering the question presented in this case, i.e., may a resort hotel hold a guest to his contract for a stay of fixed duration when that guest has, without cause, breached his contract.

In 1883, the year of statutory enactment, transportation in our nation was slow and limited. Few persons travelled great distances for the sole purpose of recreation and pleasure. Small inns proliferated the countryside, frequented by travellers requiring rest and sustenance during the course of long and arduous journeys. Such travellers might briefly stay at a convenient inn along their route, refresh themselves, and continue on to their destination. Too often, they had limited choices en route and frequently the traveller would be easy prey to unscrupulous innkeepers, who might exact unreasonable charges and enforce collection via a friendly constable and utilization of the innkeepers' lien.

Section 206 was enacted to provide some protection against such exploitation.

The automobile, fast trains, and air transportation, a developing affluent and mobile society in which an increasing number of people began to seek diversion and recreational regeneration in utilizing their expanded leisure time, have resulted in a total transformation of the nature of modern hotels.

A vast hotel and recreation industry has since developed to meet the expanding needs of our citizenry. Most resort complexes were created to cater to various recreation inclinations. Our countryside is presently dotted with countless enterprises ranging from the simple and primitive campsite or bungalow to the most luxurious and opulent hotel, providing a quality of accommodation, food and recreational facilities unavailable to even the very rich of ninety years ago. All of these enterprises compete for public patronage. Even the most expensive are frequented by persons of modest means who find they can afford to indulge themselves for periods of limited duration.

Adoption of plaintiff's statutory construction in this case would have far-reaching consequences with impact well beyond this case or this defendant. Changes during the past 90 years have transformed the conditions which required urgent redress by statutory enactment in 1883, into a rarity in the year 1973. Absurd results would follow were the statute to be literally and strictly construed in the manner urged by plaintiff. The statute could then become an instrumentality for the infliction of grave harm and injustice, rather than a buffer or shield against the activities of rapacious hotelmen. Plaintiff's construction would create the anomaly of rendering a proper contract illusory while unjustly continuing to obligate only one of the parties to the performance of the contract. The defendant, and most similarly situated hotel keepers have utilized their minimum reservation contracts as a means of achieving economic survival. Chaos and financial disaster would result from the invalidation of such agreements.

A hotel such as the defendant's services thousands of guests at a single time. The maintenance of its facilities entails a continuing large overhead expenditure. It must have some means to legitimately ensure itself the income which its guests have contracted to pay for the use of its facilities. The minimum-period reservation contract is such a device. The rooms are contracted for in advance and are held available while other potential guests are turned away. A guest who terminates his contractual obligations prior to the expiration of the contract period will usually deprive the hotel of anticipated income, if that guest cannot be held financially accountable upon his contract. At that point, replacement income is virtually impossible. Indeed, on occasion, some hotels contract out their entire facilities to members of a single group for a stipulated period many months in advance. No great imagination is required to comprehend the economic catastrophe which would ensue if all such guests were to cancel at the last minute or to check out prior to the end of their contract period without continuing contractual liability. I cannot believe that the public policy of the state sanctions such contractual obliteration.

The construction sought by the plaintiff could result in other consequences which are equally bizarre. The defendant has contracted to supply the plaintiff with a room, three meals a day, and access to the use of its varied sports, recreational or entertainment facilities. As long as these are available to the plaintiff, the defendant has fulfilled its contractual commitment. If the plaintiff's construction of the statute is tenable, he might also argue with equal force that unless a guest receives an appropriate rebate or adjustment of bill, the defendant would incur statutory liability, if such guest visited a friend in the vicinity;

slept over and failed to use his room for one or more nights of his contracted stay; became enmeshed in an all-night game of cards and failed to use his room; was dieting and failed to avail himself of all the offered meals; did not play tennis, golf, or swim; or became sick and made no use of the available recreational or entertainment facilities.

I conclude that plaintiff may not recover because he has not proved a cause of action based upon a violation of Section 206 of the General Business Law. The evidence does not prove the existence of the type of wrong for which redress was provided in the 1883 enactment. The statute was not intended to prevent a hotel from insisting that its guests comply with the terms of a contract for a fixed minimum stay. There can be no statutory violation by a hotel which fulfills its part of the contract by making its services and facilities available to a guest who refuses to accept them. Such act of refusal by the guest does not justify imposition of the penalties set forth in the statute.

Judgment is accordingly awarded to the defendant with costs.

The Freeman case represents a small legal incident in New York state, yet it allows us to examine three legal situations that innkeepers often encounter in the operation of their businesses.

1. First, examine Figure 3.1. Because the hotel had a minimum reservation requirement on weekends, Freeman made a reservation for the three-day weekend and sent a $20 deposit payment. After checking in and finding that the singer would not perform each of the three evenings, he checked out after two days. He then sued under the statute prohibiting innkeepers from receiving funds for services not actually provided, which statute allows for treble damages.

FIGURE 3.1   Freeman case: First situation.

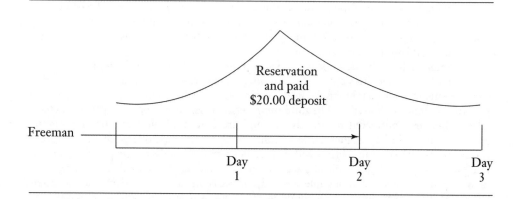

If, after Freeman checked out, the hotel had sold the room to another, Freeman then would have a valid claim for a refund of the applicable portion of his payment. If the hotel was unable to sell the room, the hotel would be entitled to keep his payment for all three days even though the room sat empty for the last day. This represents the first situation.

2. Change the facts now to show that Freeman made the three-day reservation and deposit but never showed up at all. Examine Figure 3.2.

FIGURE 3.2   Freeman case: Second situation.

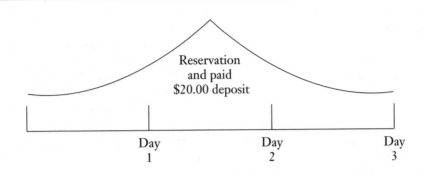

Now the hotel has a duty to "mitigate"—to keep down the damages for the benefit of Freeman. This means the hotel must make a good-faith effort to sell the room to someone else. If the hotel succeeds in doing so, Freeman need not pay for the three nights. If the room cannot be sold, the hotel is entitled to be paid for the unsold days. This then leads to a third possible situation.

3. There was no minimum stay involved, and Freeman reserved his room for one day only and paid for one day in advance. Examine Figure 3.3.

FIGURE 3.3   Freeman case: Third situation.

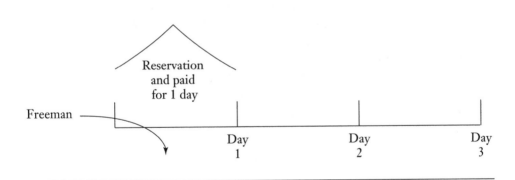

After checking in and finding that the singer would not be available over the three-day period, Freeman checked out. The legal relationship between Freeman and the hotel has ended, and nothing is left to be settled between them.

SUMMARY

Three entities and persons make the legal system function: lawyers, judges and juries. In practice, each performs distinct functions, but become joined in the ultimate conclusion of disputes in the courts.

An important concept to remember is the difference between "law" and "fact." If a certain activity is a crime in a given state, it is a question of "law" to be handled by a judge. Whether or not a certain person violated that law is a "question of fact" that must be decided by a jury.

The standard of conduct that American lawyers must measure up to is of the highest order. This is facilitated by a variety of codes and rules which are enforced on local levels by bar associations working with local judges, at the state level by state bar associations working with the top court of state, and at the national level by the United States lower courts working in concert with the United States Supreme Court. Finally, the subject of how lawyers charge for their services has gone through a variety of changes as the years have gone by. A topic under discussion is the *size* of fees that lawyers charge by the hour. Rates of $500 per hour, and higher, are not uncommon.

QUESTIONS

1. Do American lawyers have anything in their legal system that compares to England's barristers and solicitors?
2. How could the determination of a question of fact in a court case be just the opposite of what acutally happened?
3. What practical effect should the Code of Professional Courtesy have on lawyers in the states that adopt it?
4. What is an example of a special retainer? A general retainer?
5. Why might a plaintiff complain about a contingent-fee arrangement?
6. What is the difference between a grand jury and a petit jury?
7. Trial juries are triers of the law, not the facts. True or false.
8. Why do appellate courts tend to refuse to meddle with jury verdicts in the absence of error?
9. Why might the giving of instructions orally by a judge be misunderstood by one or more jurors?
10. What was the legal problem with minimum bar fee schedules?

NOTES

1. Act of July 13, 1866, sec. 9, 14 St. at Large 121.
2. *Goldfarb v. Virginia State Bar*, 421 U.S. 773 (1975).
3. *Schroyer v. McNeal*, 581 A. 2d 472, (Maryland 1990).
4. *Bright v. Turner*, 205 Ky. 188, 265 S.W. 627, 628.
5. *Rhode Island Exch. Bank v. Hawkins*, 6 R.I. 206.
6. *Agnew v. Wolden*, 84 Ala. 502, 4 So. 672.
7. *Bullock v. Bullock*, 52 N.J. Eq. 561, 30 A. 676, 27 L.R.A. 216.
8. *Barlow v. Scott*, Mo. sup., 85 S.W. 2d 504, 517.
9. *Kilpatrick v. Superior*, 277 Cal. Rptr., (California 1991).
10. *Shafer Motor Freight Service*, 4 N.Y.S. 2d 526, 167 Misc. 681.
11. 390 S.E. 2d 598, (Louisiana 1990).
12. *Atkins v. Glens Falls*, 424 N.E. 2d 531, (New York 1989).
13. *Erickson v. Curtis Co.*, 447 N.W. 2d 165, (Minnesota 1989).

4

Court Application of HH&T
Cases and Statutes

OVERVIEW

WE WANT TO learn more about legal liability and what it can mean when it arises. In this chapter we will examine the application of a state statute in two federal court actions. We will then look at a wrongful death case brought against an inn under common-law principles.

As each cause of action goes into our judicial system, it becomes known as a case or lawsuit. A court has said that " . . . the word "case" or "cause" means a judicial proceeding for the determination of a controversy between parties wherein rights are enforced or protected, or wrongs are prevented or redressed."[1] The amount in controversy is not always a determinative factor, and this should be understood. Our American courts will give the same attention to the small cases as they will to the large ones.

The phrase "cases and controversies" is found in the U. S. Constitution. It means " . . . controversy of a justiciable nature, excluding advisory decrees on hypothetical facts."[2] A "case sufficient to go to a jury" is one that " . . . has proceeded upon sufficient proof to that stage where it must be submitted to jury and not decided against the state (or other) as a matter of law."[3]

At some trial-court levels, and at the appellate level of most state and all federal courts, case decisions are reduced to typed form. Afterward, these decisions are placed into printed volumes, as will be explained in a moment. Once in printed form, they are available to the public, and wide use is made of them by law schools, hotel schools, lawyers, agencies, judges, and others. Thus the "case study" of law is one that makes use of the decisions found in printed volumes: a "reporter system."

REPORTER SYSTEM

West Publishing Company has divided the United States into "reporter regions." This company accumulates the decisions from all appeals courts in these regions and places them in bound volumes. The reporter areas are as follows:

ATLANTIC (A.)
Connecticut, Delaware, District of Columbia, Maine, Maryland,
New Hampshire, New Jersey, Pennsylvania, Rhode Island,
and Vermont

NORTHEASTERN (N.E.)
Illinois, Indiana, Massachusetts, New York, and Ohio

NORTHWESTERN (N.W.)
Iowa, Michigan, Minnesota, Nebraska, North Dakota, South Dakota, and Wisconsin

PACIFIC (P.)
Alaska, Arizona, California, Colorado, Hawaii, Idaho, Kansas, Montana, Nevada, New Mexico, Oklahoma, Oregon, Utah, Washington, and Wyoming

SOUTHEASTERN (S.E.)
Georgia, North Carolina, South Carolina, Virginia, and West Virginia

SOUTHWESTERN (S.W.)
Arkansas, Kentucky, Missouri, Tennessee, and Texas

SOUTHERN (SO.)
Alabama, Florida, Louisiana, and Mississippi

In addition, New York has the *New York Supplement* (NYS), and California the *California Reporter* (Cal. Rep.). These extra reporters were created because of the large volume of litigation carried out in those states.

At the federal level are found the *Federal Supplement* (F. Supp.) that reports some, but not all, of the decisions of the federal district courts; the *Federal Reporter,* which reports cases in the U. S. Courts of Appeal; and the *Supreme Court Reporter,* whose name tells us what cases it contains.

Legal Research

To make use of the immense body of cases, which grows larger each day, one must understand something about legal research. As one begins to search for relevant cases, one has to identify areas in which the search should be conducted. This is done by use of the TAP rule: things, acts, and places. To illustrate, a guest is injured by a dog kept in an adjoining room of an inn. The guest seeks legal advice and the lawyer wants to know if the innkeeper is liable. "Things" include pets, animals, injury to inn guests, and others. "Acts" include animals, travel, boarding of animals, innkeepers liability, and others. "Places" include motels, hotels, inns, and lodging facilities. Armed with TAP, the lawyer can use the indexes to cases, reporters, and other legal treatises to find cases and thus establish the extent of legal liability if any, as developed by prior case law. Students can also use the TAP rule when writing papers and reports.

Also, appropriate statutory law will be researched. These are found in the state codes and annotations that accompany each statute. The latter are citations to cases that have been decided involving the statutes. Through this process, items may be found that lead to other sources. Legal research is one of the arts of the legal profession, and case citations become of key importance in this process.

A Case Citation Example

Case citations tell where a printed case may be found. Consider the following citation: *Gray v. Zurick Hotel Co.*, 65 Cal. 2d 263, 419 P. 2d 168, 54 Cal. Rep. 104 (1966).

The title tells us the names of the parties to the lawsuit. It does not indicate which party is the plaintiff or defendant, as the names may be reversed, depending upon who takes the appeal. The case can be found in the *California Reports*, second series, volume 65, beginning on page 263. It also can be found in the *Pacific Reporter*, Second Series, volume 419, beginning on page 168, as well as in the *California Reporter*, volume 54 beginning on page 104. The case was decided in 1966. Figure 4.1 clarifies this.

FIGURE 4.1   Case citation example.

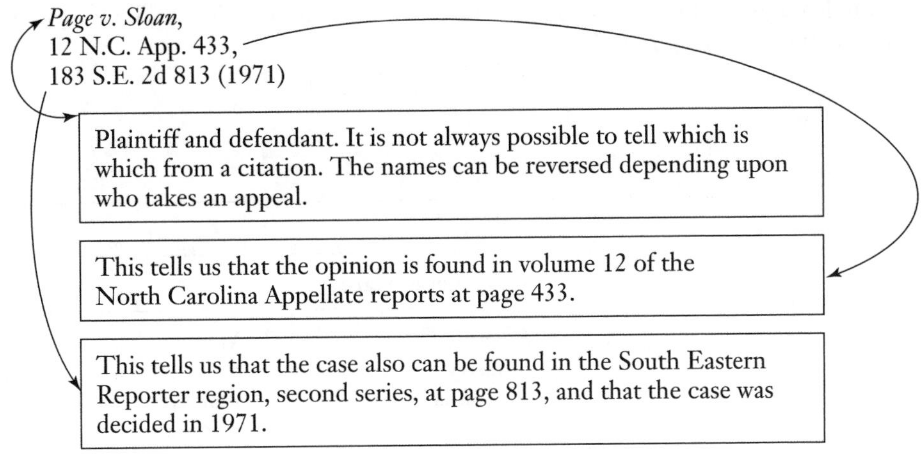

Page v. Sloan,
12 N.C. App. 433,
183 S.E. 2d 813 (1971)

Plaintiff and defendant. It is not always possible to tell which is which from a citation. The names can be reversed depending upon who takes an appeal.

This tells us that the opinion is found in volume 12 of the North Carolina Appellate reports at page 433.

This tells us that the case also can be found in the South Eastern Reporter region, second series, at page 813, and that the case was decided in 1971.

Case Briefs

To assist in understanding cases, it is good policy to create a brief for each by writing out the answers to the following questions:

1. What was the citation of the case?
2. In what state or federal court was it decided?
3. *Briefly* state the facts of the case. (How or why did it get into court?)
4. What was the decision of the court?
5. How could this decision be summarized so that it could be stated as a point of law in one short sentence?

Briefs have the practical effect of enabling one to recall the main points of a case at a future time.

Standards

Cases that are created in our courts become an extremely valuable source of legal information to us. This is especially true in the HH&T industry, and it is useful at this point become acquainted with legal standards that have been created by case decisions.

Reasonable Care

The primary standard we must meet is that of "reasonable care." This standard can be:

1. Set forth in statutes.
2. Created and followed by a particular industry.
3. Created by the common law (court case decisions).

Meeting the first two reasonable standards in a given situation may not be enough, leaving the business exposed to a claim of common law negligence. This is demonstrated in Figure 4.2.

FIGURE 4.2   Reasonable care standards.

	Reasonable Care		
Degree of Care	1. Meeting statutory requirements	2. Meeting industry standards	3. Meeting common law standards
	May not be enough →		
		May not be enough →	
			May also be required →

It is basic law that an industry cannot adopt careless reasonable standards to save time or money and thus establish its own "uncontrolled standards." The standards of care must be ". . . compared to that of the reasonably prudent [business] owner, not that of a similarly negligent one . . . ."[4]

In *Small v. McKennan*, the court ruled that a business cannot be careless in an attempt to save money and then claim that its level of care should be adopted in deciding whether it was negligent. Rather, the court pointed out that the standard was one of reasonable care—what a reasonable business person would do under the same or similar circumstances.[5]

The reasonable care standard (with the limitations for money and valuables) which has prevailed in all of our states for more than 130 years often is defined now by the "foreseeability" risk in taking certain actions. This subject is discussed in detail later. In addition, the courts now are talking about "discoverability": the duty not only to foresee but also to look actively for dangers at the inn.

The idea of foreseeability is in contrast to the idea of "direct causation," both of which relate to the proximate cause of a defendant's action. The direct causation concept (which is not followed the way foreseeability is) leads into the insurer status, as a lawsuit that results because of negligence, no matter how unforeseeable, is the defendant's responsibility.

Proximate Cause

Closely related to the reasonable care doctrine is the principle of "proximate cause." We will explore this in detail later, but it is helpful to become familiar with the concept here.

At times one can be negligent (fail to use reasonable care) and still be excused from legal liability. It has to do with proximate cause, and it works like this:

First, there must be a "primary actor." Next, the primary actor is negligent in some manner—for example, failing to upgrade room locks. A jury now must decide if the negligence was the proximate (actual) cause of the loss—for example, a theft of the guest's goods from the room. If so, the primary actor must pay.

If there is a "secondary actor," such as a thief who steals from a guest's motel room by use of an extra room key, and if this theft is unforeseeable, the causation has been broken and the primary actor is excused as a matter of law. Figure 4.3 illustrates proximate cause. The legal elements of proximate cause are (1) cause in fact, and (2) legal liability.

FIGURE 4.3   Proximate cause.

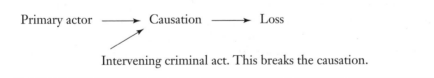

Intervening criminal act. This breaks the causation.

Words: How the Courts Look at Them

In the case-making process in court, judges constantly engage in the interpretation of words—and indeed in the creation of new words themselves. A decision of the Supreme Court of North Carolina, June 13, 1990, provides insight into how courts view the meaning of words when rendering decisions. At issue was a motorist found guilty of "driving while impaired" after visiting several inn bars. North Carolina General Statutes, Sec. 20–139.1 (b3), uses the word "readings" in reference to breathalyzer tests given to suspected drunk drivers. The argument of the convicted driver was that "readings" did not mean the same thing as "results" recorded by a state chemical analyst. The court rejected this argument.[6]

Leaving the subject of court cases, let's turn to statutes, or acts of legislation.

STATUTES

To illustrate what a statute looks like, and to see how some of them are used in the lodging industry, examine Figure 4.4.

Will a Statute Survive in Court?

Several things can happen to a statute after it is enacted by a legislature.

1. The courts may apply the statute and, thus, achieve the purpose of the legislature.
2. The statute may be "watered down" by court interpretation. In this instance, the court applies its understanding of what the words of the statute say, which may be different from what the legislature intended the words to mean.
3. The courts may "abrogate," or abolish the statute by finding that it is illegal or unconstitutional, giving it no legal effect.

When courts find that statutes are properly in effect, the matter of complying with those statutes comes to the front.

Statutory Compliance, Negligence per se, and Common Law Negligence

Failing to comply with a statute can be negligence *per se* (in itself). Yet, strictly complying with a statute may still leave a business liable for common-law negligence. This could happen in a situation where the statute itself did not meet the standard of reasonable care. In the same light, strictly following a standard of the hospitality industry also may not be enough to meet the standard of reasonable care.

"A statute or regulation merely sets a floor of due care . . . . Circumstances may require greater care, if [an inn] knows or should know of other risks not contemplated . . . " by the statute or even by a trade standard.[7]

Next, let's find out something about the place where cases originate, the courts.

COURTS

A court has been defined as

> . . . a tribunal officially assembled under authority of law at the appropriate time and place for the administration of justice;[8]

> . . . an agency of the sovereign created by it directly or indirectly under its authority, consisting of one or more officers, established and maintained for the purpose of hearing and determining issues of law and fact regarding legal rights and the alleged violations thereof, and of applying the sanctions of law, authorized to exercise its powers in due course of law at times and places previously determined by lawful authority.[9]

FIGURE 4.4   Sample state statute.

CODE OF VIRGINIA
Sec. 35-10—Duties of Inn-Keepers; Limitation of Liability

It shall be the duty of keepers of hotels, inns, and ordinaries to exercise due care and diligence in providing honest servants and employees, and to take every reasonable precaution to protect the person and property of their guests and boarders. No such keeper of hotel, inn or ordinary shall be held liable in a greater sum than three hundred dollars, for the loss of any wearing apparel, baggage or other property not hereinafter mentioned, belonging either to a guest or boarder, when such loss takes place from the room or rooms occupied by said guest or boarder, and no keeper of a hotel, inn or ordinary shall be held liable for any loss by any guest or boarder of jewelry, money or other valuables of like nature belonging to any guest or boarder if such keeper shall have posted in the room or rooms occupied by guests or boarders in a conspicuous place, and in the office of such hotel, inn or ordinary a notice stating that jewelry, money and other valuables of like nature must be deposited in the office of such hotel, inn or ordinary unless such loss shall take place from such office after such deposit is made. The keeper of any such hotel, inn or ordinary shall not be obliged to receive from any one guest for deposit, in such office, any property hereinbefore described, exceeding a total value of five hundred dollars.

Sec. 35-11—Liability Where Guest Failed to Lock or Bolt Doors

If the keeper of such hotel, inn or ordinary shall provide suitable locks or bolts on the doors of the sleeping rooms used by his guests, and suitable fastening on the transoms and windows of said rooms, and shall keep a copy of this and the preceding section conspicuously posted in each of said rooms, together with a notice requiring said guests or boarders to keep said doors locked or bolted, and transoms fastened, and if said guests or boarders fail to lock or bolt said door or doors, or to fasten said windows and transoms, then the said keeper of such hotel, inn or ordinary, shall not be liable for any property taken from such room or rooms in consequence of such failure on the part of such guest or boarder; but the burden of proof shall be upon such keeper to show that he has complied with the provisions of this section, and that such guest or guests have failed to comply with these requirements. Nothing in this section shall be construed to in any wise exempt the keeper, or keepers, of hotels, inns and ordinaries from being liable for the value of any property of guests taken or stolen from any room therein by any employee or agent of said keeper or keepers.

A characteristic of the court that must be understood is that "it is a passive forum for adjusting disputes and has no power to investigate facts or to initiate proceedings."[10] It must wait until "justiciable controversies" are brought before it by lawyers and their clients.

Classifications

Courts can be "courts of record" or "not of record." In the former, court reporters record testimony and later transcribe this testimony into transcripts for use in the appeal process. Courts "not of record" do not record proceedings.

Courts can be *superior* or *inferior*, pointing out that some have powers over those below them. Thus, a state supreme court is superior to a county circuit court in that state. Courts can be *civil*, and thus handle civil matters, and others, *criminal*. Some are *equity* courts, and others *law* courts. In smaller, rural jurisdictions, one court may have many of these classifications. There are many specialized courts such as courts of admiralty, bankruptcy, claims, and others.

As to the names by which our top courts are known, there are similarities yet differences. Maine calls its top court the Supreme Judicial Court; Massachusetts, the Full Court of the Supreme Judicial Court; Maryland, the Court of Appeals; New York, the Court of Appeals; and West Virginia, the Supreme Court of Appeals. All other states call their top court the Supreme Court. Texas and Oklahoma also have a Court of Criminal Appeals at the top of their system.

The Delaware Supreme Court has three members, as does the Oklahoma Court of Criminal Appeals. The Connecticut Supreme Court has six members. Seven state supreme courts have nine members; eighteen have five members and twenty-two have seven members.

Interpretation of a State Statute

Let's take a look at some cases. The first two cases involve a statute that limits innkeepers' liability for loss of property and money and valuables at inns in Nevada. The statute reads as follows:

651.010 Civil liability of innkeepers limited.

1. No owner or keeper of any hotel, inn, motel, motor court, boardinghouse or lodginghouse in this state is civilly liable for the theft, loss, damage or destruction of any property left in the room of any guest of such an establishment because of theft, burglary, fire or otherwise, in the absence of gross neglect by the owner or keeper.

2. If an owner or keeper of any hotel, inn, motel, motor court, boardinghouse or lodginghouse in this state provides a fireproof safe or vault in which guests may deposit property for safekeeping, and notice of this service is personally given to a guest or posted in the office and the guest's room, the owner or keeper is not liable for the theft, loss, damage or destruction of any property which is not offered for deposit in the safe or vault by a guest unless the owner or keeper is grossly negligent. An owner or keeper is not obligated to receive property to deposit for safekeeping which exceeds $750 in value or is of a size which cannot easily fit within the safe or vault.

3. The liability of the owner or keeper under this section does not exceed the sum of $750 for any property of an individual guest, unless the owner or keeper receives the property for deposit for safekeeping and consents to assume a liability greater than $750 for its theft, loss, damage, or destruction in a written agreement in which the guest specifies the value of the property. [1:256:1953]—(NRS A 1979, 1114)

The following is a summary of two federal cases in which this statute became involved.[11] The "money and valuables" statutes found in all fifty states represent the granting of a legislative grace to innkeepers and replace the harsh common-law rule of strict liability. Nevada has such a law, and features of it have been the subject of litigation in the federal courts in Louisiana and New York. The cases involved the Sands Hotel and Desert Palace, Inc. (Caesar's Palace), located near each other on the Strip in Las Vegas.[12]

Would this statute be enforced and thus deny recovery for loss of money and valuables stolen from Las Vegas hotel rooms? How were federal appellate courts in two separate parts of the United States going to interpret a law created in Carson City, Nevada?

First, what is the meaning of "left in the room?" Does it mean the valuables are left in the room while the guests are away from the room, or does it mean valuables left in the room as opposed to a fireproof safe while the guests are, in fact, in the room? In the two cases, the guests were asleep in their rooms when the valuables were stolen. If the statute does not apply, the common-law rule of strict liability will be in effect, and the innkeepers will be responsible for the value of the stolen valuables.

The second question involves the meaning of "in the absence of gross neglect upon the part of such keeper or owner." Was there negligence on the part of the innkeepers in each case? Was there an *absence* of gross neglect, or was there gross neglect?

In both cases the guests checked into their hotels with a considerable amount of jewelry. Both hotels maintain safes for the storage of valuables and so informed the guests. Both hotels had notices of the availability of the safes posted at the front office and in the rooms.

On the night of both thefts, jewelry was taken to the rooms. Deadbolts were fastened, and the couples retired. In both cases, however, the deadbolts did not function. The Caesar's Palace maintenance staff was in the process of replacing malfunctioning bolts, but the particular door in question had not yet been repaired. No repair or replacement of bolts had been planned at the Sands Hotel.

The rooms were entered in the early hours of the morning by use of a passkey, and jewelry was stolen while the couples were asleep. One couple, William J. and Simone Levitt, sued in the federal courts in New York. The other couple, Chris and Sol Owens, sued in the U. S. District Court for the Eastern District of Louisiana.

The Nevada courts had defined the phrase "gross negligence" in a previous case. Because federal courts must apply state law in this instance, they adopted the rule of this case, which held, "Gross negligence is substantially and appreciably higher in magnitude and more culpable than ordinary negligence. . . ." It is " . . . manifestly a smaller amount of watchfulness and circumspection than the circumstances requires of a prudent man."

One court said, "The issue before us is simply whether the hotel exercised even slight care to insure the safety of its guests' property." Both courts held there was more than ample care in both instances.

The value of the cases to the *HH&T* industry is to be found in guidelines summarized as follows:

1. Comply strictly with the money and valuables and property statutes.
2. Include notification of the availability of safes on the registration forms and on notices placed in the front office, the guest rooms, and in the elevators. Also, have front desk personnel tell all guests the service is available.
3. Offer to escort them to and from their rooms when they use the front-desk safe to deposit and withdraw their valuables.

4. Take full advantage of the protection the statutes offer. If the statutes are not followed strictly, a court may hold that the common-law rule of strict liability is applicable.

The third case deals with the wrongful death of a guest.

Case Introduction: Page Case

To assist in understanding the case of *Page v. Sloan* that follows, it is helpful to understand what is meant by a "pretrial conference," "stipulations," and "depositions." A *pretrial conference* is a meeting held prior to trial, at which the judge and lawyers for both sides will:

1. Attempt to settle the case.
2. Make "stipulations" so as to shorten the trial.
3. Take care of other routine matters so as to expedite the trial.

A *stipulation* is an agreement by both sides on facts or documents to be used in the trial. For example, if a deed is to be used and both sides stipulate the deed, it can be used in trial without the necessity of calling authenticating witnesses from the county clerk's office.

A *deposition* is an oral statement of witnesses taken under oath. It works this way: The attorney wanting to take the deposition of a witness will serve notice upon opposing counsel. This notice will set the time and place for the deposition. At that time the deponent (witness) is sworn and the questioning begins. Objections can be made, thus reserving them for later ruling in trial. Cross-examination follows direct examination. After the session is completed, the testimony is transcribed (typed) and the original filed in the case file. The parties are each provided with a copy. If this witness is not able to be at the trial, the deposition can be read to the jury. This is subject, however, to objections raised previously. If a deponent should change his or her testimony later at trial, the deposition can be used to impeach that testimony.

In the following case, the person bringing the suit is the widow of a guest killed at a motel. She brought the suit as the Administratrix CTA (*cum testamento annexo*) "with the will attached." This tells us that her deceased husband had not executed a formal will but had left some document such as a letter that evidenced his wishes in the event of his death. The suit was brought in tort to recover for the loss to the estate of the future services and earnings of the deceased.

The issue in the case is this: Were there questions of fact that should have been decided by a jury in the lower court?

PAGE V. SLOAN
12 N.C. App. 433,
183 S.E. 2d 813 (1971).

In this case, the plaintiff was the administratrix CTA (*cum testamento annexo*) of the estate of Channing Nelson Page, who was killed on August 29, 1964. The death resulted by the explosion of an 82-gallon electric hot water heater located in a utility room of the Ocean Isle Motel in Brunswick County, North Carolina. She alleged that Mr. Page was a paying guest in said motel which was owned and operated by the defendants as co-partners and that Mr. Page was assigned a corner room adjoining the utility room which contained the motel's hot water heater. This electric hot water heater was installed, used, and operated by defendants for the purpose of furnishing hot water to the various guest rooms of the Ocean Isle Motel. She alleged that the explosion of the electric hot water heater was the direct and proximate cause of the death of Page and that at all times the said water heater was in the exclusive possession and control of the defendants. She further alleged that the explosion of said electric hot water heater was caused by, or due to, the actionable negligence of the defendants.

Defendants answered admitting allegations of residence, the death of Channing Nelson Page, their ownership and operation of Ocean Isle Motel, their acceptance of Page as a paying guest and assigning him a corner room adjoining the utility room containing the electric hot water heater, the water heater serving the function of furnishing hot water to various guest rooms in the said motel, and said electric hot water heater exploding at the alleged time and place. However, the defendants specifically denied negligence on their part. . . . [The following stipulations were made by the parties.]

* * *

"(i) This hot water heater unit installed by Shallotte Hardware Company at Ocean Isle Motel remained in operation and use in the new units at that place from approximately April, 1962, until the explosion in August, 1964.

* * *

"(k) In June or July, 1964, George Sloan and Rea Sloan had Olaf Thorsen check the hot water unit here in question due to a complaint of no hot water or insufficient hot water by motel guests. Olaf Thorsen removed the lower heating element of the water heater and obtained a replacement from Shallotte Hardware Company. The original heating element was of the size of 2500 watts. After the explosion it was determined that the lower heating element in the heater at the time of the explosion was an element of 4500 watt size.

"(l) The water heater in question was rated by an inscription on a plate attached thereto at 3000 watts for the upper element, at 2500 watts for the lower element, and at 3000 watts maximum.

* * *

"(p) Olaf Thorsen was a licensed plumber in Brunswick County, North Carolina.

* * *

"(r) The 82 gallon electric hot water heater was manufactured by State Stove and Manufacturing Company and installed in the Ocean Isle Motel by Shallotte Hardware Company and worked on by Olaf Thorsen and was the hot water heater which exploded in the utility room adjacent to the motel room occupied by Channing Nelson Page.

* * *

"(s) There was no inspection of the installation of the hot water heater at the time of its installation in 1962 by the N. C. Department of Labor Boiler Inspection Division as required by North Carolina General Statutes. The installation was inspected by the Brunswick County inspector who was not with the Department of Labor."

* * *

In addition to the foregoing stipulations, several depositions were considered by the trial judge at the hearing on motion for summary judgment. These depositions, which were considered by consent, included depositions of each of the defendants, the deposition of Olaf Thorsen (the plumber-repairman), and the depositions of each of the three partners in Shallotte Hardware (the original installer of defendants' electric hot water heater).

The deposition of Olaf Thorsen tends to show that he is a licensed plumber, and that he has no license or experience as an electrician. It tends to show that defendants called him to adjust or repair the electric hot water heater because there was no hot water. It tends to show that he removed a 2500-watt heating element and replaced it with a 4500-watt element, and reset the thermostat to a higher temperature reading. The stipulations show that the water heater was rated for a 2500-watt heating element, and a maximum of 3000 watts. The deposition of Alton Milliken, a licensed electrician, tends to show that the introduction of a 4500-watt heating element would heat the water faster and would draw a larger current through the thermostat, which would tend to cause its points to melt and thereby freeze the thermostat so that it would no longer control the temperature. The deposition of Glenn Williamson tends to show that the tank of defendants' electric hot water heater was blown some two hundred to three hundred feet by the explosion.

Defendants' motion for summary judgment was heard during the 18 January 1971 Session of Superior Court held in Moore County. It was stipulated that Judge Long might enter judgment out of the District and after expiration of the Session. After consideration of the pleadings, depositions, and stipulations, Judge Long by judgment filed 31 March 1971 found that there was no genuine issue of any material fact as to liability and that defendants' motion for summary judgment should be granted. Plaintiff appeals.

BROCK, Judge.

Plaintiff-appellant insists that the doctrine of *res ipsa loquitur* is applicable in this case and, being entitled under that doctrine to have the case submitted to the jury, that summary judgment for defendant was error. We agree.

Summary judgment is proper only where movant shows that there is no genuine issue as to any material fact and that he is entitled to judgment as a matter of law. Application of the doctrine of *res ipsa loquitur* recognizes that common experience sometimes permits a reasonable inference of negligence from the occurrence itself. In other words, the application of the doctrine of *res ipsa loquitur* recognizes a genuine issue as to the material fact of defendants' actionable negligence and precludes summary judgment for defendants.

The rules governing the application of the doctrine of *res ipsa loquitur* in North Carolina have been stated as follows: "When a thing which causes injury is shown to be under the exclusive management of the defendant and the accident is one which in the ordinary course of events does not happen if those in control of it use proper care, the accident itself is sufficient to carry the case to the jury on the issue of defendant's negligence."

In this case, the evidence before the trial judge clearly shows that the electric hot water heater was under the exclusive management and control of defendants, and that they had undertaken the maintenance of it. It is a matter of common knowledge that electric water heaters are widely used to fill the hot water requirements of residential, commercial, and industrial users. When in a safe condition and properly managed, electric hot water heaters do not usually explode; therefore, in the absence of explanation, the explosion of an electric hot water heater reasonably warrants an inference of negligence.

[Innkeepers' Modern Law Standard]

A hotel or motel keeper, from the nature of his occupation, extends an invitation to the general public to use his facilities. When a paying guest goes to a hotel or motel, the very thing he bargains for is the use of safe and secure premises for his sojourn. Although the hotel or motel keeper is not an insurer of the guest's personal safety [in modern times], he has the duty to exercise reasonable care to maintain the premises in a reasonably safe condition; and if his negligence in this respect is the proximate cause of injury to a guest, he is liable for damages.

[Defendant's Argument]

Defendants argue that *res ipsa loquitur* does not apply because the evidence leaves the cause of the explosion a matter of conjecture. The depositions of the two defendants which were before the trial judge indicated that a thunderstorm was in the area during the night preceding the explosion of the electric hot water heater. This testimony may constitute evidence for consideration by the jury as a possible explanation of the cause of the explosion, but its probative value is for jury determination and it does not remove the more reasonable inference that the cause of the explosion was negligence of defendants in the management and control of the electric hot water heater.

Defendants further argue that they lack the knowledge and skill to inspect and regulate the heater, that they reasonably relied upon an independent contractor for proper installation, and that they reasonably relied upon an independent contractor for repairs. The evidence before the trial judge discloses that defendants hired one Olaf Thorsen to adjust and repair the electric hot water heater. The evidence before the trial judge discloses that Olaf Thorsen is not a licensed electrician and is not experienced as an electrician, but is licensed and experienced only as a plumber. The evidence before the trial judge further discloses that the repair and maintenance on the electric hot water heater required working with, installing, and adjusting electrical wiring, electrical heating elements, and a thermostat to control the flow of electrical current. At the time of the accident in question, G.S. §87-43 provided in part as follows: "No person, firm or corporation shall engage in the business of installing, maintaining, altering or repairing within the State of North Carolina any electric wiring, devices, appliances or equipment unless such person, firm or corporation shall have received from the Board of Examiners of Electrical Contractors an electrical contractor's license. . . ."

[The Independent Contractor Rule]

Plumbers who are answerable only for the result of their work are generally regarded as independent contractors. The general rule is that an employer or contractee is not liable for the torts of an independent contractor committed in the performance of the contracted work. However, a condition prescribed to relieve an employer from liability for the negligent acts of an independent contractor employed by him is that he shall have exercised due care to secure a competent contractor for the work. Therefore, if it appears that the employer either knew, or by the exercise of reasonable care might have ascertained that the contractor was not properly qualified, then the employer may be held liable for the negligent acts of the contractor. "An employer is subject to liability for physical harm to third persons caused by his failure to exercise reasonable care to employ a competent and careful contractor (a) to do work which will involve a risk of physical harm unless it is skillfully and carefully done, or (b) to perform any duty which the employer owes to third persons." Restatement, Second, Torts, §411. The evidence of the repairs and maintenance performed on the electrical system of defendants' electric hot water heater by Olaf Thorsen tends to affirm the incompetence of defendants' independent contractor as an electrician.

This evidence before the trial judge tends to show a specific act of negligence on the part of defendants in failing to secure the services of a competent independent contractor and tends to strengthen the inference that the cause of the accident was defendants' negligence. The application of the doctrine of *res ipsa loquitur* to this case should not be denied because the evidence tends to show a specific act of negligence on the part of defendants.

The entry of summary judgment was error.

Reversed.

VAUGHN and GRAHAM, J.J., concur.

The decision of the North Carolina Court of Appeals was upheld (affirmed) by the Supreme Court of North Carolina in 1972.[13] This cleared the way for the case to be returned to the trial court for a jury trial on the points raised in the case itself.

SUMMARY

The reporter systems at the state and federal levels are different from the reporter systems that are operated as private publishing ventures. At the state level, the reporting of cases moves at a slow pace. This is caused by the fact that the top court of each state produces a limited number of decisions each year. In states with smaller populations, it may take years to fill one state volume. The various federal volumes are filled quite rapidly because these courts are spread across the nation and the volume of cases decided yearly is large. A few publishing companies gather *all* state cases and *all* federal cases and produce them in volumes for sale to libraries, lawyers, and others who have use for them.

This chapter provides an introduction to the "money and valuable" statutes that have been enacted in all 50 states. While these statutes are not uniform, they are similar in many respects. The main purpose of these statutes (laws) is to place a limit on the liability of innkeepers for money and valuables brought to hotel/motel/inn properties that are then stolen or lost. Under the common law special relationship that we encountered in Chapter 1, the innkeeper is held responsible for the full value of the property of guests that is lost or stolen while the relationship is in existence. The conditions of travel in earlier centuries and the lack of insurance and means of rapid communication made this rule reasonable and placed greater obligations on innkeepers to protect their guests and property. Poor travel conditions began to improve in the nineteenth century, and the states began to enact statutes to limit liability. This topic will be explored in detail in Chapters 19 and 20 and comprises one of the more important legal topics to be aware of for those who manage hotels, motels, and inns.

QUESTIONS

1. What does a case citation tell us?
2. How can an innkeeper lose the protection of the statutes that limit liability for the money and valuables of guests as well as a guest's property?
3. In the Levitt case (Caesar's Palace money and valuables case), the court found an absence of gross negligence on the part of the hotel. What is the significance of this finding?
4. Where in your inn would you post notices of the statutory limitations on liability? Could any harm come from *extra posting* in places not specified in the statutes?
5. How do statutes differ from cases?
6. What do the words "left in the room" mean under the Nevada money and valuables statutes?
7. True or false: Historically, the innkeeper was an insurer of the goods and valuables of guests, but this is no longer true.
8. What was the principal defense set up by the inn in *Page v. Sloan*?

NOTES

1. *Ex Parte Chesser,* 93 Fla. 590, 112 So. 90 (1920).
2. *John P. Agnew Co. Inc. v. Hooge,* 69 App. D.C. 116, 99 F. 2d 349, 351.
3. *State v. McDonough,* 129 Conn. 483, 29 A. 2d 582, 584.
4. *Edgewater Motel v. Gatzlee,* 277 N.W. 2d 11 (Minnesota 1979).
5. 437 N.W. 2d 194 (North Dakota 1989).
6. *State v. Tew,* 405 H 89-Wayne (North Carolina 1990).
7. *Miller v. Warren,* 390 S.E. 2d 207 (West Virginia 1990).
8. *In re Carter's Estate,* 254 Pa. 518, 99 A. 58.
9. *Isbill v. Stoval,* Tex. Civ. App., 92 S.W. 2d 1067, 1070.
10. *Sale v. Railroad Commission,* 15 Cal. 2d 612, 140 P. 2d 38, 41.
11. *Hotel and Casino Law Letter,* Volume 2-2, College of Hotel Administration, University of Nevada, Las Vegas, John R. Goodwin, Editor.
12. *Levitt v. Desert Palace, Inc.,* 601 Fed. Rpt. 2d 684 (1979), and *Owens v. Summa Corporation and XYZ Insurance Co.,* 625 Fed. Rpt. 2d 600 (1980).

Common-Law Contracts

OVERVIEW

FIRST THE REQUIREMENTS for the formation of common law contracts will be discussed. Then, what happens when contract promises are not kept will follow.

One of the most extensive and well-developed bodies of substantive law is the law of contract. At the outset, however, we must recognize that what is discussed in this chapter must be supplemented by what we will learn in the next chapter about sales contracts. This chapter concerns all contracts *other* than those that apply to the *sale of goods between merchants* (the subject matter of the next chapter). Table 5.1 is a preliminary comparison between common-law contracts and sales contracts.

TABLE 5.1   Comparison between common-law contracts and sales contracts.

Chapter 5 Common-Law Contracts and the HH&T Industry	Chapter 6 Sales Contracts and the HH&T Industry
The rules of these contracts have arisen out of the common law over hundreds of years. These rules apply to: 1. Contracts for the sale of real estate. 2. Contracts regarding employment. 3. Contracts involving services. The "sale" of a room for the night is an example. The six requirements to form these contracts are firm and rigid. If the terms of an offer are changed, it becomes a counteroffer and the process reverses as to the parties.	The rules of these contracts have their roots in the common law of *Lex Mercantoria*, the "Law Merchant." The courts in which these rules were administered, usually at fairs, were called "Courts of *Pie Poudire*," "Courts of Dusty Boots." Beginning in the 1960s, the states began to adopt the *Uniform Commercial Code*, Article 2 of which applies to "Sales Contracts." *Article 2 of the UCC* These rules apply to: 1. The sale of goods between merchants. 2. The sale of goods between merchants and consumers. The rules here are flexible, and changing the terms of an offer *is not* a counteroffer. If goods are received and there is a failure to inspect, reject, and state why (IRS), there is an acceptance, *even if there was no offer.*

Developed after an inquiry by Professor Roberta Alison, Department of Hospitality and Management, Newbury College, Brookline, Massachusetts.

DEFINITION

A leading authority on the subject tells us that "a contract is a promise, or set of promises, for the breach of which the law gives a remedy, or the performance of which the law in some way recognizes as a duty."[1] This definition points out that a promise or promises are needed and that the "law" is involved. A contract creates legal obligations; it usually concerns property or something of value, and it creates rights that can be addressed to a court for enforcement. If the contract requires skill, exercise of special knowledge, or judgment, it is a *personal service contract*. If it concerns property, it is a *property contract*.

[handwritten margin note: Personal service contract requires skill.]

Contract Definition and Hotel Reservations: An Example

A travel group makes prepaid reservations for fifty rooms, two weeks in advance. When attempting to check in, the group is told that no rooms are available. The translation of the above contract definition follows: "A contract is the promise of the hotel to have fifty rooms available for the travel group on the agreed day. The promise was not kept, thus giving the travel group the right to seek damages (dollars) in court, or a remedy in equity. If the promise had been kept, the law would recognize that fact as having been a duty."

Some Legal Facts About Contracts

1. Contracts are pervasive; they can do a variety of things.
2. Contracts create legal duties.
3. Contracts commit each party to perform as they have promised.
4. Contracts structure the legal relationship between the parties.
5. Contracts allow the parties to plan for the future.
6. Contracts make otherwise independent parties, dependent upon each other, as to the contract terms.
7. Contracts allow the signers to safely allocate appropriate resources while starting to meet the terms of the contract.
8. Contracts represent a large part of modern commercial and personal affairs.
9. Contracts limit independent action by those who enter into them.

Leaving these introductory items, let's become further acquainted with contract matters at the typical American inn.

Contracting Considerations of the Innkeeper

The hotel manager can legally refuse to make room reservations; can place conditions upon any contract that he or she might make; and can even refuse to honor contracts that have been made already. In the latter situation, the hotel would have to face the consequences of the breach of contract. Nevertheless, the power to refuse to honor a contract remains, even though there might not be a legal right to do so. In addition, an innkeeper may step out of his or her traditional function.

An innkeeper can assume a legal role other than that of manager in two contractual situations.

1. The innkeeper substitutes other rules in contract making.
2. The innkeeper's right to make or not make reservations is involved.

The First Contractual Situation

Here, the innkeeper begins renting rooms by the week, month, or year, or sells time-share rights to certain rooms at the inn. In these situations the innkeeper has stepped out of the traditional innkeeper's role. Persons who rent for long time periods, or who contract for time-share rights for certain weeks of the year, become tenants and the innkeeper is now a landlord as to them. A legal right lost by the innkeeper in such situations is the protection of the state statutes that limit liability. Such statutes generally do not apply to money and valuables or the property of tenants.

The Second Contractual Situation

Here, the matter of receiving requests for reservations and the making of them becomes involved. The common-law duty to receive is not applicable to the making of reservations. Thus, reservations may be made or refused as the internal needs of the hotel might dictate.

It is now useful to gain a little more understanding of what common-law contracts are in fact.

Figure 5.1 illustrates the differences between fully integrated and partially integrated contracts. The second classification supplied by law is where interpretation is encountered.

FIGURE 5.1   A comparison of fully integrated and partially integrated contracts.

Fully Integrated	Partially Integrated
Contract X	**Contract Z**
No ambiguities No uncertaintyNo conditionsAll terms clear(In addition, the essential elements of a contract are found here)(In addition, the essential elements of a contract are found here)	No ambiguities No uncertaintyNo conditionsAll terms clear(In addition, the essential elements of a contract are found here)(In addition, the essential elements of a contract are found here)
No ambiguities	Terms missing
No uncertainty	Ambiguities
No conditions	Uncertain terms
All terms clear	Conditions listed
(In addition, the essential elements of a contract are found here.)	Terms not clear

INTERPRETATION OF CONTRACTS

Common law contracts have two primary classifications, which have to do with the terms they contain.

1. *Fully integrated contracts.* These are contracts in which all of the terms needed to decide what the contract means are set forth specifically. Most carefully crafted contracts fall into this category, and it is good legal business to see that this is done.

2. *Partially integrated contracts.* These are contracts in which, for some reason, such as oversight, carelessness, or perhaps misunderstanding, terms are left out. (See Figure 5.1.)

If a dispute arises, as it often does in the hospitality industry in group bookings, the second classification, a legal mechanism, is required whereby the missing terms can be supplied. This is known as "contract interpretation."

This interpretation, of course, must be done by a judge in a court of law after a lawsuit has been filed that involves the dispute. The court (judge) now has been given, in effect, the power to say what the missing terms were as a matter of law. In making this interpretation, two primary rules must be followed:

1. The interpretation (finding) must not in any way disturb the clear meanings of the terms that had been agreed upon.

2. The court must find out the meaning of the hospitality words that had been used in the specific terms that were supplied. The court then must apply this understanding when making the interpretation of the terms that are missing.

WHAT DOES THE COMMON-LAW CONTRACT MEAN?

This is an important question, and the answer can have dramatic impact on the parties in the courts where contract disputes are decided. For centuries, the common-law rules of contract were stable, understood by lawyers and strictly enforced by judges. This remained true until the days of reliable transportation and rapid communication came upon the commercial and personal scene. These happenings, which spanned the nineteenth and twentieth centuries have played a role in altering the common law of contracts. In the hustle of the modern commercial and personal community, the partially integrated contract is often used because of time constraints, the heavy work schedules of those creating such contracts, and ignorance of the law. As a result, these contracts often wind up in court for resolution.

Basic rules have developed in the courts to interpret (explain or translate) contract terms that are ambiguous or missing. Some examples follow.

1. *Plain words* are to be given their ordinary meaning. This is why avoiding use of words or phrases that may have double meaning is so important in HH&T contracts.

2. *Technical words*, including words of legal art, are to be given their technical meaning. Words of legal art have precise meaning at law and are not subject to interpretation.

3. *Written words* are to be given priority over what printed words say. That is to say, if the printed words say "XYZ" but the written words say "ABC," the latter controls and the judge will use those words in interpreting the contract.

4. *Custom and usage* also can become involved in contract interpretation, but the plain terms of a contract will prevail over custom or usage.

5. A final rule applied, when necessary, is that of *ejusdem generis*.

This is a Latin legal term that holds that specific words used in a contract and followed by phrases such as "and the like" must include only other items in the same class as the ones described by the first words. As an illustration, assume that a contract with Hotel X and Supplier Y has the following term: "Hotel X covenants and agrees to buy all of its needs for oranges, apples, bananas, grapes, and like items from the date of this contract from Supplier Y."

Does Hotel X have to buy potatoes, onions, beans, and lettuce from Supplier Y during the coming year? The doctrine of *ejusdem generis* says "no" because "like items" means only fruits. The other items are vegetables and are thus excluded. The rule also applies to words found in statutes. Therefore, if a statute requires that " . . . motels, motor courts, RV parks, and like establishments . . . " do what is set forth in the statute, do hotels have to meet these requirements? The rule says "no."

A discussion of the basic contract classifications will be now be helpful.

CLASSIFICATIONS OF CONTRACTS

Contracts can be joint or several; bilateral or unilateral; executory or executed; express or implied; and void, voidable, and unenforceable.

Joint or Several Contracts

A joint contract is one in which A and B bind themselves to C so that both are responsible for the obligations assumed. Both must be sued by C if they fail to meet their obligations. A "several" contract is one in which either A or B may be sued for breach, at the election of C.

Bilateral or Unilateral Contracts

If A and B enter into a contract and each makes binding promises to the other, the contract is bilateral, or two-party. If an *offeror*—the one who makes an offer—does not want a promise in return, the situation is unilateral. For example, A says "Cut down that tree at the inn, carry away all debris, and I will pay you $200." This is a *promise for an act* and does not create a binding obligation on either party, at least not at that point. If B cuts down the tree and removes the debris, the act requested is completed and A must pay the sum promised. The same situation often arises in the making of room reservations.

Unilateral Room Reservation Contracts

It is late afternoon and the inn is nearing capacity. Ninety percent of the guests have checked in, and an additional 8 percent of the available rooms are held on guaranteed reservations. Assuming the inn has 300 rooms, six remain available.

If a walk-in requests a room, the common-law duty to receive requires acceptance, assuming that the person is an acceptable condition and able to pay. Five vacancies now exist.

A phone caller then requests a "room for tonight, for arrival at 5:30 P.M." The caller is an American Express card holder and guarantees payment by use of the card number.

Two options now are available. The inn can accept the reservation unconditionally, reducing the available rooms to four, or accept the reservation with the condition that the traveler arrive by a specified time. The latter is an option because the common-law duty to receive does *not* extend to phone reservations.

The inn could reply, "We will hold the room for you if you arrive no later than 6 P.M. If you don't, we will sell the room if someone wants it." In this instance, a unilateral offer has been created. The inn has promised to have the room available if that person performs the act of arriving by the stated time. If he or she arrives on time, the sale is made. If not, the room is available for others.

Conditions on Inn Room Reservations

Closely related to the making of reservations in unilateral form is the using of *conditions* when taking reservations. Some examples are a "cash deposit received in advance" and a "minimum stay of three days." If these conditions are not met, the reservation contract does not come into being. As a judge once said, "Conditions are the archenemy of the promise," for the more conditions one makes, the less the promise is worth. Thus, their use in HH&T operations makes good business sense. Conditions can be *precedent* (meaning something must first happen), *concurrent* (meaning some event must occur at the same time as another event), or *subsequent* (meaning that some event must follow an event).

Executory and Executed Contracts

An executory contract is one in which one or both parties must yet perform. An executed contract is one that has been performed with nothing left for either party to do. A promise to sell land is an executory contract. After the deed is transferred and the price paid, the contract is executed.

Express or Implied Contracts

An express contract is one in which the promises and terms are stated by the parties. Implied contracts arise "from mutual agreement and intent to promise, but where the agreement and promise have not been expressed in words. Such contracts are true contracts and have sometimes been called contracts implied in fact."[2]

Void, Voidable, and Unenforceable Contracts

A *void contract* is technically no contract at all. It may be a contract that the parties believed was valid but that has been held by a court to be invalid. A *voidable contract* is one that is valid but has built within it the right of one or both of the parties to avoid all obligations under the contract. A, a minor, buys an item from B, an adult. A can void the contract because of A's age, and B can do nothing about it. Until A voids, however, B is bound to perform with A.

An *unenforceable contract* is one that, for some reason, cannot be enforced. A contract may be unenforceable in part and enforceable in the balance. For example, A contracts with B and the contract contains six provisions. Two of these provisions are illegal but the other four are not. The contract is unenforceable as to the two provisions and valid as to the balance. This brings into play the "blue pencil doctrine." If such a contract goes before a court, the judge can "blue pencil," or take out, the illegal provisions and enforce the others.

Turning from classifications, we will next examine the legal requirements for the creation of a binding common-law contract.

STATUTE OF FRAUDS

The statute of frauds requires certain contracts to be in written form and "signed by the party(ies) to be charged." Historically, these laws, which originated in England in 1677, were called "statutes of frauds" because they were designed to prevent fraud in the use of contracts. Examples of contracts that must be in writing and signed include:

1. contracts involving the sale of real estate or any interest in real estate
2. contracts that cannot be performed in one year
3. promises of one person to pay the debt of another
4. leases for more than one year
5. contracts in which one party promises another money or property if that party will enter into marriage with the other
6. promises of those who handle deceased persons' estates to pay the debts of creditors out of their own pockets if the estate does not have enough for that purpose

A helpful way to gain an understanding of the statute of frauds is to ask, "What *isn't* covered?" If a pending contract does not fall into one of the six areas, the contract *does not have to be in writing to be binding*. A sampling of non-covered areas includes:

1. personal-service contracts, even though they are to last for more than one year
2. providing a service as contrasted to a sale
3. leases of real estate for less than one year
4. the sale of items of real estate that the seller is to remove from the real estate such as bricks from a hotel to be torn down
5. reservations on a short-term basis

Statute of Frauds at the Inn

Two inn situations illustrate the legal thinking behind the statute of fraud.

In the first situation, Guest Z causes $10,000 fire damage at an inn because of her carelessly placed cigarette. She does not have enough cash or credit availability on her charge card to pay for the damages, but promises to pay for the loss. This promise does not have to be in writing to be enforced in court. (Good inn practice, of course, would be to have her sign a promissory note for the $10,000.)

In the second situation, Guest Z causes the fire damages and calls upon her brother to assist her. The brother promises to pay his sister's debt. This promise does have to be in writing or it cannot be enforced in court. The reason? It is a promise to pay the debt of another, and this is one of the specific areas covered by the statute of frauds. Law requires a writing in this instance to prevent the possibility of fraud on the innkeeper's part by claiming that a promise had been made to pay when in fact the brother had made no promise. By requiring a writing, the law cancels out the chance of fraud in such a situation.

Form of the Contract

No particular words are necessary to show contractual promises or the intention of the parties as they relate to those promises. With the exception of contracts that must be in writing under the statute of frauds, oral contracts are as binding as written contracts. For example, a hotel manager can hire an assistant manager orally and the terms agreed upon are binding. Employment contracts are an exception to the statute of fraud's one year provision. Even if the employment may last for years, it *could* end in the first year by, for example, the death of the employee. Therefore, it is *not* a contract that *cannot be performed* in one year—a technical point.

Once a common-law contract is formed, there are limits placed upon the time in which a lawsuit may be brought for a breach of the contract.

THE STATUTE OF LIMITATIONS

In each state a statute of limitations controls the time within which one may sue for breach of a written contract. The period of five to ten years is typical and starts when the breach occurs, not from the date of the contract. If this time period expires, the legal right to ask for recovery has been lost.

We next examine the legal requirements that are needed to create a common-law contract that can be enforced in court.

REQUIREMENTS OF A BINDING CONTRACT

The common-law contract has six requirements that must come into being before it becomes legally enforceable: offer, acceptance, mutuality (or meeting of the minds), consideration, competent parties, and legal purpose. We will examine each in turn.

Offer

An offer is made by the *offeror* (promisor) and is most often a statement of what that person is willing to do if the other is willing to do what is requested. Although an offer is a promise, it is conditional. The offer may be revoked by the one who made it, provided the revocation comes before an acceptance. An offer may be rejected by the *offeree*, or the offeree may make a *counteroffer*, which is a rejection of the offer. Mere silence on the part of the offeree does not constitute acceptance.

An offer must be definite in its terms. If there is an offer and an acceptance, but the terms are so indefinite that they cannot be determined, the court will hold that there is no contract.

To assist in understanding the offer, the requirements are shown in Figure 5.2 as Step 1.

FIGURE 5.2   The offer.

Step 1:

Offeror ——— **Offer** ———> Offeree

The offeror (or promisor) has made an offer, the form of which is a question: "Here is my offer (or promise). Do you want the benefits of it?"

At this point, the offer is a mere inquiry, and the offeree has no obligation to reply. He or she may stand silent, and the silence will not constitute an acceptance.

The offer will not last indefinitely and, if made face to face, ends when the parties part. It can lapse after the passage of time; it can be revoked by the one who makes it, as long as this happens before it is accepted; it can be rejected by the one to whom it is made, thus bringing it to an end; it can end by the making of a counteroffer; it can end by destruction of the subject matter of the offer, and it can end by acceptance. An offer also ends upon the death or insanity of the offeror if either event occurs before acceptance.

Acceptance

Acceptance occurs when it is clear that the offeree wants to be bound in a contract with the offeror. If the offer specifies a time by which acceptance must be made, an acceptance after that time is ineffective. If no time limit is specified, an offer must be accepted within a reasonable time or it will lapse. Acceptance comes too late if an offer lapses, is revoked, or is rejected. If a dispute arises as to whether an offer was or was not accepted, it becomes a question of fact for a jury to determine.

An acceptance can be made in the form in which the offer is made. That is, if an oral offer is made, the acceptance can be oral. If the offer is in writing, the acceptance should be in writing. If an offer is made by mail and acceptance also is made by mail, the acceptance is effective when mailed. The offeror chose the mail, so when the acceptance was mailed, it was in the hands of the offeror's agent and, thus, effective at that time. The rule that acceptance made by mail is good when mailed was laid down in the case of *Adams v. Lindsell*.[3]

Acceptance can come about by signing a document, by requested acts where the offer is in unilateral form, by conduct, by trade usage, and even by custom. If the offeror specifies that the acceptance will not be effective until received, that provision controls. In a face-to-face situation, a nod of the head may be a good acceptance.

An acceptance must conform to the offer, and if it varies from the terms, it will fail. The offer also must be accepted in its totality or not at all. An attempt to accept part would vary the terms of the offer and is not permitted. If parties exchange letters and the terms in those letters are not on "all fours," there is no contract. The letters are merely proposals of each to contract with the other. The court will treat them as "negotiations." If the terms in the letters agree, a contract will result. Figure 5.3 gives Step 2 of the requirements of a binding contract.

FIGURE 5.3   Acceptance.

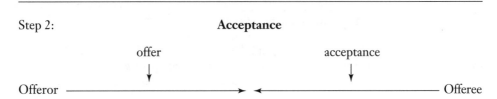

The offeree wants the benefits offered and accepts. The acceptance may be the nod of a head at an auction, a written acceptance, or some other applicable form.

Mutuality

A contract implies mutual obligations.[4] What mutuality means will vary with the types of contract situations and the intention of the parties. It at least implies that the parties have agreed to assume obligations that move from each of them to the other. In a situation involving a promise for a promise, the mutuality is provided by the promises, spoken of in law as the *quid pro quo*. Figure 5.4 shows Step 3 and illustrates mutuality.

Consideration

Consideration has been defined as "a benefit to the party promising or a loss or detriment to the party to whom a promise is made."[5] The courts think of considerations as "reasons for enforcing promises," and they do not have to be expressed in, or equated to, economic value. Consideration can be doing nothing if that is what the parties bargain for. For centuries, consideration has had to be present in common-law contracts (at least Anglo-American contracts).

FIGURE 5.4   Mutuality.

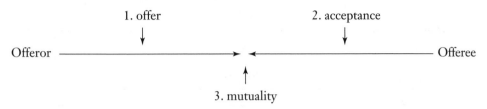

Step 3:   **Mutuality**

At the time of acceptance, this requirement is generally met.

1. offer   2. acceptance

Offeror ————————————→ ←———————————— Offeree

3. mutuality

The "minds have met" or as one book states, "there is a manifestation of mutual assent." If a meeting of the minds should fail, there is no mutuality and thus no contract.

Although consideration must be present, there is no requirement that it be adequate. The parties to a contract are considered to be the sole judges of value as it relates to consideration. A promise to sell a $10 million hotel for $1.00 would be adequate consideration if that is what the parties in fact bargained for. Contract law does not require that equal value be given for equal value, only that consideration, in some form, be present. Anything that confers a benefit on the party to whom the promise is made, or loss or inconvenience to the party making the promise, is sufficient. Consideration could be an extension of payment on a note—or giving up smoking. The consideration does not have to affect any interest of the party making the promise. It is sufficient if it affects an interest of the party to whom the promise is made.

As a black letter (established) rule, mutual promises standing alone provide the consideration to support themselves. Agreeing to do what one is already bound to do, however, will not supply consideration, as it provides no legal reason to enforce the promise. In addition, something that has occurred or has been paid before a promise is made will not support that promise. Consideration must relate to the present or future. Figure 5.5 illustrates consideration.

Consideration can take the form of an act, a promise, a nonact, a forbearance, cash, or a combination of these elements. One characteristic of it is that there must be some change, no matter how slight or insignificant, in the legal status of the parties. Other matters that supply consideration include support and maintenance, withholding competition, and giving up the right to file a lawsuit. "Failure of consideration" occurs when what is promised does not materialize as agreed.

In addition to the four requirements just discussed, a contract must be between parties of contractual capacity and have a legal purpose.

Competent Parties

Both parties to a contract must be of the age of majority; functioning free from duress, fraud, or mistake; and have no mental disabilities that would render them

FIGURE 5.5 Consideration.

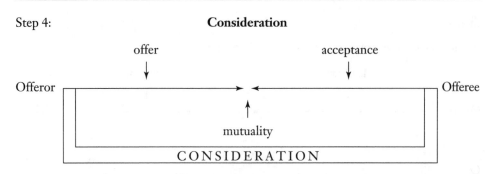

Consideration is a legal reason for a court to enforce the contract. It can be money, or it can assume other forms at law and does not have to be adequate. It simply must be present. It supports or holds up the offer and acceptance.

incapable of knowing the nature and consequences of their acts. An incompetent party can cause a contract to be void or voidable, depending upon the circumstances. The following persons are considered to be incompetent to contract: infants; those who are adjudicated as insane; intoxicated persons; those under the influence of narcotics; and those who, because of the nature of the surrounding circumstances, are not capable of exercising normal, rational judgment.

Legal Purpose

A contract must be for a legal purpose. Courts will not force parties to do illegal acts even if the parties contract to do them. Thus, if a so-called contract is for an illegal purpose, it cannot and will not be enforced in court. Illegal bargains, which often involve violations of statutes, include contracts of bribery, extortion, gambling, usury, and contracts to violate licensing laws. Once the six requirements are met, a valid contract comes into being. A list of examples at an inn follows.

Common-Law Contracts: Inn Examples

1. B requests a room at the inn and the inn accepts.
2. B reserves a room at the inn, but it is conditioned upon arrival before 6:00 P.M. B arrives at 5:45 P.M.
3. C agrees in writing to sell her inn to D for $10,000,000.
4. Guest X at a hotel gives his suit to a bellboy for cleaning, pressing, and a return the next day. The work is done and the suit is returned and full payment is made by T.
5. Travel Agent Z books T on a trip around the world.
6. Guest H deposits valuables at the front desk of the hotel.
7. Traveler Jim leaves his auto with the inn valet.

8. At a restaurant, patron U checks her fur coat at the check room and pays a $1.00 fee.

9. A hotel contracts with a band for performances on the following four weekends.

It is next necessary to learn something about contract performance and breach.

PERFORMANCE AND BREACH

Of the countless contracts entered into yearly, most are performed without problems. It is to those contracts in which disputes arise that we will now examine.

Breach

A breach of contract is anything so material and important that it will defeat the essential purposes of the parties to a contract.[6] Where a breach occurs, damages to compensate the other party for loss are generally available. The other party, however, may not be able to prove loss and, thus, recovers nothing. A breach of contract is not a criminal act. It is simply a violation of the civil duty to honor one's promises. The Thirteenth Amendment prohibits "involuntary servitude," and this keeps civil debts from being criminal in nature.

Anticipatory Breach

If one party to a contract makes it clear that he or she will not perform when the time arises, the other party can "anticipate" the breach and sue at once.[7]

Refusal to Perform

If, when time of performance arrives, one party refuses to perform, that party is guilty of breach of contract and can be held responsible for loss caused by the refusal. If one refuses to perform a minor part of a contract, however, this may not excuse the other party from performing.

If a breach occurs because of fraud on the part of one party, the injured party may sue in tort or contract. If one proceeds in a contract action for the loss suffered, a later tort action will be barred because an "election" has been made. One cannot sue twice even if the breach gives rise to two causes of action.

Damages Recoverable

What can be recovered because of a breach of contract are damages (money) that fairly, reasonably, and naturally arise in the course of such breach.[8] One will not be allowed to escape liability where the loss will be substantial but not capable of precise determination. The court will allow a "reasonable standards" measurement to be used, with the matter being a question of fact for a jury to determine. If proof of damages must be based on pure speculation, however, the proof will fail. The courts will not permit guessing in the proof of contract damages.

As a general principle of law, when a contract is breached, the damages that can be awarded in court are those that follow naturally as a result of the breach such as disappointment and perhaps mental distress.

On the other hand, if a contract, such as one for an inn reservation, is breached in a reckless and wanton manner, the person injured also can ask for damages based on the tort.[9] Otherwise, a simple breach of a reservation contract does not permit recovery of punitive or exemplary damages, attorney fees, or other damages resulting from the breach.[10] A simple breach of contract, with nothing more, never will be a tort.[11]

If a breach of a reservation contract is caused by no-shows, the inn has the right to seek damages. For a case in which a hotel recovered for the cost of 120 rooms not occupied, see *Hotel Del Cornonado v. Qwip Systems*.[12] As a general rule, damages in a court action cannot exceed the assets of the defendants, whether a corporation, chief executive officers, directors, or others.

Damages to Punish (Punitive)

If innkeeper Y overbooks deliberately and maliciously, knowing that innocent, unsuspecting travelers will be "walked," Y can be asked to pay for actual losses and possibly also be punished by having to pay an extra sum for the deliberate act of overbooking.

The courts often refer to punitive damages as being "exemplary"—designed to make an example of. Not doing something promptly that should have been done, such as mopping up rain water from umbrellas on the marble floors in the lobby, or a delay in cleaning up a plate spill in the restaurant, is not enough to allow punitive damages to be recovered. Something must be present in addition, such as maliciousness, willfulness, recklessness, or deliberateness. Punitive damages are almost never permitted in a mere breach-of-contract situation at a hospitality industry facility.[13]

Custom and Usage

Can custom and usage be used to defeat a contract action for breach of a reservation contract? A federal judge in Pennsylvania had this to say: "The plain terms of the contract prevail over trade usage or custom. . . . Custom and usage evidence cannot create an ambiguity where none exists."[14]

Nominal Damages

When nominal damages are awarded, it means the winning party has proved liability but has failed in his or her proof of loss. The typical nominal-damages verdict is $1.00. Such an award has the practical effect of placing the costs of the litigation on the losing party.

Liquidated Damages

The parties to a contract may agree in advance as to what the damages will be in the event of a later breach. Such provisions are enforceable provided they bear a reasonable relationship to actual loss and are not in the form of a penalty. "Liquidated" tells us that the damages are "set" in advance.

To illustrate, Motel Zero contracts with Ace Construction to remodel the pool. The price agreed upon is $200,000, which includes all costs and labor. The work is to be completed no later than May 31, the customary pool opening date in Eastern states.

The parties agree that, if the work is not completed by that date, the construction firm will forfeit $500 for each day the firm is late. Because the motel sells pool memberships at $100 per family, the agreed-upon damages would be reasonable and would be enforced by the court. If the pool is 30 days late in completion, the motel can deduct $15,000 from the final payment.

If a liquidated-damage clause is not included in a contract, and even if a completion date is spelled out, the passage of that time without completion of the contract generally will *not* be held to be a major breach. The exception to this would be if the contract makes "time of the essence."

"Time Is of the Essence"

If these words are used in a contract, the courts will treat the date specified as the time by which performance must be completed. In some contract situations, the legal remedy of damages (dollars) may not be sufficient. A second remedy is provided by equity.

SPECIFIC PERFORMANCE

If the subject matter of a contract is unique, upon breach by one party, the other may ask a judge to specifically require the breaching party to perform the contract. This remedy is available in real estate contracts because each parcel of real estate is unique.

Specific performance cannot be used in personal-service contracts or in any situation in which supervision of the court would be needed to carry out the contract. In such cases, the only remedy would be an action for damages.

To conclude our discussion of common-law contracts, we will examine implied contracts, illegal contracts, and contracts that violate public policy.

IMPLIED CONTRACTS

A contract can be implied in fact or implied in law. The principle involved is an equitable one that holds that one should not enrich oneself unjustly at the expense of another.

A contract implied in fact is a true contract, the terms of which will be inferred from the circumstances. When one confers benefits upon another, which the other knows of and should pay for, the law implies an agreement that such payment will be made. An express contract thus is distinguishable from one implied in fact. In the former, the terms are agreed upon. In the latter, the terms are implied from the conduct of the parties.

Contracts *implied in law* are not true contracts. Courts resort to them for purposes of remedy only. These often are referred to as "quasi-contracts." The widest application is in situations where, if they are not used, an injustice will occur. Such contracts are quite rare in practice. As a general rule, where an express contract exists, an implied contract in fact (or in law) never will arise. The express contract controls.

ILLEGAL CONTRACTS

An illegal contract is one that has as its object an illegal purpose as discussed previously. As a general rule, an illegal contract is void—not voidable—and cannot be the subject of a court action for breach of that contract. There can be no enforcement of an illegal contract in law or equity, whether the illegality existed at the outset or "intervened" later. For example, a subsequent statute may make the terms of a prior contract unlawful. In addition, "when an illegal modification of a lawful contract is attempted, the modification is a nullity and the contract is unscathed."[15]

An illegal contract should be distinguished from one that is against public policy.

CONTRACTS AGAINST PUBLIC POLICY

"Public policy" relates to the requirements of the public welfare. Whatever tends to injustice or oppression, restraint of liberty, commerce, and natural or legal rights; whatever tends to obstruction of justice, or to the violation of a statute; and whatever is against good morals, when made the object of a contract, is against public policy and therefore void and not susceptible of enforcement."[16] Contracts against public policy may be illegal, but there are also legal contracts that violate public policy.

An example of a contract against public policy is one in which a party stipulates for his exemption from liability for the consequences of his own negligence. Such a contract is not permitted at law. Other examples include contracts to influence legislation, the joining of companies to circumvent the effect of restrictive statutes, and a contract by a servant or agent promising to release the master *before* injury occurs to others.

SUMMARY

Common-law contract rules regulate our daily activities such as the purchase of gasoline or a house. These rules find their origins in earlier centuries because it was just as necessary then, as it is now, to make certain that bargains made in exchange for value were kept.

Thus, the legal meanings of "offer," "acceptance," "mutuality," "competent parties," and "legal purpose" are as important to us today as they were thousands of years ago. The common law of contract has had a profound impact on our daily affairs, and it is important to accept the importance of this vast body of law. This is especially so in the HH&T industries because they are "contract intensive." Common-law contract rules form the very means by which these industries operate and thrive. In Chapter 1, we distinguished these contracts briefly from sales contracts. This second body of contract law forms the basis of Chapter 6, and it too is of importance in the three industries under discussion.

The interpretation of contracts becomes a job for our courts when contracting parties cannot agree. Over the centuries, the courts have created rules to be used when interpreting contracts. We have rules of contract creation, and we have rules of contract interpretation, or construction, of what a contract means.

The distinction between unilateral and bilateral contracts is important at hotel front desks. The unilateral technique can be an effective tool in avoiding a later claim of overbooking. A breach of contract for a room at midnight at an isolated location can be a serious matter to the traveler. Large sums of money are often awarded when such cases go before judges and juries.

The importance of the statute of frauds also must be understood. In its simplest sense, it tells us that certain contracts must be in writing and signed, and if not, they cannot later be enforced in a court. The statute of frauds is to be distinguished from statutes of limitations. These latter statutes place limits upon the time periods in which the courts can be used to enforce contracts. This of course is also true in tort actions. Statutes of limitations do not erase or destroy a contract or a tort action; they simply do not allow the courts to enforce such actions.

QUESTIONS

1. True or false: A "several" contract is one that can be held to be binding on A and B or A or B.
2. What is the danger inherent in a unilateral contract situation?
3. Under what legal theory may a court imply a contract at law?
4. What evil was the statute of frauds designed to avoid?
5. True or false: Consideration always must have a dollar value.
6. Why do mutual promises standing alone provide consideration?
7. Why must one be careful when anticipating a breach of contract?
8. What are liquidated damages?
9. What legal impact do the words "time is of the essence" have on a contract?
10. Under what circumstances might a jury award nominal damages in a motel contract breach case?

NOTES

1. *Williston on Contracts*, sec. 1, p. 1.
2. *Williston on Contracts*, sec. 3. p. 6.
3. *Barn and Alp.* 681, 106 *Eng. Reg.* 250 (K.B. 1818).
4. *Bott v. Wheller,* 183 Va. 643, 33 S.E. 2d 184.
5. *Roller v. McGraw,* 63 W. Va. 462, 60 S.E. 410.
6. *F. A. D'Andrea, Inc. v. Dodge,* 15 F. 2d 1003.
7. *Burke v. Shaver,* 92 Va. 345, 23 S.E. 749.
8. *Krikorian v. Dailey,* 171 Va. 16, 197 S.E. 442.
9. *Dold v. Outrigger,* 501 P. 2d 368 (Hawaii 1972).

10. *Brown v. Hilton Hotels Corporation*, 211 S.E. 2d 125 (Georgia 1974).
11. *Mauldin v. Sheffer*, 150 S.E. 2d 150 (Georgia 1990).
12. N.Y.L.J., July 16, 1981, page 13, col. 4 (N.Y. Sup.).
13. *Elliott Izen v. James Winaker et al.*, 589 A. 2d 824 (Rhode Island 1991).
14. *King of Prussia v. Greyhound Lines, Inc.*, 457 F. Supp. 56 (E.D. Pa.).
15. *Tearney v. Marmison*, 103 W. Va. 394, 137 S.E. 543.
16. *Williams v. Board of Education*, 45 W. Va. 199, 31 S.E. 985.

Sales Contracts

Overview

HERE WE ENCOUNTER the contract law designed to cover the purchase and sale of goods between merchants. Because *all* purchases of food, drink, and supplies at all American hotels, motels, bars, and other HH&T components are controlled by this law, a working understanding of it is imperative.

Article 2 of the Uniform Commercial Code, Sales, is a product of the National Commission on Uniform State Laws. The UCC is the most significant law created by the NCUSL and has been adopted in full or amended form by forty-nine states, and in part (including Article 2) by Louisiana. Article 2 is a rewrite of the Uniform Sales Act, created in 1908, so the subject matter is not completely new. Yet, in relation to common-law contract rules that go back for centuries, it is quite new.

In this chapter we first present a non-legal narrative in which the features of Article 2 are set forth in nonlegal terms. This is followed by a presentation of the law. Finally, examples are offered with accompanying drawings, questions, and answers to demonstrate what this law means in practice. The following is taken from John R. Goodwin, *Hotel and Casino Law Letter,* Volume 2–3, April 1983.

THE PURCHASE OF GOODS

Let's walk toward the "back of our house" with the idea of taking a legal look at what goes on in our purchasing department. . . . While there, we might as well also take a look at our receiving department.

There are a lot of goods coming in each day and these items are worth a bundle. Thus, we need to pay the same attention to them as we would if it was cash that we were receiving and not goods.

So we have taken a look at the physical receipt of our goods, and what have we seen? A rather nondescript location with some peeling paint and hand-cart gouges in the plaster, but other than that we are in good shape. Well, we certainly hope so, but that is our reason for a look at our receiving and purchasing departments in the first place. There could be legal problems in both, and these problems could be serious indeed.

What Law Governs?

The law that governs the buying and selling of goods between merchants in all fifty states, including Louisiana, is Article 2 of the Uniform Commercial Code, known in legal circles as "sales law." Since innkeepers, restaurateurs, bar operators, and others in the HH&T industry are merchants as that word is defined in Article 2, and since they most assuredly purchase goods from other merchants, this particular law applies to them. . . .

UCC 2-104 defines a "merchant" as ". . . a person who deals in goods of the kind or otherwise by his occupation holds himself out as having knowledge or skill peculiar to the practices or goods involved in the transaction or to whom such knowledge or skill may be attributed by his employment of an agent who . . . holds himself out as having such knowledge or skill." So there it is: If the HH&T manager in fact does not have the knowledge or skill of a merchant, he or she must hire a purchasing agent who does.

What this means is that Article 2, UCC, *does* apply and that the HH&T manager will be expected to measure up to the standard of a "reasonable merchant."

What Kind of Law Is Article 2 of the UCC?

First, it is a complicated body of contract law. Second, it is new as legal matters go, being a product of the past four decades. Finally, it must be distinguished from that age-old body of contract law that we can trace back to the ancient Egyptians. If we are buying land or an inn, or hiring employees, the common law of contracts is there to guide us. If we are buying linens, foodstuffs, lamps, chairs, and other supplies, we must look to Article 2, Sales, for guidance.

We see, then, that our sales contracts involve the back of our house since that is where we receive and store our goods, and that is why we decided to take a look there in the beginning.

To facilitate our discussion of the purchasing and receiving departments, let's assume that we need to purchase 10,000 sheets for immediate and future use in our inn.

We should look to state statutes to see if our legislature has directed its attention to such matters dealing with our purchase. As it turns out, the legislatures have done just that in many states. To illustrate, Nevada Revised Statutes, 447.090, subsection 3, provides: "Sheets shall be at least 98 inches long and of sufficient width to cover the mattress and spring completely." Other states, such as Virginia, specify the size and also the substance from which they must be made.

So, being an "HH&T legal manager," and wanting to comply with laws that are binding upon us, we first go to the statutes. *Now* we turn to the catalogs and find a source for what we need.

We are in a hurry as usual, so let's get on the phone and place the order directly. That way we will get our linens shipped faster. This is all right, but there is a legal problem to consider since Article 2 does have a statute of frauds. . . .

Statute of Frauds

Article 2-201, UCC, states: "A contract for the sale [purchase] of goods for the price of $500 or more is not enforceable by way of action or defense unless there is some writing sufficient to indicate that a contract for the sale has been made between the parties and signed by the party against whom such enforcement is sought or by his authorized . . . agent." While there are three exceptions to this, the basic rule remains. So back to that oral order. Since our 10,000 sheets will cost more than $500, must we use a "writing?" We had better do so, because the seller is going to insist that we do—and, in the end, we will want to do so too. There are two ways we can [create a "writing"].

First Choice

We can place our order by use of a written purchase order, signed by our authorized agent. That will solve the problem. We will have our purchase order forms prepared by counsel and will use multiple copies for receiving, accounting, and one for the boss, or we may use computer forms. It would still be nice if we could also use the phone in order to speed things up and there is a way we can do this so long as we do it right. [We also can use the universal fax service.]

Second Choice

We place the order by phone: "Please ship us 10,000 sheets, size 100" x 96", catalog item XYZ, at a per-unit price of $16.00 each, FOB our inn, delivery needed by June 1." So this speeds it up—but what about UCC 2–201? It is still there and we do need to comply with it.

Written Confirmation

There is a way we can comply with the statute of frauds: . . . by *confirming* the oral order, in writing, and *our agent signs it.* Now under UCC 2-201 (2), if we send the confirmation within a reasonable time, it satisfies the statute of frauds. . . .

Our Policy in Purchasing Goods

First, we are going to place our orders of goods of $500 or more in writing.

Second, if we do place orders by phone or fax, we are going to confirm them in writing, over our agent's signature, and we are going to do this in due course.

So, now that our order has been placed, where are we? Well, we might receive a written acknowledgment of our order, and if our seller is being careful, we can be certain that we will receive one. Does it matter if we do? It certainly does, because the acknowledgment may change our order and if this occurs, the UCC places responsibilities upon [us as the buyer].

What Must We (the Buyer) Do?

Once we receive notice of a nonconforming shipment, we have two choices: (1) object and tell why we cannot use the substituted goods or (2) pay the price.

Are we saying that we may be held responsible for goods *that we did not order?* That is exactly what we are saying, and the law that creates this particular situation will be explored in a moment. Suffice it to say that we must take a look at our acknowledgments as we receive them, and check them against our purchase orders. To do otherwise is to court legal problems. For example, what if the price is *higher* on the acknowledgment than it is on the purchase order?

We must remember that the acknowledgment is a written confirmation of *our* order. Thus, we have to object to it within 10 days [under UCC terms]. If our objection arrives before the goods are shipped, then no harm has been done if what we object to is corrected. Change the facts, however, and assume that we do not receive an acknowledgment. We must now await the arrival of the goods.

The Shipment Arrives

Assume that the delivery is different from what we ordered and is, thus, "nonconforming." Now what? Several things can happen. First, if we were to become angry about the misdelivery, we might instruct our sales personnel to set the goods aside and not let the seller have them back. That would teach them a lesson, wouldn't it? Not at all, because "acting inconsistently" with someone else's merchandise *constitutes an acceptance* and we now must pay for something that we did not order! So we would be the ones who learned a lesson. We cannot act inconsistently with goods that belong to someone else.

A second choice is to place the goods in stock and use them. We might well decide to do that if the goods are an acceptable alternate to what was ordered, but hold on a minute. The goods we received are *cheaper* than what we ordered. What now? No problem because, by accepting the goods, we have bought them at the lower price so that is what we must pay. If the nonconforming goods had been at a *higher price* and we accept them, we do so at the higher price. Since this is something that we usually do not want to do, what now?

How to Handle Nonconforming Goods

. . . The Code makes it clear that, if nonconforming goods are received, we must do three things. First, we must inspect the goods; second, we must reject the goods if we do not want them; and, third, we must state why we cannot use the goods. . . . If we fail to meet this three-part test, *then we have accepted the goods!* . . . But why such a rule?

The reasoning behind the rule is this: Since Article 2 applies to merchants, such persons should have knowledge of what types of goods can be substituted for others that have been ordered. If such a substitution is made and the other merchant does not object, then why shouldn't there be an acceptance? If the seller is incorrect about the substitution, then that person has a right to be told why the substitution is not acceptable. . . . Once the seller is told why the nonconforming goods are unacceptable, the seller has the right to "cure"—that is, send conforming goods.

In legal circles, this process is known as the "perfect tender-cure" rule. The buyer is entitled to a "perfect tender": exactly what was ordered. But if this is not received, the seller has the right to "cure." The only way a seller can cure is to be told why the goods are not acceptable.

Does this mean that if we receive nonconforming goods and fail to inspect, reject, and state why, we have accepted those goods and must pay for them? The answer is "yes" as the U. S. Army found out with a large amount of hams (*Max Bauer Meat Packer, Inc. v. United States*, 458 Fed. 2d 88, 10 UCC Rep. 1056 (U. S. Court of Claims, 1972)), and Eastern Airlines with nonconforming 727 jet aircraft (*Eastern Airlines, Inc. v. McDonnell Douglas Corp.*, 532 F.2d 957, 19 UCC Rep. 353 (5th Cir. 1976)). The law applies to big orders of goods as well as small. . . .

How quickly must we inspect, reject, and state why? In the ham case, the army rejected the hams in less than five hours. The court held that *that was too long* and thus the army had to pay for hams it did not order, did not want, and could not use. In the airline case, Eastern waited a few weeks before it discovered that its new fleet of jet aircraft was not what was wanted. The court held that a few weeks was too long and Eastern wound up with jet aircraft that did not meet its specifications.

The Code says that the rejection must be "seasonable" and that seems to mean "in due course." With food that is going to be placed into preparation, such as the U. S. Army hams at Thanksgiving time, it would mean a short time indeed.

It is clear that our policy on all incoming goods must be to inspect in due course. If any items are nonconforming, we must reject and state why as part of the same time frame. Having done that, we have not accepted the goods and have no contract obligation to pay for them.

What About the Goods Themselves?

True, we still have the goods in our possession, but we now hold them under the law of bailment and not the law of sales. As a bailee, we must use ordinary and reasonable care to protect and safeguard them for disposition by the owner, namely the seller. If we use ordinary care and the goods are stolen or destroyed by fire, the loss falls on the seller and not us. This makes the rejection rules even more important to us, as can be seen.

If the rejected goods are perishable and we cannot safeguard them, we should tell the seller at once. The seller may instruct us to sell them at a loss or to ship them elsewhere. We are expected to follow such orders, but *at the expense of the seller.* . . . Does this law mean we are going to have to spend every minute of every hour looking at each item we receive to make sure each is conforming? For example, there is our order of new sheets packed three to a box. Do we have to open each box and inspect each linen for size and quality?

Scope of Inspection

All we have to do is to inspect *by sample*. A box or two from different parts of the shipment will meet the legal requirement of inspection.

What if our shipment is in sealed containers that we cannot open until we are ready to use them, such as canned food? If we open them later and find that the contents are nonconforming, are we stuck with them? Not at all, because the Code covers this situation too.

Revoking an Acceptance

If defects are hidden or sealed and are not likely to be discovered until use, which may not come until later, then we can revoke our acceptance. By revoking our acceptance, and doing so seasonably, the seller then has the right to cure. If the seller cannot cure, the goods belong to the seller and we hold them as a bailee.

We have had a look at the laws that control our [purchase of goods]. . . . When one considers that merchants are involved, the rules are not unreasonable at all. These rules represent a special contract law that has been designed to cover the sale of goods between merchants. If we conduct ourselves in our buying as a reasonable merchant would be expected to do, in most instances we would be complying with the rules.

Good faith and honesty are, of course, involved because merchants should so conduct themselves. Failure to act [in this manner] can trigger many of the rules of Article 2. . . .

In our discussion, we have left many topics unmentioned, such as late delivery, insolvency of a buyer, recapture of goods, and others. Suffice it to say that Article 2 covers all of these and more, and if they become involved in our buying and receiving, legal advice must be sought.

Otherwise, if we act in good faith and honesty and watch what we are doing in our purchasing and receiving department, and provide instruction in the form of house policies, we can get along nicely in the company of a contract law called "sales."

With the above in mind as an introduction, let's turn to some of the more technical aspects of the law.

Article 2 covers "transactions in goods," and this is what is so important to the HH&T industry.[1]

The courts recognize that if a seller/merchant does not disclose defects known to exist in the goods to be delivered to the buyer, and if such defects cause loss to guests and or patrons of the buyer, the seller will be held accountable for the loss to guests or patrons.

The defect, however, must not be one that is clearly visible to the buyer or agents of the buyer. In that instance, it becomes the duty of the buyer to refuse the goods or negate the dangers that they pose to guests or patrons. Failure to do either would be negligence, and this could place legal responsibility upon the buyer.[2]

Where there are ambiguities or gaps in a sales transaction, the courts will interpret the contract by using course of performance and usage of trade. In this regard, philosophy merges with law, and we are held to what we actually do in the marketplace and not what we *should* do there.

The standards of performance under Article 2 are "reasonableness," "commercial reasonableness," and "seasonably." The "reasonable person" standard of the common law does not apply, however. The reason is that what a reasonable person might do in a given sales contract situation might not at all be what a "reasonable merchant" would do under the same circumstances.

What Goods Are "Merchantable"?

Under the UCC Article 2–314, subsection (2), for goods to be merchantable, they must be at least such as:

(a) pass without objection in the trade under the contract description; and
(b) in the case of fungible goods, are of fair average quality within the description; and
(c) are fit for the ordinary purposes for which such goods are used; and
(d) run, within the variations permitted by the agreement, of even kind, quality, and quantity within each unit and among all units involved; and
(e) are adequately contained, packaged, and labeled as the agreement may require; and
(f) conform to the promises or affirmations of fact made on the container or label if any.

States that have varied from the official text of 2–314 include Alabama, Maryland, Minnesota, Mississippi, and South Carolina.

Warranties Under Article 2, UCC, Section 2–318

An important part of the UCC has to do with "warranties" or promises made by sellers, and these are found in this section. When the UCC was offered to the states for adoption, alternatives were provided for Section 2–318. Eighteen states accepted the provisions as written. All of the other states accepted alternatives or did not adopt the section at all.

Today, there is no uniformity in the states as to the express and implied warranties. On the other hand, when judges in the nonconforming states are called on for decisions, it is obvious from the cases that they use Section 2–318 of the UCC as a guideline. *Warranties*, whether express or implied, are promises that the law expects to be kept. This subject will be discussed in detail in Chapter 21.

A helpful way to continue with technical aspects of Article 2 is by examining key terms encountered in the law of sales.

KEY TERMS

A buyer is any person who buys or contracts to buy goods. A seller is one who sells or contracts to sell goods. A merchant is one who deals in those goods and has knowledge or skills of those goods and practices of the transaction. A merchant also can be one who has this skill and knowledge attributed to him or her because of the use of agents. An innkeeper ordering food supplies for the restaurant is a merchant. So is the supplier of those goods. This brings us to the definition of *goods*, and related terms.

Goods means all items that are movable at the time they become the subject of a sales contract.[3] The following are quoted from Article 2.

Lot means a parcel or a single article which is the subject matter of a separate sale or delivery, whether or not it is sufficient to perform the contract.[4]

A *commercial unit* may be a single article (such as a machine) or a set of articles (such as a suite of furniture or an assortment of sizes) or a quantity (such as a bale, gross, or carload) or any other unit treated in use or in the relevant market as a single whole.[5]

Contract and *agreement* are limited to those relating to the present or future sale of goods. *Contract for sale* includes both a present sale of goods and a contract to sell goods at a future time. A *sale* consists of the passing of title from the seller to the buyer for a price. A *present sale* means a sale . . . accomplished by the making of the contract.[6]

Goods or conduct including any part of a performance are "conforming" or conform to the contract when they are in accordance with the obligations under the contract.[7]

Termination occurs when either party pursuant to a power created by agreement or law puts an end to the contract otherwise than for its breach.[8]

Cancellation occurs when either party puts an end to the contract for breach by the other, and its effect is the same as that of termination except that the canceling party also retains any remedy for breach of the whole contract or any unperformed balance.[9]

A contract for the sale of timber, minerals, or the like or a structure or its materials to be removed from realty is a contract for the sale of goods if they are to be severed by the seller.[10]

Now we need to learn how a sales contract is formed.

FORMATION OF A SALES CONTRACT

Statute of Frauds

A contract for the sale of goods for $500 or more requires some writing sufficient to indicate the contract, and it must be signed by the one against whom enforcement is sought. It can be signed by an agent. Such writing is not insufficient if it omits a term agreed upon. If it states a quantity of goods incorrectly, the writing is not effective beyond that quantity.[11] The statute does not apply at all if (1) specially manufactured goods are involved, if (2) one admits in court that a contract had been made, or if (3) one receives the goods and pays for them. If a sales contract is in written form and then is modified, the modification also should be in writing and signed. Article 2 makes it clear that an oral modification *does not* satisfy the statute of frauds, although it may constitute a waiver.[12] To rely upon the waiver, however, is not a good idea.[13]

Examples

Certain Alabama farmers contracted to sell their crop of cotton one year for prices in the 3 cents to 35 cents per pound range. At the time the crop was in, the price was 80 cents on the market, and the farmers refused to honor the contract to sell. Because the original contract had been oral, the court ruled that the statute of frauds governed and the farmers were free to sell as they pleased.[14]

In a case that arose in Minnesota, a supplier on the witness stand stated in part

> . . . I was interested in buying up to fifty million gallons a year (of heating oil). I
> said we were interested in selling the product, and we agreed to sell it—or to put
> it in the singular, I agreed to sell it, subject to credit clearance and other clearances
> back at the home office.

The court held that this admission was sufficient to hold the supplier to the oral
sales contract.[15]

Avoiding Statute of Frauds

If one is in a situation in which the other party refuses to place anything in writing, can something be done to avoid the statute of frauds problem? Under UCC
Article 2-201(2), if one party sends the other a letter of confirmation of the oral
deal, and if the other party does not object within ten days, that letter meets the
requirements of the statute. Thus, the sales statute of frauds can be met by the
party who wants to play it safe by getting the agreement in writing—even if the
other party does not.

Parol-Evidence Rule

Related to the statute of frauds is the parol-evidence rule. The parol-evidence rule
is based upon the common-law principle that, when two persons reduce their agreement to writing, neither can vary or alter that agreement later by oral testimony.
This rule has been carried into sales contracts in a modified form. What is reduced
to writing cannot be altered by oral testimony—but it can be explained by course of
dealing, usage of trade, and prior performance between the parties. The rule does
not prohibit oral testimony as to terms not included in the written contract.

A contract for the sale of goods may be made in any manner sufficient to show
agreement, including conduct that recognizes existence of the contract.[16] One must
not forget, however, the effect of the statute of frauds or the parol-evidence rule.

The precise time of the making of the contract is not essential,[17] and the fact
that one or more terms are left open does not cause it to fail for indefiniteness.[18]
These rules are contrary to common-law contract principles.

OFFER AND ACCEPTANCE

A sales offer invites acceptance in any reasonable manner. If one offers to buy
goods that must be shipped, a prompt shipment or promise to ship will be an
acceptance. If the offer indicates that the offer is to be accepted by beginning to
perform, and the other person does not begin the performance, the offeror may
treat the offer as having lapsed before acceptance.[19]

An offer can become "firm"—cannot be revoked—if a merchant promises
another in writing to hold the offer open for a period not to exceed three months.
Such an offer takes the form of an *option*, and no consideration is required to make
the option binding on the one who made it.[20]

If Acceptance Changes Offer

If one accepts an offer but changes the terms, *it still may be a good acceptance.* The additional terms are treated as a proposal to make additions to the contract and will become part of the contract unless:

1. The offer limited the terms of the acceptance.
2. The changes alter the offer *materially.*
3. The other party gives prompt notification of objections to the changes.[21]

If the writings of the parties do not establish a contract, yet the parties recognize the existence of one, the contract will be treated as one that contains the terms upon which there is agreement. The UCC then will provide the lacking terms. Article 2 contains provisions for modification, rescission, and waiver of a sales contract, and all of these should be reduced to writing.[22]

Battle of the Forms

Quite often, the buyer uses a written purchase order when ordering goods, and the seller, in turn, uses a written acknowledgment. This is a good business/legal practice on both sides, for it removes the statute of frauds from any future legal disputes. The use of such documents, which should be initialed or signed by the parties or their agents, satisfies the sales statute of frauds. But what happens if the forms do not agree as to the terms found on them?

For example, the buyer's form says, "You (the seller) pay the freight." On the seller's acknowledgment is found the phrase "FOB our warehouse." This means the buyer must pay the freight from the seller's warehouse to the destination. Thus, the forms do not agree. This is not unusual in sales contract situations and has become known as the "battle of the conflicting forms." Does such a state of facts destroy the sales contract? It certainly would destroy a pending common-law contract.

As it turns out, Article 2 covers this situation. Here is how it works. First, examine Figures 6.1 and 6.2. Notice that the number of units has been reduced on the acknowledgment; the size and price are different; and while terms 1 and 2 are the same on both forms, terms 3, 4, and 5 are not.

The UCC says there *is* a contract as to the terms upon which the parties agree. As to the terms upon which they disagree, "course of performance" controls, supplemented by "course of dealing" and "usage of trade." Here, there is not only a contract between the parties, but its terms are there even if a court has to determine those terms.

These situations often arise in HH&T operations. Carpeting at an inn may stretch, causing a dispute over quality. Glass in windows may stain and have to be replaced. Air conditioners may fail when placed into use. What did the contracts have to say about such contingencies? Probably nothing at all, yet the law provides the terms to cover these situations.

Revocation of a Sales Offer

One who makes a sales contract offer can revoke it before acceptance. The exceptions are when it is a "firm offer" or when the other party had timely started

FIGURE 6.1   A purchase order.

To: Zero Corporation
Ship: 10,000 units ABC, Model S, 1½" × 8" at $9.00 per unit
Terms: 1. A
           2. B
           3. C
           4. D
           5. E

Hotel,
s/s Ace/, Inc.

FIGURE 6.2   An acknowledgment.

            Hotel
To: ACE/, Inc.
Thanks
Will ship 9,000 units ABC, Model S, 1¼" × 8" at $9.50 per unit.
Terms: 1. A
            2. B
            3. F
            4. G
            5. H

s/s Zero Corporation

---

performance. The UCC does not change prior contract law in this area. Unless displaced by the particular provisions of Article 2, the principles of law and equity, including the law merchant and the law relative to capacity to contract, principal and agent, estoppel, fraud, misrepresentation, duress, coercion, mistake, bankruptcy, or other validating or invalidating cause shall supplement its (Article 2) provisions.[23]

OBLIGATIONS OF THE PARTIES TO A SALES CONTRACT

Tender of Delivery

The seller has a duty to make a proper tender of delivery under the terms of the contract. This is done by placing conforming goods at the buyer's disposal and by notifying him or her so the buyer can take delivery. Tender must be at a reasonable hour and under reasonable circumstances. The goods must be held by the seller or seller's agent for a reasonable time to give the buyer opportunity to take possession.

Stopping Goods in Transit

Under certain conditions, a seller can stop goods that are in transit to the buyer. If it is learned that the buyer is insolvent or has missed a payment due the seller, shipment can be stopped. If the goods are in the hands of a common carrier, shipment cannot be stopped unless it is a truckload, carload, or planeload. A seller cannot stop a UPS truck and demand that the driver sift through a thousand packages to find one. The order to stop shipment must be made timely. If it is made after the goods are delivered, it comes too late.

When a proper stop shipment order has been made, the one who has the goods (bailee or shipper) must hold the goods and deliver them according to the seller's instructions.

The right to stop shipment applies only between seller and buyer. If the buyer has resold the goods to others, those goods cannot be stopped in transit.

In a Missouri case, A sold goods to B, who assigned the shipment to C on a nonnegotiable bill of lading. (A bill of lading is a list of goods received for shipment. A nonnegotiable bill is one that cannot be transferred to others, cutting off the original shipper. A negotiable bill can do just that.) The check from B to A bounced, and A stopped shipment to C. The court held that since C was not a bona fide purchaser for value, A could stop the shipment.[24] But if C had been a bona fide purchaser for value, A could not have stopped the shipment. If a stop shipment is unlawful in any respect, the seller must bear the responsibility for any loss to the buyer caused by the improper stop order.[25]

Buyer's Right of Inspection

Once the goods are tendered, the buyer has the right (and duty) to inspect the goods before accepting them.[26] This must be done at a reasonable time and place and in a reasonable manner.

If the parties agree that payment is to be made before inspection, the buyer must pay before inspection even if the goods are nonconforming. This occurs in COD[27] payments against documents of title and CIF[28] contracts. The burden is now shifted to the buyer, who must pay the price and then sue for any loss. Buyers should resist efforts to make them pay before inspection for this reason, and this should be a policy of HH&T buyers.

Improper Delivery

If an improper delivery is made, such as a shipment of nonconforming goods, the buyer must do one of three things:

1. Reject all of the goods.
2. Accept all of the goods.
3. Accept any commercial unit or units and reject the rest.[29]

If the buyer decides to do item 2, above, prompt notice should be given to the seller that the buyer demands an allowance for the failure to conform.[30]

If the buyer decides to reject the goods, two extremely important principles must be followed:

1. After prompt inspection, the buyer must notify the seller in a reasonable time that the goods are being rejected.[31] A wait of as long as an hour may be too long in some deliveries. Failure to so notify is treated as an acceptance.[32]
2. If the defects are such that they can be "cured" (corrected), the buyer also must tell the seller what these defects are.[33]

After rejection and notification, the buyer must act reasonably with the goods and follow reasonable instructions from the seller as to their disposal. These instructions might be to reship to the seller or a third party, or to sell the goods as salvage. The buyer is entitled to compensation for services performed with rejected goods.[34] If the seller fails to provide instructions in a reasonable time, the buyer can store, ship, or sell the goods for the account of the seller.[35] These are the options of the merchant-buyer. A nonmerchant-buyer has only the duty to hold the goods for the seller.

In any rejection, the buyer never should do anything that could be construed as treating the goods as being his or her own property. A court might treat such acts as an acceptance. For example, if an inn rejects an air conditioner, then refuses to allow the seller to pick it up, that would be an acceptance and render the inn liable for the price.[36]

Revoking an Acceptance

In instances where defects cannot be discovered by an immediate inspection, and where such defects are uncovered later, sometimes years later, is the buyer stuck because of the prior acceptance? No, because the buyer can, in some cases, revoke an acceptance.[37] In an Arkansas case, a court held that a defective air conditioner could be rejected three years after purchase, as it had not worked properly all along and efforts to repair it had not been successful. Thus, the right existed to revoke the acceptance.[38]

SELLER'S RIGHT TO CURE

If a seller makes an improper delivery, the seller has the right to be told why the delivery is improper. For example, a delivery of 1,000 cruise ship excursion tickets arrives and the buyer discovers that the name of the ship is wrong. The buyer must reject and state why. The seller now has the right to cure or remedy the defect by delivering new tickets.[39] If the cured goods arrive by the deadline for their use, the contract is complete and the price must be paid. If goods cannot be cured timely, the defective delivery and the rejection then would be a contract breach by the seller, and a right of the buyer to be compensated for any loss caused by the seller's improper delivery and failure to cure would exist.

If the goods arrive late in the beginning, must the buyer still reject timely and tell the seller why? A Florida case involving jet airliners answered this question "yes."[40] So the two steps of rejection should be made for *any* improper delivery that the buyer does not want to accept—even a delivery that comes too late for use.

PASSING OF TITLE

"Passing of title" (ownership) was an abstract legal concept that caused many problems prior to the UCC. Now the code contains specific provisions that regulate passing of title. Title cannot pass on goods that are not in existence and identified to the contract.[41] Title cannot pass until goods are made, if they are to be manufactured. Even after they are completed, title does not pass until the seller indicates that these goods are intended for the buyer.[42] Subject to rules such as these, the parties are free to agree at which point title is to pass.[43] The passing of title is always related to the risk of loss.

RISK OF LOSS

The parties are free to make any agreement between them as to risk of loss.[44] The agreement, however, cannot be unconscionable. The risk can be divided if they choose.[45] If a shipment contract is involved, the risk of loss normally passes to the buyer when the goods are delivered to the carrier.[46] Examples of shipment contracts include FOB,[47] point of shipment, FOB vessel or car, FAS,[48] CIF,[49] or C and F.[50]

 If the contract is a "destination agreement," risk of loss shifts to the buyer when a proper tender is made at the agreed-to point of destination.[51] "FOB destination" is a destination agreement. Common sense tells us that both buyers and sellers must be conscious of risk of loss, because it means just that. If the goods are lost, stolen, or damaged by fire or other cause, someone must bear the loss. As a policy matter, it is sound business practice to agree on the risk and then buy appropriate insurance to cover that risk. A discussion of risk of loss would not be complete without a discussion of the right to recapture goods.

RECAPTURE RIGHTS

If goods are sold on credit, tender is made, and acceptance follows but the buyer refuses to pay for the goods, can the seller "recapture" the goods? If goods are delivered to a buyer who is found to be insolvent, recapture is limited to the following ten days unless there is proof of misrepresentation of insolvency; then it is extended to three months.[52] What happens after these time periods is that the Code shifts the "goods" to a "debt," leaving the seller the right to take legal action on the debt—not the happiest thing for the seller.

MISCELLANEOUS SALES-CONTRACT CASES

Statute of Frauds

As we have seen, contracts for the sale of goods of $500 or more must be in writing. If not, and if one of the exceptions does not arise, the contract cannot be enforced. One court went beyond the exceptions and ruled that where one party has so changed his position in reliance on the oral contract that an unconscionable loss would result to the other, that person should be "estopped" to deny the contract,[53] thus enforcing the oral agreement.

Can a down payment satisfy the statute of frauds if made by check? Article 2 provides that it can do so only with respect to goods for which payment has been made and accepted.[54]

In a Maryland case,[55] a party to an oral contract wound up on the witness stand and then admitted the contract. That satisfied the statute.

Statute of Limitations

A glass wall had been installed in 1966. In 1972, a boy fell through the glass and was killed. The court held that the breach of warranty occurred at the time of installation, if it occurred at all, and because more than four years had passed, the manufacturer of the glass had no liability. This left the responsibility squarely on the buyer of the glass.

The UCC normally allows a four-year period in which to bring a suit for breach of sales contract.[56] This does not always mean what it says. Martin Becker bought a car in 1969 and sued for breach of warranty within four years. The California court held that, in that state, action for injuries caused by a wrongful act or neglect must be brought in one year.[57] It should be pointed out, however, the courts are split in such instances. This question has not been settled.

Trade usage can severely shorten the statute of limitations. Because a sales contract not only means what it says, but also is supplemented by trade custom and practices, the result can be surprising. A buyer purchased certain glass and insisted on a 100 percent guarantee against "staining." After resale to others, the glass stained and the buyer refunded the price to *his* buyers. He then turned to the seller for recovery on the guarantee. The court held that it was too late because, in the trade of glass selling, such complaints customarily were made between seven and thirty days. The contract was silent on the period of limitations, so trade practice controlled.[58]

Definiteness

In a Georgia case, the buyer agreed to buy more than $58,000 worth of goods and made a down payment of $4,000. The agreement was in writing, and all seemed in order. However, there was no payment schedule, no time for performance, and other terms were lacking. Did it fail for "indefiniteness" when the buyer wanted out? The court said no, pointing out that, because the parties had intended to make a contract, Article 2 would supply the price,[59] decide when payment was due,[60] and provide for the method and place of delivery.[61] The contract did not fail for indefiniteness even though these terms were missing.[62]

EXAMPLES

Leaving the technical discussion of Article 2, some examples provide a way to place the material of this chapter into perspective. The following symbols are used:

MB-Merchant-buyer (this would be the HH&T manager.)
MS-Merchant-seller
C-Consumer
IRS-The obligation to "inspect, reject, and state why"

Looking at Illustration 1, the goods are now on the loading platform of MB, where they had been inspected and found to be nonconforming.

ILLUSTRATION 1

MB   ①Sends written order for $10,000 in hotel supplies   → MS

②Ships nonconforming goods

MB ③ Inspects,
         Rejects,
         and States Why

---

1. As a matter of law, what is the legal relationship of MB and MS at this point in time?
2. Is there a contract as to the goods?
3. The goods now are stolen, and there is no fault on the MB. Who must bear the loss?

(Answers: (1) MB is a bailee and must exercise ordinary care for safety of the goods; (2) MS now has the right to cure by shipping conforming goods; (3) MS must bear the loss because MB was not at fault.)

Examine Illustration 2.

ILLUSTRATION 2

MB   ① $10,000 order for hotel supplies   → MS

Nonconforming goods shipped ②

③ Inspects,
    Rejects,
    and States Why

---

1. Is there a contract?
2. What are the rights of MS?
3. What if MS cannot cure for the reason that conforming goods are not available?

(Answers: (1) There is no contract at this point; (2) MS now has the right to cure; (3) if MS cannot cure, the matter is at an end and MB is free to go on the market and deal with another MS.)

Examine Illustration 3. Assume that the confirmation lists nonconforming goods that MB does not want. What is the danger to MB if he or she remains silent? (Answer: If MB does not object to the confirmation and ten days pass, the confirmation not only satisfies the statute of frauds but also may be held by a court to be an acceptance of the nonconforming goods for failure to object to them.)

ILLUSTRATION 3

MB ——————① Oral $10,000 Order for Hotel Supplies——————→ MS

←——————Written Confirmation ②——————

Examine Illustration 4. Who bears the loss? The answer will depend upon varying factors. If the goods had become identified with the contract, the loss probably will fall upon MB. If FOB terms are involved, the terms could affect the answer. The thing to learn here is always to provide for risk of loss and cover it accordingly, one way or the other.

ILLUSTRATION 4

MB ——————① Written order for $10,000 hotel supplies——————→ MS

③ Lost in transit ←——————② Ships conforming goods

If food in raw form is involved, a court might hold, as in the Max Bauer case, that the rejection was not seasonable. Thus, the delay in inspection could well be an acceptance of the goods (Illustration 5).

ILLUSTRATION 5

MB ——————①————Written order for specific food in raw form——————→ MS

←—————— Ships nonconforming goods ② ——————

③ MB waits three days to inspect and then rejects. ——————————→

SUMMARY

Article 2, Sales, of the Uniform Commercial Code is a highly technical, difficult-to-understand, statute. Nevertheless, some understanding of this law is essential to those in the HH&T industries.

The restaurant and bar operator are merchants and, thus, the rules of Article 2 apply to them. Actually, when any business person or corporation sells "goods," this comprehensive law applies. On the other hand, if one supplies a "service," such as rooms at an inn, Article 2 would not apply. This would be controlled by the rules of common-law contracts.

A good way to get a handle on this subject is to make an assumption. Assume that you, personally, were called upon to draft a law designed to regulate the sale of goods between merchants, or such sales by merchants to others. What words would you choose? What features would you place in the proposed law? How would you define just who a "merchant" would be? How would you provide for misdelivered goods, or loss of goods in transit, or cases where nonconforming goods are shipped and no objection is made to them?

The answer to these questions, and many more like them, are that you would use words similar to those found in Article 2. This law, extensive and complicated as it is, becomes "user-friendly" to us, and it was created to be just that way. It regulates us when we buy and sell goods, and we are not going to have too many problems with it in practice.

QUESTIONS

1. Why must goods be existing and identified before a present legal interest in them can pass to another?
2. What are the three exceptions to the sales statute of frauds?
3. Compare the sales statute of frauds with the common-law contracts statute of frauds in Chapter 5. How do they differ?
4. What must a buyer do who receives nonconforming goods?
5. Under what conditions may a seller stop goods that are in transit?
6. Under what conditions may one revoke an acceptance?

7. Define FOB, FAS, CIF, and C and F. What is the importance of knowing which of these controls a sales contract?

8. Why does the sales law require that a written confirmation be objected to quickly?

9. What are three ways in which a sales contract can be accepted?

10. What is one way that custom may become involved in a sales contract case?

NOTES

1. UCC 2–102.
2. *Nolen v. Blodget*, 278 Cal. Rptr. 794 (California 1991).
3. UCC 2–107.
4. UCC 2–104 (5).
5. UCC 2–104 (6).
6. UCC 2–106 (1).
7. UCC 2–106 (2).
8. UCC 2–106 (3).
9. UCC 2–106 (4).
10. UCC 2–107.
11. UCC 2–201.
12. UCC 2–209 (4).
13. *Double E. Sportswear Corp. v. Girard Trust Bank*, 488 F. 2d 292 (3d. Cir. 1973).
14. *Cox v. Cox*, 289 So. 2d 609, 14 UCC Rep. 330 (1974).
15. *Oskay Gasoline & Oil Co. v. Continental Oil Co.*, 19 UCC Rep. 61 (1976).
16. UCC 2–204.
17. UCC 2–204 (2).
18. UCC 2–204 (3).
19. UCC 2–206.
20. UCC 2–205.
21. UCC 2–207.
22. UCC 2–209.
23. UCC 1–103.
24. UCC 2–703 (b).
25. *Clock v. Missouri—Kansas—Texas Railroad Co. v. Crawford*, 407 F. Supp. 448 (E.D. Mo. 1976).
26. UCC 2–513.
27. "Cash on delivery."
28. "Cost of goods, insurance, and freight."
29. UCC 2–601.
30. UCC 714 (2).
31. UCC 2–602 (1).
32. UCC 2–606.

33. UCC 2–605 (1) (a).
34. UCC 2–603 (2).
35. UCC 2–604.
36. UCC 2–709 (1) (a).
37. UCC 2–608.
38. *Dapierlla v. Arkansas Louisiana Gas Co.*, 225 Ark. 150, 12 UCC Rep. 468 (1973).
39. UCC 2–508.
40. *Eastern Airlines, Inc. v. McDonnell Douglas Corp.*, 532 F. 2d 957, 19 UCC Rep. 353 (5th Cir. 1976).
41. UCC 2–401 (1).
42. UCC 2–501.
43. UCC 2–401 (1).
44. UCC 2–509 (4).
45. UCC 2–303.
46. UCC 2–509 (1).
47. FOB: "free on board" (this can be at shipping point or at destination).
48. FAS: "free alongside," referring to shipping vessel or other means of transportation.
49. CIF means that the quoted price includes the cost of goods, insurance to the designated destination, and freight charges to that destination.
50. C&F means the quoted price includes costs of goods and freight to destination, but not insurance.
51. UCC 2–509 (1)(b).
52. UCC 2–702 (2).
53. *Dangerfield v. Marhel*, 222 N.W. 2d 373, 15 UCC Rep. 915 (N.D. 1974).
54. UCC 2–201 (3) (c).
55. *Lewis v. Hughes*, 346 A. 2d 231, 18 UCC Rep. 52 (Md. App. 1975).
56. UCC 2–725 (1).
57. *Becker v. Volkswagen of Am., Inc.*, 18 UCC Rep. 135 (Cal. App. 1975).
58. *Jazel Corp. v. Sentinel Enterprises, Inc.*, 20 UCC Rep. 837 (N.Y. Sup. Ct. 1976).
59. UCC 2–305 (1).
60. UCC 2–310.
61. UCC 2–309.
62. *Deck House, Inc. v. Scarborough, Sheffield & Gastin, Inc.*, 228 S.E. 2d 142, 20 UCC Rep. 278 (Ga. App. 1976).

HH&T Agents and Independent Contractors

OVERVIEW

THE LAW OF agency plays a major role in the operation of all businesses, especially those that are "people-oriented," such as in the HH&T industries. The day-to-day need to deal with third parties creates the need for the use of agents.

The portion of American law called "agency" finds its roots in earlier years. Not so long ago, merchants and others did their commercial transactions face to face. All of that had to change, of course, with the coming of the transcontinental railroads, privately owned automobiles, the trucking industry, the interstate highway system and jet aircraft. Merchants who once dealt face to face with their customers soon would never see their customers at all. When this came to pass, it meant that merchants would have to rely upon others to carry out the duties the merchants had shouldered personally in years past. These persons became known as agents.

With the birth of this new way of doing business came the need to set parameters for the courts to follow in deciding disputes that arose as a result. This led to the rules we know today as the *law of agency*.

BASIC POINTS

Some basic points of agency law will be of assistance in understanding the discussion that follows.

1. Agents normally do not assume personal liability for contracts entered into on behalf of their principals (employers).
2. Principals and agents may become jointly liable for torts committed by an agent when carrying out the authority granted by the principal.
3. Principals seldom are liable for criminal acts committed by an agent.
4. One business may have more than one principal, and the number of agents may be in the hundreds or even thousands, depending upon the size of the business. This is especially so with large hotels.
5. The authority granted to an agent is generally not permanent in that it will end at some point as the agent completes each day's work.
6. Employees are not automatically agents, although they may become so if they have contact with and deal with third parties.

7. The usual agents found in business often are employees of that business also. These agents must be distinguished from professional agents such as lawyers, accountants, insurance men and women, and others who serve business.

8. Innkeeping is "people-intensive" and at the same time, is "agent-intensive," making this a key law in the HH&T industries.

9. Liability in contract, vicarious liability under agency law in tort, and liability under public policy are all different and can reach different results.

10. Agency law will cause liability to attach to a manager even though the manager did not know of the acts being done by the agent. That is why the liability is "vicarious" or indirect.

11. Innkeeper P hires Agent A to accomplish duties at the inn we will label "AB&C." To accomplish these duties, Agent A also must do "DE&F." Thus, A has express authority to do "AB&C" and implied authority to do "DE&F." Both sets of authority are "real authority," as one is required to achieve the other.

12. Those who carry out room-service duties at the inn, such as food service, housekeeping and maintenance, are agents and have direct contact with third parties. Any acts committed by them, such as theft or tort, can well bind the innkeeper.

Leaving these preliminary points, we next will look at some basic legal points about the law of agency.

First, if an agent plans and carries out a robbery, the principal has no responsibility for the crime.[1] If in the scope of the agent's employment, however, the agent robs or commits fraud upon an innocent third party, such as a guest at a motel, the principal can be liable for the damage done—but not for the crime itself.[2] (The principal pays for the loss; the agent goes to jail.)

Once an agent leaves work, the responsibility of the principal generally ends. Figure 7.1 shows this timing. In a car-bailment case, the employee left work at the parking lot, returned, stole a parked car, and wrecked it. The court held that the principal was not liable even though the agent had a criminal record and was on probation at the time.[3]

In a hotel case, a guest turned over his car to a bellhop, who parked it in the hotel parking lot. The bellhop went off duty, returned, took the car, and wrecked it. The facts are almost identical to the above situation, yet here the court held that misdelivery to the bellhop imposed absolute liability on the hotel for damages, regardless of whether the misdelivery was in good faith, through negligence, or otherwise. The court further said this was a bailment for hire and the bailee hotel promised to redeliver the car in good shape and failed to do so.

Hospitality units often are held liable for injuries and losses suffered by passersby from their agents. One example is an agent releasing keys of a valet-parked car to an obviously intoxicated patron, who then hits a passerby with the auto. For a striking case example see *Muniz v. Flohern.*[4]

A good way to continue is by examining the traditional reach and scope of the law of agency.

AGENCY

Agency has been defined as the relationship that results from the manifestation of consent by one person to another that the other shall act on his or her behalf and

FIGURE 7.1   Timing in agency law.

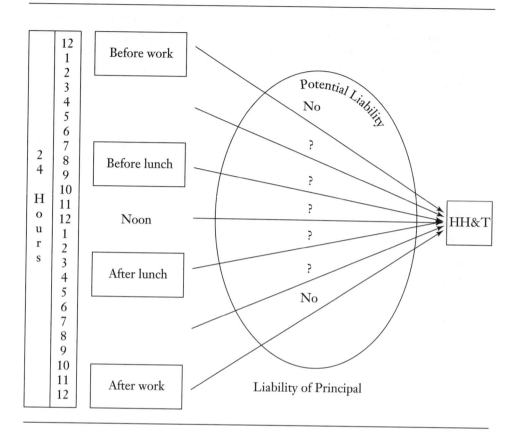

subject to his or her control and the agreement by the other so to act. The definition leads itself to an outline. In practice, P is called the "principal," A the
"agent." These letters will be used throughout the chapter. It follows that the acts
of the agent will in some manner involve third parties, which we will call T.

1. P consents that A shall act for P.
2. A agrees to act for P.
3. A agrees that P shall control A while A is so acting with third parties (T).

The relationship then brings into being four legal consequences:

1. A contract of agency exists between P and A.
2. When A acts with T, a contract may come into being between P and T, even
   though P did not deal with T personally.
3. When A acts for P, and while so doing causes injury to T, P may be held
   responsible for that injury if it occurred in the scope of the employment of A.
4. When A contracts with T for the benefit of P, A incurs no personal responsibility on the contract.

Therefore, an agent is one who acts for another, who must account to the other, who binds the other in contract and tort, and who usually does not benefit personally from the specific act performed. Rather, the agent is compensated by the principal for the act, or a continuous series of acts. Examples of agents are lawyers, bank cashiers, brokers, insurance agents, front-desk clerks, waiters, auctioneers, agents of corporations, and employees who deal with third parties. Figure 7.2 illustrates the circle view of agency law.

FIGURE 7.2   The circle view of agency law.

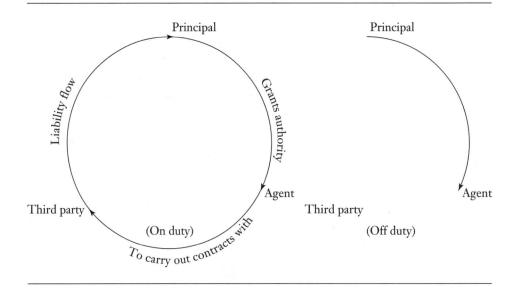

Differences Between Agents and Servants

By the nature of the law of agency, an agent acts with third parties, whereas a servant performs mechanical or manual acts under the direct control of the principal-master. Servants can create liability for the master, just as the agent can for the principal. Many employees have the characteristics of servants, whereas others will act with third parties and are agents.

Types of Agents

Agents can be private, public, special, or general agents. A special agent performs a single act or tries to accomplish a single objective. A general agent handles continuing, general affairs of the principal. One authorized to purchase all goods needed to keep an inn in operation is a general agent. One authorized to sign one deed for a principal is a special agent.

A private agent may bind the principal even when the agent acts beyond the scope of the authority given to the agent. An example of a private agent is one hired to determine if thefts are occurring at the inn bar. A public agent binds the principal only if the acts are within the authority granted. Examples of public agents are governors, police officers, sheriffs, and fire marshals. One who is injured by a tort or breach of contract committed by a public agent may find the scope of recovery sharply reduced because of the limit of liability upon the state. On the other hand, one injured by a private agent can almost always look directly to the assets of the principal.

Agents Distinguished from Trustees

In most instances a trustee has no principal. The trustee handles estates or *powers* and is in a fiduciary (high position of trust) capacity. The agent does have a principal, as we have seen.

FORMATION OF THE RELATIONSHIP

An agency relationship is formed by a contract between the principal and the agent. These relationships are express agencies because they arise from the terms expressed orally or placed in writing by the parties. In addition, agencies can be implied and, in rare cases, may arise by estoppel. We will begin by looking at the express agency, the most common type found in HH&T businesses.

Express Agency

The agency contract may be oral or written. No specific legal form is required other than a clear statement of the authority granted and an assent on the part of the agent to act as an agent. If, however, the authority granted will require a formal legal act, such as the execution of a deed for the principal, the authority granted must have the same "dignity" as the act to be performed. That is, the grant of authority also must be written and signed by the principal.[5]

In earlier times, such as the last century, a formal grant of authority to an agent had to be sealed; the word "seal" or "L.S." had to appear following the signature of the principal. This requirement has been abolished in most states and under the Uniform Commercial Code as well, when the "sale of goods" is involved.[6] Today, when agency agreements are placed in writing, they seldom are sealed.

If a court is called upon to construe (decide what the parties intended) a written agency contract, the subject matter of the contract, the acts of the parties, and the surrounding circumstances will be examined in determining the intent of the principal and agent.

Implied Agency

An agency may be implied from the conduct of the principal and the agent, and from the nature and circumstances surrounding that conduct. This means that an agency may exist even though neither party stated expressly that one was in existence. What the parties call themselves is immaterial. The courts will look to the actual relationship between them,[7] and if that relationship is in fact an agency, the courts will apply agency law to it.

Agency by Estoppel

An estoppel can be used by a court in instances where one has misled another in an "agency-type" situation to the extent that harm will result if the misled party is not provided some legal protection. This protection comes in the form of a court stopping (estopping) the one who misled the other, from denying that the two of them were in fact bound in an agency relationship. In short, a court can "close a person's mouth" in certain situations.

To illustrate, assume that P, in some manner, leads T to believe that A is P's agent. In fact, no express or implied relationship exists between P and A. If T is misled, and consequently assumes a position of liability, P will be "estopped" to deny the agency. The effect of this is that T can hold P responsible just as though an agency had in fact existed between P and A. However, if A leads T to believe an agency exists between P and A and P in fact knows nothing about it, the estoppel principle will have no application because an agency cannot be proven by statements of the alleged agent standing alone.

Statutory Agencies

A hybrid type of agency is found in relationships created by statutes. A good example is found in the "long-arm statutes." These permit nonresident corporations headquartered in one state to be sued in a state where they have transacted substantial business. In such cases, these "foreign" corporations can be sued in a local court and served process through the secretary of state of that state. The nonresident corporations, by doing business in the state, have, by statute, appointed the secretary of state their agent for this purpose.

Another statutory example is found in laws that require a newly forming corporation to name in the corporate application an agent for service of legal process.

Leaving the types of agencies, let's examine the scope of an agent's authority.

SCOPE OF AGENT'S AUTHORITY

An agent's authority to act for a principal may be express, implied, or "apparent"— sometimes called "ostensible." Express authority presents no problems. It simply involves doing those things that the principal expressly gave the agent the authority to do. The law does not stop there, however. With any grant of express authority, there is also authority that can be "implied" from the express grant itself. To illustrate, if P grants A the authority to lease apartment units in Zero Hotel, A has the implied power to advertise the rentals, enter into lease agreements, and collect rent for the benefit of P. Conversely, A does *not* have the implied power to sell the building. A restaurant manager would have the implied power to hire employees; an accountant for an inn would have the implied power to charge the principal for the books necessary to carry out the bookkeeping. On the other hand, a hotel manager would have no authority to enter into a contract to sell a used hotel van in the absence of an express grant of such authority.

The duties to be carried out and the nature of the surrounding circumstances become relevant in determining whether implied authority exists on behalf of an agent, and the courts will take such factors into consideration.

In New Mexico, under SCRA 1986, 18–407, an act of an employee is within the scope of employment if:

1. It was something fairly and naturally incidental to the employer's business assigned to the employee, and
2. It was done while the employee was engaged in the employer's business with the view of furthering the employer's interest and did not arise entirely from some external, independent, and personal motive on the part of the employee.[8]

When called upon to determine the extent and nature of an agent's authority, the courts will consider other factors. Three examples taken from a case will illustrate:

1. Requiring agents to attend seminars.
2. Reimbursing agents for trips they take to attend seminars.
3. Reimbursing agents for social expenses incurred while attending seminars.[9]

This brings us to apparent authority. Whereas an implied grant of authority falls within the real scope of the authority granted, apparent, or ostensible, authority falls outside the express and real scope of the authority granted. Figure 7.3 illustrates this kind of authority. The test of apparent authority is whether or not a third party, knowing the usages of business, is justified in supposing that the agent is authorized to perform the act because of the nature of the known duties.[10] This rule is necessary in the laws of agency to cover fringe matters that may arise as agents carry out their duties.

FIGURE 7.3   Agent's authority.

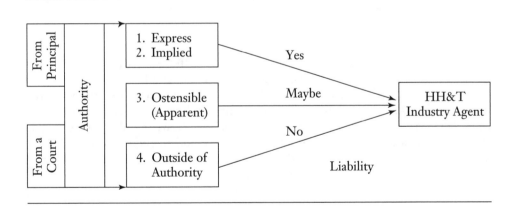

To establish apparent authority, three legal requirements must be met:

1. There must be some representation by the principal to the third party.
2. The third party must rely upon that representation.
3. There must be a loss on the part of the third party because of the representation, which in practice is called "misrepresentation."[11] If the misrepresentation

is intentional, it is fraud, which is a crime punishable by fine and/or imprisonment.

If the misrepresentation is a result of negligence that takes the form of an assurance to an invitee or a guest, legal action is confined to a lawsuit for damages suffered.[12]

When a franchise hotel of a national chain uses the sign of the parent franchisor, advertises itself as part of the chain, and leads the public to believe the hotel is part of the national chain, this is sufficient to allow a jury to decide whether an injured guest could expect to receive the same service at the franchised operation as at the others in the chain. This is another example of apparent authority.

Agency relationships can be dangerous to third parties.

Third-Party Peril

When one deals with an agent, that person is held responsible to determine the nature and extent of the authority of the agent. The law presumes that the third party knows the scope of the authority granted to the agent. If the third party is wrong in its estimation of the authority that party must bear the risk of loss. To translate this principle into commonsense terms, anyone who deals with any agent and who is in doubt of the authority of that agent should immediately make inquiry to the principal. If a third party is confronted by an agent, who is asking that the debt owing to the principal be paid in cash—not check—the third party obviously has a duty to make inquiry.

In many situations, an agent will act outside the range of actual, implied, or apparent authority. In these instances, upon learning of this, the principal should repudiate such acts of the agent. In so doing, the principal will not be bound by those acts. In other instances, however, the principal may want to adopt such acts of the agent. Now the principal must take a different action at law, called *ratification*.

Ratification

If the principal learns that the agent has done acts with third parties that are outside of all authority, and if the principal wants to gain the benefits of such acts, they must be ratified. If management allows sexual harassment, to continue after learning of it, this constitutes ratification of the conduct. This, in turn, is imputed by law to the business, making it responsible for the wrongful conduct.[13] The effect of ratification is that the principal now is bound to the third party on the unauthorized acts of the agent and, conversely, the third party is bound to the principal. Figure 7.4 shows the flow of duties.

FIGURE 7.4   Flow of duties.

P ⟶ A
A ⟶ P
P ⟶ T
T ⟶ P

Rights, Duties, and Liabilities

Duties of Agent to Principal

The agent must follow the reasonable instructions of the principal. In the event of emergencies, agents are permitted—and expected—to deviate from instructions. For example, P may expressly tell A "under no circumstances are you to borrow money in my name." If P should be absent on vacation and floodwaters have damaged the carpets in P's motel, A could borrow money in the name of P and do other reasonable acts necessary to correct the problem. In fact, the agent would, as a matter of law, be expected to do such acts.

An agent must exercise a reasonable amount of care, caution, and discretion. The "reasonable person" test is applied. If an agent acts as he or she would have if the subject had been his or her own property, that person generally will not be held personally responsible for subsequent loss if it should occur.

An agent must act in good faith with the principal and be loyal to the principal. An agent must not profit personally from the acts done for the principal. If this were to happen, such profits would be held by the agent, in trust, for the benefit of the principal. An agent must make full disclosures at all times and not withhold information of value. This disclosure is carried out best by periodic written reports—which, by the way, is a good management practice. Figure 7.5 gives an agency formula that shows how agents can use subagents to help the principal.

An agent never should sell the goods of the principal to himself or herself except upon express authority. A position of delicacy arises in such cases, so the agent must be careful. Nothing is wrong, however, with one agent buying goods from another agent of the same principal. Most principals insist that this pattern be followed.

FIGURE 7.5   Agency formula.

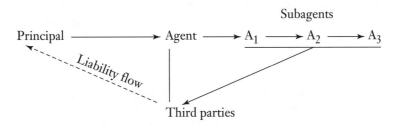

The formula of subagents: P to A to A_1, to A_2 to A_3 to T to P.

It follows that an agent never should represent a second principal so as to be in conflict with the interests of the first principal. Nor should an agent commingle the principal's funds with its own. Separate accounts always must be maintained. Collections made by an agent on behalf of a principal and deposited into the agent's account could lead to a charge of embezzlement. Care is in order. In instances where an agent collects and maintains accounts for the principal, the agent must be ready at all times to give a full accounting.

In retrospect, these duties are reasonable, designed to strip agents of temptations to take advantage. They represent rules that a reasonable person would conclude should be the duties of an agent to his or her principal.

Duties of Principal to Agent

The principal has a duty to compensate the agent for services rendered. The rate usually is set at the time the relationship is created. Further, the principal has a duty to *reimburse* the agent for expenses and advances made while carrying out the scope of authority granted. If the principal fails to compensate or reimburse, the agent would have a lien (claim) against goods or property of the principal that are in the hands of the agent. In such circumstances, legal advice should be sought before enforcing the lien against such goods.

Duties of the Agent to Third Parties

Generally an agent is *not* liable to third parties on any contract entered into on behalf of the principal. An agent *may* be bound if the agent intended to be bound, but the presumption is otherwise. If a principal remains hidden, or unknown (referred to as an undisclosed principal), the agent would be bound on any contract made. This is true even though the contract had been made for the benefit of the principal, and it is true for the reason that the agent is the contracting party in such instances. Once the principal is disclosed, a third party also can look to the principal for performance of the contract.

If an agent acts within the limits of the authority granted and is not aware that an apparent wrong or tort is being caused to others, the principal will be responsible for the tort. If the principal commands the agent to commit a tort, such as a trespass, both the principal and the agent will share the liability. If the agent commits a tort knowingly, and without any participation by the principal, the agent can be looked to for any loss suffered by third parties. If the intentional tort occurs within the scope of the authority granted, the principal also may be held accountable for the tort.

Duties of the Principal to Third Parties

As long as an agent acts within the scope of the authority, the principal has a duty to fulfill any and all obligations created by the agent with the third party.

In an undisclosed agency, when the third party enters into a contract with the agent, not knowing of the existence of the principal, both the agent and the principal have a duty to the third party on the contract—but only after the principal is disclosed. The third party then can look to either for performance—but not both. If the third party sues the principal on such a contract, the principal has a duty not to establish any greater claim against the third party than the agent could have. For example, T may have a set-off claim against the agent. Thus, P would be subject to this set-off, and have a duty to extend to the third party the benefits of this set-off.

To illustrate a set-off, assume that T buys, for $10,000, an item that A is selling as an agent for an undisclosed P. At the time of the sale, A owed T $5,000 for some outside transaction. P now comes forward and seeks payment of $10,000 from T. T has the legal right to offset the $5,000 and thus is responsible for only $5,000.

A principal has a duty to compensate third parties who are injured by tortious conduct of the agent while the agent is carrying out the scope of the authority granted. It is not material whether the tortious act was in accordance with instructions, only whether it was done in the scope of authority granted.

An exception to these rules is found where injury is caused by the *fraud* of the agent. In the usual instance, the principal is not liable to the third party for lies, untruths, fraudulent statements, or deceitful acts—unless the principal acquiesced or encouraged such acts in some manner.

If an agent exceeds his or her authority, the principal has no obligation to discharge the agent upon the demand of the third party, but in many instances that is just what happens. Principals do not appreciate agents who do not follow instructions, ignore house rules, or create liabilities.

Duties of Third Parties to Principal

Generally, the third party has a duty to honor all contracts entered into with the agent on behalf of the principal. As mentioned, however, fraud, deceit, or other such acts impair the right to claim the benefit of a contract that arose out of such acts. These acts provide the third party with a legal defense against the agent—and thus provide a legal defense against the principal.

Notice

An important part of agency law has grown up around the concept of notice. The principal is bound by notice or knowledge that the agent receives while in the conduct of authority granted. *This is true whether it is passed on or not.* The notice or knowledge must bear, however, upon the scope of authority. Agents are expected to pass on relevant information acquired while carrying out their authority.

For example, A unloads a shipment of goods at a hotel and discovers that the goods are nonconforming. A fails to pass this along, and an unreasonable amount of time elapses, so the right to reject is lost. P is bound to pay the price for the goods, even though they are not what was ordered.

Principals must create a system of "notice routing" and train their agents in how to use this system.

Termination of the Relationship

If an agency is created to last until a specified time, or until a certain act is completed, the agency ends at that time. Other agencies, called *agencies at will,* continue for indefinite time periods until the principal or agent decides to end the relationship.

Once an agency is terminated, the principal must give notice to third parties to make certain that subsequent acts of the agent do not bind the principal. Direct notice, such as by letter, should be given to all those with whom the agents had transacted business on behalf of the principal. General notice should be given to all others. A general notice that the prior innkeeper is no longer on the job might read: "We invite you to stop at our hotel and meet our new innkeeper."

INDEPENDENT CONTRACTORS

Turning from agency, let's briefly examine a relationship related closely to agency, yet different in its legal consequences. It has to do with persons so often used in the hotel, hospitality, and tourism industries: independent contractors. A helpful way to proceed is to compare agents with independent contracts in their major forms, as is done in Table 7.1.

TABLE 7.1   Agents compared with independent contractors.

Agents	*Independent Contractors*
Who are they?	*Who are they?*
They can be in-house employees or outside professionals.	They are those outside businesses who operate independent from the inn and have no in-house connection to it. They generally work under contract.
What are their functions?	*What are their functions?*
They serve at the will of their principal; thus, they are "supervised."	They serve under the terms of the contract they sign; thus, they are *not* "supervised" and are independent of supervision by the inn.
If they cause loss to others?	*If they cause loss to others?*
If they operate within the scope of the authority given to them and breach contracts or are negligent, the principal must answer: "*Respondeat Superior*—Let the master answer."	They must respond to such losses out of their assets and not the assets of the inn. (Note: If the inn does exercise control over them, this makes them "supervised," and they are now agents.)

In many business situations a principal wants a specific job to be accomplished but wants the job carried out by one who is neither an agent nor an employee. The laws of independent contractors (IC) cover this type of situation. The test applied to determine if an independent contractor relationship exists is twofold:

1. Is the one doing the job being paid a fixed price or rate for a completed project?
2. Is there an absence of control over that person or firm by the principal?

If the answer is "yes" to both, an independent contractor situation is in existence. In determining if this relationship exists, as a general rule, common, not statutory, law prevails. If the answer to one of these questions is "no," then, in all probability, an agency exists and the law of agency will be applied.

If, under a contract, one can dictate the result and direct the means by which it is reached, it *is not* an independent contractor situation. This does not mean, however, that a principal cannot make periodic inspections in person or by agents and employees to make certain the specifications are being met. This is permitted and expected. Yet, one must keep in mind the distinction between mere inspection and active supervision. The latter may convert an independent-contractor relationship into an agency—something that the principal may not want to happen. If it does happen, the principal faces the risk of loss to third parties in addition to falling under wage compensation laws. This is the reason for creating the relationship in the first place.

Another test often applied by a court is whether the principal can terminate the services of the other at will. If so, it usually is a master-servant or principal-agent, not an independent contractor relationship.

The method of payment is another test applied: Payment based upon time often denotes an agency relationship; lump-sum payment usually denotes a principal-independent contractor situation.

An innkeeper-principal contracts with an independent contractor to accomplish certain work at the inn. The independent contractor then uses his or her agents to go about completing the work. Two possible legal results that can emerge from this situation are illustrated in Figure 7.6.

FIGURE 7.6   Losing the IC protection.

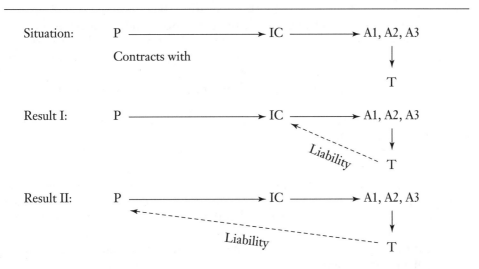

Result II was caused because in some manner the innkeeper (P) lost the benefit of the contract with the IC and was held by a court to be a principal. This is a result that must be avoided.

Losing the Independent Contractor Protection

The most common way to lose the protection of the independent contractor relationship is for the innkeeper to exercise day-by-day control of the activities of the independent contractor. When this happens, the courts, when called upon to decide where legal liability must fall, invariably will hold that the innkeeper had, in fact, become the principal of the independent contractor and must face agency liability.

An exception to this is found where a union hall sends workers to work a banquet at the inn. Here, the innkeeper must exercise direct control over the union employees but, as a matter of law, the workers remain agents of the union hall and not the inn.

Liability of Principal

Normally, if a principal uses care in selecting an independent contractor, the principal is not liable for negligent, careless, or wrongful acts of the independent contractor. If an independent contractor brings into being a situation for which the principal has primary responsibility, however, the principal cannot use the relationship to escape that responsibility. For example, a hotel must make certain that fire exits are not blocked. If an independent contractor, while doing repair work in the hotel, blocks an exit, the hotel will be responsible for injury or death caused by the blocked exit.

As another example, the common law places legal duties upon innkeepers that must be met in the operation of the inn. A collateral rule developed that an innkeeper cannot escape these duties by delegating them to others.

Thus, it would be no legal defense in an elevator accident to claim that the elevator was maintained by an elevator company. The courts would reject such a position on the ground that the elevator was a part of the inn and that the innkeeper retains responsibility for safety at all times.

If the elevator company should be found negligent in maintaining the elevator, and if it can be shown that the negligence was the proximate cause of the injuries to those in the elevator, the innkeeper would have a cause of action against the elevator firm for any sums lost.

In *Page v. Sloan*, Chapter 4, the innkeeper claimed the person hired to make repairs to the water heater was an independent contractor. The innkeeper was saying, "If this person repaired the water heater in a negligent manner, and if this negligence was the proximate cause of the death of the guest, I am not responsible as a matter of law." The problem is that the courts hold that an innkeeper cannot delegate his or her innkeeping duties to third parties. In addition, if the innkeeper is negligent in hiring, employing, or selecting an independent contractor, *that* negligence is actionable.

Generally, a principal is not liable for injuries suffered by *servants and agents of the independent contractor.* This presumes, of course, that the injuries arise while the injured party is in the services of the independent contractor, and also assumes that the principal in no way contributes to the injury. As a commonsense rule, a principal should treat servants and agents of an independent contractor just as any other third parties. Care and caution are always good business.

An independent contractor is not an employee of the principal as defined in the workers' compensation laws, and therefore is not insurable under such laws. It is the responsibility of the independent contractor to subscribe to these funds and to make certain all servants and agents of the independent contractor are covered properly. Conversely, the independent contractor is responsible for withholding, fringe benefits, and the like for its agents and employees. These are not the responsibility of the principal and represent one of the reasons for using the independent contractor relationship. State law must be examined on this point, however.

In most states the use of an independent contractor to carry out business projects relieves the one who has contracted for the services of the responsibility of carrying workers' compensation coverage on the employees and agents of the independent contractor. Thus, when an innkeeper hires Zero Construction Company to repair the pool at the inn, the company, not the inn, will be responsible for compensation coverage on its employees. This is to protect them in the event they are injured while on the job. The State of Nevada, however, has an unusual provision in its Industrial Insurance Act (the equivalent of workers' compensation coverage in other states). It is found in NRS 616.085 and reads as follows: "Subcontractors and their employees shall be deemed to be employees of the principal contractor."

NRS 616.115, goes on: "Subcontractors shall include independent contractors."

A literal reading of these two provisions from the Nevada Revised Statutes could lead one to the conclusion that one (such as an innkeeper) who contracts with an independent contractor would be responsible for compensation coverage for workers of the independent contractor.

When the inn contracts with an independent contractor, such as to replace carpeting, the contractor commonly pays for use of a room or rooms at the inn for its employees while the work is being done. In that regard, the employees of the contractor who occupy the room or rooms are guests and inn law applies to them. Conversely, a duty is placed upon the innkeeper to make certain these "guests" do not cause injury or loss to other guests.

A legal problem can arise in these situations where the inn exercises control over the independent contractor. The courts may find that the inn is a "special employer" and hold the inn liable for the defaults or transgressions of the independent contractor and its employees.[14]

As a rule, three situations can arise in which the inn can be held liable for the acts or omissions of independent contractors:

1. When the inn exercises control over the independent contractor.
2. When the responsibility for the work to be done is something that cannot be delegated, because of basic innkeeping law.
3. When the work done is inherently dangerous, thus giving rise to the rules of strict liability.

In the absence of these exceptions, the legal liability is that of an independent contractor.

MECHANICS' AND LABORERS' LIENS

One risk confronted by owner-principals who contract for services from independent contractors is the danger of third-party suppliers and laborers gaining the right to file mechanics' and laborers' liens. Such liens are filed against the real estate of the owner-principal that has been improved by materials supplied and labor performed.

All states have laws permitting such liens provided they are filed promptly. Usual time periods are sixty or ninety days after the last material was supplied or the last labor performed. When filed properly, they become a lien against the real estate of the owner-principal. It is possible for an innkeeper who contracts with an independent contractor to build a pool to wind up with liens against the inn for debts owed by the independent contractor.

One can guard against such liens by making certain the laborers and suppliers are paid out of proceeds due to the independent contractor. It is practice for principal-owners to require proof of payment before distributing funds.

If a lawyer is able to convince a court that an alleged independent contractor is not actually an independent contractor, agency law will be applied. This in turn makes the one who contracted for that person, or firm's services, responsible for any defects or defaults in such service that resulted in injury or loss to others.

SUMMARY

Those who are active in the three industries that we are discussing must be aware of the laws and regulations that control them and do all that is reasonably necessary to comply with these laws.

The law of agency involves a relationship between one or more persons or businesses who provide services for one or more other persons or businesses and receive payment for this. While this is not a special relationship, it is an important relationship. It is in perpetual use in the HH&T industries. Agents are distinguished from employees or servants who merely work for a person or business but who do not have contact or perform services with third parties. Thus, an agency is a three-party relationship while an employee is in a two-party relationship with the employer.

The law of agency was not needed in earlier centuries such as at the early English inn. The innkeeper met the guests as they arrived, saw them to their quarters, provided them food and drink, and personally saw to the safety of their persons and property so long as they remained on the inn premises. While there are many small, family operations where the use of agents is limited, that is no longer true with the giant hotel and motel operations, the airlines that span the world, and other hotel, hospitality, and tourism operations. Indeed, the HH&T industries are truly agent intensive just as they are contract intensive.

Independent contractors, on the other hand, are persons or businesses who contract to reach a result, such as building a new motel for an agreed upon price, but who are not employees or agents of the one for whom the work is being done. The distinguishing feature of an independent contractor relationship is the absence of control by the one for whom the work is being done. The independent contractor, of course, must use agents and employees to carry out the agreed performance.

Agency law has been developed primarily in the courts over the past two hundred years, and there are some statutes that create statutory agents. The law of agency is quite complex, yet it is based upon common sense and simple principles. It is in the application that it can become difficult to understand.

QUESTIONS

1. What is the distinction between agents and servants?
2. What is an example of an agency by estoppel in the hotel business?
3. What is the difference between implied and apparent authority?
4. True or false: An agent can ratify unauthorized acts of another agent, as long as both agents serve the same principal.
5. What is the effect on a principal of fraud on the part of an agent to a third party that the principal knows nothing about? Why?
6. What information items would you want your salesperson-agents to place on their customer-call reports?
7. What is the basic difference between an agency relationship and an independent contractor relationship?
8. Name three reasons why an inn owner would want work to be done by an independent contractor and not by agents.
9. True or false: An independent contractor will use agents to carry forth his or her work, and the rules of agency will apply to *that* relationship.
10. True or false: Mechanic's lien laws can be triggered by using independent contractors.

NOTES

1. *International Trucking v. U. S. (Ct. Claims)*, 281 F. 2d 457.
2. *Turner v. Zip*, 65 N.W. 2d 427.
3. *Morse v. Jones*, 223 La. 212, 65 So. 2d 317.
4. 568 N.Y.S. 2d 725 (Ct. App. New York 1991).
5. *Forrest v. Hawkins*, 169 Va. 470, 194 S.E. 721 (1938).
6. UCC 2-203.
7. *Chandler v. Kelley*, 149 Va. 221, 141 S.E. 389 (1928).
8. *Valdez v. Warner*, 742 P. 2d 517.
9. *Carroll Air v. Greenbaum*, So. 2d 914 (Florida 1994).
10. *Richmond Guano Co. v. E.I. Dupont*, 284 Fed. 803 (4th Cir. 1922).
11. *Holiday Inns, Inc. v. Shelbourne*, 576 So. 2d 322 (Florida 1992).
12. *Howard Johnson v. Fair*, 575 So. 2d 723 (Florida 1991).
13. *Hogen v. Forsyth*, 340 S.E. 2d 116 (Florida 1990).
14. *Cappo v. Vinson Guard Service*, 400 So. 2d 1148 (Louisiana 1981).

8

HH&T Employer-Employee Relations

OVERVIEW

IN THIS CHAPTER, we want to take a look at the fundamental laws that come into play between management and their agents/employees. This view is important because the laws that regulate the guest/traveler/patron relationship often are affected by the management/staff relationship. When one relationship goes bad, the other can suffer too.

A modern business can be viewed in various ways, and the outcome of the view often depends upon who is standing in what pair of shoes. A manager sees things one way; a guest at an inn may have a counterview. The employee/agent, in turn, tends to view both management and guests or patrons from a different, unique point of view. Sometimes, the view of the agent/employee can be detrimental because his or her own personal interests, rather than the interests of the business, may be at stake.

In addition, the legal demands and commands of the law that concerns employees/agents can place financial burdens on the business. This is especially so when these legal requirements are not understood, are misinterpreted, or, worse yet, are ignored. We want to become exposed to enough of the more important laws of the management/employee/agent relationship so as to be able to function more effectively as HH&T personnel.

MANAGEMENT AND LAW

A diversity of laws, both common and statutory, are involved in managing a hotel, restaurant, hospitality, or tourism facility. Included are the laws of agency, estoppel, tort, those found in the Uniform Commercial Code, civil rights acts, and the Consumer Credit Protection Act, to name a few, as well as principles of criminal law. These laws, in turn, have a direct effect upon the responsibilities of employers and employees alike and, by necessity, control the relationship that exists between them. If the employer violates these laws, legal consequences may follow. The same is true if the employee ignores or violates the laws. The result is a legal balance that must be achieved for the good of all concerned.

Maslow's hierarchy theory,[1] with its five stages that lead to self-actualization, does not fare badly when analyzed from a strict legal point of view in relation to this legal balance. In addition, the theories of McGregor[2] contain points that match up reasonably well with legal realities. By combining features of both, one could arrive at what could be called "legal aspects of traditional motivational theories."

First, McGregor's theory X holds that employees do not like to work. In some instances, this is probably closer to the realities of the business world than is his theory Y. The latter holds that work is natural. Theory Y has some truth, but people still prefer leisure to work. The ready acceptance of the shorter workweek and the increasing success of the hospitality-recreation-tourism industry are proof of this.

If it is true that employees do not like to work, even if it is natural to do so, it also is true that employers do not like to pay wages. The reasons are many: dissatisfaction with job performance, insufficient economic return for services performed, theft on the job, misuse of company property, and resentment of unions and other outside pressures that have relegated the employer to a "partner status" with the employee.

Therein lies a legal factor of importance: The employer is obligated contractually to pay the wages agreed upon, provided the required services are performed—which they often are not. In addition, once the status of employer-employee arises, the laws of agency come into play, placing precise duties on both: on the employee, the duty of loyalty, care, caution, productivity, and others; upon the employer, the duty to provide a safe place to work, the duty to compensate as agreed, and others.

Maslow's first level, "survival," is just as much the legal responsibility of the employee as it is of the employer. The second level, "security and safety," is primarily the responsibility of management, but only insofar as it relates to the employee's safety. Under the Occupational Safety and Health Act,[3] the employer must supply a safe place to work and keep it that way. In turn, the employees have a legal duty to make use of all safety devices supplied and to follow all safety instructions.

Maslow tells us that the worker needs to "belong." Employees must feel they are part of the formal organization. It is said that informal organizations and company-supplied recreational programs can provide at least part of this need. When management is called upon to provide recreational programs, however, the law of tort must be considered as a byproduct. Will an employee be injured during the activities? If so, is this injury one obtained "on the job" so as to place it under workers' compensation coverage, or will it be covered under traditional tort principles? What if a *third party* is injured by the employee during the activities, such as at an inn picnic? Tort principles then are solely in operation.

The "ego need" of the employee perhaps can be met best through the simple expedient of a job well done. After all, this is an obligation in all employment contracts. One can hardly argue that an outstanding job is beyond what was expected at the time the contract was entered into. Management should not accede to such an argument. Superior job performance certainly should be rewarded. Poor job performance should be handled by demotion or dismissal for the reason that it is a breach of contract. Although management can do much to promote superior job performance, the employee remains legally obligated to provide it.

Self-actualization naturally follows from attainment of superior job performance and also is an extension of the contractual obligation. It is logically not a permanent status. The employee must strive constantly to maintain it.

EMPLOYEES AS GUESTS AT THE INN

Normally, employees are not guests of the inn while carrying out their jobs, nor would they become guests if they were to remain at the inn bar after their shift ended.[4] If, after the shift of an employee ends, management decides the employee should remain on the premises for safety reasons, such as a severe snowstorm in the area, the employee is still not a guest. The same is true if the employee occupies a room as part of his or her contract of employment.

On the other hand, an employee can become a guest if that person intends to assume guest status and the innkeeper agrees. This could happen when an employee is given a reduced room rate as part of employee vacation benefits.

THE LEGAL RELATIONSHIP BETWEEN EMPLOYER AND EMPLOYEE

The motivational aspects of management indeed have serious legal overtones. We have touched upon the topic and will look more specifically to the laws that affect the employer-employee relationship.

The At-Will Doctrine

The at-will doctrine has been used for decades in the United States to describe what can be called the "traditional legal relationship between employers and employees." It means the employee can leave the employment as she or he sees fit, but it also means the employer can fire the employee for any reason, or for no reason at all. Only where there is a collective bargaining agreement or other contract in effect between the parties is an exception found.

Most states are "at-will" employment states if the employee is hired for an indefinite term. This means the employer or employee may end the employment at any time. On the other hand, if other promises are made, such as those found in employee handbooks, the courts may refuse to apply the at-will doctrine and instead look to those promises to resolve the situation.

More than forty states have modified the right of employers to fire at-will without stating cause. This modification has given rise to numerous court cases brought to protect fired employees. In addition, a Plaintiff's Employment Lawyer's Association now exists.

The most common theories to support the right of fired employees to recover their jobs or damages are (1) promises contained in the employee manual (if any), (2) implied contract, (3) violations of public policy, and (4) oral promises of continued employment coupled with provisions found in employee handbooks. The latter can create a legal issue of whether an employee can be fired at will, making it an issue to be determined in court by a jury.[5] In relation to the at-will doctrine, the Texas Supreme Court has called it "a relic that belongs in a museum and not in the law."

In North Dakota, if an employee handbook contains a proper disclaimer, even if that same handbook contains provisions for "progressive discipline," which may tend to look like promises to discipline prior to termination, the right to fire at will is preserved.[6]

The Term-of-Years Principle

The opposite of the at-will doctrine in employment is the term-of-years principle. This refers to situations in which the right to fire at will has been replaced by a contract promise.

Contract promises can be express, such as hiring an employee for a one-year term, or they can be implied as a matter of contract interpretation. An example of an implied contract promise of "a term of years" could be found by a court in the language used in employee handbooks. A phrase such as, "We are one big, happy family here, and we look forward to a longlasting relationship" could be held to be a promise of a "term of years." This would negate the right to fire at will. Whether such a statement does or does not indicate a promise of long-term employment becomes a question of fact for a jury to decide.[7]

APPLYING FOR A JOB

It is a good legal idea to include in job applications a clause such as the following: "I agree that the inn shall have the right to contact my former employers, the persons whom I have given as references, and those involved in my education as set forth in this application for employment." This constitutes a *legal waiver* and may be useful if the job application becomes an issue in court at a future date.

It is permissible to ask all applicants about criminal convictions and periods of incarceration but not about arrests. All other relevant background information can be asked for. References must be provided, and no laws at the moment prohibit this. Details of the applicant's education can be requested, as well as information about previous job activity. Questions must not be asked about issues protected in the federal and state civil rights acts, including race, color, religion, national origin, age, pregnancy, and disability.

An unusual "proscribed area" or "protected class" is found in the Human Rights Ordinance, passed by the City Council of Cincinnati, Ohio, in November, 1992. Included as a protected class in that ordinance are "Appalachian Americans": those who come from an area associated with poverty. That area reaches from Northern Alabama to Southern Quebec, an area of more than 1,500 miles in length. Hospitality industry operations in Cincinnati could violate the ordinance by asking a job applicant the place of her or his birth, if such place was located in Appalachia.

When facts emerge from prior employers or references that the applicant has "vicious propensities," it is essential that that person not be hired.[8] A hotel in Las Vegas violated this principle and hired a person who had tendencies to commit arson. The references from prior employers disclosed this. A fire at the hotel that resulted because of the actions of this person cost the hotel $38,000,000.

Application forms should contain a term stating that, by accepting the form and filling it out, the company gains the right to investigate the applicant's background. The form also should have a warning that what is stated on the form is considered to be the truth and, if it is not, the employer has the right to terminate employment on that ground. The courts recognize falsity on job applications as legal grounds for firing. For example, when a security company applicant falsified a job application, she could not sue her employer for firing her for that reason.[9]

Negligent Hiring and Retention

A prime concern of those who hire in the HH&T industry is what applicants have done at other jobs in the past. Job application forms ask for references, and, as can be expected, the applicants will list only those who will say good things about them. Relying on such references may not be enough as a matter of law. A good technique is to ask the applicant for the names of towns and cities in which they have worked before. A call to police departments there may disclose useful information. On the other hand, if a local law prohibits asking an application of his or her origin, such as is found in the previously mentioned Cincinnati ordinance, this information must not be requested.

Failure to screen job applicants properly can devastate a business where losses can be attributed to negligent hiring. Related to negligent hiring is the retention of an employee after information comes to light that shows that dangers exist in allowing that person to remain on the job.[10] Deciding if there was negligent hiring, and later retention, is a question of fact to be decided by a jury.

> In order to support an instruction on negligent hiring and retention, there must be evidence that the employee was unfit, considering the nature of the employment and the risk he posed to those with whom he would foreseeably associate, see Restatement (Second) of Agency sections 213 comment d (1958), and that the employer knew or should have known that the employee was unfit.[11]

The liability flows from a direct duty running from the employer to those members of the public whom the employer might reasonably anticipate would be placed in a position of risk of injury as a result of the hiring.[12] When an employee was given access to a townhouse passkey, the employer had a duty to make reasonable inquiry about the employee's background.[13]

For an employer to be liable for negligent hiring and retention, there must be a connection between the employer's business and the injured plaintiff.[14] Frequently, this connection is established by the fact that the injury occurred on the business premises while the employee was on duty and while the plaintiff was there for business reasons.

A related legal principle may arise in a negligent hiring-retention situation.

Ratification of Wrongful Conduct

An example of a ratification of wrongful conduct is having knowledge of sexual harassment by an employee and then allowing that conduct to continue without taking steps to eliminate it. This is ratification of the misconduct and, thus, the wrong would be imputed by law to the business, making that business responsible for the wrongful conduct.[15]

Other Pre-Hiring Matters

A variety of other legal matters arise before the employer/employee relationship begins. A discussion of some of these follows.

Background Checks

Contrary to misconceptions, no laws prevent a potential employer from making background checks on job applicants. Many laws, however, such as those covering sex offenders of the young, require that thorough background investigations be made of all job applicants.

Laws created by the courts and some legislatures proscribe unreasonable intrusions into one's privacy, yet such laws do not prevent reasonable inquiry for private business use. The Fourth Amendment, for example, gives a hotel guest the assurance that his or her hotel room will be free of "unreasonable searches and seizures" by state agencies. It does not give a job applicant with something to hide the right to demand that the potential employer be denied the right to uncover that past.

The false resume. A practical problem that confronts one who carries out background checks is the false resume. The use of false information on job applications has been common in the past and is on the increase. Studies show that about 30 percent of all job applications contain information that is not true.

In addition, facts disclosed on applications often contain information that is true but misleading. This creates practical problems for the manager. Laws provide penalties for those who give false information on job applications, but these laws do not assist the employer when making hiring decisions. To offset this problem, can employers make use of lie detector tests to uncover false resumes?

Polygraph tests. A federal law, effective December 27, 1988, bans the general use of polygraph lie detector tests by private employers.[16] More than forty states have passed statutes that reach the same result. This law generally prohibits use of a psychological stress evaluator or a voice stress analyzer for preemployment or random testing of employees. Some polygraph tests are permitted, but their use is limited to matters of economic loss or injury to the employer's business, and many requirements must be met by the employer prior to their use.

The federal law is enforced by the U. S. Department of Labor, Wage and Hour Division. It requires all employers to post a sign alerting employees to the ban on polygraph testing in the workplace.

Immigrant Employees

Once the background check is completed, hiring decisions must be made. These decisions are influenced by a variety of legal matters. One concerns immigrants. The Immigration Reform and Control Act of 1986 lays down rules that must be followed when hiring immigrants. The basic rule is that a form called "I-9" must be completed for each such employee, and maintained as provided in the act. Substantial penalties are provided for those who fail to comply.

Employers must make certain that Form I-9 is filled out completely and accurately. Judging from its numerous audits, the U. S. Department of Justice,

Immigration and Naturalization looks closely at the HH&T industry, because it attracts and utilizes illegal immigrants in increasingly large numbers.

The Civil Rights Act of 1964/72/92 prohibits discrimination in hiring on the grounds of "national origin." For this reason, *all* employees should be handled the same in regard to Form I-9. Potential employees never should be turned away, or existing employees fired, because of "foreign appearance" or foreign language.

When an HH&T manager files the papers to allow an illegal immigrant to remain in the United States, the employer is the *petitioner* and the employee is the *beneficiary*. The petitioner can revoke the petition at any time and for any reason.

"Business Necessity" in Employment and Human Resources

Associated with the hiring of employees is the doctrine of "business necessity." Business reasons upon which management decisions are made usually are accepted by American judges if they are reasonable. Such decisions, however, should be documented in in-house records. This is important if the decisions have to be justified in court at a later time. As an example, a hotel located near the United Nations might decide to hire a desk clerk who speaks four languages, rather than a more highly trained person who speaks only one language.

Those in charge of personnel offices must be able to give reasons for hiring certain employees. These reasons generally must *not* be based upon race, color, religion, national origin, sex, age, or physical handicap. If based upon solid business reasons, any claim of discrimination usually will fail in a court action brought by one denied employment.[17]

In reference to this matter, the terminology in current usage is "bona fide occupational qualifications." This phrase becomes important when deciding hiring criteria.

Discrimination in Hiring

Refusing to hire applicants who have criminal records where time has been served for offenses may lead to charges of discrimination. On the other hand, if there is a good *business reason* for such refusal, that refusal may pass legal muster. An example is to refuse to hire a convicted car thief to handle valet parking.

The EEOC, which has jurisdiction over these matters, suggests that employers faced with such circumstances consider the following:

1. the time that has passed since the criminal conviction
2. the nature of the job in question
3. the seriousness of the offense that led to the conviction

An Arizona court discussed the matter in this fashion:

> Hotels aren't like other businesses. Hotel employees have easy access to guests and their property, and given that access, hotels must check employee backgrounds. That takes time and money, but avoiding just one negligent hiring lawsuit will be repayment 1,000 times over.
>
> One Arizona case saw $6 million ($1 million in actual damages and $5 million in punitive damages) awarded to the husband of a woman murdered by a new employee. During the trial it became apparent the hotel had done practically

nothing to verify the background of the assailant-employee. The husband's lawyer argued it would have been easy to discover the employee had a history of violence with only a minimum background check.

The jury decided the inn was reckless and grossly negligent in failing to conduct a sufficient background check. That check would have disclosed a history of violence, aggravated assault and attempted rape.[18]

Discrimination against persons with disabilities is prohibited by the Americans with Disabilities Act unless a reasonable accommodation of that person cannot be made in the employment.[19]

Discrimination in a Hiring Suit

To establish illegal discrimination, a female applicant had to prove the following:[20]

1. that she was a member of a protected class
2. that she applied for the job in issue
3. that she was qualified for the job
4. that she was not hired
5. that the employer filled the job with a person not of the class in question

Probationary Periods

One final matter to be considered in relation to hiring employees is the use of probationary periods. The constant need for employees often mandates hiring before complete background checks can be carried out. A protective measure is to hire on a probationary basis, reserving the right to terminate the employment if harmful information is subsequently discovered.

NEW EMPLOYEE ISSUES

Once the employer-employee relationship becomes operational, other legal matters come to the front. The unionization of employees is one, and the use of employee manuals, handbooks, or policy manuals is another.

Many other examples of business reasons may justify the refusal to hire an applicant for a job.

Unions at Inns

Whether a business does or does not become unionized is a matter of bargaining and decision making. Litigation, however, has made it clear that in dealing with those who are seeking to unionize a particular hotel, care is in order as to what the hotel says or promises.[21]

One strong point for management emerges: One and only one management person should be designated to handle union matters. All other managers must be instructed to pass on such matters to that person. The designated person, in turn, must consult with counsel and be trained in the area of labor relations and union negotiation.

The attorney with whom that person consults must be chosen for his or her skill in the subject of unionization. Not all American lawyers are expert in union legal matters. An in-depth legal discussion of union organization and labor law is beyond the scope of this text; however, it is vitally important that management gain an understanding of labor, union, and management relationships and the laws that apply.

Employee Manuals

Related to unions at the inn, often as a result of collective bargaining, are employee manuals, handbooks, or policy manuals.

In the absence of a union, the well-intentioned manager usually does not intend for an employee handbook to be binding upon anyone. The courts, however, almost always view such a document in a different light. If handbooks are given unilaterally to the employees, the courts will allow them to be introduced into evidence as part of the contract that exists between the business and the employee. This is so because the courts view the handbook as a *unilateral offer*, one in which only one side made promises but in which the other side relied upon those promises by accepting the employment.

Example

Employee X is hired to work at a hotel, and no written employment contract is involved. The employer presents to Employee X an employee handbook that contains details on health, accident, and vacation benefits, and also contains a statement that "no employee will be fired unless procedures are followed." Employee X then is fired for not doing her job. No formal procedures are followed. Many courts would hold the handbook to be a unilateral contract: The hotel made a promise and the employee relied upon it. By not keeping its promise to "follow procedures," the firing was a breach of contract.

A Wisconsin court ruled in 1985 that the terms found within the handbook given to an employee at the time of hiring were contractual and were binding upon both the inn and the employee. When the employee was fired, the Wisconsin court sustained the validity of the handbook.[22]

As stated previously, handbooks also can be used against an inn if the terms within them favor the fired employee.[23]

Employee Manuals and Inn Security

Having employee manuals in use, especially when they relate to security, is not enough. Employees and agents must understand what these manuals say and be trained to carry out the mandates contained in them. Failure to do so may prompt a court to hold one responsible for an injurious incident in spite of the manual.[24] It follows that security and other measures set forth in employee/agent manuals be made the subject of employee training sessions.

States that have recognized employee handbooks as unilateral contracts include Idaho, Illinois, Massachusetts, Michigan, Minnesota, Nevada, New Jersey, and Washington.

North Dakota, on the other hand, has refused to find a unilateral contract in an employee handbook where the handbook itself contained a conspicuous disclaimer that stated: "This Employee Handbook has been drafted as a guideline for our employees. It shall not be construed to form a contract between the company and its employees."[25]

Employee Goals and Standards

Once the employer/employee/agent relationship becomes operational, a variety of other legal matters come into play. One of these involves employee goals and standards. Standards that employees are expected to meet must be clear and capable of being measured accurately. Goals established for employees also must be attainable. If either or both of these rules are violated, employees are penalized and tend to become frustrated in their job performance. This is legally dangerous because poor job performance may result in legal liability. The liability could be on several levels possibly endangering guest welfare and safety, or later trying to terminate the employee and not having sufficient documentation because of a pattern of "tacit approval."

Employee "Value"

The courts are holding that an employee who stays on a job and who does not seek other employment is giving something of value to the employer. Remaining on the job, especially in the face of adversity such as poor or unsafe working conditions, may well provide sufficient contract consideration to support promises, direct or indirect, that may have been made by or implied from the employment relationship. This is especially so of the terms in employee handbooks.

Employees and Security

It is good practice to instruct all employees and agents to keep a close watch for any activities or conditions on the business premises that appear out of the ordinary. If the activities are observed, a report must be made to that employee's superior immediately. That superior, in turn, must see to it that the information is relayed to the proper personnel and acted upon as quickly as possible.

Employees and Luggage Keys

In the HH&T industry, many employees handle countless items of luggage of guests. It is known that theft-inclined employees will arm themselves with a variety of keys that can be used to enter luggage. Management has to take reasonable steps to locate and fire those who have such keys.

As part of the security involving keys, luggage, and guests, periodic checks are made of employees' lockers. These checks are permissible, especially if this is provided for in the employee handbook.

Concessions to Employees

Supervisory personnel must be cautioned that making exceptions for one employee may prompt a court to use that concession against the business when another employee is disciplined for the same infraction. For example, if Employee X is late for work habitually but is forgiven routinely by his or her supervisor, it could well cause legal problems if Employee Y is disciplined later for being late for work. Supervisory personnel must be trained to avoid differential treatment.

Defamation of Employees

At law, defamation is an offense that, when proven, can lead to damages against the offending person. It can take one of two forms: *libel*, use of the printed word, or *slander*, use of the spoken word. For either to be actionable, a two-part legal test must be met:

1. A false statement about the employee in question must be made knowingly.
2. That false statement must be "published": brought to the minds of one or more other persons.

It should be house policy never to discuss with others what an employee did, failed to do, or is suspected of doing.

A Drug-Free Workplace

A topic of concern is the drug testing of employees and agents. In drug testing, it is not wise to single out groups for testing, such as hourly employees or those who work from "midnight until eight A.M." Such a policy creates a reason to challenge the testing when employees are fired because of it. If a testing program looks as though it might have discriminatory overtones, it should be rethought and redesigned to avoid that impression.

Unions and Drug Testing

It is important to insert a clause in the union contract that allows the testing of employees for drugs and alcohol under reasonable circumstances. This can be repeated in employee handbooks. If public safety is involved, the courts may approve random testing, such as the testing of gun-carrying guards, lifeguards at swimming pools, and the like.

Harrah's Hotel in Reno, Nevada, issued an order requiring all employees to wear a ribbon at work stating they were "drug-free." Several employees refused to comply, and they were suspended without pay. A court upheld the suspensions. In Las Vegas, the refusal of an employee to take a drug or alcohol test after the employee's discharge was held to be conclusive evidence that the termination was proper.[26]

Terminating Employment

Contrary to the "at-will" employment doctrine, firing minority employees, older employees, pregnant employees, female employees, disabled employees, and others has led to many lawsuits. Because of federal and state laws, many employees have become members of "protected classes."

If it is determined that there is sufficient reason to fire an employee, the termination should be carried out promptly. To delay the firing could lead to problems if the delay results in injury or loss to a guest at the inn.

A delay can cause another problem. Assume that an undesirable employee is allowed to continue working but is fired later when he or she becomes ill. The delay may prompt a jury to find the firing to be illegal. For a case in which the fired employee recovered more than $80,000 in back pay and more than $80,000 in future pay plus benefits, see *Folz v. Marriott Corp.*[27]

Firing in an At-Will State

More than 80 percent of the states have modified the "at-will employment doctrine." Hawaii has modified the doctrine to protect employees from being fired where "public policy" or "freedom of speech" are involved. Do these exceptions apply to an employee for getting drunk and swearing at an employee picnic, who, after a proper disciplinary hearing, was fired? A 1988 Hawaii decision has answered the question in the negative, upholding the firing.[28]

Although the Nevada Supreme Court has established that an at-will employee may be fired for any reason, the court says the discharge cannot be tortious and cannot violate public policy. The court explained that the essence of a " . . . tortious discharge is the wrongful, usually retaliatory interruption of employment . . . ."[29]

The actual illegal firing, or wrongful termination, of an employee is actionable, and the employee can seek job reinstatement and back wages in court. A second form of illegal firing that the courts recognize is *constructive firing* or *constructive discharge*. Here, the firing is not actual, but the facts and surrounding circumstances are such that to remain on the job would be intolerable to the employee and the employee is forced to quit. This type of circumstance is actionable, and the business must use care not to allow this to happen.[30]

In termination cases that are contested, the employer must produce creditable evidence of why the termination was legal and proper. In the absence of such evidence, not only will the employer probably lose the case at trial, but a jury verdict in favor of the fired employee will be upheld on appeal. If the lower court record provides no reason for the appellate court to reverse, the jury's conclusions must be upheld.

It is mandatory at trial to make certain that legal and otherwise proper reasons for the termination are entered into evidence. Appellate courts will assume nothing in the absence of such evidence in the lower court record.[31] As a management point, if the business is operating in a legal manner, employees will not be fired for illegal reasons, and management activities will be documented fully.

Quoted Salary at Firing Time

If a business had quoted an employee a yearly salary at the time of hiring, such as "$60,000" a year, the courts generally take the position that the business has guaranteed the employee one year's salary and will use that standard in deciding severance pay.

On the other hand, if a weekly or monthly wage was agreed upon, the courts usually will accept this wage at the time the employee is fired in deciding any benefits due the employee.

Employees Called for Jury Duty

To fire an employee because he or she is called for federal jury duty and serves, would place the employer in criminal contempt. State laws reach a similar result where employees are fired for serving on state juries.

The best policy to follow is to allow time off the job to employees called for federal or state jury duty. They should be replaced temporarily. To this end, it is good management policy to make up the difference in what the court pays the employee and what he or she would have earned by remaining on the job. To see what can happen if an opposite policy is adopted, see *Piergg v. Poulos.*[32]

An adjunct of firing of employees is the use of termination conferences. These can be of benefit to the business and the fired employee. They can lead to legal difficulty, however, if not carried out properly.

Termination Conference

Though disagreeable to the employer and the employee alike, such termination conferences can be beneficial to both sides. On the other hand, they can lead to litigation if the employee being fired believes that an injustice has occurred in the handling of the meeting.

The decision to fire an employee must be based upon substantial evidence, and company procedures must be carefully followed. A written record should be made of the conference. In addition, the now-fired employee should be informed of all benefits available to him or her. An agreement should be reached as to a letter of recommendation that will be written to future employers and what the letter will contain.

Nothing must be done to prevent the fired employee from obtaining employment elsewhere. But it must be made clear that the employer has a duty to report all facts if specific inquiry is made by others in the future, especially if the acts of the fired employee were criminal in nature or were characterized by criminal propensities.

SUMMARY

The relationship between employees and employers can often have a direct effect upon the success of any business. A good relationship can reap benefits for all concerned. A mediocre relationship can be unproductive for those same persons, and a poor relationship can lead to economic disaster.

The at-will doctrine is appearing frequently in employee court cases. Some states have the at-will doctrine by statute and other states have it as part of the state common law. Some states have curtailed the doctrine or have abolished it by court decisions or by statute. In more and more cases, employee handbooks are being used by the courts to assist employees who have been fired at will. There is a trend today to favor the employee in lawsuits when all other factors are equal. From the point of view of management, care must be exercised in the creation of written employee related rules and documents, such as house rules, job applications, forms, and employee handbooks.

Management often makes two errors in relation to employees. The first is being negligent in hiring those who cause harm to guests, patrons, and third parties because of the propensities that they brought with them to the work place. The second is the retention of such employees after their backgrounds have become known. A car thief should not manage the hotel valet service, nor should a jewel thief be placed in charge of the hotel safe.

Employee discrimination cases are on the rise and especially sexual harassment cases. The very nature of the hotel/motel industry, with the masses of employees, agents, and guests involved, renders it susceptible to such lawsuits. The costs to the industry have increased dramatically in recent years, and great care is needed by management in these areas.

QUESTIONS

1. True or false: The at-will doctrine, as it is seen in employment law situations, is now on the decline because its rationale no longer reflects the realities of the workplace of the coming twenty-first century.

2. True or false: The courts tend to treat employee handbooks or policy manuals, as unilateral contracts. This means the terms contained within them are promises made by the business which have been accepted by taking the job.

3. True or false: It is important to know what questions should *not* be included in job applications.

4. True or false: Privacy laws, both federal and state, prohibit detailed inquiry into the lives of potential employees.

5. What type of questions should not be used on the job application form a business uses? List five items.

6. What type of questions should be included on a job application form? List three items.

7. List three items an innkeeper should place into the handbook given to newly hired employees at the inn.

8. List three items the innkeeper should *not* place into the handbook given to newly hired employees at the inn.

9. Why must considerable thought be given to an exit interview of an employee, and what kind of legal dangers does an employer face at this session?

10. What does "negligent retention" mean?

NOTES

1. Abraham Arnold Maslow (U. S. psychologist, 1908–70).
2. Douglas Murray McGregor (U. S. College President, 1906–64).
3. USCA, Title 29, Ch. 15.
4. *Dutch Properties, Inc. v. Pac-San, Inc.,* 778 P. 2d 969 (Oregon 1989).
5. *Pond v. Devon Hotels,* 563 N.E. 2d 738 (Ohio 1990).
6. *Bailey v. Perkins Restaurants,* 398 N.W. 2d 120 (North Dakota 1986).

7. *Pond v. Devon Hotels, supra.*

8. *Pacific v. Frogatt*, 591 A. 2d 1386 (Sup. Ct. New Jersey 1991).

9. *Churchman v. Pinkerton's*, 756 F. Supp. 515 (U. S. Dist. Ct. Kansas 1991).

10. *Hogan v. Forsyth Country Club*, 340 S.E. 2d 116 (North Carolina 1990).

11. *F & T Co. v. Woods*, 92 N.M. 697, 594 P. 2d 745 (1979).

12. *Ponticas v. K.M.S. Investments*, 331 N.W. 2d 907 (Minn. 1983).

13. *Williams v. Feather Sound, Inc.*, 386 So. 2d 1238 (Fla. App. 1980).

14. See note "The Responsibility of Employers for the Actions of Their Employees"; Note, "The Negligent Hiring Theory of Liability," 58 Chi-Kent L. Rev. 717 (1977).

15. *Hogan v. Forsyth, supra.*

16. 29 USC 2001 *et seq.*

17. *Becker v. Wenco*, 638 F. Supp. 650 (New York 1986).

18. *Hospitality Law*, Volume 5, Number 4, April 1990, p. 1, speaking of *Gilmore v. Best Western International, Inc.*, Polls County, Florida, 1989, no citation available.

19. *Davidsons v. Shoney's Big Boy Restaurant*, 380 S.E. 2d 232 (West Virginia 1989).

20. *Badeen v. Burns*, 765 F. Supp. 341 (Texas 1991).

21. *Georgetown Hotel v. N.L.R.B.*, 835 F. 2d 1467 (D.C. 1987).

22. *Ferraro v. Kolesch*, 368 N.W. 2d 666 (Wisconsin 1985).

23. *Thompson v. American Motors Inns*, 623 F. Supp. 409 (Virginia 1985).

24. *MacQuarrie v. Howard Johnson Co.*, 877 F. 2d 126 (Delaware 1989).

25. *Bailey v. Perkins Restaurants*, 398 N.W. 2d 120 (North Dakota 1986).

26. *Fremont Hotel v. Esposito*, 760 P. 2d 122 (Nevada 1988).

27. 594 F. Supp. 1007 (Missouri 1984).

28. *Pagdilao v. Maui Hotel*, 703 F. Supp. 863 (Hawaii 1988).

29. *K Mart Corp. v. Ponsock*, 732 P. 2d 1364 (Nevada 1987).

30. *Churchman v. Pinkertons', Inc.*, 756 F. Supp. 515 (U. S. Dist. Ct. Kansas 1991).

31. *Patchell v. Red Apple Enterprises*, 921 F. 2d 157 (Arizona 1990).

32. 542 So. 2d 377 (Florida 1989).

Statutory Laws of Employment

OVERVIEW

EXPANDING ON WHAT we learned in Chapter 8, this chapter covers the statutory (legislative) laws of employment that apply to hotels, theme parks, travel agencies, airlines, restaurants, bars, and other industry businesses.

Many of the rules and policies discussed in Chapter 8 have their basis in both federal and state statutes. We need to learn more about those statutes so we can better understand what the law expects of those who manage HH&T operations. Included in these statutes are the Fair Labor Standards Act and its amendments, wage attachment provisions of the Consumer Credit Protection Act, workers' compensation acts, unemployment compensation laws, the Civil Rights Act of 1964 and its amendments, the Americans with Disabilities Act, the Occupational Safety and Health Act, and The Family and Medical Leave Act of 1993.

The major employment statute is the FLSA.

FAIR LABOR STANDARDS ACT

A good law with which to begin is the Fair Labor Standards Act of 1938, as amended. It is one of the primary and most often consulted employment laws at any business. Enacted in 1938,[1] it has been amended several times to keep in step with the development of business over the last six decades. As originally enacted, this law restricted the use of child labor; set a minimum wage of 25 cents per hour; set the standard work week at forty-four hours; provided for time and one-half pay for all hours over the standard work week, and set down recordkeeping requirements. The latter was provided so the U. S. Department of Labor could monitor compliance with the law. Coverage of the law is essentially the same today, but changes have been made in its terms and new sections have been added.

Although the FLSA was challenged early on as being unconstitutional, the U. S. Supreme Court upheld it as a lawful extension of the commerce clause of the U. S. Constitution. Today, in modified and expanded form, it represents one of the key employee-employer laws.

Minimum Wage and Overtime

In July 1996[2], the U. S. Senate approved a 90-cent increase in the minimum wage which had been $4.25 per hour up to that time. The 74–20 vote raised this to $4.75 initially and than to $5.15 per hour effective July 1997. The standard workweek is forty hours. Although more than 60 percent of the states have similar laws, and though some of their minimum wage requirements are less than $5.15 per hour, most businesses fall under the federal coverage.

A person being paid $3.35 in 1988 was, in fact, receiving $2.56 per hour in 1981 dollars. The same ratio is true with the $5.15 per hour wage. About 15 million American workers earn the minimum wage, and these persons traditionally fall victim to inflation when the minimum wage is not increased. The prior $362,500 gross-annual-income exemption provided in the federal minimum wage law allowed the states to set lower limits for businesses that grossed less than the federal minimum. Many states, including Nevada, took advantage of that exception. In 1987, Nevada decided to forgo the exemption and came into compliance with the federal law. The gross-annual-income exemption is now $500,000.

Overtime pay is required for all work over forty hours in one week at a rate of 1½ times the regular rate of pay per each overtime hour.

These provisions for overtime apply whether an employee is paid on a flat, hourly, or contingent basis such as a percent of sales. Hours for two consecutive weeks cannot be averaged to avoid the overtime. The test is whether there was overtime in one week. If so, it must be paid—or the employee must be given compensation for it in some other form—at the time-and-one-half rate.

If the employee agrees to accept time off instead of pay for the overtime worked, it must be taken off during the work period in which the overtime accrued. It cannot be taken during a different work period. The purpose of the law is, first, to provide for overtime pay and, second, to make certain the employee enjoys the direct benefit of it in money or time off during that pay period.[3]

Flat Pay

Care must be used in paying nonsupervisory or other exempt persons with a flat rate. Even though the employee agrees to the flat-rate pay, if that person works overtime, the additional pay must be provided as overtime. Before flat-pay agreements are entered into, advice is needed so overtime hours will be reflected in the actual sums paid. The flat pay has to become an adjusted rate.

Other Wage Rules

If employees or agents attend seminars or conferences, care again must be exercised. The general rule is that, if the attendance is mandatory, the hours spent, including travel, must be considered in calculating overtime pay. If attendance is voluntary and the employee has a true option of attending or not, the hours need not be counted.

Who Is Not Covered by the FLSA?

Outside of intrastate businesses, exemptions to the coverage of the law are provided for professionals, supervisors, managers, and some outside sales personnel. The legal problem, however, is in determining whether an employee-agent is in fact exempt. Having the title of "manager" or "supervisor" is not enough. The law provides legal tests that must be met. Once again, this becomes a one-on-one question that requires legal attention.

Special certificates can be obtained from the administrator of the Wage and Hour Division of the Department of Labor to exempt from coverage full-time students, as well as people with disabilities and others. This exemption provision can be useful and provides a means of cutting costs for regular and special events at hotels, restaurants, and other facilities.

Also exempt from coverage are businesses that have a gross annual income of less than $500,000.[4] The law does not require sick, severance, vacation, or holiday pay. No limits are placed on the number of hours that can be worked in any week by those over the age of sixteen years. There are limits, however, on the *type* of work that those under eighteen years can engage in.

Child Labor Rules

The FLSA sets standards for the employment of individuals under the age of eighteen years. In hazardous work, one must be eighteen or older. In nonhazardous occupations the norm is age sixteen or older. Those who are fourteen and fifteen can be employed in sales and clerical work, for short working hours, outside of normal school hours.

Numerous other provisions are found in the FLSA, many of which place burdens on HH&T operations.[5] Examples include provisions for tip pooling and tip credit, meals and meal credits, uniform allowances and maintenance, and the use of full-time students at reduced wages.

Tip Income

Tips have been the subject matter of substantial federal legislation. The 1982 federal tax act required that restaurants and bars report income employees receive from tips. Regulations of a temporary nature to implement the federal statute then were created. These rules became effective in January 1983. They required restaurants and bars to report gross receipts from sales, the total charge receipts, the tips shown on these receipts, and service charges made. The purpose of the federal law was to get a "tax handle" on tip income that otherwise had been slipping through the IRS net. Under the FLSA, "tipped employees" are those who customarily receive more than $30 per month in tips.

By 1985, the federal law required each restaurant operator to file IRS form 8027, "The Employer's Annual Information Return for Tip Income and Allocated Tips." Although the IRS expected more than 120,000 food-service operators to file the form, less than one-third complied. The modest penalties for failure to comply—$50 in most instances—indicates a possible reason for noncompliance.

The federal tax law that went into effect January 1, 1988, requires restaurants to pay taxes on tips received by foodservers—a far cry from what the tip laws required in the beginning. If foodservers report tip earnings falsely, the IRS can hold the restaurant liable for unreported income. The status of the tip laws can relegate the manager to a "co-conspirator" status when foodservers do not report total income.

Many foodservers believe they would come out ahead with a service charge in lieu of tips. The argument for a European-type service charge to replace the traditional tip is countered by pointing out that foodservers who know they will receive an automatic 15-percent service charge will tend to lose motivation. They will pay less attention to customers, and generally will deliver a reduced quality of service, claims Arnie Morton, owner of Morton's, a popular restaurant now located in the U.S.

Working for Tips Only

When an employee works for tips only, does the fact that the worker receives no salary remove that person from coverage under workers' compensation if injured on the job? If that person has a work schedule, must wear a uniform, or meet other requirements the same as those who are in fact on salary, the courts will hold him or her to be an employee even in the absence of a salary, and thus extend compensation coverage to them.[6]

Tips and Tip Allocation

Covered in the FLSA amendments are provisions for handling tips received by employees and allocation of these tips. The Tax Equity and Fiscal Responsibility Act of 1982 laid down the following rules relating to tips and allocation of tips:

1. If a business has ten or more employees on a typical business day, the food and beverage operations there are covered.
2. If a business has twenty-five or more employees, allocation of tips must be based on individual sales.
3. Employees must report all tips to the IRS.
4. If reported tips fall below 8 percent of sales, management must allocate tips to employees who fail to report that amount or less.

To avoid audit and fines, all tips must be reported. Failing to do so will result in underpayment of FICA taxes to the detriment of the employees. Criminal penalties are also possible.

In July 1989, a judge in the Federal District Court in the District of Columbia sentenced eight waiters to jail each night for three months for failing to fully report their tips to the IRS. They were further fined $1,000 each and had to pay tax on unreported tips of $145,000, plus interest and penalties.

A Change in Tip Laws

The Tax Act of 1986 made a change in tip allocation for larger employers. Starting in January 1987, employers with twenty-five or more employees had to allocate tips based on employees' share of the gross receipts. Smaller employers could allocate tips based on gross receipts or on the ratio of hours worked to all hours worked as totaled.

Can Management Keep All Tips?

In a restaurant case in Seattle, Washington, management kept all tips and then used these funds, and others, to pay wages to valet parking employees. The Supreme Court of Washington held this to be illegal, stating:

The valets were "tipped employees" under [FLSA]. [FLSA] mandates that tipped employees are to keep all of their tips before an employer can deduct even 40 percent of their minimum wage obligations [now 50 percent]. Therefore, an arrangement where the employer takes all of an employee's tips and uses this money to fulfill apparently all of his minimum wage obligation—and help to pay other expenses as well—cannot be legal under the present law.[7]

Leaving tips and tip allocations, it is useful to become acquainted with a 1963 amendment to the FLSA, which also has to do with wages.

Equal Pay Act

The FLSA was amended in 1963 to provide equal pay for men and women who perform similar or like jobs at the worksite. Under this amendment, employers cannot discriminate for equal work on the basis of sex. This amendment *does* apply to local and state governments. Thus, whether a job applicant has children or not is of no concern to the hiring business. If it is made a concern, it could be discrimination on the grounds of sex. If male and female front-desk clerks do the same work, they must be paid the same pay. Seniority and superior job performance would be exceptions to the rule, but the basic rule is firm. In addition, the higher-paid employee wages cannot be reduced to match the lower paid employee. This too would be discrimination.

The Equal Employment Opportunity Commission has the authority to enforce the Equal Pay Act.[8]

Equal Pay Act and "Comparable Worth"

In 1981, the U. S. Supreme Court endorsed the idea that men and women should be paid the same amount when they do different jobs. In June 1985, however, the Equal Employment Opportunity Commission rejected the use of "comparable worth" as a means of deciding whether job discrimination exists in any specific case. The Commission held that "comparable worth" is not recognized under Title VII of the Civil Rights Act of 1964. In this case, the Service Employees International Union alleged that "the words of the EEOC carry a ring of hypocrisy for the 49 million working women in the United States." The following illustrates the view of the courts:

> The Court of Appeals, Henley, Circuit Judge, held that: (1) finding that actual work performed by plaintiff [a female] was substantially equal to actual work performed by a male employee,... was not clearly erroneous, and (2) although unlawful sex discrimination was established when the male's base salary was raised above that of plaintiff, it was error to award plaintiff damages for the period between the date of the male's hiring and date of the salary increase where additional payments over and above the increase were not designed to compensate the male for work he had done during such period but to compensate him for his loss resulting from the unavailability of the extra work that had been promised him on commencement of his employment.[9]

WAGE ATTACHMENTS

Related to the payment of wages is a problem created by another federal law, found in Title III of the Consumer Credit Protection Act.[10] The unusual feature of this law, as it relates to wages, is that it places obligations upon the employer for defaults that have occurred with creditors of the employee or agent. This law regulates the "attachment" of the wages of employees or agents covered by the FLSA.

The attachment of wages of judgment debtors by judgment creditors is a popular method of collecting debts, as attested to by more than 100,000 attachments made each year. Under the federal Consumer Credit Protection Act, wage attachments are called "garnishments." A garnishment means any legal or equitable procedure through which the earnings of an individual are required to be withheld for payment of debt.

Although garnishment is popular with those who collect debts, what about the manager? Doesn't garnishment require extra bookwork for payroll personnel? Isn't it, in reality, a first-class nuisance? The answer to these questions is an emphatic "yes."

Why not fire the garnished employee and save all the worry and work? The problem with this is that if you fire an employee for one garnishment, you have violated the CCPA. An employer who willfully violates the CCPA (not to mention the FLSA) is subject to a fine of not more than $1,000 or a prison sentence of not more than one year—or both.

The CCPA prohibits firing for one garnishment, but can we fire the employee who has *two* garnishments? If there are multiple garnishments on one debt, the answer is "no."

So what do we do? First, we must determine that the garnishment order is from a court in which judgment has been taken against the debtor. We never should begin a wage attachment on the mere word of anyone. We must insist upon an exemplified (certified) copy of the court order.

Next, we must determine what, if any, portion of the employee's wages may be deducted each pay period.

State Law

State laws that are in substantial compliance with the CCPA may prevail if the state has been granted an exemption (Kentucky is an example). In addition, any state law *that is more favorable to the debtor* will control the percentage that can be deducted from the employee's wages. In New York the limit is 10 percent, whereas under the CCPA it is 25 percent. In New York, then, the limit is 10 percent.

Formula

With the above in mind, we can begin calculations for purposes of deductions. In doing this, we must look to the statutory formula. In the following example, we are assuming that we are in a state that follows the 25-percent rule of the CCPA and that the employee is paid weekly.

When a wage earner has wages subjected to garnishment, the amount that can be taken from those wages must not exceed 25 percent of the "disposable earnings" for the period, or the amount "by which disposal earnings exceed 30 times the federal minimum hourly wage prescribed by section 6 (a) of the Fair Labor Standards Act of 1938 in effect at the time the earnings are payable."[11]

Taking the minimum wage of $5.15 per hour and multiplying it by 30 gives us $154.50. If a worker has a weekly wage of $200 and had deductions of $45.50 for Social Security, income tax, and other items including fringe benefits, his or her "disposable earnings" total $154.50. *This sum is exempt from garnishment.* If one cent is withheld from these wages, the penalty provisions of the law become operative.

The HH&T manager receives a call from a member of the local bar, who says a garnishment order is in the mail and 25 percent of the debtor-employee's wages should be withheld starting next payday. The employee is earning the $200 per week mentioned. See the danger? The employer can make *no* deductions at all for that week, or the next, or the next after that.

The debtor-employee is earning $200.00 per week. Deductions total leaving $160 in disposable earnings. The employer can only deduct the sum above $154.50, or $5.50 for that week. This sum does not exceed 25 percent of the disposable earnings.

Raise the wage to $300 per week with deductions of $50. This leaves $250 in disposable earnings. Now we can take out $95.50, right? No. The 25-percent provision now controls, and this applies to "disposable earnings," which now total $250. Twenty-five percent of this is $62.50. This is the limit that can be deducted for this week, leaving the employee $187.50 free to take home. If the state limit is 10 percent, the deduction is reduced accordingly.

Policy Reasons

Two policies are reflected in this tricky federal law:

1. To ensure each worker unrestricted use of the minimum wage.
2. To set outside limits, by percent, to prevent the wholesale removal of large chunks of a wage-earner's salary when that person is earning a fairly substantial wage.

The Fair Labor Standards Act, as amended, makes it clear that it is unlawful to permit a wage attachment (garnishment) to deny an employee the benefits of the sum of money the federal law permits that person to take home each pay day. The same principle could apply, for example, if a business were to require employees to purchase uniforms or shoes, with deductions being made to pay for them. If these deductions were to leave an employee with less funds that the law guarantees, the minimum wage law has been violated. Those funds would have to be returned to the employee. Failure to do so would render the business subject to FLSA penalties for wage violations.

Those working in a true supervisory or executive capacity are exempt from the FLSA time and one-half wage requirements. Calling someone a "supervisor" or "executive," however, will not excuse the business from the time and one-half wage provisions if the requirements of the FLSA are not met.[12]

This brings us to workers' compensation laws.

WORKERS' COMPENSATION

Workers' compensation laws are designed to provide benefits for employees or agents who are injured while "on the job" as those words have come to be defined by law. The benefits paid for those found eligible are based on a percentage of the employee's wages and applicable state tables. The laws of each state must be looked to in this area. The benefits paid are not taxable to the employee.

Covered workers cannot sue their employers because workers' compensation is the sole remedy. If the worker is injured on the job by the negligence of third parties, however, an independent tort action may be brought against that third party. Any recovery must be used first to repay any funds received.

The first workers' compensation laws, passed by the English Parliament, placed strict liability upon employers. That policy has come down to us today. If an employee deliberately injures himself or herself on the job, however, the employer is excused from liability upon proof of the self-inflicted injury.

Today, injuries to an employee while on duty are considered a cost of operations. The policy of the law is to spread this loss among those who will benefit from the labor, and not force the employee to suffer the loss alone. Today, the compensation laws are recognized as being remedial in nature. They were created to remedy a specific social problem. Thus, under the rules of statutory construction, the courts will construe these statutes liberally and not strictly. Translated, this means that any doubt will be resolved by the courts in *favor of the injured person*. In that manner, the purpose of such laws will be achieved. Figure 9.1 is a flowchart depicting interpretation of these statutes.

Although workers' compensation laws represent the exclusive remedy for injured employees while on the job, there are exceptions. In West Virginia, for

FIGURE 9.1   Interpretation of remedial statutes.

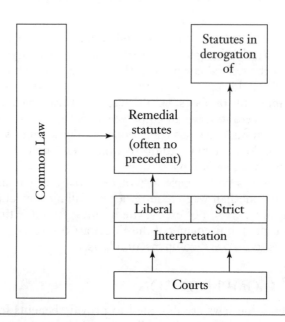

example, if an employer allows an unsafe working condition that presents a high degree of risk and results in injury, the injured employee can seek tort damages.[13]

As a general principle, workers driving to and from work where injury or death occurs at those times are not covered by workers' compensation. There is, however, an exception called the "special risk rule," created by California courts:

1. If the employee would not have been at the location of the injury or death were it not for the employment, and
2. If the risk to the employee was distinctive or greater than risks common to those the public is generally exposed to, then there is coverage.[14]

In the not-too-distant past, workers' compensation claims in the hospitality industry were limited to physical injuries. Following that came the allowance of recoveries in court for psychological claims if it could be determined that such resulted from physical injuries.

This situation has been expanded, and the courts now are looking at the following:

1. anxiety reactions
2. phobic matters
3. depressive reactions to injuries
4. post-traumatic syndromes
5. psychological injury that stands alone in its effects

When workers' compensation cases work their way into the courts, some unusual results are often seen. For example: Shelly Johns was a lounge dancer at the Dancing Sunshines Lounge in Arizona, where she performed for tips only. After slipping on a wet floor, she applied for workers' compensation. The lounge argued that she was an independent contractor and, thus, not eligible for compensation. The court found that she had a posted work schedule and had to wear a specific uniform and used these facts to hold her to be an employee for compensation purposes.[15]

Beverly Morgan quit her job as a masseuse at the Desert Inn Hotel and Casino in Las Vegas. Under directions of an agent of the Desert Inn, she filed her claim too late. Desert Inn contested both the type of injury and the late filing. The Supreme Court of Nevada granted her full benefits, holding:

> The evidence supports that Morgan's degenerative joint disease qualifies as an occupational disease which arose out of and in the course of her employment as a masseuse for Desert Inn. . . . Her job as a masseuse involved inordinate use of her hands. As she continued her employment, her problems worsened. She was diagnosed as having a disease "aggravated by overuse" in the performance of her job. . . . There is a direct causal connection between her work conditions and the aggravation of the disease; the disease worsened as a natural incident of her continued work, and her work can be "fairly traced" as the proximate cause of her worsened condition.[16]

The court pointed out,

Although Morgan's is an occupational disease claim, she erroneously filed a claim for an industrial accident at Gibbens' direction. Because its own agent gave Morgan the wrong information, Desert Inn cannot now benefit from Morgan's failure to strictly comply with the statute. . . .[17]

When Is an Accident Compensable?

In answering the question of when an accident is compensable, the courts have developed two applicable tests.

1. Was the employee on the job when placed at risk and then injured? This is called a *positional risk*. The employee was in a position to be injured by reason of being at work.
2. Was the employee in the scope of his or her employment when the injury occurred? This is called *actual risk*. The injury arose in the scope of employment and "as a result of the employment."

If one or both tests are met, the injury is compensable. Applying these two tests in court is not always clear, however.

To illustrate, Fay Jones worked at the King's Arms Tavern, where she prepared salads, cut pies, dipped ice cream, and made coffee and tea. While arriving at work one morning, she took trash from her car to deposit in the tavern waste area and fell while doing so. This happened before she had entered the tavern itself. Was she at "actual risk" when injured?

The Virginia Court of Appeals stated that when an employee chooses to go to a dangerous place outside of her place of employment, any injury sustained there is not compensable. In this case, however, the court held that

> Mrs. Jones did not choose to go to a dangerous place where her employment did not necessarily carry her. She went to what was an appropriate place provided by the employer for employees to dispose of trash. The mere fact that she stepped over to a trash receptacle for a personal need does not take the accident out of the course of her employment or cause the accident to become one not arising out of her employment. Accidents which arise out of the conditions of the workplace should be compensable if the activity which gave rise to the accident is of a nature reasonably to be expected by the employer and occurred at a place and time where an employee might reasonably be expected to be.[18]

As a general rule, if an inn maintains workers' compensation coverage, that is the sole source of recovery for injuries sustained by employees while "on the job." This includes extreme situations such as the housekeeper raped in a hotel room while trying to perform her maintenance duties.[19] This rule, however, has exceptions.

Personal Animosity Rule

In some states the courts recognize a personal animosity rule and treat it as an exception to the general rule that an employer is obligated to pay compensation to a worker injured on the job. Thus, if employee X is injured by the fall of a wall-mounted television set while cleaning a guest room, employee X is entitled to receive workers' compensation as provided by law. On the other hand, if employee X is assaulted by employee Y because of a personal dispute unrelated to the business of the inn, in most states employee X would not qualify for benefits. The reason is that, even though the injury occurred at the job site, it had nothing to do with the work being carried out there.

By statute, in some states such as Texas, after maximum payment is collected under workers' compensation, suit then can be brought against an employer if the employer had been guilty of gross negligence. To illustrate, a San Antonio Holiday Inn had to pay almost $200,000 extra to the widow of a security guard slain by a burglar at the inn. It was a house rule that security guards could not carry firearms, and that was the basis of the widow's successful claim. She argued that her husband should have been allowed to be armed.[20]

In Maryland, a court rule has developed that allows direct suit to be brought, after workers' compensation claims have been settled, for emotional distress caused by delayed payment of the claim. Both the Texas statute and the Maryland court decision represent intrusions into the common principle that, if workers' compensation is in effect, it bars all further claims.

Leaving the topic of workers' compensation, it is useful to learn something about a companion law not concerned with injury but, rather, with the loss of wages.

UNEMPLOYMENT COMPENSATION

All of the states have programs designed to compensate qualified employees who become unemployed under specified conditions. The costs of administering these programs are paid mostly by the federal government, whereas the funds for the benefits come from payroll taxes that each state levies.

Denial of Benefits

Benefits to an employee will be denied under the following conditions:

1. The employee is fired for misconduct on the job.
2. The employee is taking part voluntarily in a labor dispute.
3. The employee has not been off the job for the prescribed time period.
4. The employee has refused another job in which he or she is trained and experienced, refuses to actively seek other work, or has resigned without cause.

An employer who breaches an employment contract, which leads the employee to resign, gives cause to the employee to recover unemployment compensation in spite of the fact that the employee resigned voluntarily. The resignation must be for "good cause attributable to the employer." Breaching an employment contract meets that test.[21]

One of the more important areas of employment concern deals with the civil rights acts, both federal and state. In many instances the federal act has served as a model for the laws that state legislatures have adopted. We now turn to that federal law.[22]

CIVIL RIGHTS LEGISLATION

The Civil Rights Act of 1964, as amended, imposes two primary legal duties upon a business.

1. There must not be discrimination in hiring on the grounds of race, color, creed, national origin, or sex. Title VII covers compensation, terms or conditions of employment.
2. Title II of the act prohibits discrimination at "places of public accommodation." It is interesting to note that Title VII prohibits discrimination on the grounds of sex and Title II does not. Thus, sex discrimination is not covered at places of public accommodation, but other laws reach that result. Title II will be discussed in Chapter 21.

Before the federal civil rights laws become operative, there must be federal power over the business in question. This power can be triggered in two ways:

1. The operation of the business must have some effect upon interstate commerce.
2. It can come about when discrimination at a hotel, motel, or inn is "supported by state action."[23]

An example of this is state laws that prohibited members of certain races from occupying rooms at hotels and motels in a state. The constitutionality of the Civil Rights Act of 1964 was upheld by the U. S. Supreme Court.[24]

Equal Employment Opportunity Act

The Civil Rights Act of 1964 contained an obvious weakness: It did not give the Equal Employment Opportunity Commission (EEOC) the power to issue "cease-and-desist" orders in the federal courts. Attempts were made to give the EEOC this power, but they failed.

Instead of asking for cease-and-desist powers, the Nixon Administration suggested that the EEOC be given the power to file suits in federal court and to represent those who had meritorious employment-discrimination claims. The commission could file suit, however, only after all steps had been taken to conciliate the matter without court action.

In 1972, the House acted first, and the Senate strengthened the bill. President Nixon signed it into law on March 27, 1972, and it became effective at once. This law was an amendment of Title VII of the Civil Rights Act of 1964.

Changes in Title VII

The following areas are changes to Title VII.

1. *State and local government.* Under the original act, employees of state and local government were excluded from coverage. They now are covered, subject to the exemptions set forth below.

2. *Federal employees.* These employees are not within the power of EEOC, but the 1972 amendment makes clear that the federal government shall not discriminate in personnel matters by reasons of race, color, sex, religion, or national ori-

gin. The Office of Employment Opportunity, not the EEOC, has power to hear federal employment discrimination matters.

3. *Number of employees.* Title VII applied originally to employers with twenty-five or more employees. This was reduced to fifteen, effective March 24, 1973.

4. *Joint labor-management.* Apprenticeship training and retraining programs now are covered. In the past these programs were administered by joint committees of labor and management. Discrimination cannot now be practiced in admission to, or administration of, these training programs.

5. *Exemptions.* Teachers and religious corporations or organizations, originally exempt from the 1964 act, now are covered. A church, however, still can discriminate on the basis of religion in hiring an employee, but not on the basis of race, color, sex, or national origin. As to coverage in state and local governments, *elected* officials as well as their assistants are exempt.

6. *Use of the courts.* If the EEOC is unable to reach a conciliation with the employer, union, employment agency, or joint labor-management committee within thirty days after a charge is filed, the Commission can use the federal courts. If the Commission fails to act, or if the complaining party is not satisfied with the actions taken by the Commission, that person has direct access to the federal courts. If a state or local government is involved, the Attorney General can bring the court action. Once a suit is brought and the complaining party has set up its defense, the judge has two alternatives: hear the case promptly, or appoint a "master" within 120 days to hear the case. These deadlines were written into the law to prevent procrastination by the EEOC or the courts, or both.

7. *Employer's obligations.* An employer cannot discriminate against a job applicant, or against one who is already an employee, on the grounds set forth above. This extends to compensation, pay raises, and promotions. Likewise, employees cannot be segregated, classified, or deprived of employment opportunities on the stated grounds. For example, any test used in hiring or promotion cannot be a general intelligence test; it must relate to the job in question. A cook cannot be required to pass the same test as a cashier at the front desk of an inn.[25]

8. *Exceptions to the Civil Rights Act.* Members of the Communist Party, or a party-front organization, can be discriminated against on that ground. Religious societies can discriminate on the basis of religion, as mentioned. If a government program requires security clearance, one who does not have that clearance can be discriminated against. A motel operating on a reservation can show preference toward American Indians in its hiring practices. If an inn has a bona fide seniority system in operation, or a merit-award system based on quality of work, different compensation can be paid under those conditions. These must be "good-faith" programs.

The question of employee imbalance is something the courts are beginning to clarify. Imbalances existing as of the date of passage of the law are not affected. The *continuation* of previous imbalances, however, must be guarded against. Affirmative-action plans (plans to eradicate prior discrimination) for government construction and manufacturing by private contractors have been upheld.[26]

The business should create and be able to demonstrate that an affirmative-action program is in operation that complies with these laws. Many businesses hire or appoint someone to carry out this function. In the small business, it can be a part-time job.

When confronted with a charge of violations of the CRA, one should do the following: seek legal advice; reply at once on Form 131, which will be provided the employer within ten days of the charge; conduct an independent investigation; and, finally, draft and maintain a detailed written report of the incident that gave rise to the charge of discrimination. The report can be used in negotiations with the commission, or in court if one intends to fight the accusation. Filing an EEOA complaint or charge is just an accusation. Proof must be forthcoming from the one claiming the discrimination.[27]

9. *Notices and recordkeeping.* Notices created by the EEOC must be posted as required, and records kept as prescribed. If an employer is covered by state fair-employment practices law, however, one set of records can meet both requirements. If one thinks the recordkeeping requirements will present an undue hardship, an application for an exemption can be made directly to the EEOC.

If a hotel that is under the coverage of the Civil Rights Act also has a casino, the casino is subject to the terms of the CRA.[28] In Nevada, a casino is listed specifically as a place of "public accommodation." Thus, not only does the federal CRA apply, but the state CRA as well.[29]

Relief for Violations

As to relief available for violations of the federal law, injunctive relief can be sought against violators. Declaratory relief also can be sought, but no direct provisions for money recovery for the complainant are available. (Many *state* civil rights acts *do* permit money recoveries.) On the other hand, violations of the federal law in some instances could trigger other federal laws that could lead to money damages. No criminal penalties are available under the law.

Normally one who complains of civil rights violations is expected to seek injunctive relief at his or her own expense against the offending establishment. If successful, the prevailing party may be awarded attorney fees and costs by the court.

Private Clubs

Bars and taverns that serve drinks only and do not use musical devices and electronic and other games are not covered.[30] Private clubs that are not open to the public are not covered. In determining if an establishment is in fact a private club, the courts will look for "selectivity" through a true-management organization with formal rules for determining membership. As one court said: "Selectivity is the essence of a private club."[31] If a club is truly private, it is exempt from the law and can engage in discrimination. "Private discrimination does not give rise to a violation."[32] The burden of establishing whether a club is private is upon management and not the one complaining of discrimination.[33]

When looking at the impact of the federal Civil Rights Act as amended, one also must take into consideration that the states have such laws as well. This tends to compound the possible penalties for violations.

Through court cases and interpretation, other matters are now associated with the Act. A few of these are discussed in the next few pages.

Akin to the Common-Law Duty to Receive

Centuries ago, the English courts created the duty to receive at inns. In effect, this also created a common-law duty not to discriminate against members of the traveling public. As a 1794 court said, innkeepers "cannot refuse to receive guests, so neither can they impose unreasonable terms upon them."[34]

An American court in 1874 spoke of carriers, whose duties are analogous to innkeepers, in this way:

> A service for the public necessarily implies equal treatment in its performance when the right to serve is common. Because the institution, so to speak, is public, every member of the community stands on an equality as to the right to its benefit and, therefore, the carrier cannot discriminate between individuals for whom he will render the service. In the very nature, then, of his duty and of the public right, his conduct should be equal and just to all.[35]

Legal Discrimination

If a good-faith employment qualification requires it, such as male attendants in the male restroom at the inn, employers may discriminate legally on the basis of sex in that instance. The same is true in relation to national origin or religion. In management situations, decisions should be made on the basis of *business needs* and not sex, race, color, religion, or other proscribed areas.

In almost all instances, employers who have claimed that sex (male) is a bona fide employment qualification have failed in court. Claims that a baseball umpire, a hunting guide, a walkway supervisor, a stenographer, a casino card dealer, a race car driver, a lifeguard, a flight attendant, and many more, must be of one sex or another, have failed in court. For example, the sex law of Title VII would be violated to insist that only men could be lifeguards because they must clean the men's restrooms.

The courts always will look with suspicion on inconsistent treatment of employees. If a house rule states, for example, that employees shall not drink on the job, and a white employee drinks but is not fired but a black employee drinks and is fired, a *prima facie* case of a civil rights violation has arisen.

Illegal Discrimination

"Race may well involve more than mere skin pigment," ruled the U. S. Supreme Court in 1987. Justice Byron R. White, writing for the court, said that "Congress intended to protect from discrimination identifiable classes of persons who are subjected to intentional discrimination solely because of their ancestry or ethnic characteristics."

In June 1989, the U. S. Supreme Court held that a simple comparison of minority and white workers is not in itself, in the absence of something further, enough to prove racial discrimination. The ruling was heralded as "a major step to the rear for civil rights." The decision said that it is not the comparison of black and white but, rather, a comparison between the racial composition of the labor market and the job to be filled. The ruling was sharply against numerical quotas in the workplace.

A Kansas case will illustrate a related matter. In this case, a member of a minority race was being interviewed for a job at a Kansas City hotel. After the interview, management determined that the applicant was too "dominant" in his thinking and had an employment background that indicated that he would not be a "team player" at the hotel. He was not hired. His suit for discrimination under Title VII was dismissed. The court ruled that the reasons for not hiring that person were legitimate business reasons and that race had not entered into the decision not to hire.[36]

In 1988, in an opinion written by Justice William Brennan, the U.S. Supreme Court ruled that a public employer could favor a woman for a particular job over a man who was better qualified in training, experience, and test scoring. It was a strong advance for the concept of *reverse discrimination*, which has the practical effect of inverting Title VII. To say it another way, a woman cannot be denied a job solely on the basis of her sex, but there is no harm in favoring a woman.[37]

A male employee at an airport inn was terminated and replaced by a female bartender. The letter given to the fired male said "Your termination was caused by a policy decision; uniforms were purchased for an all-female bar." The court found for the fired bartender, awarding back pay and attorney's fees.[38]

Sexual Harassment

Sexual harassment claims fall under Title VII and can result in injunctions that require rehiring of employees plus attorneys' fees. The court also may order payment of back wages. It is clear that males also may be the victims of sexual harassment.

An insurance policy issued to an inn provided, among other things, that the insurance company would pay all sums the inn may become obligated to pay "because of bodily injury or property damages caused by an occurrence." The policy contained definitions of "bodily injury" and "occurrence." These definitions allowed the insurance company to avoid paying the judgment against the inn. The judgment had arisen out of sexual harassment by executives of the inn against employees and, thus, did not involve "bodily injury."[39]

Where harassment is carried out with the knowledge of management, suits are certain to follow. As asked previously, will the insurance policies that provide coverage for "bodily injury" apply and give protection? A Georgia court has also said "no" because harassment in the form that it was carried out resulted in "mental damages" and not bodily injury. The policy in question provided no coverage for mental injury.[40]

Constructive Discharge and Civil Rights

When an employee quits a job voluntarily, can a claim of discrimination be brought successfully against an employer? The answer is "yes" if the employee is forced from the job because of conditions there. This happened to Elizabeth Levendos at a restaurant where she worked. The court said:

> While we can imagine a maitre d' who might not object to exclusion from management meetings, denial of authority to order supplies, false accusations of stealing from and drinking on the job, and who might not be disturbed by rumors and remarks that she would be replaced by a male, her employer's refusal to talk with her and to find wine bottles in her locker, we find that these events are clearly not trivial. It is of course plausible that a jury could decide ultimately that a reasonable person would tolerate some or even all of these occurrences without being forced to quit. It is equally plausible, however, that a jury would come to the opposite conclusion. . . . Thus we hold that Levendos . . . presented sufficient evidence to raise a genuine issue of material fact regarding whether she was constructively discharged from her position.[41]

Dealers in Casinos

Can a gambler who prefers white males to black dealers force a casino to substitute a dealer on this basis? Caesar's Hotel and Casino at Atlantic City did just that. A New Jersey administrative law judge ruled that this was both race and sex discrimination and fined Caesar's $15,600, the amount lost by the gambler. The state gaming regulators then raised the fine to $250,000.[42]

Religious Discrimination

For a case in which a court action brought by the EEOC against a hotel on the grounds of religious discrimination failed, see *EEOC v. Caribe Hilton International.*[43] The evidence showed that the hotel had "bent over backwards" to accommodate a Seventh Day Adventist whose religious beliefs prevented him from working from sundown Friday to sundown Saturday. The court found that the employee had been totally uncooperative with the hotel.

The 1866 Civil Rights Law

The 1866 Civil Rights Law, found in section 1981 of the Federal Code, was enacted by Congress to allow the newly freed slaves to negotiate and enforce contracts. Can this civil rights law of the last century be used to press claims of racial harassment on the job? In a June 1989 decision, the U. S. Supreme Court ruled in the negative.

For 102 years after the Civil Rights Act of 1866 became law, it was believed that the act that became law on the tail of the American Civil War only prohibited "officially sanctioned discrimination" such as from government. Not until 1968, four years after the 1964 CRA became law, did the U. S. Supreme Court rule that the 1866 act also prohibited "private" discrimination as well.[44]

In a case where a black person was replaced by a white person purely on the grounds of competence, a District of Columbia court (federal because DC is not a state) said this:

An unqualified employee cannot fall back on the Civil Rights Act to " . . . cure deficiencies in his or her qualifications, or to immunize potentially serious defects on the worker's job profile . . . ."[45]

The bed-and-breakfast movement is growing in the United States. Large numbers of travelers no longer are satisfied to spend the night at an interstate exit inn. Many travelers not only are seeking the comfort of a room for the night but also personal experiences of the people and customs of the areas in which their travels take them. If such operations have five or fewer rooms and one room is occupied by the owner, they are not covered by the Civil Rights Act.

A legal action brought by an inn employee for "intentional discrimination," on whatever grounds, can ask for compensation on two bases, should the evidence warrant it:

1. compensatory damages for pain and suffering and emotional distress
2. punitive damages

The two types of damages are clearly not the same.[46]

Civil Rights Act, 1991 Employment Amendment

The purpose of the civil rights enactment in 1991 was to give greater weight to the federal civil-rights protection and to discourage unlawful discrimination in employment.[47] Following closely on the heels of the 1964 CRA was an amendment that added age to the areas proscribed in the 1964 law.

Pregnancy Discrimination Act of 1978

A 1978 amendment to the 1964 Civil Rights Act expanded sex discrimination to include pregnancy. Title VII of the Civil Rights Act of 1964 prohibits a covered employer from discharging or otherwise discriminating against any individual "with respect to compensation, terms, conditions, or privileges of employment because of such individual's sex." The 1978 Amendment makes it clear that "because of sex" includes pregnancy, childbirth, or related medical problems.

An employer cannot fire female employees because they become pregnant. That is sex discrimination and violates the 1978 Act, and entitles the pregnant employee to all lost back pay, all lost benefits (such as vacation, health, and retirement), plus court costs and reasonable attorney fees.[48]

When hiring, the employer cannot ask applicants if they are pregnant. They cannot fire employees who become pregnant. They cannot refuse to rehire employees who were pregnant but who are able to return to their jobs. The main words of this federal statute are as follows:

> The terms "because of sex" or "on the basis of sex" include but are not limited to because of or on the basis of pregnancy, childbirth, or related medical conditions; and women affected by pregnancy, childbirth, or related medical conditions shall be treated the same for all employment-related purposes, including receipt of benefits under fringe benefit programs, as other persons not so affected but similar in their ability or inability to work.[49]

It is not wise to inquire about an applicant's potential plans to have children. In addition, pregnancy cannot be given as a reason to deny promotion. For an example of how the 1978 pregnancy amendment to Title VII is applied in court, see *Ensor v. Painter.*[50] In this case, two workers were fired because they "were pregnant and could not perform their duties." The court found these to be "pretextual" reasons for the terminations and found against the employer. Those words graphically illustrate the problem the amendment was designed to prevent.

Another case involved a front desk clerk who never had worn makeup at the inn. Management made no comments about it, and the employee received good job evaluations. After the clerk became pregnant, her appearance began to change (her complexion became pale and she developed a skin rash). A house rule was then issued requiring all female employees to wear makeup. Because other female employees already wore makeup, the rule, in effect, applied only to the clerk.

When the clerk refused to obey the rule, she was fired. A federal court ruled that the firing was sexual discrimination because of pregnancy, and that the employee was protected under Title VII.[51]

Pregnancy Laws in the States

In addition to the federal pregnancy law, the states also have taken action. California law requires employers to grant leave to a pregnant employee, not to exceed four months. The California law also requires that, upon returning, the employees must be reinstated to their former jobs. If the jobs are no longer available because of "business necessity," the employer must make a reasonable good-faith effort to place that employee in a similar job elsewhere. A challenge to the California law reached the U. S. Supreme Court, where the law was upheld.[52]

Maternity Leave in the States

More and more states are passing statutes that require employers to treat pregnant workers exactly as they treat employees who are sick or have a disability. If certain benefits are extended to a cook injured in a kitchen, those same benefits also must be given to the front-desk clerk who becomes pregnant. The Family Leave Act of 1993 also covers this area.

Turning from the topic of sex/pregnancy discrimination, we now will learn something about the Age Discrimination in Employment Act, ADEA.

AGE DISCRIMINATION IN EMPLOYMENT ACT

The 1967 Age Discrimination in Employment Act (ADEA) prohibits discrimination because of age for employees between ages forty and sixty-five. The law is limited, however, to employers of twenty-five or more persons.[53] In 1977, the age limit was raised to seventy, but that limit, too, was to change.

In October 1986, Congress passed legislation designed to give the elderly "new hope, new courage and a new feeling of meaningfulness." The 1986 amendment does away with any age limit, except for sensitive jobs such as CIA, FBI agents, and air traffic controllers.

This law applies to any employer who has twenty or more employees for twenty weeks of each calendar year. The law is administered by the Equal Employment Opportunity Commission.

Termination because of age is permissible in four instances:

1. when a seniority system requires certain persons to step down
2. when facts *other than age* demand that the older person be let go
3. where age is a bona fide qualification of employment at a particular business
4. when the discipline or discharge of an employee is for a good cause such as stealing or dishonesty

Where discharge does not fall under the above criteria, that person is entitled to back pay and commissions, and if the discharge was willful, the damages are to be doubled. This feature came about by an amendment to the 1967 statute.

Certain procedural matters are attached to this law. The complaining person must notify the EEOC within 180 days of the alleged unlawful employment practice. The EEOC then has sixty days to attempt to settle the dispute. If no resolution follows, the one making the complaint can go to the courts. That person then is entitled to a jury trial.

A most striking age (and sex) discrimination case involved the Las Vegas Hilton, where thirty-seven white, male workers, thirty-two of whom were over forty years of age, were replaced by twenty-four females and thirteen males, all but one of whom were under forty years of age. The jury that heard the case found age discrimination was involved and awarded the thirty-seven plaintiffs sums ranging from $7,000 to $106,000 for lost wages, $200,000 for emotional distress, and $30 million for punitive damages.

Added to those sums were prejudgment interest and attorneys' fees, boosting the total award upward of $50 million. All in all, not a good day for Hilton Hotels.[54]

The Department of Labor has found that numerous help-wanted ads violate the ADEA. Some examples are:

1. great careers for young men
2. ages 25 to 35
3. boys
4. girls
5. college students
6. recent college graduates
7. young, energetic persons

Such words and phrases must be avoided in employment advertisements.[55]

The Age Discrimination in Employment Act applies to:

1. hiring
2. firing ("outplacing")
3. classifying
4. advertising
5. membership in labor organizations

Remedies (damages) provided by the courts for those who are discriminated against because of age in their employment include:

1. reinstatement
2. back pay
3. lost commissions, if any
4. if the violation is found to be willful, the judge will instruct the jury upon request, to double the damages[56]

The best defense a manager has against any discrimination claim is to be able to produce records that document terminations, discipline taken, and detailed business reasons for such actions, which reasons must in no way be related to age.

AMERICANS WITH DISABILITIES ACT

The ADA had its beginnings in the Vocational Rehabilitation Act of 1973. This law controlled contractors and those who were receiving federal funds and had structures that people with disabilities would be using.

This law has an impact upon both design and use of hospitality facilities. At the design stage of a new inn, for example, failure to learn what this law requires, and failure to implement those requirements could result in serious losses. These losses could come from adverse jury verdicts and from the costs of redoing physical facilities.

Which Employers Are Covered?

The ADA originally included only businesses with twenty-five or more employees. That number now has been decreased to fifteen or more employees. This figure is to be calculated "on a daily basis." ADA makes it illegal to discriminate against a qualified, disabled individual in job application procedures, hiring, firing, compensation, advancement, job training, or other conditions and privileges of employment.

The ADA has been called the "world's first declaration of equality" for people with disabilities. Title I of the ADA makes it illegal to discriminate against a qualified employee because of disability. Title II covers local and state governmental requirements for the accommodation of employees and visitors with disabilities in local and state buildings. Title III applies to places of public accommodation and makes it illegal to discriminate in accommodations, services, food, privileges, or facilities against those with covered disabilities. Title III will be discussed in Chapters 21 and 22.

What Does "Disability" Mean?

Who are those with a "disability" or a "handicap" or a "mental impairment" that "limits one or more of the activities of life . . ."?

Under ADA, disabilities can take a variety of forms:

1. A disability can be physical.
2. A disability can be mental.
3. A disability can be nontraditional such as a drug or alcohol addiction problem.
4. A disability can be traditional, such as a crippling stroke or partial or complete blindness.
5. A disability can be found in one who has a history of disabilities even though that person does not have a disability currently.
6. A disability could be morbid obesity.
7. A disability could be AIDS.
8. A disability could be positive HIV status.

Those who are using illegal drugs or alcohol are not considered to have a disability or handicap under ADA, although they might actually have a disability.

ADA Guidelines

The ADA Accessibility Design Guidelines are providing new parameters as to ramp designs, stairs, surface coatings to prevent falls, and much more. These guidelines emphasize preventing slipping and falling, and thus constitute a benefit for guests with and without disabilities.

In light of obligations under the Americans with Disabilities Act, in which remodeling will have to be done at existing inns, a 1987 federal court decision could be a blessing. *Moss v. Commissioner of Internal Revenue*[57] overruled the U.S. Tax Court and held that remodeling costs were needed to keep a hotel competitive, were ordinary and necessary business expenses, and could be deducted in the year incurred. The Tax Court had held that such expenses had to be depreciated over thirty years.

Nothing under ADA guidelines prohibits legal drug- or alcohol-testing programs for employees. The tests are not considered to be "medical tests" under ADA. The ADA does prohibit using medical tests in preemployment screening of job applicants. The policy of the Act is that questions about medical conditions should not be pursued until after employment begins. Figure 9.2 gives the sequence of this policy.

Once medical questions can be asked and medical examinations carried out legally, they must be job-related. Questions cannot be asked or exams carried out without valid business reasons behind them.

FIGURE 9.2   ADA policy on medical questions.

| *Applicant* | ⟶ | Drug and alcohol testing | *Applicant Hired* | ⟶ | Some medical questions and testing okay |

Flashing Lights

The Americans with Disabilities Act requires that inns provide fire alarm systems that can be seen by those who cannot hear. An unexpected problem has arisen in regard to this requirement. People with epilepsy sometimes suffer seizures because of flashing lights. Thus, the Architectural and Transportation Compliance Board, the federal agency assigned the responsibility of drafting regulations to implement the ADA, has new issues to confront: Persons with hearing impairment need to be warned, and those with epilepsy need to be protected.

In a West Virginia restaurant case, an employee had mild seizures that passed in a minute or so. She was fired because of this "disability," and the lower court upheld the dismissal on the grounds of a reasonable "possibility of injury" to herself or others. The West Virginia Supreme Court reversed, saying that the test had to be "the probability of injury to herself or others".[58]

FAMILY AND MEDICAL LEAVE ACT OF 1993

The Family and Medical Leave Act went into effect on August 5, 1993, and created some major changes for employers. This federal law applies to employers who have fifty or more employees. Smaller inns, family-operated restaurants, and neighborhood bars will not be covered, whereas larger hotels will be.

In determining the jurisdictional number of fifty employees, the act has a "seventy-five mile radius" provision. Thus, if one company has three fast-food outlets and each has twenty-five employees, all three would be covered if they are located within seventy-five miles of each other.

Once a hospitality unit is covered, the employer must give employees up to twelve weeks unpaid leave for care of newborn children; care of an adopted child; or for the serious illness of an employee, a parent, child, or spouse of the employee.

At the end of the twelve weeks, if the employee is able to return to work, the employer must offer the job back if it is available. If it is not available, the employer must offer a comparable job to the employee. The same principle will apply if the employee is able to return to work before the twelve weeks are up.

More than thirty of our states have in effect and enforce some forms of family-leave laws. If a particular state law is more favorable to an employee than the federal law is, the state law will apply. The reverse is true, of course. In states with lesser degrees of leave laws, and in all states that have no such laws, employers must meet the standards of the national act.

1. Employers must post Department of Labor notices at the hospitality property. A fine of $100 per offense is provided for failure to do so.
2. To qualify, an employee must have been on the job for one year and have worked 1,250 hours during the preceding twelve months.
3. Those who are in the top 10 percent in terms of salary are not covered. The rationale here is that the employer should not have to do without the services of these persons.
4. If both husband and wife work for the same company, they will share the twelve weeks leave time per year equally for leave related to children.

SUMMARY

The Fair Labor Standards Act (FSLA) created the original minimum wage of 25¢ per hour. In those days, employees were paid with silver quarters that now sell at about the amount of the present minimum wage. The FLSA and its amendments are the basic employee statutes.

The tip income laws have had a rapid development in recent years. Both the federal and state governments have a monetary stake here, and refinements can be expected. Tip income is a natural part of the HH&T industries. The typical traveler has no problem leaving tips for good service provided. The handling and reporting of these tips then becomes a concern to management and the governments at both state and federal levels.

The federal Equal Pay Act poses serious legal overtones for management. The spirit of this law is that employees should be treated equally in the payment of wages. To violate this objective is to ask for problems in court.

When wage attachments are made, the FLSA and the minimum wage become directly involved. When faced with having to honor such an attachment, the first person to call is the accountant of the firm.

Workers' compensation and unemployment statutes must be distinguished. The former is designed to compensate employees injured on the job. The latter gives relief to employees who are out of work for reasons not due to their personal affairs and not associated with job site injuries. The many employee statutes discussed in this chapter are important to both employees and employers.

QUESTIONS

1. What is one probable reason the number of "jurisdictional employees" was reduced from twenty-five to fifteen persons under EEOA, as well as ADA?
2. What was the weakness in the 1964 Civil Rights Act as it related to employment?
3. What is one example of lawful discrimination in employment at a travel agency?
4. Why can't the same employment test be used for all applicants for employment at a motel?
5. What is an "affirmative action" plan? An ADA "assessment program"?
6. Why are private clubs exempt from civil rights laws coverage although "private discrimination" is not?
7. List three unlawful business employment practices.
8. How do Title VII of the CRA rules differ from workers' compensation laws?
9. Who is covered by the ADA federal statute?
10. How would you define a "disability"?

NOTES

1. 29 USC 201, *et seq.*
2. It went to $4.75 per hour initially.

3. *Brock v. Claridge Hotel and Casino*, 711 F. Supp. 779 (New Jersey 1989).

4. As of April 1, 1991.

5. *Wirtz v. Healy*, 227 F. Supp. 123 (1964).

6. *Sunshine Lounge v. Commissioner*, 720 P. 2d 81 (Arizona 1986).

7. *Winans v. W.A.S. Inc.*, 772 P. 2d 1001 (Washington, 1989).

8. 29 USC sec. 213(b)(8)(A).

9. *Ridgeway v. United States*, 563 F. Supp. 123 (1964).

10. P.L. 90–321, 82 Stat. 146 *et seq.* Act of May 29, 1968.

11. Title III, Section 303 (a) (2).

12. *Brock v. Claridge Hotel*, 711 F. Supp. 779 (New Jersey 1989); *Dole v. Papa Gino's*, 712 F. Supp. 1038 (Maine 1989).

13. *Mayles v. Shoney's, Inc.*, 450 S.E. 2d 15 (West Virginia 1991).

14. *Johnson v. Stratlow, Inc.*, 274 Cal. Rptr. 363 (California 1990).

15. *Dancing Sunshines Lounge v. Industrial Commissioner*, 720 P. 2d 81 (Arizona 1986).

16. *Desert Inn Casino & Hotel v. Morgan*, 792 P. 2d 400 (Nevada 1990).

17. *Desert Inn Casino, supra.*

18. *Jones v. Colonial Williamsburg Found*, 392 S.E. 2 D 848 (Virginia 1990).

19. *Twin City v. Home*, 650 F. Supp. 785 (Pennsylvania 1986).

20. *Lori v. San Antonio Inn*, 454 So. 2D 964 (Louisiana 1984).

21. *Baker v. Fanny Farmer*, 394 N.W. 2d 564 (Minnesota 1986).

22. 42 USC sec. 2000 e-2000 (15).

23. Ibid.

24. *In Heart of Atlanta Motel v. United States*, 379 U.S. 241 (1964).

25. Civil Rights Act, 1964, Title II, sec. 201 (b).

26. *Griggs v. Duke Power Co.*, U. S. Sup. Ct., 3 FEP Cases 175 (1971).

27. *Contractors Ass'n. of Eastern Pa. v. Hodgson*, 3rd Cir. 1971 3 FEP Cases 395, cert. denied, U.S. Sup. Ct., 3 FEP Cases 1030 (1971).

28. *Rosado v. Maysonet v. Solis*, 400 F. Supp. 576 (DPR 1975).

29. Nevada Revised Statutes, 651.050.

30. *Selden v. Topaza*, 447 F. 2d 165 (Fifth Circuit, 1971).

31. *Bell v. Denwood*, 312 F. Supp. 251 (D. Maryland 1970).

32. *Moose Lodge v. Irvis*, 407 U. S. 163, 92 S. Ct. 1965 (1972).

33. *U.S. v. Richberg*, 398 F. 2d 523 (Fifth Circuit, 1968).

34. *Kirkman v. Shawcross*, 6 East. 519, 101 Eng. Rep. 410, 412 (King's Bench, 1794).

35. *Messenger v. Pennsylvania R.R.*, 37 Nev. 531, 534 (1874).

36. *Clay v. Hyatt Regency Hotel*, 724 F. 2d 721 (1984).

37. 42 USC sec. 2000 *et seq.*

38. *Airport Inn, Inc. v. Nebraska EEOC and Michael Sump*, 353 N.W. 2d 727 (Nebraska 1984).

39. *Presidential Hotel v. Canal Insurance Co.*, 373 S.E. 2d 671 (Georgia 1988).

40. *Presidential Hotel v. Canal Insurance Co., supra.*

41. *Levendos v. Stern Entertainment, Inc.*, 860 F. 2d 1227 (Pennsylvania 1988).

42. Heard on national news stations.

43. 821 F. 2d 74 (Puerto Rico 1987).

44. *Jones v. Mayer Co.*, 392 U.S. 409 (U. S. Sup. Ct. 1968).

45. *Hardy v. Marriott Corp.*, 670 F. Supp. 385 (District of Columbia 1987).

46. 42 USCA, section 1981 a(a)(1), (b)(2).

47. 42 USCA, section 1981 *et seq.*

48. *EEOC v. Newton Inn Association*, 647 F. Supp. 957 (Virginia 1986).

49. Ibid.

50. 661 F. Supp. 21 (Tennessee 1987).

51. *Tamini v. Howard Johnson Co.*, 807 F. 2d 1550 (Alabama 1987).

52. *California Federal v. Guerra*, 107 S. Ct. 683 (California 1987).

53. 29 USC 621 *et seq.*

54. *Brooks v. Hilton Casinos*, 714 F. Supp. 1115 (Nevada 1989).

55. *EEOC v. Marion Motel Associates*, 763 F. Supp. 1338 (North Carolina 1991).

56. ADEA, Sec. 4, 29 USC 623.

57. 86-7398 (U. S. Ct. App. 9th cir. October 28, 1987).

58. *Davidson v. Shoney's Big Boy Restaurant*, 380 S.E. 2d 232 (West Virginia 1989).

Credit and Debit Cards and Electronic Money

OVERVIEW

A HIGH PERCENTAGE OF the income at hotel, hospitality, and tourism operations comes from credit cards, debit cards, and electronic money. We will explore each of these monetary devises in this chapter.

DIFFERENTIATING MONETARY DEVICES

To begin with, we have to distinguish credit cards from debit cards, for they are not the same. Whereas credit cards are used to create credit and to charge purchases, debit cards are designed to *deliver money* that already is in existence in an account. Examples are the ATM cards used at bank terminals to make cash withdrawals. The credit card, on the other hand, creates credit where none existed before the charge was made. Legally, the card charge slip is a promise to pay for the credit extended at an agreed point in the future. Yet it is more than that.

Whereas the credit created by the credit card often is used to pay for services, the cash from the debit card is used less frequently for such purposes. The reason for this is that debit card holders more often use the card locally, and travelers often prefer to use a credit card. Automated teller machines (ATMs) have become important in debit card usage in the United States. In February, 1994, the Bank of America announced that its ATM cardholders could use their cards in a major Western city at five fast-food establishments.

Associated with credit and debit cards, yet distinct from them, are *transfers of funds* carried out by electronic means. Here, no cards are involved. For some time, the hardware has been in place nationally for paying bills and debts without using cards, and without using checks or other paper. Years ago it was predicted that this new concept would make banking and credit cards obsolete. This did not come to pass because the average person is quite concerned—and cautious—about any system that can strip him or her instantly of personal funds. In spite of this wariness, many banks are using electronic money and have actively marketed it by developing measures to assure customers of the safety of this means of paying the bills. Widespread acceptance has not yet come, but it most likely will.[1]

The use of electronic money is important because, where terminals are available, guests who are arriving or leaving hotels can transfer funds for services directly to the account of the business. The transfers could mean vast savings on credit-card charges and interest on the "float" time of checks—and even cash—used to pay the bills. Cash accepted in the evening loses interest before it can be deposited in the morning. This is not so with electronic transfers.

The U. S. Congress enacted the Electronics Fund Transfer Act which created a national commission on electronic transfers and set down rules for the operations of EFTs. The Board of Governors of the Federal Reserve System created regulations to implement this law, which is part of Title II of the Consumer Credit Protection Act. Possible uses of EFTs are numerous. Examples of transfers include telephone transfer of funds, payment of bills by preauthorized debits, and direct deposit of funds to accounts. Debit cards and EFTs are two methods by which bills may be paid. Credit cards comprise the third method.

CREDIT CARD USE

Credit cards are accepted at most HH&T facilities across the United States and around the world. The law that controls their use is associated in some ways with the laws of commercial (money) paper. Yet credit-card charge slips are *not* commercial paper. They do represent a way of transferring funds, however, and thus are another form of credit money.

Credit cards represent a revolution that struck the credit industry following World War II. Although credit cards had been issued by oil companies prior to that time—such as Amoco with the first oil card in 1914—the movement did not gain momentum until American Express, Diner's Club, and Carte Blanche entered the picture. By 1969, there was about $2.5 billion outstanding on credit-card accounts. By 1980, the sum had reached $120 billion, and today the amount far exceeds that sum, which does not include another $85 billion on "in-house" cards such as those issued by some hotels and charges on a multitude of oil company cards.

Most business operations accept credit cards. What is not so widely known are the rules of law that control their use. The typical hotel has a credit-card manual that guides employees in the use of credit cards. Yet, such a manual falls far short of what one must know to gain a legal understanding of the nature of credit cards and their use. Credit cards can be a profit-making device, or they can become an instrument of loss.

Around the world today the most visible credit cards are those issued by the American Express Company.

> The 1950s were a golden era for American Express, as they were for much of American business, a time when more and more wealthy suburbanites discovered travel and came to identify American Express as the company to help them do it. Cheque [travelers' checks] sales topped a billion dollars a year as Ralph Reed continued his ceaseless efforts to promote tourism, harvesting all manner of medals from thankful European governments and leaping onto the cover of *Time* magazine in 1956 as "The Grand Poohbah of Travel." Two years later, as Americans continued to flex their new economic muscles, the company joined a tide of new charge cards by introducing one of its own, the American Express Card, in its early days a frightfully ugly little rectangle of purplish paperboard. Overcoming steep initial losses and a series of accounting nightmares, the Card ultimately became a

mainstay of the company's profits, overtaking the travelers cheque itself as a symbol of the company in the public's mind.[2]

Providing us with a little more background on early credit cards is the following:

In March of 1950, McNamara and Schneider founded the Diners Club. The bylaws were straightforward. Cardholders would receive interest-free credit as long as they paid their bill in full each month.

The company had a rocky start. As it celebrated its second anniversary, the new card company was losing $60,000 a year. Restaurants were howling about slow payments. And the Diners Club, buried under an avalanche of paper, was falling further and further behind in its billing schedule.

The only success it had was in membership. The 1950s marked the dawn of the corporate expense account, and business executives were tired of stuffing their wallets with cash and checks every time they ventured away from home for a day or two. The card became a convenient device. Indeed, Diners Club would go down in history as the first travel and entertainment, or T&E, card.[3]

In light of the EFTs and increasing use of computers, the credit-card system is beginning to show its age. It is cumbersome in many ways, can be an actual inconvenience at the front desk or to the restaurant cashier, and results in delays in final payment. When a knowledgeable person sees some of the legal characteristics of credit cards and looks at them realistically, it becomes apparent that they are not the final solution at all. Let's look at a couple of their legal features.

1. The credit-card system operates on offer and acceptance of the common-law contract.
2. Although these cards often are used to buy items of personal property or "goods," the law of Article 2 of the UCC does *not* apply to them because the credit extended by their use is a *service* and not a sale.
3. Credit-card systems can exist on a two-contract basis and a three-contract basis as well.

Understanding these contract systems will assist us in understanding the true nature of credit cards and their use.

Three-Contract System

Most credit-card companies operate on a three-contract, and thus a three-party, system.

First Contract

The first contract arises between the applicant for the card and the card issuer. In the terms and conditions of issuance of the card, the issuer customarily makes written terms a part of the contract between the issuer and the cardholder. Figure 10.1 is an example of the credit terms of Union Oil Company of California.

Through this offer-and-acceptance process, the cardholder becomes bound by the terms of the agreement, if the card is issued and then used. The holder has no obligation to use it, however.

FIGURE 10.1 Example of a company's credit terms.

NEW TERMS

Union 76 Revolving Credit Plan*

Terms: Cardholder agrees to pay Union Oil Co. of Calif. within 25 days of your monthly Closing Date either of the following, as shown on your monthly statement:

1. The New Balance, or
2. An amount not less than the Minimum Due. Payment of less than the New Balance will result in the addition of a **FINANCE CHARGE.**

Calculation of Minimum Due:

I. If your New Balance is less than $500, the Minimum Due is:
   1. The full amount of the New Balance if under $25, or
   2. 10% of the New Balance or $25, whichever is greater, plus
   3. Any unpaid portion of the previous statement's Minimum Due.
II. If your New Balance is less than $500, the Minimum Due is:
   1. $50, plus
   2. Any unpaid portion of the previous statement's Minimum Due, plus
   3. Any amount of the New Balance that is more than the total of (a) $500, and (b) the unpaid portion of the previous statement's Minimum Due.

Revolving privileges may be withdrawn at any time. Total amount owing may be declared immediately due and payable, for failure to pay at least the Minimum Due each month. (Cardholders residing outside the state of purchase will be assessed a FINANCE CHARGE rate determined by the laws of their state of residence).

---

* These terms apply notwithstanding any conflicting terms that may appear on the delivery ticket received at time of purchase.

The face or back of the card also often contains contractual terms such as, "This card remains the property of the issuer and must be surrendered upon demand," "The issuer reserves the right to cancel this card at any time," and similar provisions.

Second Contract

The second contract has its beginning when the cardholder offers the card in lieu of cash or other payment, for services and food and drink received. It now is necessary to accept the offer or reject it. In most instances, use of the card has been invited, and it will be accepted after verifying its validity.

Some operations, however, will not accept credit cards, and no law says they must do so. An exception is found in those instances in which cards appear to be accepted and a guest or patron relies upon that representation. Refusal to accept a card under those conditions might lead to an actionable complaint, especially if the cardholder suffered embarrassment or other discomfort as a result of the refusal.

Otherwise, there is no common-law duty to accept credit cards. If they are accepted, the third contract arises and becomes operational.

Third Contract

The third contract comes into being when the charge slip is tendered to the issuer—or an independent issuer—and is accepted for payment. This acceptance creates two contractual obligations within the third contract. The issuer now is obligated to pay (in part) the charge slip to the one tendering it, and the cardholder is obligated to repay the issuer the full amount charged to the card.

The profit to the issuer comes by the deduction of "points" from the amount of the original charge. These points range from 2 to 5 percent. The cardholder remits the full amount, giving the issuer the profit from the difference. In the usual situations, the system works well, and everyone, in theory at least, benefits from the transaction. The cardholder gets the benefit of the extension of credit; the one accepting the charge gets the profits from the sale, less the points; and the issuer profits from the points deducted. Figure 10.2 shows this process.

The charge slips made by the impression from the credit card have some characteristics of checks. For example, those who have accepted the charges often use them to pay *their* bills. This is common at service stations and other

FIGURE 10.2 The three contracts of credit cards in operation.

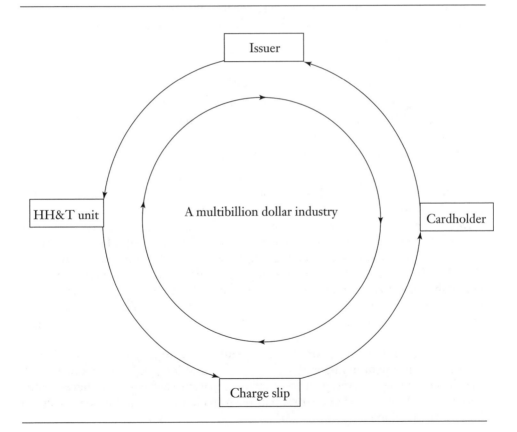

businesses that have a high volume of credit-card transactions. This generally will work, however, only where a two-contract system is in operation.

Two-Contract System

Large companies often issue credit cards designed to be accepted at captive outlets. Service-station credit cards are the best example, although department stores do this, and so do some hotels. The charges made on these cards are billed to the cardholder, who pays directly to the home company. No third parties are involved. This is essentially an accounts-receivable system and is profitable for many companies.

Because the charge slips often are used in the two-contract system much like money, such as when a service station operator pays for the new delivery of gas with charge slips, the question arises as to whether these slips have taken on aspects of money. Might these charge slips be negotiable so as to meet the requirements of commercial paper under the UCC?

Negotiability

Do these charge slips meet the requirements of negotiability? If so, they are commercial paper. Let's test a Visa charge receipt against the five requirements of negotiable paper as found in the UCC. If the charge slip meets these requirements, it is negotiable.

1. It is signed.
2. It contains the words "I promise to pay."
3. It is for a sum certain (if the charge, tip, and tax are filled in and totaled).
4. It is payable at a definite time because of the terms of the cardholder's contract, "payable in full upon receipt of invoice."
5. It is *not* payable "to the order" of anyone.

The charge receipt fails the test of negotiability on the fifth requirement.

The words "payable to the order of . . . ," on commercial paper mean that the person to whom the paper is transferred *has the right to order the sum of money on it paid to someone else.* Clearly, this right is not found on a credit-card charge slip. If it were, it could cause legal problems. Assume that X charges her motel room to her American Express card and an impression is made on a completed charge slip. The front-desk clerk keeps the top copy and gives X her copy. If it were negotiable, the motel would have the right to endorse the charge slip and order the sum of money represented by it paid to someone else. The motel could use the charge slip to pay its bills. (This is done in two-party credit-card arrangements.)

That right is not there, nor does the credit-card company want it to be. Thus, the fifth requirement of negotiability is missing, and for good business reasons. If the slips could be ordered paid to others, the parent card company never would know at any moment what charges had been made or the standing of any credit limit of the cardholders.

The charge slip is then sent to the parent card company, which, in turn, will issue its check for the charges made, less the "points." The motel or hotel then can use the issued check to pay its bills to third parties—but the charge slip cannot be used for that purpose. When we issue a check, it is an "order to pay" funds already in existence. When a cardholder signs a credit charge slip, no funds are behind it. It is simply the creation of a credit obligation.

Independent Card Companies

In addition to the regular card companies are "independents." Independent credit-card companies purchase charge slips at a discount and then collect them from the persons who made the charges. The disadvantage of this is that the value decreases the more hands the charge slips go through.

Managers should closely examine the credit-card systems in use at each facility, for a change in procedures might result in substantial savings. Alternatives are available to credit-card use.

Lost Credit and Debit Cards

Under the terms of the first contract, cards that are lost by holders must be reported at once to the issuer. The cardholder's responsibility for unauthorized charges made before notice is given is $50 under federal law. If unauthorized charges are made after notice, the cardholder has no liability as to those charges. Under regulations that became effective May 10, 1980, if a *debit* card is lost or stolen and the bank involved is given notice within two working days, the limit on liability for unauthorized use is $50. If the cardholder waits more than two days, but less than sixty, the limit increases to $500. If more than sixty days goes by without notice being given, the debit cardholder has open-ended liability, and this could mean loss of the personal funds withdrawn by unlawful use of the debit card. The loss rules on credit cards and debit cards are not the same, yet they provide substantial protection for the cardholder if the terms are followed.

Business Cards

Many companies subscribe to large numbers of credit cards for use by their employees in the field. The $50 limit is in effect for each card issued. Any losses to the company cannot be passed back to the employee who lost the card. An issuer of ten or more business cards to one company can negotiate with that company to raise the limit of loss higher than $50 per card.

Cancellation of a Card

Normally the decision to cancel a credit card is an internal matter for the issuer. Care must be exercised so that canceled, expired, lost, or stolen cards are not accepted for charges. Normal authorization procedures will take care of these problems.

Cancellation by the company, however, still may lead to litigation. In *Miller v. American Express Co.*,[4] a card was revoked upon the death of the cardholding husband. When the wife tendered it for an automobile rental charge, the charge was refused. Suit was brought for humiliation and inconvenience, basing the cause of action upon the Equal Credit Opportunity Act, which is the 1972 amendment to the Civil Rights Act of 1964. The case was settled pending remand for trial for the amount of $23,484 actual damages, $10,000 punitive damages, and $16,516 attorney fees.

Credit Cards and the Civil Rights Act

The Civil Rights Act of 1964, with its subsequent amendments, has found application in the credit-card industry. Soon after the CRA became effective, the Federal Trade Commission began an investigation to see if the credit practices of the issuers discriminated against card applicants.

Amoco Oil Company was targeted and charged with discrimination in the issuance of its oil company cards. The company was caught in a unique manner: It was using the ZIP codes of applicants to make it difficult for minorities in designated areas to obtain credit cards. In a consent decree, Amoco agreed to settle the charges for $200,000.[5]

Credit Cards and Criminal Law

Evidence may be introduced in a criminal trial of the "illegitimate value" of credit cards so as to give them a value for prosecution for theft purposes. In one case, the person accused of theft argued that by stealing a credit card, he had stolen nothing of value until a charge was made with it. This he had not done. The court held that evidence could be offered to show the street value of a stolen credit card which ranges from $25 to $500, depending upon the locale in which it is offered for sale. Thus, the card *itself* has value even if it is not used.

Two matters of importance remain for discussion. Both are involved directly in all operations that accept credit cards. The first has to do with Truth-in-Lending and the Fair Credit Reporting Act, and the second with the payment of rewards for picking up "bandit" credit cards from guests and patrons.

TRUTH-IN-LENDING AT THE FRONT DESK

The Consumer Credit Protection Act,[6] was enacted by Congress to provide assistance to consumers in areas involving credit. The law originally was intended to control the professional credit-reporting industry found throughout the nation. It also applies to any business that becomes involved in consumer-credit reporting. The law has been amended to include additional titles, one of them being the Electronic Fund Transfer Act mentioned previously.

Fair Credit Reporting Act

The Fair Credit Reporting Act has two primary features. First, if credit information *furnished by others* is passed on, the person or firm giving out that information is a credit-reporting agency under the act. This means the rules and regulations of the law must be followed. Care must be taken when passing along second-hand credit information about employees, agents, guests, patrons, and others.

Second, if credit is denied, the consumer must be told who supplied the information upon which the credit refusal was made. This will be explored in a moment.

Now we have to distinguish two points so we can understand the FCRA better. First, it applies only to persons or firms who pass on credit information *supplied by others*. Second, it does not apply to information gained from personal experience. If a guest causes damage at a motel or refuses to pay, that information can be given to another motel who inquires about it. The inquiring motel, however, *cannot give that information to others*, for it is not based on its own experience. This distinction is important.

What this means, in practice, is that care must be exercised in credit information situations. Not only does the FCRA require this, but so do the privacy laws. Personnel must be trained carefully not to give out credit information except under legal advice. The dangers are apparent, and silence is very much in order.

Denial of Credit

If consumer credit is denied, the consumer must be given the name and address of the person or firm that supplied the information upon which the refusal was based. There is no requirement that the consumer be told *why*, because, once the consumer has the name and address of the reporting agency, he or she has specific rights in reference to getting full information from that source.

So, when a would-be guest tenders an American Express card at a hotel front desk and the card charge is refused, the Act is in effect. The hotel now has a legal obligation to tell that person the source of the information upon which the denial was based.

This information, of course, should be given to the cardholder in a quiet, private manner so as not to cause unnecessary embarrassment. It also would be well to do it on a written form such as seen in Figure 10.3. A copy should be made and retained by the hotel. The original should be given to the cardholder without comment. It may be a good idea to have forms printed in several languages. Alternate arrangements can be made for payment.

This is a developing area of law, and the suggestions made here may have to be modified as the case law develops. Caution is in order in all credit denials, and use of the form might keep the facility out of litigation that may arise later because of the denial of consumer credit. If a business person is denied credit, these rules do not apply.

Nonacceptance of Credit Cards

Many leading hotels and resorts do not accept credit cards. Some accept checks, but only upon arrangements being made in advance for that purpose.

Figure 10.3 Credit card refusal form.

_____ 19 ___

Your Card Company has refused to accept any charge on your credit card account with:

_____

This information was given to us by:

_____

_____

_____

We would be pleased to accept another form of payment.

_____
Signature
Clerk, Zero Motel

Note: On the hotel copy, it would be good practice to have the clerk note the time that the original was handed to the cardholder. The cardholder should also be asked to initial the copy, which should be retained.

Unlawful Use of Credit Cards

New York Penal Law 155.00 (found in the McKinney Supplement 1978) has a provision that relates to credit cards. This law makes the unlawful use of a credit card a misdemeanor. "Unlawful use of a credit card" is defined as "use or display of a credit card known to have been revoked or canceled to obtain or attempt to obtain services." Most states have similar pieces of legislation.

"Smart Cards"

"Smart cards" contain a 64/K computer chip, an internal display screen, and a calculator-like keyboard. Of particular interest is that these cards can be used to control entrance to specified places where an ID number is required to gain access. If a card is stolen, it cannot be used without the ID number. These cards can be used to pay bills at the inn, and they also can be used in connection with a variety of other services.

CREDIT-CARD REWARDS

Card companies are willing to pay rewards to employees who recapture credit cards that have been canceled, lost, or stolen. These rewards usually are $50. Figure 10.4 is a reward check paid to a student at the College of Hotel Administration, University of Nevada, Las Vegas, for picking up a card. Nothing is inherently wrong in card companies' requesting that their bandit cards be returned to them. The danger lies in personnel becoming more interested in the reward than in customer relations. The Wood case is a striking example.

Figure 10.4 Reward check.

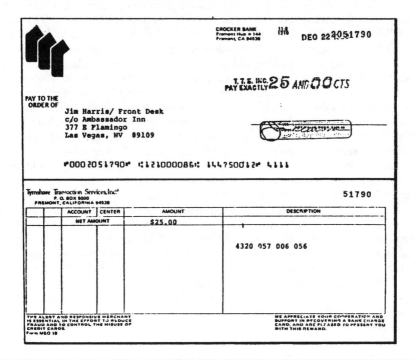

Case Introduction: Wood Case

The case involves a franchise holder of a Holiday Inn located in Phenix City, Alabama. The inn was owned by Interstate Inns, Inc., a South Carolina corporation, which held the franchise with Holiday Inn, Inc., a corporation formed in Tennessee.

At the time of this case [1975], Gulf Oil Corporation, a Pennsylvania corporation, had a credit-card arrangement with Holiday Inns, Inc., whereby Gulf credit cards could be used at Holiday Inns for room and other charges. [That arrangement now has been terminated.] One of the defendants in the case was the front-desk clerk, Goynes, an agent and employee of the South Carolina corporation.

The suit was filed in an Alabama federal court under "diversity jurisdiction," as the parties in the suit were from different states and the amount in controversy exceeded $10,000. If the parties all had been from one state, or if less than $10,000 had been involved, the suit would have been brought in an Alabama state court. What happened is set forth in the opinion of the court. (The $10,000 figure has been raised to $50,000.)

WOOD V. HOLIDAY INNS, INC., ET AL.
508 F. 2d 167 (5th Cir. 1975).

On the evening before the morning in question, Plaintiff checked into the Inn at Phenix City and submitted his Gulf credit card for the purpose of having it imprinted on a credit memorandum of the motel. After the imprint was taken, the card was returned to him, and he retired. While the evidence was in conflict as to the transactions between the Plaintiff and the Defendant Goynes on the following morning, there was evidence from which the jury might have found, and apparently they did find, the following: That, at 5:00 A.M. the following morning, the Defendant Goynes called the Plaintiff's room, awakened the Plaintiff from his repose, and informed him that he would like to obtain the Plaintiff's credit card for the purpose of making an imprint on a credit memorandum of the motel as the imprint made the night before was indistinct and another imprint was needed; that after some conversation it was agreed that Goynes take the card, secure the imprint, and return it within a few minutes to the Plaintiff; that some thirty minutes later, Plaintiff, not having resecured his card and feeling that for some purpose someone had fraudulently secured his card, dressed and went to the front desk and was informed by the Defendant Goynes that his credit had been revoked and that Goynes had telegraphic authority from National Data Processing, Inc., a computerizing service for Defendant Gulf Oil, to pick up Plaintiff's card and terminate his credit. It was conceded that Goynes obtained the credit card and asked Plaintiff to arrange to pay his bill in cash.

The credit manager of Gulf Oil testified that, on the previous day, he had reviewed the credit file of the Plaintiff; had found that the Plaintiff had been charging in ever-increasing amounts on his Gulf credit card; that he had during the current month paid to Gulf a substantial bill and charged to Gulf another bill which charges almost equaled the Plaintiff's total monthly income; that in the last three months the Plaintiff had paid his bill more than thirty days after the time the bill was sent to him; and that these facts caused him to suspect that the Plaintiff would soon be unable to pay his Gulf account. He, therefore, ordered the credit terminated and the card revoked or picked up.

The method for terminating the credit and picking up the card was that, on order of Gulf, National Data Processing sent out a communication to all Gulf agents and all desk clerks of Holiday Inns, in short, those most likely to come into contact with such credit cards, a list of all credit cards revoked and asked them to secure possession thereof for Gulf for a reward to be paid by Gulf. Suggestions as to how such cards might tactfully be repossessed had been sent out by Gulf, and there was no evidence that Gulf authorized use of rudeness or false pretenses in securing the credit cards.

After repossession of the card, the Defendant Goynes was paid by Gulf a reward for the same.

Wood's anger and frustration continued to build. Three days later, while he was relating the incident to a friend, he had a heart attack, precipitated apparently by the stress of the incidents surrounding the revocation of credit.

Wood sued the Gulf Oil Corporation, Holiday Inns, Inc., Interstate Inns, Inc. (the owner of the Phenix City Holiday Inn), and Jessie Goynes. Interstate and Goynes denied any negligence or wrongful conduct and asserted by way of cross-claim that they were acting under the direction of Gulf and were therefore entitled to indemnification by Gulf.

After trial, the jury returned a verdict in favor of Wood but apportioned damages in the amounts of $25,000 compensatory damages against Gulf, $25,000 punitive damages against Interstate and Goynes, and $10,000 punitive damages against Holiday Inns. The court then granted the motions of Gulf and Holiday Inns, Inc., for judgments notwithstanding the verdict and granted the motion of Interstate and Goynes for a new trial.

[These motions, made in writing and usually argued orally to the court, fix the right of appeal.]

Findings

Wood's primary claim against Gulf is based upon the Fair Credit Reporting Act, 15 U.S.C. §§1681-1681a(f) (1974). The Act charges "consumer reporting agencies" and users of "consumer credit reports" with various responsibilities. Gulf argues that it was not a consumer reporting agency as defined in 15 U.S.C. §1681a(f), and the district court so held, apparently as a matter of law.

The Act defines a consumer reporting agency as: " [A]ny person which, for monetary fees, dues, or on a cooperative nonprofit basis, regularly engages in whole or in part in the practice of assembling or evaluating consumer credit information or other information on consumers for the purpose of furnishing consumer reports to third parties. . . . 15 U.S.C. §1681a(f)."

[It can be seen at this point how important it is for the inn to comply with the FCRA.]

Wood next maintained that Gulf is liable under 15 U.S.C. §1681m(a) as a user of a credit report. This section provides:

"Whenever credit or insurance for personal, family, or household purposes, or employment involving a consumer is denied or the charge for such credit or insurance is increased either wholly or partly because of information contained in a consumer report from a consumer reporting agency, *the user of the consumer report shall so advise the consumer against whom such adverse action has been taken and supply the name and address of the consumer reporting agency making the report.*" [Emphasis added by author.]

Wood stipulated at the pre-trial hearing of October 4, 1973, that one of his allegations was based upon the breach of the innkeeper's duty. However, the pre-trial order indicates Wood also averred that he was subjected to "offensive, abusive and insulting conduct, action and language" by Goynes and that Gulf's liability is predicated "upon the actions of Jessie Goynes, if Goynes is determined to be the agent of Gulf Oil." Therefore, we do not believe that Wood's allegation against Gulf was based upon breach of the innkeeper's duty. Rather, we believe that Wood's alleged cause of action sounds in tort, at least as against Gulf, and *it is therefore appropriate to consider the question of the agency relationship between Goynes and Gulf. . . .* [Emphasis added by author.]

[Here the court steps away from the question of the innkeeper's duty and looks to tort liability under the law of agency.]

The existence and scope of a principal-agent relationship is generally for the jury to determine and the burden of proving agency rests upon the party asserting its existence. . . .

An agency relationship may arise from acts and appearances which lead others to believe that such a relationship has been created. . . . This concept of apparent authority is based upon manifestations by the alleged principal to third persons, and reasonable belief by those persons that the alleged agent is authorized to bind the principal. . . . *"The manifestations of the principal may be made directly to the third person, or may be made to the community, by signs or advertising. . . ."* [Emphasis added by author.]

Questions of apparent authority are questions of fact, and are therefore for the jury to determine. The license agreement between Holiday Inns, Inc. and Interstate provided that the Phenix City facility should be constructed and operated so that it would be "readily recognizable by the public as part of the national system of `Holiday Inns.'" Indeed, the Phenix City facility was required to use the same service marks and trademarks, and exterior and interior décor as the Holiday Inns owned by the parent company. A jury could therefore reasonably conclude that the license agreement required the Phenix City facility to be of such an appearance that travelers would believe it was owned by Holiday Inns, Inc.

We believe that reasonable men could differ regarding Wood's evidence of apparent authority and that the issue should therefore be determined by the jury. . . . The district court charged the jury below that the relationship of agency between Goynes and Holiday Inns, Inc. could be implied if the jury found that Holiday Inns, Inc., through its advertising and control, held out to the general public that Interstate Inns in Phenix City, Alabama, was its agent. On the basis of these instructions, the jury held Holiday Inns, Inc. liable for Goynes' actions. However, the jury manifested its confusion as to the proper application of law to the facts by holding Holiday Inns, Inc. liable in an amount different from that of Interstate Inns, although the liability of both alleged principals was based upon the same act. Rather than merely reinstating the jury's verdict, then, we believe the interests of justice would be better served by remanding Wood's action against Holiday Inns, Inc. to the district court for retrial.

Cross-appellants Interstate and Goynes appeal the lower court's decision denying indemnification. We believe the district court was correct.

Under Alabama law, an agent is entitled to indemnification for any amounts he has been required to pay for his principal in the performance of his agency. . . . However, the principal is not required to indemnify the agent for harm resulting solely from the agent's negligence.

Hence, in the absence of agreements to the contrary, an agent has no right to indemnity for damages suffered by reason of his own fraud, misconduct or other tort, even if the wrong was committed within the scope of the agent's employment. . . .

The theory of Wood's case is based upon the harm he is alleged to have suffered because of the manner in which his card was revoked. Any harm to Wood must have resulted solely from the actions of Goynes, since Gulf has not been shown to have been negligent. We therefore believe no substantial evidence has been presented which would justify the indemnification of Goynes and Interstate.

For the reasons set forth above, we affirm in part, reverse in part, and remand for proceedings not inconsistent with this opinion.

SUMMARY

In these days of e-mail, voice mail, the Internet, fax machines, and personal computers, we see a world of information that flows on a true superhighway. This process has carried over to the monetary systems of the world.

The credit card provides the convenience of creating instant credit at points of sale of goods and services. The debit card gives access to funds that are already on deposit. The system of Electronic Fund Transfers (EFTs) allows credit and debit cards to function in an even more spectacular fashion. A combination of credit and debit cards and EFTs provides enormous opportunities for those who are planning for the future.

Credit and debit cards and electronic transfers are ideal for use in the hotel, hospitality, and tourism industries. Legal dangers occur, however, when management and personnel are not educated in the care and caution that must be exercised in the use of these systems.

The Wood case discusses the dangers of not handling a credit card matter in a proper manner. The case should be required reading for innkeepers, hotel financial managers, and all front-desk personnel. The role of the law of agency as covered in Chapter 7 plays a predominate part in this case, and the judge who wrote the opinion refers to the law of agency in a variety of ways.

QUESTIONS

1. EFTs have not caught on to the degree that had been anticipated. What are two reasons for this?

2. Why would Amoco voluntarily pay $200,000 rather than contest the charge of credit-card discrimination?

3. What house rules can be placed into effect to discourage a credit-card reward syndrome on the part of employees? Why should this be done?

4. Why does the FCRA not require that the consumer be told why consumer credit is being denied?

5. True or false: The federal CCPA applies to business credit transactions just the same as consumer credit transactions.

6. If innkeeper X tells innkeeper Y that guest Z did damage to X's motel, has the FCRA been violated? Why or why not?

7. What is required to make one a "credit-reporting agency under the FCRA?"

8. Why do courts hold that a stolen credit card has a value even if it has not been used to make an unauthorized charge?

9. How does American Express make a profit from the charge slips that come to it from HH&T operations?

10. Why is a credit-card charge slip not "commercial paper"?

NOTES

1. *First National Bank v. Mularkey*, 385 N.Y.S. 2d 473 (Civ. Ct. Queens Co., 1976).

2. Bryan Burrough, *Vendetta*, (New York: HarperCollins, 1988).

3. John Friedman and John Mechan, *House of Cards: Inside the Troubled Empire of American Express* p. 54.

4. 26 ATLA L. Rep. 117, 688 F. 2d 1235 (9th Cir. 1982).

5. Reported in *U.S. News & World Report*, May 19, 1980.

6. P.L. 90.321: 82 Stat. 146 *et seq.*, act of May 29, 1968.

11

Basic Legal Duties of Innkeepers

OVERVIEW

IN THIS CHAPTER we will examine in depth the subject of legal duties of innkeepers. What we see here has particular importance in the hotel, hospitality, and tourism industry because of the sheer number of hotels, motels, and inns in the United States.

The business of innkeeping is public in nature and, therefore, duties arise that are influenced by the public need. These include the duty to receive guests and the property of guests; the duty to provide suitable accommodations; the duty to treat all guests with a reasonable standard of care and courtesy; the duty to care for the person as well as the property of guests; and the duty to comply with applicable health laws. In turn, the guest has duties to the innkeeper, principally conducting oneself with reasonable decorum and paying for services received. Here is what a judge had to say about travel and innkeeping:

> In the past, many courts have viewed travel as a privilege and as a luxury. And until comparatively recently it was true that travel was for the rich and leisure classes. However, the last two decades have seen an extraordinary increase in the demand for travel services from all sectors and classes of our society. Travel by vacationers has become accepted as a necessity which can be and should be enjoyed by all citizens in this country. The concept of travel as a right is very old and is a fundamental part of our culture.
>
> A corollary principle is the right of all travelers to receive the quality of travel services contracted for and reasonably expected without deviation. Hotels should not be relieved of liability for the damages which they cause through breaches of contract, fraud, negligence, and illegality.[1]

It was said in St. Augustine, in relation to travel, "The world is a book and those that do not travel read only one page." Sydney J. Harris may have been thinking of travel when he said, "The time to relax is when you do not have the time for it." Travel and how we accommodate travelers are what we are concerned with in this chapter.

It becomes important to make certain that travelers' expectations are met. In addition, requirements of law (and equity) have to be met because mandates are found there as dictates of law. Failure to meet these mandates may lead to legal liability, and losses may follow in court. A good place to begin is by examining the sources of the legal duties placed upon innkeepers, as illustrated in Figure 11.1.

Figure 11.1 Innkeeper's legal duties.

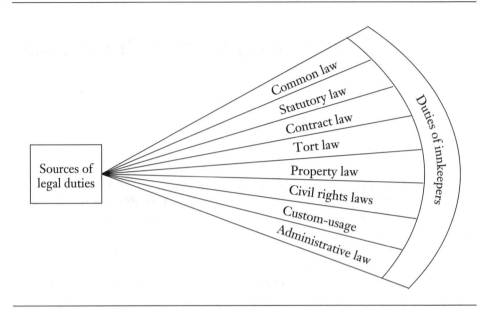

Sources of Legal Duties

Legal duties of innkeepers can be traced to eight sources. First are those principles of law that developed through court rulings during the past centuries. This is the common law that we have encountered previously in this text.

The second source is found in statutes. The following excerpt is from the Virginia Code. This appeared in 1849—a century and a half ago, making it one of the first state codes to deal with innkeeping:

> Every person licensed to keep an ordinary, or house of public entertainment, shall constantly provide the same with lodging and diet for travellers and their servants, and . . . with stableage and provender, or pasturage and provender (as the season may require) for their horses. Any such person may, at the place of a muster or public sale, distant a mile or more from another ordinary, with the consent of the proprietor of such place, vend meat or drink as at his ordinary.[2]

Found in this partial quote of a much longer statute is a little of the color of another age.

A third source of duties is found in contract law, both common law and sales. When an innkeeper becomes bound contractually, the legal duty arises to honor the terms whether it is a common law or sales contract.

Fourth, the demands of the law of tort give rise to corresponding duties to see that such are not committed against guests, employees, and third parties. "Tort" involves an injury or other loss, usually because of negligence.

Property law enters the picture as the fifth source, and it will be developed in detail in Chapters 19 and 20.

A sixth source is found in the federal and state civil rights laws. These laws raise the legal duty not to engage in discrimination in hiring, in receiving travelers at the inn, in serving patrons at other facilities, and other matters.

A seventh source is found in the ancient customs and usages of innkeeping. Many legal duties of innkeepers are based on the practices of inns across the centuries. The courts look to these practices to establish standards in modern cases. These standards also are modified and broadened through court decisions.

In Medieval and earlier times, most people were illiterate, and signs were needed to inform the population of services offered. In the ruins of Pompeii, Italy, a sign in the form of a checkerboard was found outside of what was determined to be an inn. A mule on a sign represented a baker; a goat, a dairy; a bottle of wine, a winery; and a checkerboard, an inn. Signs prompted Ben Jonson to write, "It even puts Apollo to all his strength of art to follow, The flights, and to devine, What's meant by every sign."

During the nineteenth century, beginning with the completion of the first transcontinental railroad, it was realized that common law would not be able to regulate railroads and the other industries that would develop as a result of them. There was a need for a hands-on system of law that would regulate, or "administer," these industries. It had to be a system that could be created quickly and applied rapidly. This need was met by the creation of administrative law, the eighth source of duty. The main characteristic of administrative law, as we first saw in Chapter 2, is that it is based on rules and regulations made by appointed bodies or panels that had no relationship with the courts.

The Legal Burden of Innkeepers

Innkeepers at the smallest bed and breakfast, the motel at the interstate intersection, the hotel downtown in a large city, the cozy resort in the mountains of New York, the islands of Georgia, the beaches of Florida—all bear a common legal burden: They must be aware of and comply with the laws and standards that apply to them.

Court cases for the past decade show that hotels and motels were the second largest target for major litigation filed in the American courts. (The number-one target was multi-unit operations such as condominiums.) One fourth of the verdicts against hotels and motels topped $1 million. The service industry indeed has become a major player in our courts.

A 1994 survey disclosed that there also are common events at hotels and motels that have resulted in litigation. Some examples include:

1. Failure to protect room numbers of guests, such as announcing at the front desk, "Ms. Jones, you are in room 123 . . . ."
2. Failure to maintain a proper key control system including failure to remove room numbers from room keys given to guests at inns.
3. Improper hiring of employees that results in loss to guests.
4. Failure to provide proper security.

Ontario, Canada, has enacted an Occupier's Liability Act, a statutory law much like the common-law duty of care, that requires an innkeeper, restaurateur, or bar operator to make certain not to expose guests, patrons, or invitees to ". . . unusual dangers. . . ." These dangers include:

1. behavior of those under the influence of alcohol
2. the condition of the premises in question

The duties set forth in this act extend to premises owned by others that adjoin the inn, restaurant, or bar.

In earlier days in the American Colonies and later in the United States, committees were formed for the purpose of providing for the safety of the general public. The initial concern was for fire protection, and this concern reached eventually into numerous other areas. The same principle exists today in a variety of forms, including the now-famous 911 phone call. The principle also extends to those engaged in the hotel, hospitality, and tourism industries.

It is necessary today to have contingency plans to cover disasters such as tornados, cyclones, floodings, fire, and others. Montana, North Carolina, Oregon, and a few other states have statutes requiring that safety committees be formed and made operational in the workplace.

Classes of Legal Duties

Legal duties relating to the hospitality industry can be differentiated according to two fundamental classifications:

1. Essential services: duties imposed by the common law, statutory law, custom, trade usage, or other laws. The hospitality industry cannot escape the responsibilities imposed by these laws.
2. Nonessential services: duties assumed or taken on voluntarily.

Nonessential services, or support services, have taken the front of the stage today. Many inns offer weight rooms, jogging tracks, game rooms for kids, horseback riding facilities, golf courses, fax machines, medical doctors, registered nurses, shoe repair services, a pharmacy, a travel agent, physical fitness programs, supervised swimming areas at the beaches, sliding boards, diving boards, and water chutes. Inns that once provided "a tight roof, a safe stable, and food and drink" have become miniature entertainment capitals.

The legal importance of this is that courts of today are hearing and deciding issues that were unknown even fifty years ago. All of this is a part of the sales or marketing strategies of inns in an effort to attract a larger share of the travel dollar. The management side of the question is whether the expense of the support services and the increased legal exposure is worth the increased share of the travel dollar.

A person in the hospitality industry may assume a legal duty even though that duty is not otherwise a responsibility of that person, unit, or corporation. In the latter case, the standard that must be met is the same as if the duty were imposed by law: to exercise ordinary and reasonable care, taking into consideration *foreseeability*.[3]

If an innkeeper assumes a duty not mandated by law, such as the duty to rescue, failure to use ordinary, reasonable care, can render the innkeeper liable for losses that may result to the person who is injured or killed in the rescue attempt.[4]

DEGREE OF LIABILITY

Innkeepers' duties are owed primarily to the traveler as he or she becomes a guest at the inn. Yet the law extends duties to other classes of persons, including invitees, locals, trespassers—and even thieves. The *degree* of liability, however, *decreases* as the legal standing of each class moves downward. Figure 11.2 illustrates this principle. The degree of legal duty owed to one who is attempting to rob an inn is slight, yet the innkeeper could not cause unnecessary harm to that person, for there is a legal duty not to do so. A trespasser no longer is barred automatically from recovering for injuries negligently inflicted by a landowner. Rather, one's status in relation to liability is a jury question, not a question of law.

A combination of common law, statutory law, custom, and the public nature of inns, brings into play duties that are public in nature. This is so because these duties are designed to protect the public in general.

FIGURE 11.2 Variable degrees of legal liability.

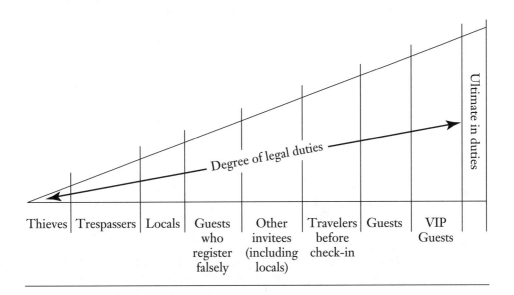

PUBLIC LEGAL DUTIES

It has long been recognized that when one enters the innkeeping business, he or she assumes duties of a public nature. Thus, what may have been private property at the outset assumes a public character. If A inherits $500,000 from his grandfather, that money is private and can be controlled solely by A. If A invests the money in a small inn, the character of the money (property) has been changed in two ways: (1) personal property has been converted to real, and (2) the property now is affected by the public interest, need, and control. One can withdraw such money and regain private control, but as long as the public use continues, the control is mandated by public need. Many of these publicly related duties arise out of the common law as well as custom, but some of them are statutory.

By far, the most important duty is to receive guests. It then becomes important as to how to treat them. Each state, by statute, provides health requirements that must be met by those who serve the public in travel, lodging, and other hospitality functions, such as restaurant food service.

In many instances these statutes are old, often having been adopted when the states were formed. Although some of these seem quaint by modern standards, they make up an important part of the duties that fall upon innkeepers, restaurant operators, and others. The statute that follow is old, and only a small portion of it is set out.[5] It was enacted in Nevada in 1919 and amended in part in 1943 and 1969.

447.020 Cleanliness of bedding; wornout and unfit bedding.

1. All bedding, bedclothes or bed covering, including mattresses, quilts, blankets, sheets, pillows or comforters, used in any hotel in this state must be kept clean and free from all filth or dirt.

2. No bedding, bedclothes or bed covering, including mattresses, quilts, blankets, sheets, pillows or comforters, shall be used which is worn out or unsanitary for use by human beings according to the true intent and meaning of this chapter.

447.030 Extermination of vermin. Any room in any hotel in this state which is or shall be infested with vermin or bedbugs or similar things shall be thoroughly fumigated, disinfected and renovated until such vermin or bedbugs or other similar things are entirely exterminated.

447.080 Air space, floor area and ceiling height of rooms. No room for sleeping purposes shall have less than 500 cubic feet of air space for each occupant. The floor area of each sleeping room must be at least 80 square feet and at least 7 feet in width. All rooms must have a ceiling height of at least 8 feet.

447.090 Amount of bedding required; furnishing clean sheets and pillow slips; size of sheets.

1. Every bed kept or used in any hotel in this state for the accommodation of any person or guest must be provided with a sufficient supply of clean bedding.

2. Clean sheets and pillow slips shall be supplied for each bed in a hotel as often as the bed is assigned to a different person.

3. Sheets shall be at least 98 inches long and of sufficient width to cover the mattress and spring completely.

447.100 Fumigation of room after occupation by person having contagious, infectious disease. Whenever any room in any hotel shall have been occupied by any person having a contagious or infectious disease, the room shall be thoroughly fumigated under the direction of the health authority, and all bedding therein thoroughly disinfected before the room shall be occupied by any other person. In any event, such room shall not be let to any person for at least 48 hours after such fumigation or disinfection.

447.110 Bathing facilities.

1. In every hotel in existence prior to October 1, 1945, at least one bathtub or shower shall be installed in a separate compartment on a public hallway or court for every 20, or fractional part of 20, guestrooms, on the same floor as the hallway or court which are not provided with private baths.

2. In every hotel built after October 1, 1945, at least one bathtub or shower provided with hot and cold water shall be installed in a separate compartment on a public hallway or court for every 10, or fractional part of 10, guestrooms on the same floor as the hallway or court which are not provided with private baths.

447.120 Towels to be furnished.
1. Every hotel within this state having a public washstand or washbowl, where different persons gather to wash themselves, must keep a sufficient supply of clean, individual towels for the use of such persons within easy access of or to such persons and in plain sight and view.

Even though inns are associated with public need and are public houses, are they such in regard to statutes that prohibit solicitation of prostitution in "public places?" The answer is "yes" in those instances where an innkeeper knows of the activity and allows it to continue. In such a case, the innkeeper could face loss of a bar license, restaurant license—and perhaps the license to operate the inn itself. The prostitute, at the same time, could be prosecuted under criminal law.[6]

DUTY TO RECEIVE PERSONS

Those engaged in the public venture of innkeeping must receive all who seek accommodations, up to the limits of their capacity. The duty is almost, but not quite, absolute, for there are exceptions. An important point, however, is that the duty extends to *travelers* and does not necessarily extend to "locals" who may use services provided at the inn. A local, however, *could* be a traveler and it has been so held.[7] The test applied to determine whether a person is a "traveler" is the transient nature of the stay. This classification is important because, as a general rule, an innkeeper does not owe special duties to those who are not "travelers."

Control of the Inn

Although the courts gave the innkeeper the duty to receive, the right to exclude remains under certain circumstances. In a New York case, two ministers of Jehovah's Witnesses were going door-to-door at a hotel but were asked to leave. Their claim to a First Amendment right to practice their religion was rejected. The court could not see a right to go freely upon private property [even though public in orientation] to advance their personal religious beliefs.[8]

In considering the innkeeper's right to control the hotel, adjoining passageways become involved. If solicitation is for religious purposes, the First Amendment comes to the front. If the solicitation is for purposes unrelated to religion, attention shifts to the Fifth Amendment.

Solicitations in Passageways

In larger cities and indeed in some smaller ones, our hotels, restaurants, bars, and other hospitality functions share passageways with other hospitality components and other businesses. The question of whether such passageways can be used lawfully for solicitations has required the courts to reexamine older doctrines of the common law that had to do with "purpose" and "use."

Today, the courts recognize two types of passageways. First are those that permit the public to carry out day-to-day passage as required in our daily lives. These passages are recognized as "public forums," which the public uses as a necessity, and thus, they fall under the protection of the Fifth Amendment:

> No person shall be . . . deprived of life, liberty, or property, without due process of law. . . .

Second are passageways that exist solely to permit members of the public to carry out special endeavors such as catching a subway, or bus, or taking an airline flight or entering a hotel to check in for the night. The courts say these nonpublic forums are used to meet a special purpose and, thus, have no constitutional protection to solicitors.[9]

Minors and the Duty to Receive

The duty to receive extends to those who normally are unable to contract, such as persons under eighteen years of age. An innkeeper, however, would have the right to determine if the minor is capable of paying for the services. There is no requirement that one furnish free lodging to a minor. The minor would be liable for the reasonable value of necessities furnished and would not be able to disaffirm the obligation later on the grounds of incompetency. The liability of the minor would be in *quasi-contract* (and not in true contract). In establishing the legal duty to receive travelers, the early courts never were concerned with whether the traveler had the legal capacity to form a binding contract. If that had been the test, minors and others would have been denied services. The duty to receive was extended to minors and others regardless of their legal capacity.

In 1984, fifteen-year-old Jenny Morgan checked into the Westin St. Francis Hotel in San Francisco with a forty-three-year-old drug addict. Morgan wound up a paraplegic and unable to speak because of a drug overdose that night.

The lawyers for Morgan, Melvin Belli and Stephen Fabbro, used a little known San Francisco ordinance in their attempt to recover $12 million from the hotel for what happened to Morgan. A city law dating from the 1930s required hotels to report to the police those under eighteen years of age who attempted to check into hotels when they were "not accompanied by parents, a guardian, or another adult with custodial authority." The defense the hotel used was that it had summoned police but was told that they (the police) had no procedures for enforcing the ordinance. Although the jury found the hotel innocent of negligence, the hotel paid $400,000, which it said it would do if it won the case. The lawyers for the plaintiff have appealed the 11-1 jury verdict, claiming the trial judge gave improper instructions to the jury.

Refusing to sell a room to an underage person who has the ability to pay is breach of the common-law duty to receive. There must be some other legal reason for refusal, such as a city ordinance requiring that the police be called immediately when an underage person requests a room at the inn.

In contradiction to the common law, the statutes of Wisconsin make it clear that the inns there can lawfully refuse to accept minors who apply for rooms at the inn. The basis of these laws is that minors can refuse to honor the contracts they made, and the courts will uphold the refusal. Under Wisconsin law, a sign must be posted stating that one must be eighteen or older to rent a room.

Let's assume that a seventeen-year-old has been driving all day and has crossed into Wisconsin. She now is confronted with the "eighteen-year-old" law. Can this person lawfully be turned away? Refusal would be violation of the common-law duty of innkeepers to receive. This, in turn, may give a valid cause of action to the teenager to sue for damages.

Hotels across the nation always are concerned about teenagers who want to use the inn for party purposes after high school graduation and the like. These concerns are legitimate. A house rule that says teenage locals will not be received at the hotel will pass legal muster.

When those under eighteen ask for a room, the courts permit the innkeeper to require two things:

1. Advanced payment for one day can be required.
2. The driver's license of that person can be requested so a copy of it can be made.

If either or both are refused, the applicant can lawfully be turned away in Wisconsin and other states as well.

Once those under age are received at the inn, another legal problem may arise. It has to do with young persons, and others for that matter, becoming intoxicated on the inn premises and causing disturbance or damage to inn property or guests. Although these persons may lawfully be excluded from the inn, the danger is that they almost always will turn to their motor vehicles as a means to leave the inn after being ejected. The answer to this, of course, is to involve local police in the ejection, thus letting the police decide whether the underage person will be allowed to drive after leaving the inn.

This problem often is magnified when major sporting events are taking place in close proximity to the inn. In such instances, if groups of underage persons apply for rooms, two house policies can be implemented to help control the problem.

1. An adult who agrees to be responsible can be required to stay in each guest room occupied.
2. Extra security personnel should be hired to serve during the course of the sporting event and aftermath.

Those under the age of majority often can avoid the obligations of contracts they enter into. On the other hand, minors can be held responsible for their torts. Thus, if a minor uses deceit and cunning in misrepresenting his age, he can be sued for the tort. The recovery for the fraud is not the subject of contract.[10] In Mississippi, however, a child of seven to fourteen years of age is presumed to be incapable of contributory negligence in tort cases unless the contrary is proven in court.[11] When such minors are involved, the issue of "attractive nuisance" may come forward. This doctrine holds that if one attracts these persons, one must pay for any injuries or loss they sustain while on the premises.

CASE INTRODUCTION: REX CASE

Must an innkeeper be prepared to receive guests twenty-four hours a day? In the *Rex v. Ivens* case that follows, Williams, a law clerk (called "prosecutor" in the case), tried to gain admission at the Bell Inn, in Chepstow, England, at a time when the husband and wife who operated the inn had retired for the night. What happened after that is spelled out in the court's opinion.

REX V. IVENS
7 Car. & P. 213, 173 Eng. Rep. 94 (1835)

". . . With respect to the non-tender of the money by the prosecutor, it is now a custom so universal with innkeepers to trust that a person will pay before he leaves an inn, that it cannot be necessary for a guest to tender money before he goes into an inn; indeed, in the present case, no objection was made that Mr. Williams did not make a tender; and they did not even insinuate that they had any suspicion that he could not pay for whatever entertainment might be furnished to him. I think, therefore, that that cannot be set up as a defense. It however remains for me next to consider the case with respect to the hour of the night at which Mr. Williams applied for admission; and the opinion which I have formed is, that the lateness of the hour is no excuse to the defendant for refusing to receive the prosecutor into his inn. Why are inns established? For the reception of travellers, who are often very far distant from their own homes. Now, at what time is it most essential that travellers should not be denied admission into the inns? I should say when they are benighted, and when, from any casualty, or from the badness of the roads, they arrive at an inn at a very late hour. Indeed, in former times, when the roads were much worse, and were much infested with robbers, a late hour of the night was the time, of all others, at which the traveller most required to be received into an inn. I think therefore, that if the traveller conducts himself properly, the innkeeper is bound to admit him, at whatever hour of the night he may arrive. The only other question in this case is, whether the defendant's inn was full. There is no direct evidence on the part of the prosecution that it was not. But I think the conduct of the parties shows that the inn was not full; because, if it had been, there could have been no use in the landlady asking the prosecutor his name, and saying, that if he would tell it, she would ring for one of the servants."

The verdict under the misdemeanor (criminal) statute under which this case was brought was "guilty," pointing out the innkeeper's duty to receive holds true even in the "wee hours" of the morning—as long as space is available. This rule is firm in modern innkeeping law.

Current Practice

The usual practice at inns located in high-crime areas is to lock outside doors at designated times of the night. Yet admittance must be possible by the use of a bell or key or other device to alert those on duty. The duty to receive remains, regardless of the time of day or night, and even more so if one has a reservation. In the latter instance, not only is there a common-law duty to receive but a contractual one as well. This duty is not restricted to normal business hours.

State Laws and the Duty to Receive

Many states have criminal statutes providing that an innkeeper who wrongfully refuses to receive can be indicted and brought to trial for violation of the statute. (*Rex v. Ivens* shows us the early English view.) Refusing to receive one who has a seeing-eye dog or "service dog" would not be a valid refusal even if the inn does not have facilities for the animal. For example, Nevada has a statute that creates a legal duty to receive dogs under the stated circumstances. The statute follows:

1. It is unlawful for a place of public accommodation to:
   (a) Refuse service to a visually handicapped person because he is accompanied by a guide dog; or
   (b) Charge an additional fee for such guide dog.
2. A place of accommodation may require proof that a dog is a guide dog. Such requirement may be satisfied, by way of example and not of limitation, by exhibition of the identification card normally presented to a visually handicapped person upon his graduation from a guide dog school.
3. A guide dog shall not be presumed dangerous by reason of the fact it is not muzzled.
4. This section does not relieve a visually handicapped person from liability for damage which may be caused by his guide dog.
5. Visually handicapped persons accompanied by guide dogs shall be subject to the same conditions and limitations that apply to persons who are not so handicapped and accompanied.[12]

Excuses to the Duty to Receive

At times an innkeeper can refuse to receive. Indeed, in some instances *there is a duty not to receive.* If all of the rooms of an inn are occupied, this is reason enough to refuse to receive. Yet, if the inn is full and one presents himself with a valid *reservation* for that night, the inn must still receive. If a potential guest appears in an intoxicated, filthy condition, this is a valid excuse not to receive. If one with a communicable disease attempts to register, that person *must* be refused. In many instances, however, one seeking a lodging room may well be sick and in need of assistance. In these instances, the innkeeper may refuse to receive but should seek outside help for that person.

One can refuse to receive for other reasons. One is the absence of baggage. As a general rule, though, when rooms are available, the innkeeper should receive, as long as it is determined that the would-be guest will be able to pay for services. No longer is it legal to refuse on the grounds of race, color, religion, or national origin, and it is unwise to refuse on the grounds of "lack of apparent stature." For example, a well-groomed traveler dressed in blue jeans should not be refused admittance at the resort hotel, even though this was common practice in the immediate past. A soldier should not be turned away because other soldiers caused problems at the inn. Selective discrimination is unwise today, and unlawful as well, as we saw in Chapter 9.

DUTY TO RECEIVE GOODS

Related to the duty to receive is the corresponding duty to receive normal "traveling goods" of the guest-to-be. Because an innkeeper has a duty to receive, it follows that the goods of a guest also must be received. This is a general statement and has limitations. For example, a guest must be permitted to bring in baggage and other items customarily taken into inns. A more difficult question arises in reference to goods, such as a truckload of sound equipment that a guest wants to place inside of the inn. The duty to receive goods might not extend to equipment, and those goods could be refused.

Travelers often bring property to the inn that they do not own. The innkeeper has no right to question ownership. That is not his or her business. On the other hand, if suspected contraband is in a hotel room, other rights of the innkeeper may become involved; these will be examined in Chapter 13.

Two of the more encompassing duties of the innkeeper are the duty to provide a safe place to work and the duty to provide a safe place to stay. The former is discussed next, and the latter in Chapter 12.

A Safe Place to Work

Tort (negligence) rules mandate that the inn be a safe place for those who work there. This is especially so under provisions of the Occupational Safety and Health Act, known as OSHA. This law provides standards that must be complied with at each covered place of business. A growing danger for inn employees is found in bloodborne pathogens.

Bloodborne Pathogens or Viruses

Although hotels today cannot lawfully refuse to receive persons who have AIDS, and though potential employees cannot be given tests to determine if they have AIDS, a serious problem remains in regard to this subject. It has to do with guest room maintenance personnel, whose eyes, skin, or mucous membranes may come into contact with an infected source such as syringes left under a mattress, soiled sheets, or discarded condoms in the guest room.

As a matter of law, at least two things are required.

1. Those at risk must be given suitable warning about the dangers, as well as provided with training designed to protect them while carrying out their duties.
2. The hotel must provide suitable safety equipment such as eye protectors, gloves, aprons, or gowns, as may be appropriate to protect personnel.

Hazard Communications Standard (HCS)

The requirements of "Hazcom," which became effective May 23, 1986, have had direct application to hospitality industry operations since that date.

1. A list must be made of chemicals on the premises, and factory labels must be left on such chemicals.
2. A program must be written and communicated to inform all employees of such chemicals and how they must be handled.
3. Proper training must be provided in regard to such substances.
4. A "library" of "Material Safety Data Sheets" (MSDS) must be maintained. These sheets are to be supplied by those who manufacture the chemicals, maintained by the inn, and made accessible to all employees.

"Hazardous chemicals" include any chemical agents that could cause health or physical hazards. Other hazardous materials include toxic chemicals used in the engineering department degreasers, solvents, swimming pool chemicals, toilet bowl cleaners that contain acid, and detergents used in hotel laundry facilities. In restaurants, for example, sanitizers, flammables, cooking fuels, and even 151-proof rum used to prepare cherries jubilee would be covered.

Occupational Safety and Health Act (OSHA)

All establishments that have more than 20 employees must maintain OSHA Log Form 20. Once each year in February, the log must be closed out and all employees given the opportunity to see it during that month.

All work-related *illnesses* must be entered in the log, but work-related *injuries* are recorded only if they require medical treatment. OSHA defines "illness" as:

> any abnormal condition or disorder, other than one resulting from an occupational injury, caused by exposure to environmental factors associated with employment. It includes acute and chronic illnesses or diseases which may be caused by inhalation, absorption, ingestion, or direct contact.

In a case where a worker died of carbon monoxide poisoning in a company van, both the Michigan trial court and the court of appeals held that the federal OSHA statute prevented the state from bringing a criminal charge of involuntary manslaughter in the case. The Michigan Supreme Court reversed both lower courts, saying that, while OSHA seeks to "preserve safe and healthful working conditions and to preserve our human resources," the state has a right under its police power to prosecute for the death under its own criminal laws.[13]

SUMMARY

The most important duty of the innkeeper is the duty to receive. This duty was nurtured by the early courts and was based upon the realities of the dangers of travel in earlier times. Today, this duty can be thought of as the point around which all laws of innkeeping developed initially and around which all laws of innkeeping exist today.

The early English courts pointed out that travelers on the road, regardless of the reason for being there, had a legal right to be received at the nearest inn, especially in the waning hours of the day. Another essential service was that the inns had to provide protection for travelers and their property once they became guests. Related to these primary duties was the duty to provide food and drink for the travelers and their horses.

The historical legal duties of innkeepers allow us to see how the common law grew. It was not a well planned or carefully thought out process. It grew in bits and pieces as litigants fought out their disputes in the courts. It was a colorful process, and vestiges of those early cases flavor and color the laws of HH&T today.

QUESTIONS

1. What is the importance of the duty to receive in hotel operations today? How would you explain this duty to a younger brother or sister?
2. Why did early innkeepers use signs? What was on the sign used for inns?
3. Why did the early courts hold that innkeepers had to protect travelers who came to their inns and became their guests?
4. When an innkeeper assumes a legal duty that he or she did not need to assume, why do the courts hold that there is a legal duty to honor the duty assumed?
5. Minors pose a special problem to innkeepers. Why is this so?
6. What are the differences between essential and nonessential services?
7. Innkeepers must provide their employees with a safe place to work as a matter of statutory and common law. Is it possible that a new "employee bill of rights" is developing? Would this be a good idea?
8. Explain in one short sentence why custom can be, and is, a source of innkeeping law.
9. As a matter of law, why is it important to know that when a loss occurs at an inn, the one who suffered the loss is or is not a guest?
10. What might have been the result today, if the judge in *Rex v. Ivens*, 1835, had held that innkeepers only have a duty to receive travelers during daytime hours?

NOTES

1. Thomas A. Dickerson, *Travel Law*. Law Journal Seminars Press, New York, sec. 106(1).
2. Virginia Code, William F. Ritchie, Richmond, Virginia, 1849. Title 28, Taverns, Travel and Highways and Patrols, sec. 4.
3. *E. H. v. Overlook Lodge*, 638 So. 2d 781 (Alabama 1994).
4. *Ellcott v. Iyenn v. James Winokeon, et at.*, 589 A. 2d 824 (Rhode Island 1991).
5. Nevada Revised Statutes, 447.020 to 447.210.
6. *Italiano v. N.Y.*, 59 A.D. 2d 820, 399 N.Y.S. 2d 727 (1977).
7. *Walling v. Potter*, 35 Conn. 183, 185 (1868).
8. *People v. Thorpe*, 101 N.Y.S. 2d 986 (New York 1950).
9. *International v. Walter Lee et at.*, 925 F. 2d 576 (S.D. New York 1991).
10. *Byers v. Lemay*, 282 S.W. 2d 512 (Missouri 1955).
11. *Steele v. Holiday Inns, Inc.*, 626 So. 2d 593 (Mississippi 1993).
12. Nevada Revised Statutes, 651.075.
13. *People v. Hegedus*, 443 N.W. 2d 127 (Michigan 1989).

12

Duties of Innkeepers to Guests, Patrons, Invitees, and Third Parties

Overview

IN THIS CHAPTER, we continue the topic that was under discussion in Chapter 11. Almost all of the matters of law encountered here find application in all hotel, hospitality, and tourism enterprises. The primary duty of all operations is to use ordinary and reasonable care taking into consideration "foreseeability."

In *Rogers v. People*,[1] an old New York state case, the judge said that ". . . the inn is regarded as part of the house of the innkeeper . . . ." And an old adage tells us that "the devil will enter the safest of homes." This happens most often because of negligence of the innkeeper, acting through her or his employees and agents.

Negligence, synonymous with carelessness, forms the basis for the vast majority of lawsuits filed in our courts today. An example of negligence is a statement to an arriving traveler that "it is safe to park your car and U-Haul trailer in our back lot" when in fact security personnel go through the back lot only every two hours. This, then, is a misrepresentation, and if the trailer is looted during the night, the responsibility for the loss could well be placed on the hotel.

Negligence takes many forms in HH&T operations. It often poses dangers to guests, patrons, invitees, and third parties.

Dangers Facing Walking Guests and Patrons

Mr. X, a guest at a motel, is walking around, and no signs warn him to watch his progress. What legal dangers may await him?

1. An "open space illusion" may exist. He thinks his path is clear, and he walks into a plate glass window that shatters, causing injury.
2. "Dark shadows" obscure the path he is taking, and he does not see a 4-inch step that causes him to step out and fall forward, causing injury.
3. The "sun-bright" glare of the afternoon sun obscures his vision. He falls into a hole and is injured.

4. The carpeted exit from the restaurant appears level, but ten feet from the door there is a wheelchair ramp that slopes downward. He steps out, falls forward, and is injured.

5. The sidewalk outside of the motel contains a hole that is not readily noticeable, and it causes a fall with resulting injuries.

6. A step that had a yellow stripe painted across its edge as a warning has become so worn that the yellow no longer shows, and Mr. X falls down the step.[2]

A variety of other legal dangers can arise in unexpected situations, giving rise to a claim of negligence against a business. A family vacationing at the Caribbean Beach Hotel in the Virgin Islands was having dinner on New Year's Eve. The ten-year-old son of the family agreed to bring a flaming cherries jubilee to his father. As the boy watched, the waiter started to pour 150-proof rum on the flame out of a slow-pour cap on the rum bottle. The flame climbed the flow of rum, blew the spout out, creating a miniature flame thrower, which burned the boy severely. It had been prior practice to pour a small amount of rum into a separate container and add it to the flame carefully. The direct pour was negligent, and a large verdict was returned against the hotel.[3]

The following excerpt is from *The Hotel and Casino Law Letter*, written by James O. Eiler, Esq. It has to do with the legal duty of providing a safe place to stay.

> The innkeeper is not an insurer of the safety of the guest. The only duty is to use ordinary, reasonable care in providing a safe place to stay. "Owner or operator of motel is not insurer of customer who uses premises, but only owes duty to maintain premises in reasonable safe and suitable conditions," *Buck v. Del City Apartments Inc.*, 431 P. 2d 360.
>
> With this in mind, the innkeeper must act as a reasonable person would in the maintenance of his or her property. And in the absence of this reasonable care, the innkeeper could be held liable to the guest in the event of injury under the law of torts, "a violation of a duty imposed by general law," *Blacks Law Dictionary*, 5th ed., or negligence, "the omission to do something which a reasonable man would do," *Blacks Law Dictionary*, 5th ed.
>
> "A hotel proprietor is not an insurer of safety of customers, and is only liable for injuries resulting from his negligence and is bound to exercise reasonable care to keep premises in reasonable safe condition for customers and others invited expressly or impliedly to enter," *Alsup v. Saratoga Hotel*, 229 P. 2d 985.
>
> This brings us to the question of the relationship between the innkeeper and persons injured. There are three [primary] classes of persons who can be injured: invitees, licensees and trespassers. Invitees, which include the inn guest, *Wagner v. Coronet Hotel*, 458 P. 2d 390, are invited onto the premises for the advantage of the innkeeper. To this type of person the innkeeper owes the highest duty of care, and must inform these persons of any latent or known danger. Therefore, the innkeeper must use reasonable care "to discover actual conditions of premises and make them safe or warn business visitor of any dangerous condition" *Silverton v. Marler*, 389 P. 2d 3.
>
> The second type of person is a licensee, "any person who comes upon the land with a privilege arising from the consent of the possessor," Prosser, *Law of Torts Hornbook*, 4th ed. This type of person comes onto the land for the advantage of themselves and not the innkeeper. This could include guests of guests. For this person, too, the innkeeper must warn of dangers. But once a licensee becomes aware

of dangerous conditions, does not adhere to such warnings and injury occurs, the inn may not be liable under the assumption of risk doctrine, "where plaintiff assumes consequences of injury occurring through fault of defendant" *Blacks Law Dictionary*, 5th ed., or under the doctrine of contributory negligence, "the act of omission amounting to want of ordinary care on part of complaining party" *Blacks Law Dictionary*, 5th ed.

In either case, the "proximate cause," "that which . . . produces the injury, and without which the result would not have happened" *Blacks Law Dictionary*, 5th ed., would be the deciding factor of liability, *Dempsey v. Alamo Hotel*, 418 P. 2d 58, and in most states this is decided by a jury, *Worth v. Reed*, 384 P. 2d 1017.

The third type of person is a trespasser, "a person who enters or remains upon land in the possession of another without a privilege to do so" (*Second Restatement of Torts*, Sec. 329). This person is not a guest of the inn. In this case, the innkeeper is not obligated to warn the trespasser of dangers that might exist. The "duty of hotelkeeper to exercise ordinary and reasonable care [is] to keep in reasonable safe condition those parts of the hotel where guests are invited or expected to go" *Balin v. Lysle, Rishel Post No. 68, American Legion, Hutchinson*, 280 P. 2d 623.

Not only must the innkeeper act as a reasonable person would and warn of dangerous conditions, the innkeeper must "foresee" what might happen if he does not correct dangerous conditions. "Proprietor of hotel has duty to warn invitee of latent dangers of which he knows or in exercise of reasonable care should have known and to take reasonable precautions to protect invitee from dangers which are foreseeable from arrangement or use of premises" *Mickel v. Haines Enterprises, Inc.*, 400 P. 2d 518.

If drunk, the plaintiff might still have claimed the protection of his host as did Falstaff when he fell asleep "behind the arras" and might say with him: "Shall I not take mine ease in mine inn, but I shall have my pocket picked?"[4]

LEGAL STATISTICS AND RISK ASSESSMENT

Studies show that 50 percent of the verdicts against hotels now exceed $100,000. Verdicts against hotels now are 70 percent in favor of the plaintiffs and, more frightening, 40 percent of jury verdicts against hotels exceed $1 million. This heavy legal assault requires that many practical matters be carried out at the place of business. An example is "risk assessment."

Today, management must draw upon observations from professionals outside of the business itself. Insurance agents, police officers, firefighters, and others should be invited to visit the operation and give their views of what they observe as they tour the business. This assessment should be carried out twice a year, or at least annually, and the innkeeper always should accompany these visitors. Examples of potential dangers include areas where persons may hide unnoticed while waiting to assault guests and others; inadequate lighting that increases the danger of falling; overgrown vegetation on the hotel grounds and on adjoining premises as well; areas where there may be open access to the hotel; and a lack of security plans.

Evaluations should be ongoing, and records must be kept of the suggestions made. In turn, steps must be taken to give fruition to these suggestions. The records should show who made the assessments, the date, and what was done to correct any deficiencies found. The records could prove valuable in later court actions brought against the hotel.

The innkeeper should review any accident reports, reports of suspicious persons, police printouts made available to the hotel, reports of security personnel, restaurant and bar reports, and others for the previous twenty-four hours. Armed with this information, the hotel premises should be walked at least once a day, a report made, and deficiencies corrected. This amounts to a mini-risk assessment program, but it can have great value if the hotel is charged with negligence in court.

The walking routine is akin to the airline captain who leaves the cockpit during flight and walks to the rear of the plane and back to the cabin. While he or she extends goodwill on the way, he or she will be looking at the wings, the bulkheads, the locked doors, and in general, things that could cause problems during the flight.

Another method of detecting problems is to require employees in their daily route to report problems to management. After learning of potential dangers, whether learned by professionals or the innkeeper, failing to take immediate steps to correct such known problems or dangers can be negligence in itself.

OPEN AND OBVIOUS DANGERS

A viable defense to the claim that an innkeeper failed to warn of dangers is that those dangers were open and obvious to the injured person. In *Much Ado About Nothing*, William Shakespeare wrote, "Let every eye negotiate for itself and trust no agent." This phrase has legal application to guests, patrons, invitees, and others in the HH&T industries. If these persons have a clear view of dangers but fail to notice them, the legal burden may shift to them for their losses. On the other hand, if a danger that cannot be perceived is known to management and a warning is not given, the hotel can be looked to for any economic loss that results.[5]

When a danger is open and obvious to a reasonable, careful, prudent person in charge of all of his or her faculties such as sight, hearing, touch, and smell, that person should not be able to place responsibility upon the business. The Michigan court, however, does not see it that way. It has held that there is still an affirmative (positive) legal duty to warn of open and obvious dangers.[6]

Some dangers, of course, are not in plain view and yet might be known to those who live in the locale of the hotel. In those instances, a positive legal duty arises to warn guests who are not locals. Prominently posted at the front doors at the Holiday Inn at Kearney, Nebraska, is a sign that says "High winds often pull doors from guests' hands as they are opened."

WHAT IS "REASONABLY DETECTABLE"?

The cases developing make it clear that they will hold businesses responsible for any dangers that could have been discovered by applying a reasonable amount of thought, insight, and energy. This is a heavy burden and probably will increase as the courts require higher standards.

Will innkeepers and other industry managers have to consult a crystal ball to predict the future? Must they now begin to predict the unexpected? Must one foresee what cannot be foreseen? Further court action will have to be taken to answer questions such as these, but more stringent standards certainly will develop in the future.

What is certain is that dangers *are* foreseeable if there are any existing means of finding them out. The means of discovery may not in fact be within the innkeeper's personal knowledge, but if the information is available, the courts are going to hold that the dangers should have been foreseen.

GRIDS

Police Grids

A major source of information that can be of great value to any business today consists of records of crimes and other incidents maintained by police departments across the nation. These are known in law enforcement circles as *police grids.*

As standard practice in police work, the geographical areas of police jurisdiction are divided into grids or squares and are given appropriate number and letter designations. These grids follow police precinct lines such as are found in New York City, or block designations in cities or magisterial districts in counties.

As crimes are reported and investigated, the police reports are tied to the grids within which they occurred. This information is computerized and made available so projections can be made about possible crimes in the future. On a state level, serial killers have been tracked down using such data in joint cooperation with other states.

Theme parks, inns, motels, hotels, and others can develop a similar grid system on a smaller scale. The source of data to establish grids would be the reports that must be created and filed for injuries, thefts, muggings, and other losses.

A Grid System at a Hotel

Innkeeper Smith, being a careful, observant person, obtains an architects' drawing of the hotel and its confines and then creates a list of "areas" such as the following:

        Area A: front desk and lobby
        Area B: elevators
        Area C: meeting rooms
        Area D: guest rooms and corridors in East Wing
        Area E: guest rooms and corridors in West Wing
        Area F: kitchen and associated areas
        Area G: restaurant(s)
        Area H: bar(s)
        Area I: receiving and storage
        Area J: maintenance, heating, cooling, garbage collection

If Smith increases the detail of the areas, such as subdividing them, a numbering system should be added to the letters to accommodate the greater number of grids.

To activate the developing system, a copy of the letter/number list should be circulated to all persons who have the responsibility for making crime and accident reports. These persons must be instructed to add the "grid designation" to the "location" on these reports.

The same idea can be carried over to individual rooms via room-security charts, assembled in a looseleaf notebook. If properly analyzed, they can provide the basis for increased room security.

Guidelines and questions have been laid down to create a room security chart:

1. Have crimes occurred in this room before?
2. If so, what type of crimes?
3. How frequently have these crimes occurred?
4. Did these crimes occur when the room was occupied or vacant?
5. What type of crimes occurred?[7]

Creating room security charts means nothing, of course, if they are not analyzed and if actions are not taken to implement the corrective steps indicated.

Two other questions arise in reference to room-security charts and other grid areas as well.

1. Do property crimes alert management to the possibility that crimes of violence may follow?
2. Might the absence of arrests by the police encourage those committing the crimes to increase their activities to include acts of violence?

This process will also assist in locating areas where injuries such as falls are likely to occur again in the future. The grid principle and room-security chart systems do not stop at the business itself: they extend to adjacent properties as well.

Crime and Theft Grids, Adjacent Properties

In a 1979 case, the court held that if a hotel knows of crimes committed at other places of businesses in close proximity to the hotel, a positive duty arises to warn guests, patrons, and invitees of these dangers.[8]

INNKEEPERS AS POLICE OFFICERS?

The innkeeper's primary duty is to summon police assistance as quickly as possible and lend help as may be needed by the professionals. There is one time, however, when an innkeeper should perform a police-like function. This is at a crime scene at the inn before the police arrive.

Preservation of a Crime Scene

If a crime occurs at the inn, three things must be done immediately.

1. Notify the appropriate authorities, providing enough detail to guide them to the scene.
2. Secure the areas where the crime occurred. Order persons milling about out of the area. Warn those present not to touch any object or pick up any item lying at or near the scene.

3. Detail a specific person to meet the authorities as they arrive and guide them to the scene.

Once the authorities arrive, management and employees should revert to their business postures and allow the authorities to seal off the crime scene formally.

Detention of Suspected Criminals and Suspicious Persons

Related to the crime scene issue is the matter of suspected criminals and suspicious persons, before crimes actually are committed. On-premises security guards, or employees in some instances, sometimes confront suspected criminals and suspicious persons. Can these persons be detained lawfully while summoning outside professional assistance?

Louisiana has a procedure that must be followed to detain a guest, patron, invitee, or other person while police authorities are being called. First, the detention must be "authorized." To be authorized, a four-point test must be met:

1. The detention must be carried out by an authorized employee or agent, such as an in-house security guard, or a guard hired from a security agency.
2. There must be reasonable cause to believe the detained person has committed a crime.
3. The detention must be carried out without using unreasonable force.
4. The detention has a deadline of sixty minutes. Police authorities must be summoned and arrive to take over by that time, or the detained person must be released.

The Louisiana "detention rule" is valid only in that state. As part of the in-house grid, and room-security room chart systems, it must be determined what the detention rule is in the state in question. The greatest danger is a future civil claim by a wrongfully detained person of "false imprisonment." A successful legal claim on this grounds has led to large civil verdicts against a variety of businesses. Another police-like matter that faces innkeepers is the use of in-house security personnel.

Security Guards

Another police-like matter involves whether security guards at the business should be armed. This question faces many hospitality personnel, especially when the facility is located in high-crime areas. Innkeeper Smith needs both legal and practical advice in answering this question. Guns carried by guards are used more often on the guards and on innocent bystanders than they are on those who commit crimes.

The policy on armed guards followed by Marriott Hotels, Resorts and Suites provides one possible answer. This business allows only off-duty police officers who are serving as security guards to carry arms, and then only during special events when difficulties are foreseeable. At all other times, security guards are not allowed to be armed.

At an extremely profitable and popular Las Vegas hotel and casino, a different policy is followed as to arming security personnel. They are present at all entrances, around the lobby, in the hallways, at the elevators, and all around the parking lots. The guests, invitees, and patrons can see that these personnel carry no weapons at all. What guests, invitees, and patrons cannot see, however, is a five-person contingent, fully armed, helmeted with bullet-proof vests, dressed in solid black, and located at a central point at the hotel. This is a "flying squad" that can be summoned by a secured phone call. This squad is rotated at appropriate times and is on duty around the clock. The expense of such a set-up is prohibitive to most businesses, yet it does provide an alternative to visible security guards carrying weapons.

All appropriate personnel must have an available "menu" of phone numbers by which professional personnel, including police, fire departments, and paramedics can be summoned. This menu must be available twenty-four hours a day and be utilized immediately as required. This is now recognized as legal duty. Failure to comply with this requirement, where it becomes the cause of death or unnecessary injury, can render the business responsible in later court actions.[9]

Incident, Crime, and Injury Reports

What we have seen thus far in this chapter can mean little if we do not create and carefully analyze incident, crime, and injury reports. It is good business legal policy to have an attorney create a report form that can be used in making records of incidents, crimes, and injuries. A variety of such forms need not be created, but they must contain appropriate spaces and directions on how they should be used. A good house policy is to designate a person on each work shift who will have the responsibility of filling out the forms immediately.

A certain amount of judgment must be exercised in using these forms. Routine and trivial matters need not be reported. If doubt arises, however, the doubt should be resolved by filling out the form. In all injury, theft, assault, or death cases, the forms become mandatory. Filling out reports is a large part of the job of all law enforcement persons across the nation. This is also true of HH&T personnel.

As part of the job description of the people who must fill out these reports, there should be a requirement that they review the reports once a day and add their analysis—even hunches they may have gained. The reports, and the additions, then must be passed on to management for further analysis. In this process, follow-up action that is needed must not be forgotten.[10]

The following is concerned with alcohol sales, designed for those actively engaged in the day-to-day operation of hotels, hospitality, and tourism functions.

> Document every step, not just cutting off a drinker. If you call a cab for someone, if you provide a room for lodging, if you call a spouse to come and get someone, if you work closely with a designated driver—all of those things should be recorded. That will make a difference to a plaintiff's lawyer should an incident occur.
>
> A plaintiff's attorney who doesn't have a property to pick on is going to be more reluctant to file a lawsuit. If a lawsuit is filed, that attorney will be far more reasonable in negotiating a settlement if there is a paper trail that speaks to the property's concern and past history of decisive action to prevent alcohol-related accidents" [and other incidents.][11]

As to filling out reports, an excellent management attitude to adopt is this:

> Records mandated by statutes such as guest registration, elevator and escalator repairs, and records that the common law could reasonably expect to be kept, such as theft, injury or death records, will be preserved for a reasonable time. Thus, what the statutes require, we will provide. What the common law expects, we will also provide.

Record Retention

Once reports and records are created and used properly, a final question arises: How long should we keep these records? The five-year statute of limitations provided by the IRS and the four-year statute of limitations of the Uniform Commercial Codes provide an answer.

OTHER EXAMPLES OF INNKEEPERS' LEGAL DUTIES

The duty of the innkeeper to keep the business premises safe for guests, patrons, invitees, and third persons has long been held to be nondelegable. This duty cannot be passed on (delegated) to others, so as to relieve the innkeeper of legal responsibility. Breach of this duty has been a constant source of court action including negligently building a front door that causes an injury;[12] spilling sulfuric acid on a dance floor, causing a patron to slip and suffer acid burns;[13] absence of smoke alarms and sprinklers, resulting in harm to guests;[14] unsafe window latches, allowing a child to fall to his death;[15] failing to keep outside areas lighted, resulting in a fall of a guest;[16] and failing to provide door locks that cannot be opened from the outside.[17]

On the other hand, an innkeeper does not have to guard against the abnormal or unusual;[18] does not have to provide a fireproof hotel;[19] need not be a nurse for a child;[20] or have screens in windows.[21] The law does not expect perfection, but it does expect ordinary and reasonable care, taking into consideration all of the facts and surrounding circumstances including foreseeability.

The law *does* expect the innkeeper to warn of known, concealed dangers[22] and to warn not only those who make ordinary use of facilities—such as a swimming pool—but to warn those who make customary use of a facility, when use is known to the innkeeper.[23] An example of this was observed at an inn where the neighborhood kids would climb the fence and swim in their clothes after the pool closed for the night. The duty to warn of hidden dangers would extend to them because the innkeeper was aware of their actions.

The State of Georgia enacted a statute requiring that hotels post exit instructions in all "sleeping rooms, meeting rooms and other rooms open to the public."[24] These regulations specifically require that a warning notice be placed above each elevator button in hotels and motels in that state, saying, "In the event of fire, do not use this elevator." The regulations then provide that "evacuation routes be shown" by arrows disclosing the nearest route to the exit.

When operations provide parking facilities for their guests, or patrons, they must realistically take into consideration the surrounding facts and circumstances. Must those who park there walk through an unlighted area? Is there dangerous traffic on a street they must cross? Is the parking lot located in a high-crime area? Are there other reasons why a person parking in the lot should be on the lookout for his or her personal safety? The common-law requirement that innkeepers exercise reasonable care comes to the front in such circumstances.[25]

Does an innkeeper have a duty to warn guests after another guest has been robbed at gunpoint? What if no warning is given and the robber remains on the premises and then robs again later? Does the second victim have a cause of action against the hotel in negligence for failing to warn? Case law in Arizona indicates that no such duty exists, but common sense dictates that, until it is certain that the robber has departed, the innkeeper should assume the robber is still on the premises and guests should be warned accordingly.

The courts tend to excuse innkeepers from the duty to warn of dangers where those dangers are so obvious as to alert guests to stay away from them. As a situation in point, a snow- and ice-covered hill is located behind a motel. A guest tries to climb the hill, then falls and is injured. Most courts would excuse the innkeeper from liability.[26] When the hotel wants to claim that a danger resulting in an injury to a guest was "obvious," it must be remembered that if such danger was obvious to the guest, it also should have been obvious to the hotel. In that regard, a court might hold that the hotel should have removed the danger.

Many lawsuits were brought against the former MGM Grand Hotel in Las Vegas as a result of a fire there in 1980, leaving eighty-seven dead and hundreds injured. A little-noted side issue of this disaster was the claims filed against the hotel alleging failure to provide fire warnings in Spanish. The complaint alleged that, while MGM solicited foreign-speaking guests, it did not provide multilingual signs for fire drills or safety information.

The dangerous character of chemicals and equipment used at the pool must be communicated in English, and other languages if appropriate, to users of that facility. Signs must be posted, and employees must be trained to provide such warnings. A court may well hold failure to do so to be negligent.[27]

Management of Sam's Town Hotel and Casino, located in Las Vegas, Nevada, came to realize that, although the property was popular and successful, room security was a serious problem. The old hotel portion of the complex had been constructed in a giant "U" with the two open wings pointing away from the casino and the front-desk area. This design enabled those who were so inclined to have direct access to first-floor rooms from outside windows. These persons would be out of sight of those in the front portions of the hotel. Being knowledgeable businesspersons, and also being innkeepers who endeavor to use ordinary care in the operation of their business, management had steel bars installed across all first-floor windows to prevent entry from the outside. These bars are welded into squares to cover each window. Making that decision eliminated one legal danger but created a second one: Would those bars deny window exit to guests who may become trapped in their rooms because of smoke or fire? This problem was recognized and solved by installing a release device on each window that allowed the bars to swing outward, giving clear exit to anyone in the room.

Thus, an initial legal problem was solved by creating a second problem, which in turn also had to be resolved. As it turned out, the second problem led to yet another: What if occupants of the rooms were not aware of the release? Was it foreseeable that some guests in the rooms, confronted by fire or other emergency, might think the bars on the windows would prevent them from ready exit to the outside? The management thought so and created signs made of brilliant red plastic material with white letters, measuring 7" by 13"; each first-floor room has such a sign located on the wall near the window with a large arrow pointing toward the release button. The sign says, in large letters, "In Case of Fire, Push Button to Open Security Bar." These signs are not particularly attractive and may in fact cause concern to some persons who occupy these rooms. Management would have avoided their use if an alternative had been available. Unfortunately, there was no alternative; the facts and the duty to warn require that those signs not only be there, but, also, in case someone should decide to remove one for a souvenir, that it be replaced promptly.

One court expanded this duty to a higher level. It held that "there is an affirmative [positive] duty not to increase the peril of guests . . . ."[28]

Adjacent Properties

Not so long ago, the courts viewed a hotel as an independent operation, divorced from businesses adjacent to it, and having no concerns about other businesses in the vicinity. This began to change a few years back.

The criminal problems of society in general become the criminal problems of each state. These problems then become of concern to the counties and cities in the state. Police grids kick in, and the problems of one part of the city become warnings to another. The problems on one city block, then, can become the problems of all on that block. It naturally follows that the problems of an adjacent business become of concern to the inn contiguous to it.[29]

Liability of the innkeeper, in some instances, can extend to injuries of guests that occur on adjacent properties. This usually happens when exits from the inn property do not warn of dangers that exist on the adjacent property, such as boulders on the state-owned beach in front of the inn.[30]

Constructive Notice

Assume that an ice maker is leaking water on the floor at the bottom of the stairs at the hotel, and guests have tracked that water up the stairs. The steps are not lighted properly and those going up and down do not notice the water on the stairs. This condition exists for several days but is not reported to the innkeeper, although the employees notice it.

Under these facts, the courts will hold that, though the hotel did not have actual notice of the danger, it still had "constructive knowledge" of it. The condition existed for such a time that it should have been reported and corrected. When someone is injured because of this dangerous condition, the hotel will be held responsible.[31]

Imputed Knowledge

Related to constructive notice is inputed knowledge. If an employee at a hotel knows of the violent nature of a guest or patron but fails to convey that information to the innkeeper, the law says that "what the employee knew, the hotel knew." This rule imputes (attributes) the knowledge of the employee to the innkeeper, and if there is a failure to warn others or to call promptly for police assistance, the hotel can be held responsible for losses, injury, or death that follows.[32]

Duty to Warn: An Extreme Example

At a hotel that is part of a national chain, located less than one mile from the international footbridge that separates El Paso, Texas, from Cuidad Juárez, Mexico, a sophisticated warning system is in operation. The parking areas contain large signs warning of the dangers of theft of property from autos. As one checks in at the front desk, the information and warning are given verbally of the high-crime situation there each day and night. As one enters the elevator, wall signs warn "to have the room key in hand when the elevator stops and to proceed quickly to the guest room and lock one's-self in." Upon entering the room, a warning from the El Paso Chief of Police about the crime situation is posted on the dresser mirror.

Duty to Inform

Related to the duty to warn is the duty to inform. Opening and closing times of swimming pools, weight rooms, game rooms, and check-in and check-out times are not matters for the traveler/guest to decide. These are house matters that must be part of the house rules. Establishing such rules, however, is not enough. The traveler/guest must be informed of them.

A court writing in the 1950s said it this way:

> The traveler should know precisely what he has to do before he can be chargeable with negligence for not doing it.[33]

Duty to Supervise

The duty to warn and to inform is complemented by the duty to supervise. This duty often involves minors and people with disabilities. Once the duty to warn has been met, the duty to supervise has commenced. If the activity warned of concerns continuing danger, or if children or invalids are involved, the duty to supervise arises. The hotel then must send sufficient personnel to ensure that that duty is met. The duty to warn and supervise increases when small children who are mobile, and infants who are not, are guests.[34]

When it becomes evident that numerous children are present, the standard of care must be upgraded until that condition returns to normal levels.

An excellent house rule to implement is that children who use game rooms or video rooms must be accompanied by an adult. A conspicuous sign to that effect should be posted at the entrance of the room or arcade, and the rule should be enforced.

Duty to Protect Guests from Employees and Others

A primary duty of employees is to see that guests are not injured from any cause. This duty rests squarely upon the innkeeper by virtue of both common law and agency law. If an employee negligently or deliberately injures a guest, tort liability falls on the employee. Liability also may fall upon the innkeeper. The liability on the innkeeper would be for the full extent of the loss and would be based upon *respondeat superior* (let the master answer) or upon the contract theory of liability.

For this rule to work, the employee must be on duty and acting in the scope of his or her employment. Yet, it has been held that an innkeeper was responsible for molestation of a 15-year-old guest by an employee who was *not* acting in the scope of his employment at the time, but, nevertheless, was on the premises when the attack took place.[35] The responsibility of the innkeeper in this area is approaching strict liability and comes close to the duty the law places on common carriers for injuries caused to passengers by employees.

Conversely, the innkeeper has a duty to protect employees from guests and others as well. This places the innkeeper in a position where he or she must protect guests from employees, other guests, and third parties; protect employees from guests and third parties; protect third parties from guests, third parties, and employees; and provide the security to see that all of this is done.

Guests often invite others to their rooms or to dinner at the hotel's dining facility. This compounds the responsibilities of the innkeeper, especially when an employee injures guests of guests. Yet, these persons are not "guests" within the innkeeping meaning, as they have not been accepted by the innkeeper. The law is not quite as strict in this area and provides some protection for the innkeeper.

When one comes to visit a registered guest for a lawful purpose, that person, at law, is an invitee of the guest. The innkeeper owes to that person some of the legal duties owed to the registered guest.[36] A visitor of a guest, thus, is entitled to be warned that the doors lock automatically once a person steps outside. When a guest of a guest was raped because she could not get back inside, the hotel was held responsible.[37] In a pool drowning case, the court held that the guest of a registered guest was entitled to the same protection as the guest, holding the hotel liable for the death of the social guest.[38]

Obligations imposed by the courts will be measured by the legal status occupied by the plaintiff the time of injury, death, or other loss. For example, if the plaintiff was a guest when the loss occurred, one standard of measurement will be applied. If the person was an invitee at the time of loss, another legal measurement will be applied.[39]

If a guest invites a nonguest to the hotel, the innkeeper should use care and caution before excluding that person. Even though such a person would not in fact be a guest, the duties of the innkeeper could well come into play. This is especially true if the innkeeper is aware of the facts. Care and diplomacy are in order. If the invited nonguest is there for immoral or illegal purposes, or if the invited nonguest engages in obnoxious or undesirable conduct, the innkeeper could exclude on those grounds.

CASE INTRODUCTION: CAMPBELL CASE

In the following case, an innkeeper wound up in court because of the refusal to admit the wife of a guest to the guest's room. The court spells out the law, and the innkeeper prevailed in the end. But it might have been better to have admitted the wife after determining that the husband was expecting her. Still, caution is in order. If the wife had been admitted and if she had removed property of the husband, the innkeeper might have been held responsible for that property. This case was decided in a "community property" state, Louisiana, which also is a "civil-law" state. Under community-property law, husbands and wives are deemed to jointly own all property acquired during marriage. It makes no difference who pays for it. Although community-property rights are mentioned in the case, they have no effect on the outcome.

CAMPBELL V. WOMACK
345 So. 2d 96 (Louisiana App. 1977)

EDWARDS, Judge.

This suit was brought by Elvin Campbell and his wife for damages resulting from breach of contract and embarrassment, humiliation and mental anguish, sustained by Mrs. Campbell as a result of the defendants' refusal to admit Mrs. Campbell to her husband's motel room. The defendants' motion for summary judgment was granted and the action was dismissed. From this dismissal, plaintiffs have appealed.

Plaintiff, Elvin Campbell, is engaged in the sand and gravel business. Since the nature of his business often requires his absence from his home in St. Francisville, Mr. Campbell generally obtains temporary accommodations in the area in which he is working. For this purpose, Mr. Campbell rented a double room on a month to month basis at the Rodeway Inn, in Morgan City, Louisiana. The room was registered in Mr. Campbell's name only.

From time to time, Mr. Campbell would share his room with certain of his employees; in fact, he obtained additional keys for the convenience of these employees. It also appears that Mr. Campbell was joined by his wife on some weekends and holidays, and that they jointly occupied his room on those occasions. However, Mrs. Campbell was not given a key to the motel room. On one such weekend, Mrs. Campbell, arriving while her husband was not at the motel, attempted to obtain the key to her husband's room from the desk clerk, Barbara Womack. This request was denied, since the desk clerk found that Mrs. Campbell was neither a registered guest for that room nor had the registered guest, her husband, communicated to the motel management, his authorization to release his room key to Mrs. Campbell. Plaintiffs allege that this refusal was in a loud, rude, and abusive manner. After a second request and refusal, Mrs. Campbell became distressed, left the Rodeway Inn, and obtained a room at another motel. Shortly thereafter, suit was filed against the motel and the desk clerk, Barbara Womack.

Plaintiffs' main contention is that Mrs. Campbell was entitled to a key to her husband's room since she had acquired the status of a guest from her previous stays with her husband in the motel room. The leading pronouncement in Louisiana on the creation of a guest status is found in *Moody v. Kenny,* 153 La. 1007, 97 So. 21 (1923). There it is stated at page 22:

> . . . a mere guest of the registered occupant of a room at a hotel, who shares such room with its occupant without the knowledge or consent of the hotel management, would not be a guest of the hotel, as there would be no contractual relations in such case between such third person and the hotel. . . .

Plaintiffs would have us conclude from this statement that once the motel management gained knowledge on the previous occasions that Mrs. Campbell was sharing the motel room with the registered occupant, the motel was thereafter estopped to deny Mrs. Campbell the key to that room. The fallacy of this argument is apparent, since under it even a casual visitor to a hotel guest's room would be entitled to return at a later time and demand a key to the guest's room, so long as the hotel management had knowledge of the initial visit.

The motel clerk was under no duty to give Mrs. Campbell, a third party, the key to one of its guest's rooms. In fact, the motel had an affirmative duty, stemming from a guest's rights of privacy and peaceful possession, not to allow unregistered and unauthorized third parties to gain access to the rooms of its guest (cf. LSA—C.C. art. 2965-67).

The additional fact that Mrs. Campbell offered proof of her identity and her marital relation with the room's registered occupant does not alter her third-party status; nor does it lessen the duty owed by the motel to its guest. The mere fact of marriage does not imply that the wife has full authorization from her husband at all times and as to all matters, (LSA—C.C. art. 2404). Besides, how could Mrs. Campbell prove to the motel's satisfaction that the then present marital situation was amicable? This information is not susceptible of ready proof.

The plaintiffs further contend that since the rental contract was entered into during the existence of their marriage, it was therefore a community asset, and that Mrs. Campbell was entitled to the use of the motel room based on her rights in the community. We need not reach the issue of Mrs. Campbell's community property rights in the motel room, since under the clear language of LSA—C.C. art. 2404, she had no right to enforce the rental contract.

Having found that Mrs. Campbell was not entitled to demand a key to the motel room, and further that no authorization to admit her was communicated to the motel by her husband, there was no breach of contract.

Accordingly, the trial court properly granted defendants' motion for summary judgment. For the reasons assigned the judgment of the trial court is affirmed at appellants' cost. AFFIRMED.

MISCELLANEOUS DUTIES

A variety of other duties arise in innkeeping. The following are some final examples.

Suitable Accommodations

An innkeeper must furnish the kind of accommodations and other services that reasonably could be expected to be found at that particular location.

Courteous Treatment

A guest has the right to receive courteous treatment from the innkeeper, the employees, and agents. The duty of courteous treatment is as old as the law of innkeeping itself and will be implied in the hotel-guest relationship. An innkeeper must school employees and agents on the need to be courteous to arriving and departing guests while they are in, as well as outside of, the hotel.

Solo Travelers

Some basic house rules have to be created and implemented for all solo travelers, and all employees and agents should be instructed accordingly. The following guidelines have been adapted from court cases in which solo travelers have suffered injury or property loss at hotels.

1. Once the hotel employee sees that he or she is dealing with a solo traveler, a second employee should be alerted to monitor the check-in process.
2. The location of the hotel room assigned should not be disclosed verbally.
3. The guest should be accompanied to the room.
4. Before the employee departs, it should be determined that no one else is in the room.
5. Once the guest is in the room, a call should be made from the front desk to make sure that everything is okay. During this call, it should be made clear that assistance is always available.

In most instances, the offer of assistance is declined. When that occurs, the burden of any losses or injuries to the guest shifts to the guest.

A Legal Duty to Rescue?

Does an innkeeper, through his or her agents, have a duty to rescue a guest who has gotten into a life-threatening situation? As a general legal principle, the common law does not place a duty upon the industry to rescue those who may get into a position of peril unless the peril was caused by the innkeeper or its agents.[40] If a fire breaks out, professional help must be sought as quickly as possible. There is, however, no duty on the innkeeper to attempt to enter a burning room and assist a guest.

If rescue is attempted by hotel personnel, as it might well be under certain circumstances, and if the rescue attempt is carried out carelessly, that could well give rise to a cause of action in tort for the negligent rescue attempt.

Because of the latter situation, many states have enacted "Good Samaritan" laws designed to hold harmless one who steps forward in an attempt to rescue but who perhaps does so in a careless manner. As a general legal rule, however, rescue is best left to the professionals. A judge had this to say about rescue:

> Whether a duty initially exists to come to the aid of another, it is clear that once the hotelkeeper does come to the aid of the guest or patron, he will be liable to the guest if through his negligence he puts him in a worse condition than that in which he found him or causes the guest to refrain from taking any steps for his protection by causing him to rely on the hotelkeeper's assistance.
>
> Because of the possibility of fraud occasioned by the above rule, a number of states have adopted "Good Samaritan" statutes which bar recovery against the rescuer in the absence of proof of willful or wantonly inflicted harm. The New York Education Law, section 6527, exempts from civil liability licensed physicians who gratuitously render first aid or treatment at the scene of an accident or other emergency to a person who is ill, unconscious, or injured except in the case of gross negligence. Section 6611 applies this exemption to dentists, and section 6908 applies it to registered nurses and licensed practical nurses.[41]

Duties of Guests

To close the chapter, let's briefly examine the duties owed by guests. Breach of these duties gives rise to the right of the innkeeper to remove such persons as well as to sue for any losses caused. The principal duty a guest owes to an innkeeper is to conduct himself or herself in a courteous, reasonably dignified manner at all times. Guests should, but do not always, refrain from riding the tops of outside elevators; throwing furniture into pools; hanging from balconies; or running through the hotel with abandon. Such conduct can be used as a defense against actions brought against the innkeeper for injuries that grew out of such activities.

In *Gore v. Whitemore Hotel Co.*,[42] the court held that the guests were under a duty to refrain from unlawful and disorderly conduct that endangered the safety of others; that a willful violation of that duty forfeited the right of a guest to possession of the room; and that when the innkeeper became aware of the disorderly conduct of the guest, the innkeeper had a duty to exercise reasonable care to abate or keep down the condition, and had the right to remove the guest from the hotel.

Other duties of guests include the duty to pay for services and food and drink,[43] not burn down a hotel room, and not steal from the hotel.

Summary

The law is constantly raising the standards that must be met when it comes time to decide who must pay for an injury, property loss, or death. This has placed increasing legal responsibility upon owners, managers, agents, and employees of the HH&T industries. Police-type procedures must be used at HH&T properties to protect crime scenes; accurate reports of losses and crimes must be created and maintained; there is a duty to warn of dangers on adjacent properties; and a duty to protect guests from employees and employees from guests, patrons, and third parties.

The *Campbell v. Womack* case has taken its place as another "legal landmark," along with *Page v. Sloan* which was discussed in Chapter 4. Both of these cases provide major guidelines for hotel/motel/inn managers. The primary message of *Campbell v. Womack* is the legal right of the motel to deny admission to an unregistered person to the room of a registered guest.

Questions

1. List three dangers that face guests at hotels, motels, and inns.
2. Why must lodging facilities be properly maintained? Name two things that can be a danger to the facility if they are not so maintained.
3. What does "reasonably detectable" mean at law?
4. What is a "grid system" as it relates to hotel/motel law?
5. What does "open and obvious" mean as discussed in this chapter?
6. What are the police duties of innkeepers, if any?
7. Should security guards at hotels carry guns? Why or why not?

8. In two sentences, explain the duty to inform and the duty to supervise.
9. List three legal duties that guests owe to innkeepers.
10. True or false: The innkeeper/guest relationship is like the relationship of a landlord to a tenant.

NOTES

1. 86 N.Y. 366.
2. *Sherman v. Arno*, 383 P. 2d 741 (Arizona 1963).
3. *Young v. Caribbean Associates*, 358 F. Supp. 1220 (Virgin Islands 1973).
4. *Jalie v. Cardinal*, 35 Wis. 118 (Wisconsin 1879).
5. *Sistler v. Liberty*, 558 So. 2d 1106 (Louisiana 1990).
6. *Noumey v. Burger King Corp.*, 470 N.W. 2d 93 (Michigan 1991).
7. *MacQuarrie v. Howard Johnson Co.*, 877 F. 2d 126 (Delaware 1989).
8. *Walkoviak v. Hilton Hotels*, 580 S.W. 2d 623 (Texas 1979).
9. *Chestnut v. Ithaca*, 528 N.Y.S. 2d 723 (New York 1988).
10. *Churchman's v. Pinkerton's, Inc.*, 756 F. Supp. 55 (U. S. Dist. Ct., Kansas 1991); *Pelican, Inc. v. Downey*, 567 N.E. 2d 847 (Indiana 1991).
11. From *Hospitality Law*, volume 9, number 8, August 1994, page 2.
12. *Bardwell Motor Inn, Inc. v. Accavallo*, 381 A. 2d 1061 (Vt. 1977).
13. *Ott v. Faison*, 287 Ala. 700, 255 So. 2d 38 (1971).
14. *Mazer v. Sememza*, 177 So. 2d 880, 882 (Fla. App. 1965).
15. *Baker v. Dallas Hotel Co.*, 73 F. 2d 825 (5th Cir. 1934).
16. *Withrow v. Woozencraft*, 90 N.M. 48, 559 P. 2d 425 (1976).
17. *Garzilli v. Howard Johnson's Motor Lodges, Inc.*, 419 F. Supp. 1201 (E.D. N.Y. 1976) (the Connie Francis case).
18. 15 *supra.*
19. 16 *supra.*
20. 16 *supra.*
21. *Tarshis v. Lahaina Investment Corporation*, 480 F. 2d 1019 (9th Cir. 1973).
22. *First Arlington v. McQuire*, 311 So. 2d 146 (Fla. App. 1975).
23. *Tobin v. Slutsky*, 506 F. 2d 1097 (2d Cir. 1974).
24. Georgia Regulations, Section 120-3-3.05.
25. *Warrington v. Bird*, 499 A. 2d 1026 (New Jersey 1985).
26. *Graf v. State*, 498 N.Y.S. 2d 913 (New York 1986).
27. *Tucker v. Dixon*, 144 Colo. 79, 355 P. 2d 79 (Colorado 1960).
28. *Mayo v. Hyatt*, 718 F. Supp. 19 (Louisiana 1989).
29. *Lou's Corp v. Haskins*, 405 S.E. 2d 474 (Georgia 1991).
30. *Motel Properties, Inc. v. Miller*, 425 S.E. 2d 334 (Georgia 1992); see also *Ventura v. Winegardner*, 357 S.E. 2d 764 (West Virginia 1987).
31. *Kauffman v. Royal Orleans, Inc.*, 216 So. 2d 394 (Louisiana 1968).

32. *S. G. Catlett D/B/A King's Inn v. Fred Stewart et al.*, 804 S.W. 2d 699 (Arkansas 1991).

33. *Van Wyck v. Richmond Hotels, Inc.*, 138 F. Supp. 407 (E.D. Va. 1956).

34. *Waugh v. Duke*, 248 F. Supp. 626 (North Carolina 1960).

35. 31 *supra.*

36. *Murray v. Lane*, 444 A. 2d 1069 (Maryland 1982).

37. *Zerangue v. Delta Towers LTD*, 820 F. 2d 130 (Louisiana 1987).

38. *Kandrach v. Chrisman*, 473 S.W. 2d 193 (Tennessee 1971).

39. *Hopkinson v. Chicago Transit Authority*, 570 N.E. 2d 717 (Illinois 1991).

40. *McLean v. University Club*, 97 N.E. 2d 194 (Mass. 1951).

41. Sherry, John H. *Laws of Innkeepers*, Third Edition. Ithaca, NY: Cornell University Press, 1993.

42. 229 Mo. App. 910, 83 S.W. 2d 114.

43. *Morningstar v. Lafayette Hotel*, 211 N.Y. 465, 105 N.E. 656 (New York 1914).

13

Legal Rights of
Innkeepers and Guests

Overview

THE PURPOSE OF this chapter is to become acquainted with the legal rights that the law extends to innkeepers. These rights create a latitude within which the management can operate. In addition, the law extends privileges to guests and these too will be examined.

Adjunct to the legal duties of innkeepers and others in the hospitality and tourism industries, as we discussed them in Chapters 11 and 12, are areas of management in which the law extends certain legal rights and privileges to innkeepers and other managers. As these rights are exercised, liability seldom flows from them, because the law recognizes them as a grace or special privilege. They represent a "head room" or operating space. They remove the worry of legal liability from the picture, at least in the areas covered.

At the same time, these rights often run headlong into rights enjoyed by guests and patrons. The innkeeper has the right to have the room cleaned in the morning, and the guest has the right to occupy the room until check-out time. If the rights of one are enforced, the rights of the other are disturbed. This is understood, of course, and in practice a certain blending or balancing is expected. The careful innkeeper will see to this and avoid as much conflict as possible.

A helpful place to begin is with a discussion of the rooms of the hotel, because here the legal rights of innkeepers find full measure.

Direct and Continuing Control of Rooms

An innkeeper, as distinguished from a landlord, is in direct and continuing control of his or her guest rooms.[1] Each room is considered to be private and in the sole charge of the innkeeper, even while occupied by a guest. The innkeeper will defer to the privacy and comfort of the guest as a matter of good innkeeping, but the legal control and possession remain in the innkeeper at all times. The room in the inn is regarded as part of the "house of the innkeeper."[2]

A tenant, for example, gains a property interest in the rooms or apartments that he or she rents from the landlord. This is not true, however, in innkeeping law, as the guest obtains only a "revocable license" or privilege to occupy the room for the period of the stay agreed upon.

The license can be revoked for failure to pay the room charges, for disorderly conduct, for immoral conduct on the premises, and other reasons. In sum, the guest does not gain a property interest in the room at the hotel. A guest at a hotel has a mere personal contract to the room assigned. There is no property interest in the room, nor does the innkeeper want there to be.

Because all contracts contain implied rights and duties on both sides, any deviation of these duties on the part of the guest justify the innkeepers' treating the contract as being at an end.

Once a guest has been received and is registered, legal rights of the innkeeper come to the front. These include the right to move a guest to a new room, the right to enter the room under certain conditions, the right to take extreme actions in the event of emergencies, the right to eject guests under certain conditions, and others.

With these preliminary points in mind, we will examine the legal nature of a hotel room.

Room Doors

A contemporary hotel room door typically is made of solid wood or stamped metal, outlined by decorative molding, and has a knob with key lock, or a slot for a plastic card, and a peephole so those inside can observe those outside the room. Although it is not there in fact, by legal implication there is a copy of the Fourth Amendment on the face of the door. This amendment reads as follows:

> The right of the people to be secure in their persons, houses, papers, and effects, against unreasonable searches and seizures, shall not be violated, and no Warrants shall issue, but upon probable cause, supported by Oath or affirmation, and particularly describing the place to be searched, and the persons or things to be seized.

The room door is protected by the amendment. This becomes particularly important when contemplating a police search of a hotel room. This will be discussed in a moment.

Returning to the door, the frame becomes of concern. Can a knife be inserted beside the frame so as to dislodge the bolt? Can the frame itself be pulled off so as to allow direct access to the bolt by use of a knife? The use of molded, steel frames is common in modern hotel construction, and this is true even if the doors are wood.

Ground-level inside hotel doors often have sliding doors on the opposite side of the hallway, leading to swimming pools or indoor recreation atriums. Sliding doors have led to serious legal liability if they could not be secured adequately from the inside. A defective door of this type allowed an intruder to enter a room at a Howard Johnson property, resulting in the rape of the singer Connie Francis, and a loss to the company of $1.5 million.

AAA Tour Books

The American Automobile Association (AAA) creates and publishes a Tour Book designed to provide its members with information about hotels. The AAA is placing more and more emphasis upon security and the safety of guests, focusing on guest room doors. The AAA guidelines set forth four points in reference to guest room doors:

1. They must have a deadbolt so that entry cannot be made once the deadbolt is in place.
2. The door must have a locking device so the guest can secure the room when leaving it.
3. There must be a peephole to allow a person to see someone outside the door.
4. Sliding doors should have a rod provided so they cannot be opened from the outside.

Key Control

The control of room keys, so as to keep them out of the hands of unauthorized persons, has been a serious problem for more than 200 years. A few decades back, the industry used a colored card code system: a yellow card placed into the front desk rack for a room meant a second key had been issued. A red card indicated that a third key had been issued. A great fault with this was that front-desk personnel, who always are pressured from all sides, especially at peak check-in and check-out times, ignored the cards and gave out keys to those who gave them a room number.

Today, various key-control systems are available. Perhaps the most reliable are the electronic systems. These systems make it difficult for thieves to get into guest rooms.

Electronic Lock Systems

More hotels are adopting electronic lock systems designed to leave a "computer trail" of those who enter the hotel rooms. These systems record the date and times of each entry and can be programmed to allow a guest to enter the room with the credit card that was used to register. Plastic cards also can be issued when a guest pays with cash. In addition, traditional hard keys can be used to enter the rooms.

Two types of electronic lock systems have been developed. The "stand-alone" system involves issuing to the guest a key or a card that contains a code allowing access. In the second system the room door lock is controlled from the front desk. As guests check in or out, the front desk communicates directly to the room and activates or cancels the access code. This type of system requires hard wiring and is more expensive than the stand-alone system.

In a criminal case where the computerized records were used at a trial in a hotel room theft, a challenge made to the admissibility of such records was rejected and the conviction was allowed to stand.[3]

While a discussion of guest room doors was being carried out in a class at the University of Nevada, Las Vegas, a student showed one of the authors a room key from the Mirage Hotel and Casino in Las Vegas, represented in Figure 13.1. This student was a room-service waiter. The key was made of nickel silver and had the words "The Mirage" stamped on it. It did not have a number and did not have the words "do not duplicate" stamped on it. The two slots on each side of the key contained black computer strips. The key had only two indentations, so it was not at all like the traditional hard key. The student said this one key could open all of the thousands of rooms at the hotel, provided that security clearance was given at the front desk.

This system is state of the art and requires hard wiring and a sophisticated computer layout. In many properties hard key systems will remain in effect in the future, particularly at older properties. Some legal points become involved in their use.

FIGURE 13.1 A guest room key.

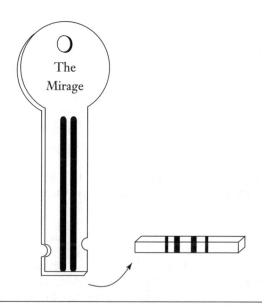

Older "Hard Key" Systems

If a hard key is used to gain unlawful entry to a room, the courts say the key has become a "burglary tool." This triggers the terms of burglary statutes. If a police officer uses a key to enter without a warrant, the key has become an instrument that has violated the Fourth Amendment. This is demonstrated by the words of a police officer holding a key to the hotel room of a murder suspect:

> All six of us have different lists of clients of Brighton Laundry, motels at the top, and we all have copies of the key found on Lumbrowski. The hardware store and the bike shops aren't much. I realize that. But they're a starting point, and that's all we're using them as. The places on my list are inside the immediate triangle formed by the shops and the store. Each of you handles a quadrant, working out away from the guest room.
>
> We try the key first. We don't talk to management; we don't announce ourselves. If the key fits, we have enough probable cause to secure the area until a

search warrant can be obtained and a search conducted. You don't go inside that room, understood?[4]

Hard keys should not have room numbers stamped on them. Most hotels today use a code system that is explained to guests as they receive the key at registration time.

Key systems may pose another problem. In a 1938 hotel case, a fire broke out near a guest room at the hotel in question. Both the guest and management tried to open the door to save the guest's belongings. The door could not be opened, and the property of the guest was lost in the spreading fire. The hotel was held responsible for the value of the property lost.[5]

Once proper guest room doors and locking systems are in place, several legal points come to the front in reference to the use of guest rooms.

Assigning New Rooms

An innkeeper retains the right to move a guest from one room to another. This should be done, however, only upon a showing of good cause. The guest has a duty to cooperate in the change, and the innkeeper should provide assistance to minimize inconvenience to the guest. The actual move must be done carefully, using due care with the guest's goods and valuables. If the guest's room is changed and, in the transfer, property of the guest is lost because of carelessness, the guest will have a right to recover the full value of those items. To guard against this, two employees should make the move in the absence of the guest.

Entry of Rooms

Once a guest is assigned a room, the legal status of the guest is as described previously. As a practical matter, however, the innkeeper will defer to the guest and step back to allow privacy consistent with good hotel practices. This, of course, must be qualified by the need to clean the room, the right to reassign a new room, and other such circumstances. In addition, the innkeeper can enter to prevent crimes from being committed, such as drug sales, gambling, and prostitution; to prevent damage from occurring to the room, and to otherwise preserve the peace and quiet of the premises, such as turning down a loud TV in a room where the guest is absent.[6]

"Do Not Disturb" Signs

Placing these signs on the outside knob of a hotel room door does not negate the innkeeper's right to enter if reasons such as those mentioned above exist. The presence of such a sign, however, makes it mandatory that the hotel have in effect, and implement, a house rule in regard to the signs. A suggested rule is as follows:

1. Two employees, one male and one female, should knock on the door.
2. If there is an answer, an employee should explain why the entry is being made.
3. If there is no answer, the door should be opened and the name of the registered guest called out loudly.

4. If there is no answer at this point, both employees should enter. This is important in the event a compromising situation is encountered.

Search of Rooms

By virtue of the Fourth Amendment, the courts hold uniformly that a lawful guest in a hotel room has "the right to be secure in . . . his or her . . . persons, houses, papers and effects" against unreasonable searches and seizures by the government. Thus, a hotel room is a home or residence during a lawful stay. However, if one obtains a hotel room with the intention of using it for illegal purposes, such as prostitution or drug sales, once this is known, the police can assert control, and the privilege to occupy can be revoked. Under these circumstances the Fourth Amendment has no application. Incriminating evidence can be admitted in court against the defendants.

As long as an innkeeper remains in the innkeeper function—doing what is reasonably necessary to run the hotel property and efficiently—the courts hold that any criminal arrests by police that might follow are valid. If the innkeeper remains in the innkeeping role, such as checking to see if a room is vacant, when in the company of a police officer, and if the guest is caught in a criminal act, the courts hold that the guest's rights have not been violated.

In the Sundum case, a manager used a hard key to enter a guest room. Check-out time had passed, and the manager first called the room. Upon not getting an answer, the manager unlocked the room door, at which time the police observed Sundum passed out on the bed with stolen goods in plain view. The arrest was upheld on appeal.

The Steven Dale Winsor case presented a different situation because check-out time had not expired. One brother was a guest in the room, and the second brother fled to that room after robbing a nearby bank. The court in Winsor, while upholding the warrantless search and the arrest that followed, made some important points:[7]

1. This was a small, two-story "residential hotel." With the police searching door to door, it increased the chance that the next room might contain the armed robber.
2. Be seeing the fleeing felon run into the hotel, the police had probable cause to believe that he was in a room, but lacked probable cause to believe that he was in a *particular* room.
3. When the police knocked on Winsor's door, they ". . . neither searched nor seized anything or anyone. . ." *Cuevas-Ortega v. INS 588*, F. 2d 1276 (California, 1979).
4. Police may approach and question an individual without triggering Fourth Amendment scrutiny, as long as the person stops and answers voluntarily. *U.S. v. Erwin*, 803 F. 2d 1505, 1508 (9th Cir. 1986).
5. The court said it would not condone such a door-to-door search at a large hotel or apartment building. Thus, the small size of the hotel in question was an important factor in the decision.
6. The court said the permissible extent of intrusion based on a reasonable suspicion is extremely limited.

7. If the clerk had given the police the room key and if they had used that key to open the door, they would have violated the Fourth Amendment. They did not do this, however. *U.S. v.Scott,* 520 F. 2d 699-700 (9th Cir. 1975), *cert. denied.* 423 U.S. 1056 (U.S. Sup. Ct. 1976).

The Fourth Amendment usually will protect the hotel guest from a warrantless police search, but there are exceptions. If a state has a statute, or if a city or county has an ordinance, that permits police to examine a guest register, the Fourth Amendment will not stop local police from examining the register.[8]

The following is an example taken from a county ordinance:

> 7.28.010   Public register required. Every person within the limits of an unincorporated town in Clark County [Nevada}, who keeps, maintains, or controls any hotel, inn, motel, motorcourt, boardinghouse or lodging house shall provide, keep and maintain a public register and shall require every person who rents or occupies a room in such hotel, inn, motel, motor court, boardinghouse or lodging house to write in such register his name and place of residence. Such registration shall be made on a page of the register properly dated with reference to the day of the year, month and week and the time of day the person rents or arranges to occupy a room shall also be therein entered. Such register shall be permanently and firmly bound and shall not be of a loose-leaf nature. (Ord. 53 § 1, 1954)
>
> 7.28.020   Registers open to inspection by law enforcement officers. Such hotel, inn, motel, motor court, boardinghouse or lodging house register so kept shall be open to the public at any and all reasonable hours and the pages thereof shall, upon demand, be open for inspection or investigation by any law enforcement officer in Clark County immediately upon demand having been made by such law enforcement officer. (Ord. 53 § 2, 1954)
>
> 7.28.030   Penalty for violation. Any violation of this chapter constitutes a misdemeanor and the offender shall be punished by a fine of not more than five hundred dollars or imprisonment for not more than six months or by both such fine and imprisonment. (Ord. 53 § 3, 1954)

If a police officer is summoned to a hotel for assistance, the officer can enter a hotel room without a warrant if the officer has reasonable grounds to believe that someone inside may be seriously injured. Once inside, if evidence of crime is discovered, an arrest can be made that the courts will uphold.[9] In another case, police knocked on an inn-room door and did not announce who they were. The occupant opened the door part way to see who was knocking. Upon observing the police, the occupant tried to close the door, but several officers with drawn guns forced entry. The entry was held to be in violation of the Fourth Amendment because the officers did not have a search warrant.[10]

Misconduct of a Guest

Misconduct of a guest, such as taking part in an illegal or immoral activity, is grounds for ejection of that person. Such activity is tantamount to a breach of contract on the part of the guest. If there is misconduct, but the misconduct ends and the guest is not ejected, the courts recognize that there is a waiver, or forgiveness, and the inn-guest relationship continues.[11]

Disorderly House

An innkeeper must not allow the hotel to become disorderly or to be used for immoral purposes. The hotel was not created for such purposes, and the innkeeper must use care to avoid being prosecuted for running a "house of ill fame." For a case in which an innkeeper was so prosecuted, see *People v. McCarthy*.[12]

Prostitutes can be legally excluded.[13] The disorderly house statutes make such exclusion possible. An example follows:

> Any person who shall keep any disorderly house, or any house or public resort, by which the peace, comfort or decency of the immediate neighborhood, or of any family thereof, is habitually disturbed, or who shall keep any inn in a disorderly manner, is guilty of a misdemeanor.[14]

Lockouts

Although there are many times when an innkeeper has the right to eject guests, what happens when a guest resists ejection? Can physical violence be resorted to? In cases of outrageous conduct on the part of a guest, such as physical violence, the answer may well be "yes." In the normal situation, the answer is "no." Nonviolent resistance of ejection cannot be met with violence because the courts will not permit it. Therefore, what can the innkeeper do?

One technique used in innkeeping is the lockout. This is carried out by double-locking the guest's room by use of a "clam device" that slips over door knobs or by changing the computer code. This is done, of course, while the guest is absent from the room. Lockouts are effective because they separate the guest from his or her belongings. They usually result in settlement at the front desk in exchange for release of the goods and departure of the guest.

Effect of Emergencies

In the event of an emergency, such as a fire, escaping gas from a derailed train, or a broken water line in the room itself, the innkeeper is given wide latitude. It then becomes a matter of acting as a reasonable innkeeper would act under like or similar circumstances. The innkeeper can, and must, enter to warn of outside dangers. Further, his or her agents can enter to stop further damage. Common sense controls. If incriminating evidence is uncovered during such an emergency, the courts will allow it to be admitted in court.

Holdover Guests

Another legal right of the innkeeper arises when the end of a guest's stay arrives and the former guest now demands to hold over, but that room has been sold to others who are waiting to check in.

> The guest who overstays the agreed time limit may be required to leave. If he (she) refuses, he may be evicted in a reasonable manner, not inflicting unnecessary injury or undue humiliation upon the guest. The usual method is to remove the guest's

luggage from his room during his absence and to double-lock the door so as to deny entry.[15]

In New York, it is not legal to evict a holdover, even if this causes a breach of contract with an arriving guest. In Connecticut, a holdover can be removed only through a landlord-tenantlike process. In Hawaii, a holdover is treated as a trespasser. In Puerto Rico, the police can be called in to remove holdovers at the request of the innkeeper. The law is not uniform on this point, so it is best to check the state law.

COMPENSATION OF INNKEEPERS

Innkeepers are entitled to be paid for reasonable charges they make to guests, invitees, patrons, and others. If they are not paid, innkeepers have the right to sue for breach of contract. The related question is: Can innkeepers ask that those who do not pay their bills be prosecuted for the crime of theft? If it cannot be shown that nonpaying persons intended to abscond in a "secretive or clandestine manner," the answer is "no." Bringing a criminal charge under these circumstances opens up the hotel to civil liability.[16] If an innkeeper does convince a prosecuting attorney to prosecute for nonpayment, the former guest has a strong weapon with which to come after the innkeeper in a civil action.[17] Caution is in order here.[18]

If there is some confusion as to the accuracy of charges, or some doubt about who has the legal obligation to pay, care is in order. In addition, if the sum in question is not large, the doubt should be resolved in favor of the guest. If such a quest or patron is detained by police, and it is later found the hotel was in error, there is the danger of a claim of false imprisonment or perhaps malicious prosecution.

The right of the innkeeper to be paid is backed up by the innkeepers' lien.

Innkeepers' Lien

At common law, the innkeeper could claim a lien against the property of a guest who did not pay for the services and goods received. This meant the inn had the right to hold property of the guest and sell it, if necessary, to obtain payment.

This is the law of all states today but in most states it is provided by statute rather than common law. The constitutionality of the lien, where the property is sold without notice, has been challenged successfully in California, Florida, Nebraska, and New York. In these states notice must be given and a hearing held before the sale can be carried out.

Nature of the Lien

The lien covers all charges the guest owes including any loans the innkeeper advanced to the guest. The lien can be enforced only during the current inn-guest relationship. A debt unpaid from last year by a guest cannot form the basis of a lien this year. Characteristics of a lien are as follows.

1. An innkeeper does not have to receive excess goods carried by a guest, but, if they are received the lien attaches to them.
2. The lien is effective against property that otherwise might be protected by the bankruptcy laws.
3. If a guest brings property owned by others, the lien attaches to the detriment of the third-party owner. With stolen goods, the prevailing view is that the lien does *not* attach and the true owner can have possession of the goods.
4. If the lien attaches and the goods then are sold to others by the guest, the lien is not defeated.

Once the lien attaches and the innkeeper takes possession of the goods, other rules control.

Care and Caution

An innkeeper must use the same care and caution with liened goods as he or she would use with his or her own goods. If the property is placed to use, credit must be given for the value of that use. An innkeeper who has a lien upon a guest's corporate stock that had been declared at a front desk would have to exercise the care and caution that would be expected if the innkeeper owned the stock. The same would be true if pets were liened: They would have to be fed, watered, and maintained properly.

End of Lien

The lien can end by payment, by the goods being returned to the owner, or by conversion of the property by the innkeeper. That, of course, would be an illegal act. It also can be waived. Although four states have held the lien to be unconstitutional in the absence of notice and a hearing, Illinois, Minnesota, and other states have upheld the lien without notice.

The procedural steps that must be followed in enforcing the lien vary from state to state, and legal advice must be sought and followed. The typical lien statute requires that notice be given, that sale be held at public auction, and that proceeds be accounted for. The statutes provide for the balance to be paid to the former guest if his or her address is known, which it often is not. In that event, excess funds forfeit to the state. The common law procedural steps for enforcement are the basis for such statutes.

Defrauding Innkeepers

Related to the right of compensation of innkeepers, and others in our industries, are state statutes that make it a crime for guests and others to steal from the innkeeper. Such thefts reduce the compensation of innkeepers. All fifty states have these laws. Most states have statutes, such as the following, that can lead to criminal prosecution of a guest:

> Any lodger who takes away, with intent to steal, embezzle, or purloin, any bedding, furniture, goods, or chattels which he is to use in or with his lodging, is guilty of

grand or petit larceny, according to the value of the property so taken, and shall be punished accordingly.

Puerto Rico, which is not a state, has a statute that makes it a felony (the most serious crime) to defraud an innkeeper intentionally of services, lodging, or food over the sum of $500. On the other hand, in Puerto Rico, if a hotel demands payment for previous charges and the hotel then grants additional credit to the person in question, the hotel cannot claim that the guest or patron intended to defraud the innkeeper.[19] If an innkeeper wants to retain the protection of the "defrauding" statutes, additional credit should not be extended. Attesting to the seriousness of the defrauding statute in Nevada is the following:

> The rhythm guitarist was a legitimate cowboy named Ci. The Bunko squad had picked him up for defrauding an innkeeper. This is a serious crime in Nevada (what Tex did was dodge out of paying a bill), which gives a good indication of the power of hotels in this gambling state. Tex got five years, perhaps as a warning to others who might consider attempting this horrible crime.[20]

Leaving the rights of innkeepers, let's take a look at some of the legal rights of guests that have not been mentioned already. We will close this chapter with a look at some cases that illustrate the principles discussed.

RIGHTS OF GUESTS

The word *right* is a noun and, taken in an abstract sense, refers to "justice, ethical correctness, or consonance with the rules of law or the principles of morals." In this signification it answers to one meaning of the Latin *jus*, and serves to indicate law in the abstract, considered as the foundation of all rights or the complex of underlying moral principles which impart the character of justice to all positive law, or give it an ethical content."[21] Taken in a concrete sense, a right is "a power, privilege, facility, or demand, inherent in one person and incident upon another."[22]

Constitutional law provides us with four basic rights: personal, natural, political, and civil. One of our primary concerns, of course, is with civil rights.

Civil Rights

Civil rights are rights ". . . as belong to every citizen of the state or country, or, in a wider sense, to all its inhabitants, and are not connected with the organization or administration of government. They include the rights of property, marriage, protection of laws, freedom of contract, trial by jury . . . ," and others.[23] Or, as otherwise defined, civil rights are rights appertaining to a person in virtue of his or her citizenship in a state or community, rights capable of being enforced or redressed in a civil action. It also is a term applied to certain rights secured to citizens of the United States by the Thirteenth and Fourteenth Amendments to the Constitution, and by various acts of Congress made in pursuance thereof.[24]

Privacy

Another right of a guest is that of privacy. It has been held that a hotel does not have a legal right to disclose to the police phone calls made by a guest without proper legal process. "A guest in a motel has a constitutionally protected right to privacy in his motel room and motel personnel cannot consent to a search (by the police) of the guest's room."[25]

This protected right ends, of course, when the inn-guest relationship ends. At that time, the innkeeper can enter freely, and can seek police help for that purpose if the need is felt.

CASE INTRODUCTION: McHUGH CASE

One of the legal rights an innkeeper has is to eject guests and non-guests who engage in disorderly, undesirable, or other unacceptable conduct. Most states have statutes similar to the following:

Eviction of disorderly persons. Every owner or keeper of any hotel, inn, motel, motor court, or boardinghouse or lodginghouse in this state shall have the right to evict from such premises anyone who acts in a disorderly manner, or who destroys the property of any such owner or keeper, or who causes a public disturbance in or upon such premises.[26]

In the absence of a statute, the common-law right to eject remains. In exercising one's rights under these laws, common or statutory, discretion and care always would be in order.

The McHugh case that follows illustrates the principle that an innkeeper has the right to exclude a guest who acts in a disorderly manner. The case goes on, however, to demonstrate the pitfalls that may arise when a guest is in fact ill and not intoxicated, as was suspected.

Mrs. McHugh brought suit against the hotel, claiming that the act of excluding her husband from the hotel was done negligently and carelessly, resulting in or contributing to his death. The case tells the legal story, and there are very important points to be learned from it.

MCHUGH V. SCHLOSSER *ET AL.*
292 A. 291 (S. Ct. Pennsylvania 1894).

WILLIAMS, J. The defendants are hotel keepers in the city of Pittsburgh. McHugh was their guest, and died in an alley appurtenant to the hotel on the 2d day of February, 1891. Mary McHugh, the plaintiff, is his widow, and she seeks to recover damages for the loss of her husband, alleging that it was caused by the improper conduct of the defendants and their employees. An examination of the testimony shows that McHugh came to the Hotel Schlosser late on Friday night, January 30th, registered, was assigned to, and paid for, a room for the night, and retired. On Saturday and Sunday he complained of being ill, and remained most of both days in bed. A physician was sent for at his request, who prescribed for him. He also asked for and obtained several drinks during the same time, and an empty bottle or bottles remained in his room after he left it.

During the forenoon of Monday he seemed bewildered, and wandered about the hall on the floor on which his room was. About the middle of the day the housekeeper reported to Schlosser that he was out of his room, and sitting half dressed on the side of the bed in another room. Schlosser and his porter both started in search of McHugh, and Schlosser seems to have exhibited some excitement or anger. He was found, and the porter led him to his room. While this was being done Schlosser said to him, "You can't stay here any longer"; to which McHugh replied, "I'll git." The porter, on reaching his room, put his coat, hat, and shoes on him, and at once led him to the freight elevator, put him on it, and had him let down to the ground floor. He then took him through a door, used for freight, out into an alley, some four or five feet wide, that led to Penn Avenue.

Rain was falling, and the day was cold. A stream of rain water and dissolving snow was running down the alley. McHugh was without overshoes, overcoat, or wraps of any description. When the porter had gotten him part way down the alley, he fell to the pavement. While he was lying in the water, and the porter standing near him, a lady passed along the sidewalk on Penn Avenue and saw him. She walked a square, found Officer White, and reported to him what she had seen. He went to the alley to investigate, and when he arrived, McHugh had been gotten to his feet but was leaning heavily against the wall of the hotel, apparently unable to step. The porter was behind him with his hands upon him, apparently urging him forward.

What followed will be best told in the officer's own words. He says: "I asked, 'What's the matter with this man, Mr. Powers?' He says, 'He's sick.' I says 'He ought to have something done for him', and at that time he fell right in the alley on his back. He had his coat open, no vest, and his shoes were untied. He had strings in his shoes, but not tied." The officer was asked if the man spoke after he reached the place where he was, and he replied thus: "He spoke to me. Somebody said he was drunk. He rolled his eyes up, and says: 'Officer, I am not drunk. I am sick. I wish you would get an ambulance and have me taken to the hospital.' Then I ran to the patrol box."

It required about 20 minutes to get an ambulance on the ground. During all this time the man continued to lie on the pavement in the alley. At length, after an exposure of about half an hour in the storm, and on the pavement, the ambulance came. He was placed on a stretcher, lifted into the ambulance, and taken to police headquarters, and thence to the hospital; but all signs of life had disappeared when he was laid on the hospital floor. The post-mortem examination disclosed the fact that the immediate cause of death was valvular disease of the heart. The theory of the plaintiff was that the shock from exposure to wet and cold in the alley had, in his feeble and unprotected condition, brought on the heart failure from which he died; and, as the exposure resulted from the conduct or directions of the defendants, they were responsible for his death.

Three principal questions were thus raised: First. What duty does an innkeeper owe to his guest? Second. What connection was there between the defendants' disregard of their duty, if they did disregard it in any particular, and the death of Mr. McHugh? Third. If the plaintiff be entitled to recover, what is the measure of her damages?

First Question

The attention of the court was drawn to the first of these questions by the defendants' third point, in which the learned judge was asked to instruct the jury, in substance, that if the deceased was troublesome to the defendants, and annoying to their guests, they might rightfully put him out of their house, if they used no unnecessary force or violence. This point was refused as framed, but the learned judge proceeded to state the rule thus: "If the annoying acts were willful, the defendants could remove decedent in the manner stated in point. If, however, they were the result of sickness, although they might, under certain circumstances, remove him, such removal must be in a manner suited to his condition."

This was saying that if McHugh was intoxicated, and the disturbances made by him were due to his intoxication, he might be treated as a drunken man; but if he was sick, and the disturbances caused by him were due to his sickness, he must be treated with the consideration due to a sick man. This is a correct statement of the rule. In the delirium of a fever, a sick man may become very troublesome to a hotel keeper, and his groans and cries may be annoying to the occupants of rooms near him; but this would not justify turning him forcibly from his bed into the street during a winter storm. What the condition of the decedent really was went properly to the jury for determination. If they found the fact to be that he was suffering from sickness, then the learned judge properly said that, if his removal was to be undertaken, it should be conducted in a manner suited to one in his condition.

Second Question

The second question was raised by the defendants' fourth point, which was as follows: "If McHugh died of heart disease, and defendants had no reason to believe that he was so sick that his removal from the house would cause his death, they cannot be held responsible in this action, even though the mere incident of his removal from the house may have in some degree contributed to bring it on at that time." This was refused. It could not have been affirmed without qualification; but its refusal, without more, left the jury without any rule whatever upon the subject.

The question which the defendants were bound to consider before putting the decedent out in the storm was not whether such exposure would surely cause death, but what was it reasonable to suppose might follow such a sudden exposure of the decedent in the condition in which he then was. What were the probable consequences of pushing a sick man, in the condition the decedent was in, out into the storm, without adequate covering, and, when he fell, from inability to stand on his feet, leaving him to lie in the stream of melting ice and snow that ran over the pavement of the alley for about a half hour in all, in the condition in which Officer White found him?

Third Question

The third question was raised by the defendants' first point. No evidence was given tending to show the earning powers or the habits of industry and thrift of the deceased. For this reason the court was asked to instruct the jury that "nothing more than nominal damages can be recovered in this action." This was refused, and the jury was told in the general charge that, as the evidence fixed his age, and gave information about his health and habits, they might from this data estimate his earning capacity, and the pecuniary loss of the plaintiff. Now, it is true, as said in *Railroad Co. v. Keller*, 67 Pa. St. 300, that since the acts of 1851 and 1855, life has a value which the law will recognize, and which the survivors who are entitled to sue may recover at law.

It is true that this value is to be fixed by the jury in view of all the circumstances, and it is not necessarily limited to what is known as "nominal damages." But it is also true that when the probable earnings of the deceased are to be taken into account in fixing the damages, it is the duty of the plaintiff to show the earning power of the deceased, or give such evidence in regard to his business, business habits, and past earnings, as may afford some basis from which earning capacity may be fairly estimated.

The true measure of damages is the pecuniary loss suffered, without any solatium for mental suffering or grief; and the pecuniary loss is what the deceased would probably have earned by his labor, physical or intellectual, in his business or profession, if the injury that caused death had not befallen him, and which would have gone to the support of his family. In fixing this amount, consideration should be given to the age of the deceased, his health, his ability and disposition to labor, his habits of living, and his expenditures.

It is very clear that the refusal of the first and fourth points without explanation left the jury without any adequate instruction on the important questions to which these points related. The consequence was a verdict based on earning power of the deceased, which the learned judge felt constrained to reduce, and without some evidence from which the calculation of the pecuniary loss of the plaintiff may be made. The judgment is reversed, and a *venire facias de novo* awarded.

This means the case now must go back for a second jury trial. At this new trial, the plaintiff must produce evidence of the earning power of the decedent under the guidelines set down by the upper court. The trial judge also must instruct the jury on the points set out by the upper court.

CASE INTRODUCTION: MORNINGSTAR CASE

A guest who refuses to pay for services—or who will not be able to pay for services when due—may be ejected on those grounds. Again, care is in order. The Morningstar case has been around since 1914 and is recognized as a leading case on point.

MORNINGSTAR V. LAFAYETTE HOTEL
211 N.Y. 465, 105 N.E. 656 (New York 1914)

CARDOZO, J. The plaintiff was a guest at the Lafayette Hotel in the city of Buffalo. He seems to have wearied of the hotel fare, and his yearning for variety has provoked this lawsuit. He went forth and purchased some spareribs, which he presented to the hotel chef with a request that they be cooked for him and brought to his room. This was done, but with the welcome viands there came the unwelcome addition of a bill or check for $1, which he was asked to sign. He refused to do so, claiming that the charge was excessive.

That evening he dined at the cafe, and was again asked to sign for the extra service, and again declined. The following morning, Sunday, when he presented himself at the breakfast table, he was told that he would not be served. This announcement was made publicly, in the hearing of other guests. He remained at the hotel till Tuesday, taking his meals elsewhere, and he then left. The trial judge left it to the jury to say whether the charge of $1.00 was a reasonable one, instructing them that, if it was, the defendant had a right to refuse to serve the plaintiff further, and that, if it was not, the refusal was wrongful. In this, there was no error. An innkeeper is not required to entertain a guest who has refused to pay a lawful charge. Whether the charge in controversy was excessive was a question for the jury.

[Note: This states the law. What happened at trial varied from the law, and the court discusses that next.]

The plaintiff says, however, that there was error in the admission of evidence which vitiates the verdict. In this we think that he is right. He alleged in his complaint that the defendant's conduct had injured his reputation. He offered no proof on that point, but the defendant took advantage of the averment to prove what the plaintiff's reputation was. A number of hotel proprietors were called as witnesses by the defendant and under objection were allowed to prove that, in their respective hotels, the plaintiffs reputation was that of a chronic faultfinder. Some of them were permitted to say that the plaintiff was known as a "kicker." Others were permitted to say that his reputation was bad, not in respect of any moral qualities, but as the guest of a hotel.

The trial judge charged the jury that they must find for the defendant if they concluded that the plaintiff had suffered no damage, and this evidence was received to show that he had suffered none. It is impossible to justify the ruling. The plaintiff, if wrongfully ejected from the cafe, was entitled to recover damages for injury to his feelings as a result of the humiliation; but his reputation as a faultfinder was certainly not at issue. The damages recoverable for such a wrong were no less because the occupants of other hotels were of the opinion that he complained too freely. In substance, it has been held that the plaintiff might be refused damages for the insult of being put out of a public dining room because other innkeepers considered him an undesirable guest.

It is no concern of ours that the controversy at the root of this lawsuit may seem to be trivial. That fact supplies, indeed, the greater reason why the jury should not have been misled into the belief that justice might therefore be denied to the suitor. To enforce one's rights when they are violated is never a legal wrong, and may often be a moral duty. It happens in many instances that the violation passes with no effort to redress it—sometimes from praiseworthy forbearance, sometimes from weakness, sometimes from mere inertia. But the law, which creates a right, can certainly not concede that an insistence upon its enforcement is evidence of a wrong.

A great jurist, Rudolf von Ihering, in his "Struggle for Law," ascribes the development of law itself to the persistence in human nature of the impulse to resent aggression, and maintains the thesis that the individual owes the duty to himself and to society never to permit a legal right to be wantonly infringed. There has been criticism of Ihering's view, due largely, it may be, to the failure to take note of the limitations that accompany it; but it has at least its germ of truth. The plaintiff chose to resist a wrong which, if it may seem trivial to some, must have seemed substantial to him; and his readiness to stand upon his rights should not have been proved to his disparagement.

The judgment must be reversed, and a new trial granted, with costs to abide the event.

WILLARD BARTLETT, C. J., and WERNER, HISCOCK, CHASE, CUDDE-BACK, and MILLER, JJ., concur.

Judgment reversed.

A cook working full time in a hotel restaurant in 1914 could expect to be paid $1.00 a day. In light of that fact, the charge of $1.00 to Mr. Morningstar probably was excessive.

CASE INTRODUCTION: RAIDER CASE

In the Raider case, the innkeeper took charge of the room of a guest based upon the negative reputation of that person. The court was not shocked by that action at all.

RAIDER V. DIXIE INN
248 S.W. 229 (Kentucky 1923)

SAMPSON, C.J. Appellant, Thelma Raider, applied to the Dixie Inn, at Richmond, for entertainment, and paid her board and lodging for a week in advance, saying that her home was in Estill County and she had come to Richmond, at the expense of her mother, to take treatments from a physician. At the end of the week, she paid in advance for another week, and so on until the end of a month, when she went downtown, and on returning was informed by the proprietor and his wife, who are appellees in this case, that she no longer had a room at that hotel, and remarked to her that no explanation was due her as to why they had requested or forced her removal.

Alleging that she was mortified and humiliated by the words and conduct of the proprietors of the hotel, appellant, Raider, brought this action to recover damages in the sum of $5,000. Appellees answered, and denied the averments of the petition insofar as such averments set forth harsh or improper conduct on the part of the proprietors of the hotel, but admitted that they had required appellant to vacate her room and to leave the hotel, and gave as their reason for so doing that she was a woman of bad character, recently an inmate of a house of prostitution in the city of Richmond, and had been such for many years next before she came to the Inn, and was in said city a notoriously immoral character, but that appellees did not know her when she applied for entertainment at their hotel, but immediately upon learning who she was and her manner of life had moved her belongings out of the room into the lobby of the hotel, and kindly, quietly, and respectfully asked her to leave: that they had in their hotel several ladies of good reputation who were embarrassed by the presence of appellant in the hotel and who declined to associate with her and were about to withdraw from the hotel if she continued to lodge there; that appellant had not been of good behavior since she had become a patron of the hotel.

Appellant moved to strike certain of the affirmative averments from the answer, but, without waiving this motion, filed an amended petition in which she set forth substantially the same facts which she had in her original petition, adding the following paragraph:

"Plaintiff says that she is advised that these defendants (the Dixie Inn) had a legal right to remove her, and that she does not question that right, but that she was removed as a guest for hire from said Dixie Inn at a time that was improper and in a manner that was unduly disrespectful and insulting, and that she was greatly mortified and humiliated thereby, and suffered indignity because of the wrongful manner in which she was removed from said Dixie Inn as herein set out and complained of." The court dismissed her petition and she appealed.

As a general rule, a guest who has been admitted to an inn may afterwards be excluded therefrom by the innkeeper if the guest refuses to pay his bill, or if he becomes obnoxious to the guests by his own fault, is a person of general bad reputation, or has ceased to be a traveler by becoming a resident.

It appears, therefore, fully settled that an innkeeper may lawfully refuse to entertain objectionable characters, if to do so is calculated to injure his business or to place himself, business, or guests in a hazardous, uncomfortable, or dangerous situation. The innkeeper need not accept any one as a guest who is calculated to and will injure his business. *State v. Steele*, 106 N.C. 766, 11 S.E. 478, 8 L. R. A. 516, 19 Am. St. Rep. 573. A prize fighter who has been guilty of law breaking may be excluded. *Nelson v. Boldt* (C. C.) 180 Fed. 779. Neither is an innkeeper required to entertain a card shark (*Watkins v. Cope*, 84 N. J. Law, 143, 86 Atl. 545); a thief (*Markham v. Brown*, 8 N. H. 523, 31 Am. Dec. 209); persons of bad reputation or those who are under suspicion (*Goodenow v. Travis*, 3 Johns, [N. Y.] 427; *State v. Steele, supra*); drunken and disorderly persons (*Atwater v. Sawyer*, 76 Me. 539, 49 Am. Rep. 634); one who commits a trespass by breaking in the door (*Goodenow v. Travis, supra*); one who is filthy or who subjects the guests to annoyance (*Pidgeon v. Legge*, 5 Week. Rep. 649; see *Morningstar v. Hotel Co.*, 211 N. Y. 465, 105 N.E. 656, 52 L. R. A. [N. S.] 740, and the notes thereto attached).

It therefore appears that the managers of the Dixie Inn had the right to exclude appellant from their hotel upon several grounds without becoming liable therefor, unless the means employed to remove her were unlawful. The petition admits as much by its averment saying:

"She [appellant] is advised that these defendants [appellees] had a legal right to remove her, and that she did not question that right."

It being conceded that appellees had the right to remove appellant from the hotel, the only remaining question is: Did they do so in a proper manner, or did they employ unlawful means to exclude her? The averments of the petition show she was not present at the time they took charge of her room and placed her belongings in the lobby of the hotel, where they were easily accessible to her; that when she came in, they quietly told her that they had taken charge of her room but gave no reason for doing so. We must believe from the averments of the petition that very little was said, and that the whole proceeding was very quiet and orderly. As they had a right to exclude her from the hotel, they were guilty of no wrong in telling her so, even though there were other persons present in the lobby at the time they gave her such information, which is denied.

The averments of the petition as amended "that appellees removed appellant from the hotel in an improper manner and were unduly disrespectful and insulting" are mere conclusions of the pleader, and are not supported by the statement of facts found elsewhere in the petition.

The petition as amended did not state a cause of action in favor of appellant against appellees, and the trial court properly sustained a general demurrer thereto.

Judgment affirmed.

CASE INTRODUCTION: JENKINS CASE

What are the rights of an innkeeper, through security personnel, to question both male and female non-guests who are using the public rooms, but have no intention of becoming guests? The Jenkins case illustrates one judge's view and discloses the attitude as he speaks of the situation. There is no inn-guest relationship, and the opinion reflects the weight the court places on that fact.

JENKINS V. KENTUCKY HOTEL
261 Ky. 419, 87 S.W. 2d 951 (Kentucky 1935)

STITES, Justice.

Appellant, Ellen Jenkins, brought this action against the appellee, Kentucky Hotel, Inc., to recover damages for an alleged assault claimed to have arisen from a request of the house detective, about 9 o'clock in the evening of June 21, 1934, that she leave the lobby of the hotel. Upon the trial of the case, the court peremptorily instructed the jury to find a verdict for the appellee at the close of the testimony for the appellant.

On the night in question, appellant says that she went to the Kentucky Hotel for the purpose of meeting her brother and sister-in-law, who were attending a meeting then in progress on the fourth floor of the hotel. She inquired of the clerk if the meeting was still going on, and, on being told that it was, she took a seat in the lobby, at a place near the elevators, where she could see who came down. While she was thus seated, the house detective approached her and asked what she was doing there. She told him the object and purpose of her visit, and she says that the detective told her, in a rude and insulting manner, that no such meeting as she claimed was being held in the hotel, and ordered her to leave the premises. She says that his manner and demeanor were so menacing and threatening that she believed that unless she followed his instructions, he would use force bodily to evict her.

Rather than be subjected to physical force, she says she left the premises and went out into the rain, where she remained for some minutes, and later came back into the hotel and went up to the meeting on the fourth floor, where she joined her brother and sister-in-law.

It is admitted that appellant was at most a mere licensee, and that if she had been requested in a proper manner to leave the lobby and had failed to do so, reasonable force could lawfully have been used to eject her. It is contended, however, that the rude and insulting manner accompanying the request to leave was an assault. With this we cannot agree. Howsoever culpable may have been the words or attitude of the detective, there was no unlawful offer of injury by force, and nothing, so far as the evidence discloses, from which a reasonable person might anticipate the exercise of more force than the law permitted.

This court has approved the following definition: "An assault is an unlawful offer of corporeal injury to another by force, or force unlawfully directed toward the person of another, under such circumstances as create a well-founded fear of immediate peril," *Smith v. Gowdy*, 196 Ky. 281, 244 S. W. 678, 679, 29 A. L. R. 1353. The words used by the detective, as recited by appellant, contained no offer of force whatever, either lawful or unlawful. While his manner, according to appellant, was rude and highly objectionable, it was nothing more. He had the right to eject appellant if she refused to leave as requested. Bad manners are not actionable.

However unfortunate this affair may have been, from the standpoint of both appellant and appellee, there was nothing in the acts or conduct complained of that constituted an assault. There was no breach of any legal duty owed to appellant.

Judgment affirmed.

CASE INTRODUCTION: SUNDUM CASE

The matter of the legal rights of an innkeeper, acting through his or her employees and agents to enter a guest room, has been discussed in detail. It now becomes important to examine the leading law case on this issue. Once a court renders a decision such as this one, the issue becomes stabilized. This is the doctrine of *stare decisis* in action. This is a primary reason why so many leading law cases date to years past.

RICK SUNDUM, APPELLANT, V. STATE OF ALASKA
612 P. 2d 1018 (1980).

MATTHEWS, Justice.

The defendant, Rick Sundum, contends that the police entry into his motel room was the product of an illegal search, and that the evidence of stolen goods found on his person pursuant to that entry should be suppressed. The superior court denied the motion to suppress[27] and we affirm.

At 5:30 A.M., May 7, 1978, Pete Heger was awakened by an intruder in his motel room at the Driftwood Lodge in Juneau. Later that morning, Heger's roommate, Roy Claxton, discovered that his watch, cash, and marijuana were missing. The Driftwood's manager, Leona Gran, was notified of the theft, and the police were summoned. In the presence of the police, Heger described the burglar to other lodgers, one of whom pointed to room 38 and said Rick Sundum was the one they wanted.

This identification was made at approximately 12:30 P.M., some one and one-half hours after the Driftwood's posted checkout time of 11:00 A.M. Gran informed the police that room 38 was registered in the name of one K. Brown, and that neither the registered guest nor anyone else had yet reregistered.

At the suppression hearing Gran testified that it was her responsibility to ascertain whether guests who had failed to appear by 11:00 A.M. were "skips,"[28] and if they were not, whether they intended to vacate their room or reregister. Her customary procedure was to telephone the occupants of the room, knock on their door, and enter their room, in that order, if such steps were necessary for the determination she was required to make. Though she had not yet done so when room 38 was suggested as the suspected burglar's quarters, the manager testified that she intended to and certainly would have followed her customary procedures even if the police had not been present.

On her own initiative, Gran telephoned room 38 and received no answer. Thereupon, Gran, Pete Heger, Dave Heger, Roy Claxton, and two police officers walked over to room 38. Gran knocked on the door, received no response, and retrieved the key from her office. She then opened the door. From the doorway, the two men could be seen, both apparently asleep. Also clearly visible, on the outstretched wrist of the man on the cot closest to the door, was a distinctive watch,[29] which Claxton immediately identified as his own. In addition, the clothing worn by the man fit the description given earlier by Heger.[30] The police officers then entered the motel room and arrested and handcuffed the suspect, Rick Sundum. They searched his person, finding sixty dollars in cash, and searched under his cot, finding a buckknife. At the station house, a bag of marijuana was found strapped to Sundum's leg.

The door of a home, even if open, presents a firm constitutional barrier to police searches unless conducted pursuant to a warrant or within an exception to the warrant requirement. *State v. Spietz*, 531 P. 2d 521, 525 (Alaska 1975). See also, *Erickson v. State*, 507 P. 2d 508, 515 (Alaska 1973). But there has been no showing that the officers opened Sundum's door or intended to do so in order to search.

Once Gran opened the door to Sundum's room and the police officers saw a man fitting the description of the burglary suspect, wearing a watch identified as stolen in the burglary, they had probable cause to arrest.[31] The officers entered in order to effectuate an arrest. The exigent circumstances presented by the sudden confrontation with the possibility of an armed and apt-to-flee felony suspect authorized the officers' immediate entry into the room. See generally, *Finch v. State*, 592 P. 2d 1196, 1198 (Alaska 1979); *State v. Spietz*, 531 P. 2d 521, 523-25 (Alaska 1975). See also *State v. Warness*, 26 Ariz. App. 359, 548 P. 2d 853, 855-56 (1976).

As a minimum, the police officers could conduct a search incident to that arrest of Sundum's person and seize evidence of the burglary. See, e.g., *Weltin v. State*, 574 P. 2d 816, 818-19 (Alaska 1978); *McCoy v. State*, 491 P. 2d 127, 132-33 (Alaska 1971); *Merrill v. State*, 423 P. 2d 686, 699-700 (Alaska), *cert. denied*, 386 U.S. 1040, 87 S. Ct. 1497, 18 L. Ed. 2d 607 (1967). Therefore, if the officers' view of the room was validly obtained, Sundum's contention that the entry was illegal and that any evidence seized must be suppressed as the product of an illegal search is without merit.

A guest in a motel has a constitutionally protected right to privacy in his motel room, and motel personnel cannot consent to a search of the guest's room. *Stoner v. California*, 376 U.S. 483, 490, 84 S. Ct. 889, 893, 11 L. Ed. 2d 856, 861, *rehearing denied*, 377 U.S. 940, 84 S. Ct. 1330, 12 L. Ed. 2d 303 (1964); *Finch v. State*, 592 P. 2d 1196, 1197 n. 3 (Alaska 1979); *Robinson v. State*, 578 P. 2d 141, 142 (Alaska 1978). But after the rental period has terminated, a guest's reasonable expectations of privacy are greatly diminished with respect to the right of motel management to enter. See *United States v. Jackson*, 585 F. 2d 653, 658 (4th Cir. 1978); *United States v. Akin*, 562 F. 2d 459, 464 (7th Cir. 1977), *cert. denied*, 435 U.S. 933, 98 S. Ct. 1509, 55 L. Ed. 2d 531 (1978); *United States v. Parizo*, 514 F. 2d 52, 54-55 (2d Cir. 1975); *United States v. Croft*, 429 F. 2d 884, 887 (10th Cir. 1970); *State v. Mascarenas*, 86 N.M. 692, 526 P. 2d 1285, 1286 (App. 1974); *State v. Taggart*, 14 Or. App. 408, 512 P. 2d 1359, 1364 (1973), *cert. denied*, 419 U.S. 877, 95 S. Ct. 141, 42 L. Ed. 2d 117 (1974); *State v. Roff*, 70 Wash. 2d 606, 424 P. 2d 643, 646-47 (1976). See also

People v. Van Eyk, 56 Cal. 2d 471, 15 Cal. Rptr. 150, 154, 364 P. 2d 326, 330 (1961), *cert. denied*, 369 U.S. 824, 82 S. Ct. 838, 7 L. Ed. 2d 788 (1962); *People v. Crayton*, 174 Cal. App. 2d 267, 344 P. 2d 627, 629 (1959); *State v. Chiles*, 595 P. 2d 1130, 1136 (Kan. 1979).

Gran testified that motel guests frequently left without paying their bill. After check-out time, she tried to contact Sundum by phoning his room and by knocking at his door, but there was no response. Gran then opened the door to his room in order to determine whether he had vacated. Her authority to do so, at the time she would normally have done so,[32] in accordance with her customary procedure, was not altered by the presence of the police.[33] Assuming the police were in a location which did not violate Sundum's rights before the door was opened, Gran's opening of the door for a legitimate private purpose did not constitute an illegal search merely because the police were present.

It is beyond dispute that the police officers were entitled to walk up to Sundum's door in order to investigate the burglary. See *Pistro v. State*, 590 P. 2d 884, 886-87 (Alaska 1979).[34] The fact that they did not avert their eyes when Gran opened the door does not convert their view of the room from a common passageway into an illegal search.

Sundum contends that the police officers' observation of him through the open door was not inadvertent and, therefore, does not come within the "plain view" exception to the requirement that no search or seizure can be made without a warrant. Inadvertence is a pre-condition to a valid seizure of evidence under the plain view exception. *Coolidge v. New Hampshire*, 403 U.S. 443, 470, 91 S. Ct. 2022, 2040, 29 L. Ed. 2d 564, 585 (1971); *Reeves v. State*, 599 P. 2d 727, 739 (Alaska 1979). But the kind of plain view to which the inadvertence requirement applies only takes place after there has been an initial search or intrusion.

[P]lain view does not occur until a search is in progress. In each case, this initial intrusion is justified by a warrant or by an exception such as "hot pursuit" or search incident to a lawful arrest, or by an extraneous valid reason for the officer's presence. *Coolidge v. New Hampshire*, 403 U.S. at 467, 91 S. Ct. at 2039, 29 L. Ed. 2d at 584. The inadvertence requirement of the plain view doctrine has never been thought to apply where the observation precedes the intrusion. It does not prevent police officers who are lawfully positioned in a public area from intentionally looking for suspects or incriminating evidence freely visible within the confines of a constitutionally protected area. 1 W. La Fave, Search and Seizure 2.2, at 242-43 (1978).

Finally, Sundum contends that seizure of the buckknife from under his mattress was the product of an unlawful search. Since the knife is but one of three allegedly stolen and identifiable items found in Sundum's possession, however, we do not see how our discussion of this point will have any effect on the plea of *nolo contendere* already entered by the defendant.

The judgment of the superior court is AFFIRMED.

SUMMARY

The legal rights of innkeepers are sometimes offset by the duties that they owe to guests, patrons, and third parties. However, if an innkeeper believes that her or his legal rights negate a legal duty and a judge rules otherwise, a serious management mistake has occurred.

The innkeeper holds control of the inn premises. The guests who come there do not enjoy the rights and privileges of property ownership. They can claim the privileges of the special relationship, but they are not owners of the property. Of growing concern today, as it was in earlier times, is the security and protection of guests and their property, patrons, and third parties. As each year goes by, the need for security increases.

A key subject in all hotel/motel/inn operations is what the law has to say about the rooms that are assigned to guests. First, of course, is the question of whether or not the room will be assigned at all. The assignment of a room becomes much like the duty to receive and occupies an important position in law. To unlawfully deny one a room that is available can lead to drastic consequences in court. The entry of guest rooms, the search of such rooms, arrests made because of items found, must be compatible with the Fourth Amendment.

The innkeeper's lien came into being as an adjunct of the court-created duty to receive. It was reasoned that if innkeepers were forced to receive travelers, they should have a corresponding right to be paid for the services and goods that they provided. Thus, the right to detain property of guests for sums owed came into being. The lien does not extend to the body of the guest or the means of the transportation by which the guest used to arrive at the inn.

QUESTIONS

1. What practical matters should be considered in deciding to move a guest to a new room?
2. What are three instances in which an innkeeper can enter the room of a guest lawfully without prior notice?
3. In the McHugh case, might the personnel have been acting in good faith? Was there any negligence on the part of the police officer?
4. Under what conditions might a lockout be considered?
5. What are the rights of innkeepers in keeping non-guests out of lobbies at the hotel?
6. What is the innkeepers' lien, and what is its purpose?
7. What does "civil rights" mean? Give a brief definition.
8. What might be one explanation for the length and detail of the McHugh case, and the Sundum case?
9. What is a hard key system at an inn?
10. How can a hotel become a disorderly house so as to be prosecuted for a crime?

NOTES

1. *Flax v. Monticello Realty Co.*, 185 Va. 474 (Sp. Ct. Va., 1946).
2. *Kane v. Ten Eyck Co., Inc.*, 175 N.Y.S. 2d 88, 92 (1943).
3. *State v. Ford*, 501 N.W. 2d 318 (Nebraska 1993).
4. Ridley Pearson, *Probable Cause* (New York: St. Martin's Press), p. 261.
5. *Knutson v. Fidelity*, 279 N.W. 714 (Minnesota 1938).
6. Adapted from California Lodging Industry Association guidelines.
7. *U.S. v. Steven Dale Winsor*, 87 Daily Journal DAR 2163 (U.S. Ct. App. 9th Circ., Pasadena, California 1987).
8. *Commonwealth v. Blinn*, 503 N.E. 2d 25 (Maine 1987).
9. *People v. Ohlinger*, 89-177 (Sup. Ct. Michigan 1991).
10. *U.S. v. McGraw*, 89-5412 (4th U.S. Ct. App. November 30, 1991).

11. *Lucas v. Omel*, 61 N.Y.S. 659 (1900).

12. 204 Misc. 119 N.Y.S. 2d 460 (New York 1958).

13. *Kelly v. United States*, 248 A. 2d 884 (D.C. App. 1975).

14. Nevada Revised Statutes, 201.420.

15. Sherry, *supra* at p. 115.

16. *State v. Snelgrove*, 384 S.E. 2d 705 (South Carolina 1989).

17. *Hodges v. Gibson*, 811 P. 2d 15 (Supreme Court Utah 1991).

18. *Thomas v. Hamilton*, 611 So. 2d 16.

19. *Uyas Sandidas v. Holiday Inns, Inc.*, 660 F. Supp. 666 (Puerto Rico 1987).

20. A quote by John Soares, *Loaded Dice: The True Story of a Casino Cheat* (New York: Dell Books) p. 60.

21. *Black's Law Dictionary*, 5th Edition.

22. *Ibid.*

23. *Winnett v. Adams*, 71 Neb. 817, 99 N.W. 681.

24. *State v. Powers*, 51 N.L. 432, 17 A. 969.

25. *Stoner v. California*, *supra* in Sundum case.

26. Nevada Revised Statutes, 651.020.

27. Sundum subsequently entered a plea of *nolo contendere* (no contest) while preserving his right to appeal the issues raised in his motion to suppress.

28. Gran indicated that guests frequently abandoned their rooms without paying.

29. The watchband was silver and was inlaid with a large turquoise stone.

30. Heger had been able to observe that the intruder had Indian features, wore his hair in a ponytail, and was wearing overalls and a striped shirt.

31. At that time AS 12.25.030 provided: A private person or a peace officer without a warrant may arrest a person:

    1. For a crime committed or attempted in his presence.

    2. When the person has committed a felony, although not in his presence.

    3. When a felony has in fact been committed, and he has reasonable cause for believing the person to have committed it.

32. Gran testified:

    Q. But for the presence of the officer would you at that time have gone up and knocked on the door?

    A. Oh, yes, definitely.

    Q. At that very time?

    A. Maybe not at that specific moment but within a very short time. I certainly would have because it was already after 12:00 o'clock [check-out time].

33. We do not conclude that the police instigated Gran's investigation or that she was an agent of the police. We note, however, that the question is a close one. She was acting in conjunction with the police and perhaps at the direction of the police.

34. At the least, Gran had the authority to consent to their entering the motel hallway to do so, because such authority derives from "mutual use of the property by persons generally having joint access or control for most purposes." *United States v. Matlock*, 415 U.S. 164, 171 n. 7, 94 S. Ct. 988, 993 n. 7, 39 L. Ed. 2d 242, 250 n. 7 (1974).

14

Liability and Management

OVERVIEW

BREACH OF THE duties described in Chapters 11 and 12, which often comes from negligent or misinformed management, can lead to legal liability. The responsibility for establishing proper legal practices falls squarely upon management. The law of agency makes this so, and one cannot use as a defense that, "My employee did it, not I."

LIABILITY AND THE COURTS

To be "liable," as that word is used in law, means to be "bound or obligated in law or equity; responsible; chargeable; answerable; compellable to make satisfaction, compensation, or restitution."[1] It is the "condition of being bound to respond because a wrong has occurred."[2] Thus liability is ". . . the state of being bound or obligated in law or justice to do, pay, or make good something; the state of one who is bound in law or justice to do something which may be enforced by action."[3]

The definitions break down into three parts:

1. Liability is involuntary as to the one who suffers it.
2. The condition is forced on the defaulting person or firm by court action.
3. The result of this court action can be enforced by "action."

Translated into simple terms, it means this: The hotel has been sued even though it did not want to be; the action in court was forced upon it and ended in a judgment against it. The judgment now can be enforced by attachment or execution against the assets of the hotel, even though the facility strongly objects to it. In short, it is an undesirable legal position to be in.

How Does Liability to Others Arise?

Legal liability can come about in a variety of ways, including but not limited to, the following:

1. breach of contract, sales or common law (contract liability)
2. negligence or carelessness (tort liability)
3. deliberate, willful acts that cause injury (tort and criminal liability)
4. acts of one's agents (contract and tort liability based on the law of agency)
5. breach of a bailment obligation (contract liability)

6. breach of warranty of food and beverages sold (contract liability)
7. statutory violations (negligence *per se*):
   a. dram Shop Act violations
   b. dire, health, and building code violations
   c. other statutes
8. fraud and misrepresentation:
   a. overreaching
   b. puffing (promising too much)
9. others, such as the rules of evidence, *res ipsa loquitur* (which raises an inference of negligence), and many others
   Figure 14.1 summarizes aspects of legal liability.

FIGURE 14.1 HH&T legal liability.

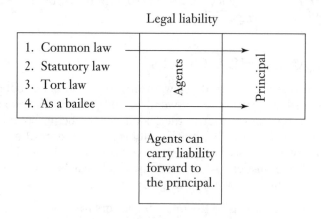

Liability can attach in three ways:

1. It can be forced upon a person or business through a lawsuit, with the subsequent award of damages by court judgment.
2. The one at fault may admit liability, thereby accepting legal responsibility.
3. Responsibility for an injury or loss may be accepted *without admitting liability*. The main reason for doing this is to maintain the goodwill of the person or persons who have suffered the loss while avoiding any admission of wrongdoing.

Decisions Needed

Managers often are faced with the need to make decisions involving legal liability situations. For instance, a guest has been injured or has suffered some other loss. Should the liability be assumed or not? Should a lawyer be consulted at the outset? If the guest brings suit, other questions arise. Should the accusation of liability be defended? Which lawyer should be retained? If the case is lost in the lower court, should an appeal be undertaken? Are there reasons for the appeal other than financial, such as the desire to avoid an undesirable precedent if the case decision is allowed to stand? These and other decisions face the manager and, though the advice of a lawyer should be sought, the final decisions in most instances are for management.

LEGAL FAILURE IN MANAGEMENT PRACTICES

Failure of management to meet the requirement of reasonable care, foreseeability, and other obligations imposed by law explains the constant flow of court cases being brought against industries today. Some examples of management failures in regard to the law follow.

1. Failing to receive travelers who do not have reservations when rooms are in fact available. This is a breach of the common-law duty to receive.
2. "Walking" (turning away) one who has a reservation contract. This is attributable to the hotel's negligence or the deliberate act of selling more rooms than are available. The former is a breach of contract that allows money recovery, and the latter is the criminal act of fraud. These conceivably could lead to fines, and perhaps imprisonment.
3. Turning away a would-be-guest because of his or her national origin. This violates federal and state civil rights acts.
4. Failing to meet statutory requirements, such as the American with Disabilities Act, and building code dictates in the construction of the hotel. In older properties, plate glass commonly was used in hotel construction. Modern building codes mandate the use of safety glass. If injury or death results from failure to comply with today's code requirements, compliance with a code of decades ago may not be accepted as a defense.[4]
5. Failing to exercise ordinary and reasonable care, taking into consideration foreseeability, in the operation of the business. This is a failure to meet the common-law standard of care.
6. Failing to give notice of the limits on liability for property loss.

LIMITS ON LIABILITY BY STATUTE

Toward the end of the last century, federal and state governments alike began to enact laws to place limits upon the liability of hospitality facilities. At the state level, the legislatures enacted statutes to limit the liability of innkeepers for the loss of guests' money and valuables. The policy reason for these laws was to lift some of the harshness of common-law liability.[5] Liability was limited in other areas also.

The State of Nevada provides an example. The following was declared as a policy of the state:

> The legislature declares that the purpose of this subsection is to effectuate the public policy of the State of Nevada by encouraging the recreational use of land, lakes, reservoirs and other waters owned or controlled by any public or quasi-municipal agency or corporation of this state, wherever such land or water may be situated.[6]

The statute then follows:

1. An award for damages in an action sounding in tort brought under NRS 41.031 above may not exceed the sum of $50,000, exclusive of interest computed from the date of judgment, to or for the benefit of any claimant. An award may not include any amount as exemplary or punitive damages.

2. The limitations of subsection 1 upon the amount and nature of damages which may be awarded apply also to any action sounding in tort and arising from any recreational activity or recreational use of land or water.

In Nevada, hundreds of hotels, motels, "botels" (where guests arrive by boat), inns, and bed-and-breakfast operations are situated along the Colorado River, at Lake Mead, and by Lake Tahoe and other bodies of water. This statute applies to all of these hospitality operations. Nevada has another statute that limits legal liability at hospitality operations. In 1983, Nevada amended its civil rights statute to limit a recovery by a prevailing plaintiff to actual damages for economic loss and exemplary damages for an act ". . . such as intentional discrimination in an amount not to exceed $1,000." The law allows the plaintiff to recover costs and reasonable attorney fees.[7]

The trend that started in the last century of placing limits on liability saw a dramatic reversal with deregulation of the airlines in 1978, effective 1983.[8] This deregulation lifted much of the protection that airlines could get through their tariffs. Airlines now face common-law liability under traditional legal rules.

The subject of liability and management requires further discussion in a variety of areas.

Beginning and Ending of Inn-Guest Relationship

Returning to innkeeping, timing often becomes involved in deciding what the liability of an innkeeper may be in a given situation. An example of this is found in the question: When does the inn-guest relationship begin and when does it end? The relationship begins when one wants to become a guest and the innkeeper accepts that offer. This becomes important in deciding the degree of liability for valuables lost at the inn, as an example. If the guest relationship is in effect, the loss-of-valuables statutes may limit the innkeeper's liability. If the relationship has ended, the matter may be controlled by the law of bailment. The latter has no limits on liability other than the value of the property itself.

A variety of cases are found in the court reports and some rules can be gleaned from them. If a guest settles the bill, although intending to return in a few days, the relationship has ended in Missouri.[9] Valuables left by the paid-up guest would be held by the innkeeper as a bailee. In a Tennessee case,[10] a guest left money with a clerk, settled the bill, and left, intending to return in a day or two. The former guest was delayed in returning. The court held that the innkeeper was not liable for the money left with the clerk.

In an early case,[11] when a guest left the inn owing 25 cents —leaving property as security—intending to return shortly, the court distinguished "dead goods" left from "live goods" such as a horse. "The property lost was "dead goods," and the same rules do not obtain as if it had been a horse. For in the latter case, the host would have had "benefit by the continuance of the horse with him." In the former, he would have "no benefit," and therefore the host would not be charged with a loss in the absence of the guest."

Clearly, the temporary absence of a guest during the day will not end the relationship.[12] Neither will eating meals elsewhere end it,[13] or going out "on the town."[14] If a guest pays early for the purpose of obtaining funds for the day, the relationship has not ended at that point.[15] Conversely, if a guest pays a bill intending to avoid a charge for the day, even if intending to return that night, the relationship is at an end. The court stated:

> The expectation thereafter to become a guest did not continue the relationship and it terminated at his instance, and for his advantage, by settling his account for entertainment. An innkeeper is chargeable as such because of the profit derived from entertaining. *The right to charge is the criterion of the innkeeper's liability* [emphasis added].[16]

Degree of Liability

Not only does timing become involved in legal liability, but so does the *extent* of liability. It can be great in some instances, moderate in others, and slight in still others. The degree or extent of legal liability will depend upon the relationship that has been formed between the hotel and the patron or guest. For example, in a bailment for hire, the bailee must use ordinary care. In a gratuitous bailment, the care might be somewhat less than ordinary care. Figure 14.2 illustrates this concept. Bailments will be discussed in detail in Chapters 19 and 20.

FIGURE 14.2 Degree of liability.

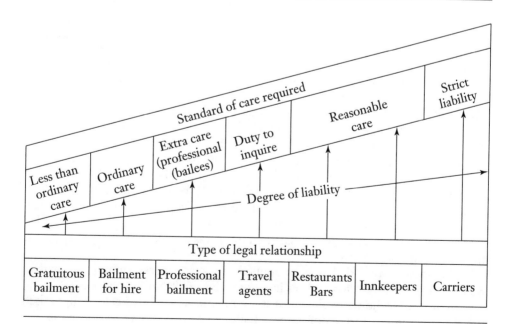

Theories of Legal Liability

The trial lawyer can look to different theories in deciding whether to take a case involving liability. Two of these are *res ipsa loquitur* (RIL) and third-party beneficiary.

Res Ipsa Loquitur

One theory of legal liability that is being called upon more often in HH&T litigation is that of *res ipsa loquitur*—"the thing speaks for itself." It has been used against guests, and it has been used against hotels, as was seen in *Page v. Sloan*, in Chapter 4.

This theory of liability is a rule of evidence

> . . . whereby negligence of the alleged wrongdoer may be inferred from the mere fact an accident happened provided the character of the accident and the circumstances attending it lead reasonably to the belief that in the absence of negligence it would not have occurred and that the thing which caused the injury is shown to have been under the management and control of alleged wrongdoer.[17]

The rule had its beginning in *Byrne v. Boadle*. In that case, Chief Judge Pollack had this to say:

> The learned counsel was quite right in saying that there are many accidents from which no presumption of negligence can arise, but I think it would be wrong to lay down as a rule that in no case can presumption of negligence arise from the fact of an accident. The present case upon the evidence comes to this, a man is passing in front of the premises of a dealer in flour, and there falls down upon him a barrel of flour. I think it apparent that the barrel was in the custody of the defendant who occupied the premises, and who is responsible for the acts of his servants who had the control of it; and in my opinion the fact of its falling is *prima facie* evidence of negligence, and the plaintiff who was injured by it is not bound to show that it could not fall without negligence, but if there are any facts inconsistent with negligence it is for the defendant to prove them.[18]

The legal effect of the RIL doctrine is that it takes from the injured plaintiff the burden of proving the cause of the injury. This is the rule in normal cases, but if this rule were universal, it would force an injured person to explain, for example, why an elevator fell in a hotel. The plaintiff would have to prove facts that may be impossible to determine after the injury occurs. The plaintiff knows nothing of the construction of the hotel and the installation of the elevator. Thus, the rule of RIL says that, if the elevator was under the care and control of the innkeeper and if the injury would not have happened in the absence of negligence, the burden shifts to the innkeeper to show that the injury was caused by some other means than his or her negligence.

The doctrine of RIL has been applied in a case where a mirror fell from a wall[19] in a suit brought for injuries in a hotel elevator[20] and other cases.

An inn guest who was scalded in a shower because of overly heated water raised the RIL theory in a tort action in an attempt to recover for the scald burns. On appeal, the lower court verdict in favor of the guest was reversed. The court said the doctrine of *res ipsa loquitur* did not apply because the guest had control of the faucets and showerhead, even though the inn had control of the hot-water source.[21]

In a similar case, where the testimony showed that the inn had set the shower controls so the guest could not control the flow of water, and the guest then was scalded, the RIL doctrine did apply.[22]

The landmark case on food service had this to say about the legal doctrine of RIL:

> A number of (court) decisions have deemed it appropriate to apply the doctrine of *res ipsa loquitur* [in food cases], where the instrumentality producing the injury was in the exclusive control of the defendant and the injury would not have occurred if due care had been exercised. We express no opinion on whether the doctrine applies in this case [Mexicali] and leave it to the lower courts to determine whether, on the facts of the particular case, the doctrine should apply.[23]

Third-Party Beneficiary

Another theory of legal liability is that of "third-party beneficiary." Travelers often are injured or caused loss in foreign nations and find it difficult to bring suit there because of the problems of distance and expense of foreign counsel. It becomes desirable, if possible, to shift that liability to hotels or others at the place of residence of the injured traveler.

One theory of law under which this is being done is that of third-party beneficiary. If a traveler is sold a travel package by a local hotel, for example, and injury occurs elsewhere, the hotel can be sued because it benefitted from the contract and thus was a third-party beneficiary. The leading case on this point is the Klakis case,[24] discussed later in Chapter 24.

Coupled with theories of legal liability is a common-law doctrine used in court when deciding questions of liability.

The "Reasonable Person"

Under this doctrine, what one did in the operation of a business in which another suffered a loss is tested against what the reasonable business person would have or would not have done under like or similar circumstances. If a jury should find that the business person met the standard of the reasonable person, that person may be excused from legal liability. If this standard is not met, the jury may find fault. If the jury then finds that this fault was the proximate (actual) cause of the loss, it can assess damages (money) against the defaulting person or firm. An author had this to say about the subject.

> The Common Law of England has been laboriously built about a mythical figure—the figure of "The Reasonable Man."
>
> It is impossible to travel anywhere or to travel for long in that confusing forest of learned judgments which constitutes the Common Law of England without encountering the Reasonable Man. He is at every turn, an ever-present help in time of trouble, and his apparitions make the road to equity and right. There never

has been a problem, however difficult, which His Majesty's judges have not in the end been able to resolve by asking themselves the simple question, "Was this or was it not the conduct of a reasonable man?" and leaving that question to be answered by the jury [a question of fact].

This noble creature . . . is one who invariably looks where he is going, and is careful to examine the immediate foreground before he executes a leap or bound; who neither star-gazes nor is lost in meditation when approaching trap-doors or the margin of a dock; who records in every case upon the counterfoils of cheques such ample details as are desirable, scrupulously substitutes the word "Order" for the word "Bearer," crosses the instrument "a/c Payee only," and registers the package in which it is dispatched; who never mounts a moving omnibus and does not alight from any car while the train is in motion; who investigates exhaustively the *bona fides* of every mendicant before distributing alms, and will inform himself of the history and habits of a dog before administering a caress; who believes no gossip, nor repeats it, without firm basis for believing it to be true; who never drives his ball till those in front of him have definitely vacated the putting-green which is his own objective; who never from the year's end to another makes an excessive demand upon his wife, his neighbors, his servants, his ox; . . . who in the way of business looks only for that narrow margin of profit which twelve men such as himself would reckon to be "fair," and contemplates his fellow-merchants, their agents, and their goods, with that degree of suspicion and distrust which the law deems admirable; who never swears, gambles, or loses his temper; who uses nothing except in moderation, and even while he flogs his child is meditating only on the golden mean. Devoid, in short, of any human weakness, with not one single saving vice, *sans* prejudice, procrastination, ill-nature, avarice, and absence of mind, as careful for his own safety as he is for that of others, this excellent but odious character stands like a monument in our Courts of Justice, vainly appealing to his fellow-citizens to order their lives after his own example. . . .[25]

To increase our understanding of liability and management, it is helpful to learn more about court procedures.

COURT PROCEDURES

First, an incident must arise that involves some alleged violation of a legal duty. As an example, guest Hayward is assaulted while staying at a Holiday Inn in Virginia, and claims there is responsibility on the part of the inn. The inn claims the injury was due to the carelessness of Hayward and is not their responsibility.[26]

Filing of Suit

Suit is filed—in this case, in a federal court in the Eastern District of Virginia. The theory of the case is that, by advertising that its inns were a "safe place to stay," Holiday Inn made an express warranty. So, when the guest was assaulted, this was a breach of that warranty and the inn was responsible.

A suit is started by the preparation and filing in court of a *complaint*, within which the theory of the case is set forth. This complaint then is served (handed to or other notice given) on the defendant, the one being sued. Under rules of procedures of the federal courts, and most states, the defendant has twenty days in which to respond and admit or deny the allegations of the complaint. This response is called the *answer*. Failing to answer before the deadline is an admission of liability.

Discovery Stage

Whereas the complaint-and-answer stage moves quickly, the next step, known as the discovery stage, takes more time. Here the parties have alternatives available designed to allow them to uncover as much information as possible about each other's case. The plaintiff may want to examine records of the defendant. The defendant may want the plaintiff to submit to a physical examination by a doctor of defendant's choosing.

Other matters take place at this stage, including the taking of *depositions* and the use of *interrogatories*. The former are oral statements taken under oath. The latter are written questions that must be answered in writing.

Case "Maturing"

In time—about one or two years in federal courts in Virginia—the case will be given a trial date, and thus it has "matured."

Trial

At the time of the trial, the burden of proof is on the plaintiff. The plaintiff must prove in court, by a preponderance of the evidence, the following:

1. That a national ad had been used by the defendant in which it promised that its inns were safe places to stay.
2. That, on the strength of this warranty, plaintiff entered into a contract with the defendant by becoming a guest at the inn.
3. That this warranty was breached, which breach was the proximate cause of the losses suffered.
4. That the plaintiff suffered money losses as the result of the breach.

If the plaintiff can produce evidence to establish the above, he or she has made out a *prima facie* (on the face of it) case. It now becomes the burden of the defendant to rebut this *prima facie* case. Figure 14.3 presents the proof process.

The Defense

The burden now has shifted to the defendant, who must come forward with evidence to rebut the presumption raised by the plaintiff's case. If the defendant cannot do this, the court will direct a verdict for the plaintiff and set a hearing on damages. In most cases, lawsuits are defended vigorously and adequate defenses are presented. The court will usually not direct a verdict in these instances.

At common law, an innkeeper has three defenses that will relieve him or her from liability to a guest:

FIGURE 14.3 Proof process in court.

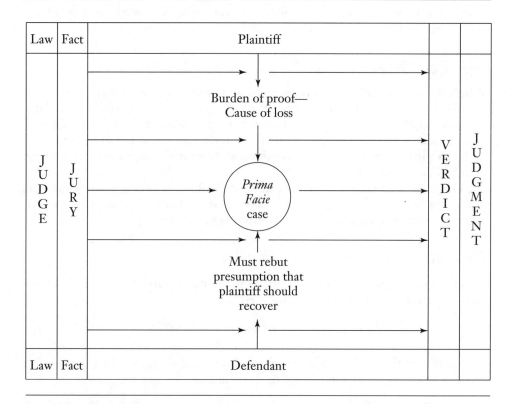

1. an act of God
2. an act of the public enemy
3. negligence on the part of the guest (The latter was the defense raised in the Hayward case.)

The Hayward case went to the jury upon a charge (called *instructions* in state courts) from the federal judge, which told the jury the controlling principles of law. The verdict was returned for the plaintiff in the sum the jury decided he should recover.

Comparative Negligence

By this process, sketched briefly here, enforceable liability arises. Other factors become involved in finding legal liability or its absence. These include comparative negligence, contributory negligence, and others.

Today, comparative fault in the states that adhere to it weighs fault and allows or denies recovery on that basis.[27] Florida follows that comparative negligence rule.[28] Pennsylvania has enacted the Comparative Negligence Act, which follows that rule also. The old common-law rule of assumption of the risk has been replaced in Louisiana by the doctrine of comparative negligence. In a Louisiana tort case, the jury found that the injured customer was 72 percent negligent and that the defendant, K-Mart, was 28 percent negligent. This barred the plaintiff from recovery.[29] In Idaho, if a jury finds that negligence on the part of the plaintiff and defendant are equal, no recovery is allowed. Also, a non-party may be included in the calculations of a jury, but the non-party will not have to pay any part of the judgment.

When comparing fault under the doctrine of comparative negligence, does responsibility have to include the deliberate act of a tortfeasor (one who caused the injury deliberately), as well as the negligence of the hospitality industry facility and the plaintiff's negligence? Thomas Blazovic was assaulted at the Plantation Restaurant and Bar and was injured severely. He sued the restaurant, alleging a lack of security, poor lighting, and negligence in selling alcohol to the person who attacked him. The New Jersey court ruled that the responsibility for the claimed injury must be apportioned according to each party's degree of fault, including the fault of the tortfeasor. The effect of this ruling is that it enlarges "comparative negligence" to include intentional conduct such as an unwarranted assault. This makes it important for the courts or legislatures to change the term "comparative negligence" to "comparative fault," as has been done in other states.[30]

In a slip-and-fall case at a seafood restaurant in Louisiana in 1990, the jury awarded the injured person (an employee) more than $645,000 in damages, plus almost $40,000 for past medical expenses. The jury apportioned the negligence (fault) as follows:

1. 60 percent was charged to the restaurant owner because moisture that accumulated on a tile floor after an air conditioner had been turned off, had not been mopped up, and

2. 40 percent was charged to the hotel corporation for the negligent operation of the restaurant on its premises.[31]

The supreme court of West Virginia described the doctrine in this way:

A party is not barred from recovering damages in a tort action so long as his negligence or fault does not equal or exceed the combined negligence or fault of the other parties involved in the accident.[32]

A unique feature of the West Virginia comparative negligence law is that the trial judge has a duty to inform (instruct) the jury of what the doctrine means if a request is made to do so.

Pennsylvania has comparative negligence by statute.[33] In Florida, when an intoxicated minor is a passenger in a car driven by an intoxicated minor, comparative negligence cannot be applied against the passenger who is injured in a car accident. The dram shop statutes of Florida say that minors are part of the class to be protected by the law. Thus, a court cannot take away that protection by applying comparative negligence rules to the minor who is a passenger.[34]

Before comparative fault began to develop, contributory negligence played a large role in the determination of legal liability.

Contributory Negligence

Fewer than one-half of the fifty states still follow the old doctrine of contributory negligence. This harsh rule of law had its beginning in the case of *Butterfield v. Forrestor*,[35] a case that involved a tipsy horseman who rode into a pole leaning across the road and was injured. The rule that came out of that case was that, if one contributes to his or her own injury because of negligence, even though slight, this bars that person from recovery. Figure 14.4 provides further illustration of contributory negligence.

In the District of Columbia this old rule is still in effect and bars all recovery by an injured plaintiff. The federal courts there do not compare the negligence (or fault) of the plaintiff and the inn where the alleged injury occurred.

As a matter of legal curiosity, has there ever been a case in which a court held a plaintiff to be 100 percent contributorily negligent? The answer is "yes." It happened in a case at the Hyatt Regency Hotel in New Orleans. Jack Mayo, fortified with over three times the legal limit of alcohol, backed up by cocaine, fell down several steps at the hotel and was injured. A security guard attempted to assist him, but Mayo jerked away and fell. It was determined that Mayo was guilty of 100 percent contributory negligence.[36] Even in a state that follows the comparative fault rule, Mayo would have recovered nothing.

> The fact that a controverted terrain is dangerous, or potentially so, does not of itself prove contributory negligence. Where a proprietor allows to develop a dangerous condition which could have been avoided, it is no conclusive defense against a person injured thereby to say that he could see the danger. *The plaintiff in the case at bar had to go home sometime* [emphasis added]. She could not remain at the business indefinitely. The question to be determined in situations of this kind is whether the danger so out-proportions the hardship of seeking ways out of it that the Court should say it was folly for the guest to enter the danger zone at all.[37]

FIGURE 14.4   Nuances of contributory negligence.

	Potential danger	Obvious peril
Guest	This is an area which, although potentially dangerous, is not prophetic of resultant mishap.	Here "the traveler is forbidden to enter on pain of culpable contributory negligence should there be an accident."

Source: *Morris v. Atlantic and Pacific Tea Company*, 384 Pa. 464, 469, 121 A 2d 135 (Pennsylvania 1956).

The Court View

To understand how the courts treat negligence, is is useful to examine it in more detail.

> Negligent conduct may be active or passive. Active negligent conduct is the commission of an act resulting in injury to another, in breach of a legal duty owed to such other, and falling below the standard of the reasonably prudent person under the circumstances. Passive negligent conduct is the failure to act, in violation of the actor's legal duty under the circumstances, resulting in injury to another.
>
> The innkeeper owes his guests or others similarly situated the legal duty to provide reasonably safe premises. The interest the law seeks to compensate is that of protecting a guest or other person against the infliction of unintentional harm.[38]

Negligence, then, may take various forms, including:

1. comparative negligence
2. contributory negligence
3. gross negligence
4. negligence *per se*
5. simple negligence

The concept includes action as well as inaction. Action indicates an act and is affirmative, such as doing something that should not have been done. Inaction means that something that should have been done was not done. Such negligence is negative.[39] Negligence that arises from improper action or by failure to act will be treated the same in court.

In a case where the absence of a handrail on stairs was the issue, the injured plaintiff claimed the failure to provide handrails was the proximate cause of her injuries due to a fall. The defendant raised the defense that it had complied with all applicable building code and safety code provisions in construction of the stairs. This proved to be correct, as shown by evidence at the trial.

The plaintiff appealed a dismissal of the case. The upper court held that compliance with statutory requirements still may not preclude the plaintiff from proving that the defendant was otherwise negligent by failing to take extra safety measures. The court cited the *Law of Torts*: "Compliance with a statute does not necessarily mean that due care was exercised."[40]

A Catch 22 situation can confront innkeepers in these situations:

1. If they fail to follow strictly the dictates of statutes, regulations, or codes, they may be held liable under the principle of negligence *per se*.
2. If they follow strictly the requirements of statutes, regulations, or codes, they may be held liable under the common-law principles of failing to exercise ordinary reasonable care, by not taking safety precautions beyond those required by the statutes, regulations, or codes.

It becomes essential for the innkeeper to comply strictly with applicable written law and, in addition, foresee other dangers and provide for them.[41]

Burden of Proof

Burden of proof can be one of three types:

1. *Preponderance of the evidence:* proof that exceeds 50 percent.
2. *Clear and convincing proof:* proof that is more than preponderance but no percentage is set.
3. *Proof beyond all reasonable doubt.*

The first two are encountered in civil actions. They are essentially the same, except that in some instances, such as product liability cases, a court may require proof greater than 50 percent. The third burden is the mainstay of our criminal system. We cannot take the freedom—and certainly not the life—of a citizen charged with a crime if there is any doubt as to his or her innocence.

Proving Negligence

> We have said many times that the law does not require every fact and circumstance which make up a case of negligence to be proved by direct and positive evidence or by the testimony of eyewitnesses, and that circumstantial evidence alone may authorize a finding of negligence. Negligence may be inferred from all of the facts plus the surrounding circumstances, and where the evidence of such facts and circumstances are such as to take the case out of the realm of conjecture, and into the realm of the field of legitimate inference from established facts, a prima facie case has been made."[42]

Proof of Damages

Not only must the plaintiff prove negligence, but the burden is on the plaintiff to prove, by clear and convincing proof, the amount of the losses suffered. In civil cases the plaintiff has to prove the loss by enough evidence to convince a jury that the loss should be compensated. In court this is spoken of as a "proof of damages." Four types of damages can be sought, depending upon the nature of the case:

1. *Actual damages* are those that result from out-of-pocket losses. If A is turned away from Motel X because of overbooking, and goes to Motel Y next door but has to pay $10 more, the actual loss to A is $10, provided the rooms are comparable.
2. *Consequential or resulting damages* are those that flow as a consequence of the defendants' acts. Here, other factors come into consideration. The courts have allowed recovery if default and its extent can be proven with reasonable certainty.
3. *Punitive or exemplary damages* can be recovered in some cases involving a tort. Such damages are designed to sting or punish the one who committed outrageous and unnecessary torts. Verdicts into the millions of dollars have been awarded for punitive damages. Punitive damages normally cannot be awarded in a breach-of-contract case. Yet, if the breach of contract is accompanied by a tort, punitives may be awarded, but only if the act was deliberate, willful, and of such a nature as to shock one's conscience. Mere negligent acts will not lead to punitive damages in tort cases.

4. *Nominal damages* are those in which the plaintiff proves liability to the satisfaction of a jury but does not convince the jury of the losses. They usually take this form: "We the jury find for the plaintiff and assess his loss at $1.00." Such a verdict has the effect of placing the costs of the lawsuit upon the defendant.

Moving from our examination of liability, we will close the chapter with some observations regarding management by agency.

MANAGEMENT BY AGENCY

The law of agency, as we know it today, is relatively new when compared with the laws of contract, property, tort, and other legal areas. This is true because the need for such a law did not exist until the coming of the Industrial Revolution. At that time and thereafter, because of expanding manufacturing of goods and perpetually increasing markets, one person or one family no longer could carry on commerce as it had been practiced over prior centuries. Those in business had to operate through others to carry on the manufacture, sale, and distribution of goods and to provide other services.

When this began to happen, a body of law was needed to regulate these new business activities. As it happened, principles of law already were in place that were destined to form the basis of the laws of agency. These had grown out of the laws of slavery.

Historically, a slave was "chattel" or personal property. Having no legal rights, the slave depended upon the master to provide the necessities of life. Thus, the master contracted as needed to maintain the slave and otherwise cared for and supported him or her. If the slave caused injury to another's person or property, the master had a corresponding duty to stand good for the damages. As the common-law judges said, *respondeat superior*—"let the master respond." It was not that the master had committed an offense. It was simply that the master had the *responsibility* for the damage done. It was liability without fault.

Today, this principle forms the basis of the law of agency and *qui facit per alium, facit per se*. "Who acts through another, acts himself" has become a frequently repeated statement in court and the law books.

Today the laws of agency form the environment or "surroundings" within which management principles must be carried out. Failure to recognize this may lead one to believe that the law of agency is a detached subject that comes into play only at prescribed times. The opposite is the truth, and agency law provides an overlay within which management principles must function. Indeed, the law of agency often determines the *form* that management principles must take. It is a case of one controlling the other.

To facilitate an understanding of this law, we will look at some principles of management and compare them with rules of agency. This will reveal how one influences the development of the other and the role played by legal liability at the inn.

Hotel Organizations

Two organizations are recognized within the hotel: the informal and the formal organizations. The former is created by the employees and operates on a "word-of-mouth" or "grapevine" basis. This organization is made up of agents and employees. The smart manager will make use of this informal organization to relay information, to permit the employee-agents to engage in self-regulation, and to permit natural leaders to play a role in running the business. Conversely, this organization must be watched carefully to make certain it is not being used in ways that may be harmful. In the latter event, movement of personnel and perhaps firings would be in order. Management must be certain that its members (the informal organization) are functioning for the good of the business.

The formal organization is something else. It is created by management and usually has five to fifteen departments. These departments are broken into classes such as line, staff, front and back of the house, and centralized and decentralized. The principles of delegation come to the front in the line departments. When one delegates, the law of agency says that what the other does is the act of the person doing the delegation. Legal responsibility flows with the delegation, and this flow is upward.

Staff departments are classed as *advisory* and *functional*. The former may be "pure staff" and have no authority over line departments. Yet the functions they perform will form the pattern that will be followed by others, who, in, turn bind the main organization by agency law. Functional staff may have some control over line staff and be in the same position as one who delegates.

The principle of *unity of command* tells us that each employee should have only one manager. This is essential under agency law to prevent an agent from being faced with conflicting orders. If this happens and loss results to third parties, management is responsible. It would not be a good legal defense to claim that a second manager had issued a valid order that, if followed, would have prevented the loss.

Finally, the principles of *division of responsibility* and *internal correlation* of data will go a long way in avoiding the theft of goods and embezzlement of funds. Theft of company funds, even by forged checks, almost always remains the responsibility of the business. The Uniform Commercial Code and the laws of agency make that so.

In this brief discussion we have seen that the law of agency does play a part in the pattern by which a business is managed. Many management principles have been arrived at by scientific study, others have developed out of the need to comply with agency law. A breakdown in principles of management can lead to what we want to avoid—legal liability.

SUMMARY

Management and employees, as well as agents, can be legally protected in their business affairs by acting as reasonable persons. The courts have never demanded perfection in business affairs—only that those who carry out these tasks and duties, do so in a manner expected from a reasonable person who occupies a similar position to the one doing the acting.

While the doctrine of *res ipsa loquitur* is not new, it establishes a method for determining liability. If an elevator falls at a hotel, "the thing speaks for itself," and a presumption arises that the hotel has neglected the elevator or was negligent in its maintenance and operation. The burden of proof shifts to the hotel to show that it was blameless for the fall and the injuries that resulted from it.

The concept that managers have a duty to foresee dangers before they happen is now well established by law. The principle is heading toward an obligation to foresee beyond what can actually be expected.

The common law doctrine of contributory negligence is rapidly losing ground to "comparative negligence." In comparative negligence, fault and the percentages, decided by the jury on both sides, is reflected in monetary awards.

"Discovery" is that part of modern civil trials in which both parties gain information about each other. Failure to participate in this process can result in legal sanctions against the uncooperative party. For example, if a hotel requests photos of an injured guest who is suing the hotel and the photos are not produced, they will not be allowed to be used against the hotel at trial time.

QUESTIONS

1. What does "liability" mean, and what concern does it raise at HH&T operations?
2. Why does the degree of legal liability depend upon the relationship of the parties involved?
3. What was, and still is, the unfair feature of the doctrine of contributory negligence?
4. What were the three common-law defenses? Are they still in use, or have they been modified?
5. What is the 50-50 rule of comparative negligence?
6. What factor should be taken into consideration when deciding whether to use brochures at an inn, keeping in mind the liability problem?
7. Who is a reasonable person?
8. True or false: Deregulation of the airlines may be the forerunner of a movement to place stronger liability on the HH&T industry.
9. Under what conditions may punitive damages be awarded?
10. What is a rational reason for limiting the liability of innkeepers for loss of money and valuables of guests?

NOTES

1. *Homan v. Employers*, 345 Mo. 650, 136 S.W 2d 289, 298.
2. *Pacific v. Murdock*, 193 Ark. 327, 99 S.W 2d 233, 235.
3. *Fidelity v. Diamond*, 310 Ill. App. 387, 34 N.E. 2d 123.
4. *Jenkins v. McLean Hotel, Inc.*, 859 F. 2d 598 (Missouri 1988).
5. Nevada Revised Statutes, 651.050 as amended in 1979.
6. Nevada Revised Statutes, 41.035.
7. Nevada Revised Statutes, 651.050 as amended January 1983.
8. Federal Aviation Act of 1958, amended October 24, 1978, 92 Stat. 1705.

9. *McKeever v. Kramer*, 203 Mo. App. 269, 218 S.W. 403 (1918).

10. *Whitmore v. Haroldson*, 2 Lea. (Tenn.) 312 (1879).

11. *Hays v. Turner*, 23 Iowa 214 (1867).

12. *Drope v. Theyar* (1650) Popham, 178, 79 Eng. Reprint 1274; *White's Case* (1553), 2 Dyer 158B, 73 Eng. Reprint, 343.

13. *McDaniels v. Robinson*, 26 Vt. 316, 52 Am. Dec. 574 (1854).

14. *McDonald v. Edgerton*, 5 Barb 562, N.Y. (1849).

15. *Brown Hotel Co. v. Burckhart*, 13 Colo. App. 59, 56, P. 188 (1899).

16. *Miller v. Peeples*, 60 Miss. 819, 45 Am. Rep 23 (1883).

17. *Hillen v. Hooker*, 484 S.W 2d 111, 115 (Tex. App.).

18. 2 Hurl. & Colt. 722 (1863).

19. *Deming Hotel v. Prox.*, 142 Ind. App. 603, 236 N.E. 2d 613 (1968).

20. *Notice v. Regent*, 429 N.Y.S. 2d 437 (1980).

21. *Simpson v. Cotton*, 396 S.E. 2d 354 (North Carolina 1990).

22. *Wolfe v. Chateau*, 357 A. 2d 282 (New Jersey 1976).

23. *Mexicali Rose et al., Petitioners, v. Superior Court of Alameda County, Respondent;* Jack A. Clark, Real Party in Interest, 1 Cal. 4th 617, P. 2d (California 1991).

24. *Klakis v. Nationwide Leisure Corp.*, 73 A.D. 2d 521, N.Y.S. 2d 407 (1979).

25. A. P. Herbert, *Misleading Cases in the Common Law*, 6th ed. (1931).

26. *Hayward v. Holiday Inns, Inc.*, 459 F. Supp. 634 (ED Va. 1978).

27. *Treichlinger v. French Lick Springs Hotel*, 102 S.W. 101 (Indiana 1917).

28. *Booth v. Abbey Road Beef & Booze, Inc.*, 532 So. 2d 1288 (Florida 1988).

29. *Crowther v. K-Mart*, 568 So. 2d 699 (Louisiana 1990).

30. *Blazovic v. Andrick*, A-36137 (Sup. Ct. New Jersey, May 22, 1991).

31. *Burton v. Berthelot*, 567 S.Q. 2d 649 (Louisiana 1990).

32. *Bradley v. Appalachian*, 256 S.E. 2d 879 (West Virginia 1979).

33. Pennsylvania Const. Stat. Ann. Sec. 7102 (Purdon Supp. 1981).

34. *Booth v. Abbey Road*, supra n. 28.

35. 11 East 60, 103 Eng. Rep. 926 (1809).

36. *Mayo v. Hyatt Corp.*, 718 F. Supp. 19 (Louisiana 1989).

37. *Morris v. Atlantic*, 121 A. 2d 135, 136 (Pennsylvania 1956).

38. Sherry, *supra*.

39. *Salt River v. Compton*, 8 P. 2d 249 (Arizona 1932).

40. W. Prosser, *Law of Torts*, *supra*.

41. *Luxen v. Holiday Inns*, 566 F. Supp. 1484 (Illinois 1983).

42. *Connolly v. Nicollet Hotel*, 254 Minn. 373, 95 N.W. 2d 657 (1959).

15

Premises Liability

Overview

In Chapter 14 we became acquainted with legal liability and saw how legal requirements and standards can place responsibility upon management. In this chapter we expand on the topics of Chapter 14 and find out how the principles discussed there apply in specific situations. The cases that have gone to court because of injury and loss have been of a remarkable variety as well as quantity.

Three quotes point out the importance of good management in preventing liability.

> Throughout the hospitality industry, litigation continues to mount. Although owners and managers do all they can to prevent occurrences which create lawsuits, and constantly attempt to purchase sufficient insurance to cover themselves, this is not always possible and sometimes, if possible, is too expensive.[1]
>
> Because inns are places of public accommodation and are obligated by law to accept virtually everyone who presents himself or herself and asks for a room, there is no opportunity to check out the guests as to their honesty or whether they are bent on committing a crime. Therefore, the hotel has to proceed as if every guest needed protection from every other guest as well as from invitees, trespassers, and hotel employees, and then provide security accordingly.
>
> The occupants . . . and those who use the facility must rely upon the innkeeper to supply their protection because they cannot avail themselves of the unusual security provided by a municipality through its police department; and the failure . . . to meet this responsibility could render it [the inn] liable in damages.[2]
>
> While second-guessing every outcome of a legal question is impossible, maintaining a basic awareness of trends is required for effective inn management. Keeping abreast of legal issues used to be a good idea for hoteliers. Now it's essential for survival.[3]

At early English common law, an innkeeper was held to be an "insurer" (insures against loss or damages) of the traveler and the traveler's property. The court recognized three exceptions, and three others developed in succeeding years. A discussion of all six follows in this chapter.

Common-Law Defenses to Court Actions

1. acts of God and Nature (an irresistible, superhuman cause[4])
2. acts of the public enemy (Losses and death caused by armed forces from another nation. Public enemy does not include criminals of the routine variety.)

3. acts of the guest:
   a. contributory negligence
   b. comparative negligence
   c. fraud of the guest
   d. acts of agents of guests who are authorized by guests
4. results of accidents that could not have been foreseen [anticipated][5]
5. crimes committed by outsiders that could not have been foreseen

As legal defenses continue to develop, the legal defenses to charges of negligence, breach of contract, and failure to exercise reasonable care will all be subject to the qualification that such defenses must be ". . . without fault . . . ."[6] If there is fault, the defense will fail.

In the eighteenth century, American courts began to rule that holding innkeepers to an insurer status was no longer reasonable or necessary in the advancing times. The courts began to agree that the legal standard should be "reasonable care," taking into consideration the facts and circumstances. This became a question of fact for a jury to decide. Under the insurer rule, it had been a matter of law for the judge to decide. This development of the common law drastically reduced the legal liability of innkeepers and others in the hospitality industry. This represented a "legal grace" and sharply reduced legal liability.

Following on the heels of this came the New York legislative act of 1855, which reduced the liability for the loss of guest property at the hotel. All of the states have such laws today, and they will be examined in Chapter 20.

The legal responsibility of innkeepers, then, started out as very severe. It was reduced in more recent times and was reduced further by statutes limiting liability for property loss.

The proprietor of a place of business who holds it out to the public for entry for business purposes, is subject to liability to guests who are upon the premises and who are injured by the harmful acts of other persons if, by the exercise of reasonable care, the proprietor could have discovered that such acts were being done or about to be done, and could have protected against the injury by controlling the conduct of the other person.[7]

The Lobby: A Legal Battleground?

A surprising number of injuries occur to guests and patrons in the lobby of the inn. A thief grabs a bag of jewelry from a guest who has just had it removed from the hotel safe. Another thief switches a briefcase with one that a guest, who is checking out, placed by her feet. A pickpocket bumps a departing guest and steals his wallet. A guest sleeping in a hotel lobby, upon being awakened by an inn employee, pulls a gun and kills the employee. In all of these instances, the innkeeper, not being an insurer, was excused from legal liability. In a Florida case, a person residing in a hotel as a tenant and not as a guest came down a stairway and tripped over the cane of a person who was seated in the lobby. A trial court verdict for the resident was reversed on appeal. The Florida Court of Appeals held that there was no evidence of any violation of a legal duty owed to the hotel resident under these facts.[8]

At times, however, liability can attach in the lobby. One example is when water accumulates from dripping umbrellas and no effort is made to clean up the water or warn of it. Another example is during peak periods of activity in a lobby when extra security is not provided, especially if large numbers of children or the elderly are present.

LIABILITY FOR CRIMES

As a general legal rule, one is not held liable for crimes committed by third parties that could not be anticipated. Liability may follow, however, in the manner in which the innkeeper responds to the crime. For example, failing to respond promptly to a call for help from a guest who was raped in her room, and though bound, managed to summon help on the phone, resulted in a verdict of almost $100,000. Even though front-desk personnel had called the police promptly, no effort was made to enter the room and assist the victim. Instead, personnel remained outside the room until the police arrived, listening to the cries for help from the guest within.[9]

Promises of Management

If a guest, invitee, or patron is injured, a tort situation has arisen. If the business promises to pay medical bills, a contract situation has arisen. As a basic rule, it is best to withhold contract promises until there has been determination of fault. Making promises before such determination may result in a business paying for injuries for which it had no legal obligation to pay. That is not a good business practice.

The E. Coli bacteria outbreak in the Northwest recently was caused by tainted Jack-in-the-Box hamburgers. The president of the company placed full-page ads in several newspapers promising to pay all medical bills associated with the bacteria outbreak. Although substantial payments were made to victims, the company began to balk at further payments, claiming the promise had been made only to "ease the concern of those involved."

A much better course to follow would have been to express concern and sympathy and leave the determination of responsibility to the courts for a later time. The stopping of payments now has placed the matter in the courts, and Jack-in-the-Box has to face the promises contained in the full-page newspaper ads.

Guest Complaints

All complaints made by guests, patrons, invitees, and others must be responded to. If someone has to be sent to a guest room upon receipt of a complaint, it is best to have that person accompanied by another. After the complaint is resolved, a written report must be prepared and retained by management. A Louisiana case illustrates what can happen when a guest complaint is ignored.

The case involved a slip and fall caused by water on unlit stairs at a hotel in Louisiana. Judge Dufrense stated:

We note that the hotel was notified twice by Lorio [the injured guest] of his fall and the conditions causing it, yet it [the hotel] made no effort to so much as investigate the alleged defects. This evidence was certainly sufficient to lead the trial judge to conclude, as he must have, that the defective conditions had existed for a sufficient time to be discovered and corrected by the hotel. Its failure to do so was breach of its duty toward a guest, and it is therefore liable for the injuries suffered by that guest.[10]

Prima Facie Rule

Under the *prima facie* rule, the injury to a guest or the loss of a guest's property raises a presumption of negligence. The doctrine of *prima facie* negligence has been adopted by court decision in some states, such as Minnesota,[11] and by statutes in others, such as New York.[12] In court decisions and statutes alike, the reason advanced for use of the doctrine is that it reduces the harshness of the ancient insurer's liability of innkeepers and the harshness of the more recent (1809) doctrine of contributory negligence.

As an example of adoption of this doctrine by court action early in this century, the state of Indiana rejected the common-law concept of insurer's liability and substituted in its place that of *prima facie* liability. Under this doctrine, the innkeeper has the opportunity to convince the jury that the loss was not due to fault of the inn.[13]

Assumption of the Risk

The common-law doctrine of "assumption of the risk" is being replaced in some states with the comparative negligence doctrine. In Louisiana, the assumption of the risk rule now has been eliminated.[14]

Assumption of the risk and contributory negligence, which are solid legal defenses in many cases, are not available when children are injured. Also, one cannot assume a risk that one is not aware of.[15]

Proximate Cause

A final legal doctrine becomes involved in premises liability cases. Proximate cause has been defined as "that cause, which in natural and continuous sequence, unbroken by an intervening cause, produces an injury that would not otherwise have occurred." It must be established by the plaintiff in premises liability cases, and its absence will be a bar to the plaintiff's case. Figure 15.1 presents the definition graphically.

HOW THE LAW AFFECTS OPERATIONS

With this background of the law of negligence and common-law doctrines, it next becomes useful to see how the law plays an active role in all aspects of HH&T operations. Numerous facilities are available, such as parking garages, swimming pools, game rooms, exercise rooms, restaurants, bars, and other facilities. The traveler who has become a guest will assume that everything offered to him or her is safe to use, is of good quality, and will not cause harm.

This, however, is not always the case. A place to begin is with balconies. These have been popular in the past, but a look at current construction will disclose that they are being used less frequently. During certain times of the year, many inns in Florida experience a rash of disorderly conduct by visitors to that state. This has

FIGURE 15.1 Proximate cause.

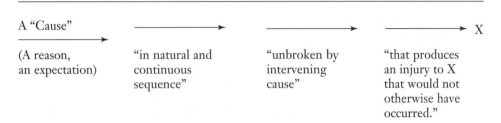

A "Cause"
(A reason,
an expectation)

"in natural and
continuous
sequence"

"unbroken by
intervening
cause"

"that produces
an injury to X
that would not
otherwise have
occurred."

Proximate cause, if it exists, is a question of fact for the jury. If the jury finds there is no proximate cause, the hotel is excused.

resulted in falls, elevator-related injuries, and death. The Florida "balcony bill" allows innkeepers who believe that disorderly conduct could lead to death or injury to take the offending person into custody and hold him or her for "a reasonable time" until the police arrive. Jail penalties are provided, and innkeepers and police are provided immunity from liability for acting under the bill.

The Florida balcony statute requires an eight-inch span between uprights on balconies in that state. This legislative act is subject to three interpretations, as shown in Figure 15.2.

FIGURE 15.2 Balcony railings in Florida.

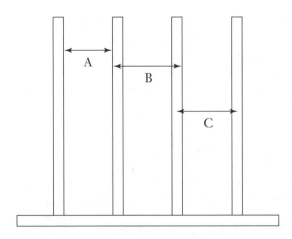

1. "A": The measurement is made from edge to edge inside the balcony bars.
2. "B": The distance is measured from the outside edge of the bars.
3. "C": The measurement is made from the center of the uprights.

A reasonable manager should resolve this conflict by simply using upright bars that are closer than the statute requires. A Louisiana case was concerned with the same subject.

If a balcony railing meets statutory requirements, if it is anchored properly, and if it is of customary height, a guest who falls over it because of his or her own misconduct of sitting backward on the rail will not be able to recover from the hotel.[16] The incident in this case took place during Mardi Gras—"Fat Tuesday"—as a guest at the Downtowner Hotel in New Orleans tried to "moon" the crowd on the streets below by lowering his trousers and then sitting backward on the balcony.

At properties located on ocean fronts, corrosion is a constant problem. Corrosion eventually will destroy the structural integrity of balconies, and this must be guarded against. Simply painting over corrosion is asking for serious legal trouble.

A balcony checklist is suggested:

1. Make timely visual inspections.
2. Make corrections as needed.
3. Learn and follow the requirements of local building codes.
4. Learn and follow the requirements of state statutes.
5. Learn and follow the standards of the hotel, hospitality, and tourism industry.

The common-law rule of reasonable care and foreseeability will control in states that do not have a balcony bill.

Elevators and Escalators

Statistics show that 15,000 Americans are injured or killed each year by elevators and escalators. If elevators and escalators are maintained by the companies that install them, can the innkeeper escape liability for death or injury caused by their use? The U. S. Court of Appeals for the Fifth Circuit has answered that question in the negative. The escalator in question connected the third floor of the inn with the lobby. At trial it was determined that the escalator created an "unreasonable risk of injury to others." The judge who wrote the opinion said, "a hotel keeper who draws a benefit from escalators, and has custody for purposes of strict liability, cannot escape liability when things go wrong by delegation of responsibility."[17]

Although the hotel cannot escape liability by delegation, it nevertheless should have had an agreement with Westinghouse, the company that installed and maintained the escalator, to hold the hotel harmless for injuries resulting from use of the escalator.

In New York state, the law allows hotels to have such a contract clause with those who maintain elevators and escalators. In a case in Manhattan where a woman fell while departing an elevator that was not level with the floor, a jury found the hotel 80 percent negligent, the maintenance company 20 percent negligent, and awarded the sum of $250,000. Although New York state recognizes that the innkeeper's duty as to elevators is nondelegable, the above clause allowed the hotel to recover $50,000 from the maintenance company.

Entertainment at the Inn

At Harrah's Hotel in Reno, Nevada, singer Paul Revere closed his show by throwing paper hats to the audience. While reaching for a hat, a spectator on an upper level fell and injured a woman below. Her suit against the hotel, for more than $450,000, resulted in a jury verdict in favor of the guest and her husband. The theory was that by allowing items to be thrown to an audience, a dangerous situation had been created.

At a Massachusetts club, a rock band placed dishes of flash powder, which were ignited as part of their performance, along the edge of the stage. An audience member thought these dishes were ashtrays, and while attempting to put out a cigarette before the show, caused the powder to explode, burning his face. Not hearing anything from the injured person, the club failed to notify its insurance company. About six months later, the injured person filed suit, and the insurance company denied coverage because it had not been told of the injury "as soon as practical," as required by the policy. The Massachusetts Court of Appeals upheld the dismissal of the insurance company, leaving the club to face liability alone.[18] Any situation in which special entertainment is present will require special precautions such as extra security, inspectors, clearances, emergency plans, and similar items.

Recreational Facilities

A small amount of sand on the hotel basketball court caused a guest to fall, with resulting injuries. A verdict of $55,000 was overturned on appeal because the hotel had been able to show that it exercised reasonable care in maintaining the surface of the court.[19] The courts will hold the hotel to the duty of using reasonable care when it supplies courts and equipment for use by its guests and invitees. Such duty is greater if children use the facilities.[20]

Part of the services furnished to guests and invitees at many places across the nation includes weight and exercise rooms. If offered, adequate supervision must be provided; instructions in the use of equipment must be given; regular inspections must be carried out; and the instructions of the manufacturers of the equipment must be followed strictly.[21]

Fire Laws

Fire codes vary from state to state and city to city, but the following example is representative. In all buildings that rise higher than 55 feet above the lowest fire department access, automatic sprinkler systems must be installed in all exit corridors, and each guest room must be protected by at least one sprinkler head. The code requires the installation of automatic sprinklers in the building's basement if the floor area exceeds 1,500 square feet, or any portion of the basement that is more than 75 feet from an opening.

This code also provides stringent standards regarding the air supply to guest rooms. Supplying air to guests' rooms from the exit corridors is prohibited, and openings between guests' rooms and exit corridors must be sealed unless: (1) approved smoke detectors are installed at specified spacing, fire dampers are installed in the air vents, and the activation of the corridor smoke detectors automatically causes the air supply system for the corridors to stop and the fire dampers to close; or (2) an approved smoke and fire damper is installed in an approved manner in the corridor; or (3) the entire building has an automatic sprinkler system.

In addition, the code states that there must be a voice communication system that is at least a one-way communication system to the guest rooms, public assembly areas, exit corridors, and stairways. There are also standards for emergency lighting, exit illumination, fire alarm systems without manual delays, and self-closing devices on doors. Other provisions include posting requirements with which hotels must comply strictly.

All fire liability insurance policies provide a time period within which the carrier must be notified before the liability of the carrier becomes fixed. In law, such a provision is known as a *condition precedent*. If the insured meets the condition, the obligation of the insurance company becomes fixed. If the condition is not met, all contractual obligations of the insurance company cease and the policyholder is thus uninsured as to that occurrence. Some policies set a specific time period, such as "30 days." Others are more general, with notice being required "as soon as practical."

In purchasing insurance, it is essential to distinguish "actual loss" from "replacement cost." A dishwasher destroyed by a short-circuit fire may have an actual value of $2,000 as of the day of the fire. The replacement cost may in fact be $5,000.

In Michigan, if a guest negligently causes a fire loss, that person cannot be charged with the amount of the loss. The reasoning of the courts is that the sum charged for the room includes some proportional part of the fire insurance policy. Thus, the guest is covered for his or her negligent act in setting the fire, just as if the fire policy had been issued in his or her name:

> Attention is called to *Faucett v. Nichols* 64 N.Y. 377 (1876), involving the application of a statute absolving an innkeeper for the loss of a guest's property by reason of an incendiary fire, wherein the court stated that a negligent act which preceded and facilitated the crime of incendiarism was as much within the statute as a negligent failure to remove and protect the property of a guest after the fire had started.[22]

The Hotel and Motel Fire Safety Act of 1990 becomes involved directly when federal employees travel. The Federal Travel Directory lists hotels approved for use by federal employees. Properties that do not comply with the 1990 law are not listed and are not approved for use by federal employees.

Part of the legal duty to use reasonable care is the duty to make certain that the physical surroundings are safe for use. Even though an innkeeper uses reasonable care, and even though the innkeeper warns of known dangers as well as those that may arise, another area of law may make the innkeeper liable. Known as *implied warranty*, it often is seen in furniture and glass liability cases.

Furniture

A hotel provided chairs for use at the swimming pool. Management was careful in the purchase of the chairs and asked for professional advice. Once the chairs arrived, and after they were placed in use, management made it a point to check them from time to time. The ones that needed it were repaired and those chairs that could not be repaired were replaced.

A guest sat down on a chair which fell apart, causing severe injuries. A lawsuit followed. The court which heard the case admitted that there was no negligence on the part of the innkeeper which could have caused the injury. Thus, there was no tort liability based on the legal theory of carelessness.

On the other hand, the court said that a guest should not be held to the duty of inspecting a chair upon which he or she was about to sit. The court held that there was a breach of the implied warranty that the chair was suitable to use. There was contract liability even though there was no tort liability.[23]

In a Georgia case, a restaurant patron sat down in a chair and the wicker covering gave way, causing the patron to fall into the chair itself. The court held the restaurant liable on the grounds that an inspection would have disclosed the deterioration of the wicker.[24]

Care must be exercised to make certain that furniture purchased is flameproof, constructed solidly, and otherwise acceptable to be used by guests and others. A special reason for this is that the courts will allow advertisements to be shown to the jury to assist in determining what standard of quality and care was offered to potential guests. The ads almost always show rooms and furniture. The displayed quality then would become a standard to be used in measuring the loss caused by the injury that resulted.[25] From time to time, chairs do collapse in restaurants and patrons fall to the floor. If the chair was in the restaurants' custody (easy enough to prove), if the chair had a defect (easy enough to prove), and if the defect caused injury to the patron, the restaurant probably is going to have to pay.[26]

Glass

In a Missouri case, a small boy slipped on wet tile and fell through the plate glass sliding door in the inn room. The jury allocated the fault at 40 percent to Howard Johnson Company and 60 percent to the franchisee. The youth was given $600,000, the mother $100,000, and the awards were upheld on appeal. Evidence was used at the trial to show that when the inn had been built in the 1960s, it was known in the industry that the use of plate glass instead of safety glass was unreasonably dangerous.[27]

Related to the plate glass problem is a doctrine of law known as the "open-space illusion." Open expanses of glass raise a legal problem in that guests and others may walk into them and be injured. Children have run into the glass and have been injured severely or killed. Open expanses of glass should have wooden bars placed across them to break the open-space illusion or have decals placed on them to alert guests to the fact that the glass is there. Another possibility is to arrange furniture so as to turn foot traffic away from the glass. A statute in Minnesota requires that open expanses of glass be marked in some manner to prevent persons from walking into them.[28]

In the absence of a statute such as Minnesota's, an injured guest still can proceed on the common-law theory of negligence for allowing the open-space illusion to exist in the first instance.[29] Glass panels should never be located in places where guests and patrons are likely to turn into them. Such a space becomes a dangerous area.[30]

Lights

Lights of proper intensity must be in place and kept operable at all times of darkness. Many interior stairs should be kept lighted twenty-four hours a day and keeping the front-desk area constantly lighted is always a good idea. Room corridors should be lit with high-efficiency fluorescent bulbs; public areas should be in a warm, white fluorescent; stairwells in cool white; and baths in high-quality fluorescent white. Using improper lighting may lead to the claim that the insufficient lighting caused some loss or injury.

Worse yet, failure to replace lights can lead to even greater losses. The Rappaport case in Chapter 1 is an example. In this case, the injured guest was attempting to reach her "temporary home-away-from home" at the time the injury occurred. She had every right to have been making the attempt because, as the judge who wrote the opinion observed, "her only alternative was to stay in her car until daylight before attempting to proceed to her room." The judge did not think this alternative was consistent with the circumstances. Thus, the failure to adequately light and keep lit the access way from the parking lot to her room becomes a jury question of probable cause. The jury also must determine if Mrs. Rappaport was guilty of contributory negligence (provided the case is tried in a contributory negligence state). This factor could bar her from recovery. If the case is tried in a comparative negligence state, the percentage of Mrs. Rappaport's negligence, if any, would be decided by the jury and her dollar award reduced accordingly.

In a Myrtle Beach, South Carolina, case, a guest returned after dark, and no lights were on in the area where his room was located. After using his car lights to allow access to his family, he started toward the room and fell over a rock. The summary judgment granted by the trial court was reversed on appeal, the court holding that there was a breach of the duty to ". . . provide sufficient illumination to enable a guest to use the walkway in safety."[31]

If adequate lighting is in place but is not turned on, liability can follow. A restaurant patron entered a room marked "rest rooms," in which she found herself in darkness. As she felt for a light switch, she fell down a flight of stairs. The trial court dismissed the case because of her contributory negligence. On appeal, the Pennsylvania Supreme Court reversed that decision and sent the matter back for a jury trial, holding that, "Those entering a dark toilet room to which they are invited cannot be adjudged negligent as a matter of law."[32]

The duties to provide adequate lighting can extend off the premises in some cases. An example of this is where a public road must be crossed to leave a restaurant parking lot and return to it. In a New Jersey case, liability attached to a restaurant where two invitees were struck by an auto while crossing the road, killing one and severely injuring the other. The inadequate lighting was held to be the proximate cause of the death and injuries.[33]

Phones

Even though no existing laws require that a hotel provide guest room telephones, it is still good policy to have them available in the lobby, in the public rooms, in each guest room, and perhaps in the elevators as well. The phones should be accompanied by decals giving a reminder of the 911 emergency number. The installation of such phones is evidence of reasonable care, just as their absence might be looked at as a lack of reasonable care.

Two phone-related legal problems follow. One has to do with guests making calls to others outside of the inn. The other has to do with outsiders calling to talk to guests. In the first situation, the privacy laws apply to records of calls made by guests. These records should not be released except upon a court order or a search warrant. The privacy laws also apply to the second situation, and that has to do with the location of the guest at the inn. Care must be utilized to protect the privacy of that location. For example, a call that requests the room number of Guest X should be replied to with a refusal to grant that request.

An incoming call that requests that a specific room number be called can be responded to safely, as would an incoming call requesting, "Guest X is staying at your inn. Would you please ring his room?" The room number always should be protected. The guests can give out their room numbers if they choose to do so, but the innkeeper must not be the one to do it.

Slip-and-Fall Accidents

One of the most common causes of liability is the "slip-and-fall" accident. More than 3 million Americans are victims of falls each year. Of these, more than 12,000 die from the injuries sustained in the falls. Many of these occur on floors that have some slippery substance on them. It is not usually the presence of such substances that gives rise to legal liability but, rather, the negligence in allowing the substances to remain. If there is grease on a stairwell and it is allowed to remain there until someone slips on it and falls, the inn must pay for the injuries that result.[34]

In bars, the most common fall injuries are caused by poor lighting, as well as unremoved slippery substances, and the failure to turn on lights.

There are areas where spills or leaks result in slippery floors. The condition is aggravated if the floor is made of tile. A solution is to assign someone to watch over these areas. If the employee sees that a dangerous situation has occurred, that person must respond immediately.[35]

In some cases, the guest or patron involved does not actually fall but catches himself or herself in such a violent manner that injury still results. The legal consequences could well be the same.

What if a nondefective product, such as soap sold by Georgia Pacific, leaks onto the floor, is not cleaned up, and an accident results? Is the inn entitled to contribution from Georgia Pacific? In a Florida case, the court said "no," leaving the inn responsible for a verdict of over $1 million.[36]

In humid parts of the nation, fallen leaves that become wet may result in liability for an accident they cause.[37]

Once a slippery condition, such as leaking water from an ice machine, or food dropped from room-service trays, comes into being on stairs, a common-law duty arises to correct that situation at once. If maintenance personnel leave work on Friday and do not come back until Monday and an accident occurs in between, the inn is going to be held liable.[38]

A variety of other substances and conditions often result in liability, including wet stairs,[39] drippings from a grill,[40] butter spilled from a plate of sauteed mushrooms,[41] accumulation of water and sand around a beach shower,[42] and many other situations.

Once a fall occurs, care must be exercised as to what is said or promised to the injured person. A patron leaving a restaurant in a Georgia town tripped, fell, and suffered serious injuries. The restaurant manager told her at the scene to "get medical care, and we will pay the costs." The medical bills reached $3,000, and the restaurant refused to pay, claiming that the promise was "naked" (unsupported by consideration and unenforceable). The Georgia Appeals Court ruled otherwise, holding that the restaurant gained a benefit from the promise in the form of goodwill, and that the question of liability was for a jury to decide.[43] In that case, what started out as a tort matter wound up as a breach of contract. That gives the injured person two ways to seek recovery.

A legal defense in these cases is that of "trivial defects." In a California Tort Claims Act case, the court dismissed the suit on the grounds that the claim was "trivial" and not covered by the California statute.[44] California law permits a court (judge) to decide if what caused an injury was "trivial" or "substantial," thus making it a matter of law and not one of fact for a jury.

Snow and Ice

Special policies must be developed to be used in inclement weather. Further, these policies must be implemented with precision and authority when the inclement weather arrives. To have a policy but not place it into effective use is an actionable form of negligence.

Subtle variations of legal rules find their way into all HH&T operations. Examples are situations in which one recognizes a legal obligation, takes action to correct the problem, and then discontinues that action before the situation is resolved. For example, during a heavy snowfall, an inn had personnel shovel snow and ice from the walkways from the time the snow started until 10:00 P.M. At that time the employees were told to go home, but the snow continued to fall. After the snow and ice removal was discontinued, a guest slipped and fell and was injured severely. The court ruled that the discontinuance was negligence. The jury found that the negligence was the proximate cause of the injury to the guest, and the inn had to pay for the losses sustained.[45]

In an Indiana case involving a slip-and-fall on ice and snow at a restaurant, the judge read the following instruction to the jury on behalf of the plaintiff: "The duty of the owner or operator of a business that is open to the public is to exercise reasonable care in keeping that part of the sidewalk in proper condition for the passage of customers rightfully using it." The defendant challenged this instruction, but it was upheld on appeal.[46]

Illinois is one of a very few states that absolve an innkeeper from liability for accidents due to a "natural accumulation of snow and ice." On the other hand, in that state if some *other* condition accompanied the accident, such as lack of adequate lighting, the courts will allow a jury to determine the proximate cause of the fall.[47]

Resort hotels that maintain ski areas also have had their share of liability cases. A 1978 Vermont case involved a resort that advertised its ski runs as being "fairway-like trails." The resort was held liable for over $1 million for injuries sustained by a skier who hit an obstruction on a ski run and became a quadriplegic.[48] Inns in ski areas have been held liable for failing to maintain sidewalls high enough to keep toboggans away from obstructions on a toboggan run,[49] for failing to operate a ski lift properly,[50] and for allowing sharp roots to protrude through the snow on a ski run.[51]

After parking in the parking lot provided, a guest walking toward the lobby fell on ice and snow and was injured severely. The court stated that:

> Because Holiday Inns invite guests to stay in its hotel and is aware that its guests will park in its lot and walk from the lot to the hotel, Holiday Inn has a duty as a matter of law to its patrons to provide safe access from its parking lot to its building.
>
> It was entirely reasonable for the jury to consider Holiday Inn's failure to salt and sand a breach of its duty of reasonable care under the circumstances, particularly in Minnesota after a substantial snowfall in early spring where the temperature was fluctuating above and below freezing.[52]

Thus, in Minnesota, the courts will examine the following factors to determine if "reasonableness" was present:

1. the duty to warn
2. the duty to inspect and repair if necessary
3. foreseeability of possible harm
4. the opportunity for repairs found necessary
5. the reasons for entry of the injured person upon the premises

Ordinances enacted by many city councils in snow territory, specify the time within which snow and ice must be removed and the extent of removal that must be met. A typical time period is twenty-four hours, and innkeepers in snow country must know this time period and act within its timeframe. Failing to do so would be negligence *per se*. If such negligence is the proximate cause of injury to a guest, invitee, passerby, or others, the inn is going to have to pay. The ordinance becomes the "ground-level" standard a court will apply.

In severe weather conditions, this basic standard may not be enough, however, and a court may hold an innkeeper to an even higher standard of care in snow and ice removal. When snow removal is undertaken, care must be exercised to make certain that piles of snow do not block the view of motorists both on and off the property. If the blocked view becomes the proximate cause of a car accident or injury to a pedestrian, liability may follow.

In Maryland, a state that has severe snow and ice conditions in its higher elevations, a court has held that snow and ice is a "natural condition" on the property of the innkeeper.[53] Given that fact, if the inn uses reasonable snow and ice removal procedures, assigns rooms away from the dangerous areas, and gives reasonable warnings that snow and ice is present, the inn usually will be excused if a guest falls and is injured.

In a fall case involving the Holiday Inn at Granstville, Maryland, a guest was assigned a room at the far end of a hallway. This was against normal procedures, but the guest said she wanted close access to her room so she could transfer items, including her cat, to the room from her auto. The inn did not warn her of the dangers of the four inches of ice and snow at the entrance nearest the room assigned to her and did not offer to provide her assistance in the move to her room. Her fall resulted in a broken ankle and a $50,000 jury verdict. The upper Maryland court ruled that whether she was or was not contributorily negligent under these circumstances was a question of fact for the jury to decide. In this case, there had been complete snow and ice removal at the front entrance to the inn. At the side entrances, however, where the guest was assigned her room, the removal was only partial. Legal liability fell on the inn primarily because of its failure to warn her of the dangerous conditions, even though those conditions were in plain view to her. The jury verdict was upheld.

Stairs and Handrails

A Kentucky Ramada Inn had three stairs leading to an outside door. A guest slipped on a substance at the top step, reached for a guardrail only to find that none existed, and was injured. The Kentucky Court of Appeals held that the Lexington Building Code required handrails on "stairs." The court held that the inn did not comply with the code; thus, the new trial was ordered to be held under the doctrine of negligence *per se*.[54]

In a case at a restaurant in Corvallis, a patron descended four steps to a landing, which then had two steps leading downward in a different direction. It was at the two steps that she fell. The Uniform Building Code of Corvallis requires handrails for stairways but exempts stairways with fewer than four risers. The court viewed the double set of stairs as being separate, thus finding for the restaurant.[55]

Waterslides

When a nationwide movement began to remove diving boards from inn pools because of the losses they caused, inns began installing waterslides to replace them. This proved to be a mistake as far as legal liability was concerned. For example, should slides be installed in the deep or shallow end? Either choice is fraught with legal dangers. In addition, the courts make it clear that users of waterslides must be warned of dangers known by the innkeeper as such dangers relate to their use. This duty to warn also includes dangers that could reasonably be foreseen.[56]

Water Temperature

The courts are in agreement that in-room water temperature should not exceed 102 degrees. Some state health departments raise that limit to 104 degrees, but that may be too high. Sediment buildup that prevents thermostats from functioning can cause water temperatures to rise dramatically. That, in turn, can result in scalding and burns. Sediment also can close up cold water lines, resulting in a slower flow of cold water at points where it should mix with hot water. Anti-scald devices are available for bath and shower tub facilities. These are single mixer control valves. What they do is ensure that the water temperature never exceeds a designated temperature.

This subject is important to hospitality industry operations and can lead to vast losses. The following list has been taken from court cases in which the question of water temperatures was an issue.

1. Limit for human use, such as in saunas, should be 102 degrees.
2. Human skin begins to burn at 120 degrees.
3. Two minutes of exposure to water of 130 degrees will result in third-degree burns to human skin.
4. At 150-degrees temperature, human skin burns within a second or two.

A variety of other legal matters have led to liability, including power failures that result in a fall[57]; a bright glare off tile that obstructs the view of a guest[58]; an unguarded drain[59]; an elevator fall[60]; an attack on a guest while in a guest room[61]; and injuries to a guest caused by an unsupervised revolving door.[62]

SUMMARY

In many instances, liability is caused by a simple human error, such as telling an injured motel guest that "we will take care of you." The slip-and-fall and related cases provide a danger to management as the statistics show. Unlit stairs, leaking ice machines, and items dropped by servers in restaurants and bars are the primary culprits. Every precaution must be taken to avoid such occurrences and this must be done on an ongoing basis.

The Florida balcony bill is a good example of how legislatures try to solve social ills by the creation of statutory laws. This particular law is in its infancy and will be refined in coming years. An immediate effect can be observed at construction sites of new hotels, motels, and inns. Balconies are no longer being constructed at such locations. They have simply been eliminated because of the legal dangers that they pose.

QUESTIONS

1. Jury Verdict Research, Inc., reports that plaintiffs in slip-and-fall cases are successful more than 50 percent of the time. What reasons might be suggested for this and what message do these reasons carry to the HH&T industries?
2. The courts uniformly agree that an innkeeper should not be allowed to delegate her or his duties to others and then claim that they have no responsibility in the matter. In a short sentence, is this view correct?
3. What is the legal danger in making promises to those who have just suffered some injury or loss at a place of business?

4. In many of the liability situations discussed in this chapter, the courts favor the injured plaintiffs. The courts seem to be saying, "It is your inn, and the guest is only a temporary visitor, so let's resolve legal doubts in favor of the guest." Might there be developing a new "public policy" in reference to the operation of American hotels?
5. What are the dangers inherent in the use of plate glass?
6. The Illinois rule on the removal of snow and ice favors the innkeeper. What reason might have prompted the courts there to have assumed this legal position? (Would the courts in Florida ever have occasion to do the same thing?)
7. What does the California "trivial defects" rule say?
8. True or false: Legal liability can arise in a variety of ways.
9. Briefly, why is it a good business practice to paint the varying depths of swimming pools a different color?
10. True or false: On the matter of avoiding liability, new issues can be expected to arise in the future.

NOTES

1. *Lodging Hospitality*, March 1988, p. 24.
2. *Florida Hotel & Motel News*, March 1983, p. 26.
3. Sheila Murphy, Vice President, Reservations, Ramada Inn, 1991.
4. *Johnson v. Chadbourne*, 89 Minn. 310, 94 N.W. 874 (Minnesota 1903).
5. *Roueche v. Hotel Braddock*, 164 M.D. 620, 165 A. 891 (Maryland 1933).
6. 28 Am. Jur. 585, "Innkeepers," section 67.
7. *Coca v. Arceo*, 71 N.M. 186, 189, 376 P. 2d 970, 973 (1962) accord; *Lindsay v. Hartog*, 76 N.M. 122, 412 P. 2d 552 (1966); *Pittard v. Four Seasons Motor Inn, Inc.*, 101 N.M. 728, 688 P. 2d 888 (Ct. App. 1984). The term "third persons" includes employees acting outside the scope of their employment (Restatement [Second] of Torts sections 344 (1965, comment b.)
8. *Sussman v. Tutelman*, 455 So. 2d 1081 (Florida 1984).
9. *Boles v. La Quinta Motor Inns*, 680 F. 2d 1077 (Texas 1982).
10. *Lorio v. San Antonio Inn*, 454 So. 2d 964 (Louisiana 1984).
11. *Asseltyne v. Fat Hotel*, 222 Minn. 91, 23 N.W. 2d 357 (1946).
12. *Faucett v. Nichols*, 64 N.Y. 377 (1876).
13. *Treichlinger v. French Lick Springs Hotel*, 196 Mo. 686, 102 S.W. 101 (1917).
14. *Murray v. Ramada*, 521 So. 2d 1123 (Louisiana 1988).
15. *Hooks v. Sheraton*, 578 F. 2d 313 (District of Columbia 1977).
16. *Eldridge v. Downtowner Hotel*, 492 So. 2d 64 (Louisiana 1986).
17. *Blansit v. Hyatt Corp.*, 874 F. 2d 1015 (Louisiana 1989).
18. *Powell v. Fireman's Fund*, 529 N.E. 2d 1228 (Massachusetts 1988).
19. *Ginsberg v. Levbourne Realty*, 298 N.Y.S. 2d 80 (New York 1969).
20. *Dillon v. Keatington Racquetball Club*, 390 N.W. 2d 212 (Michigan 1986).
21. *Burkhardt v. Health & Tennis Corp.*. 730 S.W. 2d 367 (Texas 1987).
22. *Wausau v. Underwriter's Inc. Co. v. Crook*, 455 N.W. 2d 309 (Michigan 1990).

23. *Schnitzer v. Nixon and Heath, d/b/a/ Cavalier Manor Motel*, 439 F. 2d 940 (Virginia 1971).

24. *Gary Hotel Courts, Inc. v. Perry*, 2515 F. 2d 37 (Georgia 1978).

25. *Tobin v. Slutsky*, 506 F. 2d 1097 (2d Cir. 1974).

26. *Perkins v. Rick's*, 514 So. 2d 180 (Louisiana 1987).

27. *Jenkins v. McLean Hotels, Inc.*, 859 F. 2d 598 (Missouri 1988).

28. *Peterson v. Haule, d/b/a/ Chisholm Dairy Queen*, 230 N.W. 2d 51 (Minnesota 1975).

29. *Waugh v. Duke*, 248 F. Supp. 626 (1960).

30. *Karna v. Reed*, 374 F. Supp. 687 (1974).

31. *Bowling v. Lewis*, 261 F. 2d 311 (South Carolina 1958).

32. *McNally v. Liebowitz*, 445 A. 2d 716 (Pennsylvania 1982).

33. *Warrington v. Bird*, 499 A. 2d 1029 (New Jersey 1985).

34. *Ashley v. Oclean*, 518 So. 2d 943 (Florida 1987).

35. *McGinnis v. Sunbelt*, 326 S.E. 2d 3 (Georgia 1985).

36. *Georgia Pacific Corp. v. Reid*, 501 So. 2d 653 (Florida 1990).

37. *Luxen v. Holiday Inn, Inc.*, 566 F. Supp. 1484 (Missouri 1983).

38. *Lorio v. San Antonio Inn*, 454 So. 2d 864 (Louisiana 1984).

39. *Lorio, supra.*

40. *Wilkins v. Truck Stops of America*, U.S. Dist. Ct. (New Mexico 1986).

41. *McGinnis v. Sunbelt*, 326 S.E. 2d 3 (Georgia 1985).

42. *Taylor v. Tolbert*, 439 So. 2d 991 (Florida 1983).

43. *Folk's Inc. v. Dobbs*, 352 S.E. 2d 212 (Georgia 1986).

44. *Orsino v. Big Boy*, 237 Cal. Rptr. 413 (California 1987).

45. *Robinson v. Paul*, 248 F. Supp. 632 (District of Columbia 1965).

46. *Poe v. Tate*, 315 N.E. 2d 392 (Indiana 1974).

47. *Weber v. Chen Enterprises, Inc.*, 540 N.E. 2d 957 (Illinois 1989).

48. *Sundday v. Stratton*, 390 A. 2d 398 (Vermont 1978).

49. *Bazzdlo v. Placid March Co.*, 422 F. 2d 842 (New York 1970).

50. *Trigg v. City and County of Denver*, 784 F. 2d 1058 (Colorado 1986).

51. *Brewer v. Ski Lift, Inc.*, 762 P. 2d 226 (Montana 1988).

52. *Supra*, n. 46.

53. *Schroyer v. McNeal*, 581 A. 2d 472 (Maryland 1990).

54. *Whitehead v. Ramada Inns, Inc.*, 529 S.W. 2d 366 (Kentucky 1975).

55. *McNamara v. The Night Deposit, Inc.*, 659 P. 2d 440 (Oregon 1983).

56. *Twardowski v. Westward Ho*, 476 P. 2d 946 (Nevada 1970).

57. *Ottimo v. Posadas de Puerto Rico Associates, Inc.*, 721 F. Supp. 1499 (Puerto Rico 1989), *La Vallee v. Vermont Motor Inns Inc.*, 569 A. 2d 1073 (1990).

58. *Sherman v. Arno (Flamingo Hotel)*, 383 P. 2d 741 (Arizona 1963).

59. *Benandi v. Shoney's, Inc.*, 526 So. 2d 338 (Louisiana 1988).

60. *Scott v. Churchill*, 15 Misc. 80 (1895).

61. *Kiefel v. Las Vegas Hacienda, Inc.*, 404 F. 2d 1163 (7th Cir. 1981).

62. *Schubert v. Hotel Astor, Inc.*, 168 Misc. 431 5 N.Y.S. 2d 203 (Sup. Ct. 1938).

16

Guests, Patrons, Invitees, and Third Parties: Injury and Ejection

OVERVIEW

MUCH OF WHAT we have examined thus far has been based on tort law, and a considerable amount on contract principles too. We now direct our attention to injury to guests and third parties, and also to ejection and related issues. Criminal law is touched upon occasionally, but contract law is only incidental to our discussion here. At issue is tort law.

In this chapter we will examine the principles that become involved when a guest is injured in his or her person, reputation, or mind, as contrasted to the injury to that person's goods. Although the law often limits the liability for loss or injury to *goods*, here we encounter an area that usually has no statutory limits. Recovery for injuries to one's person, reputation, or mind is controlled (1) by the skill of defense counsel and (2) reluctance of a jury to assess damages at too high a figure. These are intangibles, and one cannot afford to assume that counsel will do a good defense job, or that a jury may be restrained when arriving at a verdict. The opposite is often true.

The principles of Chapter 15 are applied also in injury cases. Proof of loss, burden of proof, defenses available, and the types of damages that can be sought are the same in injury cases as they are in contract and other loss cases. In all businesses, the premises that are made available to guests, patrons, invitees, and others must be maintained in a safe, clean, habitable condition. If they are not, injury often follows and litigation results. The business has to face the double-edged sword of failing to meet statutory requirements and failing to meet industry standards, as pointed out in Figure 16.1.

Modern law imposes a set of boundaries within which one must operate. These boundaries include what should be done, what can be anticipated there, what a court is going to say should have been done, and what in fact does happen. The innkeeper is faced with a myriad of situations that represent a flow of happenings requiring perpetual decisions to handle them properly. Is this decision better than that one? Is a report required of that particular incident? If this is done, what is likely to be the legal consequences? What might be the consequences if it isn't done?

These boundaries of the law often are tested in court, where the rules of substantive and procedural law predominate. The jury considers all facts, inferences, and impressions. In addition, the fact that a national chain is doing business in a particular state gives the courts of that state jurisdiction.[1] As to the degree of

FIGURE 16.1 The double-edged sword of legal liability.

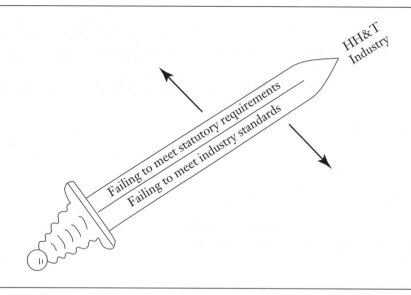

proof, the "preponderance of the evidence" rule will apply in almost all injury cases. Figure 16.2 illustrates the "funnel concept." This concept demonstrates that as we function within society, a million matters occur each minute and each day. Not all of these matters are legal in nature, and thus they never become subject to responding to law or equity. However, many of these matters are legal in nature and thus work their way into the funnel. They pass through and reach the judges and juries. In this process, every favorable inference that can be drawn from the evidence will be given to the plaintiff. This is a right that American courts traditionally extend to those who bring injury cases to the courts. What it means is that disputed questions will be given to the jury to decide. If judges in the lower courts dismiss injury cases where there were such disputed questions, the upper courts almost always will send the cases back for trial by jury. Perhaps the most constant source of injury cases is failure to provide safe premises.

SAFE PREMISES

Innkeepers have a legal duty to maintain safe premises at all times, not only for guests and patrons but employees as well. Floors, stairways, and walkways must be kept clean and free of slippery substances;[2] stairwells and outside areas must be kept well lighted at night;[3] elevators must be kept in good repair because responsibility for them cannot be delegated to third parties;[4] window screens, where they are used, must be fastened adequately to prevent children from falling from windows;[5] and large glass spans must be closed off with protective railings or furniture to prevent persons from walking into them. Rooms and furnishings must be inspected constantly to prevent unsafe conditions from occurring—such as loose

FIGURE 16.2 The "Funnel Concept."

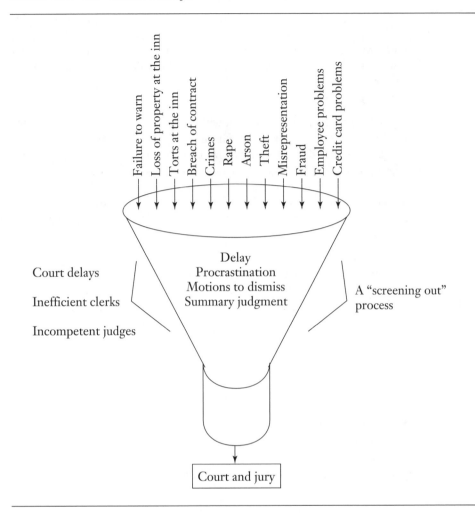

legs on chairs, unsafe wall television mounts,[6] and defective shower or tub fittings that may lead to scald burns.[7] Rollaway beds and child beds must be offered in a safe, sanitary form, and proper vermin control must be utilized.

Certain locations are more likely to produce injuries or crimes than others. Balconies and stairways are two examples explored in the previous chapter. In addition, repeated occurrences such as elevator robberies create a "track record" that requires a response. Assume that an inn had sixteen reported cases of nonviolent crimes on the premises during the past four years. Because there were no reported instances of violent crimes, the inn had taken no steps to prevent them. If a violent crime now occurs, can the series of nonviolent crimes be used to show that a violent crime could reasonably have been foreseen? A Delaware court answered that question in the affirmative.[8]

Multiple Causes of an Incident

Guests, invitees, and patrons have been injured in incidents ranging from a slip and fall to foodborne illness from eating in a restaurant. When multiple reasons for injury are possible, the courts hold that the jury must be given an opportunity to consider and decide the questions of liability.[9] The following cases illustrate.

An Obscured Step

A woman was attending a social gathering in which large numbers of persons were present. A step down from the floor where she was talking to others was obscured by the large numbers in attendance. As she moved about, she came to the step down and fell, causing injuries. She sued on the ground that this constituted an inherently dangerous condition and there was a duty to warn of the danger. The lower court said that, upon these facts, there was not enough evidence of an inherently dangerous condition and dismissed the case. The Supreme Court of Florida agreed.[10]

Falling Objects

A broom was thrown from an upper floor in an Atlanta hotel, causing injury to a guest below who was waiting for an elevator. The court called the broom "an ordinary object" and said that to impose liability on the hotel as a result of such an instant and unpredictable event would be the same as making the hotelkeeper an insurer for the safety of guests and others.[11]

Public Area Attack

Although hospitality operations may be held responsible for injury or loss to passersby, the courts usually hold these operations not responsible for loss in public areas. The reasoning is that such losses are out of the range of foreseeability as it relates to the inn.[12] The legal question remains: What if the danger is in fact known and no steps are taken to prevent injury or loss? The legal rule of "assumed duties" is triggered, and legal liability may well follow.

When Injuries Occur to Children

Injuries involving children must be given immediate, detailed attention. Reports must be written up, witnesses must be identified and addresses recorded, photos must be taken if relevant, and diagrams must be made of the accident scene.

The doctrine of *res ipsa loquitur* applies when children are injured. The injury raises an inference that what happened to the minor would not have occurred in the absence of negligence.[13] One who deals with minors must exercise more care than when dealing with adults. Thus, when an innkeeper sees that more than the usual number of minors are present, more caution is in order. The acts of minors are always unpredictable, so "childproofing" is in order to make danger areas safe for minors.

If minors are locals, the inn may, and probably should, refuse to receive them, especially if it is expected that the intent of the stay is for partying purposes. Almost all inns have a house rule in this regard.

When injuries occur to any person, minor or adult, the innkeeper should always ask an immediate question and find and record the answer to it: "Why was the injured person at that particular location when injured?" The answer could well provide a strong legal defense later. To illustrate, "Why was a guest using the iced stairs when the elevator was at hand?" Or, "Why was the guest walking through the kitchen when the accident took place?" Or, "Why was the guest in an area that had been closed for the night?" In addition, the entire area surrounding the location of the injury should be scrutinized immediately by someone assigned to make that inspection. Anything out of the ordinary should be observed and recorded, such as a tipped-over suitcase ten feet away, or a broken branch on a nearby potted plant.

Many other things occur that may cause the premises to be unsafe and that can lead to injury to guests and others. Unruly persons are an example.

UNRULY PERSONS

An innkeeper has a right to eject persons who are creating a disturbance, or who conduct themselves in such a manner as to make their continued presence undesirable. But what might be the legal consequences if an innkeeper fails or simply overlooks the right to eject and does nothing when the circumstances indicate that the offending person should be removed? A 1970 Kansas case provides some insights. To begin with, the judge stated that the general rule of the common law is as follows: "A proprietor [sic] of an inn . . . is liable for an assault upon a guest . . . by another person . . . where he [she] has reason to anticipate such assault, and fails to exercise reasonable care under the circumstances to prevent the assault or interfere with its execution."[14] In this case, the court was satisfied that the bar operator (called "proprietor" above), acting through agents, had more than ample notice that trouble was brewing and that ejecting the offending parties was needed to prevent it. Failure to exercise the right to eject resulted in liability for failing to act. What started out as a legal right ended up as a violation of a legal duty.

A related question is: "What happens if the unruly person is removed lawfully and then causes injury or death to outsiders?" Might ejection of that person be held to be the proximate cause of what happened to the outsiders? When an ejected friend of a guest killed a third party four miles from the inn, a court ruled that, "In this case, no duty of the [inn] can be found . . . to supervise the activities of the [inn] guest's visitor after he left the premises. The [inn] had fulfilled any duty it had to passersby to keep the premises reasonably safe. It has no further duty . . . " to outside third parties.[15]

A Louisiana case in which a person was killed just four feet from the front door of a hotel provides some further insight into the matter. Though the case did not involve an ejected guest, it indicates that proximity might make a difference in the legal results when unruly guests are ejected and then cause injury to others. Four miles is far different from four feet. The judge in the Louisiana case said that "Dr. Banks did not make it through the entrance doors to the complex. We refuse to transform those doors into an impregnable legal wall of immunity. . . ."[16] When ejecting an unruly guest, a wise house policy would be to have a security guard escort that person to his or her automobile, provided he or she is in a condition to drive, and see to it that he or she exits the premises. That should satisfy a court. Ejecting a person who is too intoxicated to drive, however, is going to require assistance and the police should be called for that purpose.

Related to the problem of unruly guests are those who are disturbed, distressed, angry, or who may be acting suspiciously.

Suspicious Persons

Personnel must be trained to watch for individuals who are disturbed, irritated, angry, or who are acting in a suspicious manner. When these characteristics are observed, immediate reports must be made so someone with authority may enter the picture. Even though it may amount to nothing more than a few words of inquiry, it may defuse a potentially dangerous situation. If persons are seen where they should not be, that gives rise to a suspicion.

In situations where large numbers of people gather, particular attention should be paid to them. It is a matter of continuing to assert control, because the law allows this. Traditionally, personnel such as room maids have been reluctant to say anything to suspicious persons for fear of offending a guest. This is understandable, but they should notify a superior when unusual behavior or activity is observed. The superior, in turn, must approach the person and ask if assistance can be given. In the case of persons who are acting suspiciously, identification can be asked for. Although some guests may be offended by this, the law recognizes that the house is that of the innkeeper, and long has said that the innkeeper has the right, and indeed the duty, to take all reasonable steps to maintain the sanctity and security of the inn. A court will not fault an innkeeper for doing that. As a court said, it is necessary for the innkeeper, at all reasonable times, to "have control over every part of the (inn), even though separate parts thereof may be occupied by guests for hire."[17] If a bar or restaurant operator knows personally, or knowledge can be imputed from employees, that a patron is likely to cause harm to others, a positive duty arises to exclude that person or to control his activities.[18]

Security experts believe that 99 percent of the time a person intent on a criminal act will leave immediately if asked for identification.[19] These persons are naturally concerned about future identification.

Nonguests

Those who enter a hotel who are not guests or are not patrons of the restaurant or bar have no legal standing to be there. At most, they can claim an implied license, but the innkeeper or her or his agents can revoke it at any time.[20]

What about those persons who are intent on taking their own lives? Does the innkeeper have responsibility in that regard?

THE POTENTIAL SUICIDE

If notice of a possibility of suicide is received, immediate notice must be given to the police, security personnel, and management. In a 1975 Atlanta case, it was alleged in court that the hotel had been warned that a guest had threatened to commit suicide and the hotel had failed to take action to avert that possibility. The evidence at trial, however, failed to convince the jury that those claims were true, and the hotel was exonerated.[21] The legal point is, of course, if the jury had been convinced of the allegations, the hotel could well have been held responsible for the death. The subject of "potential jumpers" is a current topic of training at Atlanta hotels that have atriums and other hotels where deaths have occurred by jumping from a roof or window.

OTHER INJURY MATTERS

Louisiana Revised Statutes require inns to post, on the inside of the door to each guest room, a map that sets out the routes to follow to the fire exits.[22] New York state has a similar law. Effective January 1, 1982, the New York legislature added the following to section 204 of the New York General Business Law:

> 204-a. Safety chain latches required. Every person, firm or corporation engaged in the business of furnishing public lodging accommodations in hotels, motels or motor courts shall install and maintain, on the inside of each entrance door to every rental unit for which there is a duplicate or master key which would afford entry to said unit by one other than the occupant, a safety chain latch.[23]

VERMIN CONTROL

Failure to control the presence of vermin can cause the premises to be unsafe in the eyes of the courts.[24] Examine Figure 16.3. Although an innkeeper is not an insurer of the guest's safety,[25] one must meet certain requirements such as providing a safe and clean inn, especially one free of insects.[26] Other state laws impose duties on innkeepers to provide a sanitary inn[27] and impose penalties[28] if these requirements are not met. It is a misdemeanor in Nevada not to comply with the sanitary regulations imposed by law. One must keep the premises free of "vermin or bedbugs or similar things."[29] If such things are found or known to be found on the property, especially guest rooms, the innkeeper must "thoroughly fumigate, disinfect and renovate until such vermin or bedbugs . . . are entirely exterminated."[30]

When the weather changes, so do the habits of insects and vermin. All towns, unfortunately, sometimes become home to bedbugs and beetles. When this happens, one must combat the problem to comply with state law. But what exactly does "fumigate, disinfect, and renovate" mean? According to *Webster's New Twentieth Dictionary*, to fumigate means "the act of smoking or applying smoke or gas, as in disinfecting . . . apartments; disinfection." *Black's Law Dictionary*, 5th edition, states that disinfected means "made free from *injurious* or contagious diseases; immunization" and to renovate means "to renew, make over, or repair, or to restore to freshness, purity, a sound state, or newness of appearance."

If such a condition exists and one does not remove it, or at least warn the guest of its existence and the actions for correcting it, a foreseeable action in negligence could arise. A Michigan court awarded an injured guest $25,000 for being bitten by a rat.[31] The court decided that the Michigan housing law did not impose

FIGURE 16.3 Summary of injury picture at inns.

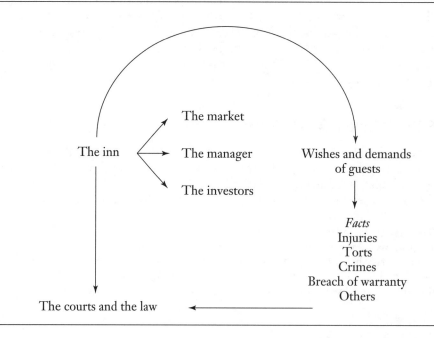

"absolute liability on hotelkeeper for failure to keep premises free from rats but *rather imposes liability only if he knew or should have known of such dangerous conditions*" (emphasis added).[32] It is this foreseeability about which one must worry. If an innkeeper has had problems in the past, or if a whole town is infected, one must correct the problem and warn the guest or be party to a negligence suit if injury results. A related issue has to do with giving notice that fumigation is taking place. New York state has such a law.

Other Considerations

An innkeeper cannot escape liability for a falling elevator that causes injury to a guest, even though the innkeeper employs experts to keep the elevator in safe condition. This duty and others like it cannot be delegated.[33] Liability was attached for sending a "nurse" to examine an injured guest, when the person sent was not in fact a nurse, had no qualifications, and did not diagnose the injury properly, to the detriment of the guest.[34] Again, even the suicide of a guest can give rise to legal liability in cases where the inn had notice of suicidal tendencies of a guest and did not react properly to this information.[35] In literally hundreds of cases, innkeepers have been held responsible for attacks on guests while in their rooms,[36] and even for the murder of a guest during a robbery attempt.[37]

Walkways must be kept free of ice and debris. Railings must be provided at elevated portions of walkways and alongside pools and recreation areas. Parking lots must be well lighted and, if autos are handled by agents, the lot should be fenced and adequate security provided for the safety of guests and patrons and their autos.

An injured guest, patron, or invitee may be barred from recovery, of course, if that person in some manner contributed to his or her injury, the same as contributory negligence will bar recovery for loss of or damage to goods. Also, as more and more states adopt the doctrine of comparative negligence, this too will become a factor to be considered. If the proximate cause[38] of the injury is the negligence of the innkeeper or an agent or employee, even if there was contributory negligence, the innkeeper may be held liable for the loss sustained.

EMOTIONAL DISTRESS

A developing area of law has to do with emotional distress, sometimes spoken of as "mental injury."

The state of West Virginia pioneered the concept of "mental injury" in the 1920s, and the California Supreme Court in 1968 established the first ground rules to be applied to determine if such claims should be allowed to go to the juries. The early cases involved mental suffering of persons who saw members of their families or close friends injured by others. Today, the doctrine has been expanded into new areas and applies to HH&T operations. The standards set by the California court are as follows.

1. There must be a close relationship between the one injured or killed and the one who observes the incident.
2. The one who witnesses the injury or death must be in close proximity.
3. There must be "sensory and contemporaneous observation" of the incident.

If these factors are present, the court will permit the case to go to the jury on the question of emotional distress.[39] In New York state, such a claim is not allowed unless the claimed mental or emotional injury is accompanied by some "impact" to the plaintiff. As a simple example, if a bottle fell and exploded near the plaintiff, causing fright because of the noise, the claim would be disallowed. On the other hand, if the bottle struck the plaintiff, then exploded, causing fright, the case would be allowed to proceed. The question of actual injury and mental/emotional injury then would become a question of fact for the jury.

Traditionally, and for good reason, the courts have been reluctant to allow recovery for mental injury standing alone. The doctrine, however, now is finding favor in more American courts as medical evidence tells us that such injuries, although often difficult to determine, have a sound basis in fact. On the other hand, the courts still resist such claims in many instances.

In Oregon, as in New York, the courts will not uphold a claim that a breach of contract resulted in emotional distress, or mental injury, without proof of physical injury accompanying it. This is true even if the purpose of the contract in question was to provide emotional security.

The first case in which this basis of recovery in tort was allowed came in 1984, in Maryland. The courts there began to establish standards that had to be met before such a tort claim would be allowed.

1. Was the plaintiff peculiarly susceptible to emotional distress?
2. Is the setting where the claimed emotional distress occurred consistent with the claim?
3. Is the personality of the plaintiff likely to be harmed by the claimed emotional distress?
4. Was there outrageous and extreme conduct on the part of the defendant?
5. Was there a reckless or intentional act on the part of the defendant?
6. Was there a direct connection between points 4 and 5 and the emotional distress claimed?
7. Did severe mental distress result to the plaintiff?

If the answers to these questions are "yes," the court can find liability for emotional distress.[40]

Leaving our look at emotional distress, we come to an area of the hotel, motel, or inn that causes many injuries to guests, invitees, and others: swimming pools.

SWIMMING POOLS

If one were to devise a way in which guests and others could be injured in a perpetual fashion, it would be difficult to improve upon the swimming pool. Guests are constantly falling, diving into partly filled pools after dark, falling from diving boards, colliding with one another in the water when diving, and, in general, injuring themselves and others.

One should consider a pool as a high-risk area and treat it accordingly. If it is beneficial to maintain a pool, it is mandatory that enough funds be allocated for proper maintenance. For example, what might be the liability of one who permits a pool to become unsanitary, resulting in serious sickness to those who use it? All states have health laws that regulate swimming pools, and so do most larger cities. One must comply with these laws.

Lawsuits arising out of pool injuries are not always successful, but many are. Lawsuit losses often result for the following reasons:

1. defective design of the pool
2. failure to maintain the pool properly
3. failure to erect suitable fences
4. failure to post signs stating that lifeguards are not on duty
5. failure to supervise the pool adequately

1. *Defective design.* The traditional pool has a shallow end, a middle-depth area, and a deep end, which usually includes a diving board. The shape of the pool often is dictated by the effect desired by the architect, and the edges of the pool are rounded, molded concrete, or ceramic tile.

The *use* of the pool always must be kept in mind during the design phase. Does a fancy curve in a pool project into an area where one would dive? Is the diving board too strong for the size of the pool? Does the shallow portion of the pool extend too closely to the diving board? Is the lifeguard tower likely to be used for diving if it is unattended? Are the safety rope and floats located too far beyond the shallow zone? Does the material on the surface around the pool become slippery when wet?

These questions have been drawn from cases in which inns were found liable. In one case, a new diving board was installed that was too strong for the pool. As a result, a diver was injured, resulting in paraplegia. The inn was found liable for $5 million.[41]

2. *Improper maintenance.* Loose tile or concrete edges may result in tort liability for failure to make repairs. In one case, a man was found dead in a pool and the evidence disclosed the concrete rim was loose. It was theorized the fall had been caused by the loose tile. A recovery for the death was allowed under the doctrine of *res ipsa loquitur.* Failure to clean up broken glass or hard plastic immediately, or to remove slippery substances also has led to legal liability. Proper and consistent pool maintenance is mandatory. If it is economically important to have a pool, proper maintenance is legally necessary.[42]

3. *Failure to erect fences.* Suitable fences are essential to prevent young children, intoxicated guests, and others from entering the pool area after it is closed. All states and most cities have statutes and ordinances that require such fences, and they must be included in the design of the pool and properly maintained.

4. *Failure to post signs.* Legislatures, as well as the courts, recognize swimming pools as high-risk areas, but having lifeguards on duty at all times is not mandatory. Some states, such as California, leave the decision to the pool operator. If a lifeguard is not on duty, however, a sign must be posted to warn the users. Failure to post a sign can result in liability in the event of injury. See Figure 16.4. In locales where foreign visitors use the pools, the warning signs should be printed in both English and the appropriate foreign language. For example, in Orange County, California, the home of Disneyland and Knott's Berry Farm, warning signs are found printed in Japanese and Spanish as well as English.

5. *Failure to provide adequate supervision.* Failure to supervise a pool adequately, especially when a lifeguard is not on duty, could result in a tort action. A system of inspection must be enforced consistently to demonstrate adequate supervision to the courts if it should become necessary later.

FIGURE 16.4 Pool signs.

—No Lifeguard on Duty.	Statutory requirement
—Swim at Your Own Risk. —The hotel is not responsible for injury or loss.	Disclaimers
—Those under 14 must be accompanied by an adult. —Pool closes at 10:00 PM.	House rules

PROTECTION FROM EMPLOYEES AND THIRD PARTIES

Innkeepers have a duty to protect guests, patrons, invitees, and others from acts of employees that may cause harm. The legal duty to protect is strong and requires that employees be schooled in the necessity of maintaining courteous, safe conduct toward all persons at all times. Some statutes and case decisions exonerate innkeepers from liability for willful acts of employees or agents toward guests while *off* duty.

Innkeepers also have a duty to protect guests and patrons from injurious acts of third parties. Liability has attached where a third party became intoxicated and injured a guest;[43] where boisterous banquet patrons knocked down guests while running in the lobby; where, by the spinning of revolving doors left unattended, a guest is injured. Failure to provide adequate security to prevent such injuries can lead to liability. Indeed, providing security that is adequate *and then reducing it for economy reasons* could lead to the same result. In the Wisconsin case of *Weihert v. Piccione* the court stated that:

> The proprietor of a place of business who holds it out to the public for entry for his business purposes is liable for harm caused by the accidental negligence or intentional acts of third persons, if the proprietor by the exercise of reasonable care could have discovered that such acts were being done and could have protected the members of the public by controlling the conduct of the third persons, or by giving a warning adequate to enable them to avoid harm.[44]

The rule of this case is now in Wisconsin Jury Instruction 1027.5. This instruction reads in part as follows:

> When one assembles a crowd or a large number of people upon his property for purposes of financial gain to himself, he assumes the responsibility of using ordinary care to protect the individuals from injury from causes reasonably to be anticipated. In the exercise of this duty, it is incumbent upon him to furnish a sufficient number of guards or attendants and to take other necessary precautions to control the actions of the crowd.

Liability has attached to a bar for the bartender's failure to call the police after a fight broke out,[45] by having patio doors on rooms that can be entered from the outside, leading to an attack on a guest,[46] by permitting sex deviants and known criminals to wander around,[47] and in other ways.

The innkeeper must use reasonable care to control or avoid things that could go wrong even though, at best, this can be a difficult job. The law does not expect miracles, only that one act as a reasonable person would act under like or similar circumstances. Yet, the things that can happen cannot always be anticipated. The following news item illustrates:

> CHATTANOOGA, Tenn. A federal court jury has awarded $25,000 to a man who said he suffered a serious neck injury when he walked into a motel room occupied by a "skimpily clad" woman.

James L. Hardy Jr. of Needville, Texas, claimed in a federal court lawsuit that a clerk at a Days Inn motel gave him the wrong key during a family vacation trip in July 1981 [and he injured his neck while taking a second look].[48]

Before turning to cases to illustrate the principles discussed in this chapter, three final topics will be examined: defamation, crisis planning, and the "Sally Board" principle. In all three, injuries come into focus.

DEFAMATION

Defamation is a legal term that includes both libel and slander. The former involves printed/written words. The latter involves spoken words. Three elements must be proven to allow one to gain a civil recovery on the claim of defamation.

1. The printed/written or spoken words must have been untrue.
2. Those words must have been "published" or communicated to another person or more than one person.
3. The published untruth must have caused injury to the person in question.

If a jury hearing such a case finds that this three-part test has been met, appropriate damages can be awarded. The Moricoli case later in this chapter is an example of what the law of defamation can mean. Although that case involved an entertainer, the principles apply to guests as well as employees. The following employee items illustrate.

Employers have a qualified privilege in most states to discuss employees. When a corporate officer discusses actions of an employee with another corporate officer, there has been no "publication" or communication.[49] In the case cited in footnote 49, the claim that bartenders had been stealing was addressed to all of the bartenders in question. The court held that, since all of those persons who heard the accusation were also the accused, there had been no "publication." If the accusation had been directed toward a particular person in the group, and had been false, a cause of action would have existed. Also, if an accusation against all of the bartenders was heard by an outside party, the entire group might have a valid claim of defamation except those in fact guilty of stealing.

Another example of defamation is found in *Columbia Sussex Corporation, Inc. v. Hay.*[50] In that case, a Best Western Hotel at Richwood, Kentucky, was robbed by a person who seemed to have inside information about the alarm system that was attached to the cash register. The president of the corporation demanded that the manager, Hay, take a lie detector test. The president said to her, in front of others, "You will be surprised to find out who gave the robber the information," hinting that Hay was a suspect.

It was later established that there was no connection between any employee and the robbery. Hay was fired shortly thereafter and brought a successful defamation suit against the hotel. Although the appeals court sent the case back for retrial, the circumstances indicate that care must be used when discussing employees and guests in front of others. The confidential privilege that employers have with employees will work to the advantage of the employer as it did in the Hay case on appeal, but it never will work where guests are concerned. The policy of the house always must be to avoid defamation.

Defamation can also arise if an inn provides false credit information to others about former guests or former employees. Such an action also could be a violation of the federal Fair Credit Reporting Act. Telling the truth is very much in order under both federal and state laws.

Turning from defamation, a matter that requires consideration is that of preparing for a crisis. The irony of this is that a crisis never may occur at a business in a normal lifetime, yet failure to prepare for a crisis probably would be held to be negligence if a crisis should arise.

CRISIS PLANNING

Personnel will not respond properly to a crisis unless they are trained for that contingency. It is important to provide that training, and a crisis plan should be in effect. This plan should include phone numbers to be called, which doors are to be used when ambulances arrive, who is to be at those doors to direct police and ambulances to the location of the crisis, and other applicable matters. A crisis is something that no one expects or wants, but it is going to strike somewhere and at some point in time. Perhaps the most dramatic example was the collapse of two walkways at the Hyatt Regency in Kansas City that took over 100 lives.

One way to alert personnel to what must be done if a crisis strikes is through clauses in the employee handbook. Other methods include bulletin board postings, group training sessions, and person-to-person instruction.

THE "SALLY BOARD" PRINCIPLE

One final matter has to do with that period of time just after an injury has occurred. Does one have any legal matters to consider at that point in time? Many years ago, the senior author had a client by the name of Sally Board, who resided in an inn near the university, where she taught English. She was injured severely at the inn when an old-fashioned, brass door closer fell, striking her on the head. She filed suit for her injuries and recovered more than a quarter of a million dollars. She told the author later that she would not have filed the suit if someone had taken a few moments to visit her at the hospital and express condolences. No one had seen fit to do that.

The business must not insult injured guests by ignoring them, regardless of where the fault may lie. Steps must be taken to assure the injured person that the inn is concerned about him or her. This is not to say that a representative should confess liability. That should never be done. Concern can be expressed without making promises.

Attorney William English of Oakton, Virginia, said:

> What occurs after an accident [at the inn] is sometimes of great importance too. . . .
> People are looking for justice; sometimes just being sympathetic will avoid a lawsuit. . . . Injured guests are particularly vulnerable and quick to anger when they

perceive [correctly or incorrectly] a "don't give a damn" attitude on the part of the [inn] and its staff.[51]

CASE INTRODUCTION: MORICOLI CASE

It is useful now to examine some cases in which the matters discussed in this chapter became involved in live situations. In these opinions, one gets an opportunity to see what the courts have to say about injuries that happen to guests, patrons, invitees, and others. As discussed previously, a way in which injury can be caused to another is by "defamation." Words of general abuse, or mere "insulting words" usually are held to be nonactionable. Some states, though have insulting-word statutes. Words that tend to cause violence toward another, even when the words are not published, become actionable under such laws.[52] "Publication," as it is used in defamation, refers to communication of the words, written or spoken, to third parties. But, as was just stated, publication is not required in the insulting-word statutes. The latter are intended to supplement the defamation laws and not to replace them.[53]

Some states, such as Illinois, apply what is called the "innocent-construction test" when deciding if defamation has occurred. This principle and others are discussed in the Moricoli case. The importance of this case is obvious.

MORICOLI V. SCHWARTZ
361 N.E. 2d 74 (Illinois 1977)

STAMOS, Justice.

Plaintiff, Thomas Lane Moricoli, brought an action to recover damages for slanderous defamation of his character allegedly resulting from certain statements uttered by defendant, James L. Schwartz, and republished by defendant, Barbara T. Reid. Count I of the complaint contained an allegation of slander. Count II prayed for damages allegedly arising from a tortious interference with prospective economic advantage. Count III sought damages allegedly arising from a breach of contract. Plaintiff appeals from that part of an order of the Circuit Court of Cook County, dated August 8, 1975, that granted defendants' motion to dismiss Count I of plaintiff's complaint for failure to state facts upon which a cause of action may be predicated. The trial court found that the alleged defamatory words upon which the action was predicated are subject to being innocently construed and hence not actionable.

Plaintiff's complaint alleged *inter alia* that plaintiff is a singer and nightclub entertainer using the name of Tommy Lane for his performances; that he auditioned and contracted with defendant Reid, on behalf of defendant P&S Management, Inc., to appear at two of that corporation's hotels; that on September 16, 1974, at a meeting of the corporation's officers and staff and in the presence of defendant Reid and others, defendant Schwartz maliciously spoke of and concerning plaintiff in the following false and defamatory words: "Tommy Lane is a fag and we don't want any fag working for us."; that defendant Reid, on September 17, 1974, in the presence of plaintiff and others republished the statement of defendant Schwartz in the following false and defamatory words: "The contract is being canceled because Mr. Schwartz says Tommy Lane is a fag"; and that thereafter the contract was canceled. Plaintiff alleges that the aforementioned statements are slanderous *per se* inasmuch as they allege that plaintiff is a homosexual.

According to *Webster's Third International Dictionary of the English Language* (unabridged ed. 1966), the word "fag" admits of four commonly used meanings:

1. *fag / n* -s [ME *fagge* flap, knot in cloth] 1: FAG END 2: CIGARETTE;

2. *fag / vb* [obs E *fag* to droop] *vi* 1: to become weary: TIRE, FAG: 2: to work to exhaustion: DRUDGE, TOIL 3a: to be a fag: serve as a fag (*fagging* for older boys during his first year) b: to serve as a fag in the field in British school games; *vt* 1: to compel to serve as a fag 2: to exhaust by toil, drudgery or sustained heavy activity—often used with *out* 3: to make (the end of a rope) frayed or untwisted

3. *fag / n* -s 1: chiefly British; a fatiguing task; DRUDGERY 2: an English public-school boy who acts as a servant to another boy in a higher form b: MENIAL, DRUDGE, SERVITOR.

4. *fag* or *fag-got / n* -s [origin unknown] slang: HOMOSEXUAL.

In construing the meaning of the word "fag," we note that Illinois follows the innocent-construction rule. That rule holds that the statements in question are to be read as a whole and the words given their natural and obvious meaning, and requires that allegedly defamatory words which are capable of being read innocently must be so read and declared nonactionable as a matter of law. Such words will be given an innocent construction if they are reasonably susceptible of such construction or if the allegedly defamatory matter is ambiguous. Whether language is susceptible of an innocent construction is a question of law for the court, to be resolved by reading the language stripped of innuendo. This doctrine has been held to be applicable to both libel and slander actions.

When the words of the statements uttered in the instant case are given their obvious and natural meaning, we do not see how these words can be given an innocent construction. Although characterized as "slang," the aforementioned published authority indicates that the sole occasion upon which the word "fag" is commonly used in the United States, in the form of a noun and to connote an adult-human being, is with reference to a homosexual.

Moreover, defendants' reference to plaintiff as "fag" in conjunction with the assertion that this status served as ground for terminating plaintiff's term of employment may not be characterized as mere objectionable but nonactionable name-calling. At common law, words of abuse do not give an action for slander. However, where such words serve to mark their peculiar target as an object of scorn and reproach, they cannot be dismissed as mere terms of general abuse. We conclude that the trial court erred in finding that the statements in question are non-actionable as a matter of law upon application of the innocent-construction doctrine. Therefore, the judgment of the circuit court in this regard must be reversed.

This means that the plaintiff must go back to the lower court for trial and prove the losses suffered because of the defamation. If successful, the inn is facing a substantial loss in the way of damages. This case did not reappear in the appellate records and perhaps was settled before or during the retrial.

CASE INTRODUCTION: HOOKS CASE

In the Hooks case, we have the opportunity to see what can happen when the dictates of a statute were not followed in the construction of a swimming pool. We also have a chance to see how the courts use testimony of economists to assist in setting the amount of damages that should be awarded to injured persons. It is important to read notes 54 through 60 with the case, because they contain key information.

HOOKS V. WASHINGTON SHERATON
578 F. 2d 313 (1977), No. 76-1958, (District of Columbia 1977)

ROBB, Circuit Judge:

This diversity case arose out of the injuries suffered by 18-year-old Thomas Hooks when he dove from the three-meter diving board at the Sheraton Park Hotel in Washington, D.C., in June 1971. The pool was equipped with a high-performance aluminum "Duraflex" board that propelled Hooks, who was not an experienced diver, into shallow water, where he struck his head on the bottom. As a result, Hooks is a quadriplegic. Hooks and his parents sued the operator of the pool, the Washington Sheraton Corporation (hereafter Sheraton), and its parent, ITT, alleging negligence in the construction and operation of the pool.[54] Specifically, plaintiffs alleged that the depth of the water in the diving area of the pool did not comply with applicable District of Columbia regulations and that it was too shallow for a three-meter Duraflex diving board.

The District Court held a bifurcated [separated] trial on the issues of liability and damages. The jury found Sheraton liable to the plaintiffs and awarded $6,000,000 to Thomas Hooks and $1,000,000 to his parents. On motion by Sheraton, the District Court ordered a new trial on the issue of damages unless plaintiffs filed remittiturs of the amounts exceeding $4,500,000 and $180,000, respectively. Plaintiffs filed the remittiturs.

In its appeal from the finding of liability, Sheraton contends that the District Court improperly instructed the jury on the standard of care owed by hotelkeepers to their guests, and on the issue of negligence *per se*. Sheraton also contends that the damages awarded to Thomas Hooks are grossly excessive for three reasons: (1) the inclusion of evidence of the effect of inflation on Hooks' future expenses; (2) the exclusion of evidence of the impact of income taxes upon Hooks' future earnings; and (3) the closing argument by plaintiffs' counsel, which Sheraton says was inflammatory.

We conclude that only one of Sheraton's complaints is valid: the evidence concerning income taxes should have been received. Nevertheless, for reasons hereinafter stated, we affirm the judgment.

I. Liability—Instructions

Sheraton contends that the District Court improperly instructed the jury on a hotelkeeper's duty of care, that contrary to the law of the District of Columbia, the instruction required Sheraton to give what Sheraton calls an "absolute warranty of safety" to its guests. Sheraton cites *Bellevue v. Haslup*, 80 U.S. App. D.C. 181, 182, 150 F. 2d 160, 161 (1945) *(Per Curiam)*; *Picking v. Carbonaro*, 178 A. 2d 428, 429 (D.C.C.A. 1962). Appellees argue that the doctrine of implied warranty is now the law of the District of Columbia. Whether the *Bellevue* decision remains the law of the District of Columbia is an issue we need not reach because, read in context, the instruction here is not a warranty charge.

The District Court began its instructions on the issue of negligence by properly instructing the jury that . . . the owner of a hotel is liable for failure to use reasonable care to keep safe such parts of the premises as he may retain under his control either for his own use of for the common use of the guests or tenants of the hotel.

It is the duty of the tenants or guests to exercise ordinary care for their own safety. In other words, the owner of a hotel is not an insurer of the safety of his guests, but he does owe to them the duty to exercise reasonable care for their safety. [Emphasis added]

The court then proceeded to instruct the jury on the general law of negligence, negligence *per se*, contributory negligence, and assumption of risk. The court's reference to warranty came in the context of the instruction on assumption of risk. [The instruction follows:]

"Before this rule [assumption of risk] is applied to defeat the plaintiff's claim, however, you must be satisfied by a preponderance of the evidence that the danger or hazard which caused the injuries of the plaintiff was open and apparent, that he was aware of it, or that in the exercise of reasonable care should have been aware of it, and that he voluntarily exposed or subjected himself to whatever hazard or danger might reasonably have been involved. *You are instructed that the owner or the operator of a hotel warrants to its patrons that the facilities of said hotel are safe for the use by its patrons, free from defects and dangerous designs, and that such facilities can be used in the use and manner for which they were intended without danger or risk of injury and that such facilities are reasonably fit and suitable for their intended use." [Emphasis added.]*

When a patron of such a hotel uses such facilities in the manner and method they were intended to be used, he does not assume the risk of injury and is not chargeable with contributory negligence if he sustains an injury in so doing. It is apparent from the language before and after the sentence relating to warranty that in this sentence the court was explaining to the jury that when using the defendant's pool in the manner for which it was intended, Thomas Hooks did not assume the risk of injury from defects or dangerous design, of which he was not aware, and that he was entitled to rely on the hotel's representation that there were no such hidden perils. We think the jury could not have understood the one sentence, delivered in the course of seven pages dealing with negligence, to mean that the hotel owed an "absolute warranty of safety" to its guests. This we think is plain in light of the clear statement at the outset, that the hotel is not an insurer and that it owes its guests a duty of reasonable care. Accordingly, we reject the argument that the instruction improperly imposed upon Sheraton a duty to give its guests an absolute warranty of safety.

Sheraton also contends that the District Court erred in instructing the jury on the issue of negligence *per se* because Sheraton had explained that any possible violations of the applicable District of Columbia regulations were consistent with due care. At trial Hooks offered evidence from which the jury could conclude that the pool failed to meet District of Columbia regulations concerning the depth of water required to be directly under as well as extending out from the end of the three-meter diving board.

Padlock, the third-party defendant, introduced evidence on the dimensions of the pool, which showed that there might have been minor violations of the regulations.[55] In an effort to explain any violations, Sheraton called Mr. Brink, the chief of the District of Columbia Bureau of Air and Water Quality, to testify that the plans for the pool had been approved by his Bureau.

In *H.R.H. Construction Corp. v. Conroy,* 134 U.S. App. D. C. 7, 411 F. 2d 722 (1969), this court drew a distinction between cases in which the defendant offers no explanation of a violation of a statute or regulation[56] and those in which the defendant introduces evidence tending to show that its failure to comply with the statute or regulation is consistent with the exercise of due care.[57] The instruction on negligence *per se* is proper only when no explanation is made, 134 U. S. App. D. C. at 9, 411 F. 2d at 724. Sheraton urges us to hold that its evidence of the approval of the plans, the custom of inspection during construction, and the issuance of the operating license for the pool was enough to negate the inference of negligence *per se.* We disagree.

Mr. Brink testified that he personally approved the plans for the pool in 1960. He also testified that it is the custom for inspectors to check compliance during construction, and that a license to operate the pool would not have issued unless the pool had been built according to the plans. Mr. Brink did not testify from personal knowledge that the pool was so constructed, nor did anyone else. As it turned out, the pool was not so constructed. The approved plans called for a wooden diving board. In 1968 Sheraton replaced the original board with a high-performance aluminum "Duraflex" board. Several experts, including the 1976 U. S. Olympic diving coach, testified that this type of board at the three-meter height is unsafe for the inexperienced divers likely to use a hotel pool. A college diving coach said that a Duraflex board "has a great deal more of elasticity and projects people higher in the air. . . . [I]f a person's balance is forward at the time [he leaves] that board, it's going to send him a lot farther out." Moreover, the aluminum board extended five inches farther into the pool than the original wooden board. This seems at first a small modification, but it is of particular importance to the question whether the pool depths violated District of Columbia regulations. The regulations require ten feet of water directly under the board and extending out from it for twelve feet. Thereafter the bottom may incline toward the surface at a rate of one foot of depth for every three feet of distance from the board. Obviously, as the board extends farther over the water, the distance from the end of the board to the point where the bottom inclines toward the surface is reduced. The area where the bottom slopes up is where the injury occurred. Finally, plaintiffs introduced evidence that on the day of the accident, the pool's water level was several inches low. This, too, would reduce the depth of the water under and out from the diving board. There was no showing that the District of Columbia approved these deviations from the plans approved by Mr. Brink in 1960.[58] We conclude, therefore, that the negligence *per se* instruction given here was proper under the circumstances.

II. Damages

On the question of damages, Sheraton contends that the jury award was so grossly excessive that it indicates a "runaway" jury motivated by passion and prejudice. The remittiturs, argues Sheraton, were insufficient to remedy the problem. Specifically, Sheraton objects to the admission of evidence of estimated future inflation, to an allegedly inflammatory closing argument, and to the exclusion of evidence of the effect of income taxes upon Thomas Hooks' future earnings.

We note at the outset that the District Court has broad discretion to order a remittitur in lieu of a new trial, and we find no abuse of that discretion here. *See H.R.H. Construction Corp. v. Conroy, supra*, 134 U.S. App. D.C. 7, 8, & n.1, 411 F. 2d 722, 723, & n.1 (1969). With respect to Sheraton's specific allegations of error, two are not properly before this court. Appellants conceded at oral argument that the issue of inflation had not been raised in the District Court; therefore, it will not be considered here. Similarly, the objection to counsel's closing argument is not properly before us. Sheraton first raised this objection in its motion for a new trial, too late to preserve the point. We have reviewed the arguments in question and find no basis for treating them as plain error.

Sheraton's third contention with respect to damages is more troublesome. The District Court permitted Sheraton to cross-examine plaintiffs' expert economist and statistician on the effect of income taxes upon Thomas Hooks' lost future earnings. In a subsequent ruling on plaintiffs' objection to this line of questioning, however, the court ordered the testimony stricken and admonished the jury to disregard it.

In *Runyon v. District of Columbia*, 150 U.S. App. D.C. 228, 231, 463 F. 2d 1319, 1322 (1972), we held that in determining a decedent's projected future earnings, probable income taxes are to be deducted. Hooks attempts to distinguish the *Runyon* case upon the ground that it was a death case in which the jury could award only the amount available to the estate after deducting taxes and the costs of maintenance of the decedent and his dependents. We are unable to perceive any distinction between death cases and personal injury cases in computing lost future earnings. In both situations the compensation is for future earnings lost as a result of a defendant's tortious act. That the estate in a death case receives only a net amount after taxes and expenses are deducted whereas the personal injury plaintiff is himself being compensated for his lost future earnings is a distinction without legal significance. "The primary aim in measuring damages is compensation, and this contemplates that the damages for a tort should place the injured person as nearly as possible in the condition he would have occupied if the wrong had not occurred." C. McCormick, Law of Damages 560 (1935).

Both sides rely on the Second Circuit's *en banc* decision in *McWeeney v. New York*, N. H. & H. R. R., 282 F. 2d 34 (2d Cir.), *cert. denied*, 364 U.S. 870, 81 S. Ct. 115, 5 L. Ed.

2d 93 (1960). In the *McWeeney* case the Second Circuit concluded that juries should not be instructed to consider the effect of income taxes in determining awards for middle- to low-income plaintiffs.[59] The court reasoned that determination of future tax liability would be too speculative and confusing to the jury, and that countervailing factors of inflation and attorneys' fees reduce the recovery and offset the failure to consider taxes, 282 F. 2d at 36-38. We are not persuaded by these reasons.

The existence of income taxes is hardly more speculative than is the assumption, indulged here, that Thomas Hooks would attain his dream of being a Boy Scout executive and that he would continue in that employment for forty years at ever increasing salaries.[60] To allow a plaintiff to attempt to prove what he would have earned, yet to shut off as too speculative the defendant's attempt to show what he would have been taxed is in our opinion unjust. The second factor cited by the Second Circuit, jury confusion, is a more weighty consideration; but we think expert testimony, presented under the watchful eye of the experienced trial court, see Fed. R. Evid. 403, can reduce confusion to a minimum. Moreover, expert testimony will avoid the possibility of a tax-conscious jury attempting to include in its award its own uninformed allowance for income taxes. The third consideration, that excluding evidence of taxes offsets the effects of inflation and attorneys' fees, has no application here. Hooks presented extensive evidence of the effects of future inflation. As for attorneys' fees, they are typically borne by the parties. If we are to depart from this rule, it should be a step taken consciously by the legislature, not one blended into a judicial opinion under the guise of excluding tax evidence to offset plaintiffs need to compensate his attorney.

We are told by plaintiffs that in holding that income taxes should be considered, we part company with the considered opinions of the vast majority of jurisdictions which have followed the *McWeeney* case. We question whether this is so, for Thomas Hooks would probably qualify as a high income plaintiff under the *McWeeney* rule. We note too that support for the *McWeeney* rule has begun to erode. See *Burlington Northern, Inc. v. Boxberger*, 529 F. 2d 284, 288-94 (9th Cir. 1975), applying the "high income" exception; *Felder v. United States*, 543 F. 2d 657, 665 (9th Cir. 1976).

We conclude that evidence of probable income taxes on lost future earnings should have been admitted.

The question remains whether a new trial on the issue of damages is required by our holding. For the reasons set forth below, we believe that the remittitur already filed by Thomas Hooks in the amount of $1,500,000 more than compensates for any error in excluding evidence of the effect of income taxes.

Plaintiffs' expert on economics and statistics, Dr. Miller, testified as to Thomas Hooks' potential future earnings. Using alternative career patterns, Dr. Miller estimated Thomas Hooks' potential lifetime earnings, assuming a 40-year work life and a salary growth rate of 4.5 percent. These totals were discounted to present value assuming investment at seven percent. Sheraton did not offer any testimony on Hooks' probable earnings. Sheraton did, however, cross-examine Dr. Miller on the effects of income taxes on the various lifetime earnings that he had projected. Dr. Miller computed the taxes on the witness stand, assuming that with a standard deduction and one personal exemption, Thomas Hooks would pay 20 percent of his gross income in taxes. The estimate of taxes ranges from $70,000 to $225,000.

Sheraton points out, correctly, that for some of his hypothetical career, Thomas Hooks would be in a much higher tax bracket than the 20 percent used by Dr. Miller. With a general verdict we cannot know which potential income the jury decided Hooks would have realized. But a new trial is unnecessary because the trial court has already required and Hooks has accepted a $1,500,000 remittitur. Treating every variable most favorably to Sheraton, we assume that the jury believed Hooks would have had a career as a $40,000 Boy Scout executive, and we further assume that Sheraton could have demonstrated conclusively that the tax rate would have been 40 percent. This would result in only $450,000 in taxes, less than one third of the amount already remitted by Thomas Hooks.

We have no doubt that we have the power to order a further remittitur as a condition of affirmance, but we are persuaded that the remittitur below is sufficient. It reduced the jury verdict by 25 percent and was more than three times the maximum amount assignable to the trial court's error. The District Court arrived at an amount of recovery which it found in conformity with the interests of justice. We are not inclined to upset that conclusion.

The Judgment is Affirmed.

SUMMARY

One of the primary legal duties of hotels, motels, and inns is to provide safe premises for guests, patrons, employees, and third parties who may be merely passing by. A vast variety of ways exist in which injuries can occur and which then result in the violation of this legal duty. Many injuries occur in a routine manner such as the slip-and-fall cases. Others arise in a more novel fashion, such as items thrown from hotel atriums. It makes no difference how they occur; the legal question is the same. Was the duty to provide safe premises violated?

Because of the ways that premises can become unsafe, it is essential that inspections be made at all levels on an ongoing basis.

Emotional distress, also known as "mental injury," has no early common law precedent. It is a product of this century and persons who suffer fright, shock, or emotional trauma, even if no physical injury occurs, form the majority of these types of claims today. Employers should ask themselves such questions as "How could such things happen and what can be done to prevent them?" A gun fired in an inn lobby by a robber cannot be anticipated. A ceiling fixture that becomes loose and falls can be anticipated.

Defamation cases are also on the increase, and they often lead to large damage verdicts by juries. A constant area of concern is when managers make untrue accusations or insinuations about employees in front of other employees and others. Care must be used to avoid this.

QUESTIONS

1. What are three reasons why any manager must learn to be liability-conscious where injuries are involved?
2. What was the legal issue in the Moricoli case?
3. What role did "assumption of the risk" play in the Hooks case?
4. Why is the duty to keep stairways in safe condition *implied* in law?
5. What suggestions might you make about how a convention in a hotel can be controlled so as to prevent unnecessary injuries?
6. Why does the law place duties on businesspersons to protect those who are not guests?
7. What are three areas of danger at a hotel that has a swimming pool?
8. Draft a notice to limit liability at a swimming pool that has no lifeguard on duty. Should a lawyer review this notice before it is placed in use?

NOTES

1. *Wronicowski v. General,* 716 F. Supp. 5 (Minnesota 1989).

2. *Mizenis v. Sands Motel,* 362 N.E. 2d 661 (Ohio 1975).

3. *Jenkins v. Missouri State Life Ins. Co.,* 334 Mo. 941, 69 S.W. 2d 666 (1934).

4. *Trulock v. Willey,* 187 F. 956 (8th Cir. 1911).

5. *Baker v. Dallas Hotel,* 162 Wash. 289, 298 P. 465 (1931).

6. *Lyttle v. Denney,* 222 Pa. 395, 71 A. 841 (1909).

7. *Parson v. Dwightstate Co.,* 301 Mass. 324, 17 N.E. 2d 197 (1938).

8. *MacQuairie v. Howard Johnson,* 877 F. 2d 126 (Delaware 1989).

9. *Wilson v. Circus Circus Hotels, Inc.,* 710 P. 2d 77 (Nevada 1985).

10. *Cosby v. Flint,* 70. 143 (Sup. Ct. Florida, Feb. 25, 1988).

11. *Taylor v. Atlanta Center Ltd.,* 430 S.E. 2d 841 (Georgia 1993).

12. *Van Blargam v. El San Juan Hotel and Casino,* 759 F. Supp. 940 (U.S. Dist. Ct., Puerto Rico 1991).

13. *Zimmer v. Celebrities,* 615 P. 2d 76 (Colorado 1980).

14. *Kimple v. Foster,* 469 P. 2d 281 (Kansas 1970).

15. *Upthergrove v. Myers,* 299 N.W. 2d 29 (Minnesota 1981).

16. *Banks v. Hyatt Corporation,* 722 F. 2d 214 (Louisiana 1984).

17. *People v. Thorpe,* 101 N.Y.S. 2d 986 (New York 1950).

18. *McGill v. Frasure,* 790 P. 2d 379 (Idaho 1990).

19. Jury Verdict Research, Solon, Ohio, *supra.*

20. *Kelly v. U.S.,* 348 A. 2d 864 (District of Columbia 1975).

21. Peachtree Hotel, Atlanta (Georgia 1975), no citation available.

22. Section 40: 1580 (1981).

23. N.Y. Labor Law, section 473-a.

24. The following discussion and documentation are derived from the "UNLV Innkeeper's Duty to Provide a Safe Place to Stay," by James O. Eiler, in *Hotel and Casino Law Letter,* Volume 2-1, November, 1983.

25. *Buck v. Del City Apartments, Inc.,* 431 P. 2d 360.

26. For statutory requirements as to keeping a clean and sanitary hotel, see NRS 447, *et seq.*

27. See NRS 447.030 with respect to "extermination of vermin."

28. See NRS 447.210.

29. NRS 447.030.

30. *Ibid.*

31. *Harvey v. Switzerland General Insurance Co.,* Mo. App., 260 S.W. 2d 342, 344.

32. *Deluce v. Fort Wayne Hotel,* 311 F. 2d 853 (1962).

33. *Scott v. Churchill,* 15 Misc. 80 (1895), 36 N.Y.S. 476, *affd.,* 157 N.Y. 692, 51 N.E. 1094 (1898).

34. *Stahlin v. Hilton Hotels Corporation,* 484 F. 2d 580 (7th Cir. 1973).

35. *Sneider v. Hyatt Corporation,* 390 F. Supp. 976 (N.D. Ga. 1975).

36. *Kiefel v. Las Vegas Hacienda, Inc.*, 404 F. 2d 1163 (7th Cir.), *cert. denied*, 395 U.S. 908, *reh. denied*, 395 U.S. 987; *Garzilli v. Howard Johnson's Motor Lodges, Inc.*, 419 F. Supp. 1210 (E.D.N.Y. 1976).

37. *Banks v. Hyatt Hotel Corp.*, (Docket No. 81-3377, 5th Cir. Court of Appeals), *supra.*

38. That which, in a natural and continuous sequence, unbroken by any efficient intervening cause, produces the injury, and without which the result would not have occurred—*Swayne v. Connecticut*, 86 Conn. 439, 85 A. 634, 635.

39. *Dillon v. Legg*, 441 P. 2d 912 (California 1968).

40. *Weatherby v. KFC*, 587 A. 2d 569 (Maryland 1991).

41. *Hooks v. Washington Sheraton Corp.*, 578 F.2d 313 (1977).

42. *Brown v. Southern Venture Corp.*, 331 So. 2d 207 (La. App. 1976), *cert. denied*, 334 So. 2d 211 (1976).

43. *Reibolt v. Bedient*, 562 P 2d 99 (Wash. App. 1977).

44. 273 Wis. 448, 78 N.W. 2d 757 (1956).

45. *Kowalczuk v. Potter*, 63 Wis. 2d 511, 217 N.W. 2d 332 (1974).

46. *Garzilli v. Howard Johnson*, *supra* n. 27.

47. *Kiefely v. Las Vegas Hacienda, Inc.*, 39 F.R.D. 529 (N.D. Ill. 1966).

48. *Las Vegas Sun*, April 7, 1983.

49. *Jones v. Golden Spike*, 623 P. 2d 970 (Nevada 1981).

50. 627 S.W. 2d 270 (Kentucky 1982).

51. *Hospitality Law*, volume 5, number 7, July 1990, p. 4.

52. 361 N.E. 2d 74 (Illinois 1977).

53. *Manuch v. City of Martinsville*, No. 14888, WV., July 7, 1981.

54. The builder of the pool, Paddock Corporation, was joined as a third-party defendant by Sheraton but the jury absolved Paddock of any responsibility for the accident.

55.

Distance from end of diving board	*Depth (Paddock)*	*Depth (Hooks)*	*Depth (D.C. regulation)*
0'	10' 5"	—	10' 0"
12'	9' 10½"	9' 7³⁄₁₆"	10' 0"
14'	9' 3⅞"	9' 0"	9' 4"
15'	9' 0"	8' 8³⁄₁₆"	9' 0"
17'	8' 5"	8' 1¹⁄₁₆"	8' 3⅝"

(Sheraton Brief at 5.)

56. See, e.g., *Ross v. Hartman*, 78 U.S. App. D.C. 217, 139 F. 2d 14 (1943), *cert. denied*, 321 U.S. 790, 64 S. Ct. 790, 88 L. Ed. 1080 (1944); *Richardson v. Gregory*, 108 U.S. App. D.C. 263, 281 F. 2d 626 (1960).

57. See, e.g., *Hecht Co. v. McLaughlin*, 93 U.S. App. D.C. 382, 214 F. 2d 212 (1954); *Karlow v. Fitzgerald*, 110 U.S. App. D.C. 9, 288 F. 2d 411 (1961).

58. Sheraton contends that semiannual inspections were carried out after the operating license was issued and after the board had been changed. These inspections, however, appear to have been limited to testing water quality and could not explain any violation resulting from the change in the diving board.

59. The court suggested that income taxes might be considered properly in cases of high-income plaintiffs (282 F. 2d at 38). Subsequent decisions have followed this

suggestion—*LeRoy v. Sabena Belgian World Airways*, 344 F. 2d 266, 276 (2d Cir.), *cert. denied*, 382 U.S. 878, 86 S. Ct. 161, 15 L. Ed. 2d 119 (1965); see *Petition of Marina Mercante Nicaraguense S. A.*, 364 F. 2d 118, 126 (2d Cir. 1966), *cert. denied*, 385 U.S. 1005, 87 S. Ct. 710, 17 L. Ed. 2d 544 (1967).

60.

Hypothetical career	*Present value of life earnings*	*Tax (20%)*
High school graduate	$ 352,000	$ 70,000
Two years college	402,000	81,000
College graduate	536,844	107,844
Boy Scout executive ($25,000 yr.)	700,000	140,000
Boy Scout executive ($40,000/yr.)	1,125,348	[225,000]

Tr. 53, 87-88, 90, 104 (5/22/75). The $225,000 was not testified to by Dr. Miller but represents 20 percent of the $1,125,348 earnings for a Boy Scout executive averaging $40,000 per year over a lifetime.

17

Hotel-Made Standards, Practices, and Policies

OVERVIEW

IN PREVIOUS CHAPTERS, we have seen how our legal system grants a significant leeway or latitude to the innkeeper. In this chapter, we want to expand on those rights because a hotel, hospitality, or tourism business, can increase this legal freedom by its use of in-house policies and practices. When in-house policies and practices are set up intelligently, legal liability can be reduced sharply. This will increase the business' legal freedom.

Looking backward for a moment, we find that twelfth-century England had no constitution. The inns that flourished in those times were not under constitutional law. Yet there existed the foundation upon which a sophisticated government would evolve in time. Privilege was the order of the day, and it came from the crown, from the law-makers, and from status itself. It was a system of feudal hierarchy. In those days it was a refined political theory, much more subtle than mere allegiance. All of this influenced inn law as it developed in those early centuries.

The Magna Carta was a product of war and it was not unique. In 1183, Emperor Frederick Barbarossa, in the Treaty of Constance, granted liberties to towns in Northern Italy. Others followed with such grants, including King Alphonso VIII in 1188, Emperor Frederick II in 1220, and King Andrew II of Hungary in 1222. Along with the Magna Carta, other factors, including practical and regal matters, influenced the development of inn law.

As an example of a practical matter, people had to travel from their homes to the marketplaces.

> The lodging industry was born, thousands of years ago, to facilitate commerce. Ancient tribesmen moved down from the hills to Mediterranean shores to barter their wares. They were housed—transiently—in huts and dugouts by the side of the sea. They paid the hairy innkeepers of ancient times in barter: They exchanged polished flints, horn and bone. They were exchanging goods. That has always been the key purpose of lodging: to extend the boundaries of the world wherein men and women in commerce exchange goods—and, in more civilized societies, services.[1]

A sample of a regal matter was the rule of St. Edward the Confessor: the "awn hinde" proclamation. This law provided that on the "forman night"—the first night—a traveler who stayed at an inn, or at the home of another, was an "uncuth." In Saxon language, that meant "stranger." If that person remained a "twa night"—

second night—he or she became a "guest." If the guest then remained a third night—"awn hinde"—the law said this person now was a member of the family of the host. This placed legal responsibility upon the host for offenses, such as tort or crime, committed against others by the guest. The practical effect of this early proclamation was to encourage innkeepers to see to it that their guests resumed their travels after two days. Thus, innkeeping became a transitory business and is distinguished today from landlord/tenant relations in that regard.

Today, in the great Sahara Deserts, the Bedouin people will receive, shelter, and entertain any traveler, at no cost, for two nights. That person must then move on. The same principle is found in all modern hotels. If the innkeeper permits a guest to remain for an extended time, the innkeeper becomes a landlord and the courts will then apply that body of law in legal disputes that may arise. In Virginia, by legislative act, one who stays for more than seven days becomes a tenant. This statute applies only in that state, of course. Perhaps this seven-day period will be accepted in time as the standard separating a guest from a tenant.

Although the workings of early English kings, the Magna Carta, early decisions of English courts, and practical factors shaped innkeeping law, the opportunity, limited in early centuries but almost unlimited now, has been present for one to create his or her own system of "law." This "making of law" has found approval in cases before modern courts and there is every reason to expect that this will be true in the future.

Table 17.1 compares "hotel-made laws," policies, and practices with law and the courts.

TRAVELERS

The purpose of innkeeping is to facilitate travel and to accommodate travelers to that end. The function of the laws is to lay guidelines and provide the standards by which innkeeping is to be carried out, and to lay the basis by which to resolve disputes that arise. The former exists because of the need to facilitate a system of travel; the latter, to ensure that the goal of the former is realized. Sixty percent of the innkeeper's time is spent undoing mistakes, and this simply should not be so. The problems begin as travelers arrive and seek to become guests there. What is their legal right to do so?

It is a general rule that:

> . . . an innkeeper gives a general license to all persons to enter his house. Consequently, it is not a trespass to enter . . . without a previous actual invitation but, where persons enter . . . not as guests, but intent on pleasure or profit to be derived from intercourse with its inmates, they are there, not of right, but under an implied license that the landlord [innkeeper] may revoke at any time. The respondent did not enter the inn as a guest or with the intention of becoming one and it was his duty to leave peaceably when ordered to do so, and in case of his refusal to leave on request appellant was entitled to use such force as was reasonably necessary to remove him."[2]

The right of the traveler to enter, when seeking to become a guest, must be honored by house policy, and nothing must be done that runs counter to it. Further,

TABLE 17.1   Comparison of hotel-made law, policies, and practices with law and the courts.

Hotel-Made Law	*Law and the Courts*
Quality standards	Common law
House policies	Statutory law
Treatment of travelers	Case precedents
Care in design and construction	Rules
World inn trends and their legal implications	*Stare decisis*
	Custom
Contracting away liability:	Trade usage
Disclaimers	History
Waivers/Releases	Constitutions
Releases after the injury	Contracts
House rules	Tort
Trade usage	Property law
Inn customs	Administrative regulations
Foreseeability	Employment law
Attitude of innkeeper	

it must be house policy to treat the traveler, once accepted as a guest, as a temporary member of the household, because the law for centuries has said just that.

The conduct of the innkeeper, acting through agents, requires that many hotel-made standards be adopted and enforced. Unprofessional comments are always out of order because they tend to distract the traveler or guest, which in turn could cause a loss or injury. Those who know how to operate equipment and amenities, which, in turn, will be used by guests, should be in charge of such equipment and amenities. Included are ice machines, elevators, escalators, equipment in fitness rooms, and equipment at the pool. Nurses who are sent to rooms upon request, must be qualified and licensed.[3] Many other traveler-oriented house policies are desirable and arise in practice. Failure to implement such policies can well result in lawyers entering the picture later. Consider what Roy M. Cohn had to say:

> I know a family whose vacation was an abomination. Everyone was in a terrible mood until they began to plan the lawsuit during the vacation. They vied with each other to see who could come up with the best and most creative evidence for a future lawsuit. This turned into a family sport, and they began to root for everything to go wrong so they could document it. They even suffered a sense of disappointment at the few things that were delivered as promised. They returned home armed to the teeth, and the travel agent gave them most of their money back, for a "ruined" vacation, which in retrospect was one of their most successful and fun-filled.[4]

In developing hotel-made standards, quality standards need to be considered.

QUALITY STANDARDS AND LEGAL STANDARDS

Quality standards must be contrasted to legal standards. These are not the same, yet meeting quality standards can satisfy requirements of law. As examples of legal standards, consider the following quotes, one from a court and the other from a legal treatise. Considered together, they provide the standards that one must measure up to as a matter of law.

> HUSKINS, J.: What standard of care is required of innkeepers with respect to their guests?
> An innkeeper is not an insurer of the personal safety of his guests. He is required to exercise due care to keep his premises in a reasonably safe condition and to warn his guests of any hidden peril. [Citation omitted.] The duties thus imposed . . . for the protection of his guests are nondelegable, and liability cannot be avoided on the ground that their performance was entrusted to an independent contractor.[5]

The statement from the legal treatise is:

> Sec. 341. Activities Dangerous to Licensees
> A possessor of land is subject to his licensees for physical harm caused to them by his failure to carry on his activities with reasonable care for their safety, if, but only if,
> (a) he should expect that they will not discover or realize the danger, and
> (b) they do not know or have reason to know of the possessor's activities and of the risk involved."[6]

Now, compare these legal standards with the quality standards to distinguish them. Standards of quality involve the policies and practices carried out as a matter of good management. The innkeeper's state of mind is reflected through the attitudes, actions, and even emotions of the employees, agents, and others. Quality standards refer to doing things, not so much because the law requires them, but, rather, because management desires them. They are the actions and attitudes designed to please and provide comfort and promote the confidence of the guest.

Quality standards include many legal duties, of course, such as the duty to warn, the duty to receive travelers, and the duty to protect guests. They satisfy legal requirements but do more than that. That is what makes "quality" something that is created by the hotel and not by law. Quality represents standards that are basically the same—no higher, no lower. It is a constant condition.

Franchise agreements of national hotel chains require that quality standards be maintained even though the law does not make that demand. Quality thus can be a matter of contract between franchisor and franchisee. Many national chains have a system of unannounced inspections. Days Inns, Holiday Inns, and Howard Johnson's Motor Lodges see the inspection as a "communication tool," a public relations opportunity, and a means of control. Quality standards then are of importance, represent good practices, and almost always exceed the legal standards.

HOTEL ACTIVITIES AROUND THE WORLD

At Kissimmee, Florida, Days Suites offered a "price-is-right" package that allowed a family of four to spend an entire week visiting Disney World for "about $1,000." This suggests both a marketing ploy and a quality image.

TABLE 17.2   Hospitality error: Occurrence frequency and discontinuance rate.

	Male		Female	
	Freq. (%)	Disc. Rate (%)	Freq. (%)	Disc. Rate (%)
Unsatisfactory food service	19	20	13	18
Tired facility—poor maintenance	18	27	13	35
Slow check-in, check-out	18	15	18	31
Employees not friendly	12	32	9	48
Room not ready upon arrival	10	11	13	15
Poor overall service	9	48	10	58
Requested room type	7	14	7	16
Morning wake-up call not made	5	14	3	19
No record of reservation	4	31	5	27
Overbooked—guest walked	2	59	1	81
Overall:				
Frequency rate per trip	1.035		.909	
Discontinuance rate	24%		31%	
Trip per discontinuance	4.0		3.5	

Information compiled from a 1988 Citicorp Diner's Club Study.

In Paris, overlooking the Place de la Concorde, the Hotel de Crillion, billed as the "Palace on the Place," is the epitome of French elegance and impeccable taste. With a restored Ancient Regime splendor, its staff is considered in the service world to be razor-sharp. The Crillion has become a symbol of classical French taste and culture. Its facade, facing the Egyptian obelisk that marks the spot where a guillotine stood during the French Revolution, was built in 1758 by Louis XV's architect. Out of respect for the building's history, its owners (the Taitinger family) have restored the original Bourbon decor with faultless taste.

Quality at this hotel represents the ultimate and far exceeds the legal requirements for hotels in France—or any other nation of the world, for that matter. Such an extreme level of physical surroundings and service might be used *against* the hotel when a deviation from the quality standards results in an injury or a loss. The French courts might well adopt the quality standards of the hotel as the ones to be applied, thus making them legal standards.

A unique form is found in "rolling hotels"—those operated on trains. There are three in Europe: The Al Andaluz, the Royal Scotsman, and the Orient Express, and one in the United States: the American European Express, which runs from Chicago to Washington, D.C. The legal and quality standards in train operations are unique, as are the logistical needs.

A hotel in a unique market can set itself off from the pack. Here is one example.

The Omni San Diego Hotel stresses service, and as a result ranks fifth in service among the 43 Omni Hotel properties. One service program used is the "Omni Service Tradition Program," which strives to involve employees in the hotel's future by making them more aware of the product and encouraging them to create good guest experiences. Ambassadors are elected to advise hotel management on how to improve services, facilities, and the working environment.[7]

HUMANITARIAN TRENDS

A special motel is offered by the National Institutes of Health at Bethesda, Maryland. It is called the "Children's Inn" and is a place where the family can walk down the hill to one of two spacious 24-hour kitchens and make its own sandwiches—with food the parents brought themselves and stored earlier in a refrigerator.

Here, parents can cook and care for their children much as they do at home. The two sunlit playrooms make it easy for parents to keep an eye on their kids. One even has special glass that filters out ultraviolet rays.[8]

Humanitarian standards set by the Children's Inn are reflected in actions that benefit homeless people or low-income renters.

Two New York City motels were ordered to rent rooms to homeless families. The motels had had empty rooms but had turned homeless families away in Bulls Head, Staten Island, and Sheepshead Bay in Brooklyn.[9]

At least one national chain, Days Inns of America, decided to do something about homeless persons by hiring them. The program was started in 1988 and, as of 1990, the chain had hired thirty-five homeless persons. As Richard A. Smith, vice president of human resources said, "Traditional hiring practices are dying." The program of Days Inns includes hiring elderly and disabled persons in addition to the homeless. Today, the inn accepts referrals from shelters, pays up to $7.00 per hour, and provides rooms for these persons for a small daily charge. On the inn-law side of this dramatic program is the development of a covenant that sets rules that those persons must follow in use of the rooms. Of the first thirty-five homeless hired, sixteen remained on the job and proceeded in the direction of obtaining their own homes.

IMPLEMENTATION OF HOTEL-MADE STANDARDS

One of the more far-reaching ways that hotel-made standards can be brought into being is by creating and implementing house rules, disclaimers, waivers, and releases.

House Rules

The early common law placed a heavy legal burden upon the innkeeper by making her or him an "insurer," and modern law creates a variety of pressures on the operator, too. Nevertheless, the law recognizes that the innkeeper has a right to create "rules of the house" and consequently to expect that guests and others will follow those rules. The courts tend to uphold such rules if reasonable, if proper notice is given of them, and if they are applied uniformly. The basis of this concept is found in the early case of *Rogers v. People*,[10] in which the court said "The room in the inn is regarded as part of the 'house of the innkeeper.'" Consequently, reasonable house rules are in order.

Rules and Religion

Many inns provide Bibles in guest rooms as a rule of the house. A group in Madison, Wisconsin, known as "Freedom from Religion," was unable to force innkeepers there to remove Bibles from inn rooms. On the other hand, can a house rule be enforced that prohibits in-house, room-to-room solicitation by religious groups? In *People v. Thorpe*[11] the court held that "the hotel manager, in stopping (their) preaching activities and in requesting them to leave the hotel, infringed no rights of the defendants since the Constitution does not guarantee them any right to go freely onto private property for such purposes."

Rules Limiting Access

If certain areas are to be off-limits to employees, guests, invitees, and others, conspicuous notice must be given of that rule. In the case of workers' compensation coverage, the courts tend to hold that an employee is "on the job" for purposes of coverage if he or she is on the premises and has a right to be there. Failure to give notice of off-limit areas can be tantamount to approval for employees to be there.

Check-In Identification Rules

Many inns have a rule that two items of identification must be produced at check-in time, especially those inns located in high-crime areas. Some inns use the rule as a means of controlling use by locals. Prostitution, drug dealing, and other criminal acts often are carried out by locals on the inn premises. A few states have the double-identification rule by statute, called "true-name registration" laws. A house rule to the same effect accomplishes the same purpose and will be upheld by the courts if uniformly applied.

Check-In, Check-Out Rules

For many decades, an almost universal rule was for the check-in and check-out hour to be 12:00 noon. The coming of the "megahotels" in New York City, Los Angeles, Las Vegas, and elsewhere changed all that. Could the innkeepers make the check-in time 2:00 in the afternoon and the check-out time 11:00 in the morning? As it turned out, the common law never defined what a "room for the night" means in actual hours, and now it is common practice industrywide, to use the variable-hour pattern. It is of great assistance to room personnel, and it results in a more smoothly running house for all concerned.

Rules Regarding Minors

It is a good house rule to provide that children under a certain age, such as eight or ten, are not to take part in hazardous recreational activities such as horseback riding, water skiing, or other such activities. For this rule to be held enforceable in court, direct notice of the rule must be given to the parents. Failure of the parents to comply where injury or death to a child results will be looked at as contributory negligence, or at least as providing mitigating circumstances.

Dress Codes for Guests and Invitees

Dress codes for guests and invitees tend to be upheld in court if they are reasonable; if notice is given; if they are uniformly applied; and if they do not discriminate on the basis of sex, age, color, or other civil rights grounds. In *Moolemaar v. Atlas Motor Inns, Inc.*,[12] the court said, "Dress codes of varying degrees of formality are common at restaurants and nightclubs and insistence upon them by proprietors is not unusual, extreme or outrageous."

Dress Codes for Employees

Members of the various professions have a "standard look," and that goes for the employee and management levels in the hospitality industry, too. One practical way to handle the matter is to require all employees to comply with a "uniform" requirement. In the hotel industry, uniforms sometimes are referred to as "costumes" because they often turn out to be just that. This amounts to an industry "dress-code house rule" for employees.

Not all house rules are accepted without complaint, especially in hotels that are unionized. A major hotel in Las Vegas attempted to implement a house rule that set forth standards of dress and appearance of employees. The house rule was a "spruce-up regulation" and touched on points of employee neatness in regard to perfume, makeup, jewelry, hair style, fingernail care, and related items. The rule also required that employees maintain a body weight "proportionate to their height and body structure." The union representing the employees affected by the rule mounted a successful attack against it. The union argued that the house rule was too extreme.

Rules on Employee Parking

A reasonable house rule is one that requires employees to park their autos in specific parking areas. Whether such areas are attended or not might raise legal problems if an employee's auto is stolen, but if the rule is a reasonable one, it will be upheld in court.

Rules on Employee Dating

A rule found at many hotels is that supervisory personnel shall not date employees in lower worker classifications. A challenge to this rule has been overruled by a federal court. The court found that the rule has legitimate business reasons in that it will tend to prevent sexual harassment, especially when the upper-level employee has the power to grant or deny raises or promotions to the lower-echelon employee.[13]

The creation and implementation of employee-related house rules should always be reviewed by counsel because they may lead to claims of a tort for the invasion of privacy, or a breach of fair dealing and good faith. The latter two are implied in all employment contracts. Such rules may also violate the civil rights laws if there is a "dissimilarity in treatment between the sexes."[14]

House rules may be written, or they may be unwritten. The question is: Will the courts give legal effect to one or the other, or both? A lot will depend upon the facts and circumstances in individual cases, but some unwritten house rules have become so well established that they become standards through trade usage. Thus, in some instances the courts may uphold unwritten rules just as they will written ones.

On the other hand, reliance upon so-called unwritten rules can be avoided by placing them in writing, giving proper notice of them, and enforcing them. This is true whether they are posted in guest rooms, posted on bulletin boards, or handed out at guest registration time.

Disclaimers/Waivers/Releases

A final in-house way to limit or eliminate liability is found in the use of contracts to limit liability: disclaimers, waivers, and releases. Disclaimers and waivers become entwined both in practice and in the courts. They often are hard to differentiate. In addition, releases are of two types: those that waive a legal right and are thus waivers, and those that surrender an accrued legal right upon payment of money and are releases.

Because of the danger of a court ruling that an employee handbook is in fact a unilateral contract, many businesses are using disclaimers. A typical disclaimer states, "The handbook shall not be treated as a contract between the hotel and the employee. Rather, it represents the policies and practice of the inn *in re*, the philosophy of the inn." In *Bailey v. Perkins*, the North Dakota court upheld the disclaimer, which was conspicuous, to the detriment of the employees there.[15]

A source of considerable litigation is the health and fitness areas that have become popular in recent years. Providing such amenities raises the question: Who is to be responsible for injuries that occur there? Lack of supervision is an issue in many of these cases.

There is a legal difference between supervising such facilities and providing instruction at them. Providing instruction is no defense to the claim of lack of supervision. One technique is to limit the number of users at the facility by use of a house rule. This may anger some guests, but the courts will uphold it if proper notice is given and the rule is applied uniformly. This house rule will facilitate supervision, which in turn will reduce injuries. Also, disclaimers and waivers can be prepared and used at such facilities.

A jogging trail is another amenity that can lead to court claims. Inns in major cities are even allowing jogging on their roofs. The cases abound with instances of falls, robberies, rapes, and other crimes against joggers for which claims are being filed. If such activity is permitted, disclaimers and warnings must be given to potential users of these facilities. It must be made clear that the hotel cannot guarantee safety for those who engage in use of the facilities. Rules should specify that joggers use the trails at their own risk and that the hotel assumes no responsibility for use. If a minor is involved, the parent or guardian should sign a waiver. Without that, the minor should be denied use of the facilities.

The legal effectiveness of waivers is not uniform from state to state. Many courts reject them on public policy grounds as being an unfair form of bargaining. Other courts reject them if they are not clear or if the guest did not in fact know of them. In a New York case, horseback riding was available for guests. When signing up for the rides, a disclaimer-waiver-release was inserted inside the receipts given to each guest. After a guest was killed by a horse, the court held the waiver to be ineffective because the guest had never, in fact, seen the disclaimer.[16]

A disclaimer folded into a receipt given to a guest who buys a bus tour in the city, which is not called to the attention of the guest or not actually seen, will receive no legal recognition in court. New York law prohibits the owner or operator of a "recreational facility" from using disclaimers to absolve the owner of liability for injury or other loss to those who use the facilities in question.

Another situation in which disclaimers will not be upheld by the courts is where they attempt to transfer all risk to the guest. The reason for this is that, as a matter of public policy, the law does not allow one to contract away all responsibilities for one's acts. Thus, the disclaimer must contract away normal risks and not all risks.

Generally, if the innkeeper has a signed waiver or disclaimer or release, and if the judge allows it to be considered by a jury, it usually will favor the innkeeper. It will show the jury that the injured guest was aware of the dangers before the injury or loss occurred. Using disclaimers, waivers, and releases involves paperwork, time, and care, but almost always represents good practice. Drafting a good disclaimer, whether for the parking lot, the fitness room, or other recreational facilities, should be done by an attorney.

The following list, summarized from several court cases, shows reasons disclaimers often do not survive legal muster.

1. Failure to use bold, conspicuous type to alert as to restrictions.
2. Disclaimers not positioned effectively, such as being placed on the back of a ticket receipt folder that goes unnoticed.
3. Too-small type used to spell out the terms of the disclaimer, which go unnoticed.
4. Lack of contrasting color, or background, that otherwise would have drawn attention to the disclaimer.
5. "Artfully camouflaged" disclaimers buried inside of something else.
6. Concealed disclaimer, such as being inside of an envelope that was not opened.

An example of a disclaimer-exculpatory clause that was approved by a Georgia court follows.

> Member agrees . . . use of all club facilities shall be undertaken at the member's own risk . . . and that the corporation which owns the club and/or any affiliated companies and/or their respective agents and employees shall not be liable for any claims, demands, injuries, damages, actions or causes of action . . . which arise due to the negligence of the corporation which owns the club and/or their respective agents and employees to member. . . arising out of or connected with the use of any of the services and/or facilities of such corporation. . . and the member does hereby expressly forever release and discharge said corporation and any affiliated companies, and their respective agents and employees, from all such claims, demands, injuries, damages, actions or causes of action. . . .

Such clauses in Georgia are both binding and valid.[17]

COURTS LOOK AT HOTEL-MADE STANDARDS

Various courts have taken a close look at a variety of hotel-made standards. We will close the chapter by a look at some of them.

"Adults-Only" Policy

An adults-only policy violates the federal Age Discrimination Act, if the hotel is a "place of public accommodation," which in most instances it certainly would be. In California, the Unruh Act prohibits such a policy in the Golden State. The Unruh Act also provides that one who is successful in proving a violation can recover three times the amount of actual losses. Multiple recoveries are referred to as *treble damages.*

Creating Advertisements

Two legal matters become of primary concern in creating ads. First, the advertisement must not be worded in a way that would prompt a court to hold that the ad was an "offer." If it were couched in such words, an attempt to accept the offer, such as tender of the funds for a scheduled event at the hotel, would be an acceptance. The inability of the hotel to fulfill the contract would render the hotel liable for losses. This situation can be avoided by qualifying all advertisements with words such as "subject to availability"; "supplies limited"; "first come, first served"; "this advertisement is not a contractual offer."

Care is always in order in these situations because, if a judge sees there has been an offer and it has been accepted, the common-law rules of contract must be applied.

The second legal matter has to do with words that constitute promises that cannot be met later. Such promises are called *express warranties.* Some examples are: "sugar-free dessert," "boneless fish," "Sanka coffee," and the advertisement that Holiday Inns International used. Two words were used in this warranty: "No surprises." The use of these two words became the subject of litigation against the chain. A person who had been a guest at the time of his injury claimed that what caused his injury was a "surprise" and was a breach of warranty. The court agreed and allowed a substantial recovery for the breach of warranty (promise).[18]

Reasonable Inspection

Reasonable inspections of the premises are essential. If dangerous conditions exist that are discoverable in the exercise of reasonable care, the business can be held liable for injuries or death caused by failure to discover such dangers. Whether reasonable care is exercised is a question of fact for the jury. Thus, it is an error to dismiss a plaintiff's complaint without instructing the jury of the law and allowing the jury to decide the issue as a question of fact.[19] Inspection becomes a matter of hotel-made law.

Nurseries

Nurseries are not always provided, yet they sometimes are offered as an amenity. If nursery services are provided, properly trained personnel must be on hand and caution must be exercised at all times. The courts have long held that when dealing with children, one must exercise greater care than when dealing with adults. The court will instruct the jury to that effect. In a child injury case, the court instructed the jury that, because a child was involved, there was a presumption of negligence, as this was an injury that would not have occurred if there had been no negligence. The instruction was upheld on appeal.[20]

Mini-Liquor Bars

Hotels often provide mini-bars in rooms from which guests may serve themselves. Beverages that are used are added to the room bill. Mini-bars are in locked containers that can be opened only by a room key, magnetic card, or similar device. A challenge to in-room sales as violation of a state constitution was overruled in *Miller v. Alcoholic Beverage Laws.*[21]

Shoplifting or Theft

Shoplifting is usually associated with shopping malls and supermarkets. It often happens, too, in hotel shops and in the hotel itself. Some states and cities have statutes and ordinances that provide that a hotel accusing a person of theft is immune from legal liability for a later charge of "false imprisonment" or "false arrest." To gain this immunity, there must be evidence showing that an innkeeper of "reasonable prudence," acting through agents, would conclude that another is stealing. The question of guilt or innocence then becomes a question of fact for the jury.[22]

Guests, patrons, invitees, and others cause great theft loss each year. One court referred to the situation as "runaway theft." By far the largest dollar loss by theft is caused by employees and the greatest opportunity for theft is with food and beverage personnel. Strict house rules and policies are required to counter this disturbing practice.

Miniature Steps and Cones

Because of sloping terrain, small step-downs often have to be created that are not deep enough to qualify as stairs. Often these steps are only 3 or 4 inches in depth. Miniature steps should be edged in yellow or red paint to alert walkers to them. This, in turn, raises another problem. At certain times of the day, the glare of the sun may make the warning strips difficult to see, and a person using the small steps may step out and fall. The courts call this "glaring bright"—an obstruction by nature that prevents one from seeing. The answer is to treat small steps just as other steps: Install handrails beside them.[23]

Warning cones sometimes appear along our highways where streetwork is being done. These are made of red or yellow plastic with square black bases and are shaped like dunce caps. The cones are also used at hotels to warn of wet floors. They represent a legal problem when they are left in place after the need for them ends. In such circumstances, if one falls over a cone, liability may attach.[24] It must be house policy to remove them promptly after they are no longer needed.

Failing to Follow Hotel-Made Standards

If a hotel regularly hires off-duty police when conventions are held, this creates a hotel-made standard. If the hotel then fails to hire off-duty police for a convention during which a guest is attacked in the parking lot, the hotel has failed to meet its own standard. A court would treat this as negligence, and if this negligence was the proximate cause of the injuries suffered, the hotel will lose the case.[25]

SUMMARY

The law which normally finds its origins in constitutions, statutes, case decisions, regulations, ordinances, and other sources, can also come from legal standards that are created within the hotel itself. This is also true in other businesses in the hospitality and tourism areas. As long as these "in-house rules" do not violate the law, the courts almost uniformly uphold them.

The distinction between quality standards and legal standards is important because they are not the same. A hotel could meet all legal standards in its operation but fall short on quality standards; the reverse could also be true. Increasing quality can increase costs, but it can also increase the volume of business. Guest expectations play a role and travelers today are no longer satisfied with complacency, average service, or accommodations that lack quality. It is not enough to create hotel-made standards. They must be implemented on a regular and even-handed basis.

The careful and judicious use of disclaimers, waivers, and releases can be good business practice. This is true at parking lots, recreation areas, and at many other locations at the hotel. Such documents, if properly executed, can provide protection from liability that is lacking in the common law.

QUESTIONS

1. What does the term "hotel-made law" suggest to you? Explain in a short sentence.
2. What is the difference between a legal standard and a quality standard?
3. From the activities described here, can you think of a new legal issue that may arise in the future in relation to hotel-made standards?
4. If a hotel has extraordinary in-house standards, such as the Crillion in Paris, why might a court decide to use those standards to measure house conduct when guests suffer a loss? Would this, in your opinion, discourage the creation and implementation of quality standards at other hotels?
5. What is the legal danger in trying to rely upon an unwritten house rule as a defense in a court case against the hotel?
6. What is the legal logic of including disclaimers in the handbooks given to employees?
7. Hospitals are entering the innkeeping picture in a positive manner. What legal consequences might result from this? Could the spreading of diseases from the hospital to guests become an issue?

8. Sketch an instance in which the careless use of a disclaimer could result in a court holding that it was ineffective.

9. True or false: The fact that the courts hold that the hotel is the house of the innkeeper provides protection for guests.

10. In the future, is the desire to assist the homeless and low-income families likely to play a larger role in hotel law? Provide one *pro* and one *con* thought on this issue.

NOTES

1. *Lodging*, May 1982, p. 2.

2. *Hopp v. Thompson*, 72 S.D. 574, 38 N.W. 2d 133, 135 (1949).

3. *Stahlin v. Hilton Hotels Corp.*, 484 F. 2d 580 (Illinois 1974).

4. In Cohn, Roy. *How to Stand Up for Your Rights and Win!* (New York, Simon Schuster: 1986, p. 177).

5. *Page v. Sloan*, 281 N.C. 697, 190 S.E. 2d 189 (North Carolina 1972).

6. *Restatement of Torts*, A Hornbook published by West Publishing Co., St. Paul, for use in law schools.

7. *Successful Hotel Marketer*, volume 3, number 19, p. 2.

8. In *Las Vegas Review Journal*, Sept. 16, 1990, p. 10B.

9. In *New York Times*, October 24, 1986.

10. 86 N.Y. 360.

11. 101 N.Y.S. 2d 986 (New York 1950).

12. 616 F. 2d 87 (Virgin Islands 1980).

13. *Sears v. Ryder*, 596 F. Supp. 1001 (Maine 1984).

14. *Zentiska v. Pooler Motel, Ltd.*, 708 F. Supp. 1321 (Georgia 1989).

15. 398 N.W. 2d 120 (North Dakota 1986).

16. *Di Maria v. Coordinated*, 526 N.Y.S. 2d 19 (New York 1988).

17. *My Fair Lady v. Harris*, 364 S.E. 2d 580 (Georgia 1988).

18. *Hayward v. Holiday Inns, Inc.*, 459 F. Supp. 634 (Ed Virginia 1988).

19. *Sandoe v. Lefta Associates*, 559 A. 2d 732 (District of Columbia 1989).

20. *Zimmer v. Celebrities, Inc.*, 615 P. 2d 76 (Colorado 1980).

21. 797 P. 2d 1013 (Oklahoma 1990).

22. *Bi-Lo, Inc. v. McConnel*, 404 S.E. 2d 327 (Georgia 1991).

23. *Sherman v. Arno*, 383 P. 2d 741 (Arizona 1963).

24. *Luthy v. Denny's Inc.*, 782 S.W. 2d 661 (Missouri 1990).

25. *Walkoviak v. Hilton Hotels*, 580 S.W. 2d 632 (Texas 1979).

18

Reservations, Registration, and Rates

Overview

I N THIS CHAPTER we will examine some of the legal basics that become involved in the making of reservations, as well as in check-in procedures. The emphasis is on creating the hotel-guest relationship, pricing, and overbooking. Case examples are provided, with particular attention to the landmark Rainbow case.

Forming the Hotel-Guest Relationship

The relationship that comes into being between the innkeeper and the traveler who becomes a guest has long been recognized as "special." The courts give stronger attention to "special relationships" than they do to the more ordinary kind. The point of time at which the relationship becomes operational is of legal importance, and it is not always the time of actual registration. Although that act is *prima facie* evidence that the relationship has come into being, it can arise before that point in time. This is so because it is based upon consent and not contract in all instances. It *may* be based on contract, and the consent often results in a contract, but that is not the legal test.

The intent of the traveler to become a guest must be coupled with the agreement of the innkeeper to accept that person. Thus, if X, who is registered, gives his key to Y, who does not register, and the innkeeper knows of the exchange of the key and does not object, Y is also a guest at law. Faced with this situation, the innkeeper, of course, should make it clear that the acceptance of Y is subject to proper registration.[1] Figure 18.1 illustrates the formation of the hotel-guest relationship.

The innkeeper must have an opportunity to accept or reject the traveler. One can never become a guest by unilateral action. The consent usually comes through actions of agents and arises most frequently by registration. There is no need for a formal contract, although there usually will be one because the law will imply the contract if the consent is given. The consent can be evidenced by furnishing a room key, providing food and drink, or extending other services to the traveler. Meeting a traveler at the entrance and providing assistance with his or her luggage can supply the consent. If the consent is given, the relationship begins immediately. No lapse of time is required.

FIGURE 18.1 Formation of the hotel-guest relationship.

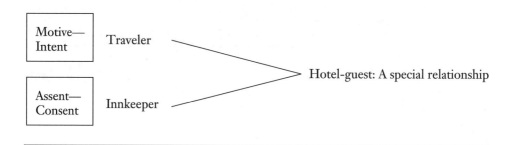

The law has placed reliance upon consent for so long that if the refusal to grant the consent is wrongful or even illegal, the courts still find that there is no hotel-guest relationship.[2]

One can become a guest without ever intending to take a room, and it was so held in *Overstreet v. Moser*.[3] On the other hand, in a 1409 case, a traveler asked to be accepted but was wrongfully turned away. While he was furnished a key, the agreement was that he was to look out for himself. The court held that there was no inn-guest relationship.[4]

The telling point, where a traveler does not take a room but may be held to be a guest, is that the traveler is in the course of a journey and the inn is used temporarily to further the journey. Resorting to the inn for drink only created the relationship,[5] as did remaining in a public room while waiting for a train.[6] The act of leaving goods with the intent of returning for them later also created the relationship.[7]

Where the head of a household registers and does so for his family, all become guests although only one registered.[8] A business luncheon at the inn, attended by locals, does not make those who attend its guests, though. They are not in the "course of a journey." Conversely, if a local is received with intent for him or her to be a guest, that person is then a guest.[9] Many hotels refuse to rent rooms to locals, and the common law recognizes the right to do so as they are not in the class that the law was designed to protect in the beginning.

MAKING A RESERVATION

Making a reservation is the act of contacting a hotel, hospitality, or tourism facility in advance of arrival and gaining in return the assurance that accommodations will be available on the date and at the time requested. Making reservations has become routine and reliable. Yet, problems often arise, and the problems often are legal in nature. To illustrate, does a phone reservation for a motel room, or a table at a restaurant not accompanied by an advanced payment create a binding contract on the part of the business? Conversely, does there even have to be a binding contract to hold either of the parties to their promises: the one to provide the service and the other to use it as promised?

The Reservation Contract

A good way to begin is by equating the six requirements of a common-law contract with the steps that take place in making reservations both with and without deposits. The contractual elements of a hotel reservation appear to be as follows:

1. Offer: made by the traveler "I will need a room on August 3, 4, 5, 19—, double beds." (It is communicated, made in good faith, and is definite.)
2. Acceptance: the agreement to hold the room.
3. Consideration: payment of the deposit, or exchange of the promises.
4. Mutuality: apparent.
5. Legal purpose: presumed. (If not, the contract would fail. An example is a room reservation made for the purpose of engaging in immoral activity.)
6. Competent parties: a duty to receive minors as well as adults. (This seldom causes legal problems in practice.)

Now assume that the reservation is by fax in the morning for a 6:00 P.M. guaranteed arrival, given with an American Express Card number. The inn accepts by immediate fax reply.

1. Offer: made by the traveler.
2. Acceptance: an indication by fax of the willingness to be bound. If the traveler is told, "Sorry, we are full," the matter ends there.
3. Consideration: a promise by the traveler to take the room and the inn's promise to provide it. These mutual promises provide the consideration, *quid pro quo*, and so does the guarantee with the credit card.
4. Mutuality: apparent.
5. Legal purpose: presumed.
6. Competent parties: no problems, as indicated previously.

In both instances, a binding contract has come into being.

If the room is not available when the guest arrives, this would be a breach of contract by the inn. If the traveler does not cancel by 6:00 P.M. and does not show, that would be a breach of contract by the traveler.

Contract Counterpart

The *common-law duty* that innkeepers must receive all guests has a counterpart in the law of contract where, under the facts, there is a *contractual duty* to receive. In the latter, the innkeeper cannot use the normal excuses *not* to receive because to do so would breach the contract. In the case of the common-law duty to receive, the usual excuses, such as a full house, would be valid.

The distinction between the common-law duty and the contractual duty was recognized by a leading author on the subject of contracts:

> The obligations of an innkeeper arising from the common-law relation of innkeeper and guest are imposed by law irrespective of contract, and may arise when no contract is or can be made. There is, nevertheless, frequently a contract

between the parties fixing the terms of their relation within the limit which the law allows.[10]

Computer and Fax Reservation Systems

Look Ahead Interflow (LAI) is a reservation system developed by AT&T and related to the Integrated Services Digital Network (ISDN). LAI automatically sends reservation requests at booked reservation centers to other centers. Multiple locations are treated as being one location, reducing the costs of finding accommodations for travelers asking for rooms in a certain area. These systems are of great value not only to travelers but also to hotel, hospitality, and tourism operations that subscribe to the service.

Overbooking

A troublesome practice found at hotels, motels, inns, restaurants, bars, car rental agencies, and even theme parks, is overbooking. The major cause is those who make reservations but do not show as promised and who fail to give notice of cancellation. One major credit card company found that an estimated 500,000 of its card members made reservations at hotels each year and not only failed to show up as agreed, but also did not give timely notice of cancellation. This company estimated that its credit cardholders cost the hotel industry more than $35 million in profits each year.

The industry has compensated for the huge losses by overbooking, selling more rooms than are available. This, in turn, has led to thousands of cases in which travelers with binding reservations have been "walked" to other hotels, creating breaches of contract.

As a matter of contract law, a no-show can be held responsible for the room that remains empty all night. Nevertheless, attempting to use the courts to collect on that loss is uneconomical because the sum involved will not support litigation. Most hotels ask that reservations be backed up by major credit card numbers. The no-show traveler then can be billed for the price of the room.

The credit card company mentioned above instituted a program that has a beneficial impact on no-shows who carry its credit card. This company guarantees the arrival. If the company has to pay the hotel because of the no-show, it bills the cardholder on her or his next monthly statement. If the cardholder fails to pay the card issuer, he or she faces cancellation of the credit card. Table 18.1 gives the forms of overbooking and the legal consequences.

Courts tend to frown upon overbooking for a simple legal reason: It is usually a breach of contract. If there were no contract, there never could be overbooking. When breach occurs, the law must give the offended person a legal remedy if that person asks for it in court.

In overbooking situations personnel must use caution in talking with would-be guests who are being "walked." A front-desk person, for example, would be unwise to admit the overbooking. If this is done, a court may hold it to be an admission that can be used against the innkeeper as proof of the breach of the reservation contract. It would be much better to take all reasonable steps to place the bumped person elsewhere, saying nothing at all or as little as possible about why the walking became necessary.

TABLE 18.1 Variances of overbooking.

How It Happened	Damages Faced
1. Mistake	Actual
2. Negligence	Actual
3. Misunderstanding	Actual
4. Deliberate act	Punitive
5. Bait-and-switch	Punitive
6. Fraud	Punitive

If an inn carelessly overbooks, that act gives rise to a cause of action for the negligent wrong. If a hotel unit overbooks, *knowing in advance that it cannot honor the reservations,* that is fraud. Punitive damages can be sought in fraud cases.

Although some courts recognize that mere overbooking that is not carried out by design and results from an unexpected cause is a breach of contract, the jury may consider the circumstances when awarding damages. In the Wells case[11] there was expert testimony of an average overbooking rate nationwide of one-half of 1 percent, and the walk rate at the Holiday Inn in question was much lower. Although the plaintiff recovered, the damages were limited.

Florida specifically prohibits overbooking by regulation. If overbooking does occur, the inn must make every effort to find comparable accommodations. If the traveler does not accept the substitute, all deposits must be returned. Rules have been written in that state to enforce the regulation, and a fine of up to $500 can be levied, while the travelers are free to pursue their legal remedies for the breach of contract.

Bait-and-Switch

Overbooking often arises from a deliberate bait-and-switch effort, and that seems to have been the motive in *Dold v. Outrigger Hotel.*[12] First, the travelers were baited in their reservations with a promise of ocean-front rooms. Upon arrival, the switch was made to an inn off the beach. The hotel was receiving money for each referral. The court allowed recovery to the travelers who refused to accept the substituted premises.

Many of the 40,000-plus American hotels, motels and inns, engage in overbooking at one time or another. Certain operations do this continually, causing injury to large numbers of travelers. It is to this class of business operators that the courts now are applying harsher penalties. The Rainbow case in this chapter is an example of the attitude of courts that is developing in reference to overbooking. The striking feature of that case is that it deals with breach of contract, which is a civil matter, and fraud as well, which is a criminal matter.

When a hotel baits potential guests with the promise of ocean-front rooms, or special hotel amenities, and then switches accommodations to a less desirable location, fraud has occurred. Fraud has been defined as "an intentional misrepresentation of a material existing fact, upon which one relies to his/her detriment "or loss." The intent makes a fraud a crime so, in theory, a hotel that deliberately overbooks could be sued for breach of contract as a civil matter, and then prosecuted for the fraud. That could lead to criminal fines and perhaps prosecution.

Owners of two moderate-size motels in West Virginia stated, "We know it is legally wrong to do this, but we want to make certain that we fill up as often as possible even though it causes inconvenience to ten or twelve travelers. The loss to those travelers will be small, so they aren't going to hire a lawyer to sue us."

If innkeepers are not going to adhere to solid legal and ethical standards, would-be guests cannot be expected to overlook this lack of standards and allow it to pass without doing something about it. That brings us to a final question: Is there a way to assure that we have a full house, yet not encounter the legal and ethical problems we have been discussing? Figure 18.2 presents an overbooking diagram. The large triangle represents the rooms available for, say, July 4th, as sales are made by reservations or by requests from walk-ins. As sales are made, the number of available rooms decreases. At some point in this process, the inn will pass the break-even point. Beyond that point, we show a profit, subject, however, to the problem of no-shows.

FIGURE 18.2 Economic aspects of overbooking.

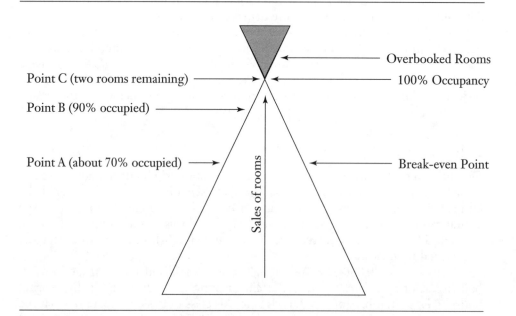

A workable answer that will benefit travelers and hotels is suggested. Points A, B, and C are listed on the left side of the figure, and the "break-even point" and the "100% occupancy point" on the right. First, it is our house policy on reservations and walk-in sales to freely make sales up to Point A. We will have to draw on our business experience to determine this point. It probably will be around 90%, which will be above the break-even point.

Next, from that point to Point B, we will use the principles of unilateral contract law. We can do this in two ways: (1) accept the reservation, provided that the traveler arrives no later than 6:00 P.M. on July 4th, or (2), require the traveler to send us a wire payment for one day, which must be received no later than 6:00 P.M. If neither is done, there is no contract. (If a traveler guarantees a room with a credit card and the card company accepts the charge, or the card company guarantees payment, there *would* be a contract; these forms of payment would be included in sales up to Point A.)

Now, we have sold July 4th at perhaps 98%, and none of our sales at this point can result in a claim of overbooking. This brings us to the third step. For the balance of this July 4th, we will make "conditional promises" and nothing more. A caller requests a room, and we state, "We will try to provide you a room, but we cannot promise it at this time. If we have a room when you arrive, we will provide it for you." This language is not an acceptance of a request for a room and does not create a contract. Many hotels use waiting lists, and these, too, are conditional as a matter of contract law.

Any late walk-ins can be accepted freely, and we also will accept other arrivals to whom we have made conditional promises until we reach 100% occupancy. At that point in time, we can hang out the "No Vacancy" sign. In this process, we will not have breached any contracts nor committed fraud.

A system such as the one described in Figure 18.2 is effective at hotels that enjoy frequent full occupancy. What it does is prevent the selling of excess rooms.

Even with a careful operational system such as this one, a mistake sometimes occurs and we sell a room we do not have available. Many American hotels have the policy of finding a traveler a room elsewhere, paying for the room, and transporting the traveler there at no cost. Some hotels throw in a complimentary breakfast at the replacement hotel the next morning. In Florida, a regulation makes this policy mandatory. This regulation requires hotels that overbook to make every effort to obtain suitable accommodations for the traveler elsewhere. If demanded, all deposits must be returned to the traveler. A fine up to $500 is provided for each person who is turned away. That person still retains the common-law right to sue for breach of contract. In a case in which a Holiday Inn accidentally overbooked and did not have a policy of doing so, the resulting award was limited to the price of a room elsewhere.[13]

In a Fort Worth, Texas, rape case, which cost Motel 6 and its insurer $10 million, depositions of managers disclosed that the Motel 6 was offered financial rewards if it maintained a more than 100% occupancy rate each night. This could be done only by renting "hourlies," which a former Houston Police Chief identified as rooms rented to "dope fiends" and "whores."

Minimum-Period Reservation Contracts

A final registration matter also has to do with reservations. Resorts and many other lodging facilities have the custom of requiring that reservations be made for minimum time periods, such as three days, even if only a one-day advance payment is required. This is true in Florida during certain months and at lodging facilities close to major sports events. What is the contractual obligation of a guest who checks out before the minimum time period has expired? If the accommodations cannot be rented, which is often the case, the former guest would have a contractual obligation to make up the loss.

In *Cardinal Consulting Company v. Circo Resorts, Inc.* (Circus-Circus in Las Vegas),[14] the plaintiff was awarded $71,500 in damages for loss of profits resulting from the defendant's breach of reservations.

Excuses for Nonperformance

Under contract rules, once a contract is in being, a court will accept few excuses for nonperformance. A "mutual mistake" might be one. Another might be "impossibility." What is impossible at law, however, is not the same as an impossibility in the normal sense. If an inn is full, it is "impossible," in the normal sense of that word, to give a room to a late arrival who has a reservation. Yet this is not a *legal impossibility* and could not be used as an excuse for nonperformance. Sealing off an inn by police agencies because of poisonous gas leakage from a train derailment would provide an excuse at law. So would the destruction of a lodging unit by fire.

If there is a breach of a contractual relationship, the guest must allege and prove the existence of the contract. A complaint that fails to allege a contract would be defective. The guest also would have the burden of proving the damages (losses), if any, that were suffered. In an increasingly large number of cases being decided each year, two facts are emerging: Guests are more willing than ever to sue, and they are succeeding in carrying the burden of proof in court.

The terms of a reservation contract must be clear because the law requires certainty. In a California case, a travel business made a reservation for 250 rooms. An exchange of letters followed, and the travel business changed what it had first called a "tentative reservation" to one it confirmed in a letter. The 250 rooms were not used as agreed. In the lawsuit by the inn, the court found that there had been a contract, that it had been breached, and awarded the inn $15,300 in damages.[15]

In *Freeman v. Kiamesha Concord Inn*, the court held that: "The solicitation of a reservation, the making of a reservation by the transmittal of a deposit and the acceptance of the deposit constituted a binding contract in accordance with traditional contract principles of offer and acceptance."[16]

In addition to the requirement of contract certainty, the courts will not allow the plain terms of a contract to be changed by custom or trade usage.

> The court did not err by charging that plaintiff's liability evidence was not ambiguous. What the court charged was that the purpose of the evidence concerning custom and usage was to help understand what the parties intended and understood *if* there was uncertainty or ambiguity. The court said that the plain terms of the contract prevail over a trade usage or custom, that evidence of custom or usage cannot be considered to destroy a contract, or to make the rights and liabilities of the parties to a contract other than those created by the contract terms. The court also said that custom and usage evidence cannot create an ambiguity where none exists and that where the terms of an express contract are clear and unambiguous, they cannot be varied or contradicted because they differ from those usually found in a particular trade or business. Whether or not there was ambiguity was left to the jury.[17]

Making a binding reservation contract does not create the inn-guest relationship. To illustrate, if a traveler in Los Angeles makes a reservation by phone in Las Vegas, that person would not be a guest until he or she arrives and is accepted there. Any other rule would subject the innkeeper to unnecessary and unneeded responsibilities. The traveler now arrives and is turned away. There has been a breach of contract. In this instance the inn-guest relationship did not come into being.[18]

REGISTRATION

Once a traveler with or without a reservation arrives at the hotel, the next step of the legal process under discussion comes to the front. It has to do with registration, commonly referred to as check-in. It is here that the hotel-guest relationship most often comes into being. It occurs when the innkeeper, acting through front-desk personnel, accepts the traveler, making him or her a guest.

If the traveler has a valid reservation but is refused, that would be a breach of contract, yet there would be no hotel-guest relationship. If a walk-in without a reservation is refused a room, wrongfully, that would be a common-law tort or wrong. Again, in that event there would be no hotel-guest relationship.

A variety of legal matters arise as the traveler is greeted at the front desk and the registration or check-in process begins. This is so whether the traveler has a reservation or is seeking to be admitted under his or her common-law right to be received. Included in this process are the keeping of guest registers, the matter of false registration, true-name registration, and related topics.

Guest Registers

In centuries past, hotels and inns commonly kept and maintained guest registers, although there was no common law duty to do so. Several decades back, a front-desk "ledger" was in vogue. As travelers checked in, their names were entered into the log. As they left the premises, appropriate notations were made as to time of departure and payments received. At the Hotel Del Coronado in San Diego, a turn-of-the-century register used there is on display. It shows who came in, at what hour, what deposits they made, and the time and date they left. It was maintained in beautiful cursive handwriting.

Some states today require that a registration system be maintained as travelers check in and become guests, and as they check out and become travelers again. New York has two statutes addressing the subject.

> The owner, lessee, proprietor or manager of any hotel, motel, tourist cabins, camp, resort, tavern, inn, boarding or lodging house shall keep for a period of three years a register which shall show the name, residence, date of arrival and departure of his guests. Such record may be kept within the meaning of this section when reproduced on any photographic, photostatic, microfilm, microcard, miniature photographic or other process which actually reproduced the original record.[19]
>
> Every keeper of a hotel, lodging house, boarding house or rooming house in a town or city, shall cause to be kept for a period of one year a record showing the name and residence and the date of arrival and departure of his guests or lodgers

and the room, rooms or bed occupied by them, which record shall have a space in which each guest or lodger shall sign his name. The keeping of but one person as a guest or lodger in any building shall not constitute such building either a boarding house or a rooming house within the meaning of this section.[20]

In contrast, the registration rule prevailing in Louisiana, a civil law state, is that a guest may be accepted there without any registration at all. A register does not have to be signed to prove the contract between the parties. The hotel-guest contracts in that state are matters of oral assent and no further formality is needed to make them legal.

Massachusetts has a statute requiring all hotels in that state to keep a register and to record the "true name" and other data. Such registers must be kept for one year. The statute also requires that such register shall be ". . . open to the inspection of licensing authorities, their agents and the police. . . ."

This statute was challenged as being in violation of the Fourth Amendment when a manager at a hotel in that state refused the request of a police officer to look at the guest register. The Massachusetts court said the statute was constitutional.[21] The court stated, "In business premises a person [the manager] enjoys less of an expectation of privacy than in a home. . . ." If the manager personally was a suspect in a crime, that would have triggered the protection of the Fourth Amendment.

A related question is whether a guest register is open to police inspection without a search warrant. Although the U.S. Supreme Court has held that a guest's room is entitled to the protection of the Fourth Amendment,[22] it is not clear if the same rule applies to the register.

It becomes necessary for the innkeeper to seek a legal opinion of what must be done in this regard in a city, county, or state. Being uninformed on this issue is not a good idea.

Preregistration

More and more hotels, especially the larger ones, are using systems in which the registration is done before the traveler arrives at the front desk. Two variations are seen today. At the Las Vegas Hilton, for example, travelers in the check-in line are contacted by an automated radio check-in system in which their room needs and other data are obtained and recorded before the traveler reaches the desk. In the second variation, the registration is completed before the traveler arrives. The legal concern in such systems is in regard to the actual time the hotel-guest relationship begins.

False Registration

It is not uncommon for persons to register under false names. Entertainment personalities and others do it as a matter of course, and in such cases no legal problems are encountered because management takes part in the false registration. A better question arises when someone registers falsely at the hotel for an immoral purpose. Over the years the courts have come to agree that even though a guest may register falsely to carry out an illegal or immoral purpose, this in itself does not excuse the innkeeper of the duty to use ordinary care in reference to that person. In short, the false registration, standing alone, is not a defense to a negligent injury of the guest. The Rappee case later in this chapter illustrates this point, which seems to be the majority view.[23]

True-Name Registration

The state legislatures have at times expressed concern about false registration. It is a means of taking up spurious residence for fraudulent voting purposes. It is a means of skipping out on the support of families. It is a means of avoiding obligations due to creditors. This concern has found expression in statutes that place a burden upon innkeepers to prohibit those checking in from using false identities.

These laws are designed to aid law-enforcement agencies in tracing criminals, "skips," and others. Arkansas, Massachusetts, New Hampshire, North Carolina, Ohio, and Vermont are states that have such laws. Positive identification is required at registration time. In true-name registration states, is a signature required in addition to positive identification? In all of the listed states, the answer is "yes."

When Does the Hotel-Guest Relationship End?

In a New York case, a couple checked out, retrieved jewelry from the front-desk safe, and were about to enter a cab at the front entrance to the hotel. The woman placed the bag with the jewelry in it on the middle of the back seat as she started to enter the cab. Someone tugged on her sleeve, pointed to money lying on the ground, and suggested it was hers. She hesitated, looked back, and said the money was not hers. Entering the back seat, she found her bag missing.

The couple sued for loss of the jewelry, claiming lack of proper security. The hotel defended on the grounds that the hotel-guest relationship had ended and the hotel had no further liability. The hotel also claimed the loss was not *infra hospitium*—inside the confines of the hotel.

The court refused to accept either defense, ruling that even though a guest has retrieved valuables, paid the bill, and left the lobby with the intent of not returning immediately, the hotel-guest relationship had not ended until the guest had an opportunity to remove their baggage. As to the *infra-hospitium* claim, the court said it was a matter of architecture: If the hotel wall had been built on the other side of the cab, the loss would have occurred in the lobby.[24]

Leaving the subject of registration, creation of the hotel-guest relationship, guest registers, and related subjects, it becomes necessary to learn what the law has to say about what hotels and motels can charge for the services and goods they supply to guests.

HOTEL ROOM RATES

In the matter of rates charged, the law makes a distinction between rates that are quoted when one makes a reservation and the rates that are charged to the arriving traveler who has no reservation. The reason for the difference is legally important. When one calls for a reservation, the matter of rates is one of agreement (contract). Even if the rate quoted is exorbitant, no harm comes to the traveler because the room is not going to be used until a later date. The inquiring traveler can refuse to agree to the rate and seek accommodations elsewhere.

On the other hand, when the traveler arrives after a hard day's travel and is in need of the room for the night, quoting an exorbitant rate would have the practical effect of forcing the traveler to pay the price or seek another inn. These situations are what the law has long sought to prevent. Thus, the law has long held that the price quoted must be "reasonable." If the law were otherwise, the unreasonable rate would be a form of extortion and at the same time would tend to hinder travel. Because the law mandates that an innkeeper make "reasonable charges" for rooms, services, and food and drink furnished to travelers, it becomes a logical question to ask. Just what price is that?

The answer will be determined as an accounting function in many instances in which one is alleged to have made unreasonable charges. Or a court may look to rates charged at like or similar inns. Where the accounting approach is used, the court, acting through a "master"—an accountant appointed by the court—will determine overhead costs for the previous year. Factored in would be part-time help, utility costs, thefts by guests, percent of no-shows, and the like. A sum for a reasonable profit will be added. Once a total is reached, the master will look at the occupancy rate, taking into consideration the break-even point and the seasonal-occupancy variance. It then will become a matter of determining what rates for rooms, food and drink, and other services must be charged to equal the total sum. If these figures come close to the charges that were made, courts would find that those rates were "reasonable."

Another factor that could be considered in such calculations would be the "amenity creep" that may have occurred in the year under investigation. This is a new term that describes the upgrading of services and the adding of new facilities, which in turn may justify the charging of higher rates. The courts could be expected to make an allowance for more than just the costs of such upgrading because what may have started as an economy-oriented operation now may be classified as a mid-class operation.

Amenity creep is an economic principle that logically drives rates higher and increases the legal duties of innkeepers as well. The "creep" creates a void as the inn is upgraded. It has a dynamic impact on rates and should be explained to the court if an inn is ever accused of charging unreasonable rates.

Today, the amount charged by innkeepers is rarely challenged in court, but in light of the Rainbow case (presented later) that may change in the future. In an early King's Bench case, the court said the charge the innkeeper made would be upheld if it were not extravagant; "a person residing at an inn cannot live so cheaply as at his own house."[25]

> The requirement that the compensation should be reasonable is a necessary corollary of the requirement that the guest should be received, for if it were open to the innkeeper to charge what he pleased, he might exclude such applicants as he did not care to entertain by the mere device of demanding from them an unreasonable payment. They [innkeepers] do not deal upon *contracts* [emphasis in original] as others do. They only make bills, in which they cannot set unreasonable rates; if they do, they are indictable for extortion.[26]

Hotel Rates and Statutes

The legislatures of the states have enacted a variety of statutes concerned with hotel rates. Most of these require that the rates be posted in each guest room showing prices per day for one person, two persons, and more. None of these statutes observed to date tell the innkeeper what the rates charged must be. The common law plays that role, as we have seen. The innkeeper is free to set the rate, as long as it is reasonable, and to vary the rate during different seasons of the year or during local events when that becomes prudent.

It has been observed that the highest seasonal rate is posted but lower rates are charged during the slow periods of business. No legal harm seems to be involved in this practice. However, charging more than the posted rate could cause legal problems. It certainly would not be appreciated by guests who take notice that this has happened. Following is a sample of a posting statute.

651.030 Posting of rates; liability for overcharge.
1. Every keeper of any hotel, inn, motel or motor court in this state shall post, in a conspicuous place in the office and in every bedroom of such establishment, a printed copy of NRS 651.010 to 651.030, inclusive, and a statement of charge or rate of charges by the day for lodging.
2. No charge or sum shall be collected for any greater or other sum than he is entitled to by the general rules and regulations of such establishment.
3. For any violation of this section, or any provision herein contained, the offender shall forfeit to the injured party 3 times the amount of the sum charged in excess of what he is entitled to charge.

The statutes of some states, such as California, Florida, and Nevada, prohibit advertising hotel and motel rates and the rates on outdoor signs. These statutes do not prohibit advertising of Nevada rates outside of the state, and such advertising is seen in California, Arizona, Utah, Idaho, and near the borders of Nevada. The statute does not prohibit television, newspaper, and radio ads stating rates, and these are seen and heard throughout Nevada and near the borders.

The sign statute in Florida states:

No person shall display or cause to be displayed any sign which may be seen from a public highway or street, which sign includes a statement or numbers relating to the rates charged at a public lodging establishment renting by the day or week, unless such sign includes in letters and figures of similar size and prominence the following additional information: the number of rental units in the establishment and the rates charged for each, whether the rates quoted are for single or multiple occupancy if such fact affects the rate charged, and the dates during which such rates are in effect.

Motel 6 wanted to erect two types of signs in that state. One was to read "Motel 6, $20.95 single, all rooms, all year." The other was to say "Motel 6, $20.95 single." The Florida Department of Business Regulation and the Division of Hotels and Restaurants of that state both ruled that these proposed signs violated the above statute. These agencies based their decision upon the fact that the signs were misleading, as higher rates would be charged depending upon the circumstances, and "all rooms" did not cover dates in which the rates would be in effect. On appeal, this holding was upheld.[27] This decision resulted in the removal of price signs at Motel 6 units in Florida.

Turning from the statutes that apply to rates charged, a look back at a former time can provide some insight into rates charged today.

> Inns were intended for the middle class merchants, small landowners, itinerant packmen, etc. A certain number of beds were placed in one room. . . . Each man bought separately what he wished to eat, chiefly bread, a little meat, and some beer. Complaints as to the excessive prices were not much less frequent then than now. . . . The people petitioned Parliament, and the King interfered accordingly with his accustomed useless goodwill. Edward III promulgated, in the twenty-third year of his reign (1350), a statute to constrain "hostelers et herbergers" to sell food at reasonable prices; and again, four years later, tried to put an end to the "great and outrageous cost" of victuals kept up in all the realm by innkeepers and other retailers of victuals, to the great detriment of the people traveling through the realm.[28]

Preferred-Rate Contracts

Preferred-rate contracts are those negotiated at the time reservations are made. These contracts usually result in a lower room price being agreed upon than will be charged to the walk-in traveler who seeks a room for the night. The courts see no problem with this as long as the granting of a preferred rate is available on a uniform basis. Preferred rates frequently are granted to businesses that wish to use the inn for business reasons, and the preferred rate tends to attract business.

Advance Payment

At early common law, the law permitted the innkeeper to collect one day's payment in advance, and one day's payment on the beginning of each succeeding day. In times when cash was the only means of payment, the rule was fair and was founded on common sense. In these days of credit cards, debit cards, lines of credit, electronic funds transfers, access checks, and much more, the rule seldom is used. Yet it remains as a part of the common law of our states.

If a hotel requests that the reservation be paid in advance, the other party has a duty to comply. This is true for the simple reason that there was never any common-law duty to make a reservation. Thus, when one requests a down payment or places some condition upon the reservation, it becomes a matter of contract and contract law will apply. If the guest-to-be fails to meet the condition, no contract results. Table 18.2 compares express conditions placed on reservations with implied conditions that arise by operation of law.

In addition, it is the practice for front-desk personnel to require that the credit card that will be used for payment be tendered at check-in so an imprint may be made of it on a charge slip. Upon checking out, the guest is asked to sign after the charge amount has been added. If the guest should leave without checking out, the hotel would, at law, have implied permission to enter the charges, adding the guest's name to the charge slip.

TABLE 18.2 Conditions on reservations.

Express Conditions	*Implied Conditions*
1. "Payment for one day in advance."	1. Must be in acceptable condition on arrival.
2. "Payment for three days in advance."	
3. "Minimum stay required."	2. Must make satisfactory arrangement for payment.
4. "Must arrive by 6:00 P.M."	
5. "Two nights only on weekends."	3. Will not overstay.
6. Others such as in group bookings.	4. Will act in a reasonable manner while at the inn.
	5. Others.

A problem associated with taking credit-card numbers or impressions as assurance of payment is the possibility that the person using the card will call the credit-card company and demand that the company not honor the charge. Most credit-card companies, and notably American Express, refuse to honor such requests.

Refunding Deposits

When advance deposits are made by cash or check, and the one who made the deposit does not show up as agreed, should the deposit be returned? In answering this question, the rules of contract law become involved. First, one who has a contract breached by the other party must mitigate (keep down) the losses of the one who breached the contract. In the case of a reservation, this means selling the room or rooms to others, if possible. If this is done, there has been no loss, so the deposit should be refunded, less any handling costs.

If the hotel does not fill up, then the hotel has lost the profits that would have been made if the promise had been kept. In that event, the deposit can be retained as part of the damages suffered because of the breach. If the deposit was for more than a routine sum, however, it is best to consult legal counsel about whether to retain the full amount.

In many instances, such as when the inn agrees to hold large numbers of rooms for conventions, sports teams, and the like, advance deposits are requested. If the request is not met, the pending contract fails and the inn is free to sell the rooms to others. When deposits are made and the contract arises, a concern of the innkeeper is that the balance be paid as agreed. Another legal technique is to require a guarantee from another to cover the contingency of the contracting party failing to pay the balance.

Guarantees of Payment

Guarantees of payment can be one of two forms:

1. guarantee of payment
2. guarantee of collectibility

The first guarantee is the best, of course, because the one guaranteeing payment can be looked to as soon as it becomes certain that the primary party is not going to pay. In the second situation, one must exhaust all efforts to collect before the guaranteeing party can be looked to for payment.

CASE INTRODUCTION: RAPPEE CASE

In this first case, a guest registered falsely. The guest then was injured because of a failure of the innkeeper to use due care in the maintenance of an elevator. The inn also failed to warn the injured guest of the hazard of the elevator door. Can the false registration of the guest be used as a defense against the tort action the guest brought for the resulting injuries?

RAPPEE V. BEACON HOTEL CORPORATION
293 N.Y.S. 196, 56 N.E. 2d 548 (New York 1944)

LOUGHRAN, Judge.

Plaintiff and his fiancee registered at the defendant's hotel as husband and wife under an assumed name and then went out for the evening. On their return at an early hour the next morning, there was no response to his repeated ringing of the elevator bell at the ground floor, because the elevators were not operated below the mezzanine at that time of day. Eventually, the plaintiff leaned against the shaft door of an elevator to listen more closely for what seemed to be the sound of an approaching car. His weight caused the door to slide open and he fell into a pit below. A judgment for his damages has been affirmed and is now challenged by the defendant in this court.

[The Judge Instructs (Charges) the Jury]

In his charge the Trial Judge said to the jury: "It was the duty of the defendant to see that the elevator doors were properly closed. The gates or doors leading to the shafts of the elevator were required to be locked or bolted or securely fastened on the shaft side, that is, from the inside. . . . The duty which I have charged you the law imposes upon the defendant in the maintenance and operation of passenger elevators is not diminished by the fact that the plaintiff may have intended to occupy a room with a female not his wife or that he imposed upon the hotel authorities by misrepresenting some person to be his wife, or by making use of an assumed name. I charge you that for the purposes of your consideration of this case the plaintiff was a guest of the hotel and that the obligation of due care as I have charged it to you was applicable to this plaintiff in the same manner as to other guests and to other persons lawfully on the premises."

To these instructions, counsel for the defendant took the following exception: "I respectfully except to that part of your Honor's charge in which you stated that the plaintiff was a guest of the hotel and the same duty which was owing to any guest of the hotel was due and owing to him. . . ."

Whether the plaintiff's trickery was nevertheless enough to disable him from maintaining this action was an additional question. . . . The defendant insists there was error in the negative answer that was given thereto in the passage we have quoted from the charge of the Trial Judge. But so much of that excerpt as asserted the plaintiff's position as a guest was sound,—or so we have said; and a general exception to an instruction that is correct in part cannot be sustained. For that reason, the defendant's exception to the charge is of no avail at this point. The defendant did not in its answer set up the plaintiff's imposture as a defense. More than that, the motion for dismissal of the complaint made by the defendant at the close of the case did not mention that matter at all. Thus, there is no formal warrant in this record for the defendant's demand that the plaintiff forfeit his recovery for his misconduct.

The defendant invokes the statute against keeping houses of ill-fame, Penal Law, §1146, Consol. Laws, c. 40. The provisions thereof have not persuaded us that we should dismiss this complaint on some theory of public policy.

The judgment should be affirmed, with costs.

Judgment affirmed.

CASE INTRODUCTION: RAINBOW CASE

The Rainbow case is a landmark decision, and one that will set standards for overbooking cases in the future. The court found that not only was the overbooking damaging to the goodwill of the plaintiff, but that it was also fraud because of the manner in which it was carried out. Curiously enough, the court did not allow damages for breach of the reservation contract, but that finding must be examined carefully. What the court was saying was that, because damages were allowed for injury to goodwill, double damages cannot be recovered for breach of contract.

The court repeatedly found that the reservation was a contract; that it was breached; that jurisdiction of the court was proper; and thus upheld the damages as a result of the breach of contract. This decision comes as close as any court has in holding that a reservation is a binding contract and that breach of it will allow a jury to award damages. The discussion that follows is by James O. Eiler, Esquire.[29]

OVERBOOKING-BREACH OF CONTRACT AND FRAUD DAMAGES
Rainbow Travel Service, Inc. v. Hilton Hotels Corp., 896 F.2d 1233 (10th Cir. 1990).

A Federal Court of Appeals . . . affirmed a federal trial court jury verdict which awarded a travel agency $37,500.00 for loss to its goodwill for the misrepresentations made by employees of the Fontainbleau Hilton Hotel.

In *Rainbow Travel Service, Inc. v. Hilton Hotels Corp.*, 896 F. 2d 1233 (10th Cir. 1990), the Court of Appeals agreed with the trial court judgment that sufficient evidence existed that the Hilton Hotel misrepresented the hotel's room availability when it confirmed the reservations of the travel agency for a block of rooms for its tour.

A. A Hotel Reservation Is a Legally Enforceable Contract:

Hotel reservation contracts can be in writing (see *Rainbow Travel Service, Inc. v. Hilton Hotels Corp., supra*) or, oral (see *Dold v. Outrigger Hotel and Hawaii Hotels Operating Co.*, 54 Haw. 18; 501 P. 2d 368 (1972), and will be valid and enforceable. If the hotel fails to comply with the terms of the reservation, the hotel can be sued for breach of contract.

B. Damages for Breach of the Reservation Contract:

In California, the measure of damages for breach of a contract "is the amount which will compensate the party aggrieved for all detriment proximately caused thereby, or which, in the ordinary course of things, would likely to result therefrom," (California Civil Code, section 3300). . . .

C. Overbooking and Fraud Damages—The Rainbow Travel Case:

According to the decision, the Rainbow Tour Service had entered into a contract for room reservation with the Fontainbleau Hilton Hotel in Miami Beach, Florida, for several rooms. The tour agent is a tour operator in Oklahoma and contacted the hotel because of advertisements the hotel had sent to Oklahoma. The hotel had sent contracts which called for the hotel to reserve 105 rooms for the tour operator for one weekend, and a second contract which required the hotel to reserve 45 rooms during the same weekend. The tour operator signed the contracts and returned them to the hotel. Several months before the arrival dates, the hotel confirmed the tour operator's reservations by mail and requested prepayment for one night for the rooms. The tour operator sent a payment of over $6,000.00. The hotel sent another confirmation a few months before the arrival and requested the remainder of the first night's payment. The tour operator then sent a final customer list and the remainder of the down payment.

The president of the tour operator went to Miami a few days before the arrival of his group to make sure all the arrangements had been made. The first group arrived and was accommodated as planned. The tour operator's president met with the hotel tour representative four times within a three-day period to make sure all had been properly arranged for his group's arrival. Each time he was told everything was fine and all the rooms would be available. When the second group arrived . . . the next day, they were told . . . that no rooms were available. The hotel made arrangements for the group to stay at another hotel ten blocks away from the Hilton. The tour operator sued the hotel, alleging breach of contract and fraud.

The jury found in favor of the tour operator and awarded $37,500.00 in damages for loss of goodwill. The jury believed there was sufficient evidence to find that the hotel had committed fraud when it confirmed that everything was fine and that all rooms were available. The evidence submitted by the tour operator was that the hotel . . . should have known that a substantial number of people would overstay their announced departure date. It also showed that the hotel gave a block of rooms on that same day to another group that had not reserved any rooms. The hotel did not inform the tour operator of its practice of overbooking and was not told there was a possibility that "guaranteed" reservations might be dishonored.

The hotel argued that the overbooking situation was due to facts beyond its control such as guests extending their stay at the hotel, and rooms being out of order for repairs. However, the tour operator offered into evidence the hotel's own policy manual which indicated that the hotel never told a guest that they were "overbooked" and that if such a situation arose, that they were to inform the guest that something occurred outside the control of the hotel such as:

1. Scheduled departures do not vacate their rooms.
2. Engineering problems with the room (pipe burst, thus water leaks, air conditioning, heating out of commission, broken glass, etc.) . . . .

Evidence was also offered that the hotel was extremely busy during the week of the tour operator's group's visit, and that for several days before the arrival, the hotel was sold out and had to dishonor other reservations.

The hotel argued that it needed to sell 115 percent capacity of the hotel based on a 15-percent no-show factor. The night clerk's summary for the night before the intended arrival date of the group indicated that the hotel would be short of rooms even if the 15-percent no-show factor was taken into account. . . .

Finally, the court was under the opinion that the hotel's explanation concerning its treatment of the tour group's reservations lacked candor in that the hotel had indicated that it had not become aware of the shortage of rooms until after the president of the tour operator went to the airport to pick up the tour, even though when the group arrived they already had assigned specific rooms at the hotel to which they had been relocated.

The court took all of the evidence into consideration and held that there was sufficient evidence for the jury to find that the hotel committed fraud, and, thus, the award for the loss to the goodwill of the tour operator was justified. The appellate court was of the opinion that a reasonable juror could find that the hotel recklessly made statements without knowledge of their truth, and that the hotel did so with the intention that the tour group rely upon those representations and that in fact that the tour group did rely on them to their loss. . . .

D. The Hotel Can Also Sue for Breach of Contract:

Hotels can also sue for breach of contract when the guest does not show up or the tour operator cancels the reservation after the hotel had reserved rooms for the group. In *King of Prussia Enterprises, Inc. v. Greyhound Lines, Inc.*, 457 F. 2d 56 (E.D. Penn., 1978), a hotel sued a travel agent when the travel agent breached a room block contract at the hotel. The hotel was located near Philadelphia during the 1976 Bicentennial time period and also during the 41st International Eucharistic Congress. The tour operator had contracted directly with the hotel for all of the hotel's 200 rooms instead of going through the Housing Bureau for the Eucharistic Congress. A deposit of $10,000.00 was sent to the hotel, indicating that it was a deposit for 200 rooms. When the hotel requested the balances due on the deposits for the rooms several times, the hotel was informed that the checks were forthcoming. Approximately one month before the arrival of the group, the group operator informed the hotel that it was canceling its reservations and asked for a refund of all deposits made. The jury believed there was an enforceable contract between the parties and awarded the hotel $58,900.00 for damages. The tour operator's motion for new trial was denied as the appellate court was of the opinion that there was sufficient evidence for the jury to conclude that there was a contract and that it had been breached. See also, *Hotel Del Cordono Corporation v. Food Service Equipment Distributor Association*, 783 F. 2d 1323 (9th Cir. 1986).

CASE INTRODUCTION: THOMAS CASE

In the Thomas case that follows, we see an older breach-of-reservation case (1955). In this situation, a man attempting to check in at a front desk was turned away when the hotel had *three* duties to receive that person. Mr. Thomas waited more than two years to bring his lawsuit against the hotel, so the statute of limitations became involved. Two of his three causes of action were barred by the statute of limitations. The first of these alleged that the innkeeper breached his common-law duty to receive. If true, this would be a tort and was barred in Kansas courts after two years. Second was the allegation that by turning him away because of his color, the Kansas Civil Rights Act was violated. This cause of action was also barred.

His third cause of action alleged a breach of a reservation contract. Here, the statute of limitations in Kansas was three years, and the court held that he could go to trial on this cause of action. Figure 18.4 summarizes this.

At trial the burden of proof will be on Mr. Thomas to prove the following:

1. That there was a binding reservation contract between himself and the hotel.

2. That the hotel, acting through its lawful agents, broke this contract.

If Mr. Thomas carries the burden on these two points, he then will have to prove what he lost because of the breach.

FIGURE 18.3 Causes of action in Kansas.

	Statutes of Limitations		
	1 Year	2 Years	3 Years
1. Common-law duty to receive		——→	
2. Kansas civil rights law—duty to receive regardless of color	——→		
3. Contractual duty to receive			——→

THOMAS V. PICK HOTELS CORPORATION
244 F. 2d 664 (10th Cir. 1955)

MURRAH, Circuit Judge.

Earl D. Thomas, a Negro, sued the Pick Hotels Corporation and others for damages resulting from a denial of hotel accommodations.

The trial court sustained a motion to dismiss the amended complaint on the grounds that the action against the appellee was barred by the Kansas two-year statute of limitations, Kansas G.S.1949, 60-306(3), as one "for injury to the rights of another, not arising on contract. . . ."

As we understand appellant's contentions on appeal, they are to the effect that his claim is governed by the Kansas three-year statute of limitations, Kansas G.S.1949, 60-306(2), as (1) one upon a contract, express or implied, or (2) one based upon the common-law duty of an innkeeper to provide nondiscriminatory accommodations to all, or (3) as one upon a claim, the liability for which is created by the Kansas Civil Rights Statute, Kansas G.S.1949, 21-2424.

The second section of the Kansas statute of limitations provides that "an action upon contract, not in writing, express or implied; an action upon a liability created by statute, other than a forfeiture or penalty" can only be brought within three years after accrual. Kansas G.S. 1949, 60-306(2).

[How the Case Got Into Federal Court]

The action against this appellee hotel corporation based on *diversity of citizenship* and requisite amount in controversy, was commenced within three years from the accrual of the asserted claim. And if by a liberal interpretation of the pleadings, they can be said to state a claim or claims upon which relief, not barred by the three-year statute of limitations, can be granted, it is our duty to so construe them, although they may be alternatively or inconsistently stated.

There is nothing in the common law to preclude the parties from entering into a valid and enforceable contract for hotel accommodations. Certainly a contract of this kind is not against public policy of the State of Kansas. Indeed the statute and the common law sanction the contract by forbidding the innkeeper from making any distinction on account of race or color.

The complaint pleads a written contract to provide hotel accommodations on a given date subsequently modified by a telephone conversation, and it pleads an arbitrary refusal to provide such accommodations. The prayer is for damages, compensatory and punitive. But if the demand or prayer is for relief in tort, it in no way affects the right to recover on the contract, for the dimensions of a lawsuit are measured by what is pleaded and proven, not what is demanded.

We conclude that the complaint states a claim on an express contract to provide hotel accommodations and a breach of that contract. The claim is therefore governed by the Kansas three-year statute of limitations as one arising under a contract express or implied.

The judgment is accordingly reversed.

CASE INTRODUCTION:
STATE OF CONNECTICUT CASE

In the next case, we have the opportunity to see how criminal law can blend with innkeeping law. Note what the court had to say about the accused being a transient guest and the importance of that decision to this man's freedom. This also points out the importance of statutory terminology to the outcome of a case. The case raises warnings. After this decision, the accused has a good cause of action against the inn for injury to his name. The defendant is anonymous in the case style and probably was a person under the age of majority.

STATE OF CONNECTICUT V. ANONYMOUS
34 Conn. Sup. 603, 379A 2d 1

DAVID M. SHEA, Judge.

The defendant was found guilty of larceny in the third degree by theft of services in violation of General Statutes §53a-124. Although the defendant filed twelve assignments of error, he has abandoned all except that relating to the failure of the court to warn him adequately about the hazards in his decision to act as his own attorney at the trial and that relating to the conclusion of guilt reached by the trial court upon the evidence. Since our resolution of the latter is dispositive of the appeal, we need not consider the former issue.

General Statutes §53a-119(7) provides, in pertinent part: "A person is guilty of theft of services when: (1) With intent to avoid payment . . . for services rendered to him as a transient guest at a hotel, motel, inn, tourist cabin, rooming house or comparable establishment, he avoids such payment by unjustifiable failure or refusal to pay, by stealth, or by any misrepresentation of fact which he knows to be false. . . ." The question which is decisive of this appeal is whether there was sufficient evidence that the defendant was a "transient guest" within the meaning of this statute.

There was testimony that the defendant rented an efficiency apartment at a motel on a weekly basis for four weeks. The efficiency apartments of the motel were not rented on a daily basis, as were the regular motel rooms. They were provided with cooking facilities and did not receive maid service, unlike the other units. There was no provision for renting the efficiency apartments for a period of less than one week. The rent of $58.35 per week was payable in advance on the first day of each weekly period. The defendant paid the rent as it fell due each week. On the day when the next weekly payment was due and was not made, the room of the defendant was checked and some of his belongings were still in the room. Two days later a woman came to the motel, removed the remaining property of the defendant and left the key at the motel office. The next day the complainant telephoned the defendant at an address which was obtained from his room registration card and informed him that he owed the rent for one week. The defendant claimed that he had vacated his motel room and was not responsible for rent for an additional week.

Who Is a "Guest" at Law?

It is fundamental that the state had the burden of proving every element of the offense charged beyond a reasonable doubt. *State v. Brown*, 163 Conn. 52, 64, 301 A. 2d 547. Proof that the defendant was a "transient guest" at the motel was essential for a conviction under the statute. The word "transient" means "[a] person passing through a place or staying there only temporarily." *Ballentine's Law Dictionary*, p. 1293 (3d Ed.). "To be a guest of an inn or hotel it is essential, at least at common law, that the person should be a transient, that is, that he should come to the inn for a more or less temporary stay, for if he comes on a permanent basis he will be deemed a boarder or lodger rather than a guest." 43 C.J.S. Innkeepers §3, p. 1140. Although it has been said that a guest must be a traveler, that is meant in a broad sense to include anyone away from home who enjoys the same accommodations which are offered to travelers. *Walling v. Potter*, 35 Conn. 183, 185. The length of stay, the existence of a special contract for the room, the fact that a person has another abode and the extent to which he has made the room his home for the time being are material circumstances in determining whether the relationship is that of a guest or a lodger. 43 C.J.S., *supra*, p. 1138.

The defendant, who acted as his own counsel, never raised any claim that he was not a "transient guest." It was essential, nevertheless, that the evidence establish beyond a reasonable doubt that he had that status. That standard has not been met in this case. The testimony bearing upon this issue indicates that the defendant may have been a roomer rather than a "transient guest." Apparently he was not a traveler in the literal sense. The rental arrangement and the nature of the accommodations differed from those pertaining to the regular motel rooms. The duration of the occupancy was not so brief as to justify a conclusion that it was merely temporary in character. Whether the defendant intended the room to be a more or less permanent residence or whether he had a home elsewhere are questions unanswered by the testimony. In sum, there is insufficient evidence to support a conclusion that the defendant was a "transient guest."

There is error, the judgment is set aside, and the case is remanded with directions to render a judgment of not guilty.

Summary

A few states, such as Florida, regulate rates that can be charged at hotels, motels, and inns. Other states have laws that regulate the making of reservations and the practices that must be followed at the time of guest registration or check-in.

The precise time of the formation of the special relationship of innkeeper-guest can play a key role in court cases. A waiver signed by a guest while using a hotel recreation facility will not apply if that person is injured at the facility after the guest status has ended. The formation of the relationship is governed by the common law contract principles of "offer" and "acceptance." That is, the traveler must offer to become a guest, and the innkeeper or an agent must agree to that offer. Until that point in time, the relationship is not legally in effect.

Reservations made by travelers are controlled by common law contract principles. In the not too distant past, hotel colleges in the United States taught that reservations could be dishonored if the hotel had a good reason for doing so, such as a full house. That is a dangerous management policy if followed today.

QUESTIONS

1. Do you know why mutual promises provide "consideration"?
2. What legal problems does the hotel face in overbooking?
3. Why did the court refuse to allow the false registration in the Rappee case to be used as a reason to deny recovery?
4. What was the main point the court made in the Rainbow case?
5. What is the difference between "consequential" and "punitive" damages?
6. Why does the law refuse to allow punitive damages in contract cases?
7. How could a breach of contract develop into a tort situation? Use an example.
8. True or false: Group bookings should be handled with the same informality as customary bookings.
9. What is one implication of a federal law on overbooking if such is created?
10. Can you think of a legal problem that may arise when taking an unsigned impression of a guest's credit card at check-in?

NOTES

1. Williston on Contracts, A Horn Book, West Publishing Co., St. Paul, Second edition, 1950.
2. *Bird v. Bird*, 123 Eng. Rep. 47, 337 (C.P. 1558).
3. 88 Mo. Ct. App. 72 (Missouri 1901).
4. *Y-B Anon*, 11 Hen. 4 (England 1409).
5. *McDonald v. Edgerton*, 5 Barb 560 (Sup. Ct. New York 1849).
6. *Overstreet v. Moser*, 88 Mo. Ct. App. 72 (Missouri 1901).
7. *Bennett v. Mellor*, 101 Eng. Rep. 154 (King's Bench 1793).
8. *Holland v. Pack*, 7 Tenn. 151 (Tennessee 1823).
9. *Walling v. Potter*, 35 Conn. 183 (Connecticut 1868).
10. *Williston on Contracts*, Vol. 5 sec. 1070.
11. *Wells v. Holiday Inn*, 522 F. Supp. 1023 (Missouri 1981).
12. 501 P. 2d 368 (S. Ct. Hawaii 1972).
13. See *Wells v. Holiday Inn*, 522 F. Supp. 1023 (Missouri 1981).
14. 297 N.W. 2d 260 (Minnesota 1980).
15. *Hotel del Coronado v. Quip Systems*, 186 N.R.L. lower (New York 1981).
16. 76 Misc. 2d 915, 351 N.Y.S. 2d 541 (New York 1974).
17. *King of Prussia Enterprises, Inc. v. Greyhound Lines, Inc.*, 457 F. Supp. 2d 56 (E.D. Pa. 1978), affirmed 595 F. 2d 1212 (3rd Circuit 1979).

18. *Brown v. Hilton Hotels Corporation*, 211 S.E. 2d 125 (Georgia 1974).

19. Section 204 of New York General Business Law.

20. Section 61(1) of New York Election Law.

21. *Commonwealth v. Blinn*, 503 N.E. 2d 25 (Massachusetts 1987).

22. *Stoner v. California*, 376 U.S. 483, 490, *rehearing denied*, 377 U.S. 940 (U.S. Supreme Court 1964).

23. *Rappee v. Beacon Hotel Corp.*, 293 N.Y.S. 196, 56 N.E. 2d 548 (New York 1944).

24. *Penchas v. Hilton Hotels Corp.*, 590 N.Y.S. 2d 669 (New York 1992). This decision, as to the *infra-hospitium* issue, follows the 1957 case of *Halliman v. Federal Parking Services*, 134 A. 2d 382.

25. *Proctor v. Nicholson*, 173 Eng. Rep. 30, 31 (King's Bench 1835).

26. *Newton v. Trigg*, 89 Eng. Rep. 566 (King's Bench 1691).

27. *Motel 6 v. Dept. of Business Regulation*, 560 So. 2d 1322 (Florida 1990).

28. *English Wayfaring in the Middle Ages*, 4th ed., by J. Jusserand, 1961.

29. Featherstone & Eiler, Attorneys at Law, San Bernardino, and Santa Ana, California, 1-909-381-1869.

19

Property of Guests

Overview

THE PROPERTY OF hotel guests, invitees, third parties, restaurant and tavern patrons, and others has been classified by court cases into three categories:

1. Goods.
2. Money and valuables.
3. Transportation.

In this chapter, we will examine these classifications, find out about their origins, subclassify them, and learn how important the laws of property can become to our HH&T operations.

Classifications

For at least 1000 years the English common law has recognized two primary classes of property. The first is *real property* (real estate), which is the earth and everything attached to it in permanent fashion. The second is *personal property*, all other items that are loose on the face of the earth. These classifications, from two very old common-law forms of action, take their names from the type of court actions required to recover for losses involving them.

1. Actions *in rem:* court cases brought against the real estate itself. Because realty cannot be moved, the action is against the "thing itself."
2. Actions *in personum:* court actions brought against a person who caused the loss of "movables" owned by another. If S stole a cow from T, butchered it, sold off part of the meat, and ate the rest, a court action had to be brought against S "personally." This was an action *in personum.* An action against the "thing" was not possible because the thing no longer existed.

Today, these two classifications are firmly in place in the American legal system, and an additional one has been added: mixed property. Mixed property is that which is not "real" or "personal" but has characteristics of both. An example is drapes in the guest rooms. Although the drapes are not "permanently attached" to the real estate, they hang from curtain rods that are attached. Thus, the rods are real property but the drapes are mixed property.

The issue of mixed property and the application of mechanic's liens came up in a Missouri case. Mechanics liens are provided by law and provide one who does work on real estate, or provides fixtures to it, an enforceable claim against the real estate itself so they can collect the value of the labor or fixtures provided. The Revised Statutes of Missouri, Section 429.010, provides:

> Every mechanic or other person who shall do or perform any work or labor upon, or furnish any material [or], fixtures . . . for any building . . . under or by virtue of any contract with the owner, . . . upon complying with the provisions of sections 429.010 to 429.340, shall have for his work or labor done, or materials [or] fixtures . . . furnished, a lien upon such building . . . and upon the land . . . .

The issue in the case was whether drapes and bedspreads furnished by Sears Roebuck to a motel were subject to a mechanic's lien. The court held that the drapes attached to sliding rods were subject to the lien, but bedspreads or comforters, which were attached to nothing, were not.[1] Mechanic's liens are used to collect debts owing to creditors, and their success is tied directly to the classifications of property. They will not work against the auto of a guest but will work against the real property of a travel agency, a theme park, a car rental property, a hotel, motel, or inn.

At any given moment, the amount of cash, jewelry, clothing, goods, automobiles, and other property belonging to guests represents a substantial value. At any major hotel, such value will reach into the multimillions of dollars regardless of the time of day or night. At smaller locations, the value may not be so great yet always will be substantial. The manager must keep this in mind because of the constant danger of loss, theft, or damage to such property. This is true since marketing efforts brought about this accumulation of wealth and value. The accumulation has been for the benefit of the business, and the law says that when one benefits, one also must carry any burdens that may result.

The law early directed its attention to this matter. The question was: Who has the legal liability for the loss of goods, autos, and valuables? The question is important in practice because, in every loss of property, *someone* has to bear that loss. The courts must make this determination. If a defaulting innkeeper knows he or she will lose in court, it makes good sense to pay the loss and avoid the litigation.

If existing statutes limit liability, or if a disclaimer (or waiver of liability) is involved, the words of the statute or the terms of the disclaimer or waiver will play a role in determining who shall bear that loss.

We can eliminate real and mixed property from our discussion, as guests normally are not involved with such property. What a guest brings into the confines of the hotel, including automobiles, is personal property. This category must now be subdivided.

Classes of Personal Property

The personal property of guests can be subdivided into three categories (See Table 19.1.):

1. *Goods.* This is a catch-all category and means all general property of guests, but does *not* include automobiles or money and valuables.

2. *Money and valuables.* In this category we encounter rings, watches, jewelry of all types, ornaments, money, and other items of more than casual value. The category has been held to include business papers and the work product of professionals. This subclassification now must be divided further into valuables a guest *uses* and valuables *in excess* and not necessarily used during the guest's stay. Valuable jewels often fall into both categories. When the guest wears them, they are "in use." When the use ends, they are "in excess."

Valuables in excess can be divided further into valuables that are "hidden" and valuables that are "not hidden." An example of the former is an heirloom watch carried in the guest's luggage of which the innkeeper takes custody. If the luggage is lost, the innkeeper may be responsible for the luggage but probably not the watch. If the innkeeper knew the watch was there, liability for it might follow.

3. *A guest's means of transportation.* An automobile, while being personal property, has not been treated the same as "goods" and money and valuables. The legal reason for this will be explored later in this chapter.

When determining liability for loss of a guest's property, the *location* of the loss, as well as its *cause*, will have a bearing upon the outcome.

Classification by Location and Cause of Loss

The location where property is lost can have a legal bearing upon the responsibility for the loss. For example, a suitcase left in a hallway and stolen is legally different from a suitcase left on the back seat of the guest's automobile, that is valet-parked.

In addition, the *cause* of the loss becomes important. If a guest leaves a room unlocked and goods are stolen, that is one thing. If an innkeeper fails to have

TABLE 19.1   Classes of personal property and governing laws.

Types of Goods	*Law that Governs*
1. *Goods*	
Baggage	Common law
Clothes	Negligence law (tort law)
Cameras	Bailment law
Jewelry being worn	Contract law
2. *Money and Valuables*	
Money and valuables (not being carried by the guest)	Statutory law (all 50 states have these laws)
3. *Transportation*	
Autos	Common law
Bikes	Bailment law
Trucks	Negligence law
Horses	Statutory law
	Contract law

electrical wiring repaired and this causes a fire that destroys a guest's goods, that is another.

Classifications of Intent

In addition, the courts have classified property by what the guest *did* with that property. These categories can be called "classifications of intent."

1. *Mislaid property.* This is property the guest placed at a certain location, such as a drawer in her room, and then forgot where she put it. In this situation, the guest had no intent to give up the property.

2. *Lost property.* This is property that has left the guest's possession through the guest's carelessness or inadvertence, and the location of it is not known to the guest. The guest had no intention to lose the property, yet it happened.

3. *Abandoned property.* Here, the guest gives up title and ownership intentionally. This happens frequently as guests check out leaving partially filled whiskey or soft-drink bottles in the room or tossing a broken umbrella into a garbage can.

In a "treasure trove" situation, money or valuables (or both) of unknown ownership are found. In such cases the courts usually hold that the true owner had no intention to give up the goods.

In the case of *Jackson v. Steinberg,*[2] while cleaning a guest room a chambermaid found eight $100 bills under the lining of a dresser drawer. She delivered them to the innkeeper. The owner of the money could not be found, and the maid sued the innkeeper for the money. After the maid received a verdict in the lower court, the innkeeper appealed. The upper court had this to say:

> From the manner in which the bills were carefully concealed beneath the paper lining of the drawer, it must be presumed that the concealment was affected intentionally and deliberately. The bills, therefore, cannot be regarded as abandoned property.
>
> With regard to plaintiff's contention that the bills constituted treasure trove, it has been held that the law of treasure trove has been merged with that of lost goods generally, at least so far as respects the rights of the finder. Treasure trove, it is said, may, in our commercial age, include the paper representatives of gold and silver.
>
> The natural assumption is that the person who concealed the bills in the case at bar was a guest. . . . Their considerable value, and the manner of their concealment, indicate that the person who concealed them did so for the purposes of security, and with the intention of reclaiming them. They were, therefore, to be classified not as lost, but as misplaced or forgotten property and the defendant [innkeeper], as occupier of the premises where they were found, had the right and duty to take them into his possession and to hold them as a gratuitous bailee [bailment] for the true owner.
>
> It would seem that, as to articles voluntarily concealed by a guest, the very act of concealment would indicate that such articles have not been placed "in the protection of the house" and so, while the articles remain concealed, the innkeeper ordinarily would not have the responsibility of a bailee therefore. Upon their discovery . . . , however, the innkeeper's responsibility and duty as bailee for the owner becomes fixed. [Thus, the maid lost the case. The innkeeper must find the owner or surrender the money to the state.][3]

The rule developed that an innkeeper was responsible for the loss of goods, transportation and valuables of a guest, once those items were brought within the confines of the inn. The innkeeper, much like a common carrier today, became an insurer of the goods and valuables of each person who became a guest.

As with many rules of law, the English courts recognized three exceptions.

1. If the loss was due to the traveler's carelessness, the innkeeper was excused from liability.
2. If the loss was due to "an act of God," the innkeeper also was excused.
3. If the loss was caused by "the public enemy," the innkeeper again was excused.

An act of God was defined as an accident that "could not have been occasioned by human agency but proceeded from physical causes alone," such as a severe storm. "Public enemy" meant armed persons from an invading force originating outside of England. The term was not broad enough to include an armed robber, and the courts so hold today. Out of this process came the principle of *infra hospitium*.

It became necessary for the courts to decide at what point in time the liability of the innkeeper arose and at what point in time it came to an end. Thus came into being the rule of *infra hospitium* (pronounced "infra hospish-e-em"). This rule marked the beginning as that point in time when the traveler and the traveler's property came within the confines of the inn. At that time, as a matter of law, the property was in the care and custody of the innkeeper, and the duty to safeguard it arose. The burden ended when the guest and the property left the confines of the inn.[4]

Through interpretation over the years, the courts have extended the "confines of the inn" rule to include adjacent fields where a traveler's horses were placed and then lost[5] and parking garages detached from a hotel where goods were stolen from guests' automobiles parked there for the innkeeper's convenience.[6] The confines of the inn at law may, depending upon the facts, include real estate that is not part of the hotel or even close to it. The *use* of the real estate by the innkeeper is what controls the result.

The important point to learn about this old English legal doctrine is that, in relation to the loss of property, an innkeeper's liability can find application in areas outside of the physical boundaries of the inn and, indeed, even after the hotel-guest relationship has ended. In Figure 19.1, Hotel X is surrounded by two streets and two avenues. Therefore, the "confines" include an entire city block. To the east of the hotel is a parking lot operated by an independent contractor. Here, overflow autos are taken from the hotel lot. When a guest's auto is taken there, this parking lot is in the "confines of the inn" by law.

As Traveler Z goes north on Avenue A at point 1, she is not *infra hospitium*, and innkeeping law does not apply to her. As she crosses the threshold at point 2, she is in the confines of the hotel. When her auto is taken to the overflow lot, it still is *infra hospitium*, even though it is on real estate owned by others. When she checks out and resumes her travels at point 4, the doctrine comes to an end. This, however, is subject to an exception.

In a 1992 New York case introduced in Chapter 18, two former guests had settled their bill and loaded their baggage into a taxi that was to take them to the airport. They were hit by a grab-and-run theft and lost a bag containing jewelry. The court held that at the time of the loss, they were still *infra hospitium*.[7]

FIGURE 19.1 Hypothetical situation illustrating *infra hospitium*.

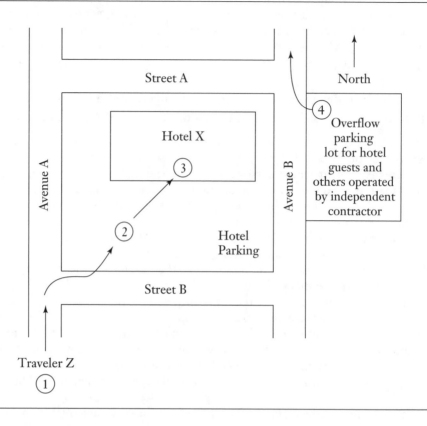

This doctrine can become important in two instances:

1. When deciding whether the statutes limiting liability for lost property apply.
2. In deciding if the business should be held responsible for property loss under the legal principle of bailment.

BAILMENT

We now turn our attention to the subject of bailment. First, a review of the five primary bases of legal liability for the loss of property of guests, patrons, invitees, and others will be helpful. These areas of liability apply at all hotel, hospitality, and tourism operations.

1. *Common-law strict liability.* This basis finds application in those instances where a business makes use of a substance or an item that is inherently dangerous, such as flammable liquid or items with explosive propensities. If such items cause a loss, the business is going to be responsible no matter how much care was exercised in their use. Also, a hotel may be strictly liable for guest goods if the statutes that limit liability are not followed strictly.

2. *Liability based upon negligence of the business.* This is tort liability, which we encountered in Chapter 2.

3. *Liability based upon the principle of negligence* per se. Here, the loss of property occurs because the manager, acting through agents, failed to comply with the requirements of statutes, regulations, ordinances, or other written law.

4. *Liability based upon breach of contract.* As an example, a patron at a hotel restaurant delivers a mink coat to a checkroom. When the patron tries to redeem it, it cannot be found. Although some states, such as New York, limit liability for loss of patrons' goods in checkrooms, this is still a breach of contract.

5. *Liability based upon the law of bailment.* The one creating the bailment is the *bailor.* The other party, who takes custody of the property, is the *bailee.* The bailor most often is a guest, a patron, an invitee, or a third party. The bailee is the hotel, motel, inn, restaurant, car rental agency, theme park, and others.

Even though a bailment is based upon principles of common law, it has distinctive characteristics that must be understood in the HH&T industries, especially because these are all "bailment-intensive" businesses (bailments arise constantly). Bailments even arise in situations in which they are not recognized at the time they occur.

Classifications of Bailments

Bailments are of five classifications. Following each is the degree of care the law requires of the bailee while in possession of the property.

1. *Voluntary bailments.* These arise out of a desire to create them, and each party agrees to the creation. Degree of care: ordinary and reasonable care.

2. *Involuntary bailments.* Inadvertence, such as when a patron leaves something behind upon leaving the premises. Once management, through agents, takes custody of the item, there is an involuntary bailment as to that property. Degree of care: ordinary and reasonable care.

3. *Gratuitous bailment.* Here, no payment for the bailee's service is expected. This type of bailment is not found in the HH&T industries for a simple economic reason: The courts say the price for a bailment in a hospitality situation is part of the price paid for goods and other services. An example is a hotel that accepts the auto of a guest. This acceptance has marketing value to the hotel and is considered a bailment for hire, even though no charge is made for the service. Degree of care: slight care.

4. *Bailment for hire.* This is a bailment in which a charge is required for the service. This is common at valet parking lots. (This classification also includes bailments in the HH&T industries in which the courts infer the price to be factored into the price of goods and services, as mentioned in item 3).

   A bailment is for the mutual benefit of the parties, although nothing is paid directly by the bailor, where property . . . is delivered to and accepted by the bailee as an incident to a business in which the bailee makes a profit. . . .[8]

   This economic principle may be thought of as "value included"; that is, if a guest pays nothing to valet-park her car, the cost of the parking is included in the sum paid for the room for the night. Degree of care: ordinary and reasonable care.

5. *Professional bailments.* These are bailments carried out as a separate business matter, such as a parking concession contracted out to a professional bailee. One might argue that innkeepers who do their own valet parking are in fact professional bailees. A judge may so hold if faced with that issue. In a state where such a case may be decided in that manner, innkeepers would face the higher standard of care. Degree of care: extraordinary care.

Actual and Constructive Bailments

The above classifications can be subdivided in two additional types: actual bailments and constructive bailments.

Actual Bailments

In this subclassification three legal requirements must be met.

1. There must be a delivery of property from the bailor to the bailee. The delivery can be actual, such as leaving valuables at the front desk, or it can be "constructive," leaving a package on a chair at a restaurant, which is found by a bus girl and delivered to the cashier.

2. The bailee must use the degree of care that matches the classification above. Failure to meet that degree of care would render the bailee/innkeeper liable for the value of the property should it become lost.

3. There must be a return of the bailed property to the bailor. An example of an improper return is giving the property to someone who is not the owner of it.

If these three requirements are met, the legal responsibilities of the bailee have been met.

Constructive Bailments

Understanding constructive bailment requires an analysis of what they consist of. First, we must recognize that we are not talking about "constructive deliveries." That is something entirely different. Next, we find that here *there is no delivery at all.* The bailee never has possession of the property.

An illustration will explain this type of bailment: X offers to sell his Swiss Army watch to Y for $10 dollars. The $10 dollars is paid, but X will not deliver the watch. Under these circumstances, the law implies a bailment between X and Y even though there has been no delivery. X is the bailee of the watch owned by Y and must meet the degree of care for it provided by law. This is a constructive bailment.

This would be an unusual situation in restaurants, bars, and stores, but it does arise between HH&T operations and those who supply goods to them. It often comes into being as a result of dispute over goods ordered and paid for but not delivered.

Miscellaneous Bailment Issues

Possession by the bailee is the essence of a bailment. Without possession, there can be no actual or constructive bailment .[9] The courts have held that in a private club, as opposed to a public hotel, the club has exclusive possession of all property brought within it.

The terms *constructive delivery* and *constructive bailment* have their origins in the old legal principle of *construction juris*. This maxim means that at times when acts are not actual, they should be held to have the same validity as acts that are actual. When Y parks his car and goes into a restaurant, he does not have actual possession of his car while in the restaurant but does have constructive possession of it. The law treats this possession with the same dignity that it does actual possession, such as when Y is behind the wheel of his vehicle.

The law does not require an intent to deliver the property. When Mrs. Z left her purse on a chair at a restaurant as she departed, and the bus boy took the purse to the cashier, Mrs. Z did not intend to make a constructive delivery. Yet the intent is not required to bring the bailment into being. (Bailments in which there is a constructive delivery are actual bailments; they are *not* constructive bailments.)

Situations

The following situations and the questions and answers that relate to them will aid one's understanding of these bailment concepts.

Situation One

A sells her ring to B, who pays cash for it, but A refuses to deliver the ring to B.

1. Is there a bailment? (yes)
2. What type is it? (constructive bailment)
3. Has there been an actual or constructive delivery? (There has been no delivery at all.)

Situation Two

S leaves a gift-wrapped package in a booth at a bar where he has been spending an hour with a friend. He departs the bar, leaving the package in the booth, where an employee notices it and gives it to the bartender.

1. Is there a bailment? (yes)
2. Was there a delivery? (yes)
3. What type of delivery was it? (constructive delivery)
4. Was there a constructive bailment? (no)
5. Was the bailment voluntary or involuntary? (involuntary)

Situation Three

Y arrives at a restaurant with X and, as a courtesy, waiter S hangs their coats in a public coat rack. Both coats then are stolen.

1. Is there a bailment? (no)
2. Why was there no bailment? (The establishment took no exclusive possession.)

Assume that Mr. Smith, who is a guest at a hotel, loses $20,000 in valuables by theft at the hotel restaurant. Assume further that it is found in court that there had been an actual bailment, and that the hotel restaurant did not meet the legal duties required of it, and is responsible for the loss. Can the restaurant then claim the protection of the money and valuables statutes that limit liability to $300 dollars for loss of money and valuables of guests in that state? The courts say "no" because these statutes apply to guests in hotels, not patrons in the hotel restaurant, even when such patrons are guests in the hotel.

Checklist for Avoiding Bailment Legal Liability

1. Exercise ordinary and reasonable care, or extraordinary care, in a professional bailment situation.
2. Avoid appearances that may mislead patrons and guests. Does it appear that someone is guarding property when that is not the case?
3. Avoid actual bailments, if possible. (Many restaurants and taverns refuse to create voluntary bailments.)
4. Use conspicuous disclaimers that make it clear that no bailment is contemplated at the checkroom, parking lot, or elsewhere at HH&T operations.
5. Provide safe areas for property of patrons and guests, but avoid taking exclusive possession.
6. Screen patrons, guests, invitees, and others as they enter and leave. Make it known that this is being done.
7. Train employees to keep a sharp lookout for the activities of persons at the place in question.
8. Use signs that give clear instructions as to the disposition of property while on the premises.

One requirement of law in a bailment situation is that the bailee must redeliver the property to the bailor at the time agreed upon. If, at the time, the bailee delivers the property to a third party who absconds with it, there has been a misdelivery. This would be a violation of the duty of care owed and would render the bailee liable for the full value of the property at the time of its loss. The value of such property is a matter of proof in court.

Burden of Proof

The burden of proof initially is on the bailor, who must prove that the bailment, in fact, came into being. The burden of proof then shifts to the bailee, who must prove the degree of care required by law and overcome the presumption of negligence. The bailor must overcome any claim that he or she was guilty of contributory negligence.

In about half of the states, contributory negligence will bar recovery to one who has suffered the loss. Nevertheless, where there is contributory negligence that ended and then there is subsequent negligence on the part of the bailee causing the loss, the contributory negligence does not bar recovery. Thus, when X leaves her purse at the restaurant as she leaves, she is negligent. She also is a "constructive bailor" at law. When the restaurant takes possession of her purse, it becomes liable if the purse is lost or misdelivered, because X's contributory negligence has ended.

Lost-and-Found Records

When a guest departs, leaving money, valuables, or other property in the guest room, the innkeeper becomes a bailee of this property. Once one becomes a bailee, the property must be safeguarded and returned to the bailor. Failing to do so will render the hotel-bailee liable for the full value of the property. Property of departed guests first must be deposited at the front desk so a record can be made. If the property consists of valuables, these should go to the safety deposit boxes. Other items can go to housekeeping for storage.

At the front desk, a record should be maintained describing the property, the number of the room in which it was found, times and dates, and names and addresses of the room occupants. Once such property is turned in and recorded, it must be safeguarded because that is one of the legal obligations of a bailee.

In a bailment lawsuit, proof of (1) contract of bailment, (2) delivery of the item to the innkeeper, (3) demand for return of the item, and (4) failure of the innkeeper to redeliver the item, makes a *prima facie* case for the plaintiff.[11] The burden then shifts to the innkeeper, who must show that he or she exercised reasonable care for the property that was lost.[12] If the innkeeper does not carry this burden, the innkeeper can be held responsible for the full value of the lost property.

LIMITING LIABILITY

When the early courts made the innkeepers insurers, the innkeepers naturally began to look for ways to cut down on the dangers of this common-law rule. The innkeeper often greeted incoming guests and saw to the safety of their horses, coaches, and baggage. In addition, the innkeeper often dined with the guests, which gave him or her an opportunity to learn of their wishes and complaints. This gave the innkeeper the control that parents exercise over a family. This personal attention went far toward meeting the requirements of the common law. The law said the hosts had to care for the guests and their property, and they did just that. It was the golden age of innkeeping—but it was not to last.

As inns began to grow in number and size, the personal control enjoyed by early innkeepers began to fade. With more rooms and with guests arriving in increasing numbers both day and night, the innkeepers began to lose control. They no longer could keep their entire operation in view. They were forced to use employees and agents to do what they previously had been able to do themselves. When this happened, the incidence of loss of property of guests began to rise. It was natural to look for ways to reduce the common-law liability because of the heavy burden it placed upon them. This search led to house rules (the topic of Chapter 17), as well as disclaimers which we will discuss further in this chapter.

House Rules

Innkeepers began to use "rules of the house" that affected travelers and employees alike. This was an attempt to reassert some control over what the courts had declared to be a "public house." If the rules were not obeyed, it was reasonable to expect the courts to pass some of the blame or loss along to those who did not obey them. Before the courts would allow recovery to be barred for this reason, however, two tests had to be met. First, the rule had to be reasonable and, second, the one to be bound by it had to know of it. If an innkeeper tried to use house rules to avoid the duty to receive, or the duty not to negligently cause loss of property or injury to a guest, the courts would refuse to honor them, and this is true today.

Innkeepers did not stop in their quest for limits on liability with house rules, however. They began to use the contract in an attempt to limit their liability. Today, such contracts or agreements are known as disclaimers or "exculpatory clauses." The latter means "clearing or tending to clear from alleged fault or guilt."[13]

Disclaimers to Limit Liability

Although the courts have accepted reasonable house rules as a way to limit liability, they have frowned upon contract disclaimers in many instances. Thus, some courts have held that "contracts that limit liability are void as being contrary to public policy."[14] In other jurisdictions the courts become disturbed with them when guests have no choice but to agree to them.

On the other hand, if disclaimers are used in a reasonable manner and if notice of them is given, the courts will allow them to be used as a defense. When a guest is given a disclaimer, it has the practical effect of alerting that person to the limit on liability. This, in turn, encourages the guests to exercise more care and caution with their property. Disclaimers, then, serve two purposes: They may give the innkeeper a defense, and they may prevent loss in the first place.

Sample Disclaimers

The parking ticket in Figure 19.2 is from the parking lot of a hotel in New York City. It contains forty-five words, four periods, two commas, and one dash. Translating the legal words into common English, here is what it has to say:

FIGURE 19.2   Parking lot disclaimer.

NOTICE

THIS CONTRACT LIMITS OUR LIABILITY—READ IT

WE RENT SPACE ONLY.
No bailment is created and we are not responsible
for loss of, or damage to, car or contents. This ticket is not transferable.

Ticket covers only day purchased.

NO IN AND OUT PRIVILEGES

You are hereby notified that this piece of paper is legally binding upon you under provisions of American contract law, and if you fail to read it, you will be bound by what it says. We are landlords, not bailees, and we are leasing to you an eight by twenty foot space in our parking lot. We do not care what you place on that space, but whatever you do place there is at your risk, and we accept no responsibility if what you place there is damaged or lost. This ticket cannot be used by any other person and is good on this day only. This is a short-term lease. You have no right to leave this space and return. If you do leave, this lease is at an end.

The disclaimer in Figure 19.3 is self-explanatory. This mission is a major tourist attraction in California.

FIGURE 19.3   Disclaimer at tourist attraction.

Mission San Juan Capistrano
FOUNDED NOV. 1st, 1775

CALIFORNIA

THE PERSON USING THIS TICKET ASSUMES ALL RISK OF
PERSONAL INJURY AND LOSS OF PROPERTY. MANAGEMENT RESERVES
THE RIGHT TO REVOKE THE LICENSE GRANTED BY THIS TICKET.

VAYA CON DIOS

The disclaimer in Figure 19.4 was taken from one of the leading theme parks in the United States. The ticket is given when paying for admission to the parking lot. The same terms also are painted on signs located at the driver's eye level at each of the entrance ticket booths. These signs have in large letters across the top, "PLEASE READ THIS CONTRACT." The combination of notices makes it hard for a patron who suffered a loss of property there to say that he or she did not know of the disclaimer. In the state where this double disclaimer is used, California, a state statute requires the double use.

FIGURE 19.4   Theme park disclaimer.

THIS CONTRACT LIMITS OUR LIABILITY—READ IT

This ticket LICENSES the holder to park ONE VEHICLE as directed. The management hereby declares itself NOT RESPONSIBLE for and assumes no liability arising from fire, theft, damage to or loss of the vehicle or any article left therein. ONLY A LICENSE OF SPACE IS GRANTED HEREBY AND NO BAILMENT IS CREATED. Acceptance of this ticket constitutes acknowledgment by holder that he or she has read and agrees to the provisions of the foregoing contract.

Disclaimer Cases

In an Oklahoma case, a guest checked baggage at a hotel and was given a receipt. On the reverse of the receipt were the following words:

> In consideration of the receipt and free storage . . . for which this check is issued, it is agreed . . . that the hotel shall not be liable for loss or damage to said property unless caused by the negligence of the hotel in which event only the hotel shall be liable for a sum not to exceed $25.00. The hotel shall not in any event be liable for loss or damage to said property by fire, theft or moth, whether caused by its own negligence or otherwise.[15]

Following a loss of a guest's goods, the guest sued and won in the lower trial court. The hotel then appealed to the appellate court. The upper court held that "such alleged contractual limitations are contrary to public policy and void."[16] In a more recent case, the bailee of a fur coat was allowed recovery in spite of a $100 limitation on liability found on the storage papers.[17]

In a hotel parking lot case,[18] a guest had baggage and other property stolen from his automobile, which had been parked by a hotel attendant upon a detached parking lot. The lot was not a part of the hotel property and the hotel simply leased parking space there for overflow business. The case was decided in favor of the guest on the grounds of *infra hospitium*, negligence of the innkeeper, and bailment for hire. This happened even though the guest had been given a disclaimer at the time the auto was surrendered to be parked. Here is what the court had to say when it refused to give legal effect to the disclaimer:

> We therefore . . . remand the case for a determination of the reasonable value of the lost property and the costs of repairs to the automobile, and for entry of judgment for the appellant [plaintiff] in such sum against the hotel. In so doing, we are mindful that the court has many times ruled that the printed notice of limitation of liability on the claim check is not binding *unless the terms are known to the bailor (guest)*.[19] The complete absence of testimony as to the knowledge of the limitation and agreement to it makes any contention of limited liability untenable. Reversed with instructions. [Emphasis added].

This case tells us two things: First, we must have our employees call attention to our disclaimers. Second, if we ever go to trial on such matters, we must put testimony into the record to show that our employees had been trained to alert persons to applicable disclaimers.

RESPONSIBILITY FOR LOSS OF ONE'S OWN PROPERTY

At times a guest has sole responsibility for the loss of his or her property. Four examples will illustrate.

   1. *Instructions given by the guest.* The guest gives instructions in reference to the property that the innkeeper follows. The property is then stolen. In all prob-

ability a court would place the responsibility on the guest—unless the innkeeper knew of some danger of theft and failed to warn the guest of it.

2. *Loss caused by roommate.* A guest's roommate steals from the guest. The guest would have to carry the loss. In those rare instances when guests are doubled up by the innkeeper, the result could be different.

3. *Guest uses outsider.* A guest authorizes someone from outside the inn to handle his or her goods, and that person damages, steals, or loses them. The innkeeper would have no liability because the outside party would be the agent of the guest. Of course, the guest would have legal recourse against such agent.

4. *Contributory negligence.* A guest can incur personal liability through contributory negligence. Negligence has been defined as "the failure to use such reasonable care and caution as would be expected of a reasonable person."[20]

Contributory Negligence Revisited

Contributory negligence is "the act or omission amounting to want of ordinary care on part of complaining party, which, concurring with [the innkeeper's] negligence, is the proximate cause of [the loss]."[21] When goods of a guest are lost, contributory negligence will bar recovery.

Comparative Negligence

Contributory negligence is different from comparative negligence. In the states where the comparative negligence rule is in effect, the guest shares the responsibility for loss when both the innkeeper and the guest have been negligent.

More than twenty states have adopted the rule of comparative negligence to replace contributory negligence. Some states have passed statutes to adopt this rule, and others have done so by rulings of the courts. Therefore, one may find comparative negligence in one state by legislative act and in another by doctrine or the common law of that state.[22]

Let's look at how the laws of property are applied in the courts in relation to transportation of guests.

LIABILITY AND TRANSPORTATION

The innkeeper long has been held to be responsible for the loss of a guest's means of transportation once the item was *infra hospitium.* In a 1965 auto loss case, a statute limited liability for "loss of money, jewelry, wearing apparel, baggage or 'other property' brought onto the hotel premises." The court held that "other property" did not include transportation of the guest.[23] The older cases were concerned with saddle horses, carriages, drays and their teams,[24] so this decision was correct and stands until this day.

The early cases extended the "confines of the inn" to include not only in-house storage areas, but also adjacent areas that guests used. In an early case, a field near an inn was held to be within the confines when the innkeeper placed the saddle horse of a traveler there to pasture and the horse subsequently vanished.[25]

The plaintiff, upon driving to the hotel, was asked by the doorman if he wished his car parked. Among other things, the doorman was authorized to have a guest's vehicle driven to a nearby garage for parking if the guest so desired. Plaintiff did wish to have his car parked and gave the doorman the auto keys. The doorman, instead of making the necessary arrangements for parking, took the car on a frolic, in the course of which he looted the glove compartment and damaged the car. Plaintiff sued the hotel for damage and the value of the articles taken from the glove compartment. After trial, judgment was entered for the defendant. Plaintiff appealed. On appeal, the Supreme Court of Colorado held defendant liable and reversed the judgment.[26]

Contents of Autos

An offshoot of the problems caused by loss or damage to a guest's means of transportation is found in the theft of goods from within those vehicles. An innkeeper's responsibility for the goods of a guest is quite different than that for goods left in a vehicle. If an innkeeper does not know that diamonds are in the vehicle, there probably would be no innkeeper's or bailee's liability as to the diamonds. The car may be within the confines of the inn, but a court may hold that the diamonds are not. If an attendant accepts the vehicle, parks it, and retains the keys, liability for auto loss may attach. If the guest self-parks the vehicle, it probably would not. If the damage or loss is caused by an agent or employee, such as theft of the diamonds, liability would attach.

To complicate matters, the courts make a distinction between "ordinary" bailees and those who are "professional" bailees. The standard of care is much higher for the latter.

> The courts, while recognizing that an ordinary bailee may contract to exempt himself from liability for loss of or damage to the goods, occasioned by his own negligence or that of his employee, exhibit a strong tendency to hold contracts of this character, when entered into by bailees in the course of general dealing with the public, to be violative of public policy, and this tendency becomes more pronounced in the more recent decisions.
>
> These bailees, who are termed "professional," as distinguished from "ordinary," bailees, are those who make it their principal business to act as bailees and who deal with the public on a uniform and not an individual basis, such as owners or proprietors of parcel checkrooms, garages, parking stations, and parking lots, carriers, innkeepers, and warehousemen. The basis for denying the right of such bailees to limit their liability for their own negligence is that the public, in dealing with them, lacks practical equality of bargaining power, since it must either accede to the conditions sought to be imposed or else forego the desired service. It is said that a bailee who is performing services for which the public has a substantial need should not be permitted to use this circumstance to coerce the members of the public into contracts of this kind. . . .[27]

Innkeepers who regularly take custody of the autos of guests fall into the professional category. Because of this bailment liability, many hotels and, in particular, motels, forego all contact with guests' autos, making it clear that they are accepting no liability for the safety of the autos or their contents.

There is a natural interest in limiting liability for autos and contents, and it can be done in certain ways. Some possibilities include the use of disclaimers, getting autos under the protection of the property statutes, and having the states pass special statutes to cover autos and contents. In the absence of statutes that limit liability an innkeeper *cannot* limit liabilities that arise out of his or her various duties. Because of the public nature of this calling, it would be against public policy to allow the innkeeper to do so. As to the automobile of a guest, however, the innkeeper is generally a bailee. In the absence of a statute to the contrary, a bailee can limit liability if it is done properly.

Disclaimers often take the form seen in Figures 19.2 and 19.3. The bailment is specifically disclaimed. In addition, the ticket says that space only is rented. Such provisions have been upheld on the ground that, because the words are on the ticket, there is just a lease of land.[28]

Are Autos and Contents "Money and Valuables"?

Do the statutes that limit liability for money and valuables apply to autos and their contents? Under Missouri Revised Statutes,[29] the statute limits liability for "any money, jewelry, wearing apparel, baggage, or other property of a guest." In *Phoenix v. Royale*,[30] the innkeeper's lawyer argued that "other property of a guest" included the auto and contents, and thus the innkeeper's liability was limited to $200 under the Missouri statute.

The court applied the rule of *ejusdem generis*, a rule of court interpretation. Under this rule, where general words follow an enumeration of specific items, the general words are to be held to apply to the class of items specifically listed.[31] The statute lists:

1. money
2. jewelry
3. wearing apparel
4. baggage
5. other property of a guest

The courts read number 5 as meaning watches, coats, shoes, ornaments, cash, coins, rings, briefcases, and other such items. Autos would *not* be included, and the protection of the statute is lost. Figure 19.5 depicts the rule of *ejusdem generis*.

A statute relieved an innkeeper of liability for loss of personal baggage other than valuables. When a guest failed to deposit such baggage in a checkroom for storage provided by the innkeeper, a guest whose automobile was stolen from the hotel garage was precluded, in *Savoy Hotel Corp. v. Sparks*,[32] from any recovery for certain articles of personal baggage left in the automobile. The garage was not an authorized agent for storing any personal property other than cars.

By far the best protection for liability of autos and the contents thereof comes from statutes that specifically cover such items. Unfortunately, at the present time, few jurisdictions have enacted such laws.

FIGURE 19.5 Rule of *ejusdem generis*.

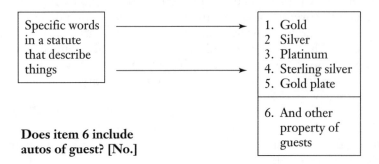

Statutory Limits

On August 2, 1956, "by the Queen's most Excellent Majesty, by and with the advice and consent of the Lords, Spiritual and Temporal, and Commons," the Nova Scotia Parliament enacted the following statute:

> Without prejudice to any other liability or right of his with respect thereto the proprietor of a hotel shall not as an innkeeper be liable to make good to any guest of his any loss of or damage to, or have any lien on, any vehicle or any property left therein, or any horse or other live animal or its harness or other equipment.[33]

The statute of Puerto Rico provides as follows:

> No innkeeper shall be liable to any guest, or other person, for any loss sustained by reason of theft of, or damage done to, any motor vehicle or other conveyance while parked in any free parking lot maintained by such innkeeper, or for any loss sustained by reason of the theft of, or damage done, to any personal property left in such vehicle or other conveyance while so parked; provided, however, that nothing contained in this section shall be construed as to relieve any person of liability for his own willful act.[34]

The Puerto Rico statute goes on to state that, if free parking is provided, regular hotel services will not make the relationship one for hire or mutual benefit. Thus, the statute strikes down the common-law position on this point.[35]

In Iowa, the following statute is found:[36]

> No keeper or owner of any hotel, inn or eating house shall be liable by reason of his innkeeper's liability or his responsibility as innkeeper to any guest for the loss of or damage to the automobile or other conveyance of such guest left in any garage not personally owned and operated by such hotel, inn or eating house or the owner or keeper thereof.

The Iowa statute makes it clear that innkeepers, restaurant operators and others who operate parking areas are bailees for hire, but liability is limited to the sum of $50 for the auto and contents. Under this statute, the guest can gain addition-al protection by placing a value on specific items.[37]

CASE INTRODUCTION: CARLOCK CASE

Another possibility for limiting liability for autos is by using closed lots with "ticket spitters" and check-out lanes to collect fees. Ticket spitters became the subject of a blistering legal opinion in *Carlock v. Multiple Parking Services, Inc.* Selected portions of what the court had to say about the theft of an auto there provide guidelines for considering the use of such automated devices at HH&T facilities.

CARLOCK V. MULTIPLE PARKING SERVICES, INC.
103 Misc. 2d 943, 427 N.Y.S. 2d 670 (Buffalo City Ct. 1980)

In our society today, the use of the automobile as the main mode of transportation is irrefutably established (with the possible exception of the City of New York). A person does not really choose where to park; he parks as close to his destination as possible. The fee he pays depends more on the distance he must then walk to the main business district or other specific area of attraction, rather than the perceived amount of security offered by supposedly competing operators. . . .

All of this exploration and analysis leads this Court to one conclusion: the "bailment theory" as a basis for recovery in parking lot cases is no longer appropriate. We assume this was the state of mind and conclusion reached by the Court of Appeals in 1976, in regard to the archaic distinctions between the status of persons on real property, and the conse-quent duty of care owed them.[38]

The new standard to be followed . . . was to be ". . . reasonable care under the cir-cumstances whereby foreseeability shall be a measure of liability."[39]

Therefore, this Court need not decide whether a bailment was created in the instant case. The measure we will apply is that of "reasonable care under the circumstances where-by foreseeability shall be a measure of liability. . . ."

The plaintiff's burden is met by his showing that the defendant failed to exercise ". . . reasonable care under the circumstances, whereby foreseeability shall be a measure of liability."

Free Parking Lots and Spaces

Will the use of free parking lots or parking spaces solve the problem? It has been held that free parking is an invitation to park there. When a guest accepts that invitation, this brings the auto *infra hospitium* with the attending liability.[40] Other courts have held just the opposite, letting the case be decided on negligence or bailment grounds.[41]

Others enter into contracts with independent contractors to operate parking lots in an attempt to escape liability for autos and contents. This arrangement has been held, however, not to change the basic obligations, and the courts generally hold the private garage to be the agent of the innkeeper.

If there is in fact no inn-guest relationship, the *infra hospitium* rule would not be applied at all. A plaintiff who was attending a banquet at a hotel was held not to be a guest.[42]

The apparent authority of agents who take custody of autos usually is said to be enough to bind the inn as to the safety of both the auto and its contents.[43] The guest-to-be does not "have to search behind the uniform of the valet" for actual authority to accept the auto on behalf of the innkeeper.

SUMMARY

The American legal system (civil law) contains three major divisions: (1) contract, (2) tort and, (3) property. Property can be real (the earth and things fixed permanently to the earth), personal (all items that can be moved about freely), or mixed (property that has characteristics of both real and personal property).

For purposes of the HH&T industries, the primary classifications of property are: (1) goods, (2) money and valuables, and (3) a guest's means of transportation. All are personal property, and real or mixed property classifications are not involved.

In the early days of common law, the legal duties of an innkeeper arose when a traveler and his or her property came *infra hospitium* (within the confines of the inn), and the innkeeper agreed to accept that person as a guest. This doctrine is still important in modern property–loss cases. Today money and valuables statutes, as we will see in Chapter 20, can sharply reduce liability for certain property loss. In addition, the use of disclaimers, waivers, and releases create hotel-made legal standards and can also reduce liability.

The principles of "bailment," grew out of the common law of contract. Bailment law plays a constant role in the resolution of cases in which property is on deposit at a hotel checkroom and is then lost or stolen. The owner of such property is known as the "bailor"—the one depositing the property—and the HH&T facility receiving the property is the "bailee."

QUESTIONS

1. What do you think prompted the courts to hold early innkeepers responsible for the loss of transportation of guests?
2. Might the "confines of an inn" include a distant parking lot? If so, under what circumstances?
3. How would you define "reasonable care"? How would this standard be applied in a court?
4. What effect does the negligence of a guest have upon the innkeeper's liability for loss of the guest's auto?
5. Why might an innkeeper try to claim the status of bailee if an auto is stolen when, in fact, there may be no bailment?
6. How does a court use the "confines" rule to real estate that is, in fact, not a part of the inn? When courts make such rulings, might they be in the process of developing a new phase in law?

7. What are examples of "real property," "mixed property," and "personal property"? Why is it important legally to be able to distinguish them?

8. If a guest accidentally loses a watch that she is wearing and there was no fault on the innkeeper, should the innkeeper be held responsible? Why or why not?

9. What is the legal difference between mislaid and abandoned property? What effect might this difference have in a case in which a guest is suing for the value of lost property?

10. Regarding the case of *Jackson v. Steinberg*, several years have gone by and no one has claimed the eight $100 bills. What happens to the money now? Should the innkeeper have kept the money in an interest-drawing account? Why or why not?

NOTES

1. *Sears Roebuck and Company v. Seven Palm Motor Inn, Inc.*, 530 S.W. 2d (Missouri 1975).

2. Donald Dale Jackson, *Gold Dust* (New York, Alfred A. Knopf, 1980), p. 146.

3. 186 Or. 129, 200 P. 2d 376 (Oregon 1948).

4. *Davidson v. Madison Corporation*, App. Div. 421, 247 N.Y.S. 789, 795 (New York 1931).

5. *Cayle's Case*, 8 Co. Rep. 32a, 77 Eng. Rep. 529 (K.B. 1584).

6. *Park-O-Tell v. Roskamp*, 203 Okl. 493, 233 P. 2d 375.

7. *Penchas v. Hilton Hotels Corp.*, 590 N.Y.S. 2d 669 (New York 1992).

8. *Wilson v. Hooser*, 573 S.W. 2d 601 (Tex. Cir. App. Texas 1978).

9. *Wentworth v. Riggs*, 159 App. Div. 899, 143 N.Y.S. 455 (First Department New York 1913).

10. *Apfel v. Whytes, Inc.*, 110 Misc. 670, 180 N.Y.S. 712 (Sup. Ct. New York 1920).

11. *Right Way Laundry v. Davis*, 98 Okl. 264, 255 P. 345.

12. *Smith v. Maher*, 84 Okl. 49, 202 P. 321, 23 A.L.R. 270.

13. *Baird v. State*, 246 S.W. 2d 192, 195.

14. *Scott Auto & Supply v. McQueen*, 111 Okl. 107, 226 P. 372.

15. *Oklahoma City Hotel Co. v. Levine*, 189 Okl. 331, 116 P. 2d 997, 999 (1941).

16. *Oklahoma City Hotel Co. v. Levine*, *supra*. n. 15.

17. *Carter v. Reichlin Furriers*, 21 U.C.C. Rep. (Conn. Supp., June, 1977), applying U.C.C. 7-204(2).

18. *Hallman v. Federal Parking Services*, 134 A. 2d 382 (1957).

19. *Manning v. Lamb*, D.C. Mun. App., 89 A. 2d 882, *Palace Laundry Dry Cleaning Co. v. Cole*, D.C. Mun. App., 41 A. 2d 231.

20. *Hamrick v. McCutcheon*, 101 W. Va. 485,133 S.E. 127, 129.

21. *Honaker v. Critchfield*, 247 Ky. 495, 57 S.W. 2d 502.

22. See NY CPLR 1411 (McKinney Supp. 1975).

23. *Phoenix Assurance Co. v. Royale Investment Co.*, 393 S.W. 2d 43 (Ct. App. 1965).

24. *Hulett v. Swift*, 33 N.Y. 571, 88 Am. Dec. 405 (1865).

25. *Cayle's Case, supra*, n.5.

26. *Bidlake v. Shirley Hotel*, 133 Colo. 160, 292 P. 2d 749 (1950).

27. *8 Am. Jur. 2d*, para. 131, page 1026.

28. *Wall v. Airport*, 40 Ill. 2d 506, 244 N.E. 2d 190 (1969).

29. 419.010.

30. *Supra*, n. 23.

31. *U.S. v. La Brecque*, D.C. N.J., 419 R. Supp. 430, 432, *Aleksich v. Indus.*, 116 Mont. 127, 151 P. 2d 1016, 1021.

32. *57 Tenn App.* 537, 421 S.W. 2d 98 (1967).

33. Hotel Proprietors Act, 1956, 26 & 27 Vict. c. 41(2), repealing the Innkeepers Liability Act of 1863.

34. Ch. 35, sec. 715.

35. Sec. 711 (e).

36. Nonliability for Conveyance, sec. 105.7.

37. Sec. 105.8.

38. *Basso v. Miller*, n. 39.

39. *Basso v. Miller*, 40 N.Y. 2d 233, 352 N.E. 2d 868, 872.

40. *William v. Linnitt*, 1 K.B. 565 (C.A. 1950).

41. *Lader v. Warsher*, 165 Misc. 559, 1 N.Y.S. 2d 160 (Columbia Co., 1937).

42. *Edwards Hotel v. Terry*, 185 Misc. 824, 187 So. 519 (1939).

43. Bidlake, *supra*, n. 26.

20

Property: The Statutory View

OVERVIEW

I N CHAPTER 19 we took a close look at common-law liability for the loss of property, as well as the theories upon which that responsibility can be based. In this chapter we will examine statutory limits on liability for property loss. These limits had their beginning in 1855 in New York and now are part of the law in all fifty American states.

In the last century, American innkeeping began to spread from coast to coast, and it has not ceased. The early expansion paralleled construction of the railway system. During that century, the legislatures of existing, and later forming, states began to enact statutes to place limits upon liability for the loss of property of guests. New York state took the lead with its statute of 1855. Many reasons prompted this. First, the realities of earlier centuries were fading. Travelers of the 1800s did not need the protection that was needed 500 years before.

> The statutes defining the limits of an innkeeper's liability for loss of or injury to his guest's property represent a legislative intent to soften what has been termed an unduly harsh common-law rule.
>
> In former times, there were a number of sound reasons to justify the public policy of imposing a strict rule of liability on innkeepers. And so, at common law, the innkeeper was an insurer of property brought by a guest to his inn and he was relieved of liability for the loss of such property only where the loss occurred through an act of God, through an act of a public enemy, or through the fault of the guest himself.
>
> Since the passing of years has erased much of the need for such absolute liability, the modern innkeeper is often permitted by statute to lessen his responsibility to certain limits, if he provides suitable locks on his guests' rooms, provides a safe for the protection of their valuables, and provides adequate notice of the presence of that safe and, in some cases, of his limited liability.[1]

Statutes such as this have a practical effect: They force some of the care for the goods and valuables upon the guest. This, in turn, "protects the inn against unrestricted liability for articles of value that can be stored conveniently in a safe or some similar secure receptacle where the inn may not even know the guest has such valuables. The liability is limited provided that the inn makes available such a secure facility and posts notice to that effect. If the guest chooses not to avail himself or herself of that facility, having notice thereof, it is surely not an unreasonable legislative decision to exculpate the inn from any liability if the guest thereafter sustains the loss of or damage to those valuable articles."[2]

Public policy becomes involved. As one judge wrote, speaking of guests:

> Those who carry with them large amounts of money or jewelry must take other measures for their protection. The added costs to the hotelkeeper of providing such protection, even as against the willful act or negligence of an employee, is in the last analysis one of his costs of operation reflected in the rates charged to all. Why should those guests who do not need such protection pay for the cost of those who do?[3]

Since 1872, California has provided for limited liability in instances where the inn provided a fireproof safe for use by guests who were notified of the availability of the safe.[4] Since 1895, in the same state, a limit on liability has been provided for other losses to personal property of guests:

> The liability of an innkeeper, hotel keeper, operator of a licensed hospital, rest home or sanitarium, furnished apartment house keeper, furnished bungalow court keeper, boarding house or lodging house keeper, for losses of or injuries to personal property, is that of a depositary for hire; provided, however, that in no case shall such liability exceed the sum of one hundred dollars ($100) for each trunk and its contents, fifty dollars ($50) for each valise or traveling bag and contents, ten dollars ($10) for each box, bundle or package and contents, and two hundred fifty dollars ($250) for all other personal property of any kind, unless he shall have consented in writing with the owner thereof to assume a greater liability.[5]

Willingness of the state legislatures to limit liability is the important point. If this change had not taken place, it could possibly have taken the courts another 100 years to have achieved the same result.

These laws usually take one of three forms. First are those statutes that limit liability for fire loss. Next are statutes that limit liability for loss of goods as they are being transported to the inn. Finally are those that limit liability for loss of money and valuables. We are most concerned about the latter category and will devote most of the chapter to that topic. The others will be examined briefly first. Many property statutes are of the "minimum-maximum" variety.

Minimum-Maximum Statutes

The states which have enacted such statutes usually have two value levels:

1. "No-value-stated" level, representing the minimum liability for loss.
2. "Value-stated" level, representing the maximum liability. Figure 20.1 shows the legal effects of these two levels.

If a guest's goods are accepted and no value is set, the minimum amount of the statute, such as $75 or $100, sets the limit of the liability should such goods be lost, destroyed by fire, or lost while in transit. If a value is stated, and if one accepts this value, the upper limit, such as $500, controls and this becomes the limit of liability.

FIGURE 20.1 Legal effect of minimum-maximum statutes.

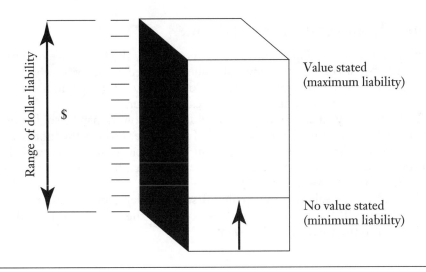

Range of dollar liability

$

Value stated
(maximum liability)

No value stated
(minimum liability)

Under the typical statute, one can refuse to accept liability for more than the maximum amount. If the innkeeper refuses the higher amount, this forces the guest to accept that limit or to make other arrangements for the safety of the goods or other items.

Loss by Fire

The statutes that limit liability for loss by fire are similar. A limit is placed on liability unless it appears that the loss was caused by the fault or negligence of the innkeeper. In the case of stored baggage, the liability limit often is doubled. If a guest who checks baggage fails to state a value, the limit on liability is set (such as $100). If a value is declared, the limit is set at another figure (such as $500).

Loss of Goods in Transit

Statutes that limit liability for the loss of property of one who will become a guest, while the goods are in transit, follow the minimum value–maximum pattern, much as stored baggage provisions.

Loss of Money and Valuables

These statutes presuppose that the loss was *not* caused by negligence of the innkeeper. If it were, the liability would be the full value of the goods and not the statutory limitation. This is so because the negligence would be the cause of the loss and the innkeeper would lose the protection of the statute. A variety of matters have arisen in reference to state statutes.

Arizona Money and Valuables Statute

Several points are found in statute 33–951, enacted by the legislature of Arizona. The words "of small size and unusual value" are used to describe what can be locked up in the safe if the guest desires to do so. These laws apply to hotels, inns, boardinghouses, lodging houses, and auto-camp keepers.

The statute says that property detained for debts owed may be sold at public auction after four months if not reclaimed. The statute provides that notice of the sale must be published once a week for four weeks before the sale is carried out. If the debt does not exceed $60, the notice can be given by posting at three locations where the debt was incurred.

Proceeds of the sale shall be applied first to the debt, and the balance to the costs of the sale. If the former guest does not claim the balance in thirty days, it is to be paid to the treasury of the county.

Arkansas

To gain the protection of the Arkansas statute, which limits liability for the innkeeper, strict posting requirements must be met. The statute says a copy shall be " . . . printed in distinct type and constantly and conspicuously posted in not less than ten conspicuous places . . . ".[6] The word "constantly" makes it clear that the notices must be replaced if stolen. In the Grimes case, ten notices were posted, but one was obscured by a potted plant at the front desk. The hotel lost the protection of the statute for that reason.

Statutory Construction in California

The courts apply basic rules when it becomes necessary to construe what the words of these statutes mean. The rules of construction are relatively consistent from state to state, although they are not uniform. The rules of statutory construction in California are representative:

1. The statute must be construed to avoid an interpretation that renders any of its language surplusage.[7]
2. The legislature is presumed to have meant what it said; thus, the "plain meaning" of the words used govern it.[8]
3. The courts must give effect to the usual, ordinary import of the language used.[9]
4. The statute must be considered within the statutory framework as a whole.[10]
5. When a word or phrase has a well known and definite legal meaning, it should be so construed when used in a statute.[11]
6. "Where a word of common usage has more than one meaning, the one which will best attain the purposes of the statute should be adopted even though the ordinary meaning of the word is thereby enlarged or restricted, and especially to avoid absurdity or to prevent injustice."[12]

The California Code of Civil Procedure, Section 341a, states in part:

> All civil actions for the recovery or conversion of personal property, wearing apparel, trunks, valises or baggage alleged to have been left at the hotel . . . shall be begun within 90 days from and after the date of the departure of the owner of said personal property, wearing apparel, trunks, valises or baggage from said hotel. . . ."

The issue before a California court in a 1991 case was the meaning of the words of the above statute. Did those words create a ninety-day statute of limitations and bar the lawsuit because it was filed more than 90 days after the loss? The court applied the rules of statutory construction, as to the plain meaning of words, and held that the ninety-day statute of limitations under Section 341a did not apply. Rather, Section 338, subdivision (c) did apply, which gave the plaintiff three years to sue for "negligence resulting from damage to property," and the two-year period of limitations of Section 339, subdivision (1), which applies to "an action upon an agreement not founded upon an instrument in writing."[13]

In the case of *Nagashima v. Hyatt Wilshire Corp.*, the guest sued for the loss of a small bag containing $72,000 worth of jewelry. The court held that Section 1860 of the California Civil Code, which placed a limitation of $500 for such loss at hotels, applied to the plaintiff's situation "where valuables were deposited at the safe, subsequently withdrawn by the guest, and [stolen] from her as she checked out of the hotel."[14]

Under California Civil Code, Section 1859, an innkeeper's liability is limited to $500 for each trunk and $250 for each piece of luggage, with total liability not to exceed $1,000. The California statutes are negated as to the extent of liability for loss of money and valuables if the innkeeper is negligent or dishonest.[15] If an employee causes loss of guest money and valuables while outside the scope of his or her employment, however, the innkeeper might escape liability.[16] California innkeepers have no duty to inquire as to the value of property that is kept in the possession of the guest or "declared" (deposited) at the front desk for safekeeping.[17] A California court has upheld the constitutionality of the Colorado money and valuables statutes. The Colorado statutes are similar to those of California.[18]

The California Code contains two forms for use by those who wish to limit their liability for property of guests and others. These are shown in Figure 20.2.

District of Columbia

The District of Columbia Code Annotated[19] allows hotels located there to limit liability for loss of guest property, if among other things, they comply strictly with the posting requirements of the statute. Failure to properly post a notice that informs guests of what the statute says will result in loss of protection of the statute. The hotel will be held responsible for the full value of lost money and valuables and other property in the absence of proper posting.

Florida Statute

A twenty-four-foot U-Haul truck containing all of the possessions of a couple moving to Florida was stolen. Upon inquiry at check-in time, the front-desk clerk

FIGURE 20.2 California forms to limit liability.

---

§ 1840. [Liability of depositary]

SUGGESTED FORM

Provision in Depositary Agreement Concerning Declared Value of Thing Deposited

Depositor hereby declares that the value of the goods deposited with ____1____ is the sum of $ ____2____ . Depositary shall not be liable to the depositor, in the event of negligence in the care of the goods, for more than this declared value.

---

§ 1854. [Termination of deposit]

SUGGESTED FORM

Notice by Depositor to Terminate the Deposit

NOTICE

To: ____1____ *[name and address of depositary]*

You are hereby notifed that the deposit of ____2____ *[nature of goods]* with you by the undersigned is terminated as of ____3____ , 19 _4_ . Please have the goods ready for delivery to me at ____5____ *[address]*, City of ____6____ , County of ____7____ , State of California, by ____8____ *[date.]*

Dated ____9____ , 19 _10_ .   *[Signature]*

---

had assured the couple that the rear parking lot was secure. The guests were not told about the high incidence of crime and vandalism in that parking lot. Suit was brought for the value of their possessions. The couple alleged that there was a failure to warn as well as failure to provide adequate security at the parking lot. The lower court held that the Florida statute limiting liability to $1,000 applied. The upper court reversed, stating that the statute does not apply when a front-desk clerk fails to warn and misleads persons, as happened here.[20] Though not ruling squarely on the point, this same Florida court said that when a hotel posted its room notices inside of the room closets, it was ". . . doubtful whether the [notice] was posted in a prominent place . . . ."[21]

The innkeeper of the motel where a loss of valuables occurred said, "We place the notice of the limit on liability inside the closet door in each room because the franchisor prefers it that way."[22] That location is not likely to be acceptable to the courts that must rule on such issues.

In Florida, the courts also make it clear that before a hotel can gain the protection of the $1,000 limit on liability for the loss of a guest's money and valuables, it must carry the burden of proving that it had complied with the requirements of the statute. The courts there base this position on "superior position and knowledge" of the hotel. The hotel is in a better position to know what Florida law requires than is a visitor from Germany, for example.[23]

The Florida money and valuables statute provides that:

1. A receipt is given to guests, stating the value of what is being deposited for safekeeping.
2. The receipt contains a clear [conspicuous] statement that the limit on liability is $1,000.
3. The guest agrees that liability will not exceed that sum.
4. The guest is told that the only exception to the limit on liability is negligence on the part of the innkeeper.
5. A notice on the liability limit is posted in "the office, hall, lobby, or other prominent place" at the hotel.

In another case, a couple deposited $85,000 worth of jewelry at the front desk of a Florida hotel. The jewelry then was stolen by an employee who had a duplicate key to the safe deposit box. Both the jewelry and the employee vanished. The lower court ruled that the limit on liability for the hotel was $1,000 because of the Florida statute. On appeal, the upper court held that the limit was lost and that the hotel had to pay the full value of the loss. The upper court ruling was based on the fact that two things had not been done as required by the statute:

1. The hotel did not give a receipt for the valuables.
2. The hotel had not posted a notice of the liability limit "in the office, hall, lobby, or other prominent place."[24]

These statutes in Florida do not apply to motor vehicles.[25] "In no event will a hotel be liable" for the loss of valuables not deposited with the hotel. Since motor vehicles cannot be "deposited," the statute does not apply.[26]

Indiana Statute

The money and valuables statute in Indiana limits liability to $200 if the property of the guest is "brought into the inn." In a 1986 case, a couple traveling west pulling a U-Haul tow-a-long, filled with their possessions, stopped at an Indiana inn for the night. Upon inquiry, they were told to park in the truck parking area and were told that a guard patrolled that lot every half hour. The next morning, the U-Haul was gone. At the trial, the court limited the couple's recovery to $200, based on the money and valuables statutes, and issued a summary judgment to that effect. The appellate court reversed and sent the case back for trial by jury. The upper court made three points:

1. Because the statute covered only property "brought into the inn," it would not apply to property left in the parking lot.
2. Whether the travelers exercised reasonable care in leaving their property in the U-Haul under the circumstances was a question of fact for a jury to decide.

3. An innkeeper in Indiana has a duty to exercise ordinary care to prevent loss or damage to the vehicles of its guests. Whether this duty was or was not breached also was a question of fact for the jury.[27]

Louisiana Statute

In a Louisiana case involving the loss of two valuable rings left in the bathroom of a departed guest, a question arose as to the amount of liability, and whether the notices of availability of the safe had been posted in a conspicuous manner. The court excused the hotel from legal liability, basing its decision on three points:

1. A notice of the limit on liability, measuring 8-inch square with 3/16-inch lettering was posted in the lobby.
2. Notices of the limit on liability, 4 1/2 inches wide and 8 inches high, had been posted on the inside of each guest room.
3. The notices were silver in color with the words printed in black.

The court found that these notices were "conspicuous" or "easy to see," so the limit of $500 applied to the rings.[28]

The New Orleans Fairmont Roosevelt Hotel was denied the protection of the Louisiana statute because no employee was on duty at 5:30 A.M. to accept deposit of a guest's jewelry. The court reasoned that, even though the safe was there, if a guest could not use it, the safe was "not available" as a matter of law.[29] Because of this decision, the Louisiana legislature amended the statute to limit liability in either of these circumstances.[30]

Nevada Statute

Does the Nevada statute that limits liability to $750 for the loss of valuables "left in the room" or "not deposited for safekeeping at the front desk" extend to valet-parked vehicles and the property that is in plain view inside the vehicle when custody is taken by hotel valet personnel? A lower Nevada court and the Supreme Court of that state agreed that the answer was "no."[31] In that state, however, the $750 limit on liability for money and valuables works perfectly if the hotel is in strict compliance with the statute.[32]

In 1983, in the Ninth Circuit of the U.S. Court of Appeals, there was a constitutional challenge to the Nevada statute. It was claimed that the statute violated the "equal protection" provision of Section 1, Fourteenth Amendment, U.S. Constitution (ratified July 9, 1868). The Ninth Circuit held that the Nevada statute was designed to foster a legitimate state interest, which was to promote tourist trade, and upheld it.[33]

New York Statute

One of the leading jewelers in Italy was waiting in the lobby of a Fifth Avenue hotel in New York to check in. Accompanied by his wife, he was carrying a leather briefcase containing $500,000 in jewelry and $5,000 in cash. The jeweler had an order he was to deliver to another jeweler in New York the next day. After the theft, he told the police that he and his wife were seated, waiting for the check-in line to shorten. He said he placed the briefcase next to him where he was seated. Someone pulled a "switch" by taking his case and replacing it with a similar one. Neither he nor his wife noticed the exchange. The jewelry, cash, and briefcase were never recovered. Under such circumstances, what is the liability, if any, of the hotel?

At the time the switch was made, the jeweler and his wife had not yet become guests at the hotel, although they were in the lobby with the intention of becoming guests. No hotel-guest relationship existed at the time of the theft. The New York statute that limits liability for loss of money and valuables did not apply, as it applied only to "guests." Thus, if the hotel is found liable, that liability is going to be for the full $505,000.

Is there any legal basis upon which the New York hotel could be held liable under these facts? Although no hotel-guest relationship was in effect, the courts would say a "special relationship" still was in being. The traveler and wife were waiting to check in and perhaps had reservations. Duties were owed to them even if they were not yet guests. Consider the following points:

1. If the hotel had been notified that the guests would be arriving with valuables, it would have had a duty to have security personnel available to escort the travelers so the valuables could be protected. Failure to provide such security would be negligence and could render the hotel liable for the full value of the loss.

2. If the hotel had no notice of the arriving travelers and their valuables, a second basis of legal liability is possible: If the "switch" activity was common at that hotel, it would have had a duty to warn all arriving travelers of this danger. Failing to warn could lead to liability.

3. If it was known that a "crime-family" was using the hotel as a base of operation and nothing had been done to stop that operation, liability could follow.

4. If there was an absence of security at the time the jeweler and his wife arrived, and if security had been present so the loss would not have occurred, liability could possibly attach.

5. If the innkeeper failed to post copies of the statutory provisions in conspicuous places as required by the statute, "he or she is liable as an insurer under the common-law rule for loss of the guest's property resulting from the destruction of the hotel by fire of unknown origin."[34]

Tennessee Statute

Whether a three-inch by six-inch notice, printed in 5-point type and placed on the back of guest room doors, was notice given in a "conspicuous" manner as required by the Tennessee statute was a question of fact for a jury to decide.[35]

THE STATUTES IN USE

The money and valuables statutes almost uniformly contain the following requirements that must be met:

1. The innkeeper must provide a safe for valuables.
2. The guest must be given notice in a prescribed manner that the safe is available and must be told the liability limit in dollars.
3. The guest must be given notice that failure to declare (deposit) valuables at the front desk may relieve the innkeeper of liability if such valuables are lost.
4. A statutory limit is set beyond which the innkeeper will not be liable for loss of declared valuables.
5. The innkeeper may accept liability for valuables beyond the statutory limit but does not have to do so.

In most states the declaration must be made in writing. In some states, an innkeeper does not have to receive valuables if "[they are] of a size which cannot easily fit within the safe or vault."[36]

Also, some, but not all, states allow the statutory limit to apply, ". . . unless the owner or keeper is grossly negligent."[37] In states that have such provisions, the benefit of the statutory limit may be lost if the hotel is grossly negligent. In some states' statutes, the word "grossly" is left out. In those states, protection of the statutes may be lost if the keeper is negligent, but not grossly so.

If the statute does not have the negligence exception, what then? Some states allow the protection of the statutory limitation if the keeper is negligent.[38] Other cases hold that if there is negligence on the part of the innkeeper, the protection is lost. This means that the innkeeper may be held liable for the proven value of lost valuables.[39]

Under 15 Oklahoma Statutes Annotated, section 503a, the guest must "advise such person [host] of the actual value of" the property being declared. If a guest signs an instrument stating the maximum value of goods as $1,500, even though the goods consist of over one quarter million dollars in cash, the innkeeper's liability is limited to $1,500. This also precludes federal jurisdiction because the amount in controversy must exceed $50,000.[40]

In many jurisdictions, a negligent innkeeper is held liable for the full value of lost valuables. Even in those jurisdictions, however, if the guest fails to carry the burden of proof, the statutory limit on liability will be applied.[41]

Statutory Limitations

In spite of the statutes, problems arise, and it is useful to look at some of them. To illustrate, A leaves a valuable watch at a front desk. The watch is sealed in an envelope and locked in a safety deposit drawer. A fire breaks out and the innkeeper removes the watch, intending to protect it from the fire but then negligently loses it. The liability extends to the full value of the watch. If the watch had remained in the safe and had been destroyed, the statutory limitation would have applied.

Another distinction is found when deposited property is stolen by the innkeeper or by an employee. In the former, liability for the full value would attach. In the latter, the statutory limitation would control. In these illustrations, we are assuming that the value of the deposited property had not been declared at a higher value. If it had been, the innkeeper had the right to refuse the risk. If the risk had been accepted, however, the statutory limitation would not apply.

In New York, failure to comply with the statutory limitations on liability revives the common-law rule, and the innkeeper has become an insurer once again.[42] An innkeeper who chooses not to take advantage of the statutes that limit liability waives the protection of those statutes.[43] Figure 20.3 illustrates this concept. In the operation of these statutes, the declaration of excess value often becomes an issue in court.

FIGURE 20.3 Losing the protection of the statutes.

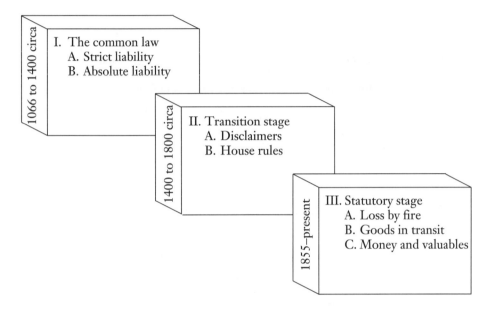

What happens if Stage III protection is lost because an innkeeper fails to comply with the statute, and Stage II protection is lost because the same innkeeper was not using disclaimers or house rules—or a court refuses to uphold those disclaimers or house rules?

Stage I applies.

Declaration of Excess Value

The burden is on the guest to declare excess value of items brought to the front desk for safekeeping. It is not the responsibility of the innkeeper to see that such declaration is made. The innkeeper is not in a position to know if excess value should be declared, so the law makes it the burden of the guest.[44] If a dispute arises later as to whether excess value had been declared and accepted by the innkeeper, the burden of proof again is upon the guest.

An innkeeper can accept or refuse (in most states) excess value when it is declared by the guest. If the excess value is accepted, most states require that it be done in writing. Figure 20.4 is an example of a form that can be used to declare excess value.

FIGURE 20.4 Sample form for declaration of valuables.

ZERO MOTEL
Declaration of Valuables

Under the provisions of (state statute), I hereby declare the following for safekeeping:

1.

2.

3.

I declare the value of the above to be $ _____ total.

I have read this form, understand it and agree to be bound by it.

_____
Guest

_____
Date

_____
Room Number

I, Innkeeper of Zero Motel, accept the above items and I DO—I DO NOT (circle one) accept the evaluation of them.

_____
Innkeeper, Zero Motel

_____
Date

Notice of Limits on Liability

It becomes important in practice to read the statute of the state in question to see how notice of limitation on liability is to be given.

Notice on Room Mirrors

One court held that placing notices on the mirrors in rooms met the requirements of the statute of the state in question.[45] Another court held that placing the notice under the glass on top of a dresser made the matter a jury question as to whether notice had been given adequately. In both of these cases, the innkeepers were challenged on adequacy of the notice. If notice had been given as prescribed by the applicable statutes, neither case would have been brought in the first place.

These notices should be made in separate, distinct writing, in large enough type to be read easily. They should not be combined with information about the location of the ice machine and the fire escapes. Those notices are important, of course, but should be kept separate from the money and valuable notices.[46]

Quantity of Posting

In a Pennsylvania case, a coin collection was stolen from a coin dealer. Notices were not posted at ten conspicuous places, as required by state statute. The notice was on the registration form and, though that is a good practice, it does not comply with Pennsylvania law. The jury found for the coin dealer in the sum of more than $34,000 but found him to have been 49 percent negligent, reducing his recovery to a little less than $18,000. To this, the judge added more than $7,700 in "delay damages," giving the coin dealer a recovery of over $25,000. If the ten signs had been posted, the recovery would have been $300. To gain the protection of these statutes, a safe must be provided.

SAFES

Full Safe

A full safe is an unusual occurrence, but it could happen. What if a guest wants to deposit money and valuables but is turned away because the safe is full? Although there is no case in point at the moment, a court may well hold that this situation would constitute having no safe available so the protection of the statute would be lost if that particular guest had property stolen. If an innkeeper should be caught in such a situation, it would be wise to take extraordinary care and see that the valuables are protected in some reasonable manner. If a safe fills up repeatedly, new safe facilities must be acquired. The movement that began a few years back to place individual safes in guest rooms has cut down on the use of front-desk safes, but has in turn created new legal problems.

In-Room Safes

Over the past several years, various companies have begun to manufacture and market a variety of safes designed to be placed in each guest room so the guest may have private access to them. Although a charge is made for the use, they are popular with guests. The trend to install such safes in older inns started slowly, but their use in remodeled inns and in new construction has become an industry standard.

The legal problem is this: Are they "safes" within the meaning of the money and valuables statutes that limit liability if a "safe" is provided and proper notice is given? This question has not yet been before a court, but there is a legal reason why a judge will probably will answer that question "no." Almost without exception, the money and valuables statutes in our states were enacted before the first in-room safes appeared on the market. Therefore, a court almost always will rule that something that was not developed until after the statutes were enacted could not have been in the contemplation of the lawmakers who wrote and enacted the statutes. The court would look to trade usage as of the time of enactment of the statutes, and what they would find would be the traditional front-desk safe. That is to say, of course, that there is no statute written specially to extend protection to the in-room safes.

FIGURE 20.5 Newspaper report concerning inn safes.

Monday Morning Briefs

A microprocessor-controlled keyless safe for use in hotels, motels and condos in Las Vegas and throughout the United States, "Elsafe," is now being distributed through a growing chain of local affiliates, including Elsafe Nevada at 900 E. Karen Ave., C-202 (369-9415).

Used in 37 countries and with nearly 6,000 in use in Hawaiian hotels, Elsafe consists of a full-size steel safe that enables guests to select their own combination by depressing numbers on a telephone-type keyboard. A microprocessor stores the combination and allows the safe to be opened only when that combination is entered.

Each new combination is displayed on a digital readout panel for 14 seconds to help the guest remember the combination. A million combinations are possible.

If the wrong combination is tried, the digital panel flashes to tell the user to try again. As a safeguard against outsiders trying to arrive at the combination through trial and error, the safe mechanism refused to function for 30 minutes after the wrong combination is tried three times.

Interior of the safe measures 18.5 gallons (70 liters)—enough to store brief cases, large purses, cameras and cassette players. Walls are ⅓-inch thick steel. Doors are ⅓-inch thick and designed to prevent jimmying. The safe is bolted to the floor from the inside to prevent removal.

Las Vegas Sun, August 8, 1983, p. 6A.

Hawaii's In-Room Safe Statute

Hawaiian inns were the first big users of in-room safes, and it seems fitting that that state would be the first one to amend its "valuables" statute to make it clear that the statutory limit on the liability extends to these special safes.[47] Until such laws are enacted in the other states, the innkeeper who decides to install the safes has a legal problem. When deciding to install such safes, legal advice should be sought. Some form of notice, or perhaps a waiver, would be in order to make it clear that the in-room safe is for the mere convenience of the guest and that the inn still maintains the traditional safe and stands on its limit on liability.

Charging for the Safe

Another problem might be found in charging for the use of in-room safes. If guests use the in-room safes, a charge such as $3 per day is made for that use. This sum is added to the guest's bill for as long as the use continues. This procedure is at variance with prior practice in which no charge was made to use the front-desk safe. Might the fact that a charge was made for the in-room safe influence the court that may have to decide the question of liability for stolen property?

To make a charge for the use of the traditional front-desk safe would be unwise, for example. The reason is that guests may claim they did not use the front-desk safe because they objected to the charge. It must be remembered that these statutes are a "grace" extended by the state legislatures. A court may well hold that if a charge is made at the front desk, the inn did not "provide" the safe! It is a subtle legal point but one that a careful lawyer would pick up on quickly.

The plus side of in-room safes, of course, is that guests who have used them have had very little loss. Another legal plus is that the courts will look upon the act of providing safes as proof that the innkeepers are demonstrating care. "Gross negligence" has been defined as "the failure to provide any care." Providing in-room safes would protect the innkeeper from a charge of gross negligence in that regard.

A Blanket Charge for In-Room Safes

A 116-room hotel in midtown Manhattan provided in-room safes and placed a daily charge of $1.50 on the bill of each guest, keeping no record of whether the safes were in fact used. This violates Section 206 of the New York General Business Law, which states, "No charge or sum shall be collected or received by any such hotel keeper or innkeeper for any service not actually rendered. . . . For any violation of this section the offender shall forfeit to the injured party three times the amount so charged, and shall not be entitled to receive any money for meals, services or time charged."

If in-room safes are of an inferior quality and if that quality becomes a factor in the loss of a guest's property, the courts probably will allow the loss to be recovered. Also, if such safes are not inspected on a regular basis and maintained properly, the courts will use those facts against the innkeeper. Safes cannot be placed in guest rooms and then ignored.

The biggest legal mistake that could be made in reference to in-room safes would be to try to substitute them for the traditional front-desk safe. The courts would never buy that one in the absence of a specific statute permitting it to be done.

Does the Front-Desk Safe Have to Be Fireproof?

Some states, such as Nevada and Oklahoma, specifically say by statute, that the safe must be fireproof. It has been held that if there is no statutory requirement that it be fireproof, it does not have to be, and the notice does not have to say that it is.[48]

This brings us to a final question about safes: Just what is a "safe"?

What Is a "Safe?"

In a New York case, two salesmen deposited $2 million in jewelry at the front desk of the Mayfair Regent, and all seemed to be in order—that is, until the safe was broken into and the jewelry was stolen. Because the hotel had provided a safe, notice had been given that the safe was available, and the jewelry had been deposited as required by the statute, it seemed clear to the trial court that the liability of the hotel was limited to the statutory amount of $500 per person. Upon appeal, the upper court reversed, holding that there was evidence that the safe deposit boxes were in an unguarded room; that there was public access to that room; that a list of those who had valuables on deposit was available at the hotel;

and that the walls of the safe-deposit room were made of mere plasterboard. The upper court in New York sent the case back for a determination of the security measures in effect at the hotel. The case then was settled without retrial.[49]

For the statutes to apply, the guest does not have to bring the money and valuables or goods. The statutes also apply where property was delivered from an airline where it had been lost and then found. The property then was placed upon a bellhop stand, from which it vanished. The $1,000 limit on liability of the New Mexico statute was held to apply.[50]

The New York statute has been held to apply even if the inn fails to place the declared valuables in the safe.[51] This was a harsh decision, as it did not take into consideration the negligence on the part of the innkeeper. Yet, the decision shows how strong these statutes are when applied in court.

For negligence to defeat the protection of the statutes, a distinction must be made between active and passive negligence. It has been held that to make an innkeeper liable for negligence, there must be some active "misfeasance." On the other hand, nonfeasance, such as failure to have additional security on hand, is not enough. As one court said, "nonfeasance has not made the situation worse." Active misfeasance does make the situation worse and is needed to hold the innkeeper liable.

By interpretation, the courts have included certain items and excluded others under the coverage of the statutes. It has been held that a watch, chain, and rosary, each being an article of use and not worn as ornaments, are not "jewels or ornaments" within the meaning of the statute.[52] The same has been held for silver tableforks, a silver soup ladle, and an heirloom watch,[53] and for a gold pen and pencil in a case[54] and a silver-mounted set in a traveling bag.[55]

Do these money and valuables statutes represent a "taking of property" as prohibited by the Fourteenth Amendment? They have been so challenged in California and Colorado but have been upheld in those states.[56]

In a Georgia case, a guest left a bag containing $9,000 in a room. The room maid then turned in the money to a supervisor. It subsequently was stolen by another employee. The Days Inn in question provided a safe and gave notice of its availability. The court dismissed the case, holding that the Georgia property statute makes no exceptions even for negligence of the innkeeper. The court said, "If the innkeeper posts notice of the availability of the safe pursuant to the statute, it is not liable for articles stolen from a guest's room even if its negligence contributed to the loss."[57] The unusual aspect of this case was that the money had not been stolen from the guest's room. It had been stolen elsewhere. Yet the statute gave the innkeeper protection as to the loss.

Nevada Statutes

The Nevada property statute provides that protection of the coverage is lost if the innkeeper is "grossly negligent." Thus, a Nevada hotel can be negligent in the loss of a guest's money and valuables and the $750 limit still applies.

The Nevada statute uses the words "any individual," so if more than one person occupies a guest room, the statute is applicable to all of them. The statute also covers boardinghouses, lodginghouses, and motor courts, but it does not mention

RV parks. Thus, if a guest should become a permanent resident at a Nevada inn, the limit on liability would still apply to that person even though he or she has become a tenant.

In the 1986 Kahn case brought in federal court in California, the court was called upon to construe the Nevada statute and found that it had "awkward language." Table 20.1 is a summary of what the statute says, including the rulings of the court.

TABLE 20.1   Interpretation of Nevada money and valuables statute.

Facts	Innkeeper Is Negligent	Innkeeper Is Grossly Negligent
1. Jewelry is left in room and it is stolen.	No liability	$750 liability
2. Notice is given and jewelry is deposited in the front-desk safe.	$750 liability	Full value liability
3. Notice is given; jewelry is not placed in safe.	No liability	$750 liability
4. No notice given, and no safe provided.	$750 liability under Kahn	$750 liability under Kahn
5. In-room safes provided, but no front-desk safe.	$750 under Kahn	$750 under Kahn

The case involved a visit to the Tropicana Hotel by Robert Kahn, a part-time jewelry broker. While Mr. Kahn was checking out, a bellman negligently allowed Mr. Kahn's briefcase, containing over $50,000 in jewelry, to be lost. It never was determined who stole it or how, but the empty case was found later on the hotel's golf course. The court held that the $750 limit applied "even when the innkeeper was grossly negligent" in spite of the fact that the statute says the limit shall not apply if the innkeeper is grossly negligent. The reason for this is that the Nevada statute is divided into three numbered paragraphs. The "gross negligence" phrase is found in paragraph 2. Paragraph 3 says in effect that "in all other instances of the loss of a guest's money and valuables, the limit shall be $750." There is no mention of gross negligence in paragraph 3. The result of this ruling is that the Nevada statute has been enlarged by court interpretation.

Two final matters that relate to the money and valuables of guests, and the statutes that limit liability for them, should be considered. The first has to do with money and valuables inadvertently left by the departing guest. The other has to do with money and valuables lost or stolen during the check-out process.

PROPERTY LEFT AFTER CHECK-OUT

Most property (including money and valuables) left by travelers is lost or misplaced and not abandoned. Most states have statutes that control the situation.

For example, one statute states, "All baggage or property of whatever description left at a hotel, inn, motor court, boardinghouse, or lodginghouse for the period of 60 days may be sold at public auction by the proprietor or proprietors thereof" under the following conditions:

1. Notice must be given as provided [by the state statute].
2. The sale must be carried out by public auction.
3. The proceeds of the sale shall be distributed as follows:
   a. storage costs
   b. costs of sale
   c. balance to county treasurer

After the funds are received by the county treasurer, they are paid into the county school district fund, subject to the right of the true owner to reclaim the balance within six months.

In some states, such as New York, the property may be retained for ten days, during which time an effort must be made to find the owner. If the owner is not located, the property must be surrendered to the police.

Under laws, all property, money, and valuables left at a hotel must be delivered promptly to management. The innkeeper then holds the property as a bailee and must use ordinary care in its security. The money and valuables statutes no longer apply, since they apply only to guests, not departed guests.

In *Spiller v. Barclay Hotel*,[58] a guest who had completed check-out gave a bellhop her bags to take to her car, which were still on the hotel premises. One bag came up missing and the court held the hotel liable for the entire value of the bag and its contents. The court said the money and valuables protection was lost as of the time check-out was completed.

SUMMARY

In the days of common law, an innkeeper was an "insurer" of the safety of all property brought *infra hospitium* by travelers who were accepted as guests. If this principle had been perpetuated, modern accommodations for travelers would require razor wire fences, patrols of armed guards with attack dogs, and much more. The character of our modern hotel, hospitality, and tourism industries would be very different than what it is today.

The use of safes in hotel rooms provides a good example of how the laws of another day can be forced to change. When the strict liability of innkeepers for the loss of property began to be limited by statutes, a "safe" was often mentioned. In-room safes began to appear in hotels.

The money and valuables statutes represent a true "grace" for the HH&T industries from the state legislatures, and this makes it especially important that their requirements are adhered to. This responsibility falls upon management, not upon employees or agents, and certainly not upon the lawyers of the businesses involved.

QUESTIONS

1. True or false: One must use care in placing into effect house rules that give property left at a hotel to the one who finds it.
2. What might be the reasoning of the lawyers who brought the lawsuits that challenged the money and valuables statutes as being unconstitutional?
3. What economic realities prompted the state legislatures to enact laws to limit the age-old liability of innkeepers as insurers of guests' property?
4. What happens in a minimum-maximum situation where no value has been stated on a guest's lost property?
5. What happens in question 4 if a value *has* been stated?
6. What is one time when a manager should seek a legal opinion on a question of liability for the money and valuables of guests?
7. Most of the statutory limits for money and valuables are under $1,000. Can you think of a historical reason why the limit in Colorado is $5,000?
8. What are the rights of an innkeeper in Nevada when property too large for the safe is tendered at the front desk?
9. What is the legal effect of failing to give proper notice as required by the money and valuables statutes?
10. What is the legal problem with in-room safes?

NOTES

1. *American Law Reports* 37, 3d 1276, 1279-80 (1971).
2. *Diamond v. Super,* 149 Cal. Rptr. 813, 85 Cal. App. 3d 885 (California 1978).
3. *Levesque v. Columbia Hotel,* 141 Me. 398, 44 A. 2d 730.
4. Cal. Civil Code, sec. 1860 (1872).
5. Cal. Civil Code, sec. 1859 (1895).
6. *Grimes v. MHM,* 776 S.W. 2d 336 (Arkansas 1989).
7. *Well v. Marina,* 29 Cal. 3d 781, 788 (California 1981).
8. *Great Lakes Properties v. City of El Segundo,* 19 Cal. 3d 152, 155 (California 1977).
9. *People v. Morris,* 46 Cal. 3d 115 (California 1988).
10. *Select Base Material v. Board,* 51 Cal. 2d 640, 645 (California 1959).
11. *People v. Hertz,* 145 Cal. App. Supp. 8, 17 (California 1983).
12. *People ex rel S.F. Bay v. Town of Emeryville,* 69 Cal. 2d 533, 543–544 (California 1968), quoting *People v. Asamoto,* 131 Cal. App. 2d 22, 29 (California 1959).
13. *Linda Taylor v. Forte Hotels International,* 91 Daily Journal DAR 13493 (C. Ct. App. 1991).
14. 228 Ca. App. 3d 1006, at page 1011 (California 1991).
15. *Gardner v. Jonathan Club,* 35 Cal, 2d 343 (California 1950).
16. *Muchlback v. Pasa Robles Springs Hotel,* 65 Cal. App. 634 (California 1924).

17. *Altman Inc. v. Biltmore Hotel*, 190 Cal. App. 2d 274 (California 1961).

18. *Pacific Diamond Company v.* Super U.S. Superior Court, 85 Cal. App. 3d 875 (California 1978).

19. Section 34–101, 1981.

20. *Fennema v. Howard Johnson Co.*, 559 So. 2d 1231 (Florida 1990).

21. *Supra*, n. 20.

22. "Hospitality Law" Magna Publications, Inc., Dec. 1989, p. 7.

23. *Garner v. Margarey Lane, Inc.*, 242 So. 2d 776 (Florida 1970).

24. *Florida Sonesta Corp. v. Aniballi*, 463, So. 2d 1023 (Florida 1985).

25. Florida Acts, Ch. 16042, section 40 (1933).

26. *Johnson v. Fair*, 575 So. 2d 723 (Florida 1991).

27. *Plant v. Howard Johnson's*, 500 N.E. 2d 1271 (Indiana 1986).

28. *O'Rourke v. Hilton Hotels Corp.*, 560 So. 2d 76 (Louisiana 1990).

29. *Durandy v. Fairmont Roosevelt Hotel, Inc.*, 523 F. Supp. 1382 (E.D. Louisiana 1981).

30. Louisiana Civil Code Annotated, section 2971. See also *Kraaz v. La Quinta Motor Inns, Inc.*, 410 So. 2d 1048 (Louisiana 1982).

31. *Tienda v. Holiday Casino, Inc.*, 853 P. 2d 106 (Nevada 1993).

32. *Pachinger v. MGM Grand Hotel—Las Vegas, Inc.*, 618 F. Supp. 218 (Nevada 1985).

33. *Morris v. Hotel Riviera, Inc.*, 704 F. 2d 1113 (9th Cir. 1983).

34. *Swetlow v. Zindarest Park, Inc.*, 201 Misc. 116, 107 N.Y.S. 2d 786, 116 N.Y.S. 2d 208, *affd.* 281 App. Div. 369, 119 N.Y.S. 2d 446, 63 ALR 2d 503 (New York 1951).

35. *Cook et al. v. Columbia Sussex Corp. et al.*, 807 S.W. 2d 566 (Ct. App. Tennessee 1991).

36. Nevada Revised Statutes, 651.010 (2).

37. Nevada Revised Statutes, 651.010 (2).

38. Applying Florida law, see *Lazare Kaplan & Sons, Inc. v. Penascola Hotel Co.*, 153 F. Supp. 31, *affd.* 253 F. 2d 410 (D.C. Florida 1957).

39. *Edwards House v. Davis*, 124 Miss. 485, 86 So. 849 (1921), *Elcox v. Hill*, 98 U.S. 218, 25 L. Ed. 103 (1878, applying Illinois law).

40. *Kalpakian v. Oklahoma Sheraton*, 398 F. 2d 243, 37 A.L.R. 3d 1268 (Oklahoma 1968).

41. *De Panfield v. Hilton*, 33 Misc. 2d 967, 231 N.Y.S. 2d 906 (New York 1962).

42. *Insurance Company of North America, Inc. v. Holiday Inns, Inc.*, 337 N.Y.S. 2d 68 (Sup. Ct. Saratoga Co. 1972).

43. *Friedman v. Breslin*, 51 A.D. 268, 65 N.Y.S. 5 (2d Dept. New York 1900).

44. *Sagman v. Richmond Hotel*, 139 F. Supp. 407 (E.D. Va. 1956).

45. *Terry v. Linscott Hotel Corporation*, 617 P. 2d 56 (Ariz. App. 1980).

46. *North River v. Tish*, 64 N.J. Super. 357, 166 A. 2d 169 (New Jersey 1960).

47. Hawaii Revised Statutes, Chapter 486–1, subsection (5).

48. *Terry, supra* n. 45.

49. *Gonalves v. Regent International Hotel Ltd.*, 406 N.Y.S. 2d 750 (New York 1980).

50. *Albuquerque Hilton v. Haley*, 565 P. 2d 1027 (New Mexico 1977).

51. *Carlton v. Beacon Hotel*, 3 A.D. 228, 157 N.Y.S. 2d 774 (1st Dep. New York 1956).

52. *Jones v. Hotel Latham Co.*, 62 Misc. 620, 115 N.Y.S. 1084.

53. *Hoorise Waters & Co. v. Gerard*, 189 N.Y. 302, 82 N.E. 143, 24 L.R.A. N.S. 958.

54. *Briggs v. Todd*, 28 Misc. 208, 59 N.Y.S. 23.

55. *Rosenplaenter v. Roerssle*, 54 N.Y. 262.

56. Diamond, *supra.* Note 2, and 18, 589 N.Y.S. 422 (New York 1966).

57. *Gooden v. Days Inn*, 395 S.E. 2d 876 (Georgia 1990).

58. *Spiller v. Barclay Hotel*, 60 Misc. 2d 400, 327 N.Y.S. 2d 426 (Civ. Ct. New York 1972).

21

Restaurants

Overview

IN THIS CHAPTER, we will take a look at state and federal laws, regulations, and other legal matters that arise in the operation of restaurants. These laws are relatively uniform from state to state. The laws of innkeeping do not necessarily apply to restaurants. This is true of restaurants located inside hotels, motels, and inns, as well as those that are freestanding. There are common areas, of course, such as the law of bailment, yet the law of restaurants stands as a distinct area in itself.

Food Service at Common Law

The early common rule was that the inn had to furnish food and drink in addition to shelter and protection. This rule still prevails in New York and a majority of the states as a requirement to be classified as an inn. A trend growing in the courts, however, is toward removing food and drink as a requirement.

One of the first laws enacted in the American Colonies had to do with food and drink. In the year 1646, the General Court of the Massachusetts Bay Colony set forth by decree just how much bread a person should receive for a penny. The first general food law, enacted in Massachusetts on March 8, 1785, prohibited the sale of "diseased, corrupted, contagious, and unwholesome" food and drink and provided penalties including "fine and imprisonment, standing in the pillory" or "some or all of these penalties."

In the late 1800s, chemical analysis by the U. S. Department of Agriculture shocked the nation with disclosures of adulteration in alcoholic beverages, butter, oleo, margarine, and other food and drink products. The Bureau of Animal Industry likewise was concerned about the unsanitary conditions known to exist in the meat and other food packing operations.

It took a book to bring the whole situation into focus. *The Jungle*, by Upton Sinclair, published in 1906, horrified the nation by disclosing what was taking place at Chicago slaughter and packing plants. President Theodore Roosevelt appointed a three-person commission, whose report and recommendations resulted in the Pure Food and Drug Act of 1906. This law required that enforcement be carried out at all levels of processing and packing of food and drink. If the laws were to be meaningful, they had to apply across the board, and so they do today.

There are more than twenty federal food laws. The importance of these laws is that they ensure that the food and drink consumers purchase is wholesome and free from dangerous defects.

Today, producers and packers of food and drink, both retail and wholesale, are part of what is one of the most regulated industries in the world. This massive regulation carries over to the serving of food and drink at restaurants and has an effect at those operations. The bulk of legal control, however, comes from general law.

What Is a Restaurant?

A restaurant is a place of public accommodation where food is prepared, sold, and consumed on the premises or in carry-out form. The term is broad enough to include cafeterias, fast-food shops, grills, coffeehouses, cafes, and others, but does not include eating places at private clubs. Although private clubs will be able to escape the strictures of the civil rights laws, they still are subject to statutory restaurant law and the common law as well.

Restaurant operators (restaurateurs) have duties, liabilities, and rights that are distinct and separate from those of innkeepers. This also is true of bar operators, as we will see in Chapter 22. It is helpful to see how a court has defined the word *restaurant* and then see a legislature's definition.

Definition by a Court

"A restaurant is an establishment where meals and refreshments are served."[1] This definition is short but serves its legal purpose. The definitions in court cases vary, but this one is typical.

Definition by Statute

The West Virginia Code defined a restaurant in this manner in 1966: "Every place where food without lodging is usually furnished to patrons and payment required therefore shall be deemed a restaurant. The provisions of this article shall not apply to temporary food sales, not exceeding two weeks in length, by religious, educational, charitable, or nonprofit organizations."[2]

In this definition we see additional legal points:

1. It is a place "without lodging" (although lodging may adjoin it).
2. The food furnished is to "patrons." (They are not called "guests.")
3. Payment is required. (Thus, one's home would not be a restaurant by this definition.)
4. The exemptions exclude temporary food sales not exceeding two weeks in length, by religious, educational, charitable, or nonprofit organizations. (This has one unfortunate legal side effect: It makes the provisions of the West Virginia food service sanitation regulations inapplicable to such organizations. This would be true when sales are conducted by the exempt organization in connection with carnivals, church activities, banquets, and fairs that involve the public.)[3]

Definitions of restaurants by statute also are found in the Civil Rights Act of 1964 as amended in 1972, as well as in state civil rights laws. The Nevada Revised Statutes[4] provides:

Unless the context otherwise requires, "place of public accommodation" means: 1. Any inn, hotel, motel, or other establishment which provides lodging to transient guests, except an establishment located within a building which contains not more than five rooms for rent or hire and which is actually occupied by the proprietor of such establishment as his residence; 2. any restaurant, cafeteria, lunchroom, lunch counter, soda fountain, casino, or any facility where spiritous or malt liquors are sold, including any such facility located on the premises of any retail establishment.

The Nevada statute then provides:

All persons are entitled to the full and equal enjoyment of the goods, services, facilities, privileges, advantages, and accommodations of any place of public accommodation, without discrimination or segregation on the ground of race, color, religion, national origin, or physical or visual handicap. [This includes restaurants.]

Turning from definitions, it is necessary to notice an important legal distinction.

A Distinction

Some restaurants are constructed and operated as single, freestanding businesses. This is especially true with the fast-food chains and many local and higher-quality restaurants. On the other hand, almost all hotels have restaurants as part of the premises. The law does not have a separate body of rules for "attached" or "detached" restaurants. An innkeeper must keep this in mind, for it would be a legal mistake to assume that laws that *protect the innkeeper* would also protect the innkeeper as a restaurateur. This is not so.

Turning from these preliminary matters, we will begin an examination of the legal duties of those who operate restaurants.

DUTIES OF RESTAURATEURS

To begin with, does a restaurateur have a common-law duty to receive all persons who present themselves in presentable condition and are able to pay for the services they may request? Contrary to the common-law innkeeper rule, a restaurant operator does not have to receive all who seek services there. The early courts did not equate the need for food and drink by nontravelers in the same light as they did the need of protection for the traveler. The nontraveler could go home for supper. Once the traveler was received, it was necessary to provide food and drink. Indeed, in the early American West, the room was $1.00 for the night, but the food and drink were free. The duty to receive applied to the inn, not to the restaurant.

The fact that the common law developed in this way gives the modern restaurant operator leeway in establishing house rules, setting dress codes, and establishing opening and closing hours. It allows the operator to close the restaurant for a day or a week if that is the business decision. The law affords wide latitude in the operation of restaurants as to opening and closing times.

Although restaurants do not have to remain open twenty-four hours each day and there is no common-law duty for them to receive, at times the operator has a duty to receive on other legal grounds. Examples include the civil rights laws, both federal[5] and state,[6] and the duty to receive based upon contract.

Duty to Receive Under the Civil Rights Laws

Civil rights laws make it clear that a restaurateur cannot refuse to receive on the grounds of race, color, creed, national origin, sex, and disability. The legal effect of these laws is that, as long as the restaurant remains a place of public accommodation, these laws must not be violated. Thus, there is a "civil rights duty to receive." Yet, this duty would apply only while the restaurant is open.

Antidiscrimination laws, however, apply only to public, as contrasted to private, places. A true private club can establish its own qualifications for membership and set whatever standards it may choose without fear of a civil rights violation. As an example of one standard, to be a private club, there must be an internal plan for the election of officers who have the power to control the organization. A hotel could not circumvent the civil rights laws by claiming its restaurant is private and available only to members.

It is unwise business policy to use a dress code to keep minorities out while allowing others to enter who do not conform to that code, or to require minorities to stand in a line and admit others without hesitation or to place a cover charge on minorities and no charge to others. The Red Onion chain of Mexican food restaurants had such facts brought to its attention in a 1980 lawsuit. The restaurants would turn away minorities by claiming that they did not meet the standards of a "dress code" that in fact did not exist. The Carson, California, restaurant had to pay twenty-three persons $15,000 each for following this line of conduct.[7]

Attorney Clyde L. Griffith, then legal counsel for the National Restaurant Association, was asked this question a few years back: "If a prospective customer appears at your restaurant in an objectionable manner—drunk, disorderly, barefoot, in improper dress—can you [legally] refuse to serve him [or her]?" His answer was "yes."[8]

CASE INTRODUCTION: HARDER CASE

If one has a reservation contract at a restaurant and is refused service, that is another matter. There has now been a breach of the contractual duty to receive.

The following illustrates how the courts view this type of breach. This court is deciding whether the complaint filed stated a cause of action.

HARDER V. AUBERGE DES FOUGERES
46 App. Div. 2d 98, 338 N.Y.S. 2d 356 (3rd Dept. 1972)

PER CURIAM.

This is an appeal from an order of the Supreme Court at Special Term, entered March 7, 1972, in Albany County, which granted defendants' motion to dismiss the complaint for failure to state a cause of action.

The first cause of action alleged by appellant states, in part, that respondent "unlawfully, willfully, deliberately, and without just cause, refused to admit or seat plaintiff and his guests for dinner service even though plaintiff and his guests (a) had made a bona fide reservation, (b) requested service, and (c) were ready, willing and able to pay any reasonable charges imposed by defendants for such meal." And further that, "By reason of defendants' actions and failure to furnish plaintiff and his guests with appropriate accommodations in this restaurant, plaintiff and his guests were subjected to great inconvenience, humiliation, and insult and were exposed to public ridicule in the presence of a number of people in such restaurant. As a result of the activities of defendants, its officers, agents, representatives or employees, plaintiff and his guests, were forced to leave this restaurant and proceed to another place for their meals. Because of the commotion caused by defendants, plaintiff was injured in his good name and reputation which was absolutely uncalled for and unwarranted." . . .

The order should be modified, on the law and the facts, so as to deny the motion to dismiss the first cause of action, and, as so modified, affirmed, without costs.

Duty to Protect Property

The next duty of restaurant keepers has to do with the property of patrons. The liability of a restaurateur for loss of the property of patrons is based upon one of two legal theories: actual bailment or constructive bailment. In a fast-food carry-out restaurant, there seldom would be a bailment because patrons never stay long enough to check a coat or a handbag. Yet, such property might be left there by accident, bringing into play the constructive legal theory of bailment. In better-quality establishments, checkrooms are made available.

If loss of property does occur, the burden of proof is on the patron to prove the bailment and to prove failure to redeliver the goods. The burden then shifts to the operator to prove that he or she exercised ordinary care as a bailee. If this burden is not carried, then the loss will fall on the restaurant operator. Because of these rules, the property of patrons must be handled with care when acting as a bailee, and also when property left by a patron is found by employees or agents. There must be a firm house rule that such property must be taken at once to the person in charge. That person must, in turn, take reasonable steps to safeguard the property until the patron can reclaim it. Failure to take such steps can lead to legal liability if the property is lost before it can be reclaimed.

Except in New York, the statutory limits on liability that protect innkeepers for the loss of money and valuables of a guest, do not apply to restaurants, for they are not "hotels or motels." This is true even if they are within a hotel or motel.

Duty to Protect Patrons and Others

Not only must property be protected, but the persons of patrons and others as well. It has long been a rule of restaurant law that those who are given service have the right to be safe and secure in their property as well as in their persons while obtaining service. They are entitled to a reasonably calm atmosphere and safe surroundings that would be expected in that particular establishment. Yet, the fast pace of a Hard Rock Cafe or a Planet Hollywood would be perfectly acceptable as long as the premises are safe.

Duty to Protect Patrons from Patrons

If X becomes unruly and threatens to injure Y, a duty falls upon management to prevent that injury. The duty to protect extends also to third parties and, in some instances, those who are not patrons at the property.

Duty to Protect Patrons from Employees

The duty to protect patrons extends to employees and agents of the establishment. The courts make this doubly so because the place of business hired the agent or employees in the first instance. The courts view that as placing additional duties of care on the one doing the hiring. When employees cause injury to guests and patrons, the law places additional responsibility on management for failing to screen out such employees. When a room-service clerk started a fire at the Las Vegas Hilton in 1982, which resulted in eight deaths and many injuries, civil suits resulted against management for negligence in hiring that employee. (The employee was found guilty of murder.)

When employees cause injury to restaurant patrons, problems also can arise with insurance coverage. In a Pennsylvania case, an employee assaulted a patron, "striking her with fists, and with great force and violence repeatedly shook, cast and threw the patron to the ground." The court ruled that this was a deliberate attack (tort). Because the insurance policy covered accidents only, the insurance company was excused from payment for the tort.[9]

At a Hardee's Restaurant in Independence, Missouri, off-duty police officers were hired as security guards and were instructed to control the loitering of teenagers. A guard arrested three persons without having just cause to do so, and the loitering charges were dismissed. The three persons then brought a civil action against the restaurant for false arrest. One settled out of court for $10,000, and the jury awarded the other two $7,500 each. The court ordered the restaurant to pay attorney fees of over $11,000.[10]

Duty to Protect Employees from Patrons and Third Parties

The duty to protect does not stop with patrons and third parties. It extends to employees and agents of the business itself. There is a legal duty to protect employees who are being threatened or injured by patrons or third parties.

Duty to Provide Merchantable Food and Drink

One of the major duties of the restaurant has to do with the quality of food and drink. To understand this legal duty, let's examine some features of the law of warranties, as found in the Uniform Commercial Code, Article 2, Sales.

Warranties

A warranty at law is a *promise*. Here we are concerned with the warranties found in the retail sale of food and drink. At common law, the courts held serving of food and drink be a service and not a sale. It has been a rule of law for centuries that warranties arise only with a sale. At common law, serving food and drink carried no legal warranties with it. This may have been a satisfactory rule in earlier centuries, but it is unsuitable in modern times. Thus, when patrons were served a meal at an early inn, they were buying the service and not the food. The food and drink not consumed remained the property of the inn.

This has been changed. Today the Uniform Commercial Code, Section 2-314(1) makes it clear that the sale of food and drink is just that, a sale involving a contract. Because it is a sale, the sale carries with it promises [warranties] that become part of the contract.

The warranties can be express or they can be implied. When the Code provisions went into operation as state after state adopted them, there was legal controversy over whether an implied warranty of wholesomeness of the food attached between a restaurant operator and patrons who sought service there. Some courts held that the sale of food was a service and no warranties attached. This became the minority view. The majority view was that the service of food and drink was a sale because of 2-314(1) of the UCC, and that is where we are today.

Today, the serving of food and drink is a sale under the Uniform Commercial Code. This carries an implied warranty that the food is wholesome and fit for human consumption.

Express Warranties

Express warranties can be made by the use of words "we serve the world's finest beef," and they can be made by pictures on menus. In restaurant keeping, just as in any other business, it is important not to make unnecessary express warranties. If the sale does not measure up, or if the product is inferior, there would be a breach of the express warranty.

UCC 2-313(1) states that there is an express warranty that the goods will conform to photos in advertisements. A New York case held that an ad that showed a photo did not conform to what was sold; thus, there was a breach of warranty.[11] Other examples of express warranties include "boneless fish," "Sanka coffee," "hand-picked," "sugar-free," "100% hamburger," "home-cooked," "the best," "unsurpassed," "top quality," and "finest in town." Such statements become the standards by which a court will measure what in fact was served. Even though such statements appear to be good marketing techniques, the legal aspects of using them must be considered when drafting advertisements and writing menus.

Implied Warranties

First, there is the implied warranty of title. The law says that when a supplier sells furniture, the seller must have a rightful and valid title to what is sold. The parties to the sale do not have to state this because the law says it.

Second, there is a warranty against infringement. If a business buys a copier for use in its accounting department, the machine must not infringe upon legal rights of third parties, such as patent and copyright holders.

Third, there is the implied warranty of fitness for a particular purpose. When a restaurant serves a prime rib dinner, the restaurant impliedly promises that the dinner is fit for the purpose for which it was intended: human consumption. If the dinner should carry a foodborne illness, there would be a breach of this warranty. The patron has a legal right to assume that the food provided meets this warranty. This is especially true because the patron cannot control the source of the food, the preparation of it, or the service of it.

Statutory Warranties

The federal Magunson-Moss Warranty Act was passed in 1975. Its primary purpose is to protect consumers who are buying goods at shopping malls or by mail order. It requires posting signs in stores, a disclosure as to whether the warranty offered is "full" or "partial," and sets forth procedures by which disputes in purchases may be decided. It has little application at hotel, hospitality, and tourism operations except where merchandise is sold.

Disclaiming Warranties

The Uniform Commercial Code allows one to disclaim implied warranties if it is done in the manner specified in Article 2. The disclaimer must be conspicuous and must mention "fitness" and "merchantability." It is a good idea to use such disclaimers on menus when serving seafood or exotic items that may have possible side effects. For example, at times in the Caribbean, certain fish contain toxins that cause problems to persons who are unused to them. Natives of that region are not affected by the toxins, but that is not necessarily so for the tourist from Kansas. Thus, a warning in disclaimer form is in order.

The implied warranty rule under Article 2 (1) does not apply if there is no "sale" of the food and drink, (2) may not be applied by a court if a proper disclaimer is used, and (3) usually becomes of no legal consequence when adequate care is used in the preparation and serving of food and drink.

If express warranties are made, there is very little at law that can be done to get rid of them. One cannot expressly warrant that food is "home-cooked" and then, in small print, claim that it is not home-cooked and, by doing so, escape the express warranty.

Objects that are foreign to food and drink could give rise to a breach of the implied warranty of merchantability. A foreign object is something not found in nature. Such objects could lead to litigation in tort for the negligence in allowing them to get into the food or drink. Some examples are glass in a bowl of soup, a pebble in a spinach salad, caustic acid in a beer bottle, and a nail served in food.

Yet, what if the object served is natural and causes injury? Examples include an olive pit in a martini,[12] a cherry stone in a slice of cherry pie,[13] a chicken bone in a chicken pot pie,[14] and a pearl in a can of processed oysters that resulted in broken teeth.[15] The courts are not so quick to place responsibility upon the restaurant in such instances. The one who consumes the items should exercise some care because he or she would be on notice that these items could be found. Yet, in all of the cases mentioned, the injured patron was able to recover.

Fish bones in fish, chicken bones in fried chicken, and clam shells or fish bones in fish gumbo or clam chowder are clearer examples of the type of cases in which the courts place greater responsibility upon the one consuming the food.

However, in some situations a patron could not be expected to be looking for a natural substance in a food. A cherry pit in cherry ice cream is an example. Although the pit is natural to the cherry, it should not have survived the processing of the ice cream. The question of whether the one who consumed the ice cream acted reasonably while eating it was held to be a jury question and the case that had been appealed was returned to the lower court for determination of that issue.[16]

Thus, two tests are applied by the courts:

1. the *natural test*
2. the *reasonable-expectation test*

The latter places a higher standard of care upon the patron. Regardless of the legal theories, however, they place upon the restaurant operator an increased duty of care.

The U. S. Department of Agriculture (USDA) has defined a "natural product" as one that contains no artificial ingredients and was processed minimally. The courts have discussed this matter time and again.

If a part of food, such as a walnut shell, could not reasonably be expected to be found in walnut ice cream, for example, the manufacturer, as well as the server of that ice cream, may incur legal liability for injuries that may result from consuming it. Oklahoma follows this rule.[17] California has just adopted it.[18]

"'Natural' refers to bones and other substances natural to the product served and does not encompass substances such as mold, boutulinus bacteria or substances (like rat flesh or cow eyes) not natural to the preparation of the product served."[19]

In *Kilpatrick v. Holiday Inns, Inc., et al.,*[20] the court held that, in light of the above case, *vibrio cholerae non-1* is not a natural substance in raw oysters but, rather, a deadly bacteria that is foreign to it. The hotel was held liable to the injured patron because the bacteria was considered to be a foreign substance.

The case that created the "foreign-natural" test is *Mix v. Ingerson Candy Co.*[21] States that follow this rule include Ohio,[22] North Carolina,[23] and Louisiana.[24]

States that follow the "reasonable expectation" test in place of the "foreign-natural" test include Maryland,[25] Texas,[26] and California.[27]

Perhaps the most frequent basis of legal liability for breach of warranty is found in foodborne illness cases. Previously, this was called "food poisoning," until it was decided that the food itself did not cause injury. Rather, it was the bacteria that the food carried.

FOODBORNE ILLNESS

If food contains bacteria because of improper preparation or lack of sanitation and illness results to patrons, the restaurant is going to find itself in court and in the newspapers. Jury Verdict Research reports that the average recovery exceeds $70,000 per case. Such illness can come from food handlers who have an intestinal organism known as shigella. It is similar in effect to salmonella, but its source is the human body and not food. When suits are brought, the burden is on the plaintiff to show that the illness was carried by the food. In the case of shigella poisoning, the evidence almost always will be devastating to the restaurant. Symptoms include diarrhea, nausea, abdominal pain, and vomiting, and the presence of the bacteria can be established by laboratory testing. The organisms can be carried in the patron's body for weeks after the food consumption and can be passed on to others by physical contact. This increases the legal risk to the restaurant because others may gain the right to sue.

At a Southland Motor Inn in Tulsa, Oklahoma, a patron dined one evening, became violently ill the next day, and was admitted to a hospital. The diagnosis made (in error) was that he had colitis. In the meantime, the innkeeper was notified of an outbreak of foodborne illness among guests. Tests made of the employee who had prepared the food showed that that person had shigella. The inn made no attempt to notify the patron and others of that fact.

The patron sued and recovered $375,000 compensatory damages and $500,000 in punitive damages. Both awards were upheld on appeal. The court ruled that the evidence showed that the inn

> . . . had repeatedly violated health department regulations by permitting unsanitary conditions to exist in the restaurant. . . ; there was also evidence that [the inn] took no steps to notify guests that they had been exposed to shigella, apparently because [the inn] feared that the publicity would hurt its business. We believe that this evidence justifies submitting the issue to the jury and that the jury could have found that [the inn] acted in reckless and conscious disregard for the rights of [the patron].[28]

When a restaurant is sued for foodborne illness, a "food history" of the plaintiff must be obtained. Although patrons try to place the blame for their illness on the most recent meal that they ate, the actual source may be in the past because of incubation periods. If such facts can be presented to the jury, the restaurant has raised a viable defense to the claim.

Another common cause of food poisoning is salmonella. Sources of this microorganism include chicken and raw eggs. (Pasteurizing eggs prevents this.) Complaints from those affected include diarrhea, dizziness, fainting, nausea, stomach pains and vomiting. Carriers of salmonella, such as restaurant employees, may show no signs themselves, but the poisoning is still "cast-off" (shed) into the bodily wastes of the carriers. The wastes can be passed on to others by failure of food handlers to wash their hands adequately, as one example. Some actual case situations follow.

Case Number One

A chef at a restaurant kept sauce at room temperature instead of placing it in refrigeration. As a result, twenty-six customers developed staphylococcus intoxication, and one customer suffered permanent paralysis. The cost was in excess of $1 million, and the restaurant was closed permanently as a result of this case.

Case Number Two

A restaurant manager decided to use home-canned peppers. As a result, fifty-two persons were hospitalized with botulism; the restaurant was closed for more than five months, and the costs went over half a million dollars.

When a lawsuit claiming injury from a foodborne illness is brought against a restaurant, it is proper to allow evidence to go to the jury to show:

1. how the patron ordered the food
2. how the food was delivered to the patron
3. how the food had been stored before preparation
4. how the food had been prepared after being ordered
5. how others who consumed the same food suffered no adverse effects[29]

Case Number Three

"Elsie" had been released from the hospital earlier in the day in question. She then had dinner at the L.K. Restaurant & Motel and became very ill. The state health inspector had cited the restaurant for food infractions twenty-nine days earlier. The report contained no mention of illness resulting to patrons at that time. The issue at trial was whether the inspector's report had "probative value." If so, the jury could consider it in deciding whether the restaurant should be held liable for the illness. The court held that the report was too remote and that it would not allow the jury to know of it. This decision was sustained on appeal.[30]

To defend such cases, the restaurant must produce witnesses to testify to the following in addition to the above:

1. how the food was handled when it arrived from suppliers
2. how the food then was stored at the inn
3. how the food was prepared at the inn
4. how the food was served when ordered by patrons (Such servings are known in restaurant language as "covers.")

A patron has become hospitalized after eating at the restaurant. The manager now is visiting that person at the hospital. Some legal suggestions for the manager to follow are:

1. Let the ill person tell her or his story.
2. Do not introduce symptoms of the illness into the discussion.
3. Do not say "I'm sorry our food made you ill." (That is an "admission against interest.")
4. Do not say: "Don't worry—we'll pay all of your hospital bills." (Those words create a contract the courts will enforce.)
5. It is permissible to say, "We're sorry you're not feeling well, and we hope you feel better soon."

After such a visit, the manager should take the time to record the time, date, and the conversation.

Liability to Whom?

If A invites B to have dinner at Restaurant X, and B is injured by a foreign substance in the food, is Restaurant X responsible even though A intended to pay for the food? The courts answer this question in the affirmative, holding that there is an implied warranty to furnish suitable food to both of them, even though the contract is with A alone.[31]

Duty to Comply with State and Federal Statutes

Other state and federal laws must be complied with. Two examples of state statutes and one federal law will illustrate. Two have to do with food and food preparation, the third with entertainment.

Microwave Ovens

The wide usage of microwave ovens has resulted in statutes to protect those who might suffer harm because of their use. These statutes can be local, state, or federal. The following is an example of a state statute.

> Any restaurant, hotel, motel, dining room, hospital, snack bar or any food dispensing facility utilizing a microwave oven shall prominently display a public notice in the following words:
> "NOTICE TO PERSONS HAVING HEART PACEMAKERS: This Establishment Uses a Microwave Oven."
> The state director of health shall be responsible for administering this section. He may delegate the duties to any county boards of health or combined local boards of health.
> The state health department shall purchase such notices assuring a uniform size and color of the notices.
> Any person, firm or corporation who shall violate any provision of this section shall be guilty of a misdemeanor, and, upon conviction thereof, shall be fined not less than one hundred dollars nor more than five hundred dollars.

Accuracy-in-Menus

The states desire to make certain that the food and drink served to the buying public is of a proper quality. An example is found in Accuracy-in-Menu laws (AIM), also known as "Truth in Menus." A policy memorandum issued in Los Angeles County started this movement. The Los Angeles memo first sets forth the goal of the policy: to guarantee that buyers of food and drink get what they are supposed to. This is followed by examples of violations and concludes with enforcement provisions. Some examples are adulteration of products, hamburger not meeting specifications, imitation hamburger being offered as real hamburger, and dairy products not meeting specifications. Other guidelines are provided. "If food is prepared in the restaurant kitchen from a recipe under conditions and with ingredients similar to those used at home, the food may be advertised as 'home-style' or 'homemade style'." Consequently food that is not being so prepared cannot be advertised in that manner.

Some states and many cities have such menu laws. An Albany, New York, restaurant was fined because its "fresh brook trout" had in fact been refrigerated. A Long Island restaurant was caught serving "Long Island duckling" that had come from Wisconsin. (In both of the above instances there also would be a breach of the express warranties.) When the issue of accuracy-in-menus came up in New Jersey, the state inn association published AIM guidelines and suggested that members submit copies of their menus so they could be screened to see if they were in compliance with AIM requirements. The National Restaurant Association also has an AIM code. As part of this movement, it must be remembered that disclaimers and warnings on menus are not out of order. In addition to alerting patrons to possible dangers, such disclaimers also assist in describing the food and drink being offered at the restaurant. That is what the AIM laws are all about.

Related to AIM is a trend to require restaurants to make information about ingredients and nutritional value of the food available to patrons. McDonald's Corporation began a voluntary disclosure program in 1986 in New York. States that now have this requirement by statute include California, New Jersey, New York, Pennsylvania, and Texas. A McDonald's outlet in Orange County, California, got into legal difficulty when it advertised that it sold "fresh orange juice" when in fact the juice used had been frozen. The principles of the National Restaurant Association often are cited in such cases.

AIM statutes follow similar patterns. The following is adapted from a document prepared by the National Restaurant Association.

1. *Brand names.* Examples include "Sanka," "Chase and Sanborn Coffee," and "Miracle Whip." If brand names are used on a menu, the product served must comply with the brand name. A ketchup bottle with a brand name, placed on a table, cannot be refilled with generic ketchup.

2. *Food preparation.* Strict compliance is a must when a menu contains words such as "fried in butter," "charcoal-broiled," and "barbecued."

3. *Merchandising terms.* This has to do with "puffing," such as, "Our prime rib is the best in town." Using such terminology creates an express warranty under the UCC, Article 2. Phrases of this nature should be avoided in menus.

4. *Nutritional claims.* Terms such as "sugar-free" must be strictly complied with. This statement also is a warranty under Article 2, and if a diabetic suffers injury from a breach of such a warranty, legal liability could follow.

5. *Points of origin.* If "Wisconsin cheese," "Alaskan King Crab," and "Gulf Shrimp" are offered on the menu, the source must comply with what the menu says.

6. *Preservation of food.* The restaurant industry has well developed standards, such as freezing, frying above a given temperature, and chilling, and these procedures must be complied with.

7. *Price.* If extra charges are to be made, such as for extra ice, the menu must state this.

8. *Product identification.* If there is a substitution of products, such as powdered eggs for fresh eggs, the menu must state this.

9. *Quality.* State and federal laws both address the matter of quality of eggs, dairy products, ground beef, and more. When terms such as "Grade A," "Choice," and "Fancy," are used on menus, the product served must comply.

10. *Quantity.* A "16-ounce steak" is one that weighed one pound before it was cooked. A "three-egg omelet" requires three eggs, not two. "All you can eat" has a clear meaning and must be honored if that statement is made on the menu.

11. *Visual presentations.* Menus that contain pictures, almost always in color, must display accurately what will be served. An example of a violation would be a picture on the menu showing a single thick slice of beef when what is served are several small slices of beef.

An attempt to enact an accuracy-in-menu statute in Nevada was defeated in 1988. The state motel and hotel association argued that the Federal Trade Commission regulations on truth-in-advertising preempted the area, and the state legislature agreed. In states and counties where accuracy-in-menu rules have been adopted, the content of menus at restaurants also falls under federal control.

State statutes that prohibit defrauding of innkeepers also become involved with menus. All of the states have statutes that make it a crime to defraud a business for the cost of goods, services, food, and fuel. Menus become involved in the fraud statutes. Wyoming Laws, Chapter 44, Section 1, describes what activities shall constitute fraud:

> (b) "Agreement with such public establishment" means any written or verbal agreement as to the price to be charged for, and the acceptance of, food, beverage, service or accommodations, where the price to be charged therefor is printed on a menu or schedule of rates shown to or made available by such public establishment to the patron, and shall include the acceptance of such food, beverage, service or accommodations for which a reasonable charge is made.[32]

A New York state law requires labeling of imitation cheese, as well as requiring notice on menus that imitation cheese products are being served. A federal court struck down the labeling requirements on the ground that it was in conflict with its federal counterpart. The requirement of such notice on menus was upheld, however, on appeal. The court said the lack of action by Congress was ". . . at least a sturdy buffer against the Commerce Clause."[33]

The California legislature passed a bill requiring restaurants to give a warning that those who eat raw oysters from Mexican warm Gulf water may be subject to injury or death from that consumption. This warning must be given to all members of the "at-risk population." Oysters from cold-water areas are not covered, including California, Oregon, Washington, and East Coast sources of oysters. Oysters from the Gulf of Mexico, labeled "hot," are covered. It is known that "hot oysters" can be tainted with vibrio cholera bacteria (*vibrio unlnifificus*). Most California restaurants no longer serve raw oysters from the Gulf of Mexico. Where such oysters are served, warnings must be placed on "table tents" and on menus. Bacteria are carried by all raw oysters, whether the source of the oysters is hot or cold water oceans. Failure to so warn on menus can give rise to strict liability.[34]

The same is true of toxins carried by red snappers throughout the Pacific and amerjack in Hawaii and surrounding areas. This toxin, ciguatoxin, is found in fish that feed on coral reefs, as well as in other fish that consume the reef feeders. The toxin is produced by a free-swimming dinoflagellate that attaches itself to algae growing on coral reefs. The small fish that feed on it are, in turn, consumed by larger fish. The danger is that, as the toxin passes up the food chain, it becomes more concentrated. Its existence has been known since Spanish explorers in the area of Cuba described it in the 1550s. It was found in the South Pacific by Captain James Cook, who reported it in the 1770s. After the famous "Mutiny on the Bounty," the toxin came close to killing Captain Bligh and the ship's physician in 1789.

Early in 1994, the Food and Drug Administration implemented regulations designed to protect the public from tainted seafood. A system was created called Hazard Analysis Critical Control Point (HACCP) inspections, which calls for scientific inspections of all seafood from its source to the dining table. The 5,000 seafood-processing plants in the United States have to be able to prove that they handled seafood properly and that they tested for contaminants or pollution. This proof is required when cases come to court involving injury or death from seafood consumption.

The Food and Drug Administration revealed regulations designed to prevent contaminated or tainted seafood from reaching the American public. These rules place the responsibility on seafood processors to assure that seafood offered for sale:

1. is chilled properly
2. is cleaned properly
3. comes from clean water
4. is handled properly

In addition to the laws of food service, the operators of restaurants and bars must know the laws that regulate the playing of music. Let's first find out what role 17 United States Code 101, as amended, plays when the manager wants to use recorded or live music for entertainment of patrons at the restaurant or bar.

FEDERAL COPYRIGHT STATUTES

The federal copyright law can cause legal problems at restaurants and bars where music is played. Figure 21.1 gives an account of one case. To understand this, it is necessary to learn something about the legal rights of composers, publishers, and performers of music.

First, copyright laws protect composers and publishers just as they protect authors, poets, and others who produce creative material. For a restaurant to have the legal right to use music in a "public performance for profit," royalties must be paid to the composers and publishers of the music.

FIGURE 21.1 Account of lawsuit involving copyright.

Bogie's Faces Lawsuit

A New York music licensing organization has filed suit in U.S. District Court against Bogie's, . . . charging the Las Vegas nightclub with violation of federal copyright laws.

The suit, filed by Broadcast Music Inc., alleges that BMI-copyrighted songs were performed at Bogie's without the company's authorization in violation of the U.S. Copyright Act.

The company is seeking statutory damages in addition to attorney's fees and court costs.

Las Vegas Sun, April 26, 1984, p. 8C

To facilitate collecting these royalties, the composers and publishers belong to performing arts societies, such as the American Society of Composers, Authors, and Publishers (ASCAP), and Broadcast Music, Incorporated (BMI). These organizations use the contract to grant the legal right to use the works of their members. In this way, the composers and publishers receive royalties from the vast network of radio and television stations and other organizations that play the music for profit.

The courts have held that playing music for the enjoyment of customers in a restaurant is a public performance for profit. This makes the operator liable for the payment of royalties. Some choices are available to meet this mandate of federal law. We will look at four of them.

1. One simply may decide to forgo music.
2. If it is desirable to provide the music, one way is to play the music of only one organization. In this manner, a contract can be entered into, bringing the matter into compliance with the law.
3. One may use a programmed system such as MUZAK. The operator of the restaurant pays a fee to MUZAK (or other system operator) which, in turn, pays the royalties to the national organizations.
4. One may use "jukebox" or other systems that are exempt from copyright laws. To gain this exemption, however, these systems must be owned by someone other than the person who uses them. (The owner must pay royalties.)

In *Twentieth Century Music Corp. et al. v. Aiken*, the U.S. Supreme Court held that small restaurant operators (1055 square feet in the Aiken case) could use "homestyle" speakers to broadcast music without liability for royalties. On the other hand, if an elaborate system of speakers is used, the courts hold that this is a copyright infringement.[35]

A two-part test is used to decide if the federal law has been violated.

1. There has to be a "transmission." If a restaurant operator buys an audiotape and plays it at home for her own entertainment, there would be no transmission. If she plays the same audio at the restaurant for her patrons, there would be.
2. There must be a "performance for profit." In most restaurants, no charge is made for the music, yet the courts hold that it is a "performance for profit" because the charges made for the food and drink include the entertainment.

"Jukebox police," also called "loggers," are people who work for Broadcast Music, Inc., (BMI), and the American Society of Composers, Artists, and Publishers (ASCAP). Their job is to find persons who make profits from music without paying royalties to composers and performing artists. Favorite targets of loggers are bars and restaurants. At Joey's Bar and Grill in Charleston, West Virginia, a logger made a playlist that resulted in the bar owner paying $12,000 to keep from going to court. The owner said, "I had no idea that the machine [that played the music] had to have a license on it."

HOUSE RULES AND OTHER LEGAL ITEMS

Because restaurants do not have a common-law duty to receive, they can create and place into use reasonable rules of conduct. An example is the "no shoes, no service" policy seen around the nation. On a higher level, one finds the dress codes at better restaurants. If patrons fail to meet the requirements of these rules, they can be excluded and service refused. The courts enforce in-house rules and do not extend to would-be patrons at restaurants the same privileges they do to guests at hotels.

California law requires that each restaurant post first-aid instructions on how a choking patron can be provided assistance. The statute does not require the restaurant to apply such aid, but the restaurant must, of course, call for outside assistance promptly. If that is done and even if no first aid is given and death results, the courts will exonerate the restaurant from liability.[36] There must be a firm rule as to whether first aid is to be attempted. Aside from the humanitarian aspects, legal advice is required when making this decision. If aid is provided, proper training must be given to ensure that the aid is carried out properly. If the aid is attempted and the patron dies, the restaurant has a legal problem. The estate of the deceased probably will claim that the attempted aid was not carried out properly.

In states or cities that have adopted the Restatement of Torts position on patrons choking in restaurants, as drafted by Professor Prosser, restaurants not only must summon medical assistance within a reasonable time but also must provide first-aid assistance until emergency help arrives. In such states or cities, specified employees must be given first-aid training in CPR and know how to make proper use of the Heimlich maneuver. It would be a good house policy to provide this training to designated persons and have this duty set forth in their job descriptions. The legal danger in jurisdictions that require that restaurant employees be trained to handle choking patrons is that such a trained person may not be available when needed and patron injury or death may result.

In Wyoming, the rule is that restaurants do not have a duty to provide this training to employees and employees have no duty to provide assistance, if, in their discretion, they decide not to do so.[37]

Restaurant No-Shows

Although hotels have had to contend with no-show reservation holders for decades, the problem has not been so pronounced at restaurants. Yet, it happens. Restaurants who hold tables for those who do not show lose income. As a result, there is an increasing willingness to sue defaulting persons for the breach of contracts.

Illegal Immigrants

Another house rule addresses whether to hire illegal immigrants. If immigration agents have a search warrant, they can proceed with the search for such immigrants. If the search is warrantless, under the Fourth Amendment the operator can refuse to allow the search. If the operator consents to the search, that satisfies the Fourth Amendment.

Searching for illegal immigrants is a criminal matter and must be distinguished from an administrative search, such as a health inspection. In a criminal search, someone ultimately may go to jail or be deported. In an administrative search, the result is a reprimand or a civil fine. A warrant is required in the criminal search unless permission is given, but none is required in an administrative search.

Restaurant operators at times may want to assist certain illegal immigrants in gaining lawful status. In doing this, there could be a tax advantage. The manager at Ernie's Diner, located in the lobby of the No-Show Inn, decides to assist an illegal immigrant employee in getting her immigration visa. Although the costs for this process can be as much as $10,000 per person for court and attorney fees, this expenditure may be a plus in the long run. To encourage this, an income tax deduction is allowed for "ordinary and business expenses" for the restaurant, giving the operator a tax deduction. If, however, these costs are paid to the immigrant with instructions to pay them over, the immigrant will have that money taxed as income. Thus, such payments should not be made directly to the employee when assisting illegal immigrants.

Meals Furnished to Employees

When the restaurant furnishes meals to employees during working hours, the value of such meals is not subject to social security, federal unemployment, and workers' compensation taxes. On the reverse side, this value is subject to the income tax law and must be reported on the tax returns of the restaurant employees.

SUMMARY

An ever growing body of law (federal, state and local) applies to restaurant operations. This is true whether such establishments are part of a hotel, motel, or inn, or are free standing such as the many fast food operations that dot the country. However, the legal duties that courts place on restaurant operators are not the same as those that are placed on inns. This is true even if the same person operates the inn with the restaurant located within it. The innkeeper thus has certain legal duties when serving food and other duties when bedding down guests for the night.

Legal duties of restaurants and inns have common grounds in regard to safe premises, and protection of persons and their property, but the similarity breaks down on the question of the duty to receive. This common law duty applies only to inns, even though they might also have a duty to provide food.

In modern food service, warranties, both express and implied, are two primary legal obligations that must be met. Implied warranties are provided by law, and there is no need for them to be expressed to the customer. Express warranties, however, are expressed to the customer in one form or another.

In many cases in this century, the courts have been called upon to decide claims by those who have been injured or killed while consuming food products in restaurants. Two rules prevail in these situations. The first is the "foreign/natural" rule: the second is the "reasonable expectation" test. In the foreign/natural situation the courts look to see if the item in the food that caused the injury was natural or was foreign to it. A small stone in a bowl of bean soup would be "foreign" to the bean soup. A fish bone in a bowl of fish chowder would be natural to the soup.

The second rule concerns what one can reasonably expect to find in the food. A walnut shell is natural to the source of walnut ice cream, and thus is a natural and not a foreign substance. Yet one eating walnut ice cream cannot reasonably expect to find a piece of walnut shell in such ice cream. Its presence would be a breach of warranty under the reasonable expectation test.

QUESTIONS

1. Why does the common-law duty to receive not apply to restaurants?
2. What is required to make a restaurant dress code legal?
3. What is the legal difference between a *tort* and an *accident* in liability insurance language?
4. What is the problem with advertising frozen food as "fresh"? Isn't all frozen food fresh to begin with?
5. Does the federal copyright law apply to in-room video shows where royalties are not paid to the copyright holders and a fee is charged to the viewer? If no fee is charged, might a court find that the fee is included in the room rate and that royalties are due the copyright holder?
6. "Privity of contract" is defined as "that connection or relationship which exists between two or more contracting parties" (*Black's Law Dictionary*, Fifth Edition, p. 1079). Under what circumstances does this old legal doctrine become involved in the operation of a restaurant?
7. The duty to receive at common law did not extend to restaurants. Would the operation of modern restaurants be different if it had? What major difference would we notice?
8. The courts in the United States are beginning to develop the idea that the common-law duty of innkeepers to receive should be extended to restaurants. What will be a benefit to travelers if this happens? What will be a detriment to restaurant keepers?
9. The legal standards that must be met when serving food and drinks for a price are set forth in Article 2 of the UCC. Why did the drafters use so much detail in these laws? What problems were they trying to cure?
10. True or false: If a substance is natural to a particular food, such as a clam shell in clam chowder, injury caused by its presence is excused automatically as a matter of law.

NOTES

1. *Alpaugh v. Wolverton*, 184 Va. 943, 36 S.E. 2d 906.
2. Chapter 16, Article 6, Section 3 (1966).
3. Opinion, West Virginia Attorney General, January 9, 1970.
4. 651.050, 651.060 and 651.070.
5. Title II, Civil Rights Act of 1964, 42 U.S.C. 2000, as amended in 1972.
6. In New York, for example, see McKinney's Supp. 1972, section 296(2).

7. 92 Daily Journal DAR 12031 (California 1992).

8. Weekly newsletter, *Motel/Hotel Insider,* May 19, 1980.

9. *Gene's Restaurant v. Nationwide,* 548 A. 2d 246 (Pennsylvania 1988).

10. *Woodward v. Hardee's,* 643 F. Supp. 691 (Missouri 1986).

11. *Rinkmasters, Inc., v. City of Utica,* 348 N.Y.S. 2d 940, 13 UCC Rep. 797 (New York 1972).

12. *Hochberg v. O'Donnell's Restaurant Inc.,* 272 A. 2d 846, (DC App. 1977).

13. *Musso v. Picadilly Cafeterias, Inc.,* 178 So. 2d 421 (La. App. 1965).

14. *Mix v. Ingersoll Candy Co.,* 6 Col. 2d 674, 59 P. 2d 144 (Colorado 1936).

15. *O'Dell v. DeJeans Packing Co.,* 24 UCC Rep. 311 (Okl. App. July 1978).

16. *William v. Braum,* 543 P. 2d 799 (Oklahoma 1974).

17. *William v. Braun, supra.* n. 16.

18. *Mexicali Rose et al., Petitioners v. The Superior Court of Alameda County, Respondent Jack A. Clark, Real Party in Interest,* 1 Cal. 4th 617 (California January 1992).

19. 1 Cal 4th at page 630, footnote 5, majority opinion.

20. 92 Daily Journal DAR 12031 (California 1992).

21. Cal. 2d 674, 681, 683 (California 1936).

22. *Allen v. Grafton,* 164 N.E. 22 167 (Ohio 1960).

23. *Coffee v. Standard Brands, Inc.,* 226 S.E. 2d 534 (North Carolina 1976).

24. *Title v. Pontchartrain Hotel,* 449 So. 2d 677 (Louisiana 1984).

25. *Bryer v. Rath Packing Company,* 156 A. 2d 442 (Maryland 1959).

26. *Matthews v. Campbell Soup,* 535 S.W. 2d 786 (Texas 1974), and Jim Dandy Fast Foods Inc., 536 S.W. 2d 786 (Texas 1976).

27. *Mexicali Rose, supra* n. 18.

28. *Averitt v. Southland Motor Inn,* 720 F. 2d 1178 (Oklahoma 1983).

29. *Orlando v. Herco,* 505 A. 2d 308 (Pennsylvania 1986).

30. *Gallegher v. L. K. Restaurant & Motel,* 481 So. 2d 562 (Florida 1986).

31. *Conklin v. Hotel Waldorf Astoria,* 5 Misc. 2d 496, 169 N.Y.S. 2d 205 (N.Y. City Ct. 1957).

32. Laws 1969, Ch. 44, section 1.

33. *Grocery Manufacturers v. Gerace,* 84-6141 (Second Circuit, Feb. 14, 1985, New York).

34. *Kilpatrick v. Superior,* 227 Cal. Rptr. (California 1991).

35. *Twentieth Century Music Corporation, et al, v. George Aiken,* 422 U.S. 151, 95 S. CT. 2040, 1975.

36. *Breaux v. Gino's,* 200 Cal. Rptr. 260 (California 1984).

37. *Drew v. LeJay's Sportsman's Cafe, Inc.,* 806 P. 2d 301 (Wyoming 1991).

Bars, Lounges, Taverns, Pubs, and Dram Shops

OVERVIEW

RESTAURANTS ALMOST ALWAYS have a bar or tavern adjunct. The primary legal topic that has emerged in recent years in reference to bars is that of liability for the sale of alcohol.

A BRIEF HISTORY

Historically, there were three classes of persons or businesses that sold alcoholic beverages to travelers and others:

1. The "taverner," the Jewish seller of wines. This ancient occupation gave us the word "tavern."
2. The "publican," the English and Greek brewer and seller of beer. From this we get the word "pub." This is "the most compressed piece of shorthand in the world. The village pub is a drinking house, a parish parliament, and a club rolled into one," wrote Timothy Finn, in *The Camara Beer Guide.*[1]
3. The "dram shop," where hard liquors were sold by measure. Courts have adopted this term to describe the statutes and case decisions that make bar operators liable for injuries, loss, or death caused by persons who have become intoxicated by illegal liquor sales.

The past 1,000 years are replete with accounts of the sale and consumption of alcoholic beverages and the enactment of laws to control that consumption. The royal courts of earlier times were constantly on the move, traveling 20 to 35 kilometers per day. Hundreds and perhaps thousands of persons accompanied those rulers. In *Annalista Saxo,* it was reported that in the year 968, a royal court in Europe consumed "ten tuns of wine, and as many tuns of beer," and "one thousand pigs and sheep." It was said in this year that "many an involuntary host saw his wine cellar depleted." There was a demand for drink, and the taverner, publican, and dram shop provided it.

In the tenth century, under King Edgar, drinking vessels were required to have eight pegs placed inside of them at equal distances apart. If one would drink past a peg in one draught, there was a fine of one penny. The old saying of "taking one down a peg or two" came from this old edict. One of these tankards was found in recent years at the Glastonbury Abbey. It could hold two quarts of liquid and was made of oak wood.

The "Assize of Bread and Ale" was held in 1267 under the auspices of Henry III. The price for good ale was set at a penny and a half per gallon. "Weak ale" was to be sold at one penny per gallon.

The laws regulating the operation of taverns, pubs, and dram shops go back many centuries and have been associated historically with the laws of merchants. The Magna Carta of 1215, for example, discloses the interest of the British in promoting the activities of merchants as they went about their business both within and outside of the island nation. They regulated the activities of those merchants and developed a system of courts (*lex mercatoria*) and enacted laws to make certain that value was given for value.

An example is:

> There shall be standard measures of wine, ale and corn throughout the kingdom. There shall also be a standard width of dyed cloth, russet, and haberjet, namely two ells [yards] within the selvedges [the specially woven edges]. Weights are to be standardized similarly.[2]

Here, we see the forerunner of our weights and measures laws.

When Columbus discovered America, there were more than 300 brewers of beer in the city of London. Regulations were enacted to ensure that casks of beer held the amount they were supposed to. Casks at that time—or "barrels," as we know them today—were made by "coopers." It was known then as the "cooperage industry," and the laws required the coopers to place marks on the casks to identify who had made them. By 1500, this industry was in decline because of the introduction of glass bottles and the invention of machines that could create cask staves.

In 1531, the English Parliament passed an act that prohibited brewers from making the casks in which their own beer and ale was sold. This act stated:

> Whereas the ale brewers and beer brewers of this realm of England have used, and daily do use, for their own singular lucre, profit and gain, to making in their own houses, their barrels, kilderkins and firkins of much less quantity than they ought to be, to great hurt, prejudice and damage of the King, liege, people, and contrary to divers Acts, Statutes, Ancient Laws and customs heretofore, made, had, and used, and to the destruction of the poor craft and mystery of coopers."[3]

The standard for beer casks in those years was 36 gallons, and ale casks, 32 gallons. Ale was much stronger than beer, which was hopped and also sweeter. A character in Green's *Tu Quoque* (an Elizabethan comedy), Sir Lionel Rash, said: "I have sent my daughter this morning as far as Pimlico to fetch a draught of Derby ale that it may fetch a colour into her cheeks." Derby was noted for its brewers.

In 1728, the English Parliament created an act that prohibited wine to be imported in "flasks, bottles, or small casks." The purpose of this law was to prevent smuggling. The statute was repealed in 1802. At that time, wine bottles as we know them today were becoming popular, and thus was born the corkscrew.

After the turn of the nineteenth century, the English laws were directed toward seals. An early 1900 law required that bottles of beer have a seal over the top. The alleged purpose was to keep children from taking a swig. Those early laws also were concerned with labels.

The best known of all beer labels is the Bass red triangle for its pale ale. An executive of the brewery sat all night on the steps of the registrar's office when the first trademarks were being allocated, and thus the Bass red triangle is Trade Mark No. 1. Its diamond trademark was the second entry, and became Trade Mark No. 2. The trademark achieved further fame when a bottle of Bass showing the red triangle was included in a painting dated 1821, entitled "Bar at the Folies Bergere," by Edouard Manet.

The British Licensing Act of 1902 required something that is related to our modern dram-shop laws. For centuries the drinking places were used to post proclamations, advertising, and legal notices because they were the places where the local population gathered. One of the notices that had to be posted under the 1902 law had to do with habitual drunkards.

> At this time it was customary, when a person was convicted of being an habitual drunkard, to pin up a notice in the public house where he or she had been arrested and on this notice would be a front and side view picture rather like those photographs taken of prisoners today. This was posted as a warning that the person was banned from drinking in that pub and, in some cases, in any pub in the district for a period of up to three years. The recent new regulation (1982) known as the "Ban the Thug" Act, endeavors to emulate the regulations of eighty years ago, and one wonders why the earlier law was ever allowed to lapse.[4]

Just after World War I, an alcoholic beverage known as absinthe was being sold in France. This was a strong spirit marinated in wormwood. It could cause blindness, impotence, alcoholism, and death. In 1919, France banned its consumption.

STATE CONTROL

Today, the power to control the sale of intoxicating liquors resides solely with each state. This came about as a result of the Eighteenth Amendment, which prohibited "the manufacture, sale, or transportation of intoxicating liquors within, the importation thereof into, or the exportation thereof from the United States and all territory subject to the jurisdiction thereof for beverage purposes." Ratified in 1919 and effective in 1920, this amendment opened up a period of lawlessness in the nation. The ultimate result was its repeal in 1933 by the Twenty-First Amendment, which states: "The transportation or importation into any State, Territory, or possession of the United States for delivery or use therein of intoxicating liquors, *in violation of the laws thereof*, is hereby prohibited." (Emphasis added.) The sale of alcohol became a privilege that had to be granted by the states. Thus, the states may regulate or suppress such sale, and such regulation or suppression in no way interferes with any rights of citizenship.[5]

The sale of alcoholic beverages is controlled by the states in a variety of ways:

1. By the rules embodied in the Uniform Commercial Code, Article 2, Sales, especially the law of warranties.
2. By the common-law rules of negligence.
3. By the rules laid down by state statutes including alcohol beverage control laws, "dram shop" laws, and laws as established by state court decisions.

Uniform Commercial Code

Under the UCC, in all fifty states, the "serving for value of food or drink to be consumed on the premises or elsewhere is a sale."[6] Thus, "unless excluded or modified, a warranty that the goods shall be merchantable is implied in a contract for their sale if the seller is a merchant with respect to goods of that kind. . . . Goods to be merchantable must be at least such as . . . are fit for the ordinary purposes for which such goods are used."[7]

All operators of taverns and bars and other sellers of intoxicating liquors, in package or otherwise, are merchants under the Uniform Commercial Code. As this law makes the serving of drink a "sale," warranties arise that the seller must meet. In this manner, the law provides standards for such sales and serves as a liquor-sales control measure. The UCC lays down one set of guidelines to control liquor sales, and common law lays down the other.

Common-Law Rules of Negligence

The legal theory of common-law negligence has been used in court successfully time and again to recover damages from the sellers of alcoholic beverages where the one who consumed the drinks caused injury to himself or herself or to third parties. In a Michigan case,[8] recovery was allowed against a bar that had served alcoholic beverages to an alcoholic who subsequently fell to his death from a bridge while attempting to return home. By making the sales on the night of his death, the seller was negligent, or had engaged willingly in misconduct by making the sales. Either activity will give rise to a common-law action for the loss sustained, and the court so held.

The New Jersey Supreme Court recognized a common-law action for negligence where a tavern served alcoholic beverages to a minor who subsequently caused injury to a third party.[9] Because it is important here, we will revisit negligence and how it is proved in court.

The plaintiff (the one bringing the action in court) must prove four elements in a negligence case:

1. that there was a duty owed to the person who was injured or killed
2. that there was a failure to live up to that duty
3. that the failure was the proximate (direct) cause of the injury that resulted
4. that monetary damages resulted as a consequence

Thus the courts have standards by which to test conduct to see if it is actionable or to see if it is excusable.

Standard of Care

The test is whether a reasonably prudent person at the time and place where drinks were served should have recognized an unreasonable risk or likelihood of harm to others. Thus the standard of care becomes the conduct of a reasonable person of ordinary prudence under the circumstances, and is a question of fact to be answered by a jury under instructions of the judge.

Serving alcoholic beverages to a person who is visibly intoxicated or to a minor does not meet the standard. If a jury determines that a reasonably prudent bartender, in similar circumstances, would have refused service, then the bartender (and the bar) was negligent.[10]

Courts have found liability when they believed a bartender should have known a person was intoxicated or a minor.[11] The standard of care has become strict.

> When alcoholic beverages are sold . . . to a minor or to an intoxicated person, the unreasonable risk of harm not only to the minor or the intoxicated person but also to members of the traveling public may readily be recognized and foreseen; this is particularly evident in current times when traveling by a car to and from the tavern is so commonplace and accidents resulting from drinking are so frequent.[12]

Drunk drivers are killing more than 20,000 people per year in the United States, injuring 600,000 more, and costing an estimated $20 billion per year in medical, burial, and other costs. Groups around the United States are directing massive efforts toward removing drunk drivers from the American highways. This movement has had an effect upon state courts and legislatures as well. "Many states have made penalties against drunken drivers more harsh, and numerous organizations have been formed to make people aware of the drunk driving problem." Some examples of the organizations that seek to stem this carnage are MADD (Mothers Against Drunk Driving), SADD (Students Against Drunk Driving), and RID-USA (Remove Intoxicated Drivers).

Liability has been found even in instances where drinks were refused but the intoxicated person was handled in such a manner that injury resulted. As an illustration, a would-be drinker was refused service because of his intoxicated condition. After the refusal, he asked if he could use the phone. There was an unlighted stairway on the way to the phone, and the bartender should have realized there was danger of the person falling down the stairs. No assistance was offered, however. The drunk fell down the stairs, and the jury gave him $25,000 in damages in a subsequent court action. The presence of negligence

> . . . is tested by whether the reasonably prudent person at the time and place should recognize and foresee an unreasonable risk or likelihood of harm or danger to others. And correspondingly, the standard of care is the conduct of the reasonable person of ordinary prudence under the circumstances.[13]

Negligence standing alone, however, cannot form the basis of recovery. Something else is required.

Proximate Cause

The negligent act complained of, and not some other act must be the direct or actual (proximate) cause of the injury.[14] Many cases have held that the sale of alcoholic beverages to an intoxicated person or to a minor was the proximate cause of injury to such persons, or others injured by them.[15]

Dram-Shop Laws

At common law, a dram shop was an establishment in which hard liquors were sold and consumed on the premises. From early centuries, the laws regulating such sales held that consumption of the alcohol and not the sale of it was the proximate cause of injury or death that resulted to third parties. That early view has been reversed in many states. These laws, court-created or statutory, are known today as "civil liability acts" and give rise to a presumption of negligence by the sale of alcoholic drinks to an intoxicated or a minor person. As one court said:

> In view of the fact that the statute prohibiting furnishing drinks to an . . . intoxicated person was adopted to protect the general public from injuries resulting from the excessive use of intoxicating liquor, a presumption of negligence on the part of the bar keeper arises when the statute is violated.[16]

Under these laws, the seller that causes or contributes to intoxication is held liable for injury to others by the intoxicated person. These laws protect against an assault by that person as well as injury or death from the use of an auto or other means. The laws also give a cause of action to the family of the injured or deceased person for lost income.

The liability imposed in the states that have these laws has wide variation. In some, the liability is severe; in others, less so. Bar operators thus must learn the nature and extent of legal liability of their particular states. This is especially so because these laws play a direct role in establishing closing times and policies that will be followed in the day-to-day operation of the bar. These laws can be by statute or by court decision.

If a modern tavern keeper allows a patron—minor or adult—to become intoxicated, or serves drinks to one who is intoxicated already, legal liability may arise if that person causes injury or death to another. The proximate cause of the injury or death would be the sale of the alcohol. If the intoxicated person had visited several bars, in some states the liability will be spread among those who sold alcoholic beverages to that person.

Suit can now be brought for losses sustained or, if the person is killed, by his or her spouse or children. In some states, an employer has a right to sue.

Some states place a limit on recovery; others do not. This, too, is important for the tavern keeper to know for insurance purposes.

These laws are beneficial to society because they force tavern keepers to train their bartenders to use caution and discretion when serving drinks. It is a situation in which a good bartender can reduce legal liability sharply.

Historically, the dram-shop laws did not provide protection for the one who becomes intoxicated and injures himself or herself. The reasoning was that the person would have to shoulder some of the blame for the injury or loss. Thus, the right to sue where an intoxicated person killed himself, but no one else, did not survive to the widow or children. The courts have looked at this common-law position.

The Michigan Court of Appeals held that a wrongful death complaint stated a common-law cause of action for gross negligence for willful, wanton, and intentional misconduct independent of the Michigan Dram-Shop Act, when it alleged that the death that occurred when the deceased fell from a bridge while intoxicated was caused by the actions of defendant tavern owner in selling alcohol to the deceased, even though he had been warned that the deceased was a hopeless alcoholic and the defendant had agreed not to serve him alcohol. The Court noted that an action under the Dram Shop Act was not available to the deceased's executrix, because it would not have been available to the deceased himself had he survived; the common-law action approved by the court, however, would be available to the intoxicated person himself.[17]

Violations of the dram-shop statutes are negligence *per se*. That is, violation of the statute itself is negligence without need for anything further. An example of such a law illustrates the nature of this principle. The New York General Obligation Law provides:

> . . . any person who shall be injured in person, property, means of support or otherwise by any intoxicated person, or by reason of the intoxication of any person against any person who shall, by unlawfully selling to or unlawfully assisting in procuring liquor for such intoxicated person, have caused or contributed to such intoxication . . . has the right to sue the seller of the intoxicants, and nothing further need be proven to recover.[18]

Normally, the dram-shop laws do not give a cause of action against the seller where injury results to the one who consumed the drinks and not a third party. Yet, such suits have been brought, as the Mitchell case illustrates.

Miss Mitchell, along with her escort, became intoxicated at a tavern. After passing out, she was helped to the auto of her companion, who then proceeded to run the auto into a wall. The court allowed recovery against the seller of the intoxicants and in favor of Mitchell. If she had bought the intoxicants for her companion, the result might have been different, but this was not the case.[19] (In Michigan and Illinois, the result of this case would have been different.)

Suits brought under the dram-shop laws are separate from wrongful-death actions and do not replace those laws. To say it another way, if a tavern operator is sued under the dram-shop laws for the death of a third party caused by the serving of drinks to a minor or an intoxicated person, that operator still can be prosecuted by the state for the wrongful death, which is a criminal offense.

An examination of the dram-shop laws of several states, follows. It can be seen that there are variations in these laws from state to state. See Figure 22.1.

Some State Laws

Arizona had followed the early common-law rule that a tavern could not be held responsible for death or injuries to third parties by having served alcohol to the one who caused the injuries or death. In 1983 the Supreme Court of Arizona rejected the common-law rule and joined the other dram-shop states.[20] Thus, Arizona has dram-shop liability by court decision rather than by legislative act.

In 1978 the California legislature abolished dram-shop liability, making it law that consumption of alcohol, and not the sale of it, is the proximate cause of injuries or death to third parties. What if a California bartender holds the car keys of a drinking patron with an understanding that the keys are not to be returned to the patron if he or she becomes intoxicated? If the keys then are released and a

FIGURE 22.1 A dram-shop law in action.

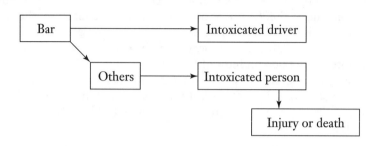

Source: *Carillo v. El Mirage Roadhouse*, 793 P. 2d 121 (California 1990).

third party is injured or killed by the intoxicated person, does liability attach? A California appellate court has ruled that such an arrangement is "a special relationship" and brings into play Section 324 A of the Restatement Second of Torts, creating a question of fact to be decided by a jury.[21] Other states reject dram-shop liability. The Supreme Court of Delaware had this to say about the vendor's liability for sale of alcohol to one injured by the intoxicated person:

> There is no cause of action, sounding in negligence or in willful and wanton conduct, against a commercial vendor of alcohol by a third party injured by actions of an intoxicated driver who was served by the vendor.[22]

The Florida statute grants an exemption to alcohol servers where the intoxicated person causes injury to a third person. The state law, however, provides an exception that states:

> A person who knowingly serves a person habitually addicted to the use of . . . alcoholic beverages may become liable for injury or damage caused by or resulting from the intoxication.[23]

For a Florida case in which the court found that the exception applied, see *Sobo v. Shamrock*.[24] In Florida also, if an underage person rides in an auto operated by an alcohol-impaired person who is also underage, the passenger is still a member of the protected class and cannot be held responsible, under comparative negligence rules, if injured.[25]

As with other American states, persons who suffer losses by intoxicated persons can sue those who sold the alcohol or contributed to the sale of the alcohol that caused the intoxication, if such sales were illegal. Illinois has an exception to this rule, however, called "complicity." If Patron A encourages Patron B to consume alcohol and if Patron B becomes intoxicated and causes loss to Patron A, there is no cause of action by Patron A against the seller of the alcoholic beverages because of the "complicity."[26]

Liquor licensees in Iowa can bring an action against other licensees for "contribution" [help in paying a dram shop judgment], if others contributed to the intoxication of the person who caused injury or death to third parties. The Iowa court ruled that Iowa code Sec. 123.92, which provides a cause of action for injured persons against liquor licensees, does not limit the right of one dram shop hit with a judgment from bringing an action for contribution against another dram-shop that contributed to the intoxication of the one who caused the loss.[27]

In Connecticut the Supreme Court held that an adult who served liquor to a minor at a party at an adult's home was responsible for the death of the minor and injuries to another with him when the minor attempted to drive his car home.[28]

In Minnesota, if an injured plaintiff has taken part in causing the intoxication of the driver who caused the injuries to that person or others, the seller of the alcohol is excused from legal liability.[29] The finding of that court is consistent with a Ohio case that held that one who encourages a bartender to serve excessive drinks to an intoxicated person was not liable for injuries or death caused by the encouraging person after the intoxicated person left the tavern The bartender was solely responsible and should have stopped the sales.[30]

What if a bartender refuses to serve a person who had become intoxicated elsewhere and, instead, tries to sober up that person with food while detaining him? If the intoxicated person resumes driving over the bartender's objection and kills himself and another in a head-on car collision, will liability attach to the "Good Samaritan" bartender? A Maine appellate court ruled on this issue, making two points;

1. No special relationship existed between the bartender and the intoxicated person.
2. The bartender did nothing to increase the risk to others.

Does a bar operator who refuses to serve alcohol to a would-be-patron, have a legal duty to stop that person from driving after the refusal? If the intoxicated person is not stopped and injures or kills others, is there liability upon the bar operator? "No," says *O'Gorman v. Rubinaccio*.[31]

Michigan has a "non-innocent party" rule in dram-shop cases. The courts there say that the drunk person and those who contributed to the intoxication have no cause of action under the dram-shop laws, but the family of the deceased does. Therefore, when intoxicated Deborah Warnica died in a car crash, she had no cause of action against the bar that served her the drinks, but her family did. In seeking recovery against the bar, the damages the family claimed included (1) loss of financial support, (2) services of the deceased, (3) parental training since birth of deceased, (4) love and affection, (5) "society," (6) companionship, (7) grief, (8) shock, and (9) mental anguish.[32]

Missouri and other states enacted statutes stating that before dram-shop liability can be sought, it must be proven that the alcohol server had been convicted in the past of selling to an intoxicated person or to a minor. The Missouri Appellate Court overturned a dismissal of a dram-shop case on the basis of the statute, saying that "the plaintiff's constitutional right to access to the courts must be taken into consideration."[33]

Illinois passed a bill to prohibit "lady's night" promotions, "happy hours," and "two-for-one" drinks, often a contributor to injuries and death. In Nevada, a bar is not liable if a parking lot attendant surrenders keys to the owner of a valet-parked car when the car owner was intoxicated.[34] In New Jersey, a bartender is allowed to testify as to the habit of the defendant getting intoxicated when the bar is prosecuted for aggravated manslaughter and death by auto. [35]

The dram-shop laws vary from state to state. Some states do not have them, and others provide liability not only to bar owners but also to bartenders and those who own the premises that are leased to the bar. The latter is true in Illinois. Some states had such laws and then repealed them. Other states have such laws but provide that they shall apply only to minors who become intoxicated and injure themselves and others.

The states that have such laws require an "illegal sale"—a sale to an intoxicated person or to a minor. The New Mexico statute is representative:

> *Section 41–11–1:* Civil liability shall be predicated . . . in the case of the licensee who: (1) sold or served alcohol to a person who was intoxicated; (2) it was reasonably apparent to the licensee that the person buying or apparently receiving service of alcoholic beverages was intoxicated; and (3) . . . knew from the circumstances that the person buying or receiving service of alcoholic beverages is (was) intoxicated. Furthermore, . . . no licensee is chargeable with knowledge of previous acts by which a person becomes intoxicated at other locations unknown to the licensee . . . (that) as used in this section, "licensee" means a person licensed under the provisions of the Liquor Control Act and the agents or servants of the licensee. . . . A licensee may be civilly liable for the negligent violation of Sections 60–7B–1 and 60–7B–1.1 NMSA 1978. The fact-finders [jury] shall consider all the circumstances of the sale in determining whether there is negligence such as the representation used to obtain the alcoholic beverage. It shall not be negligence *per se* to violate Sections 60–7B–1 and 60–70B–1.1, NMSA 1978.

Because of the wide variance in these laws, a legal opinion as to what the laws of any state say and require is worth the money. Some of these laws protect bars from lawsuits where an intoxicated person is refused service at the bar and provide nothing further. As an example: after a bar has refused to continue to sell alcohol to X, who is intoxicated, Y continues to buy drinks and slips them to X unnoticed by the bar personnel. If X then causes death or injury to others after leaving the bar, Y can be looked to for recovery under the complicity doctrine. This legal principle is a defense if the bar is charged with dram-shop liability. This assumes, of course, that the complicity of Y could be proven in court.[36]

In New Mexico, the legislature set a $50,000-dollar limit for those injured by intoxicated persons where illegal sales were involved. The New Mexico Supreme Court stated:

> We are distinctly unable to rationalize a legitimate or substantial reason for limiting the liability of a tavern-keeper who has a duty not to place drunks behind the wheel of a vehicle on the highway, when by contrast, a rancher or farmer is fully liable for negligently allowing his livestock to meander dumbly into the path of oncoming vehicles. . . . The liability cap works a manifest injustice on innocent victims and lacks any of the redeeming features entitling it to constitutional validity.[37]

In Oklahoma, one who becomes intoxicated voluntarily and injures himself, but no one else, has no common-law cause of action against the bar that sold the drinks.[38]

If a bar allows an employee to remain on the premises after her shift has ended and she becomes intoxicated before leaving, there is liability even though the employee goes to other bars and drinks before the injury to others.[39]

In a 1988 Texas case, a court ruled that those who serve alcoholic beverages have a duty to the general public and not just to those who drive motor vehicles. The court held that if unlawful sales of alcohol to an intoxicated person result in the rape of another, the server can be called upon to provide compensation for that assault.[40]

The Supreme Court of Washington ruled that the sale of alcohol to a minor is illegal, and if the sale causes death of the minor, the sale is negligence *per se*,[41] and the seller must pay. The state of Utah agreed with this decision,[42] but Nevada disagreed.[43]

The common law of Wyoming held, since statehood in 1890, that a "liquor vendor is immune from liability to a third party for the illegal sale of alcohol to a patron." This principle was overruled in *McClennan v. Tottenhoff*.[44] Thus, Wyoming has dram-shop liability by court decision.

In the past two decades, three types of state statutes were created to provide relief for servers of alcohol. These were designed to protect them from lawsuits brought by third parties.

1. Statutes were enacted that said consumption of the alcohol, and not the serving of it, was the proximate cause of injury or loss to the third party. (This also was the early common-law rule.)
2. Statutes were enacted to protect servers of alcohol to minors and obviously intoxicated persons unless they, the servers, had a criminal conviction for such activity.
3. Statutes were enacted to place limits on the amount of money such third parties could recover from servers.

Court decisions now have eroded away these statutes to one degree or another.

Generally, the dram-shop laws impose strict liability upon the sellers or servers of alcoholic beverages. Thus, the defense of contributory negligence of the drinker is not available to the seller.

A few states, such as Virginia, have no dram-shop laws or alcoholic beverage control (ABC) liability laws. No licensee to date has been held liable in that state for injury to third persons caused by an intoxicated person. Missouri, like Virginia, does not have a dram-shop law, yet has allowed recovery by an injured third party against the seller of alcoholic beverages. This came about by court decision, so the absence of a formal dram-shop law in itself is not absolute protection.

Repeal of Dram-Shop Laws

A few states have repealed their dram-shop laws: Nebraska in 1935, Oklahoma in 1959, Nevada in 1969, North Carolina in 1971, and California in 1978. In most instances, the reasons can be traced to unpopular court decisions which in turn promoted the repeal.

> In all too many states, Dram Shop liability has become outrageously unfair, exposing licensees to extraordinary hazard. It is a problem that must be addressed by

state legislators. One logical way is a reasonable but firm cap on awards that juries may make. Meanwhile, licensees must make their personnel keenly aware of this hazard and institute cautions to minimize the likelihood of suit.[45]

Alcoholic Beverage Control Laws

A final control of alcohol sales is found in the ABC laws. In the states that permit the wholesale, retail, and pouring sales of alcohol, one will find liquor-control administrative agencies. These agencies are charged with regulating alcohol sales, and the administration is carried out by county and state control boards. The primary control is the requirement of a license before alcoholic beverages can be sold legally.

In this manner, the issuance of a license initially, and the retention of it, are subject to supervision, and subsequent investigation by the licensing authorities. Transgressions of the control laws can result in loss or suspension of such license, plus fines.

Liquor-control laws have a variety of requirements that each license applicant and licensee must meet, including posting notices at the place of sales,[46] reporting changes in ownership and management, rules that prohibit employing minors, and training employees in alcohol-awareness programs.

State and other legal regulations must be complied with or one may face the loss of the privilege to engage in the sale of alcoholic beverages. These laws form a firm set of standards. Some examples of what is happening follow.

Intoxicated persons pose a threat not only to themselves, but to guests and third parties as well. Protecting them from their own actions is not the same as protecting others.[47] Since 1969, Louisiana has had a rule that one who becomes intoxicated voluntarily must use the same degree of care for his or her own safety as one who is sober.[48] That rule does not solve the third-party problems. In Idaho, if a bar operator knows of the propensity of an intoxicated patron to cause harm to others and gives no warning, it becomes a question of fact for a jury as to whether the operator, acting through agents, should be held liable for injuries caused by that person to others while on or near the bar premises.[49] In 1989, the Supreme Court of South Dakota ruled that when a dispute arises as to the proximate cause in an alcohol-related case, it becomes a question of law and fact for the courts and juries and not the legislatures. The statute there says that the consumption of alcohol rather than the serving of it is the proximate cause of losses to third parties. Thus, the Supreme Court of South Dakota overrode the South Dakota legislature on this legal point.

MANAGEMENT POLICY RELATED TO ALCOHOL SERVICE

If an alcohol server decides a patron should not be furnished further drinks, the manager must back up the bartender, not the patron. In a Pennsylvania case, a bartender refused to serve further drinks to a patron. The manager ordered further drinks to be served, but the bartender refused and was fired. The bartender then sued for wrongful discharge. Being successful in her primary suit, the question then arose as to whether she also can get punitive damages if she can prove that the discharge was done "with a reckless indifference to the interest of the employee, or for a bad motive." Many states had said "yes" to this question, but Pennsylvania had not. This federal court ruled that a federal judge could predict how a state court would rule if confronted by such a situation. The award of punitive damages was allowed to stand because the federal court believed that a state court would do likewise in this case. So, failing to back up the alcohol server became expensive indeed for the bar.[50]

A few other suggestions can be made about effective bar management based upon other court rulings. A good management policy is to rotate bartenders at designated times. This will reduce opportunities for collusion with cocktail servers, failing to collect for drinks, working with prostitutes, gambling, and other detrimental things that can take place at bars. Although this policy may be resisted, the rotation policy does have sound legal basis.

Proportionate Liability

When more than one bar becomes involved in dram-shop court judgment payouts, a wise provision to include is that each bar reserves the right to litigate its proportionate liability. In this manner, the plaintiff is removed from the picture. Then, if evidence arises that the sharing had not been correct, it can be litigated as a separate matter between the bars that had contributed to the payouts.

Insurance Coverage

In third-party liability cases, insurance coverage may not apply. In *Shefield's Insurance v. Lighthouse,*[51] the court said, "We hold that coverage is specifically excluded by the language of the policy." That means the bar is going to have to pay the damages without being able to look to its insurance carrier.

Legal scrutiny of insurance policies being purchased is always in order. Yet, in practice, managers and even lawyers have difficulty understanding what insurance policies say. A suggested technique is to ask the one selling the insurance, "Will this policy cover us in the event of a tort as well as a criminal act?" If the agent says it will, reduce that representation to writing and attach it to the policy. In a later court dispute over what the policy does or does not cover, that letter might be nice to have. Most agents carry malpractice insurance. If their representations later prove wrong and the insurance does not cover the occurrence, an action will remain against the agent.

Lesser legal matters are involved in the operation of bars, but they, too, affect management decisions.

Number of Bars

Many cities in the United States, such as Henderson, Nevada, limit the number of bars that can be located within the city limits. The city ordinance there limits bars to one for every 3,500 residents. With a 1995 population of 55,000, that works out to about fifteen bars. Under this law, if the population reaches

150,000—and it is predicted that it will do that by the year 2000—there still will be a limit of forty-three bars. Bars there also must be at least 1500 feet from churches and schools.

The Name Problem

Two persons in Albany, New York, by the names of Mickey Colarusso and Mickey Vish, decided to use their first names on the sign outside of their bar. They had a sign created with a mouse dressed in a jacket and top hot, and called it "Mickey's Mousetrap." Walt Disney Productions brought an injunction against them. The two Mickeys then added sunglasses and a moustache to their mouse, but it did not satisfy the Disney lawyers or the court.

Minors

The bar often serves as the entertainment center for the community in which it is located. This, in turn, means that people of all ages can be expected to turn up there on a typical evening. This makes it important, as a legal matter, that under-age persons be kept away from bars. Techniques that are popular are "color-coded" wrist bracelets issued when admission fees are paid, and wrist stamps.

At the beginning of the 1980s, state law varied in regard to age of majority, with ages running from 18 to 21, plus related rules that made exceptions for those who were married. Action by Congress was necessary to place these state laws into a uniform position. This is how it happened.

FEDERAL DRINKING LAW

In 1983 and the first part of 1984, leaders of the hospitality industry and the U.S. Congress were engaged in a fierce argument on the *pros* and *cons* of a proposed federal drinking bill that would force the drinking age to twenty-one in all of the states. Proponents of the bill wanted the age raised to twenty-one. Opponents cited many reasons why this should not be done. Those in favor of the bill spoke of the laws that created "blood borders" as young people traveled across state lines to purchase alcoholic beverages in states where the legal age was lower. Statistics were produced to show that increases in the legal drinking age reduced alcohol-related deaths in some instances. Statistics from Florida and Maine, however, displayed the opposite result.

Among the reasons that prompted bar executives to oppose the law was that 1 million youths would lose their jobs because they would not be able to work as bartenders until they reached the age of twenty-one years. Another reason was the loss of tax revenues. At the time of the hearings, twenty-three states had set the drinking age at twenty-one, and four raised it in 1983. After the arguments, hearings, debates, and other action, the law became effective in June of 1984.

In 1987, by a vote of 7 to 2, the U.S. Supreme Court upheld the constitutionality of the law. The law had been challenged by South Dakota as being in violation of the Twenty-first Amendment, which had given the states powers to control liquor distribution within their borders. The point of the U.S. Supreme Court ruling was that different drinking ages prompted young persons to cross state borders to purchase alcohol where age limits were lower. This created an interstate safety problem that Congress had the constitutional power to control. South Carolina and Colorado then set the age limit at twenty-one. The last two hold-out states were Ohio and Wyoming, and they now have joined the other states. (As might have been expected, one state has now dropped its drinking age to 18 and other states may follow.)

Blood Alcohol Content

The blood-alcohol percentage used by the police in most states was well established at 0.10 percent. For a 175-pound person, this would require about one dram of 80-proof alcohol in the bloodstream. Most state statutes have followed this percentage, but that is changing. In 1989, the Vermont senate reduced the level to 0.05, requiring one-half less drinking for one to be legally intoxicated.

Robbery

The Court of Appeals of Arizona has held that a barkeeper's primary duty of making the premises reasonably safe for patrons does not encompass an additional duty not to increase the risk of criminal activity by complying with demands of a robber. The court, therefore, upheld the trial court in denying damages for injury and death to patrons that occurred when a bartender, confronted with an armed robber demanding that he turn over the money in the cash register, replied, "Go ahead and shoot me—you're not getting my money." The robber complied, killing the bartender with four shots, injuring one patron, and killing another. The court pointed out that a contrary holding would dissuade proprietors from offering resistance to armed robbers because of the constant fear of civil suit, and would not provide the desired assurance that the risk to an invitee would be reduced substantially. The only persons who would clearly benefit from the imposition of such a duty would be the criminals themselves.[52]

SUMMARY

The laws that regulate the selling and serving of alcoholic beverages are controlled by the states, and these laws vary from state to state. Most states permit such sales although some do not. The control of these sales has a long background.

In earlier years, taverns sold wine, pubs (publicans) sold beer, and dram shops sold hard liquor. Over the years, dram shops became known as "saloons" or "tippling houses." Those names are seldom seen today. On the other hand, the phrase "dram shop" predominates in modern laws that dictate whether or not one who serves alcohol to an intoxicated person (or a minor) should be held responsible for injury or death caused by that person. California has laws that cover both sides of the question. Most states now make the server of alcoholic beverages responsible for injury or death to third parties.

Under the U.S. federal drinking laws, the lawful age to consume alcohol has been made uniform at 21 years of age. However, in early 1996, Louisiana departed the ranks and lowered the lawful drinking age to 18.

QUESTIONS

1. Why is there a legal difference today between the laws of hotels and the laws of taverns?

2. The law traditionally has placed a premium upon definitions. Why is it important, as a matter of law, to know if a business establishment is a bar or not?

3. What was a dram shop under early English law? What is dram-shop law today?

4. The laws that regulate the consumption of alcoholic beverages are being developed in two primary ways. What are they?

5. What did the federal laws on the drinking age accomplish in the United States?

6. Why do you think dram-shop laws that create a third-party liability did not develop until this century?

7. What did "cooperage" mean in an earlier England? Might a person today whose name is Cooper have roots back to those years?

8. Why did early bars become places to post legal notices, proclamations, and other information?

9. What is the difference between ABC laws and dram shop laws?

10. What words in the Twenty-first Amendment gave the states the right to control liquor sales?

NOTES

1. Timothy Finn, *The Camara Beer Guides*, Vol. 1, 1931.

2. Cap. 35 (Chapter 35), "Great Charter."

3. Charles E. Tresise, *Tavern Treasures*, (Dorset, England: Blandford Press/Ling House, 1960), p. 131.

4. *Ibid.*

5. *Nevada v. Rosenthal*, 559 P. 2d 830 (1977), at p. 40-41.

6. Uniform Commercial Code, Article 2, section 314.

7. UCC, *supra.*

8. *Grasser v. Fleming, supra.*

9. *Rapport v. Nichols*, 31 N.J. 188, 156 A. 2d 1 (1959).

10. *Rapport, supra*, 9.

11. *Nevada Beverage Index*, 1983, p. E-17.

12. National Safety Council, *Accident Facts*, p. 49, 1959 Edition.

13. *Rapport, supra.*

14. *Thomas v. Bohelman*, 86 Nev. 10, 13, 462 P. 2d 1020, 1022 (1970), emphasis added.

15. *Rapport, supra*, 9.

16. *Coffman v. Kennedy*, 141 Cal Rptr. 267 (Cal. App. 1977).

17. *Grasser v. Fleming*, 253 N.W. 2d 757 (Michigan, 1977).

18. Section 11-101, McKinney Sup. 1978.

19. *Mitchell v. Shoals, Inc.*, 280 N.Y.S. 2d 113 (1967).

20. *Brannigan v. Raybuck*, 667 P 2d. 213 (Sup. Ct. Arizona 1983).

21. *Williams v. Saga Enterprises*, 274 Cal. Rptr. 901 (California 1990).

22. *Acher v. S.W. Cantinas, Inc.*, 168 S.W. 2d 13 (Supreme Court of Delaware 1991).

23. 566 So. 2d 267 (Florida 1990).

24. *Ibid.*

25. *Booth v. Abbey Road Beef & Booze, Inc.*, 532 So. 2d 1288 (Florida 1988).

26. *Sterenberg v. Sir Loin, Inc.*, 539 N.E. 2d 294 (Illinois 1989).

27. *Schreier v. Sonderleiter*, 298 186–836 (Sup. Ct. Iowa March 16, 1988).

28. *Ibid.*

29. *Dhuy v. Rude*, 465 N.W. 2d 32 (Minnesota 1991).

30. *Ibid.*

31. *O'Gorman v. Rubinaccio & Sons*, 563 N.E. 2d 231 (Maine 1990).

32. *Warnica v. Cheer's*, 464 N.W. 2d 902 (Michigan 1990).

33. *Luxen v. Holiday Inns, Inc.*, 566 F. Supp. 1484 (Missouri 1983).

34. *Mills v. Continental*, 475 P. 2d 673 (Nevada 1970).

35. *State v. Radziwic*, A–35 (Sup. Ct. New Jersey Dec. 11, 1991).

36. *Arnenson v. Bastien*, 438 N.W. 2d 151 (North Dakota 1989).

37. *Sunshine v. Commissioners*, 720 P. 2d 81 (New Mexico 1986).

38. *Ohio Casualty v. Todd*, 72 Okla. 490 (Sup. Ct. Oklahoma 1991).

39. *Dutch Properties Inc. v. Pac-San, Inc.*, 778 P. 2d 969 (Oregon 1989).

40. *S. A. Beverage Co. v. DeRoune*, 753 S.W. 2d 507 (Texas 1988).

41. *Young v. Caravan Corp.*, 672 P. 2d 1267 (Washington 1983).

42. *Yost v. State*, 640 P. 2d 1044 (Utah 1981).

43. *Yoscovitch v. Wasson*, 645 P. 2d 975 (Nevada 1982).

44. 666 P. 2d 408 (Wyoming 1983).

45. Nevada Beverage Index, *supra* at p. E-20.

46. N.Y. Alco. Bev. Cont. Law, section 65(c) McKinney Supp. 1982.

47. *Mayo v. Hyatt*, 898 F. 2d 47 (Louisiana 1990).

48. *Guss v. Jack Tar*, 407 F. 2d 859 (Louisiana 1969).

49. *McGill v. Frasure*, 790 P. 2d (Idaho 1990).

50. *Woodman v. AMF Leisureland*, 842 F. 2d 699 (Pennsylvania 1988).

51. 763 P. 2d 669 (Montana 1988).

52. *Bennett v. Estate of Baker*, 557 P. 195.

23

Travel Agents and Agencies

OVERVIEW

HERE WE WILL examine what the law has to say about those who arrange the travel upon which the hotel, hospitality, and tourism industries rely so heavily. Plaintiff's lawyers have mounted a serious effort in the past decade to force travel losses back on those who arranged the travel in the first instance. This is especially true when travelers suffer injury, death or other losses in other nations.

A helpful way to begin is by examining two paragraphs from a law book written by a leading plaintiff's attorney specializing in travel litigation. In these paragraphs we have an opportunity to see one professional discussing legal strategy with other professionals.

> In discussing reported travel cases, it should be noted that many courts focus on establishing the nature of the relationship between the parties. Once such a relationship is identified, the courts will then find duties and standards which traditionally flow from such relationships. Four different relationships are usually found. First, some courts have found that the travel agent is the agent of the supplier, wholesaler, or tour operator.[1] Second, some courts have found the travel agent to be the agent of the traveler.[2] Third, some courts have viewed the relationship between the traveler and travel agent as contractual in nature with the travel agent as the principal.[3] Fourth, some courts have viewed the travel agent as a broker in the business of assisting in the creation of bilateral contracts.[4] This latter relationship has been referred to as transactional analysis.[5]
>
> The focus on traditional relationships has generated much judicial confusion and has often generated unjust decisions. Travel cases should be decided on an *ad hoc* basis relying upon transactional analysis of the facts.[6] The facts of the case should include not only what transpired between the traveler and the middleman but also (1) facts establishing the functional relationship between the travel entities involved,[7] (2) facts demonstrating the knowledge which the middleman possesses or should possess,[8] and (3) facts and admissions identifying the standards of care which are applicable, whether self-imposed through education[9] or trade associations[10] or imposed by statute[11] and by the courts.[12]

Thus, we see an expert discussing his craft with his contemporaries. With this as a beginning point, let's make some observations about travelers and their needs.

Travelers vary from person to person in their wishes, needs, wants, and travel objectives. Some are seasoned travelers; others are novices. Many lack basic information about visas and health requirements to travel in foreign nations, and most cannot speak a second language. Thus, they are in need, as a class, of information about customs in the states and in foreign nations. They need help with currency exchange and advice about clothing and climatic conditions. They have an obvious need for someone to provide such information and assistance. This has come to pass through the services offered by travel agents and agencies.

The services that have been provided have been quite good in most instances. Yet, some of those services have formed the basis for lawsuits. Lawyers look for anything that may imply or establish a promise by a travel agent to an injured traveler. An example is an oral representation about the quality of the trip package that was purchased, or perhaps some symbol, desk sign, button, or patch that would lead the traveler to believe the travel agent was the agent of someone else.[13] All of this is part of a legal warfare that is being waged against travel agents.

In the past, travel agents operated with little fear of the consequences of their acts because seldom did an injured traveler come after them for compensation. This was so because there had been no legal effort to bring them into litigation or to have them answer for the defaults of others. This has changed, and the field of litigation is opening up against travel agents and their agencies. As long as travel agents were permitted to run their operations without fear of legal liability, the legal picture developed one way. Now that the fear of money loss is a strong reality, the legal picture is taking on new forms. To those new patterns we want to direct our attention.

A topic of growing interest is the legal liability of those who serve as "travel conduits" between one who is planning to travel and those who provide the travel, lodging, and entertainment at the destination. Such persons, or firms, are known as "travel agents"—although use of the term "agents" leaves a lot to be cleared up in the legal sense.

In the customary situation, the traveler (who in most instances is a consumer, yet may be combining business with a pleasure trip) seeks the advice and services of the travel agent. The traveler sets forth the proposed trip, providing an idea of time, destination, and desired price range, and what he or she wants to accomplish on the trip. The travel agent then makes arrangements with a wholesale travel agent, and air, rail, or sea carriers; then coordinates with those at the destination and makes reservations there. In addition the travel agent often sets up tour plans for the traveler. For these services, the travel agent charges a fee, usually a percentage of the deposits required by wholesale travel agents, hotels, and others. These deposits are forwarded to the wholesale agent and those at the destination, minus the percentage the travel agent retains per the agreement between the travel agent and the wholesale agent.

Thus, we find at least four and perhaps five persons or firms involved in this process:

1. The direct-sale travel agent, who deals with the traveler face to face.
2. The wholesale travel agent, who is contacted by the direct sales agent. (In many instances, wholesale agents are bypassed.)
3. The innkeeper.
4. The airline, railroad, or shipping line, or a combination of them, referred to as "carrier."
5. Tour operators at the destination, whom we will call "guides."

Obviously, in such a multiple-party undertaking, many things can go wrong. Funds may not be forwarded as promised; lodging may not be available upon arrival; guides may fail to materialize as planned; carriers may not meet the required timetables; and, worst of all, injury or death may occur to the traveler in the process.

SOME LEGAL BASICS

First, it is helpful to examine some of the legal basics involved in this relationship. We then will look at cases in which disputes have arisen.

"Sale" or Not?

To begin, does an agent "sell" a traveler a trip package within the UCC Sales meaning of that word? This is an important question. In the absence of furnishing food or drink, the answer seems to be "no." A "service" rather than a "sale" is provided.

Standard of Care

What standard of care is a travel agent held to? The courts hold both direct-sale and wholesale travel agents to the standards of knowledge and skill that could be expected of the reasonable person engaged in that business. Failure to meet these standards could result in legal liability just as in other areas of law.

Prior Experience

If an agent has had unfavorable experiences with those at the destination, that information must be made available to the traveler. If the agent has had no previous experience, a duty exists to make reasonable inquiry about accommodations at the destination. In the travel industry, some parts of the world are known as "hot spots." The agent must learn of them and warn of them.

Failure to Make Inquiry

The courts hold failure to make inquiry about destinations and travel routes to be negligence. After all, this is part of the services the travel agent is providing. This is true even though there is usually no direct money payment by the traveler to the travel agent. If it is found that this negligence is the proximate cause of the loss suffered by the traveler during the trip, the legal results are obvious.

Travel agents have a duty to confirm reservations being made for the traveler. In addition they are held responsible to confirm the contractual obligations of tour operators and wholesale travel agents. This latter duty approaches strict liability because few excuses are acceptable for failure to do so. Travel agents no longer are ticket sellers—although that is what they were until about two decades ago—and they are moving into a closer legal relationship with those they serve. Although increasing legal obligations place costs on the travel agent, these burdens must be considered as part of the costs of doing business.

Constructive Fraud

Courts have held that a special relationship exists between a travel agent or agency and the traveler.[14] Because of this, a case can be brought against the travel agent for constructive fraud. This type of fraud was defined in *Brown v. Lockwood*.[15]

> Constructive fraud may be defined as a breach of a duty which, irrespective of moral guilt and intent, the law declares fraudulent because of its tendency to deceive, to violate a confidence or to injure public or private interests which the law deems worthy of special protection. . . . The elements of a cause of action to recover for constructive fraud are the same as those to recover for actual fraud with the crucial exception that the element of *scienter* upon the part of the defendant, his knowledge of the falsity of his representation, is dropped and is replaced by a requirement that the plaintiff prove the existence of a fiduciary or confidential relationship warranting the trusting party to repose his confidence in the defendant and therefore to relax the care and vigilance he would ordinarily exercise in the circumstances. The law regards the making of a misrepresentation by a defendant who possesses a position of superiority and influence over the plaintiff by reason of the confidential relationship between them as a breach of duty actionable as constructive fraud. . . .

Duty to Accept

Since the courts are finding a special relationship between travelers and travel agents, what is the duty of the agent to enter into the relationship in the beginning? Even though an innkeeper must accept all of those who apply for rooms, if available, the same is not true of the travel agent. A travel agent may turn away potential travelers as he or she may choose.

Not an Insurer

In addition, a travel agent is not an insurer of the safety of the traveler—and certainly does not want to be. As previously mentioned, however, if the agent knows of risks or has reason to know of them, they must be brought to the traveler's attention. Failure to do so may create responsibility to the traveler who suffers a loss because of those risks.

The issues we have been discussing have resulted in regulations on the travel agent business.

REGULATION OF THE INDUSTRY

The travel-agent industry came in for some black eyes in the early 1970s. The result was an increased demand for controls. In the past, because of a relatively low demand for such services, there was little regulation. Today the American Society of Travel Agents serves the industry and has done all it can to protect travel agents, as well as travelers. In the past, at the federal level, the Federal Trade Commission (FTC) and others had powers but seldom used them. Such agencies now are active in controlling the activities of travel agents directly and indirectly. This is an outgrowth of the consumer protection movement that became so prevalent in the past decades.

Agents or Not?

If a direct sale agent is a true legal agent (see Chapter 7), and so long as the identity of the principal (such as a wholesale travel agent, innkeeper, carrier, or guide) is disclosed, there is no contractual obligation on the part of the agent. An agent is not responsible for contracts negotiated for the principal as long as the principal is disclosed.

As one examines the basic requirements of an agency relationship, however, it becomes clear that travel agents often do not meet the requirements of a true legal agency. These requirements are four in number:

1. Both the principal and the agent must agree to the relationship.
2. The principal must have the right to control the agent.
3. A fiduciary relationship must exist between them.
4. The agent must have the power to bind the principal.

An examination of these requirements makes it clear that in the usual travel situation, at least one and often more of them are not present. The cases that have attempted to construe this topic have not been satisfactory to date.

CASE INTRODUCTION: BUCHOLTZ CASE

If a direct sale travel agent does not disclose the wholesale agent, the contract of the traveler and the sales agent would be binding upon the agent. This follows the traditional legal liability of an agent who acts for an undisclosed principal. In the following case, the judge placed the matter squarely into the law of agency and held the travel agent responsible for the reservations that went bad.

BUCHOLTZ V. SIROKIN TRAVEL, LTD.
80 Misc. 2d 333, 363 N.Y.S. 2d 415 (1974)

Before HOGAN, P. J., and FARLEY and GAGLIARDI, JJ. *PER CURIAM.*

Judgment affirmed without costs.

In this Small Claims action, plaintiff seeks to cast defendant travel agency into damages for reservations that went awry. Since it is undisputed that the travel agency had utilized the services of a wholesaler who had put together a "package tour," defendant contends on this appeal that the wholesaler alone is liable for any default in performance.

Allocation of responsibility in the case before us should proceed upon the principles of agency law. In our opinion, where, as here, there is no proof of an independent relationship between the retail travel agent and the wholesaler, the travel agent should be considered the agent of the customer. If, in using a wholesaler to make the travel arrangements, the travel agent acts with the consent, express or implied, of the principal-customer, then, if reasonable diligence has been used in its selection, the travel agent will not be responsible for any dereliction of duty on the part of the wholesaler. If, on the other hand, the travel agent acts without such consent, he will be responsible to the customer for any damage sustained as a result of the acts of the wholesaler.

The court below, in applying these principles, found that the plaintiff did not consent to the employment of the wholesaler. Although its opinion did not so state, the record indicates that the court also declined to hold that knowledge of the practice of employing wholesalers should be imputed to the plaintiff. We see no reason to disturb this determination. The record supports a finding that plaintiff was not informed of the existence of the wholesaler until after the reservations were agreed upon and it cannot be said that knowledge of this practice is so pervasive among the public as to compel a finding of implied consent.

We find no merit in defendant's remaining contention.

All concur.

Figure 23.1 illustrates the Bucholtz case. The decision seems clear on its face, yet, as a matter of law, it is not that simple. In this case, the court finds the traveler to be the principal. In practice, this normally isn't so because the direct travel agent is the agent of the wholesale travel agent and that makes a big difference. Yet, the court holds that the travel agent is the agent of the traveler, who is the principal. The traveler, however, did not consent to use of the wholesale travel agent, and this had a key bearing on the outcome of the case.

FIGURE 23.1 Bucholtz case.

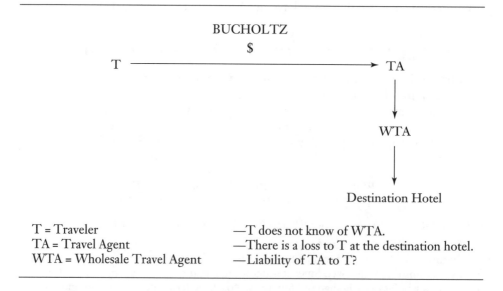

	BUCHOLTZ	
	$	
T ——————————————→		TA
		↓
		WTA
		↓
		Destination Hotel

T = Traveler   —T does not know of WTA.
TA = Travel Agent   —There is a loss to T at the destination hotel.
WTA = Wholesale Travel Agent   —Liability of TA to T?

CASE INTRODUCTION: MCQUADE CASE

The legal question raised in the McQuade case that follows is: To what extent must the travel agent go in disclosing its principal? In this case we see the consequences that can follow for failing to so disclose. Figure 23.2 depicts this case.

E.A. MCQUADE TRAVEL AGENCY, INC., V. DOMECK
190 So. 2d 3, Dist. Ct. App. Fla. (1966)

Plaintiffs filed this suit against defendant to recover damages for breach of contract. Plaintiffs alleged that, in consideration of $2,677.50 paid to defendant, defendant agreed to sell plaintiffs two tickets on a certain cruise to Europe. Defendant answered, alleging that it received the monies for the benefit of and transmittal to Caribbean Cruise Lines, Inc., a foreign corporation.

This cause came before the trial court on stipulated statement of facts to the effect that, on May 12, 1964, the defendant agreed to sell plaintiffs two tickets on a European cruise of the M/S Riviera which was to leave on September 11, 1964; that plaintiffs paid defendant the sum of $2,667.50 on or prior to July 23, 1964. All payments were made to E.A. McQuade Travel Agency, but the tickets were not delivered to the plaintiffs. It is also stipulated that there was no discussion between the plaintiffs and the defendant as to the person or corporation for which the defendant acted as agent, if any, or as to what disposition would be made of the money paid to defendant.

Prior to August 15, 1964, defendant forwarded $2,406.75 to Caribbean Cruise Lines, Inc., the company that was offering the cruise to Europe. On or about August 15, 1964, the plaintiffs and the defendant were informed that the M/S Riviera would not be making the scheduled cruise and that Caribbean Cruise Lines, Inc., had filed bankruptcy.

The plaintiffs requested the defendant to return the money which they had paid for the tickets they did not receive. The defendant has offered to pay to the plaintiffs $266.75 which was its commission but declined to pay any additional monies.

The original complaint contained a prayer for judgment in the amount of $2,057.50 plus costs. Prior to trial plaintiffs amended their complaint to reflect the exact amount they had paid defendant to be $2,667.50.

The trial court held the defendant liable because it failed to disclose its principal and awarded the plaintiffs $2,057.50 plus costs.

The main question presented for our determination is whether the defendant sufficiently disclosed the identity of its principal, Caribbean Cruise Lines, Inc., by merely revealing the name of the cruise ship, M/S Riviera.

In our research we failed to find a Florida decision directly on the question of disclosure of principal by an agent. However, the law in other states is well established that the disclosure of agency is not complete for the purpose of relieving the agent from personal liability unless it embraces the name of the principal. The disclosure of the name of the ship is merely the disclosure of a trade name, and is not a disclosure of the identity of the principal. The liability of an agent acting for an undisclosed principal is fully discussed in *Unger v. Travel Arrangements, Inc.,* 1966, 25 A.D. 2d 40, 266 N.Y.S. 2d 715, a decision involving the same cruise.

FIGURE 23.2 McQuade case.

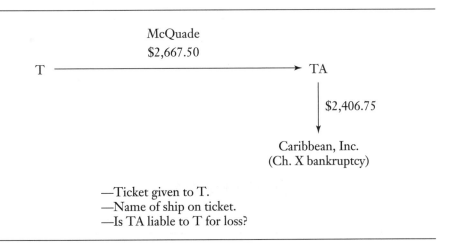

We agree with the trial court that the defense of agency does not relieve the defendant from liability. The record supports the trial court's finding that the defendant was an agent of an undisclosed principal and therefore can be held liable. *Hohauser v. Schor,* Fla. App. 1958, 101 So. 2d 169. We hold that there is sufficient evidence to support the trial court's holding that the defendant breached its contract with plaintiffs by failing to furnish the promised tickets.

The court has carefully considered the other points raised on appeal by appellant and finds them without merit.

Accordingly, we affirm as to liability and reverse as to amount of damages with direction that the judgment be amended to award damages to the plaintiffs in the amount of $2,667.50, plus costs.

SMITH, C. J., and WALDEN, J., concur.

One suggested solution to the generally unsatisfactory attempt to apply agency law to the travel agent and agency is to find that a double agency exists. The first comes about between the travel agent and the traveler. The second then comes into being between the travel agent and the wholesale travel agent. As soon as the first agent meets all legal obligations, such as contacting the wholesale agent, arranging for tickets, and paying over deposits, the first agency has been completed and liability ends there for the first agent. The second agency now comes into being between the traveler and wholesale agent.

CASE INTRODUCTION: LEVINE CASE

In the Levine case, the court found that there were two agencies, one of which came into being and was completed before the other one arose. This is illustrated in Figure 23.3. After the purpose of the first agency was completed, the second agency then came into being. The facts in the case explain how this came about.

FIGURE 23.3 Levine case.

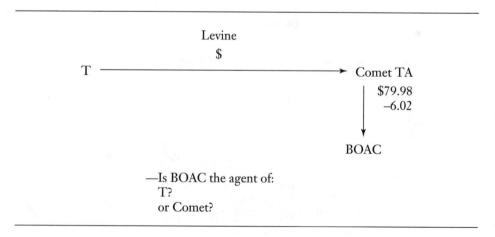

LEVINE V. BRITISH OVERSEAS AIRWAYS CORPORATION
66 Misc. 2d 820, 322 N.Y.S. 2d 119 (1971)

BENTLEY KASSAL, Judge.

Plaintiffs move for summary judgment against defendants, British Overseas Airways Corporation ("BOAC") and Leo Lazar d/b/a/ Comet Travel Agency ("Comet") to recover the sum of $86 as a refund for a portion of two airline tickets returned unused to BOAC. Comet failed to appear in this action. BOAC does not dispute that plaintiffs are entitled to the refund, but asserts in opposition to this motion that "pursuant to airline custom and regulation," it paid the claimed amount, less the travel agent's commission, to Comet, as "agent" for plaintiffs, and is thus no longer liable to plaintiffs. BOAC's answer, however, does not refer to Comet as plaintiffs' agent but states that BOAC paid the money to Comet pursuant to the said IATA regulations, contract and industry custom.

The essential facts are not in dispute; the issue to be resolved is whether Comet was plaintiffs' agent in this transaction, and, if so, whether payment to Comet discharged BOAC from further liability for the refund.

The facts are these: On September 3, 1970, plaintiffs purchased two round-trip BOAC tickets from Comet for this trip—New York/London/Amsterdam/Copenhagen/Stockholm/London/New York. On September 30, 1970, pursuant to BOAC instructions, plaintiff Robert Levine sent the two unused portions of the tickets directly to BOAC for a refund. His accompanying letter is as follows: "We are enclosing herewith two (2) tickets (BEA No. 6942777 and No. 6942778), each for a refund in the sum of $43. Kindly forward your check in the sum of $86 to me at your earliest convenience, and oblige."

BOAC, having determined that plaintiffs were entitled to a refund, sent back a form letter acknowledging plaintiffs' request and advising them that the claim had been processed through "your travel agents," who would make the final settlement with them. Simultaneously, BOAC sent a check to Comet, made to Comet's order, for $79.98, the refund due, less Comet's retained commission of $6.02. This check was negotiated by Comet on October 13, 1970, but no payment has ever been received by plaintiffs.

In January, plaintiffs again wrote to BOAC to demand the refund. On January 19, 1971, the day this action was instituted, BOAC wrote Comet enclosing a photocopy of its check and requesting that plaintiffs be paid. Since that time, BOAC has repeatedly contacted Comet to make payment to plaintiffs, without avail.

In its answer BOAC does not cite any specific regulations of the International Air Transport Association, a voluntary association of international air carriers, or any binding custom, to substantiate its claim that it has satisfied its obligation of payment by making the refund to the travel agent. Nor do I have knowledge of any IATA regulations regarding such refunds.

It is understandable, however, that BOAC and other airlines may have adopted this practice for their own benefit as the most convenient and feasible method of repayment since the travel agent retains a commission on the sale. But such practice, established unilaterally, could not bind plaintiffs or exonerate BOAC from liability to plaintiffs, simply on the ground of its being their own usual procedure. Plaintiffs returned their tickets directly to BOAC, not through their travel agent. They were not in the travel business, and no custom existed between them and BOAC or any other airline as to any further involvement of the travel agent beyond the initial purchase and issuance of the original BOAC tickets. Furthermore, the instructions in plaintiffs' letter are explicit to that effect. "Kindly forward your check in the sum of $86 *to me* . . ." [emphasis added]. Thus, the fact that BOAC might have followed its usual "custom" will not immunize it from liability to plaintiffs, especially in view of plaintiffs' express instructions.

The other theory on which BOAC relies is one of agency. It claims that its obligation has been discharged because a travel agent is the agent of the traveler and thus payment to the agent constitutes payment to the traveler, his principal. Plaintiffs, on the contrary, consider Comet to be BOAC's agent.

When a person goes to a travel agency to book transportation and other arrangements with a vague request such as "Get me a flight to London on the 15th and hotel reservations," it may very well be in that situation that the travel agent, who is essentially a "broker," becomes the traveler's agent; under those circumstances, he is not the agent of the airline, even though he may have a supply of blank official tickets supplied by them. At most, the travel broker is an agent for an undisclosed principal and the agent alone is responsible to the traveler; the airline only becomes liable if it ratifies the transaction made by the broker.

In my opinion, once plaintiffs' initial purchase of the tickets from Comet had been satisfactorily completed, any possible agency relationship which may have existed between them was thereupon terminated. Having used only a portion of their tickets, plaintiffs were entitled to a refund, whether they had purchased their tickets from Comet or across a BOAC counter. They chose to deal directly with BOAC, as a disclosed principal, to ask for a refund. They did not deal with Comet, and it was not necessary for plaintiffs to return tickets through the travel agency, as BOAC's acceptance implies; nor was it "necessary" for BOAC to return this money via Comet, except for their own convenience and sole benefit for accounting purposes to avoid the extra step of having to collect the commission Comet had retained on the ticket sale. Plaintiffs never authorized BOAC to remit the refund in this manner; Comet was not authorized to receive this payment; plaintiffs in no way held out Comet as their agent for this purpose.

Assuming *arguendo* that an agency relationship between plaintiffs and Comet continued after the initial sale of the tickets, this would not per se justify BOAC's refund payment since "an agent has no authority to receive payment merely because of the fact that he represented a principal in the transaction out of which the debt arose . . ." Restatement Agency 2d sec. 71, Comment; see also 12 Am. Jur. 2d, Brokers sec. 79. Payment to a party who has no authority, actual or apparent, to receive it does not discharge the debtor.

Accordingly, summary judgment is granted against defendant, British Overseas Airways Corporation and against defendant Leo Lazar d/b/a Comet Travel Agency, by default, and judgment may be entered in favor of the plaintiffs for the relief demanded in the complaint.

These cases illustrate the legal complexities, as well as the uncertainties that come into play, when the courts apply agency law to travel agents and agencies. It never is certain what is going to happen in the end. Therefore, travel agents and agencies are looking for ways to limit their liability. It is not unlike the situation that existed centuries ago when innkeepers began to look for ways to limit the strict liability placed upon them by the common law.

TRAVEL AGENTS AS INDEPENDENT CONTRACTORS

Direct-sale travel agents are taking legal steps to make it clear that they are not agents of the wholesale travel agents or those at the destination. This is being done by the use of conspicuous disclaimers in the contract with the traveler. Thus, the direct sales agent is bound by the contract to make the arrangements agreed upon, but makes no promises or warranties as to performance by others or quality of accommodations. This limits the legal liability of the direct-sales agent, leaving the liability based solely upon the traveler-direct sales agent contract. After all reservations are properly made, failure of those services would be the responsibility of others. On the other hand, if the traveler specifies a specific quality of accommodations and the direct sales agent fails to obtain them, or forgets to do so, contractual liability would exist.

CASE INTRODUCTION: ODYSSEYS CASE

In cases where liability attaches to a travel agent, the question arises as to what the extent and measure of damages should be. On this point, it must be recognized that not only can a disappointed traveler receive damages for himself or herself, but also for the accompanying spouse and children.[16]

> ... [W]here a person had entered into a contract for the benefit of himself and others who were not parties to the contract, he could sue on the contract for damages for the loss suffered not only by himself, but also by the others in consequence of a breach of the contract. ...
>
> Jackson was, therefore, entitled to damages not only for the loss in the value of the holiday and the discomfort, vexation, and disappointment which he himself suffered by reason of Horizon's breach of contract, but also for the discomfort, vexation, and disappointment suffered by his wife and children.

The Odysseys case that follows is a leading case on damages. It lays down principles that are being followed in travel cases. This case was tried before a judge and not a jury. The recovery the judge allowed was conservative and equals the contract price for the trip lost. Plaintiff's lawyers now have come to realize that, in such cases, not only is the contract price of the trip involved but also the loss of the trip itself, the ruined vacation, and other measurable factors.

Travel lawyers recognize that such cases must be tried before juries and not judges because juries are able to relate to disappointments others suffer in ruined travel situations. In a case similar to Odysseys, where the contract amount was $1,003, the jury returned a verdict of $15,000 for the traveler.[17] Judges tend to be more conservative because they center their rulings on legal points and not on the personal issues.

On the other side of the coin, the one being sued will opt for a trial by judge and not jury where that can be arranged. All that is required in most courts is the agreement of the parties. For the reasons stated above, however, it is now difficult to get such an agreement from plaintiffs' lawyers in travel cases.

ODYSSEYS UNLIMITED, INC., V. ASTRAL STAR TRAVEL SERVICE
77 Misc. 2d 502, 354 N.Y.S. 2d 88 (1974)

JOSEPH LIFF, Justice.

Following an earlier practice, in the summer of 1972 the Paterson and Majewski families began to plan a joint vacation over the Christmas holiday. In doing so, they relied upon Astral Travel Service ("Astral"), an agency with which they had previously dealt. They looked forward to spending a few days with their five children in the Canary Islands, of course not anticipating the discomfort, inconvenience and disappointment they would suffer.

Astral (a retail travel agent) suggested to Dr. Paterson and Mr. Majewski a package tour prepared by Odysseys (a wholesale agency). The tour, entitled "Xmas Jet Set Sun Fun/Canary Isle," was scheduled to depart December 26, 1972, by jet for Tenerife, Canary Isles, Puerto de la Cruz, staying at the "delux Semiramis Hotel" and returning on January 1, 1973, by jet. Majewski and Paterson accepted this trip costing $1,375.90 and $1,076.80 respectively and made their down payments to Astral. Astral withheld its commission and forwarded the balance along with the reservations to Odysseys, [which] in turn confirmed the reservations to Astral's Mr. Howard Pollack. Exhibit B is a handsome colored brochure illustrating the Hotel Semiramis, its location, accommodations, etc. designed to excite the eye of anyone contemplating a trip abroad. An information sheet furnished details of the trip and referred to the accommodations at the "Five-Star Hotel Semiramis."

On December 26, 1972, the group flew off to the Canary Islands. They arrived at the airport in Tenerife at about dawn and waited about two hours (one-half hour was spent in a bus) before they were taken to the Hotel Semiramis. At this point the passengers had been en route some thirty hours. While at the airport they saw Mr. Newton, President of Odysseys, who accompanied the group tour. (The inference may reasonably be drawn that he went along because he anticipated the difficulties which were shortly to be encountered.) Two hundred fifty weary but expectant guests arrived at the Semiramis and were presented with a letter from the hotel advising them that there was no space available and that he was looking for others. For about four hours, two hundred fifty people (including bag and baggage except for what was strayed) were in the lobby of the Semiramis until they were divided into groups and directed to other hostelries. The Paterson and Majewski families were brought to the Porto Playa Hotel, which was not fully ready for occupancy because it was under construction and without the recreational facilities and conveniences available at the Hotel Semiramis. Portions of the Porto Playa Hotel were enclosed in scaffolding. Paterson and Majewski testified that work was done in their rooms, water supply uncertain, electric connections incomplete, etc. throughout their stay.

The Court is convinced that prior to the group's departure, Mr. Newton was aware that there were no reservations at the Semiramis Hotel for his charges. He testified that on either December 18th or 19th, 1972, he knew of the overbooking at the hotel. Paterson and Majewski stated that Newton told them at the hotel that the reservations were in jeopardy and would not be honored but he did not share his knowledge. In his letter of January 12, 1973, addressed to tour members, Mr. Newton confirms the fact that he had been aware of some "problem with overbooking by that hotel" (Semiramis Hotel) and states that his agent (Viajes Aliados, S. A.) "had the foresight to have arranged for alternate accommodations." He is at the least disingenuous in asserting that he had assurance from the Spanish National Tourist Office that the Semiramis Hotel would have accommodations for the group because that office informed him that the Hotel Semiramis was "instructed to receive all the members of your group for whom reservations were made." However, the reservations for the tour were not confirmed and, therefore, the hotel was not obligated to accommodate the members of the group.

Majewski and Paterson sue in contract and negligence seeking recovery of their payments for their trip and for their ordeal. Their claims spring from a breach of contract by Astral for its failure to furnish the hotel accommodations agreed upon. Majewski and Paterson are entitled to recover from Astral for the breach of contract. Damages in the usual breach of contract action should indemnify a party "for the gains prevented and losses sustained by the breach; to leave him in no worse, but put him in no better, position than he would have been had the breach not occurred" (2 N.Y. PJI 907; see also 13 N. Y. Jur., Damages §38; 25 C.J.S. Damages §74). However, when a passenger sues a carrier for a breach of their agreement concerning accommodations the "[i]nconveniences and discomforts which a passenger suffers . . . are to be considered in the assessment of the damages" (N.Y. Damages Law §624). "[D]amages arising from a breach of the contract to carry, which results in inconvenience and indignity to the passenger while in transit, are not limited to the price of passage" (*Lignante v. Panama Railroad Co.*, 147 App. Div. 97, 99-100, 131 N.Y.S. 753, 754; see also *Aplington v. Pullman Co.*, 110 App. Div. 250, 97 N.Y.S. 329) and "the discomfort and inconvenience to which" a passenger was put by the breach of the carrier's contract "was within the contemplation of the parties and a proper element of damage" (*Campbell v. Pullman Company*, 182 App. Div. 931, 169 N.Y.S. 1087; see also *Owens v. Italia Societa Per Azione*, 70 Misc. 2d 719, 723, 334 N.Y.S. 2d 789 [Civil Court of the City of New York] aff'd 75 Misc. 2d 104, 347 N.Y.S. 2d 431 [Appellate Term, First Dept.]). Although these cases concerned accommodations with common carriers, the principle should be applied to the relationship between travel agent and clients. The agent should be "held responsible to: (a) verify or confirm the reservations and (b) use reasonable diligence in ascertaining the responsibility of any intervening 'wholesale or tour organizer'" (*Bucholtz v. Sirokin Travel Ltd.*, 74 Misc. 2d 180, 182, 343 N.Y.S. 2d 438, 442). Because the contract was violated and the accommodations contracted for not furnished, a more realistic view for awarding damages to Majewski and Paterson would include not only the difference in the cost of the accommodations but also compensation for their inconvenience, discomfort, humiliation, and annoyance.

Paterson and Majewski are entitled to return of the total sum each paid for the trip as damages to them and their family for the inconvenience and discomfort they endured.

The tour included a period from December 26th to January 1st. The party landed on its easterly journey on the 27th December. When the Majewskis and Patersons became aware of their predicament, they made heroic efforts to return immediately but heavy bookings in the holiday season made that impossible. They were constrained to remain and to suffer the results of Mr. Newton's callousness. Had their dealings been directly with the plaintiff, we would have considered the imposition of additional damages. However, their negotiations and dealings were with Astral, [which] might have exerted greater efforts to see that arrangements were properly made.

In all of the circumstances, we think that it would be appropriate to make the Patersons and Majewskis whole in pocket. Accordingly, they are awarded judgment against Astral in the amounts of $1,076.80 to Paterson and $1,375.90 to Majewski.

On Astral's cross-claim against Odysseys for breach of contract, concerning the Majewski and Paterson claims if successful, Astral is entitled to a judgment against Odysseys in the amount of $2,452.70 less $308.30, which Astral retained as its commission, because Odysseys failed to perform its contract and it was Odysseys which was responsible for the fate which befell Majewski and Paterson.

In an unrelated matter, Astral counterclaimed against Odysseys seeking return of a $1,345.00 deposit for a group tour also to the Canary Islands but via Iberia Airlines and with a stay at the San Felipe Hotel. Astral gave this sum to Odysseys as a deposit for a group tour of fifty persons since it was allegedly required by the San Felipe Hotel to "firm up your confirmation" (Exhibit L). Odysseys indicated that this deposit was non-refundable (Exhibits L and N). Having received cancellations by members of the group that was to take this trip, Astral was unsuccessful in attempts to substitute their vacationers and requested a refund of the deposit paid. Odysseys' proof failed to show that it suffered any loss by the cancellation or that it paid any part of the deposit to the hotel. We also found that Odysseys asked for the deposit because it was required by the hotel but no part of it was ever paid over to the hotel. Accordingly, Astral is entitled to a return of . . . deposit and may enter judgment against Odysseys for said amount.

CASE INTRODUCTION: KLAKIS CASE

As mentioned before the Odysseys case, travel agents and agencies are turning to the use of disclaimers to limit their liability for defaults by others in the travel chain. As a principle of law, parties of equal bargaining power can reach any reasonable agreement and the courts will uphold them. There is also a rule of law that says that, if the bargaining power of the parties is not equal, the courts will take that fact into consideration when it comes time to decide whether the agreement should be upheld. Thus, in looking at disclaimers used by travel agents and agencies, the courts will look to:

1. readability
2. equal bargaining power—or the lack of it
3. notice to the traveler of the disclaimer
4. unconscionability of the disclaimer, if any[18]

The leading case on disclaimers as used by travel agents is found in *Klakis v. Nationwide Leisure Corporation*, which follows. This dissenting opinion was adopted by a subsequent decision handed down by the court in 1980.[19] The case itself was eliminated because it is a legal maze of motions, orders, and opinions that are of little value to us.

MARION KLAKIS ET AL. V. NATIONWIDE LEISURE CORPORATION
73 A.D. 2d 521, 422 N.Y.S. 2d 407 (1979)

Plaintiffs purchased from defendant Nationwide Leisure Corporation (hereinafter "Nationwide") a chartered tour to Nassau which was scheduled to leave Kennedy Airport at 6:00 A.M. on January 22, 1978, and to return there at 1:30 P.M. on January 26, 1978. The tour included round-trip chartered jet flights on defendant Capitol International Airways (hereinafter "Capitol"), a certified supplemental air-carrier. In the complaint, plaintiffs charge that the flight left Kennedy one day later, on January 23, 1978, rather than January 22nd, as scheduled, and that as a consequence of the delays in their travel, they received, instead of the advertised four nights and five days, a stay of only three nights and two days. Insofar as here pertinent, the complaint states three causes of action against all the defendants. The first cause of action alleges fraud, the second breach of contract, and the third seeks rescission.

The disclaimer of liability contained in Nationwide's brochure, which was incorporated in the agreement between plaintiffs and Nationwide to the effect that Nationwide "shall not be responsible in any way for any delays, changes in departure time," while it may be viable regarding incidental delays and changes, is not a defense to delay of sufficient magnitude to vitiate the contract for the simple reason that such delay strikes at the heart of the performance bargained for under the agreement. The principal herein, Nationwide, assumed a specific duty by contract, to wit, to afford to plaintiffs a five days and four nights tour. Under the circumstances herein, Nationwide as principal might well be liable to plaintiffs for the failure of performance occasioned by the delays caused by the independent contractor Capitol (See, Dorkin v. American Express Co., 74 Misc. 2d 673, 675, 345 N.Y.S. 2d 891, 892.). No explanation is presented on this record by defendants relevant to the delays in air transportation experienced by plaintiffs regarding the return flight to New York. Thus, a viable claim for breach of contract against Nationwide and Capitol respecting the delays encountered by plaintiffs in returning to New York remains.

THE OCCASIONAL TRAVEL AGENT

Assume that a tourist destination has a visitor's center on the outskirts of town. The purpose of the center is to assist motorists in becoming oriented to what is available in town and to assist them in obtaining hotel or motel accommodations. Such centers are found at interstate entrances to the various states. Are such centers engaged in the travel agency business and, if so, what rules govern the operations? If not, what then?

For finding rooms for tourists, the hotel pays a fee to the center, such as $20.00 per room placed. This activity raises legal questions. First, what is the liability of the tourist center, if any, if it is unable to find accommodations for a traveler who wants to use these services? The answer is probably "no liability at all" for there would be no contractual agreement between anyone.

Now change the facts. The tourist center asks a motel for a room for a traveler, and the motel refuses to make the reservation. Does liability now attach to anyone? The answer probably depends upon the availability of rooms at the motel. If rooms had been available and the reservation was refused, was the common-law duty to receive violated? The problem here is that the motel refused the tourist center which is not a traveler, but at the same time, they refused the traveler. If the motel had been full, the refusal would have been lawful and that would have been the end of it.

What happens now if the tourist center takes cash from the traveler, say $10.00, with the promise to find a room elsewhere, and the tourist center fails to find a room? This changes the facts, and there would be liability on the tourist center because of the breach of contract, and damages would be recoverable.

Change the facts one more time. The center locates a room, gets the tourist checked in, and then the tourist declares the room to be unsatisfactory. Is this a breach of contract as to the center—or is it a breach of contract as to the motel or hotel?

Without arriving at answers, let it suffice to say that the activities of the tourist centers at the edge of town raise legal questions for which there are no ready answers.

SUMMARY

The laws that regulate travel agencies and the agents who operate them are in their infancy. The major laws in effect today did not come into being until the jet age arrived after World War II. Until that time, there were few cases brought against travel agencies and agents. Travelers, and lawyers as well, did not seek legal liability against those who planned and sold the trips in which property was lost, or injury or death occurred; travel agencies and agents were viewed as mere ticket sellers. This has dramatically changed.

An important contract distinction is that the "sale" of a trip around the world is based upon common-law contract rules and not upon sales contract principles. Such a trip is a sale of services and not a "sale of goods between merchants."

While the relationship between a travel agency and agent and the traveler who buys the service is not a special one, it is also not an ordinary relationship.

Thus, while the standard of care of the seller is that of a reasonable, ordinary travel agency or agent, it goes beyond that. An example is the duty to warn of "hot spots" or dangerous areas of the world where travelers might wish to go. They must be informed of the dangers that face them if they go there.

The regulation of the travel and tourism industry nationwide is increasing steadily. There have been far too many instances of fraud where planned travel failed because of the misappropriation of funds or the failure to provide services as agreed at promised destinations. It is in situations such as these that the law begins to exert control. The creation of legislation, of course, is much more rapid in attaining solutions to these problems. In the end, case decisions and acts of legislatures move in concert to solve these problems.

QUESTIONS

1. Why does a travel agent fill a positive need for travelers?
2. What is the legal problem that becomes involved when a travel agent passes on to someone else the services the traveler thought the agent was going to perform?
3. What is the legal error in disclosing only the name of a ship to a traveler who buys a ticket for a cruise on that ship?
4. What is "constructive fraud"?
5. Who is entitled to damages when the vacation of a family of five is ruined because of the negligence of a travel agent?
6. What is one problem the courts encounter when they apply agency law to travel agent cases?
7. What is an example of how one can be an "undisclosed principal" in a travel agency case?
8. How is a travel agent paid for his or her services?
9. The Levine case involved less than $100. Can you suggest how such a case got into an upper New York court in 1971?
10. True or false: One possible solution to the traveler–travel agent legal problems is for the courts to find two agencies instead of one.

NOTES

1. See *Rappa v. American Airlines, Inc.*, 87 Misc. 2d 759, 386 N.Y.S. 2d 612 (New York 1976).
2. New York: *Odysseys Unlimited, Inc. v. Astral Travel Service*, 77 Misc. 2d 502, 354 N.Y.S. 2d 88 (1974); *Seigel v. Council of Long Island Educators, Inc.*, 75 Misc. 2d 750, 348 N.Y.S. 2d 816 (1973); *Bucholtz v. Sirokin Travel Service, Ltd.*, 74 Misc. 2d 180, 343 N.Y.S. 2d 438, *aff'd* 80 Misc. 2d 333, 363 N.Y.S. 2d 415 (New York 1974). Pennsylvania: *Slade v. Cheung and Risser Enterprises, Inc.*, 10 Pa. D. & C. 3d 627 (Pennsylvania 1979).
3. Illinois: *Simpson v. Compagnie Nationale Air France*, 42 Ill. 2d 496, 248 N.E. 2d 117 (Illinois 1969). New York: *Levine v. British Overseas Airways Corp.*, 66 Misc. 2d

766, 322 N.Y.S. 2d 119 (New York 1971). Pennsylvania: *Slade v. Cheung and Risser Enterprises, Inc.,* 10 Pa. D. & C. 3d 627 (Pa., 1979).

4. *Ibid.*

5. See Wohlmuth, "The Liability of Travel Agents: A Study in the Selection of Appropriate Legal Principals," 40 *Temp.* L. Q. 29, 51 (1966).

6. See *Slade v. Cheung and Risser Enterprises, Inc.,* 10 Pa. D. & C. 3d 627 (Pa. C. P. 1979). See also, Wolmouth, N. 5 *supra,* 40 *Temp. L. Q.* at p. 56. "Even if the travel agent could be considered an agent, it merely clouds the issue to treat him as such for the purpose of liability. The issue is: Should the travel agent be held liable to the client under various circumstances? This question, aside from the problem of negligence, can best be answered by treating the travel agent as one who contracts with his client and, then, by determining what the travel agent expressly, impliedly, and as a matter of legal imposition, undertakes to do in his relations with his client."

7. See §5.02 *supra.*

8. See §5.04[4] *supra.*

9. See §5.04[2] *supra.*

10. See §5.04[3] *supra.*

11. See §5.04[5] *supra.*

12. Thomas A. Dickerson, *Travel Law,* Law Journal Seminars-Press, New York, sec. 5.05, using the author's footnotes.

13. *Maggio v. Maggiore,* 44 A.D. 2d 883, 351 N.Y.S. 2d 408 (New York 1954).

14. *United Airlines v. Lerner,* 87 Ill. App. 3d 801, 401 N.E. 3d 225, *Slade v. Cheung,* 10 Pa. D. and C. 3d 627 (Pa. C. P. 1979), *Rosen v. Porter,* 62 Ill. App. 3d 762, 379 N.E. 2d 407 (Illinois 1978).

15. 76 A.D. 2d 721, 432 N.Y.S. 2d 186, at pages 193–94 (New York 1980).

16. *Jackson v. Horizon,* 175 All. E.R. 92.

17. *Scher v. Liberty Travel,* 38 A.D. 2d 581, 328 N.Y.S. 2d 836 (New York 1971).

18. *Majestic,* 166 U.S. 375, 17 S. Ct. 597, 41 L. Ed. 1039 (New York 1897).

19. *Dupack v. Nationwide,* 73 A.D. 2d 903, 424 N.Y.S. 2d 436 (New York 1980).

24

Common Carriers

OVERVIEW

AN IMPORTANT PART of the travel chain is found in the means of transportation by which travelers get from one point to another. While a considerable amount of travel is carried out by private vehicle, a substantial part is carried out by public transportation. The laws that regulate these common carriers form the basis of this chapter.

An important part of hotel, hospitality, and tourism law is found in those rules and statutes that regulate cruise ships, passenger trains such as Amtrak, airlines, and other carriers. These rules, statutes, and treaties are of relatively recent origin, although the original control of common carriers came out of early common law. The rules of cruise ships can be traced back for centuries, when the sailing ships plied the high seas. In this chapter we will look first at the principles that regulate ship travel and then examine airline cases. The law is in a state of flux, and changes will be forthcoming, particularly in air travel. First, let's take a look at the law that regulates cruise ships.

CRUISE SHIPS

Contract of Carriage

When a breach of contract of common carriage occurs, compensatory damages are available to the traveler who can prove those damages. Punitive damages cannot be recovered unless the breach is accompanied by an intentional, wanton, and willful act of the carrier or its agents. If a willful act of an employee is outside the scope of employment, punitive damages cannot be recovered from the common carrier.[1] In most states, punitive damages cannot be recovered in a breach of contract case unless the acts also constitute an independent cause of action in tort.[2]

Contractual Duty

Once the contract of carriage arises, a common carrier has a contractual duty to transport passengers exercising the highest degree of vigilance and care for their comfort and safety.[3] This duty extends to employees and agents of the carrier even when such acts are outside the scope of employment. We are talking about contractual duties, not tort duties. Therefore, the damages recoverable are only compensatory and not punitive for breach of contract when the act of the employee is outside the scope of the employment. If an employee of a common carrier acts within the scope of his or her employment and insults or harms a traveler intentionally, punitive damages can be recovered from the common carrier upon proof in court. The act must be authorized by the carrier or ratified by the carrier later. That is to say, the act of the employee must be that of the carrier. As a general principle, a criminal act committed by an employee outside of the scope of employment does not render the employer liable—unless ratification takes place. In some states, employers cannot ratify an unlawful act of an employee.

CASE INTRODUCTION: COMMODORE CASE

In the following case, the plaintiff brought suit for compensatory and punitive damages because of an assault by an employee against her during a cruise. The upper court set aside punitive damages that had been awarded to the injured plaintiff as being contrary to the rule of common carriers.

COMMODORE CRUISE LINE LTD. V. KORMENDI
344 So. 2d 896 (Fla. App. 1977)

Before HENDRY, C.J., and BARKDULL and NATHAN, J.J. *PER CURIAM*

Appellant, defendant below, appeals from a final judgment entered pursuant to a jury verdict which awarded plaintiff both compensatory and punitive damages for an assault and battery alleged to have been committed upon Ilona Kormendi by an employee of appellant during a cruise on appellant's ship. . . .

Appellee [plaintiff], traveling without her husband, was allegedly assaulted and battered by an employee of appellant. The incident was alleged to have occurred . . . during a Caribbean cruise . . . while appellee was a passenger. The assailant apparently attempted to rob appellee's cabin but was taken by surprise by appellee's presence in said cabin. A scuffle ensued, after which the knife-wielding individual ran from the scene. This retreat was, however, not taken before appellee identified the person as a black man in crewman's garb. A subsequent investigation by the ship's captain and officers transpired; however, the identity of the assailant was never discovered.

The cause proceeded to trial upon the theory of breach of contract of common carriage. At trial there was ample testimony to suggest that the . . . investigation to ascertain the identity of the assailant was far from adequate, as there were no black passengers aboard the ship during the cruise and only two black crewmen.

At trial's conclusion, a jury returned a verdict for appellee and against appellant in the sum of Eighty-five Thousand Dollars ($85,000.00) compensatory damages and Two Hundred Thousand Dollars ($200,000.00) punitive damages. . . .

Appellant raises two points on appeal. The first challenges the sufficiency of the evidence in support of appellee's claim for assault and battery. After reviewing the record, we are of the opinion that there was substantial . . . evidence [to] support a verdict for appellee.

Appellant's second point concerns the . . . award of punitive damages. It is appellant's contention that, pursuant to a cause of action based upon a breach of contract of common carriage, punitive damages are only awardable against an employer when its employee commits an intentional, willful, wanton or malicious act while within the scope of his employment. *Subjudice*, no contention or argument was made by appellee that the assault occurred while within the official duties of the employee and, therefore, appellant argues, it was error to allow punitive damages.

For the reasons that follow, we agree with appellant's contention and reverse.

Under Florida Law, punitive damages are not . . . recoverable for breach of contract unless the acts constituting the breach also amount to an independent cause of action in tort, sustained by proper allegation and proof of an intentional wrong, insult, abuse or gross negligence.

Furthermore, under Florida law, a contractual duty arises between a passenger and common carrier obligating the carrier to transport the passenger to his or her destination, exercising the highest degree of care and vigilance for the passenger's safety. *Hall v. Seaboard Air Line Ry. Co.*, 84 Fla. 9, 93 So. 151 (1921); 5 Fla. Jur. *Carriers*, §108. The carrier's duty is transferred by and through its employees and any willful misconduct by its employees are actionable as against the carrier-employer. *Hall, supra*, 14 Am. Jur. 2d *Carriers*, §1059.

In addition, in comparison to an ordinary master-servant relationship, a common carrier is liable to a passenger for the wrongful acts of his or her employees during the contractual period, notwithstanding the fact that said acts are not within the scope of the employees' employment. Compare *Reina v. Metropolitan Dade County*, 285 So. 2d 648 (Fla. 3d DCA 1973), where the contract of carriage had terminated before the employee–bus driver assaulted the former passenger.

The only question, then, for our determination, is whether the expanded liability of a common carrier for damages occasioned by a breach of contractual duty owed by its employee to a passenger includes liability for punitive damages, over and above compensatory damages, notwithstanding the fact that the complained of act or acts were committed by the employee outside the scope of employment.

While case law and authority for awarding punitive damages against a common carrier and in favor of a passenger for the wrongful acts of an employee done within the scope of the employee's employment are ample, *Miami Transit Co. v. Yellen*, 156 Fla. 351, 22 So. 2d 787 (1945); *Atlantic Greyhound Lines v. Lovett*, 134 Fla. 505, 184 So. 133 (1938); 5 Fla. Jur. *Carriers*, §144, our research and research of counsel have failed to reveal authority from within this state for the question posed above.

Research of the law in other jurisdictions which have considered the question does reveal the following. In order for a common carrier to be liable to a passenger for punitive damages, the insulting, abusive or intentional wrong must be committed by the employee while discharging duties within the scope of his employment, or the act must be authorized by the employer or subsequently ratified by [the employer].

In that the assault was not committed by the employee while discharging duties within the scope of his employment, it was therefore incumbent . . . to allege and prove at trial that the act was subsequently ratified or initially authorized by appellant. This was never done, however, assuming *arguendo*, that the theory of ratification was attempted by appellee, this would be to no avail. The law is clear that unless the original act under scrutiny is done on the behalf of the employer, no ratification can take place. In addition, the Florida Supreme Court has stated that a criminal act committed outside the scope of a servant's authority cannot be ratified by the master, *Mallory v. O'Neill*, 69 So. 2d 313 (Fla. 1954).

In conclusion, we hold that where, as here, a passenger injured by an employee of a common carrier files suit based upon a breach of contract of carriage, punitive damages can only be awarded to the passenger upon a proper allegation and proof that the complained-of act was committed by the employee while within the scope of his employment or when the act was initially authorized by the carrier or subsequently ratified by him. . . .

Affirmed in part; reversed and remanded in part.

Classes Aboard Ship

One of the leading hotel colleges in the United States books passage on cruise ships and then conducts classes on board during the cruise. Samples of these classes include "The Economic and Political Implications of Tourism in the Caribbean," "Hospitality Protocol," and "Variations in Casino Play and Management."

A poster circulated throughout the campus of this particular university announces "Come Join Us—Sign up for a Nautical Course—January 1–8, 19XX. A six-day Cruise on the S/S Rhapsody." In the upper-left corner of this poster, in small type, is found "Paquet—French Cruises." Payment is to be made to the Board of Regents of the university.

Now assume that Joe Student signs up, pays the $999.00 "double occupancy," and then suffers a loss of goods or is injured during the cruise. He certainly would have the right to sue the shipowner, assuming the cause of the loss was the shipowner's negligence or act of an employee of the ship. Such suits normally must be brought where the ship is registered—often a foreign nation. But could Joe Student sue the Board of Regents of the university? This is much preferable to having to go to some other nation where the shipowners can be found.

Under the ruling of the McQuade case, in Chapter 23, the answer would be "yes." Although the name of the ship had been disclosed, the complete name, address, and capacity of the shipowner was not. Thus the Board of Regents, in all probability, would be held to be the agent of an undisclosed principal. Therefore, under agency law the agent assumes personal liability for all contracts (and resulting torts) that have been entered into while carrying forth the authority granted by the principal.

This undesirable legal result could be avoided in a simple manner. The owner of the ship, the legal capacity, and the address of the owner should be set forth on all ads, tickets, brochures, and other written information about the cruise. In addition, that information should be placed in conspicuous type so it will be noticed. In doing this, the principal has been disclosed and, under agency law, the agent (Board of Regents) incurs no personal liability for any subsequent breach of contract, tort, or other loss.

As to the use of disclaimers on cruise ship contracts, there is little chance of their being successful against ship owners. The courts have passed on their use negatively[4] and the U.S. Code covers them specifically:[5]

> It shall be unlawful for the manager, agent, master, or owner of any vessel transporting passengers between ports of the United States or between any such port and a foreign port to insert in any rule, regulation, contract, or agreement any provision or limitation (1) purporting in the event of loss of life or bodily injury arising from the negligence or guilt of such owner or his servants, to relieve such owner, master, or agent from liability, or from liability beyond any stipulated amount, for such loss or injury, or (2) purporting in such event to lessen, weaken, or avoid the right of any claimant to a trial by court of competent jurisdiction on the question of liability for such loss or injury, or the measure of damages therefor. All such provisions or limitations contained in any such rule, regulation, contract, or agreement are declared to be against public policy and shall be null and void and of no effect.

Turning from our look at the law of cruise ships, let's examine the laws that come to the front in the operation of airlines. This is an area in which the rules, regulations, and common-law holdings are vast indeed. A helpful place to begin is by a look at airline reservations.

AIRLINE RESERVATIONS

When breach of an airline reservation occurs, recoveries have been permitted for compensatory damages (actual loss) as well as punitive damages. In one case a federal judge permitted a "bumped" traveler to recover punitive damages, basing the decision on federal law.[6]

CASE INTRODUCTION: ARCHIBALD CASE

The Archibald case, below, shows the view of the courts on airline "bumping."

ARCHIBALD V. PAN AMERICAN WORLD AIRWAYS
460 F. 2d 14 (1972)

CHOY, Circuit Judge.

Mr. and Mrs. George B. Archibald appeal a district court order directing a verdict for Pan American World Airways, Inc. (Pan Am). The District Court found that the Archibalds had failed to present a *prima facie* case of undue or unreasonable preference or unjust discrimination in violation of 49 U.S.C. §1374(b). We reverse and remand.

. . . The Archibalds made two economy reservations for Pan Am's Flight 801 on August 6 from Tokyo to Guam. Pan Am accepted and confirmed the reservations, and told the Archibalds no further confirmation was necessary. On August 6, the Archibalds checked in . . . nearly an hour early and received seat assignments. When they attempted to board the plane, however, they and 28 other passengers were asked to step aside. Many of these passengers eventually enplaned, but the Archibalds and a dozen others did not. Three passengers who did go aboard made their reservations after the Archibalds had made theirs.

Pan Am then told the remaining passengers that the flight had been oversold, and that they would not be able to go. The airline provided hotel accommodations for the bumped passengers, tendered a voucher for payment of denied boarding compensation, which Mr. Archibald did not cash, and put the Archibalds on the next available flight to Guam.

49 U.S.C. §1374(b) reads, in pertinent part:

"No air carrier or foreign air carrier shall make, give, or cause any undue or unreasonable preference or advantage to any particular person . . . in any respect whatsoever or subject any particular person . . . to any unjust discrimination or any undue or unreasonable prejudice or disadvantage in any respect whatsoever."

This section creates a . . . federal cause of action for unreasonable preferences and unjust discrimination. *Fitzgerald v. Pan American World Airways, Inc.*, 229 F. 2d 499 (2nd Cir. 1956). An injunction against prospective or continuing discrimination is usually refused out of deference to administrative remedies before the Civil Aeronautics Board. *Mortimer v. Delta Air Lines*, 302 F. Supp. 276, 282 (N.D. Ill., 1969); *Wills v. Trans World Airlines, Inc.*, 200 F. Supp. 360, 366 (S.D.Cal., 1961). However, purely nominal compensatory damages are available, including an award for humiliation and hurt feelings when the facts warrant, and the extent and nature of the affront are established. *Flores v. Pan American World Airways, Inc.*, 259 F. Supp. 402, 404 (D.P.R., 1966). See *Wills, supra*, 200 F. Supp. at 366-367, in which the plaintiff received $1.54 for pecuniary loss and $5,000 in punitive damages. Punitive damages over and above actual injury are awardable if the defendant acted "wantonly, or oppressively, or with such malice as implies a spirit of mischief or criminal indifference to civil obligations." *Wills, supra*, at 367-368. . . .

In *Wills*, an economy passenger was sacrificed in favor of a first class passenger with a later reservation in direct violation of the airline's own bumping policy. The court held that the plaintiff was "entitled to priority in flight accommodations over all passengers who had made later reservations than he and yet were permitted to board the flight.... By disregarding plaintiff's priority, the defendant airline unjustly and unreasonably discriminated against him, and thus violated the Act." 200 F. Supp. at 365. And in *Stough v. North Central Airlines, Inc.*, 55 Ill. App. 2d 338, 204 N.E. 2d 792 (1965), the court affirmed a jury verdict that the airline had not discriminated against two passengers with reserved seats who (in accordance with company safety regulations) were not allowed to board a plane which departed with empty seats.

These . . . cases demonstrate that while overselling does not *per se* give rise to a §1374(b) action, substantial overselling is evidence of malice to be considered in assessing punitive damages. See *Wills, supra,* 200 F. Supp. at 367-368. Some overselling is an economic necessity for an airline in view of inevitable cancellations and no-shows. However, when a flight is thus oversold, the airline must fill the plane in a reasonable and just manner. *Stough* and *Wills* indicate that bumping which is outwardly discriminatory or preferential may be legitimated by proof that the airline adhered to its established policy and that the policy is reasonable. This policy is within the peculiar knowledge of the airline, which is most able to present evidence justifying the selection of one passenger over another. The passenger cannot reasonably be expected to divine at the gate, or discover later, what the airline's policy is and whether it has been obeyed. The passenger is able to prove that he possessed a confirmed reservation and a resultant right to a seat, and that this priority was not honored. This suffices to establish that a preference or discrimination has occurred. It is not unreasonable then to place upon the airline the burden of proving that the discrimination or preference was reasonable by demonstrating company policy and why, in each particular case, one passenger was chosen over another.

The Archibalds proved that they had a priority right to an economy seat because they held confirmed reservations on Flight 801, and that Pan Am allowed three passengers with later reservations to board the plane. With this, they established a *prima facie* case that Pan Am had unjustly and unreasonably discriminated against them. Since Pan Am had not demonstrated, if it could, the reasonableness of its preference of the three passengers over the Archibalds, a directed verdict for the airline was inappropriate at that stage of the trial.

Reversed and remanded.

OVERBOOKING

The Archibald case provides the historical perspective on airline bumping. The following shows what has happened since then.

Under the Deregulation Act of 1978, the Civil Aeronautics Board (CAB) did away with the tariff system as it related to flight delays. There was one exception to this, however. It had to do with oversales of seats. Under current regulations,[7] control still is maintained to balance the interests of airlines and passengers. The procedure now followed is that passengers are asked to give up their seats for appropriate compensation. The regulations require that notice be given of this practice.

The best way to understand airline overbooking is to read the terms found on U.S. airline tickets. Figure 24.1 is an example. As to deregulation in general, the CAB had been active until it was replaced.

During 1980 and 1981, the CAB took several actions to assist carriers as well as travel agents to prepare for the airline deregulation that became effective in 1983. It encouraged small carriers to enter the market, permitted discount air fares,

FIGURE 24.1 Airline overbooking notice.

NOTICE—OVERBOOKING OF FLIGHTS

Airline flights may be overbooked, and there is a slight chance that a seat will not be available on a flight for which a person has a confirmed reservation. If the flight is overbooked, no one will be denied a seat until airplane personnel first ask for volunteers willing to give up their reservation in exchange for a payment of the airline's choosing. If there are not enough volunteers, the airline will deny boarding to other persons in accordance with its particular boarding priority. With few exceptions, persons denied boarding involuntarily are entitled to compensation. The complete rules for payment of compensation and each airline's boarding priorities are available at all airport ticket counters and boarding locations.

---

eliminated the filing of tariffs—which the airlines had relied on so long for lost baggage and delayed flights—and returned the airlines to common-law control.

Now that airline deregulation is a reality, much of the regulation of airlines is coming from the courts because the airlines no longer have tariffs for protection. A look at some holdings in court cases will illustrate.

Court Changes in Regulation

The doctrine of *res ipsa loquitur* was applied to the airline industry when it was in its infancy. This has changed because of airline deregulation. It is not so important now to keep the "big brother eye" upon airlines as it was in earlier decades. The airline industry has done much to control itself, bringing the safety level of flying to an all-time high. Yet, many problems still exist. One of them is flight delays. Flight delays can lead to recovery in court for discomfort and inconvenience. One court said it this way:[8]

> [I]n an appropriate case, damages for mental distress can be recovered in contract, just as damages for shock can be recovered in tort. One such case is a contract for a holiday, or any other contract to provide entertainment and enjoyment. If the contracting party breaks his contract, damages can be given for the disappointment, the distress, the upset and frustration caused by the breach. I know it is difficult to assess in terms of money, but it is no more difficult than the assessment which the courts have to make every day in personal injury cases for loss of amenities. Taking the present case, Mr. Jarvis has only a fortnight's holiday in the year. He books it far ahead and looks forward to it all the time. He ought to be compensated for the loss of it.

Antitrust cases are making their appearance in airline cases.

Airline trade associations, ATA and IATA, monitor the sale of air transportation by travel agents and tour operators. ATA and IATA have the power to withdraw an agency appointment if the travel agent or tour operator fails to adhere to association rules. On occasion, travel agents and tour operators have commenced antitrust actions against these trade associations. These actions usually allege a conspiracy to restrain trade and drive the plaintiff out of business. All of these actions had been limited if not dismissed because of the doctrine of primary jurisdiction of the Civil Aeronautics Board. This defense, however, became no longer available in 1983, and the courts will, no doubt, see a goodly number of antitrust cases in the travel field.[9]

As a common carrier, an airline is an insurer of the baggage it carries,[10] subject to the Warsaw Convention, which we will examine in a moment. An air carrier that violates the racial laws or fails to follow its boarding plans can be sued for actual plus punitive damages.[11] Leaving this examination of actions by the courts, it is useful to learn something about the Warsaw Convention. If it is applicable, it provides protection to the airlines and strips passengers of considerable legal protection. In reading this material, it is important to also read the notes.

The Warsaw Convention

A major treaty enacted at Warsaw, Poland, in 1929, had, and continues to have, a major effect upon "international carriage by air." It has no application to flights inside of a single nation. Of all HH&T legal conventions, this one has been accepted most widely, with more than 100 nations being signatory to it today. The original articles of the Warsaw Convention were signed by twenty-three nations on October 12, 1929. The first ratifying nations were Brazil, France, Latvia, Poland, Romania, Spain, and Yugoslavia. The pact took effect on February 13, 1933, in those nations. It went into force in the United States on October 29, 1934.

Purpose of the Treaty

The convention was created to limit the liability of the fledgling airlines. Written in French, it replaced common-law liability with the limits on liability contained within the treaty. The limit on liability for death was set at $8,000, or 125,000 francs. The treaty provided that this sum was to be paid by use of the French franc, with provisions to convert this standard to any national currency.

Montreal Agreement of 1966

In 1966, at a meeting of the signatory nations held in Montreal, Canada, the limit on liability was raised to $75,000. This was not an amendment of the original treaty. It was a mere contract by the signing parties and it applies only to American citizens.

Montreal Protocol of 1975

The treaty was updated again in Montreal in 1975. Figure 24.2, taken from an airline ticket, explains the terms of the convention. These and other limitations on liability have been the subject of litigation and some examples are offered.

CASE INTRODUCTION: GREENBURG CASE

In the Greenburg case, limitations similar to those found in Figure 24.2 were challenged and formed the basis of the opinion of the judge. (This was not an international flight, so the Warsaw Convention did not apply.)

FIGURE 24.2   Terms of 1975 Montreal Protocol.

ADVICE TO INTERNATIONAL PASSENGERS ON LIMITATION OF LIABILITY

Passengers on a journey involving an ultimate destination or a stop in a country other than the country of origin are advised that the provisions of a treaty known as the Warsaw Convention may be applicable to the entire journey, including any portion entirely within the country of origin or destination. For such passengers on a journey to, from, or with an agreed stopping place in the United States of America, the Convention provides that the liability of certain carriers, parties to such special contracts, for death of or personal injury to passengers, is limited to proven damages not to exceed U.S. $75,000 per passenger, and that this liability up to such limit shall not depend on negligence on the part of the carrier. The limit of liability of U.S. $75,000 is inclusive of legal fees and costs except that in case of a claim brought in a state where provision is made for separate award of legal fees and costs, the limit shall be the sum of U.S. $58,000 exclusive of legal fees and costs. For such passengers traveling by a carrier not a party to such special contracts or on a journey not to, from, or having an agreed stopping place in the United States of America, liability of the carrier for death or personal injury to passengers is limited in most cases to approximately U.S. $10,000 or U.S. $20,000.

The names of carriers are available at all ticket offices of such carriers and may be examined on request. Additional protection can be obtained by purchasing insurance from a private company. Such insurance is not affected by any limitation of the carrier's liability under the Warsaw Convention or such special contracts of carriage. For further information, please consult your airline or insurance company representative.

NOTICE OF BAGGAGE LIABILITY LIMITATIONS

Liability for loss, delay, or damage to baggage is limited as follows unless a higher value is declared in advance and additional charges are paid: (1) For most international travel (including domestic portions of international journeys) to approximately $9.07 per pound ($20.00 per kilo) for checked baggage, and $400 per passenger for unchecked baggage; (2) for travel wholly between U.S. points to $750 per passenger on most carriers (a few have lower limits). Excess valuation may be declared on valuable articles. Carriers assume liability for fragile or perishable articles. Further information may be obtained from the carrier.

GREENBURG V. UNITED AIRLINES, INC.
414 N.Y.S. 2d 240, 98 Misc. 2d 544 (New York 1979)

BERNARD FUCHS, Judge.

Plaintiff is a school teacher who flew . . . on vacation from New York City to San Francisco and checked her bags for the flight. The bags never arrived. She sues for their value and for damages incident to the baggage loss.

At trial, . . . there was no serious contest of liability. As a common carrier, defendant bears an insurer's responsibility for the loss, 7 N.Y. Jur., Carriers §434. Defendant's principal reliance was . . . on the tariff, which limits its liability for lost baggage . . . to $750.00, Local and Joint Passenger Rules Tariff P. R.6, CAB No. 142, Rule 370.

The tariff . . . sets forth the following exception to its limitation of liability: "The above maximum liability shall be waived for an individual claimant where it can be shown that with respect to that claimant the carrier failed to provide notice of limited liability for baggage in accordance with Section 221.176 of the Civil Aeronautics Board's Economic Regulations."

The clear policy of the CAB's Economic Regulations in Section 221.176 is to require conspicuous display of the limited liability notice. They specify the size of type and language of the notice and require it to be posted on signs.

A notice of limited liability for baggage is printed on the sixth page of plaintiff's six-page ticket. That page, measuring 3 1/4 inches vertically by 7 3/8 inches horizontally, is dense from edge to edge (no margins) with 24 lines of material.

Three of those lines are distinct from the rest in capital letters of bold-faced type. One of the . . . lines is centered at the top and reads "ADVICE TO INTERNATIONAL PASSENGERS ON LIMITATION OF LIABILITY." About 2 1/4 inches down the page, in similar type at the end of the first of only two paragraphs, appear the words "SEE CONDITIONS OF CONTRACT ON REVERSE SIDE OF PASSENGER COUPON." The latter statement ends near the right edge and is followed, in the same lettering, by a line directly under and appearing to continue as part of it, reading "NOTICE OF BAGGAGE LIABILITY LIMITATIONS."

Any reasonable person, let alone a harried tourist, would conclude that the described page, under its top line, applies solely to international passengers. The format is perfectly calculated to obscure from a domestic traveler's view the presence there of an applicable limit of baggage loss liability. Even the second paragraph, where the loss limitation finally appears, applies only to international travel until the domestic passenger's eye, if it persists through the upper mass of irrelevant material, falls at last on the fourth of its six lines.

A notice so elusive cannot fulfill the office provided for it . . . . In order to succeed, defendant's communication must be positioned and identified so as to penetrate the traveling public's reasonably focused consciousness. Instead, *defendant has set before the traveler a morsel of nourishment hidden in a banquet of dust*. Authority and principle combine to deny its effect. [Note: The words in italic are considered to be a classic legal statement.]

In *Lisi v. Alitalia-Linee Aeree Italiane*, 370 F. 2d 508 (2d Cir., 1966), *aff'd* 390 U.S. 455, 88 S. Ct. 1193, 20 L. Ed. 2d 27 (1968), *rehear den.*, 391 U.S. 929, 88 S. Ct. 1801, 20 L. Ed. 2d 671 (1968), limited liability under the Warsaw Convention for wrongful death and personal injuries was disallowed because defendant's notice of the limitation (in tickets and baggage checks) was printed too small to notify passengers adequately. Our own Court of Appeals reached the same conclusion in *Egan v. Kollsman Instrument Corp.*, 21 N.Y. 2d 160, 287 N.Y.S. 2d 14, 234 N.E. 2d 199, *cert. den.*, 390 U.S. 1039, 88 S. Ct. 1636, 20 L. Ed. 2d 301 (1967), again because the carrier had failed to provide "conspicuous notice" of its limited liability. The rationale of those decisions, equally applicable in the present case, is that an inadequately communicated notice cannot alert a passenger to seek alternate protections such as insurance coverage.

Failure to deliver (or to deliver timely) a ticket bearing notice of limited liability is equally fatal to a carrier's defense against death claims exceeding the Warsaw Convention ceiling and for the same reason. *Martens v. Flying Tiger Line, Inc.*, 341 F. 2d 851, *cert. den.*, 382 U.S. 816, 86 S. Ct. 38, 15 L. Ed. 2d 64 (2d Cir., 1965); *Warren v. Flying Tiger Line, Inc.*, 352 F. 2d 494 (9th Cir., 1965). Nothing in *Martin v. Trans-World Airlines, Inc.*, 219 Pa.Super. 42, 280 A. 2d 647 (1972) limits the application of those authorities in the present case.

Plaintiff testified to the loss of a long list of clothing and personal items, both new and used, which she had packed for use in the climates of California, Washington and Alaska (not a flight destination) over a five-week period. Her claimed cost of those items and of one new suitcase is in evidence . . . . See *Lake v. Dye*, 232 N.Y. 209, 133 N.E. 448 (1921); *Warren's Negligence*, Vol. 7B, ch. 16, *Personal Property*, 1.05 (1968). Plaintiff also . . . spent over four days in San Francisco travelling repeatedly to the airport in search of her baggage.

Defendant has already paid its claimed maximum liability of $750. Accordingly, plaintiff is granted judgment [for the excess loss] . . . with interest from the date of loss, July 31, 1978, and costs of the action.

In *Maugnie v. Compagnie National Air France*,[12] an airline passenger brought an action against an air carrier to recover damages for personal injuries sustained when she slipped and fell as she proceeded down a passenger corridor leading from the carrier's gate to the main area of an airline terminal. The U. S. District Court held that, because the passenger had deplaned and reached a safe point inside the airport when the accident occurred, the injuries complained of were not suffered "on board the aircraft or in the course of any operation of . . . disembarking" within the meaning of that phrase as used in the Warsaw Convention and that the passenger therefore could not recover. The passenger appealed. The Court of Appeals held that the district court's conclusion was correct.

Under the Warsaw Convention, damages for mental injury must flow from some bodily injury and not from mental distress alone.[13] Once it is determined that an airline cannot rely on the protections of the Warsaw Convention, common-law principles of liability control.

The Convention provides for a two-year period of limitation from the date of destination arrival—or the date that arrival should have occurred. Failure to give notice of this time limitation does not extend it.[14]

Under the Convention, carriers are liable for any delays involving passengers and their luggage.[15] A court has held that this duty includes efforts to get passengers on other flights.[16] A defense provided by the Convention is that "the carrier shall not be liable if it takes all measures to avoid damage."[17] The cases that follow involve the Warsaw Convention.

CASE INTRODUCTION: COHEN CASE

A passenger who lost luggage on an international flight claimed there was "willful misconduct" on the part of the airline. If the court so finds, Article 25(1) of the Convention will not apply and the airline will be responsible for the full value of the lost luggage.

The case had its beginning in July 1974, when Charles and Hermaine Cohen left New York to begin a twenty-eight-day tour of South America.[18] On one leg of their tour, their flight to Rio de Janeiro was diverted to São Paulo, Brazil. Upon transfer to another flight, the Cohens became concerned that their luggage would not be transferred to the new flight. After being assured that the transfer had been made, they went on to Rio. At that point, they found that their luggage was on a New York-bound jet.

Because of the timetable of the remaining tour, they had to continue without their luggage, forcing them to buy clothes and other items. During the balance of their trip, they suffered inconvenience, embarrassment, and discomfort because they were not able to replace their clothing and other effects adequately.

On their return to New York, the airline, Varig, told them their luggage had disappeared. Varig offered them $640.00, taking credit for $60.00 that was advanced to them by the airline in Rio, for a total of $700.00. This was the amount the airline was obligated to pay under the 250 francs-per-kilo rule of the Warsaw Convention.

The Cohens refused the $640.00 and sued. A New York jury awarded them $6,440.65, with the award split one-half for the lost baggage and one-half for discomfort and mental suffering. The jury found that the refusal to unload was willful and thus the Warsaw Convention limitation did not apply. The airlines appealed, and in the case that follows, you can see what the appellate court did to the jury verdict.

COHEN V. VARIG AIRLINES, INC.
390 N.Y.S. 2d 515 (New York 1976)

Carriers

In action by airline passengers against airline to recover value of lost baggage checked with airline, there was insufficient evidence to support trial court's finding that airline's refusal to unload all luggage from its plane constituted "willful misconduct," so as to abrogate limitation of liability provision of Warsaw Convention.

Before DUDLEY, P.J., and RICCOBONO and TIERNEY, JJ. *PER CURIAM:*

Judgment entered . . . (Danzig, J.) modified by decreasing the total recovery to the sum of $700.00, with interest and costs; as modified, affirmed without costs.

There was insufficient evidence in the record to support the trial court's finding that the act of defendant in refusing to unload all luggage from its plane in Rio de Janeiro constituted "willful misconduct" within . . . Article 25(1) of the Warsaw Convention *(Grey v. American Airlines, Inc.,* 227 F. 2d 282 [2d Cir.]).

DUDLEY, P.J., and TIERNEY, J., concur. RICCOBONO, J., dissents in the following memorandum. RICCOBONO, Justice (dissenting):

I dissent and vote to affirm for the reasons set forth in the opinion of Danzig, J., at Trial Term.

In my view, there was sufficient evidence in the record for the Trial Court to find in the . . . factual pattern under review that the act of defendant, by its employees, in refusing to remove plaintiff's luggage from its plane in Rio de Janeiro constituted "willful misconduct" within the purview of Article 25(1) of the Warsaw Convention *(Grey v. American Airlines, Inc.,* 227 F. 2d 282 [2d Cir.]). Moreover, I agree . . . that New York law governed the elements of damages to be recovered by plaintiffs.

Plaintiffs' recovery was not limited to the loss of their personal property. Individuals and corporations engaged in quasi-public business may not contract to absolve themselves from liability for their own willful misconduct or . . . negligence.

Tishman & Lipp, Inc. v. Delta Airlines, 275 F. Supp. 471 (S.D.N.Y.), *aff'd* 413 F. 2d 1401, (2nd Cir.), relied on by appellant is not applicable. Plaintiffs' luggage contained apparel and accoutrements of vacationers, not thousands of dollars worth of jewelry.

The Cohens were not finished yet. They appealed this ruling to the intermediate appellate court of New York. That court reinstated the jury verdict for the loss of the luggage but refused to reinstate the jury award for the mental suffering. The latter part of the ruling was based on a longstanding rule in New York that recovery cannot be had for mental injury in the absence of physical injury independent of the mental injury. Such had not been the case here. The Cohen cases represents a leg in the development of the "laws of lost luggage," under the Warsaw Convention.

CASE INTRODUCTION: EGAN CASE

The next case provides one more example of what not to do with disclaimers. This was an unfortunate situation, as not only Mrs. Seiter, but scores of others as well, died in the crash in question. The Warsaw Convention was recognized, but when it came to the question of whether Mrs. Seiter had proper notice of the limitation on liability, the court ruled in favor of her estate.

EGAN V. KOLLSMAN INSTRUMENT CORP.
287 N.Y.S. 2d 14 (New York 1967)

FULD, Chief Judge.

Mrs. Eileen M. Seiter was killed when the American Airlines plane on which she was a passenger crashed as it approached LaGuardia Airport . . . . Her administrators [estate representatives] have brought this action for wrongful death, and American has raised as an affirmative defense the limitation of liability provisions of the Warsaw Convention (49 U. S. Stat., pt. 2, p. 3000, hereinafter referred to as the "Convention"). Two questions are presented by this appeal: Was the final leg of the flight—from Chicago to New York City—to be deemed "international transportation" for purposes of the Convention so as to render it applicable to the present action and, if it was, had the carrier sufficiently complied with the Convention's notice requirements to permit it to limit its liability?

Mrs. Seiter had purchased an airline ticket for a round trip between New York City and Vancouver, Canada. The ticket scheduled her on successive flights of Northwest Airlines and United Airlines with stopovers at Seattle (west and eastbound) and at Chicago (eastbound). On the face of the ticket, below the name of the passenger, the following foot-note appeared in exceedingly small, almost unreadable (4 1/2-point) print:

> "Carriage/Transportation under this Passenger Ticket and Baggage Check, hereinafter called 'ticket', is subject to the rules relating to liability established by the Convention for the Unification of Certain Rules relating to International Carriage/Transportation by Air signed at Warsaw, October 12, 1929, if such Carriage/Transportation is 'international carriage/transportation' as defined by said Convention."

Mrs. Seiter arrived in Vancouver . . . as scheduled, but . . . when she was ticketed to return to New York, she discovered that all flights out of Vancouver had been canceled because of inclement weather. Instead of waiting for the next available flight, she proceeded to Seattle by bus, obtaining a refund check from Northwest Airlines for that portion of her journey . . . .

Mrs. Seiter reached Seattle in time to permit her to take off on the Northwest flight to Chicago for which she had been originally scheduled. Reaching Chicago too late to make her . . . connection to New York City, she presented her ticket to Northwest Airlines and received a new one for passage on an American Airlines flight to La Guardia Airport. The new ticket—under the heading "COMPLETE ROUTING THIS TICKET AND CONJUNCTION TICKET(S)"—specified the origin and destination as "NY" and expressly recited that it was "ISSUED IN EXCHANGE FOR" the original ticket, the fare being listed at the figure which had initially been paid for the entire round trip. Mrs. Seiter boarded respondent American's aircraft which, as stated, crashed while attempting to make a landing at La Guardia.

The present action for wrongful death was brought against American Airlines and two other defendants—one the manufacturer of an assertedly defective altimeter and the other the assembler of the aircraft. We are, however, concerned solely with the sufficiency of American's (third) affirmative defense which asserts an "exemption from and limitation of liability in accordance with all of the applicable provisions of said Convention."

As both courts below recognized, answer to the underlying question—whether the flight from Chicago to New York City was "international transportation" under the Convention—depends upon the nature of the contract between the carrier and its passenger.[19] When it provides for "international" transportation, "whether or not there be a break in the transportation" (art. 1, subd. [2]), all flights taken under it are governed by the Convention.

The Convention's emphasis on the contract actually "made" appears to have been . . . designed to prevent any subsequent intervening circumstances from affecting the result. The reason is manifest; as one commentator put it, "[t]his prescription possesses, for the parties involved, the appreciable advantage of settling in advance the application of the Warsaw Convention, thus becoming independent of fortuitous events."

The contract embodied in the original ticket issued in this case was undoubtedly for international transportation since, in the words of the Convention (art. 1, subd. [2]), it provided for "an agreed stopping place within a territory . . . of another power." Whether or not Mrs. Seiter might have been able to rescind this contract and enter into a wholly new one of an entirely domestic character in Seattle, the simple fact is that she chose not to do so.[20] The remainder of her journey—from Seattle to Chicago and from Chicago to New York—was performed under the original contract; and since, as already noted, it provided for international transportation, it was subject to the Convention. . . .

This brings us to the . . . argument that, even if the Warsaw Convention applies, the carrier is not entitled to invoke the provisions limiting its liability because the ticket delivered to Mrs. Seiter did not give sufficient notice that the rules of the Convention relating to the limitation of liability were applicable.

Under article 3 (subd. [1], par. [e]), . . . an airline is required to deliver a passenger ticket which contains a "statement that the transportation is subject to the rules relating to liability established by this Convention."[21] The ticket before us did contain in footnotes on the several coupons, such a statement, but, as is apparent from inspection, it is in such exceedingly small and fine print as almost to defy reading.[22] Thus, although there was literal compliance with . . . article 3, the question arises whether such . . . satisfies the Convention's demands when viewed in the light of its over-all purposes. We do not believe that it does. In our judgment, a statement which cannot reasonably be deciphered fails of its . . . function of affording notice and may not be accepted as the sort of statement . . . required by the Convention.

An examination of the ticket forms which the respondent used . . . can only lead one to conclude that Mrs. Seiter was not sufficiently apprised of the consequences which would result from the fact that her flight happened to carry her outside of the United States. Despite the fact that the Convention was applicable to her journey, the carrier's failure to give the requisite notice prevents it from asserting a limitation of liability. [Thus, the estate recovered the full value for the loss of her life and property.]

CASE INTRODUCTION: RUDEES CASE

In the final case, an airline was sued for scald burns a passenger received while in flight. The "directed verdict" was set aside because the upper court believed there were questions of fact for a jury to decide. The court also distinguished negligence of the pilot, if any, from that of the stewardess.

RUDEES V. DELTA AIRLINES, INC.
553 S.W 2d. 84 (Tennessee 1977)

MATHERNE, Judge.

While riding as a fare-paying passenger on a . . . scheduled flight of the defendant airline, the plaintiff sustained . . . injuries when a stewardess spilled scalding coffee on his lap. The plaintiff sued . . . and the trial judge, at the conclusion of the plaintiff's proof, directed a verdict for the defendant. The plaintiff appeals, assigning that action of the trial judge as error.

The plaintiff boarded the defendant's DC-9 airplane at Memphis for a flight to Atlanta, Georgia. The passengers were asked to keep their seat belts fastened due to the possibility that the plane might encounter air turbulence. . . . Approximately 100 miles from Atlanta, a stewardess came down the aisle of the airplane carrying . . . an open tray which contained . . . cups of scalding coffee. The plaintiff was seated on an aisle seat with his seat belt fastened; he had not ordered coffee. The airplane . . . hit some clear air turbulence, which made the stewardess sway in the aisle and spill the contents of the cups on the plaintiff's lap. This resulted in . . . severe burns to the plaintiff's thighs and groin area.

The defendant, on motion for a directed verdict, argued that the plaintiff had not proved any negligence on its part. Counsel for the defendant argued, and the trial judge apparently agreed, that the plaintiff could not recover because he failed to prove that the pilot was negligent or that the defendant knew or should have known about the air turbulence.

The foregoing argument overlooks the basis of the lawsuit. The plaintiff alleged that the stewardess was negligent: (1) in spilling the coffee; (2) in her manner of carrying scalding coffee down the aisle of the plane; (3) in carrying the coffee in uncovered containers; and (4) in attempting to serve scalding coffee during flight. The issue is the negligence of the stewardess; therein lies the lawsuit.

Facts were proved from which the jury could have found the proximate cause of the plaintiff's injuries was the negligence of the stewardess as charged. We hold that reasonable minds could well differ on this issue and that the trial judge erred in directing a verdict for the defendant.

The judgment of the trial court is reversed, and this lawsuit is remanded for a new trial [before a jury].

CARNEY, P.J., and NEARN, J., concur.

SUMMARY

Early common law established rules concerning controlling the passage of sailing ships and the protection of the persons and the goods that they carried. In the nineteenth century, laws were developed to regulate the train systems that enveloped the eastern states, and as of May 10, 1869, linked the entire nation. This linkage changed the face of the nation and the laws of travel as well.

As the twentieth century began, laws and regulations became necessary to regulate motor vehicles such as taxi cabs, buses, tractor trailers, and privately owned motor vehicles. The nation left the waterways and the rails and took to the roads. Today, these motor vehicles are regulated by public service commissions and other state laws.

As all of this came to pass, a new body of common law developed in the American courts and is still developing today. This new segment of the common law provides guidelines that must be followed by those involved in all phases of travel and tourism. This is true even though such travel may occur outside the continental limits of the United States. American courts have the power to determine disputes involving injury, property loss, or death of travelers that occur in remote points in the world, subject of course to the Warsaw Convention.

With increasing international travel, the Warsaw Convention is of key importance to those who fly between nations who have signed this treaty. The Warsaw Convention contains liability limits, and the traveler should contact an insurance agent to assure that sufficient insurance is in place before the flight begins.

QUESTIONS

1. What did "airline deregulation" do to airline liability in the United States?
2. What does the law require before one can recover punitive damages in common carrier cases?
3. What was the legal issue in the Commodore case?
4. What is the Warsaw Convention? What is its purpose?
5. Why was "willful misconduct" so important in the Cohen case?
6. What is a "directed verdict"? What is it used for? (See *Owen v. Burn.*)
7. Can there be a directed verdict in a case where there is in fact a jury question? Why?
8. Why is the question of whether there was negligence one a jury must determine?
9. What is an "affirmative defense"?
10. True or false: The Warsaw Convention was designed to protect airlines making international air flights.

NOTES

1. *Commodore Cruise Line, Ltd. v. Kormendi.* (See accompanying case.)
2. *Country Club of Miami Corporation v. McDaniel*, 310 So. 2d 436 (Florida 1975).
3. *McManigal v. Chicago Motor Coach Company*, 18 Ill. App. 2d 183, 151 N.E. 2d 410 (Illinois 1958).
4. *Moore v. American*, 30 F. Supp. 843 (S.D. New York 1935).
5. 46 U.S.C. sec. 183c.
6. Civil Aeronautics Act of 1938, section 8404 (b). "No air carrier shall, . . . cause any undue . . . preference . . . to any person . . . in any respect whatsoever" (in the granting of air seats). Also see *Nader v. Allegheny Airlines*, civ. act No. 1346-72 (District of Columbia 1971).
7. CAB Econ. Reg., Part 250-Oversales (Reg. E.D. 1306).
8. *Jarvis v. Swan Tours*, Q.B. 233 (Queen's Bench 1973).

9. Dickerson, *supra* sec. 2.09(3).

10. *Greenburg v. United*, 98 Misc. 2d 544, 414 N.Y.S. 2d 240 (New York 1979).

11. *Mahaney v. Compagnie*, 15 Aviation Cases 17, 655 (S.D. New York 1979).

12. 549 F. 2d 1256, 1977.

13. *Rosman v. Trans World*, 34 N.Y. 2d 385, 358 N.Y.S. 2d 97, 314 N.E. 2d 848 (New York 1974).

14. *Bergman v. Pan American World Airways, Inc.*, 32 A.D. 2d 95, 299 N.Y.S. 2d 982 (New York 1969): "It follows that the carrier may not avail itself of those provisions of the Convention which exclude or limit liability. Is a statute of limitations a provision that excludes or limits liability? We think not. . . . Firstly, because a statute of limitations never limits liability, nor does it exclude it. . . . If by virtue of any state of facts the statute is tolled or waived, the liability is unaffected. . . ." 299 N.Y.S. 2d at 984 (New York 1974).

15. Article 20(1) of the Convention.

16. *Murry v. Capitol*, 424 N.Y.S. 2d 89 (New York 1983).

17. *Supra*, n. 15.

18. A detailed account of their adventures and court trials can be found in *How to Stand Up for Your Rights and Win!* by Roy Cohn (New York: Simon & Schuster, 1988) p. 154.

19. Article 1 of the Convention, which bears on its applicability, reads as follows:
"(1) This convention shall apply to all international transportation of persons, baggage, or goods performed by aircraft for hire. It shall apply equally to gratuitous transportation by aircraft performed by an air transportation enterprise.
"(2) For the purposes of this convention, the expression 'international transportation' shall mean any transportation in which, according to the contract made by the parties, the place of departure and the place of destination, whether there be a break in the transportation or a transshipment, are situated within the territories of two High Contracting Parties, or within the territory of a single High Contracting Party, if there is an agreed stopping place within a territory subject to the sovereignty, suzerainty, mandate or authority of another power, even though that power is not a party to this convention. Transportation without such an agreed stopping place shall not be deemed to be international for the purposes of this convention.
"(3) Transportation to be performed by successive air carriers shall be deemed to be one undivided transportation, if it has been regarded by the parties as a single operation, whether it has been agreed upon under the form of a single contract or a series of contracts, and it shall not lose its international character merely because one contract or a series of contracts is to be performed entirely within a territory subject to the sovereignty, suzerainty, mandate, or authority of the same High Contracting Party."

20. That she took out a $50,000 insurance policy in Seattle has, as Special Term declared, "little bearing on [the passenger's] intent relative to termination of the contract for international transportation or of the character of the trip from Seattle to New York in terms of internal or international passage." Mrs. Seiter may have purchased the $50,000 policy because she desired coverage in addition to the $25,000 of insurance (to cover the round trip) which she had procured

before leaving New York, in view of the forecast of bad weather. Its purchase certainly created no inference that she considered the round trip at an end.

21. Article 3 provides:
"(1) For the transportation of passengers, the carrier must deliver a passenger ticket which shall contain the following particulars:
(a) The place and date of issue;
(b) The place of departure and of destination;
(c) The agreed stopping places provided that the carrier may reserve the right to alter the stopping places in case of necessity, and the alteration shall not have the effect of depriving the transportation of its international character; (d) The name and address of the carrier or carriers; (e) A statement that the transportation is subject to the rules relating to liability established by this convention. (2) The absence, irregularity, or loss of the passenger ticket shall not affect the existence or the validity of the contract of transportation, which shall nonetheless be subject to the rules of this convention. Nevertheless, if the carrier accepts a passenger without a passenger ticket having been delivered, it shall not be entitled to avail itself of those provisions of this convention which exclude or limit his liability."

22. One court (*Lisi v. Alitalia-Linee Aeree Italiane*, 253 F. Supp. 237, 243, *affd.* 2 Cir., 370 F. 2d 508) (District of Columbia 1980) has described the notice in this way: "The footnotes printed in microscopic type at the bottom of the . . . coupons, as well as condition 2(a) camouflaged in Lilliputian print in a thicket of 'Conditions of Contract' crowded on [the outside back cover], are both unnoticeable and unreadable. Indeed, the exculpatory statements on which defendant relies are virtually invisible. They are ineffectively positioned, diminutively sized, and unemphasized by bold-face type, contrasting color, or anything else. The simple truth is that they are so artfully camouflaged that their presence is concealed."

Bibliography

Arnold, Emmett L. *Gold Camp Drifter, 1906–1910*. Reno, NV: University of Nevada Press, 1973.

The Association of Trial Lawyers of America. *Everyday Law*, December, 1988.

Black, Henry Campbell. *Black's Law Dictionary*. 5th ed. St. Paul, MN: West Publishing Co., 1979.

"Bogie's Faces Lawsuit." *Las Vegas Sun*. (April 26, 1984): 8C.

Bryan, J., and J. V. Murphy. *The Windsor Story*. New York: Dell Publishing Co., 1980.

Cooley's Blackstone. 1850.

Dickerson, Thomas A. *Travel Law*. New York: Law Journal Seminars-Press, 1986.

Douglas, William O. Eighth Annual Benjamin Cardoza Lectures.

Eiler, James O. *Hotel and Casino Law Letter* 2, no. 1 (November 1983).

Florida Hotel and Motel News, March 1983, 26.

Goodwin, John R., *Business Law*. 3rd ed. Homewood, IL: Richard D. Irwin, Inc., 1980.

Hospitality Law 5, no. 7 (July 1990): 4.

Hotel and Casino Law Letter 2, no. 2 (April 3, 1983).

"Law as a Liberal Art Versus Law as a Professional Discipline: A False Dichotomy," *American Business Law Journal* 15, no. 1 (Spring 1977): 68.

Lodging (May 1982): 2.

Lodging Hospitality (March 1988): 24.

Marshall, Anthony G., and Elio C. Bellucci. "Innkeeper's Security: Quo Vadis." *Florida Hotel & Motel News* 2 (March 1983): 1.

National Law Journal, May 11, 1981, 36.

New York Times, June 7, 1981, 15.

New York Times, July 19, 1981, 1.

Sherry, John E. H. *The Laws of Innkeepers*. 3rd ed. Ithaca, NY: Cornell University Press, 1993.

Successful Hotel Marketer 3, no. 19, 2.

Vallen, Jerome J., et al. *The Art & Science of Managing Hotels/Restaurants/Institutions*. Rochelle Park, NJ: Hayden Book, 1980.

Weekly Newsletter, Motel/Hotel Insider, May 19, 1980.

Recommended Readings

The listing that follows contains many books that are readily available at the news stand or a local library. Several of these entries contain page citations that refer the reader to a scene in which the legal system and often the HH&T industry is the focus. It is hoped that these make real for the readers the possible legal situations in which they might find themselves involved in the future.

Alexander, Shana. *Anyone's Daughter.* New York: The Viking Press, 37.

Alvarez, A. *The Biggest Game in Town.* Boston: Houghton Mifflin Company, 6, 8, 10, 40, 48, 61, 66, 85, 155.

Asinof, Eliot. *Eight Men Out.* New York: Pocket Books, 44.

Benet, George. *A Short Dance in the Sun.* San Francisco: The Lopes Press, 12, 13, 36, 67, 105, 125, 135, 168.

Berton, Pierre. *The Klondike Fever.* New York: Carrol & Grof Publishers, 23.

Bledsoe, Jerry. *Bitter Blood.* New York: New American Library, 547.

Brandt, Charles. *The Right to Remain Silent.* New York: St. Martin's Press, 82.

Brett, Simon. *A Nice Class of Corpse.* New York: Charles Scribner's Sons, 58.

Bryson, John. *Evil Angels.* New York: Bantam Books, 328.

Caro, Robert A. *The Path to Power.* New York: Alfred A. Knopf, 1982, 5.

Clarke, Thurston. *Equator, A Journey.* New York: William Morrow, 198, 262, 263, 365, 366.

Collins, Max Allan. *Neon Mirage.* New York: St. Martin's Press, 12.

Cook, Robin. *Fever.* New York: New American Library, 170.

Dillman, John. *The French Quarter Killers.* New York: Macmillan Publishing Company, 55.

Early, Pete. *Prophet of Death.* New York: William Morrow, 433.

Franco, Joseph. *Hoffa's Man.* New York: Dell, 162.

Gardner, John. *Nobody Lives Forever.* New York: G. P. Putman's Sons, 149.

Garrison, Jim. *On the Trail of the Assassins.* New York: Warner Books, 73,74.

Goulden, Joseph C. *The Million Dollar Lawyers.* New York: Berkeley Books, 161.

Gowans, Elizabeth. *Heart of the High Country.* New York: Bantam Books, 210.

Greene, Robert W. *The Sting Man.* New York: Ballantine Books, 1981.

Hall, Oakley. *The Bad Lands.* New York: Bantam Books, 249.

Hohl, Joan. *Nevada Silver.* Mira Books, 8, 42, 205, 250.

Jackson, Donald. *Voyages of the Steamboat Yellowstone.* New York: Ticknor & Fields, 1985, 62.

Jackson, Donald Dale. *Gold Dust.* New York: Alfred A. Knopf, 1980, 39, 70, 140.

Jenkins, Peter and Barbara. *The Walk West, A Walk Across America 2.* New York: Ballantine, 1983, 387–88.

Kakonis, Tom. *Michigan Roll.* New York: St. Martin's Press, 51.

Kennedy, Ludovie. *The Airman and the Carpenter.* New York: Penguin Books, 85, 254, 255.

Lewis, Georgia. "The Way it Was, Diary of a Pioneer Las Vegas Woman," *Las Vegas Sun,* Series 1978, 78.

Lord, Walter. *The Night Lives On*. New York: Jane Books, 38, 233.

Martini, Steve. *Compelling Evidence*. New York: Jane Books, 257, 259.

Napley, Sir David. *The Camden Town Murder*. New York: St. Martin's Press, 22.

Newman, Christopher. *Sixth Precinct*. New York: Fawcett Gold Medal, 1986.

Pileggi, Nicholas. *Wise Guy*. New York: Pocket Books, 106.

Pileggi, Nicholas. *Casino*. New York: Simon & Schuster, 13, 14, 15, 17, 80, 91, 93, 97, 211.

Pilkington, John. *An Englishman in Patagonia*. London: Century, 201, 204, 208, 217.

Pounds, Neil. *The Las Vegas Connection*. New York: Vantage Press, 3.

Roberts, Les. *Not Enough Horses*. New York: St. Martin's Press, 148.

Sandford, John. *Shadow Prey*. New York: Berkeley Books, 286, 341.

Sayer, Dan, and Douglas Booting. *Nazi Gold*. New York: Grove Press, 112, 325.

Shannon, Dell. *Destiny of Death*. New York: William Morrow, 70, 120.

Silyenat, James R. rev. ed. of *The Tides Of Power* by Bob Eckhart and Charles Black. New Haven, CT: Yale Press, 1978.

Sinclair, Upton. *The Jungle*. New York: New American Library, 1960.

Stockley, Grif. *Expert Testimony*. New York: Ivy Books, 249.

Tanenbaum, Robert K. *No Lesser Plea*. New York: New American Library, 41.

Taubman, Bryna. *The Preppie Murder Trial*. New York: St. Martin's Press, 118.

Thomas, Lowell. *With Lawrence in Arabia*. New York: Popular Library, 122.

Traver, Robert. *Anatomy of a Murder*. New York: St. Martin's Press, 35, 63, 424.

Traver, Robert. *People v. Kork*. New York: Dell, 14, 91, 92, 95, 122, 143, 263, 290, 295.

Twain, Mark. *Roughing It*. Hartford, CT: American Publishing Company, 1872, 39, 109, 115, 187, 238, 239, 240, 244, 245, 248, 249, 268.

Ure, John. *The Quest for Captain Morgan*. London: Constable, 107, 123.

Volkman, Ernest. *The Heist*. New York: Dell, 79, 177.

von Hoffman. *Citizen Cain*. New York: Doubleday, 412, 428.

Wambaugh, Joseph. *The Blooding*. New York: William Morrow, 226.

Werner, Fred H. *The Beecher Island Battle*. Greeley, CO: Werner Publications, 134.

Williams, David. *Treasure in Roubles*. New York: Avon Books, 55, 69.

Williamson, George F. *The Gold Rush*. New York: Indian Head Books, 142, 180, 181.

Wood, William. *Gangland*. New York: St. Martin's Press, 210, 211.

Index to Cases

Note: Text page numbers in this index are indicated by boldface type.

Index to Words and Topics